THE MANUSCRIPTS OF LEO
THE GREAT'S LETTERS

INSTRVMENTA PATRISTICA ET MEDIAEVALIA

Research on the Inheritance of Early and Medieval Christianity

83

THE MANUSCRIPTS OF LEO THE GREAT'S LETTERS

THE TRANSMISSION AND RECEPTION OF PAPAL DOCUMENTS IN LATE ANTIQUITY AND THE MIDDLE AGES

Matthew J J Hoskin

BREPOLS

2022

INSTRVMENTA PATRISTICA ET MEDIAEVALIA

Research on the Inheritance of Early and Medieval Christianity

---

Founded by Dom Eligius Dekkers († 1998)

D/2022/0095/149
ISBN 978-2-503-58966-4
E-ISBN 978-2-503-58967-1
DOI 10.1484/M.IPM-EB.5.120392
ISSN 1379-9878
E-ISSN 2294-8457

Printed in the EU on acid-free paper.

Table of Contents

Acknowledgements

This book is the culmination of years of study into the manuscript tradition of Leo the Great's letters, both during my Ph.D.
and in the years following. I would like to begin my acknowledge-
ments with Richard Burgess of the University of Ottawa who recommended that I edit the letters of Leo the Great. I have never
looked back. The project is not, as it turns out, an edition, for
the task before me then was much more monumental than I had
expected. Yet it is from his suggestion (on Facebook!) that made
me take the road that has led me here.

I would like also to thank the following bodies for their gen-
erous financial support: the University of Edinburgh, through
the Principal's Career Development Studentship and Edinburgh
Global Scholarship; Edinburgh's School of Divinity helped defray
the cost of research trips; the Hugh Last Fund of the Society for
the Promotion of Roman Studies helped finance a research trip to
Italy in 2014; and the Thomas Wiedemann Memorial Fund paid
for my travel to Oxford in 2012. The Erasmus Exchange Programme allowed me to spend three months in Tübingen and visit-
many libraries of Germany and Austria.

A project such as this could not be possible without the gener-
ous assistance of many libraries. In Edinburgh, I benefited from
the collections of the National Library of Scotland, New College
Library, the University of Edinburgh's Law and Europa Library,
and the University of Edinburgh's Main Library, as well as the
diligent efforts of the University of Edinburgh's Interlibrary Loan
team. In Rome, the BSR Library was a tremendous place to
conduct research. In Durham, I benefited from the Bill Bryson
Library and Palace Green Library as well as the Interlibrary Loan
system, at the University of British Columbia I made good use
of Koerner Library, the Irving K. Barber Learning Centre, yet
more interlibrary loans, and, finally, the Morrisset Library of the
University of Ottawa and the Jean-Léon Allie Library at St-Paul
University, Ottawa. I would like to thank the staff of the following other libraries in alphabetical order by city: Berlin, Staatsbibliothek Preußischer Kulturbesitz; Durham, Durham Cathedral

Library and Palace Green Library; El Escorial, Real Biblioteca de San Lorenzo; Florence, Biblioteca Medicea Laurenziana and Biblioteca Nazionale Centrale di Firenze; Leipzig, Universitäts-bibliothek Leipzig; Lucca, Biblioteca Capitolare Feliniana; Milan, Biblioteca Ambrosiana; Munich, Bayerische Staatsbibliothek; Oxford, All Souls College Library, the Bodleian Library, and Oriel College Library; Paris, Bibliothèque nationale de France, both the manuscripts section at Site Richelieu and the main collection at François Mitterand, as well as the Institut de Recherches d'His-toire des Textes; Rome, Biblioteca nazionale centrale di Roma and Biblioteca Vallicelliana; Sankt Paul im Lavanttal, Benediktiner-stift Sankt Paul; Stuttgart, Württembergische Landesbibliothek; Vatican City, Biblioteca Apostolica Vaticana; Venice, Biblioteca Nazionale Marciana; Vercelli, Biblioteca Capitolare di Vercelli; Verona, Biblioteca Capitolare; and Wolfenbüttel, Herzog August Bibliothek.

I am also thankful for the careful supervision of Professor Gavin Kelly and Dr Sara Parvis of the University of Edinburgh, my doctoral supervisors, who helped guide me on this long jour-ney and have read far more tables and charts and multiples drafts thereof than I would have thought adviseable! They have saved me from many errors and directed me to many of the best resources for this massive undertaking. Gavin has also taken time to review some of the new material for the book version, for which I am incredibly grateful.

I would like to extend my thanks to Dr Abigail Firey of the University of Kentucky who manages the Carolingian Canon Law Project. She assisted me with the use of images of Berlin, Hamil-ton 132, as well as the transcription software T-PEN that accom-panied it. She also gave me proofs of her 2015 article on said manuscript before it went to print. Her graduate student Christie Pavey has also been of assistance in transcribing Hamilton 132. I must also unburden an enormous and hearty debt of thanks to Dr Andrew Dunning, R. W. Hunt Curator of Medieval Manuscripts at the Bodleian Library, University of Oxford, whose zeal for text editing, publishing, and the software involved is infectious.

In the years since the original composition of this work, more debts have accrued. The chronological priority must go to Pro-fessor Mark Humphries of Swansea University and Dr Thomas S.

Brown of the University of Edinburgh, my external and internal examiners respectively. Their corrections and insights into the project over the course of my *viva* have made this a much better book than otherwise. I am also indebted to the British School at Rome, where I was Ralegh Radford Rome Fellow for the year 2015–2016, providing me access to the Biblioteca Apostolica Vaticana, Biblioteca Vallicelliana in Rome, Biblioteca nazionale centrale di Roma, Biblioteca Capitolare di Vercelli, and Biblioteca Ambrosiana in Milan. The staff, scholars, and artists at the BSR made for a wonderful nine months! I am further grateful to Joanne Barker and the Zeno Karl Schindler Foundation for funding my year as Barker Priory Library Fellow at Durham University, giving me unparalleled access to Durham's manuscript collection and transforming Chapter 5 into a coherent whole. In particular, I am thankful to Professor Giles Gasper at Durham who helped guide this Late Antique specialist into the realm of High Medieval intellectual history. I am further grateful to Dr Charles West of Sheffield University and Professor Rosamond McKitterick of Cambridge University, both of whom assisted me in the matter of Carolingian bibliography. Thanks are also due to Professor Stephen Oakley of Cambridge University for methodological insight and directing me to the existence of at least one manuscript.

I would finally like to extend my thanks to the patience of everyone around me who does not get excited about such things as Corbie a-b or scribes who write Latin in Greek characters. The patient endurance and support of friends and family is invaluable in an undertaking of such monumental proportions as this. I am notably grateful to my family in Canada who have supported me in many ways, both metaphysical and financial. Most especially, I must thank my wife for her understanding, support, and patience. She endured 'PhD brain' for four years, an ailment that still afflicts me. She lovingly supported me through my long absences on the Continent, hunting down the manuscripts. Many thanks to Jennifer for these years with Leo, and the many more to come.

Conspectus Siglorum, Based on ACO 2.4 Where Possible; in Alphabetical Order for Ease of Reference (Chapter and Section in Parentheses)

A – Collection of Vat. lat. 1322 (4.1.b)

Ac – Early Latin *Acta* (4.1.a)

Al – *Collectio Albigensis* (3.2.o)

Ar – *Collectio Arelatensis* (3.2.n)

B – *Collectio Bobbiensis* (5.3.a)

C – *Collectio Corbeiensis* (3.2.j)

Ca – *Collectio Casinensis* (4.1.f)

Ch – *Versio Gestorum Chalcedonensium antiqua correcta* (4.1.d)

D – *Collectio Dionysiana* (3.2.f)

D–a – *Collectio Dionysiana adaucta* (5.2.c)

D–b – *Collectio Dionysiana Bobiensis* (3.2.g)

D–h – *Collectio Dionysio-Hadriana* (5.2.a)

Di – *Collectio Diessensis* (3.2.b)

E – *Collectio Ratisbonensis* (5.3.b)

F – *Collectio Frisingensis Prima* (3.2.a)

G – *Collectio Grimanica* (4.1.g)

H–s – *Collectio Hadriano-Hispanica* (5.2.b)

I – Pseudo-Isidorian forgeries (5.2.f)

I–a – Pseudo-Isidore Class A1 (5.2.f.iv)

I–b – Pseudo-Isidore Classes A/B and B (5.2.f.iii)

I–c – Pseudo-Isidore Class C (5.2.f.vi)

K – *Collectio Coloniensis* (3.2.q)

m – *Collectio Florentina* (6.2.f)

M – *Collectio Sancti Mauri* (3.2.r)

N – *Collectio Novariensis de re Eutychis* (4.1.e)

P – *Collectio Pithouensis* (3.2.k)

Q – *Collectio Quesnelliana* (3.2.c)

Re – *Collectio Remensis* (3.2.p)

Ru – Rusticus' *Acta* (4.1.c)

S – *Collectio Hispana* (3.2.u)

S–g – *Collectio Hispana Gallica* (5.2.d)

S–ga – *Collectio Hispana Gallica Augustodunensis* (5.2.e)

Sa – *Collectio Sanblasiana* (3.2.e)

T – *Collectio (ecclesiae) Thessalonicensis* (3.2.l)

Te – *Collectio Teatina* (3.2.i)

V – *Collectio Vaticana* (3.2.d)

Y – Yale/Cluny Recension of Pseudo-Isidore (5.2.f.v)

Y–a – Ballerini Collection 21 (6.3.b)

22 – Ballerini Collection 22 (6.3.c)

23 – Ballerini Collection 23 (6.3.d)

24 – Ballerini Collection 24 (6.3.e)

73 – Collection of 73 Letters (6.3.g)

Abbreviations Used

ACO	*Acta Conciliorum Oecumenicorum*, ed. E. Schwartz
CLA	*Codices Latini Antiquiores*
CSEL	Corpus Scriptorum Ecclesiasticorum Latinorum
EOMIA	*Ecclesiae Occidentalis Monumenta Iuris Antiqua*, ed. C. H. Turner
JK	*Regesta Pontificorum Romanorum*, ed. P. Jaffé
JTS	*Journal of Theological Studies*
MGH	Monumenta Germaniae Historica
SC	Sources chrétiennes
ST	Carlos Silva-Tarouca's edition of Leo the Great

Introduction

This project is an analysis of the manuscripts of the letters of Pope Leo I (pope 440–61). These letters are among our most valuable sources for the middle decades of the fifth century, and although we can construct most events from Leo's papacy without them, with them everything enters into sharper definition. Given the major importance of the letters as sources documenting so important a figure, it is remarkable that no one has attempted a full examination of them and their manuscripts since the Ballerini brothers in the 1750s. The Ballerini did an outstanding job, and consulted more manuscripts than any previous editor of Leo. However, regardless of how good their text is, and it is good, their notes are maddeningly obscure. Furthermore, 250 years of exploration in the libraries of Europe have brought to light more manuscripts and collections of Leo's letters, some representing witnesses from within a century of his death. If a new editor of Leo were to do nothing more than provide us with a good apparatus documenting these manuscripts, we would be in good stead. If a new editor were also to apply the advances in later Latin philology we have enjoyed since then, such as the study of prose rhythm, we would be in even better stead. Leo's significance for theology and canon law has never waned, as the many manuscripts that I examine show. Even in the High Middle Ages when canonists shift their allegiance to systematic collections of excerpts rather than chronological collections of documents, Leo is consistently present in both fields. Furthermore, collections of his sermons and letters continue to be copied up to the dawn of print: we know of more than one copy of Leo's letters made for fifteenth-century popes. He is the only pope to get his own chapter in Quasten's *Patrology*. His place as a theologian and man of power have been highlighted in recent studies, from the introductory (Neil 2009) to the theological (Armitage 2005 and Green 2008) to the politico-theological (Wessell 2008).

Leo studies are not slowing down, yet his letters still lack a solid critical edition. This book, a contextual exploration of the manuscripts, is the first step on the road to providing that edition. It is also, however, a contribution to the history of canon law and intellectual history in the Middle Ages. The technical studies involved in this book are crucial for the task of the text editor. Nevertheless, the transmission of texts is not a purely natural, scientific phenomenon. We may look at this research as 'stemmatics' and 'lineage', yet it is not the case that one manuscript gave birth to another manuscript. Humans copied each manuscript, humans existing as full members of their own societies, with their own concerns, reasons for copying, materials at hand, history, politics, religion, and art. These historical contexts are not unimportant for considering the story that emerges from the technical discussions and the burgeoning lists of manuscripts. Each aspect of transmission gives the other fulness, taking the reader into an engagement with a real tradition. I believe that when we consider, for example, the Carolingian manuscripts and canonical collections, it is worth asking what the Carolingian Renaissance was, and how it produced so many manuscripts. At the other end of the story of transmission, when twelfth-century collections of Leo's letters are copied for fifteenth-century popes and for cardinals at the Council of Ferrara-Florence, the relationship between that council, those men, and those manuscripts is not unimportant. Understanding why Leo was copied will help open up the mysteries hidden in the manuscripts. Finally, the marriage of both kinds of awareness—scientific textual criticism and stemmatics on the one hand and reception on the other—make the story of transmitting Leo's letters into an adventure, into a major piece of the history of western European intellectual culture, theology, and canon law.

Chapter 1 starts this book off with a study of Leo's life and letters in context, followed by a chapter about the major printed editions of Leo's letters. Chapters 3–6 analyse the manuscripts, and Chapter 7 is a conspectus of the letters, arranged by epistle.

In Chapter 1, I begin by providing two accounts of Leo's papacy, the first from external sources, the second from the letters. Both elements together demonstrate the significance of Leo's letters.

In Chapter 2, the book continues with a discussion of the editions of Leo's letters, beginning with the few in Bussi's edition of 1461, then a select discussion of certain other editions meant to be indicative of their eras, with more detailed discussion on Pasquier Quesnel's groundbreaking work in 1675, and then that of the Ballerini in 1753. Finally, the excellent, albeit selective, editions

of C. Silva-Tarouca and E. Schwartz are assessed. It is the custom of some editors to scorn their predecessors, but I am neither
inclined, nor have grounds, to do so; whatever advantages I may
have,[1] they did well at the task set them. Our need for a better
apparatus and, at times, a better text, does not make them fail-
ures at what they did. Their work makes mine possible, and I am
daily aware of what I owe them.

Chapters 3–6 take on the task of assessing these manuscripts.[2]
Leo's letters are gathered in 45 letter collections, ranging from
two or four letters all the way to 104 letters. These collections
overlap, and many of them use each other or common sources. At
the beginning of Chapter 3, I set out the context of the earliest
collections and their common sources, no longer extant, which I
call 'proto-collections', which had little or no official, papal impetus behind them, for they do not need a pope to be made or mined.
The time was ripe and the sources fecund. Chapter 3 then analyses
the canonical collections of the pre-Carolingian era, not just cata-
loguing the manuscripts, but finding variants peculiar to certain
collections or common to multiple collections, and thereby tracing
relationships among manuscripts of individual collections and then
among the various collections. Each collection, as far as can be
done, is put into context. Chapter 4 does the same for the various
letter collections appended to the *Acts* of the Council of Chalcedon,
including a section about the Greek transmission. Chapter 5 discusses the crucial era of the Carolingians. I demonstrate the major
significance of the Carolingian era for the survival of Leo's letters
and the collections that contain them, and then discuss briefly
the Carolingian Renaissance. Chapter 6 covers the High and Late
Middle Ages, seeing the dependence of the increasing number of
collections upon the work of Carolingian collectors and copyists.

Methodology

A few points concerning the methodology of Chapters 3 through
6 are in order. First, the reader will find that throughout I have
used the Ballerini edition as a control text by which to assess the

---

[1] As Leo, *Ep.* 14, says, 'Honor inflat superbiam'.

[2] The vast majority of these manuscripts I visited myself in Austria, Britain, France, Germany, Italy, and Spain.

variants of the manuscripts and thereby trace their relationships. The result is that I cite their readings time and again. It must be stressed, therefore, that I do not assume that the Ballerini are correct when I cite a reading as being 'against' the Ballerini. Rather, by showing that it is at variance with them, I am able to bring out the unique characteristics of a reading. The same is true for those times when my control is Schwartz or Silva-Tarouca. The purpose of the control text is to give something to which all manuscripts can be compared with no question of right or wrong.

Second, I make a distinction between 'variant' and 'error' that is artificial. Obviously, all errors are variants, and many variants are errors. By 'error' in what follows, I mean those variants that are clearly and obviously wrong, due to carelessness or the slip of the pen. By 'variant' I meant those variants that are not immediately wrong and whose assessment may require more effort. Third, the assessments are accompanied by a large quantity of tables of prodigious size. These tables exist to demonstrate as fully as possible what I argue and have seen in the manuscripts. Far too often textual criticism reads like conclusions already made. I wish the reader to be able to follow my arguments and disagree where possible. Fourth, each letter collection has a siglum in **bold** and its manuscripts sigla in *italics*; a *conspectus siglorum* for the letter collections is immediately following the table of contents at the beginning of this work.

I have included in these analyses certain data that may not seem to be of much value, at least stemmatically. For example, inversions of words, such as 'petri apostoli' as against 'apostoli petri' are included. Such inversions could easily be done by any scribe at any point. Nevertheless, Leo's editor will have to decide which order these pairings go. Furthermore, I believe these inversions can be of stemmatic value if, for example, they turn up in almost every manuscript of a particular tradition (say, **Q**) and then again in manuscripts of a later tradition (say, **S–ga**) whose relationship with the first needs elucidation. I have also included variants in dates. Frankly, many of these are useless. Nonetheless, what needs to be determined is how Leo's *notarii* originally wrote the dates, as well as the wider families of readings. Given that *vi* and *iii* could be descendants of the same exemplar, paying attention to these dates is not unimportant. Furthermore, neglecting such details may make a transmission history seem 'cleaner' than it is really is. Therefore, besides recording them here, a useful place for them, since they might clutter up an apparatus with little or no benefit to the reader, would be an appendix, as Kaster does with the poorly-copied Greek variants in his edition of Macrobius.[3] A casual glance may make a reader think that I have maintained the scribal habit writing *ci* for *ti* under the same motivation. This habit is stemmatically worthless and will not help us find Leo's orthography. When it appears in the tables, it is not the variant in question but simply the honest recording of what the manuscript contains. Again, I have no desire to present the codices as 'cleaner' than they are. On the other hand, some variants of *i* and *e* being exchanged are included because, although extraordinarily common, in some occasions, this exchange produces an entirely different word, case, or voice of the word at hand. It strikes me that a good editor ought to be aware of these exchanges.

There are some scribal habits I would like to have documented, but there is never enough time. One of these is the difference between *spiritalis* and *spiritualis*, especially in Cistercian mss: *spiritalis* = 'philosophic, hermeneutic, and speculative context, and *spiritualis* referring to the action of the Holy Spirit'.[4] How a copyist might write this word in Leo, then, can reveal something about his or her interpretation of the text.

A final methodological consideration is the question of why I have not analysed the manuscripts of the systematic collections or of Peter Lombard. The systematic collections are themselves a vast quantity of manuscripts—indeed, Gratian's *Decretum* alone exists in 160 manuscripts from the twelfth century alone, and the less popular *Decretum* of Burchard of Worms exists in over eighty.[5] It is worth knowing which collections transmit Leo, so I have included these. I have also listed, but not collated, the manuscripts of Cresconius, besides the citations of Leo in Gratian. However, I do not believe that most of these manuscripts are of textual value for considering Leo's letters. When their sources are known,

---

[3] See Kaster 2011, xxx–xlv.

[4] Dutton 2010, 25, citing Gaetano Raciti, Introduction to Aelred's sermons, CCCM 2A:xiii.

[5] For Gratian, see Landau 2008, 48; for Burchard, see Fowler-Magerl 2005, 86.

we have earlier manuscripts of high quality—or the very manuscripts from which they were copied. For example, although I did do some minor collation of the *Collectio Vetus Gallica*, we know that it used the *Collectio Corbeiensis* as a source—that is to say, the manuscript Paris, lat. 12097. The high medieval collections tended to draw from Pseudo-Isidore, and we have enough manuscripts of that collection to set us in good stead for editing the Leo portions. Therefore, while they are an interesting part of the story of the transmission and reception of Leo's letters, the manuscripts of the systematic canonical collections are not analysed in this study.

Chapter 1

Historical Introduction to Leo's Letters in History, Canon Law, and Theology

1.1 Leo's Letters in History and Canon Law

Leo I was pope from 440–61 and lived through interesting times, both in terms of geo-ecclesiology (to borrow the term of Philippe Blaudeau) and of geo-politics.[1] For example, when he became bishop of Rome, Cyril was bishop of Alexandria, as the ascendant theologian in Greek Christianity. After sitting in the see of Alexandria for thirty-two years, Cyril died in 444; from 444 to Leo's death in 461, Alexandria went through four bishops, sometimes two at once, one of whom was killed by a mob. In secular politics, for the first fifteen years of Leo's episcopate, Valentinian III was western emperor; from Valentinian's death in 455 to Leo's in 461, the western empire went through four emperors. Both East and West saw the passing of the Theodosian dynasty, in the East with Theodosius II in 450 and the West with Valentinian III in 455. Moreover, in his lifetime, assuming Leo to have been born around 390, the Western Roman Empire was dismembered in different ways and at different stages; many of the places that were not alienated from Roman *imperium* in Leo's lifetime, such as Narbo and Aquileia, were nevertheless victims of war and sacking— including Rome herself. Even Rome's generals went to war against each other. Leo's letters are valuable sources for these communities as they put the pieces back together, whether Aquileia after Attila,[2] Narbo after the Visigoths,[3] or Gallaecia under Suevic rule.[4] This tumultuous political environment, this decades-long erosion of Roman control of the West, was coterminous with the careers of some of the greatest Latin churchmen, most famously Augustine of Hippo and Jerome, but Gaul was home to John Cas-

---

[1] For *géo-ecclésiologie*, see Blaudeau 2012a; 2012b; 2001.

[2] See Leo, *Ep.* 159.

[3] See Leo, *Ep.* 167.

[4] See Leo, *Ep* 15.

sian, Vincent of Lérins, and Prosper of Aquitaine, while Aurelius of Carthage and Quodvultdeus ensure Augustine was not alone in Africa, and Peter Chrysologus preached in Ravenna. The poetic life of Latin literature also continued in Leo's lifetime, seeing the end of the careers of Claudian, Ausonius, and Prudentius as well as the work of Sedulius, Paulinus of Nola, and the early career of Sidonius Apollinaris. The crisis of empire did not mean a diminution of intellectual and artistic creation in the western Mediterranean.

In fact, one barometer of intellectual vitality is theological controversy. Leo was involved in these, East and West, especially the christological controversy surrounding Eutyches, but also what we might think of as 'mopping up' of Pelagians and Priscillianists in the West, as well as a campaign against Manichaeans. One would expect a major figure such as the bishop of Rome to have important and interesting things to say in his letters, having held office during these two decades. His 143 surviving letters show that, indeed, he did. No bishop of Rome before Gregory the Great, with a surviving corpus of 860 letters, has a better epistolary survival rate. So many letters survive from Leo's episcopate for two interrelated reasons. First, Leo was an active correspondent who involved himself in the disciplinary and theological world of his day. Second, succeeding generations found Leo's statements, especially in theology, to be touchstones of orthodoxy in Latin Christianity. Therefore, both Leo's own activities and the reception of them by tradition work together to create this large body of surviving correspondence that is the subject of this book. In this chapter, we will consider their historical background and their place in the history of canon law and in the history of theology. I shall now begin with a brief outline of Leo's episcopate within the historical moment of the mid-fifth-century Roman Empire.

Leo was archdeacon of Rome at the time of his accession to the Roman episcopate. What little we know of his career as archdeacon already signals for us a few things about what sort of episcopate he would have. John Cassian's *De Incarnatione contra Nestorium* was written on behalf of Leo when Leo was archdeacon, presumably because Leo was Greekless in an increasingly Greek-free Rome. Setting aside questions of Leo's proficiency as a theologian or originality, we see that, as a member of the church

hierarchy tasked with an organisational role, he sought out someone with a known competency in both Greek and theology to
provide Rome with a response to the emerging Nestorian crisis
in the East. Leo, then, first definitively appears in the historical
record as someone interested in taking an interest in wider affairs
and even taking the initiative himself.[5] Worth noting is the fact
that, for all that people such as Leo and his predecessors such
as Siricius,[6] maintained that someone had to go through all the
ranks of the ecclesiastical *cursus honorum* before becoming bishop,
in Rome, deacons were frequently elected bishop. The church of
Rome only had seven deacons at any time, and they had a very
distinct function in the operation of church life.[7]

In 440, Xystus III died while Leo was on a diplomatic mission
to Gaul to reconcile the general Aëtius and Albinus, Praetorian
Prefect of the Gauls.[8] He came back to Rome to celebrate his
election, and the sermon that he preached on 29 September 440
survives as the first in the collection of 96 of his sermons Leo
published. He thanks the people of Rome and God for his election
as bishop and expresses his hope that the people of Rome would
'progress to salvation'.[9] In the first eight years of his episcopate,
Leo's career looked much the same as that of any previous Roman
bishop, although the sermons give us greater insight into his mind

---

[5] There is an earlier reference to a Leo, likely the same person, who was
an acolyte on an embassy from Zosimus to Carthage in Augustine, *Ep.* 191.8:
'si enim breuissimam epistulam tuam, quam de hac ipsa re ad beatissimum
senem Aurelium per Leonem acolithum direxisti'.

[6] Siricius to Himerius of Tarragona, *Ep.* ch. 13.

[7] For a recent discussion of Roman deacons and their role, see Moorhead
2015, 159–69.

[8] Prosper, *Chron.* 1341: 'At the death of Bishop Xystus, the Roman Church
was without a priest for 40 full days, awaiting with wondrous peace and
patience the presence of Deacon Leo, whom at the time the Gauls were
detaining as he restored friendship between Aëtius and Albinus, as if he had
been taken far away—so that the judgement would be reckoned worthy of
both the one elected and the ones electing him. Therefore, Deacon Leo, after
he was called by a public delegation and presented to a rejoicing fatherland,
was ordained the forty-third Bishop of the Roman Church'. See PLRE 2,
Fl. Aetius 7, ALBINUS 10. Despite the spelling of *CAH* 14, I have chosen
'Xystus' over 'Sixtus' since that is how he himself spelled the name in the
dedicatory mosaic in Santa Maria Maggiore.

[9] *Serm.* 1.23: Proficientibus ad salutem. CCSL 138: 6.

than into others', for he is the first bishop of Rome from whom we have a corpus of sermons, pointing to Leo's own image of himself as a spiritual leader and author who takes care with his work in publishing it.

The first issue that emerges in the letters is Pelagianism, a teaching the Roman Church had dealt with in earlier decades, siding with Augustine of Hippo against it, notably during the papacy of Innocent I (401–17). Leo's concern in *Epp.* 1 and 2, both from 442, is the presence of runaway Pelagians trying to insinuate themselves into the churches of northern Italy; Leo reiterates some of these concerns again in *Ep.* 18, 30 December 447. According to Leo, Pelagians are to make public confession and recantation before admission to the church's fellowship; they are also to be barred from advancement in the ecclesiastical *cursus*.

Leo shared another target with Augustine that was more important for him than Pelagianism, and that was Manichaeism. In 443, according to Prosper, Leo found many Manichaeans in Rome.[10] He tackled Manichaeism from the pulpit in *Sermm.* 9, 16, 24, 34, 42, 72, and 76. According to investigations he undertook himself,[11] Rome had a large Manichaean population that included members of the church and involved amongst its secret rites the violation of a young girl.[12] This investigation resulted in the expulsion of the Manichaeans from Rome, and in *Ep.* 7 of 30 January 444, Leo warned the bishops of Italy that these Manichaeans were now fugitive and would try to infiltrate their congregations. Leo seems to have got the imperial administration involved, for one of Valentinian III's laws from around this time was promulgated against the Manichaeans, *Novella* XVIII of 19 June 445, sent to Albinus, Praetorian Prefect of Italy, Illyricum, and Africa (443–48).[13] This letter could be read as reflecting the weakness and malleability

---

[10] Prosper, *Chron.* 1350.

[11] See *Serm.* 16, 12 December 443.

[12] These Manichaeans were likely refugees from North Africa following the Vandal invasions of the previous decade, for the most part. See Schipper and van Oort 2000, 1.

[13] Ed. Mommsen and Meyer 1905, 103–05. Edited by the Ballerini as Leo, *Ep.* 8. However, it does not belong with Leo's letters in my judgement, although MS **Q** *o*, (see below 3.2.c.ii and 6.2.c), does include it amongst Leo's letters.

of Valentinian III; on the other hand, it could also show us the weakness of Leo: if his own efforts had been effective, he would not have needed to involve the emperor in the first place.[14] Presumably this law was part of the impetus behind the discovery and prosecution of Manichaeans in Astorga who had allegedly been hiding there after having been tried by Bishops Hydatius and Turribius some years before.[15] The last certain mention of Manichaeans I have found during Leo's episcopate is in Hydatius, where a certain Roman Manichaean named Pascentius fled from Astorga and was arrested in Emerita in 448, then banished from Lusitania.[16]

The other major event for Leo's early episcopate was the death of Cyril of Alexandria in 444 upon which Leo wrote *Ep.* 9 to Dioscorus, Cyril's successor. Here Leo explains to Dioscorus that, since St Mark was the disciple of St Peter, and the Bishop of Rome is the successor of St Peter, then the Bishop of Alexandria is under the authority of the Bishop of Rome. Leo then proceeds to explain to Dioscorus the right way to conduct sacerdotal and diaconal consecrations. The document is helpful to the historian of liturgy for what it contributes to our knowledge of Roman practice at the time. It also shows us what Leo thought of his own position in the hierarchy. It has been argued that Leo saw himself as the theological successor to Cyril of Alexandria.[17] This may be true, given what would happen in a few years' time. This letter certainly sees Leo setting himself up as the head bishop of the Mediterranean world, reflecting his Petrine ecclesiology, an ecclesiology at odds

[14] This interpretation is directly at odds with the more traditional reading, represented by Gore 1880, 33, who believes that the pro-Leo *novellae* XVII and XVIII were executed through papal pressure. Jalland 1941, 48–49 sees the edict as of possible imperial origin, representing cooperation between church and secular government.

[15] Hydatius, *Chron.* 122.

[16] Hydatius, *Chron.* 130. This is not the last we hear of Manichaeans, who next appear in Rome during the episcopate of Gelasius who burned their books in front of Santa Maria Maggiore, as attested by the *Liber Pontificalis* 51.1. Their final appearances are also attested in the *Liber Pontificalis*, in the episcopate of Symmachus (53.5; pope, 498–514) and again that of Hormisdas (54.9; pope, 514–23). They are not known in Rome after these events, as attested by Moorhead 2015, 49, n. 96.

[17] Green 2008, 139.

with that of the eastern churches as would become apparent in years to come.

In early July of 445, Valentinian III issued another constitution, *Novella* XVII to Aëtius,[18] in support of Leo's authority, saying that his authority deserved to be upheld because of the merit of St Peter, the dignity of the city of Rome, and the authority accorded it by Nicaea.[19] The issue under consideration was the activity of Hilary of Arles, who, contrary to Leo's wishes, was causing trouble in the churches of Gaul by removing bishops from their sees and replacing them with others. Hilary is supporting this activity, according the imperial constitution, with an armed band and bringing about war. Such actions are against the imperial majesty and the reverence of the Apostolic See, and Hilary is banned from mixing arms with ecclesiastical affairs; people are to respond to any summons made by the Bishop of Rome and abide by his judgement. For details of the events that provoked this imperial constitution, we must combine Leo, *Ep.* 10, with the *Life of Hilary of Arles* by Honoratus of Marseille, who provides us with the other side of the debate. According to Honoratus, while Hilary was visiting the apostles and martyrs, he presented himself to Leo at the pope's command.[20] This makes it seem as though Hilary was simply on pilgrimage to Rome at the time. According to Honoratus, Hilary presented himself with respect and humility, and explained that he was simply putting affairs in Gallic churches in order following established custom. He said that certain peo-

---

[18] Ed. Mommsen and Meyer 1905, 101–03. Also ed. Ballerini as Leo, *Ep.* 11, but not really one of his letters. As with *Novella* XVIII (*Ep.* 8), outside of MS **Q** *o*, it is not transmitted with Leo's letters in the manuscript tradition and, therefore, should not be edited with them as argued by Humphries 2012, 168–69.

[19] Moorhead 2015 argues that Valentinian's decree runs contrary to the Roman view of its own position, rooting it not primarily in Petrine succession but in the status of Rome and the Nicene canons. However, Roman bishops had previously used this three-pronged argument to bolster their case for primacy. Indeed, Innocent I in his letter to Victricius of Rouen (JK 286) mentioned Nicaea alone as the basis for his authority. Furthermore, when Demacopoulos' work on the subject is taken into account, the argument for Petrine primacy is not used from a position of strength in the first place, but, rather, of weakness, when all else fails; Demacopoulos 2013, Chapter 2.

[20] 'Apostolorum martyrumque occursu peracto beato Leoni papae ilico se praesentat', *Vita Hilarii* 22.1–2.

ple who justly deserved a public sentence had entered into the church in Rome and asked that things that had been expressed publicly might be emended secretly; Hilary had not, according to his speech as recorded by Honoratus, come to Rome to be judged but to do his duty,[21] and the statements he had made on these issues had been put forward as protests not accusations. Moreover, if he wished anything more, it was that he would not be disturbed in future. Honoratus does not name the men involved, but Hilary refused to give them an inch of ground in Rome, and therefore left the city despite guards posted at his chambers and the savage harshness of winter. To put a holy ending on an unbecoming tale, Honoratus says that Hilary, prompted by piety, sent Ravennius, who would succeed him as Bishop of Arles, with Nectarius and Constantius to change Leo's mind by placating him with lowly humility. They met up with Auxiliaris, a former prefect, who felt that Hilary had been firm in his course and always level-headed,[22] and, essentially, that Hilary's forthrightness and obvious sanctity had done him no favours amongst the people of Rome.[23] Auxiliaris took their message. This is the last Honoratus says on the subject; the question of which Gallic city ought to be the metropolis of Viennensis is not mentioned, nor are Leo's and Valentinian's rulings on the subject that are so hostile to Hilary.

In Leo, *Ep.* 10,[24] on the other hand, we learn that Leo has judged an appeal to Rome against Hilary of Arles, declaring that the Bishop of Vienne, not of Arles, should be Metropolitan of Viennensis, and nullifying all of Hilary's acts as metropolitan. According to Leo, the dispute with Hilary arose because Hilary had deposed a certain Celidonius, Bishop of Besançon. Celidonius went to Rome as a court of appeal, and Hilary followed to defend his action. In contrast to Hilary's hagiographer, Leo recounts that in front of the pope Hilary seems to have lost control and behaved

---

[21] 'se ad officia, non ad causam venisse', *Vita Hilarii* 22.8.

[22] 'propositi tui tenax sis et semper aequalis', *Vita Hilarii* 22.37.

[23] Here emerges the trope of the venality of the Roman populace, well-known from Juvenal and Ammianus, amongst others.

[24] The Ballerini date it to July 445 since that is when Valentinian sent *Novella* XVII on the subject, discussed above. However, it is entirely likely that, as with the Manichaeans, Leo's letter could have been sent earlier, and that he only enlisted the emperor's help when things were not going his way.

in a way unbecoming of a bishop. As a result, Leo decided in favour of Celidonius, arguing that secular prestige such as Arles had was insufficient grounds for ecclesiastical power. The claim that Leo did this because the Bishop of Rome was suspicious of Gallic monasticism and feared that it (and therefore also Hilary, a former monk of Lérins) was Pelagian,[25] is largely groundless. The Roman hierarchy was no longer suspicious of asceticism at large,[26] and Leo, as observed already, was on close terms with Cassian, himself an ascetic who promoted precisely the sort of ascetic life practised by the monks of Lérins. From reading his letters on church discipline, it is clear that Leo was a firm believer in ecclesiastical order, and he believed that Hilary had upset this order. Therefore, he took action against him; asceticism has nothing to do with it.

A few years later, as attested by Hydatius, in 447, Leo would respond to a letter from Turribius of Astorga in Gallaecia, Spain, about Priscillianism.[27] This, *Ep.* 15, is the longest of Leo's so-called decretals and draws connections between Priscillianism and Manichaeism throughout, as Turribius also did in his surviving letter to Hydatius and Ceponius.[28] Priscillianism is, besides the end of the world,[29] one of Hydatius' great concerns, being Spain's first home-grown heresy.[30] However, it disappears from view in his *Chronicle* after the year 447, presumably because Priscillianist

---

[25] As argued by Wessel 2008, 71–84.

[26] Green 2008, 61–73. Armitage 2005, 145–51, introduces Leo's use of ascetic ideals in his preaching then lays the details bare in the following two chapters (153–83). One would expect nothing less from a man who requested theological tractates from one of Gaul's greatest ascetic writers.

[27] Hydatius, *Chron.* 128.

[28] Ed. Ballerini, PL 54.693–95. The only medieval manuscript source for this letter was lost in a fire in 1671; a copy of this letter from that manuscript exists in Toledo, Archivo y Biblioteca Capitular, 27–24 (saec. XVI), fols 3ʳ–4ʳ. See Abellán and Martín-Iglesias 2015 for the transmission history of this letter.

[29] See Hydatius, *Chron. Praef.* 6. According to Burgess 1993, 9–10, Hydatius believed that the world was going to end on 27 May 482 due to his acceptance of an apocryphal apocalypse, allegedly written by Christ himself to St Thomas. The *Chronicle* was an eyewitness account of the world's end.

[30] He details the Priscillianist controversy in *Chron.* 13, 16, 25, 30, and 127.

activity, if any, had quieted down.[31] More context is given in the undated, fragmentary letter of Turribius to Ceponius and Hydatius, appended by the Ballerini to Leo, *Ep.* 15. When Turribius finally gets around to his point, his main concern is the use of apocryphal scriptures by the presumed Priscillianists, especially a text called the Acts of Thomas which teaches to baptise not with water, but with oil—a Manichaean practice. Indeed, Turribius declares, Manichaeism is intimately tied to Priscillianism;[32] they also have apocryphal acts, such as those of Andrew and John, and another of Thomas. It is unclear to me whether the other apocryphal work, the *Memoria Apostolorum*, is Manichaean, Priscillianist, or both. Perhaps Turribius is intentionally vague so as to unite the two sects in one 'perversity'.

Later in 447, Leo penned *Ep.* 18 to Januarius of Aquileia about the ongoing Pelagian problem, one which he addressed in his first two surviving letters. This letter is substantially a copy of *Ep.* 2. Whether there were real Pelagians or rumours of Pelagians cannot be ascertained. But Leo believed they were still present in northern Italy, so he wrote to the Metropolitan of Venetia et Histria to deal with what he perceived as a danger to the spiritual well-being of the Christian populace there. Remnants of Pelagianism were soon to be a lesser issue to Leo, though, as the Christological controversy broke.

---

[31] Burgess 1993, 5, writes, 'the peaceful co-existence between orthodox and Priscillianist would seem to have been restored in Gallaecia after the witch-hunts stirred up by the zealous Thoribius'. However, to take the McCarthyist concept of the witch-hunt to its logical conclusion, I contend that perhaps there were few, if any, Priscillianists to be found by Turribius at all. This argument hinges upon their relative quiet in the surrounding decades as well as the fact that the gory details as ascribed to them in Leo, *Ep.* 15, are closer to some form of esoteric Gnosticism as caricatured by catholic Christians and not to the beliefs of Priscillian. In fact, according to Escribano 2005, Priscillian and his followers were not Gnostic at all, but more likely hard-line Nicenes who rejected the acceptance of lapsed Nicenes in Spanish sees and were ascetic rigorists. One very striking piece of evidence is that the earliest and most consistently repeated charges against the Priscillianists are not the Gnostic/dualist ideas of Leo, *Ep.* 15, but the charge of Sabellianism and the charge of Gnosticism on the grounds of rigorism.

[32] The connection between Priscillianism and Manichaeism is also asserted by Prosper, *Chron.* 1171, besides Leo, *Ep.* 15.

All theological powerhouses need controversies to test their mettle, and Leo's came in 448 when the Home Synod of Constantinople deposed the archimandrite Eutyches for heresy on 8 November. Eutyches promptly wrote to both Leo and Peter Chrysologus in Ravenna, protesting that he was as orthodox as any anti-Nestorian; Flavian of Constantinople's own letter arrived hot on its heels.[33] In *Ep.* 20, Leo had already been in contact with Eutyches whom he had praised for informing him of an alleged Nestorian revival in Constantinople in June of that year. Now, with the information given Leo by Flavian, the tables were turned on Eutyches. Rather than hunting heretics, he was now hunted *as* a heretic. Leo responded to Flavian in *Ep.* 23 on 18 February 449, expressing amazement that he'd not been informed about the Eutychian scandal sooner; he requested more information from Flavian to be able to make a sound judgement on the issue. He sent a similar letter, *Ep.* 24, to Emperor Theodosius II in Constantinople the same day. In March of that year, Flavian sent Leo his second letter explaining Eutyches' condemnation, saying that Eutyches' error, partly Apollinarian and partly Valentinian, was twofold: first, he believed in two natures before the incarnation, and in one afterwards; second, he believed that Christ's body from Mary did not possess exactly the same nature as ours. Furthermore, writes Flavian, Eutyches had lied in his letter to Leo, for there had been no written appeal to the Synod at Constantinople or to Leo. In *Ep.* 27 of 21 May 449, Leo praised Flavian for his treatment of Eutyches and promised a full response soon.[34]

The full response was the *Tome* of Leo, *Ep.* 28, sent 13 June 449. This lengthy letter is essentially a treatise on Christology, and it has been written upon extensively.[35] Although addressed to Flavian, Leo circulated it in the West and sent the *Tome* to the Second Council of Ephesus on 8 August 449, the goal being its acceptance by the council.[36] Despite Leo seeing no need to call a council to

[33] Eutyches to Leo: Leo, *Ep.* 21; Flavian to Leo: Leo, *Ep.* 22. Chrysologus' response to Eutyches: Leo, *Ep.* 25; he tells Eutyches to listen to the Bishop of Rome.

[34] However, this letter considered suspect by Silva-Tarouca 1931, 183.

[35] Useful analyses of the *Tome*'s Christology are Sellers 1953, 228–53; Grillmeier 1975, 526–39; Green 2008, 193–226.

[36] We know that this was Leo's expectation from *Epp.* 43 (26 August 449), and 44 (13 October 449).

deal with the matter of Eutyches,[37] Leo's *legati* would nevertheless go to represent papal interests,[38] and Leo commends them to various eastern persons, including Theodosius II, Theodosius' sister Pulcheria, Flavian of Constantinople, Juvenal of Jerusalem, and Julian of Cos. Leo also encourages his correspondents to hold fast to the truth against Eutychianism but to be lenient if Eutyches himself is penitent.[39] However, Second Ephesus did not go according to Leo's plans—Dioscorus never allowed the *Tome* to be read out, and Leo's *legati* were bulldozed by the Bishop of Alexandria's presidency of the council.[40] In fact, one of Leo's *legati* claimed to have been barred from entering the council at all.[41] Furthermore, Flavian of Constantinople was hauled away from the council by imperial soldiers and died of injuries incurred.[42] In response, Leo began a letter-writing campaign to the East, either encouraging his supporters or putting pressure on the imperial court, totalling nine such letters amongst the surviving corpus by Christmas 449. In February 450, at Leo's insistence, the western imperial family, Valentinian III, Galla Placidia, and Licinia Eudoxia all wrote letters to Theodosius; Galla Placidia also wrote a letter to Pulcheria.[43] Leo's personal letter-writing campaign also continued at this time, sending another six letters East before July trying to have a new council called to overturn Second Ephesus and establish the *Tome* and two-nature Christology as official orthodoxy. Theodosius remained unswayed by Leo's entreaties until his death—an untimely fall from his horse, 28 July 450.[44] He died without an heir.

[37] *Epp.* 36, 37.

[38] Leo commends his *legati* to parties in the East on 13 June, 449, in *Epp.* 29, 30, 31 (30 & 31 may be different redactions of the same letter to Pulcheria; see JK 425), 33, 34 as well as on 20 June in *Epp.* 36 and 37.

[39] See *Epp.* 31, 32, 33, 35, and 38.

[40] *Ep.* 44. All Hilarus could cry was, 'Contradicitur!', as recorded in the acts read out at Chalcedon, *Actio* I.964.

[41] See *Ep.* 46.

[42] See Chadwick 1955.

[43] Leo, *Epp.* 55–58. The western imperial court had relocated to Rome from Ravenna by this point, an important fact often overlooked. See Humphries 2012, 161–82.

[44] Theodorus Lector 353 and John Malalas XIV.71–72. See Burgess 1993, 48.

On 25 August, Marcian, formerly tribune and *domesticus,* was crowned Augustus in the East; he was fifty-one years old and gained his legitimacy from a marriage to Pulcheria Augusta, herself a consecrated virgin and sister to the late Theodosius II. Valentinian III was not informed; as sole and senior Augustus, Valentinian ought to have had the right to appoint his imperial colleague in light of the dynastic vacuum in the East.[45] Following the arguments of Burgess, it seems most likely that Marcian was the choice of the *patricius* Aspar and that Pulcheria was necessary for legitimisation.[46] The one-month interregnum was due to Aspar's negotiations with Pulcheria to ensure her compliance.[47] Nonetheless, despite the constitutional irregularities of Marcian's accession and Valentinian's lack of recognition of Marcian until March 452,[48] what would have mattered most to Leo was the presence of an Augustus and Augusta who supported his vision of orthodoxy. That said, he was careful not to address the new emperor with any official titles in his letters East until after Valentinian III recognised him. What mattered to Marcian was avoiding a civil war with Valentinian III; as senior Augustus, it was Valentinian's prerogative to appoint the new Augustus, and he had not even been consulted. Marcian himself was ready for war,[49] but we may also see the Council of Chalcedon as a kind of soft diplomacy, winning over Rome's bishop to gain influence in the West.[50] Whatever the politics of Marcian's position, Leo was glad for his support; to quote Prosper, he was 'ecclesiae pernecessarius'.[51] At the accession of Marcian, events were set in motion to have a new council called that would repeal the Second Council of Ephesus.

---

[45] See Burgess 1993, 49; he writes *contra* Holum 1982, 208–09; that Pulcheria chose Marcian has been stated as recently as Moorhead 2015, 27. I accept Burgess' view that Pulcheria did not rule alone for approximately one month after Theodosius' death.

[46] Burgess 1993, 62–65.

[47] Ibid., 65.

[48] Ibid., 63.

[49] For Marcian and Valentinian's relationship and the very real possibility of civil war of which Marcian was aware, see Jankowiak 2002.

[50] Bevan 2016, 319–23.

[51] Prosper, *Chron.* 1361. Marcian was also popular with Hydatius.

Leo's council was called to finally settle the disturbances that had rocked the church since the enthronement of Nestorius in Constantinople in 428, a task at which it did not succeed. Originally called to sit at Nicaea (a symbolic move taken again in 787), it met at Chalcedon, just across the Bosporus from Constantinople. Unlike at previous councils, such as Nicaea, which seems to have followed its own course, or the First Council of Ephesus, where two independent and mutually hostile councils met and then presented their acts to Theodosius II to ratify, the emperor took a firm hand in directing the activity of the Council of Chalcedon, with his own special lay appointees chairing many of the sessions, although formally run by Leo's delegation. Everything that had transpired at Second Ephesus was undone, even those deeds that many of those present at Chalcedon would have thought salutary, such as the deposition of Ibas of Edessa. Here, Leo's *Tome* (*Ep.* 28) was affirmed as the official teaching of the imperial church. After its reading, the bishops are recorded as hailing it with acclamations that the *Tome* is the faith of the fathers, the apostles, Peter, and Cyril, even saying, 'Leo and Cyril taught the same'.[52] Alongside the *Tome*, the dogmatic letters of Cyril of Alexandria were also acclaimed as orthodox. Cyril, who died in 444, had been the greatest and most esteemed theologian of the Greek East in the generation before Leo. He was a powerful polemicist but also sought to articulate his theology of Christ's unity with a rigorous logic rooted in the Christian scriptures. For Leo to be acclaimed alongside Cyril was a great victory for the western church; for once, the Bishop of Rome seemed to be leading the way.[53] After much debate over multiple sessions, including a secret one, the Chalcedonian delegates put forward a famous σύμβολον (*symbolon*) or *definitio* of the faith that quoted a version of the Nicene creed adopted at the Council of Constantinople in 381[54] and declared

[52] *Actio* II.25.

[53] This is in direct contrast to the interpretation provided by Moorhead 2015, 28, where Leo's acclamation alongside Cyril is seen as detrimental to the pope's rising star. In fact, Cyril and Leo are acclaimed complementarily, even when Cyril's letter to John of Antioch, *Laetentur Caeli*, is read out in *Actio* II.20.

[54] For the origins of this creed that seems to appear out of nowhere, see Behr 2004, Part 2, 372–79.

Christ to exist in two natures, 'without confusion (ἀσυγχύτως), without change (ἀτρέπτως), without division (ἀδιαιρέτως), without separation (ἀχωρίστως)'.[55] Even when its first draft was read out (this draft was later modified), glory redounded to Leo, albeit coupled with Cyril.[56] As far as the doctrinal acts of Chalcedon are concerned, the council was a great success for Leo. Cyril was held in the highest esteem by the Eastern bishops there assembled, and time and again, the Roman bishop's name was given glory alongside Cyril's. The false impression must not be made, however, that the bishops at Chalcedon were unqualified supporters of everything Leo said in the *Tome*; it has been persuasively argued on more than one occasion that their acceptance of Leo is always coupled with Cyril precisely because the bishops at the council were concerned more with preserving Cyril's memory than appeasing Leo. Leo could only be approved by them inasmuch as he agreed with Cyril.[57] The Council of Chalcedon was also a victory for Leo in that here we see Leo's enemies brought low in the depositions of Dioscorus of Alexandria and Eutyches, and his friends raised up, as in the restoration of Theodoret of Cyrrhus to his see.

However, Leo's letters demonstrate that, even setting aside eastern developments later in the century,[58] Chalcedon was not happily accepted by the opponents of Nestorius and the Eutychian position. The monks of Palestine rebelled and barred Bishop Juvenal of Jerusalem entry to the city, installing the anti-Chalcedonian Theodosius as his replacement until Juvenal regained the city and his bishopric in 453.[59] This crisis was so heated that

[55] *Actio* V.34. For Greek and Latin versions of the *definitio*, see Kinsig 2017, vol. 3, § 215, pp. 94–105. For the various other faith statements at Chalcedon, see the edition and translation in Kinzig 2017, vol. 4, § 570, pp. 417–33.

[56] *Actio* V.20.

[57] Most recently, McGuckin 2017, 561–62; however, McGuckin is mistaken that Cyril's controversial Third Letter to Nestorius was part of the wider Cyrillianism of the council—only one voice called for its approval, see *Actio* II.29. See also Price and Gaddis 2005, vol. 1, 65–75, and P. T. R. Gray 1979, 7–16. Whether the *definitio* of Chalcedon succeeded at being Cyrillian is a different question, but the argument of the above scholars is that the intent of the bishops assembled at the council was to be Cyrillian.

[58] Particularly the *Henotikon* of the Emperor Zeno in 482.

[59] Theodosius then fled to Sinai for refuge. We have Emperor Marcian's letter to Bishop Macarius and the monks of Sinai urging them to drive The-

Severianus of Scythopolis was murdered.[60] In response to the crisis and then its resolution, Leo wrote letters to the monks and to Juvenal,[61] to the former explaining his theological position under the assumption that the *Tome* had been mistranslated through malice in order to stir up trouble;[62] to the latter, congratulating him on his restoration but reminding him that it was his own tergiversations that caused his trouble, since Juvenal had been one of Dioscorus' supporters at Second Ephesus. He also wrote to his colleague and representative Julian of Cos to put pressure on the emperor to move against the Palestinian monks and to Eudocia, the widow of Theodosius II, then resident in Jerusalem, to urge the monks into orthodoxy.[63]

Palestine was not the only location of anti-Chalcedonian sentiment, for many Egyptians saw the deposition and exile of Dioscorus and the adoption of two-nature Christology as an abandonment of Cyril, whose first Council of Ephesus was enshrined as an ecumenical council by Chalcedon itself.[64] The replacement of Dioscorus as Bishop of Alexandria was Proterius, a Chalcedonian whose statement of faith Leo accepted.[65] In March of 454, Leo wrote to Proterius encouraging him to maintain vigilance against those who would lead the Egyptians into heresy;[66] at the same time he wrote to Marcian, praising the Emperor for approving of

---

odosius out (ACO 2.1.3, 490–91). He wandered about until he was caught in Antioch; imprisoned in Constantinople, he died in 457; see Ps-Zachariah Rhetor, *Chronicle* III.3–9. Evagrius Scholasticus, *Ecclesiastical History*, II.2.5, discusses the rebellion of the Palestinian monks.

[60] See Marcian's letter to Macarius again.

[61] To the monks in rebellion, *Ep.* 124; to Juvenal on his restoration, *Ep.* 139.

[62] For a discussion of the Greek of the *Tome* and how it Nestorianises Leo, see Prestige 1930.

[63] To Julian, *Epp.* 109, 118; to Eudocia, *Ep.* 123, around the same time as *Ep.* 124 to the Palestinian monks. Eudocia herself was a supporter of the anti-Chalcedonian movement at this time. In Theophanes, *Chronographia* AM 5945, Eudocia emerges as anti-Chalcedonian from the start; in John Rufus, *Plerophoriae* 10, 11 (PO 8.23–24, 27), she is a pious woman of anti-Chalcedonian bent.

[64] Dioscorus would die in exile in Gangra, northeast of Ancyra, in 454.

[65] Mentioned in *Ep.* 127 to Julian of Cos, 9 January 454.

[66] *Ep.* 129.

Proterius as archbishop.[67] The Egyptian situation was to heat up, and in 457, Proterius was killed by anti-Chalcedonian mob violence;[68] responding to this situation, Leo wrote *Ep.* 149 to Basilius of Antioch and *Ep.* 150 to Exitheus of Thessalonica, Juvenal of Jerusalem, Peter of Corinth, and Luke of Dyrrhachium.[69] In these letters, Leo laments Proterius' death and the seizure of power by 'Eutychians' in Alexandria. Leo's letters also help demonstrate the Bishop of Rome's awareness of earlier unrest in Egypt, for in *Ep.* 113 to Julian of Cos, mentioned above in relation to the Palestinian monks, he requests information on the source of discontent amongst the Egyptian monks as well. In *Ep.* 126 to Marcian from January 454, Leo rejoices in the restoration of the Palestinian monks to orthodoxy, but laments that the Egyptian monks are still in a state of rebellion. In 455 Leo inquires of Julian of Cos about the outcome of an embassy made to Egypt by a certain John,[70] and in 457 Leo sent eleven letters East discussing the anti-Chalcedonian problems in Egypt, including *Epp.* 149 and 150 mentioned above,[71] as well as two, *Epp.* 154 and 158, to Egyptian bishops in exile at Constantinople. By June of 460, Timothy Aelurus had been expelled from Egypt by Emperor Leo I, a feat upon which Pope Leo congratulates the Emperor.[72] However,

---

[67] *Ep.* 130.

[68] According to Victor of Tunnuna, *Chron.* 19, Timothy Aelurus organised Proterius' death. For the mob violence, see Evagrius, *HE* 2.8 and Theophanes Confessor, *Chron.* AM 5950. Anti-Chalcedonians say that Proterius was murdered by a soldier who felt his support for the emperor's policy was equivocal: Zachariah Rhetor, *HE* 4.2, and Michael the Syrian, *Chron.* (trans. J.-B. Chabot, II, 124–25). On the whole, mob violence is the more likely of the two scenarios, although each account is tailored to cast aspersions upon the opposing side. However, the tone of Leo, *Ep.* 145, leads one to suspect anti-Chalcedonian mob violence rather than pro-Chalcedonian assassination.

[69] These two letters are redactions of the same original sent East; see Silva-Tarouca 1926, 28.

[70] *Ep.* 141.

[71] *Epp.* 145–47, 149–50, 154–58.

[72] In *Ep.* 169, 17 June, 460. This and the final letters of the correspondence, *Epp.* 170–73, are found only in the *Collectio Avellana*; for discussion thereof, see below, 3.2.m. Leo's correspondence concerning Timothy Aelurus has been unjustly described as 'starkly reminiscent of modern colonial ideologies', in Davis 2004, 89—however, the political situation of a united Roman Empire, wherein a religious leader in one of its greatest cities engages in polemic

on the same day the pope unhappily complains to his episcopal colleague in Constantinople for allowing the anti-Chalcedonian to take refuge there.[73] Leo also wrote to Timothy Salophakiolus (that is, 'Wobble-cap'), the presbyters and deacons of Alexandria, as well as a selection of Egyptian bishops in August of that year, encouraging them to uphold the orthodox, Chalcedonian, faith.[74]

Chalcedon addressed more than Christology. Amongst its canonical enactments was the so-called 'Canon 28'. This ruling, debated in the sixteenth or seventeenth session of Chalcedon,[75] 'assigned privileges equal [to those of Senior Rome] to the most holy see of New Rome' with the right of consecrating the Metropolitans of the provinces of Pontica, Asiana, and Thracia.[76] Leo's representatives at Chalcedon responded strongly to this action, initially taken at an unofficial sitting of bishops at the council. The Roman delegates had been asked to take part in the unofficial gathering, but they declined on the grounds that their mandate from Leo did not cover the issue.[77] Thus they had a way out of approving it without having to necessarily express their disapproval of the actions of the council. Nonetheless, the Roman delegate Lucensius argued against the canon on the grounds that it ran contrary to the Nicene canons,[78] which were about the only conciliar canons accepted in Roman canon law at the time.[79] In terms of real ecclesiastical power, the canon gives Constantinople the same privileges as Rome in terms of local, metropolitan power. No doubt this is one reason why so many eastern bishops accepted it; 185 signatures are appended to it in the Greek *acta*. Another reason for its

---

against the religious leader of one of its other greatest cities is almost absolutely unlike a colonial situation. Davis's description of the battle over Chalcedon frequently turns to such imagery, and the thoroughly Romano-Greek leadership of the Egyptian church are referred to as 'Coptic' whenever they are in accord with the Cyrillian-Miaphysite tradition.

[73] *Ep.* 170.

[74] *Epp.* 171–73.

[75] It is number 16 in the Latin and 17 in the Greek *acta*.

[76] τά ἴσα πρεσβεῖα ἀπένειμαν τῶι τῆς νέας ῾Ρώμης ἁγιωτάτωι θρόνωι, ACO 2.1.3, 89.

[77] *Actio* XVI/XVII.6. Gk ACO 2.1.3, 88.

[78] *Actio* XVI/XVII.12. Gk ACO 2.1.3, 95.

[79] Cf. Nicene Canon 6, Latin in EOMIA 1.2.120–23.

widespread acceptance in the East is that it solved a number of jurisdictional problems in the relationship between Constantinople and Asia Minor. Nonetheless, however one tries to downplay the powers thus given, the phrasing runs τά ἴσα πρεσβεῖα, and could be interpreted as bringing Constantinople to the same level of honour as Rome.

Furthermore, by elevating Constantinople above Alexandria and Antioch, this action would reduce Rome's real power in theological disputes. Eastern bishops had often turned to the Church of Rome to aid them or to put pressure on their opponents, most recently in Celestine's support of Cyril against Nestorius. With Constantinople taking precedence over Antioch and Alexandria, the real power of Rome in eastern ecclesiastical polity would diminish; furthermore, with Constantinople wielding both official and actual power, Rome's importance would also decline since eastern appeals could more easily turn to the eastern imperial patriarch than the western. These reasons, succinctly laid out by Price and Gaddis, lay behind the Roman rejection of 'Canon 28',[80] alongside others mentioned in Meyendorff's discussion, that Leo's western vision of patriarchal power lay not in the imperial system but in apostolic descent: Constantinople had no apostolic descent, and therefore no legitimate claim to the same powers as Alexandria, Antioch, and Rome.[81] The two positions persist to this day in the differing ecclesiologies of the Eastern Orthodox and Roman Catholic Churches, the eastern position being the principle of accommodation—that is, ecclesiastical hierarchy accommodates secular political realities— and the apostolic principle.[82] It is difficult not to view 'Canon 28'

[80] Price and Gaddis, vol. 3, 70–72. See also the discussion in Meyendorff 1989, 156–58.

[81] Wessell 2015, 340, argues that the Constantinopolitans tried to appease Leo by demonstrating their place in Apostolic Succession but gives no reference to where this allegedly occurred. I believe she means apostolic descent, which is not the same, referring as it does to the actual foundation of the local church in question. And, while Leo argued for the necessity of apostolic foundation, I am keen to know in which documents Constantinople claimed such a foundation.

[82] For a recent discussion of the development of these two views in the ancient church with up-to-date bibliography, see Siecienski 2017, 152–71, with a discussion of Leo and Chalcedon, 171–78. An important contribution to the discussion of the 'rise' of Constantinople as an ecclesiastical power is

as an early stage on a long road to schism. The position not only of Rome as the Apostolic See descended from Peter, but of the other major sees, was thus imperilled by 'Canon 28' in the Roman view taken up by Leo. All of this, of course, cannot be explicated from the conciliar *acta*—some of it is only implied, other aspects require the sources of pre-Leonine papal history, while still more aspects come from Leo's letters themselves.

In his response to 'Canon 28', we encounter Leo the diplomat. In the spate of letters sent East in response to 'Canon 28', Leo never refers to the apostolic origin necessary, in his view, for a patri-archate,[83] but to Constantinople's overriding of Canon 6 of Nicaea and displacement of Antioch and Alexandria in rank of honour. The correspondence between Leo and the East immediately homes in on this topic, beginning with *Ep.* 98, from the Council to Leo, which encourages him to ratify Canon 28 since his *legati* opposed it. In *Ep.* 104, Leo responds to the Emperor Marcian's requests for him to ratify Canon 28 with his own grief against the ambition of Anatolius that put the canon forward. The letters continue in this vein; of the letters between Leo and the East in 451 after Chalcedon, only one of the eight does not touch on Anatolius and Canon 28. Throughout 453, Leo continued sending letters men-tioning Anatolius and this canon, and the East kept asking for his ratification of the actions at Chalcedon. However, Leo never gave his official sanction to Canon 28, although he was reconciled to Anatolius in *Ep.* 128, 9 March 454. Undoubtedly, this division

---

McLynn 2012 whose focus is the similar Canon 3 of Constantinople 381 which seems to have been unknown at Rome until the Council of Chalcedon, which is why, if we discount the alleged acts of a council of Damasus in 382, there was no firestorm in 381 but there was in 451, and it was never satisfactorily resolved. On the inauthenticity of the acts of 382, see L'Huillier 1996, 121, 290; Dvornik 1966, 44. Besides the ensuing silence on Canon 3 of Constanti-nople 381 for seventy years, my contention is that the acts are false because the situation they represent fits much more closely with the era of the *Decre-tum Gelasianum* of the late fifth or early sixth century, when Rome was no longer the seat of imperial power and Constantinople was the imperial city, than the late fourth, when Constantinople had only just recently become a permanent imperial residence, as well as the Acacian Schism wherein Gelasius scorns Constantinople as being merely a suffragan of Heracleia.

[83] A point of view that Leo's eastern correspondents would not have under-stood or shared, as argued by Meyendorff 1989, 153–54.

over the position of Constantinople weakened the imperial promotion of Chalcedon in the face of conservative Cyrillians in Egypt
and Palestine.

In the years immediately following Chalcedon, Leo's letters to
the East deal not only with the aftermath of Chalcedon but also
with the date of Easter for 455. This was a big enough issue that
not only did Leo write many letters to East and West on the question, but Prosper noted it in his *Chronicle*,[84] and Hilarus commissioned a new set of Easter tables from Victorius of Aquitaine, the
Cursus Paschalis from 457, as a result. It was the responsibility
of each metropolitan to inform his provincial bishops of the date
of Easter every year. Calculating Easter is not a straightforward
task, and the date of Easter is one of the longest-running sources of
dispute in Christianity, from the second-century 'Quartodecimans'
to this day, when western and eastern churches do not agree on
the date.[85] At some point in 443, Paschasinus of Lilybaeum, Sicily, consulted Leo, his Metropolitan, concerning the date of Easter
for the upcoming year.[86] Easter does not emerge in the existing
correspondence again until *Ep.* 88 (24 June 451). In this letter,
Leo sends Paschasinus, who was to preside over the Council of
Chalcedon in his stead, the *Tome* and asks about the date of Easter, 455. Paschasinus had a reputation for reckoning the date of
Easter well, and Leo says that he has found an irregularity in the
paschal table set out by Theophilus of Alexandria; according to
'ecclesiastical rule' (of Rome) Easter should be 17 April that year,
whereas Theophilus had 24 April.[87] Paschasinus' activities in Constantinople in 451 did not satisfactorily clear up the discrepancy
between the Roman practice and Theophilus. Thus, Leo penned a
letter to Marcian on 15 June 453, urging the emperor to look into
the date of Easter 455, and another to Julian of Cos, urging him
to encourage Marcian to look into this issue for him.[88] By 9 January 454, the situation was not resolved, and Leo wrote to Julian

---

[84] Prosper, *Chron.* 1376.

[85] For an introduction to how *computus* works, the dating of Easter, and
Paschal controversy, see Wallis 1999, xv–lxiii, and, more recently, Louth
2019, a review of Mosshammer 2017.

[86] Leo, *Ep.* 3.

[87] Theophilus' *Prologue* has received a new 2017 edition by Mosshammer.

[88] *Epp.* 121 and 122 respectively.

again in *Ep.* 127. *Ep.* 131, of 10 March 454, requested information from Julian concerning the emperor's response to these enquiries. Early in April of 454, Leo is sent a response from the official guardian of this concern, Proterius of Alexandria; Proterius tells Leo that the Roman tables are wrong—Easter 455 is to be 24 April.[89] Unfortunately for the Emperor Marcian, Leo was to send him *Ep.* 134 before receiving Proterius' answer. On 29 May 454, Leo corresponds with Marcian to thank the emperor for conferring with Proterius on the issue of dating Easter 455.[90] His capitulation is signalled in *Ep.* 138 of that July, wherein Leo tells all the bishops of Spain and Gaul that Easter 455 is to be 24 April, the date established by Theophilus and confirmed by Proterius. On 13 March 455, Leo makes sure there are no loose ends by informing Marcian that the western bishops had received the date set forth.[91] Leo had compared the Roman reckoning with that of Alexandria and found that there was a discrepancy. He wrote repeatedly to Marcian and the eastern bishops arguing that there was an error in the Alexandrian Easter tables and that the Roman date should be preferred. Here was a battle he lost. In the end, he wrote to the bishops of the west telling them that, for the sake of unity, they would celebrate Easter on the same day as the eastern church, even though they were wrong.

Outside of his letters, the early 450s see two of the most famous events from Leo's episcopate, at least as far as popular imagination is concerned: his meetings with Attila the Hun in 452 and with the Vandal King Geiseric in 455. In 451, one of the reasons for Leo to stay home in Rome and not attend the council was Attila's invasion of Italy.[92] In 452, after laying waste to much of northern Italy, Attila was met by a delegation from the emperor, the senate, and the people of Rome, consisting of Avi-

---

[89] Leo, *Ep.* 133.

[90] *Ep.* 137.

[91] *Ep.* 142.

[92] One may wonder if a wise Roman bishop also remembered the fate of Liberius, who found himself subscribing to a form of Arianism after abuse and torture. It is easier to ratify a council you agree with that you never attended than to abrogate one you were at; we see the difficulties of attendant popes in the case of Vigilius at the Second Council of Constantinople in 553.

enus, a former consul;[93] Trygetius, a former prefect; and 'the most blessed Pope Leo'.[94] According to Prosper, Attila was so delighted by the presence of the chief priest that he ceased from war and returned back across the Danube.[95] According to Jordanes, who uses the now-fragmentary history of Priscus as his source, Attila was wavering at this point in his journey because his advisers had reminded him that Alaric had died shortly after sacking Rome; therefore sacking Rome was a deed of ill fortune. When Attila met Leo (the only member of the delegation Jordanes names) at the Mincius, his mind was made up.[96] Gold probably changed hands, or was at least promised.[97] Modern scholars usually accept Italian famine and the fatigue of long campaigning as the reasons for Attila's departure in 452.[98] Hydatius, in fact, fails to mention Leo's embassy and attributes their departure from Italy to famine, disease, and a punitive expedition led by Aëtius and sent by Marcian.[99] Moreover, in a letter to Pope Symmachus (pope, 498–514), reference is made to Leo having been involved in the ransom of Christian, pagan, and Jewish captives from the Huns.[100] If this

[93] Considered one of the two most distinguished men in Rome by Sidonius, *Ep.* 1.9.

[94] Prosper, *Chron.* 1367, *l.* 13. However, Prosper makes Leo the subject of the sentence; he himself took up the business with ('cum') the others.

[95] Prosper, *Chron.* 1367.

[96] Jordanes, *Getica* 222–23.

[97] Priscus, *frag.* 17, as cited by Neil 2009, 9, suggests that there may have been some sort of treaty made with Attila, one possibly involving gold, as had been made with Attila in the past. However, this is simply the Latin paraphrase of Jordanes above and makes no mention of such things. Nevertheless, it is not unlikely that gold changed hands, given how much the Romans had been paying Attila earlier in his career to keep him from harassing; see Kelly 2015, 201–02, for these payments, as well as arguments as to why they were possibly a better investment than costly wars, 205–06.

[98] e.g. Jalland 1941, 413 n. 6; Wessell 2008, 44–45; Kelly 2015, 202.

[99] Hydatius, *Chron.* 146.

[100] Pope Symmachus, *Ep.* 6, PL 62.59D–60A: 'Si enim qui praecessit beatitudinem tuam inter sanctos constitutus Leo archiepiscopus ad Attilam tunc erronem barbarum per se currere non duxit indignum, ut captivitatem corrigeret corporalem, nec tantum Christianorum, sed et Iudaeorum (ut credibile est) atque paganorum: quanto magis ...' The inclusion of pagans and Jews amongst the captives ransomed by Leo is not so much 'unusual' to the writers (Wessell 2008, 46 n. 165) as it is being used to rhetorical effect. If Leo had set free not only Christians but pagans and Jews as well, *how much more*

ransom occurred—perhaps it was an extrapolation of Leo's role in 452 on the part of Symmachus' eastern correspondents, we do not know—it would have been part of the embassy. The involvement of bishops in the ransom of captives and slaves is not unusual; they are a logical choice, for they are meant to be representatives of the whole people, having been chosen by the people, clergy, local bishops, and metropolitan bishop.[101]

In 454, out of suspicion that Aëtius was a traitor and sought the imperial honours for himself, Valentinian III killed the patrician with his own hand.[102] The suspicious emperor was not to live long, however. On 16 March, 455, the friends and comrades (Prosper: 'amicos armigerosque eius'; Hydatius: 'duos barbaros Aetii familiares') of Aëtius slew Valentinian on the Campus Martius.[103] Petronius Maximus was now raised to the imperial purple.[104] According to Prosper, the people fled soon after when a messenger from Geiseric, the Vandal King of Africa, arrived in the city. On 31 May, the city was invaded by the Vandals, and Petronius was slain as he attempted a secret withdrawal from Rome, according to Prosper; Hydatius says that a mob assassinated him.[105] Geiseric, reports Prosper, intended to leave the entire city bare, when Leo stood in his way in front of the city gates and extracted promises from the barbarian king to refrain from fire and slaughter. Nevertheless, the Vandals pillaged the city for fourteen days,[106] acquiring

---

ought Symmachus to be involved in setting Christians free from the heresies of Eutyches and Nestorius.

[101] In several places, e.g. *Ep*. 167.1.

[102] Prosper, *Chron*. 1373, 'Aetius imperatoris manu et circumstantium gladiis intra palatii penetralia crudeliter confectus est'. Hydatius, *Chron*. 152, 'Aetius ... accitus intra palatium manu ipsius Valentiniani imperatoris occiditur'.

[103] Hydatius, *Chron*. 154, for the assassination of Valentinian. Procopius, *Wars* 3.4.36, mistakenly turns Petronius into the assassin.

[104] See Prosper, *Chron*. 1375, for the events of March and May-June 455.

[105] Hydatius, *Chron*. 162. See also Procopius, *Wars* 3.5.2.

[106] Besides the list in the *Liber Pontificalis*, discussed below, Procopius, *Wars* 3.5.3–7, lists the plunder as including all the valuables from the imperial residence and the contents of the Temple of Jupiter Capitolinus, including half of its roof; at *Wars* 4.9.5, we learn that amongst this palatial plunder were the treasures from Jerusalem brought back to Rome by Titus. Cassiodorus, *Chron*. 1263, says that Rome was emptied by Geiseric.

as part of their booty Valentinian's widow and daughter. Leo had once again stood in the gap between the people of Rome and a barbarian king, but his embassy was less effective this time, given that the invaders were literally at the gate of the city; Prosper lessens the blow by saying, 'cum omnia potestati ipsius essent tradita'—since everything had been handed over to Geiseric's power. It was not a failure on Leo's part; Rome was already in Geiseric's hands.

From the *Liber Pontificalis* we learn that:

> After the Vandal disaster [Leo] replaced all the consecrated silver services throughout all the *tituli*, by melting down 6 water-jars, two at the Constantinian basilica, two at the basilica of St Peter, two at St Paul's, which the emperor Constantine had presented, each weighing 100 pounds; from these he replaced all the consecrated vessels.[107]

The Vandal sack of Rome provided Leo with an opportunity to exercise papal largesse by attending to the maintenance of church buildings and church plate (a preoccupation of the *Liber Pontificalis*).[108] In this way, the aftermath of the Vandals allowed Leo was able to exercise a visible, temporal function of his role as spiritual head of the Roman community.

More significant for Leo's correspondence and Mediterranean geo-ecclesiology was the death of Marcian and accession of Leo I in the East in 457. Leo wasted no time in congratulating the emperor, although said letter does not survive. It is alluded to in his first surviving letter from 457, *Ep.* 145, in which he entreats the new emperor to uphold the Council of Chalcedon and put down the unrest in Alexandria. Emperor Leo's approach to the question was to solicit the opinions of the bishops on the matter of the teaching of Chalcedon. These survive in the *Codex Encyclius*, translated into Latin in the sixth century at the behest of Cas-

---

[107] *Liber Pontificalis* 47.6, trans. Davis.

[108] In the same chapter, it says that Leo renewed St Peter's and the apse-vault as well as St Paul's 'after the divine fire'; the mosaic decoration on the triumphal arch at San Paolo fuori le Mura was completed during Leo's episcopate and is presumably what was meant. To the 'Constantinian basilica' (St John's Lateran, presumably), he added an apse-vault, besides founding a church for St Cornelius near San Callisto on the Via Appia.

siodorus.[109] The *Codex* reveals to us that all of the bishops queried accept the system of the imperial church with the emperor taking an active role in protecting and promoting orthodoxy, calling councils, and stamping out heresy. Some bishops saw Chalcedon simply as a means of protecting the Council of Nicaea; others support it not simply as protecting Nicaea but as clarifying new points arising since then and producing its own important contribution; two only, Timothy Aelurus and Amphilochius of Side, rejected the council entirely. The system of the imperial church at this moment in 457 seemed, on the surface, to have succeeded at enshrining the Council of Chalcedon. However, there were clergy, monks, and laity, especially in Syria, Palestine, and Egypt, who rejected the council, besides the aforementioned Timothy of Alexandria who enjoyed this popular support. Nevertheless, with the *Codex Encyclius* in hand and Leo I on the throne, Pope Leo's own teaching enjoyed support. As part of his campaign to maintain this state of affairs, Leo wrote Emperor Leo in 458 what is called his 'second' *Tome*, *Ep.* 165, which outlines in greater detail and specificity his Christology. It closes with a florilegium of patristic excerpts to support the two-nature Christology, showing us both in its terminology and its content that Leo had learned from the failure of the *Tome* to garner support, changing his tone and his method for his audience.

Another recurring concern of the latter half of Leo's episcopate was the status of the episcopate of Arles. After the dispute with Hilary in 445, relations were calm for a while; at this time Leo sent *Epp.* 40 and 41 (22 August 449) to Gallic Bishops and Ravennius of Arles respectively in order to congratulate them on Ravennius' election to the episcopacy of Arles. In *Ep.* 42 (26 August 449), Leo also wrote to Ravennius about a certain Petronianus, who was causing mischief. However, the bishops of the province of Viennensis were evidently dissatisfied with the outcome of Leo's confrontation with Hilary back in 445. In spring of 450, the fellow-bishops of Arles' metropolis wrote *Ep.* 65 to Leo expressing their discontent with the turn of events and a desire to see Arles restored to metropolitan status. They argued that from its secular prestige as a major political centre in Gaul and from its ancient

---

[109] Ed. ACO 2.5, 9–98. The *Codex Encyclius* is analysed at length in Grillmeier 1987, 195–230.

foundation by St Trophimus, whom they believed was a disciple of St Peter, Arles was deserving of the old rights it had lost in Leo's dispute with Hilary. In response, Leo wrote *Ep.* 66 relating that the issue had already been decided. He also wrote *Ep.* 67 on the same day (5 May 450); this letter mentions the presence of Gallic legates whom Leo had detained in Rome so that they could bring information to all the bishops of Gaul. It does not in any clear way mention their mission, which was undoubtedly the same as *Ep.* 65, although Leo has sent them with an oral message giving Ravennius instructions. Thus, Leo has put the Bishop of Arles in his place without leaving a record of the action. Undoubtedly this was to help Ravennius save face, thus maintaining visibly good relations between Rome and Arles, although they would have been undoubtedly strained at this point in time. Leo corresponds with Arles again around the time his concern over the date of Easter 455 emerges, this time informing Ravennius of the date of Easter 452 to ensure there is no diversity in celebrating the feast.[110]

Leo's letters are a treasure-trove of information. As the above description of his pontificate has demonstrated, they give us insight into his thought on Christology, canon law, the episcopate, and many other issues facing the Church in the fifth century. They set out for us the major lines of the Eutychian crisis and the aftermath of Chalcedon. They show us Leo's role in establishing episcopal boundaries in southern Gaul. We can watch the playing-out of the controversy of the date of Easter 455. We see the ongoing actions against Manichaeans, Pelagians, and Priscillianists in the western church at that time. We see the effect of invasions, whether by Attila and the Huns or by Visigoths, upon the churches and communities of the western Empire. Without Leo's letters, not only would our knowledge of this pope be inestimably diminished, so would our knowledge of the theological, ecclesiastical, and secular issues affecting the Roman Empire, both East and West, during the twenty-one years of his pontificate.

Leo's Letters and Canon Law

Amongst these various interactions that can be tied to movements or persons, interactions that flesh the history of the fifth century,

---

[110] *Ep.* 96.

Leo's biography, and the story of his episcopate, is a large body of letters dealing with disciplinary and pastoral matters. Regardless of where we stand on the question of whether it is appropriate to designate some of Leo's letters as *epistulae decretales* as a separate genre from the rest, it is the case that Leo dealt with a lot of business that would come under the umbrella of canon law. His letters are recurring sources for medieval canon law. Even if we acknowledge that 'canon law' in the High Medieval sense of Gratian did not exist,[111] church regulations and texts called canons did. Leo's letters are a contribution to the growing body of disciplinary texts and were copied in their earliest manuscripts alongside other disciplinary texts, such as conciliar canons, other papal letters, and disciplinary letters from other bishops. Given this importance of Leo's letters for the history of canon law and its development, we must linger a moment with these letters and their legacy in the canons of the church. In so doing, we will be on the way to coming to grips with the story told in the manuscripts.

Besides the matters of church discipline discussed in the account above, in several letters, Leo's letters reflect the day-to-day business of a metropolitan bishop as well as the unrest of his times. On more than one occasion, he deals with the displacement of persons due to the instability of the western Roman Empire. For example, in *Ep.* 159, he deals with what to do in cases where men captured by barbarians return to Roman territory to find that their wives have remarried. Leo rules in favour of the first marriage, repeating the judgement of Innocent I in the case of Ursa, who returned to discover that her husband had remarried. The gender of the displaced person is not the concern; the sacrament of marriage is. Here, unlike Innocent, Leo is able to draw an analogy from Roman law, even as he argues against it. Under the relevant law, *ius postliminii*, a man returning from captivity regained all his property rights, but his marriage could only be regained under mutual consent. Leo argues to extend the rights to include marriage as well, although the foundation of his argument is that

---

[111] See de Jong 2005, 117. Of course, a body of documents of church regulation, the canons, exists, ready to be manipulated by unscrupulous kings (see Gregory of Tours, *Historiae* 5.18) and to be defined by Isidore of Seville, *Etymologiae* VI.XVI.1–2.

marriage is a *sacramentum*.[112] Elsewhere, in *Ep.* 167, Leo considers what to do with those who have returned from captivity and who do not recall whether they have been baptised, or those who ate at pagan feasts while in exile but did not participate in sacrifices, and what to do with persons who have migrated from Africa but do not know who baptised them. All of these cases laid important foundations for canon law and sacramental practice, whether it is the binding nature of marriage as a sacrament (and, indeed, the definition of *matrimonium* as *sacramentum* in the first place), the enduring efficacy of baptism, the possibility of Christians polluting themselves at pagan gatherings, and the validity of non-catholic baptisms so long as they are Trinitarian. What they also show us is the displacement of people in the fifth century. People had been carried into exile and slavery by those invading Roman territory—yet now they were making their way home. Others had moved from one location to another, due no doubt to invasion and conquest, such as the Vandal conquest of Africa 429–39. Thus, not only are Leo's letters sources and authorities for the canons of the western church in centuries to come, they stand as sources today for the final Roman generation and the first post-Roman generation as they lived in a new world with shifting political horizons and shifting frontiers.

Other regulatory concerns emerge throughout the corpus. In 452 Leo wrote a letter, in response to Theodore of Fréjus who had asked him about penitence. In *Ep.* 12, we learn about Leo's ideal functioning of the ecclesiastical *cursus honorum*. Leo's last decretal was Ep. 168, another letter to bishops of Suburbicarian Italy concerning the canonical times for baptism, which Leo considers as only Easter and Pentecost. This issue was one he had earlier addressed in a letter to the bishops of Sicily, *Ep.* 16, who had a practice at variance to that of Rome, in that they baptised at the Epiphany and saints' days. In the body of so-called 'dogmatic' letters, we also gain a vision of Leo's understanding of the ranking of episcopates as he argued against 'Canon 28' of Chalcedon and the rise of Constantinople. These arguments are themselves fundamental to or at least an early indication of the western view

---

[112] For a discussion of Leo, *Ep.* 167, and its relation to Roman law see Sessa 2012, 153–54. Justinian would change Roman law to reflect ecclesiastical canons on this point.

that would hold throughout the Middle Ages. This view would be part of the estrangement that would lead to the Great Schism between Rome and Constantinople in 1054.[113] It was also adopted or at least shared with other western sees. Thus, for example, Arles would continue to argue for its own position as metropolitan based upon its foundation, according to tradition, by St Trophimus, a disciple of the apostles. Likewise, Paris would grow its own apostolic connection through the identification of the martyr Dionysius with Dionysius the Areopagite of Acts and the famous Dionysian mystical corpus.

From our end of history, however, it is Leo's clear articulation of the apostolic succession and Petrine primacy, related to the dispute with Constantinople, that may be his greatest contribution to the history of canon law. The biblical heart of Leo's position, Matthew 16, was already traditional amongst bishops of Rome in his day, having been previously deployed by Damasus and Siricius. From Matthew 16, Leo moves on to a discussion in terms of inheritance. Leo is the heir to St Peter, in legal terminology and concepts from Roman law. Legally speaking, Leo holds all the rights and responsibilities that Peter held. Leo also speaks at times in hierarchical terms, admittedly also related in some sense to inheritance, that the power of Christ flows into Peter, thence to the other apostles, thence to their successors, the bishops, and so forth. Thus, the authority to bind and to loose flows from Christ to Peter's successors on down through the hierarchy. Leo's vision of the apostolic succession and the resulting authority of the Roman bishop is clear and clearly articulated. The Roman episcopate thus gained theological foundations for its own growing sphere of influence beyond Suburbicarian Italy. We must quickly be aware, however, that simply articulating Petrine primacy does not make Roman episcopal authority into a medieval papacy. Two requirements must be fulfilled in the following centuries. First, the rest of the western bishops and secular rulers must accept the Roman bishop's claims to supremacy. This process was already underway in Leo's day, seen in responses to his letters about doctrine as well as in his dealings with Arles, not to mention the letters such as

---

[113] The rift has many sources beyond their understanding of canon law and the 'patriarchates'. For a helpful discussion, see Louth 2007, 305–18.

that of Turribius of Astorga, letters that treat Leo as an authority and ask him questions that need not truly be asked. Second, the bishops themselves must gain and attempt to use effective power beyond Suburbicarian Italy. Although Leo's active letter-writing throughout the Mediterranean would make this aspect seem to have developed already, the subsequent history of the Roman episcopate and its weakness in Spain and Gaul, and then its domination in Rome in the ninth and tenth centuries, demonstrates that we must wait until the eleventh century for both developments to quicken and the 'papacy' as we understand it to emerge, especially with Leo IX and Gregory VII, despite the strengths of such earlier figures as Gregory I, Zacharias I, and Hadrian I. Nonetheless, these later developments of the Middle Ages are built upon the foundations laid by Leo in the later Roman Empire. Canon law is not the only realm where Leo's letters had a significant impact.

1.2 Leo's Letters and the History of Theology

From the above, it cannot be denied that Leo is a major figure in the history of canon law. Yet it is not his articulation of ecclesiastical canons, or of the Petrine primacy, or even his activities and ideas that helped maintain or recreate a universal vision of *Roma*,[114] that made those who come after call him *Magnus*. As the collection of these references made by Turner reveals, Leo is called Leo Magnus not because he first articulated Petrine primacy in a clear manner, not because he wrote so many letters, not because he produced *decreta* on certain subjects, but because of his theology. Indeed, in Quasten's *Patrology*, while all of Leo's predecessors together take ten pages, he alone takes twenty-three.[115]

In 444, the year of Leo's anti-Manichaean actions, Cyril of Alexandria died. Despite the modern distaste for his personality, Cyril should be recognised as a theological powerhouse in the first half of the fifth century, certainly one of the most influential and highly-regarded theologians of the eastern Church. Cyril had been involved in the dispute with Nestorius from the moment Nestorius said, '*Christotokos*'—for, as Henry Chadwick has made clear, Cyril's commitment to *mia physis* Christology and opposition to any

---

[114] As analysed by Wessel 2008.
[115] Quasten 1986, 589–612.

division in Christ's single *prosopon/hypostasis* predates the Nestorian Controversy.[116] His version of the Council of Ephesus, 431,
won imperial favour. He penned the Formulary of Reunion, a document of theological compromise known in Latin by its opening
words: *Laetentur caeli*, 'Let the heavens rejoice' (*Ep.* 39);[117] this was
a letter to John of Antioch that sought to heal the breach between
'Antiochene' bishops from Oriens and 'Alexandrian' bishops from
Egypt (and their western supporters, such as Pope Celestine I)
that resulted from Ephesus. The 'Antiochene' position was keen
to see the dual aspect of Christ's Incarnation—he was fully man
and fully God; they used language that Cyril found very dangerous, characterised in Latin by the term *assumptus homo* which,
he observes in *Quod Unus Sit Christus*, makes it seem that there
was a man Jesus separate from the Incarnate Word. At its worst,
or at least most careless, this version of Christology accidentally
made Christ into two persons, πρόσωπα/ὑποστάσεις, as Nestorius
seemed to at times, or seemed to deny the full divinity of Christ
from the point of conception, as Nestorius did in calling Mary *Christotokos* instead of *Theotokos*. The 'Alexandrian' position stressed
above all else the unity; Cyril had no room for attributing certain
acts or sayings of Christ to one nature or the other. For him, it
was all one Christ, fully man, fully God. The difficulty with Cyril
is that there is the uncompromising Cyril, favoured in the years
to come by Miaphysites, and there is the Cyril of *Laetentur Caeli*
who compromised with John of Antioch to produce a Christology
hopefully suitable to both sides. This latter Cyril is undoubtedly
the Cyril of Leo.[118]

Leo's Christology is most famously articulated in *Ep.* 28, the
Tome, whose historical course has been discussed above. In this letter, after giving a preamble about Eutyches' theological ineptitude
and unworthiness as an archimandrite, Leo presents a two-nature

---

[116] Chadwick 1951.

[117] Ed. E. Schwartz, ACO 1.1.4, 15–20.

[118] For further discussion of Cyril as christologian and his role in the
Nestorian Controversy, I recommend Russell 2000, especially 31–58, which
is a good introduction with selected writings. See also Wessell 2000 and
McGuckin 1994, who also gives a good analysis of Cyril in this period with
selected translations of pertinent documents in the latter portion of the book,
244–378.

Christology, drawing upon several of his earlier homilies and using all of his rhetorical flourish to lay out his own vision of how scripture teaches that Christ exists *in* two natures, fully human and fully divine, evident in how some of his actions are clearly divine, others clearly human.[119] One of the main purposes of the *Tome* is to attempt to steer between the two perceived extremes—Eutychianism and Nestorianism. To Leo, Eutyches has denied the full manhood of Christ, Nestorius the divinity. In Leonine Christology, Christ is still fully man and still fully God. The *Tome* has had its critics, some immediate, such as Dioscorus, and others right up to this day;[120] what these critics often fail to see is what the *Tome* means. It does not mean that there are two acting persons inside Jesus; that would be Nestorianism. Although Severus of Antioch would cast aside the statement in the early 500s,[121] Leo does declare, 'in domino Iesu Christo dei et hominis una persona sit'. Severus could doubt the logic of that in the face of 'agit enim utraque forma ...', but he could not doubt the honesty of Leo's belief. He simply felt that Leo was an honest Nestorian heretic. Nonetheless, when we consider the fact that the *Tome* does, indeed, attribute, or seem to attribute, certain actions of Christ to his humanity and others to his divinity, it comes as no surprise that conservative Cyrillians, inspired by texts such as *Quod unus sit Christus*, saw Leo as bringing back the teaching of Nestorius. Nevertheless, elsewhere in his corpus, Cyril does, in fact, say that one can see the different actions of Christ as evidence of the divinity on the one hand and the humanity on the other, but it is always very carefully balanced and accompanied by a strong sense on the unity of person.[122] We see, then, that the legacy of Cyril was itself contested in the years around and following Chalcedon.

---

[119] See especially the passages 'agit enim utraque forma ... non relinquit' and 'esurire sitire lassescere atque dormire euidenter humanum est ... diuinum est'. (ACO 2.2.1, 28.12–16, 29.1–5).

[120] For example, Jenson 2002, 19, states that the *Tome* is either Nestorian or worse.

[121] For example, *Ad Nephalium, Or.* II, pp. 14–15; trans. Allen and Hayward 2004, 62.

[122] For example, the First Letter to Succensus, ch. 6; ed. Wickham 1983, 75.

The prime difficulty regarding the thought of Leo and Cyril lies in the fact that the semantic ranges of *natura* and φύσις do not perfectly overlap.[123] Etymologically, both have to do with growth, with being born, but *natura* could, to take C. S. Lewis's suggestion, be better construed by the English *kind*—to ask what the *natura* of a hill is, is to ask what *kind* of hill it is. A *natura* does not, therefore, always mean a single, instantiated being in and of itself. It is not an ἀλήθεια, as the Emperor Marcian defines φύσις.[124] Φύσις, however, is the reality of something as we engage with it. Therefore, one can immediately see how in Latin, Christ can have two *naturae* but in Greek, it may very well sound nonsensical to say that he had two φύσεις, for φύσις, or ἀλήθεια, treads closer to ὑπόστασις and πρόςωπον than *natura* does to *persona*. Indeed, in the sixth century, John Philoponos, the Miaphysite head of the Neo-Platonist School of Alexandria, would define a monster as something that possesses more than one φύσις.[125] While Leo may not have had all the linguistic tools and categories at his disposal to realise this, he was certainly aware that his language of two *naturae* was causing problems in the East, and he shifted his vocabulary as a result.[126]

In the aftermath of Chalcedon, Leo wrote *Ep.* 124 to the rebellious monks of Palestine in 453.[127] Here, Leo's Christologi-

[123] This was first drawn to my attention by Lewis 1960, 24–42, and has recently been highlighted in Torrance 2008, 202–03. A full study of *natura* and φύσις would be fruitful not only in theology but in the relationship between Greek and Latin philosophy as well.

[124] Marcian, of course, was stripping φύσις of its philosophical content to calm the monks of Palestine, as discussed by Grillmeier 1987, 101–02. The quotation is from his letter to the archimandrites of Jerusalem, "Εντυχὸν τὸ ἡμέτερον' / 'Agnoscens nostra maiestas', ACO 2.1.3, 126 (2.1, 486), 14.

[125] *In Phys.* 201,10–202,12; trans. Sorabji 2004, 57–58.

[126] On Leo's vocabulary shifts, see Barclift 1997. As recently as Vincent of Lérins, *Commonitorium* 13, Latin Christological vocabulary was using *substantia* as the equivalent of ὑπόστασις. To take a mundane example of vocabulary and semantic shifts between language, *chaise* in French tends to unproblematically translated as *chair* in English, yet *chaise* includes both *chair* and *stool* in its semantic range, as in the discussion of Saussure in Culler 2011, 59. A signifier and its signified even in the concrete can easily vary between languages; it is no surprise that they vary in the context of the abstract.

[127] For what follows, see the very good discussion of *Ep.* 124 in Green 2008, 231–47.

cal vocabulary shifts and changes. The changes in vocabulary demonstrate to us that Leo is aware of his audience and aware of difficulties besetting the *Tome* in Greek translation. This letter is more careful in its explication of the two natures, avoiding such terminology altogether, in fact, and arguing more clearly for the unity of the person of Christ. Later, he would re-use much of this letter in *Ep.* 165 to Emperor Leo I, the so-called 'second' *Tome*. In all of these letters, as well as in his Nativity sermons, Leo explicates a traditional, western Christology. Nothing new is found in Leo; this is the Christology of Hilarius of Poitiers and Augustine of Hippo.[128] If there is genius here, it is the genius of synthesis and of oratory. He was thus easily embraced by succeeding generations in the West as a father, and as a touchstone of orthodoxy. The Council of Chalcedon, by enshrining Leo's Christology as the official orthodoxy of the imperial church, likewise became a touchstone of orthodoxy in the West.

An example of Leo's legacy as a touchstone of orthodoxy outside the Chalcedonian debate can be found in the works of Fulgentius of Ruspe, who wrote in the first third of the sixth century. In *Ep.* 14 to Ferrandus, Fulgentius addresses several questions pertinent to the doctrine of the Trinity and Christology. In the discussion of Christology, Fulgentius quotes Leo's *Tome* four times in chapter 18.[129] Most of the rest of the time, Fulgentius' sources are Augustine, Ambrose, and Cyprian. Here, though, in setting out what he viewed as the catholic faith, Fulgentius has recourse to Leo, *Ep.* 28. Elsewhere, Fulgentius demonstrates that he has drunk deeply from the well of Chalcedon. When he discusses Christology in *Ep.* 8.13–14, while his wording and examples are not precisely the same as Leo's in the *Tome*, his balancing of

---

[128] It is unjust to call Leo's *Tome* a pastiche of Hilarius and Augustine, as does McGuckin 2017, n. 40, p. 1326. For a discussion of one of the ways in which Leo engages with Hilarius, see Armitage 2005, 89–90.

[129] The passages quoted are: 'Salua igitur proprietate utriusque naturae ... et mori non posset ex altero' (Fulgentius, *Ep.* 18, ll. 686–97; Leo, *Ep.* 28, ed. Silva-Tarouca, § § 54–64); 'Assumpta est de matre ... consumitur dignitate' (Fulgentius, *Ep.* 18, ll. 709–15; Leo, Ep. 28, ed. Silva-Tarouca, § § 90–93); 'Quem itaque sicut ... obsequia' (Fulgentius, *Ep.* 18, ll. 717–23; Leo, Ep. 28, ed. Silva-Tarouca, § § 109–11); and 'Quamuis enim in Domino Iesu ... cum Patre diuinitas' (Fulgentius, *Ep.* 18, ll. 724–28; Leo, *Ep.* 28, ed. Silva-Tarouca, § § 122–25).

divine and human is a rhetorical parallel. Moreover, in chapter 26 of that same letter he explicitly rejects Nestorius and Eutyches. Even those, then, who were not involved in the controversies of the *Henotikon* or Three Chapters, as about to be discussed, were reading Leo and absorbing him. His letters were in circulation even beyond imperial control in Vandal Africa. Nonetheless, the main story of Leo's letters is found within the imperial church, so this study now returns to Emperor Leo I.

After soliciting the opinion of the bishops in the *Codex encyclius*, Emperor Leo I supported the Council of Chalcedon until his death in 474. This imperial support, however, does not mean that Chalcedon and Leo had no critics. Timothy Aelurus continued to oppose the council from exile, first in Gangra and then Cherson, after his deposition from the see of Alexandria in 459, writing letters and the treatise *Against Chalcedon* in support of the anti-Chalcedonian cause.[130] Egypt also had radically conservative Cyrillians who felt that Aelurus was too soft; this group is called the *akephaloi* (ἀκέφαλοι)—the headless. Emperor Leo's successor was his young grandson, Leo II, who died in November 474. Leo II's father, Zeno, ascended the throne in Constantinople. While Zeno was not popular overall, it is worth noting that he was accepted as co-regent by the people with no difficulty. That is to say, it was not Zeno's Isaurian origins that were the problem, but his policies as emperor. In particular, his mother-in-law, Verina, widow of Leo, was not pleased with him, and drove him into exile to be replaced by her brother, Basiliscus in January 475.

From 475 until the Arab conquests of the seventh century, the Christological controversy was a live topic in the Eastern Roman Empire. First came Basiliscus' *Encyclical*, drafted by the newly-returned Timothy Aelurus, that explicitly anathematised Leo's *Tome* and the Council of Chalcedon.[131] This was retracted and replaced by Basiliscus' *Antencyclical*,[132] but after Zeno's reinstal-

---

[130] See Davis 2004, 89. Timothy Aelurus, *Against Chalcedon*.

[131] It explicitly cites Leo's *Tome* and the Council of Chalcedon as having 'divided the churches ... and the world's peace' and anathematises them. Text in Evagrius, *HE* III.4 (Bidez-Parmentier 103, 27–104, 19), *Faith in Formulae*, vol. 3, § 548, pp. 340–46; English translation in Grillmeier 1987, 238–40, with a study of its theology, 240–42.

[132] Ed. *Faith in Formulae*, vol. 3, § 349, pp. 346–48.

lation in 476, he would produce, with the assistance of Acacius of Constantinople, the *Henotikon*, which essentially sidestepped Chalcedon, and was effectively in force until 518.[133] Alongside the *Henotikon*, Acacius of Constantinople accepted fellowship with the anti-Chalcedonian successor to Timothy Aelurus, Peter Mongus.[134] The western response to these events demonstrates their unwavering commitment to Leo's memory, and references to Leo's writings and letters demonstrate that the bishops of Rome, at least, had Leo's letters at hand. For example, Pope Simplicius came down against anti-Chalcedonian policies, and in his letter to the presbyters and archimandrites in Constantinople, he refers to Leo's 'multiplici sermone' and Leo having written to Flavian, the Council of Chalcedon, and Marcian, demonstrating that Leo's theological letters were known in Rome.[135] Simplicius' other letters in the *Collectio Avellana* are also in support of Chalcedon against Timothy Aelurus, and we find several other references to Leo's letters in this correspondence.[136] Later, Gelasius I, *Ep.* 1.18, references Leo, *Ep.* 165, in arguing why the bishops of the East should reject Acacius and uphold Chalcedon.

The period of the Acacian Schism saw the rise of the anti-Chalcedonian, or 'Miaphysite', movement's two greatest theologians. The elder was Philoxenus of Mabbug/Hierapolis (bishop, 485–23), who has left behind the largest Syriac corpus of writings in existence, and the younger was the talented Greek theologian Severus of Antioch (bishop, 512–18, *d.* 538).[137] Both of them are ascetic theologians as well as exponents of a conservative Cyrillian Chris-

---

[133] Ed. *Faith in Formulae*, vol. 3 § 550, pp. 348–50, with English translation.

[134] Gelasius I's letters make it clear that the issue of Peter Mongus was at least as important, if not more so, as the *Henotikon*.

[135] Simplicius, JK 574, ed. *Collectio Avellana*, 59, p. 134.

[136] Simplicius to Zeno Augustus, ed. *Collectio Avellana* 56, p. 127; to Acacius, ed. *Collectio Avellana* 58, p. 132; to Zeno, ed. *Collectio Avellana* 60, p. 138.

[137] The classic exposition of the theology of these two, arguing ultimately that what divides them from Chalcedon and Neo-Chalcedonians is language, not substance, is Lebon 1909. Much the same case is made for Severus in Grillmeier 1995, 21–173; Grillmeier's picture of Severus is detailed and nuanced, and here we see an able theologian seeking what he believes to be the good of his community in the face of what he perceives as dangerous heresy. On Philoxenus in more detail, see Michelson 2014.

tology. Both of them seek to maintain the unity of Christ without mixture or confusion. Severus rejects two natures in the person of Christ as well as a division of the properties. He also demonstrates a familiarity with Leo's *Tome*, engaging with the text directly, unlike many people on all sides of any controversy. If viewed through the lens of the Justinianic, so-called 'Neo-Chalcedonian' movement on the horizon, both of these Miaphysites would be considered 'orthodox' in terms of content, emphasising the full divinity and full humanity of Christ, emphasising above all, as do the Neo-Chalcedonians, the hypostatic union. As work on these theologians continues, and as editions and translations of their work continue to be made, we run the risk of seeing someone like Severus or Philoxenus as representative of the movement as a whole. However, as the dispute with Julian of Halicarnassus over Aphthartodocetism reminds us, the Miaphysite movement was not monolith—nor was that of the Chalcedonians. Indeed, it included both moderate supporters of the *Henotikon* and opponents of the document.[138] Elsewhere, we also see the disagreements between Severus and Sergius.[139]

It is, therefore, worth noting that during this time we see how fault lines were already developing in the East, and how the opponents of Leo and Chalcedon perceived what they resisted. While theologians like Severus of Antioch and Philoxenus of Mabbug produce sophisticated arguments for their position, on either side of the debate were those who knew what ideas they opposed, but what they articulate is not the view of their opponents. For example, around 482 an Egyptian credal statement,[140] similar to the *Henotikon*, was created. Its fourth chapter anathematises 'all heresies', singling out Nestorius, Eutyches, Leo's *Tome*, and 'everything that was said and done in the council held at Chalcedon'. In the chapter beforehand, the actual theological content they reject would likewise be rejected by Chalcedonians, and in similar language:

---

[138] For a discussion of these basic positions at the outset, see Grillmeier 1987, 258–60.

[139] Helpfully analysed and translated by Torrance 1988.

[140] Syriac text, PO 13.239–41; English trans. *Faith in Formulae*, vol. 2, § 219, pp. 107–08.

> As to those who divide and those who confound, or those who introduce an illusion,[141] we in no way receive them, for the sinless incarnation, that was in truth from the Mother of God, does not add another son, for the Trinity has remained a Trinity even after one of the Trinity, God the Word, was made flesh.

At other times, anti-Chalcedonians simply anathematise the council with no content whatsoever, such as Martyrius of Jerusalem (d. 486) as quoted by Pseudo-Zachariah Rhetor.[142] On the Chalcedonian side, John Moschus (d. 619) displays a similar trend. His 'Nestorians' reject the title of *Theotokos* for the Virgin Mary (ch. 27), and no content is given the Severans in his collected stories, simply miracles proving them heretics (chh. 29, 30, 36, 79, etc.). There is an implication, however, that Moschus considers all Miaphysites as Docetic, when the Chalcedonian Bishop Ephraim of Antioch says, 'Lord Jesus Christ our God, who for our sakes condescended truly to be made flesh of our Lady the holy Mother of God and ever-virgin Mary'.[143]

In 518, the 'Acacian Schism' ended, after the accession of the Chalcedonian Justin I.[144] The debate over Chalcedon, however, simply entered a new phase. The Miaphysite leaders found themselves now out of favour with the imperial powers. Severus of Antioch fled the city of Antioch by night when he learned that an order had gone out for his tongue to be cut out. He made his way to exile in Egypt.[145] Part of the agreement with Pope Hormisdas

---

[141] A reference to the Miaphysite Julian of Halicarnassus' Aphthartodocetism.

[142] Ps-Zachariah Rhetor, *HE* 5,6c-d, ed. Brooks 1919–1924, vol. 1, 221–22.

[143] *Pratum Spirituale* 36, trans. Wortley.

[144] That Justin and Justinian were Chalcedonians by conviction and not opportunists seeking western support before the conquest of Italy should be evident from how many decades elapsed, the early ascendancy of the Chalcedonian Vitalian, and the fact that the *Henotikon* was failing in its purpose, and a new direction in the pursuit of ecclesiastical unity was needed, anyway. This is not, however, to say that a return to Chalcedon was inevitable; it is simply the direction the new regime took.

[145] The order to remove Severus' tongue came from Justin under the influence of the Chalcedonian general Vitalian, against whom Severus had spoken during the reign of Anastasius; see Evagrius Scholasticus, *Historia Ecclesiastica* IV.4. Vitalian at this time held greater influence over the emperor than Justinian. For Severus' flight from Antioch, see the 'Letter on His Flight'.

that helped end the schism was the removal of Miaphysite leaders from the liturgical diptychs. This demand from the bishop of Rome led to the entrenchment of Miaphysite opposition and was one of the dynamics that helped lead to the creation of a separate Miaphysite hierarchy.[146] Justinian continued the policy of appeasing Hormisdas in the matter of the diptychs but also sought avenues of reconciliation with the Miaphysites. In the long run, these attempts would not only fail in the East, but cause schism in the West. The failure of Justinian's reconciliation plans was due not only to the enforcement of the demands concerning the diptychs but also to the entrenchment of leaders such as Severus of Antioch who would not reconcile themselves to Chalcedon in any way, since it was the formula of the council and the *Tome* of Leo to which they objected, not simply Ibas and Theodoret, to be discussed presently.[147]

The debate that would soon arise between East and West would guarantee the survival of large quantities of Leo's letters. When he became emperor in 527, Justin's nephew Justinian inherited an empire with a divided church. Since the days of Constantine, the ideal of the imperial church was for a single *ecclesia* throughout the empire with hierarchical/disciplinary and doctrinal unity.[148] The emperor was a bishop to the bishops, and he had a role to play in protecting the unity and doctrinal purity of the imperial church.[149] In the early 500s, both Leo's friends and foes were clearly reading his letters. Just as Timothy Aelurus had written his point-by-point refutation of Chalcedon, so did Severus of Antioch, the leading anti-Chalcedonian theologian of the day, produce a body of anti-Chalcedonian polemic, engaging with Leo's letters directly. Justinian's efforts to reconcile anti-Chalcedonians such as Severus

---

[146] This is the central thesis of Menze 2008.

[147] In enforcing Chalcedonian policies, the emperors from Justin onwards were cast in the role of the pagan emperors of the past and the Syriac Miaphysites in the role of early Christian martyrs, or (alleged) martyrs under Julian, thus strengthening their group identity and weakening their allegiance to the emperors in Constantinople, according to the nuanced study of Wood 2010, especially chapters 6 and 7.

[148] Meyendorff 1989, 28–38, gives a discussion of the relationship of emperor to church and thus of church unity in the post-Constantinian empire.

[149] For the emperor as bishop to the bishops, see Eusebius of Caesarea, *Vita Constantini* 4.24.

and Philoxenus of Mabbug included edicts and letters as well as disputations and debates, most prominently in 536. Given that Severus and Philoxenus had both felt that the *Henotikon* did not go far enough, these efforts were all in vain.[150] Furthermore, as already argued, the western insistence upon removing the names of prominent anti-Chalcedonians from the diptychs, such as Dioscorus and even Acacius, meant that the anti-Chalcedonian tradition would never reconcile itself to the imperial church so long as Justinian upheld that policy.

One of Justinian's attempts to reconcile the anti-Chalcedonians was a condemnation of 'Three Chapters'. The Three Chapters were the person and work of Theodore of Mopsuestia, the letter of Ibas of Edessa to Mari the Persian, and the works written by Theodoret of Cyrrhus against Cyril of Alexandria. In the later stages of the Nestorian controversy, after the Council of Ephesus in 430, it had become apparent to the opponents of Nestorianism that the source of Nestorius' teaching was, in fact, Theodore of Mopsuestia. If they wanted to destroy their opponents' theological tradition, removing Nestorius to exile and banning his writings would never be enough. Theodore was the root of the problem.[151] Ibas of Edessa's letter, which had been read out at Chalcedon and was previously part of the case for Ibas' deposition at Second Ephesus, was very anti-Cyrillian and an obvious thorn in the flesh of the conservative Cyrillians opposed to Chalcedon. Likewise, of course, the anti-Cyrillian writings of Theodoret, such as the diagolue *Eranistes*, were also an obstacle to the conservative Cyrillians, since Chalcedon rehabilitated both Theodoret and Ibas. Around 543, Justinian published his edict against the Three Chapters. The text of the original edict does not survive, but that of a subsequent edict 'On the Orthodox Faith' does.[152] By 551 when this

---

[150] For Severus and Philoxenus and their position on the *Henotikon*, see Grillmeier 1987, 269–88.

[151] For Theodore as the wellspring for Nestorius' thought, see Bevan 2016, 42–57. The fifth-century controversy over Theodore and Diodore of Tarsus is recounted by Bevan 2016, 256–79. The case in favour of the orthodoxy of the councils against Theodore and his predecessor Diodore is made, using a wide selection of fragments from their own works, by Behr 2011.

[152] This edict is most likely from 551, according to Price 2009, 122–23. Ed. Schwartz 1939, 72–111.

later edict was promulgated, Justinian was trying to win over convinced Latin Chalcedonians who supported the Three Chapters; a subtle aspect of Justinian's approach is his unsignalled quotation of Leo's *Tome* in the edict, which was given directly in the Latin version of the edict rather than back-translated out of Greek.[153] However, since Justinian was still interested in eastern unity, the quotation of Leo is still left unsignalled. This intertextuality with Leo's *Tome* would be caught by a careful reader, especially one who was also a careful reader of Leo, such as Facundus of Hermiane, Liberatus of Carthage, Ferrandus of Carthage, and other supporters of the Three Chapters. These supporters, mainly but not entirely in the Latin West, argued against the posthumous condemnation of Theodore of Mopsuestia. More to the point, they felt that a condemnation of the writings of Ibas and Theodoret was an abrogation of Chalcedon, since both Ibas and Theodoret had been reinstalled by the council. Furthermore, one of the grave concerns they raised was the fact that the letter of Ibas seemed to have been approved by the papal legates;[154] in counting the letter 'Nestorian', they argued, the authority of the Council of Chalcedon was being challenged.[155] As the letter of Ferrandus of Carthage to the deacons of Rome makes clear,[156] the council was considered perfect in all its ways. Any hint that it needed clarification or revising was considered a danger to maintaining it as the standard of orthodoxy.[157] Some also argued that the emperor was reaching beyond his bounds—revealing fault lines between

---

[153] Schwartz 1939, 76–77.

[154] Consider their statement, 'Now that the documents have been read, we know from the verdict of the most devout bishops that the most devout Ibas has been proved innocent, and from the reading of his letter we have found him to be orthodox'. (*Actio* X.161, trans. Price and Gaddis).

[155] See Vigilius, *Constitutum II* (126–36) and Facundus, *Pro Defensione trium capitulorum* V.1.8,22 and 2.17–18, as cited in Price 2009, 95.

[156] PL 67.921–28; trans. Price 2009, 112–21.

[157] Many centuries later, this sentiment was phrased succinctly by Deusdedit in 1086, 'For the Council of Chalcedon ... is of such authority and strength that whoever does not adhere to its solidity, whatever his life and conduct ... even if he appears to be a precious stone, lies outside the building of God'. See his dedicatory letter to Pope Victor III and the clergy of the Roman Church, ed. von Glanvell 1905, 4; trans. Somerville and Brasington 1998, 126.

the western and eastern views of the relationship between secular and ecclesiastical authority that had earlier emerged during the Acacian Schism, with, for example, the articulation of the Gelasian doctrine of the two spheres.[158]

To gain wider support for his condemnation of the Three Chapters, Justinian held a council at Constantinople in 553. Despite much resistance and reluctance as well as changing of position, Pope Vigilius was present at the time of the council and ultimately ratified it. A schism with northern Italy ensued. As far as Leo's correspondence is concerned, letter collections were made as fuel for controversy. These definitely include the collection of Rusticus that he appended to the *Acts* of Chalcedon. Rusticus, a supporter of the Three Chapters, put this together in his time at Constantinople in his hideaway with the Sleepless Monks, or *Acoimetae*. The heart of resistance to Justinian was in northern Italy, and it is not unlikely that *Collectio Grimanica*, with Veronese origins and a relationship with the northern Italian *Collectio Bobbiensis*, was also compiled in this context, as discussed in Chapter 3. Furthermore, as the dispute involved not only theology but questions of jurisdiction, it seems not implausible for the *Collectio Avellana* to have had a Justinianic origin, as we shall see in the next chapter.

The Christological controversy would continue, and Leo's *Tome* would remain the touchstone for orthodoxy in the Latin West. In 649, a Greek council held at the Lateran under Pope Martin I upheld not only the teaching of two natures in the one person of Christ, but also of two wills, as taught by Maximus the Confessor against the imperial policy of one will, or monothelitism. This was confirmed in 681 at an ecumenical council in Constantinople. Ultimately, however, the most important theological moment for the collection, and therefore preservation, of Leo's letters is the sixth century and the era of Justinian, for the collections gathered then were copied and transmitted to us in the manuscripts that form the discussion that follows. The Carolingians, as we shall see, preserved these collections and made some of their own, for they, too, had an interest in Christology alongside wider questions of theology and canon law.

---

[158] Vigilius argued that the emperor was going beyond his bounds in his letter of excommunication to Theodore Ascidas and Menas of Constantinople, ed. Schwartz 1940, 13.

The unifying thread that runs through the various letters of Leo's papacy, whether decretal, pastoral, or dogmatic is his vision of what the Bishop of Rome was to do and to be. Throughout all of the above, Leo is acting as the leading bishop of the western church. He involves himself in ecclesiastical disputes outside of his own metropolitan area. He strives for the recognition of himself as head over the papal vicariate in Thessalonica. He corrects episcopal abuses wherever they are found in the West—whether Suburbicarian Italy, North Africa, or southern Gaul. He gives his support to the pursuit of orthodoxy in places as geographically disparate as Gallaecia in western Spain and the diocese of Oriens bordering the Syrian Desert. He seeks the acknowledgement of his theological position from bishops in Gaul, northern Italy, and the Eastern Empire. These practical actions on Leo's part derive from his own ecclesiology, that as Bishop of Rome and successor to St Peter who sits on the Apostolic See at Rome, the imperial capital, he holds primacy of honour and power in the Church. Leo does not hold this belief because it is convenient for him or because he is a power-hungry villain. Throughout his writings, it is clear that Leo seeks the health and well-being of all the churches, from Gallaecia to Galatia, from Mauretania to Mesopotamia. As a man who takes the ecclesiastical hierarchy and episcopal duties seriously, Leo engages in the actions he does in the way that he does because he considers these activities his solemn duty as Bishop of Rome.

Chapter 2

Editing Leo's Letters

This chapter is an overview of the editions of Leo's letters from the first printed edition in the 1400s to the various partial, scientific editions of the twentieth century. From Giovanni Bussi in 1470 to the brothers Pietro and Giacomo Ballerini in 1753, the main trends in editing Leo's letters are the discovery and printing of more and more letters, as well as increasingly scientific methods of redaction. Before the Ballerini, the most important edition is that of Pasquier Quesnel, a Jansenist, in 1675; due to Quesnel's Jansenism, Pope Benedict XIV commissioned the Ballerini brothers to produce their edition as a Catholic rival to Quesnel's. This they did, taking on many of Quesnel's points of divergence from the previous tradition, but also noting where they themselves diverged from Quesnel and providing the reasons why. Moreover, the Ballerini also compiled a vast quantity of other canonical material pertinent to the study of Leo the Great and fifth-century canon law. Although new Latin printings of Leo's letters continued to be made in the following centuries, no real progress in the scientific editing and textual analysis of Leo's letters was made until the late nineteenth century. From the late nineteenth century into the 1930s, several critical editions of some of Leo's letters were made, including editions of collections of Leo's letters, broader letter collections that happen to include Leo's letters, and editions of individual letters. Of these editions, the largest and most influential was that of Eduard Schwartz, including 117 items and edited in *Acta Conciliorum Oecumenicorum* 2.4, although perhaps the best was that of Carlos Silva-Tarouca. After the 1930s, only one new edition of note appeared, Vollman's edition of *Ep.* 15 in 1965, although this same letter along with *Ep.* 8 was printed in the Corpus Fontium Manichaeorum in 2001.

The following editions were selected for overview in this chapter. Their dates and locations in this chapter are given in parentheses: Giovanni Bussi (1470, see 2.1), Petrus Canisius (1546, discussed in 2.2), Severinus Binius (1606–1638, discussed in 2.3), Pasquier

Quesnel (1675, see 2.4), the Ballerini (1753, see 2.5), Gundlach's
edition of *Epistolae Arelatenses genuinae* (MGH Epist. 3 from 1892,
see 2.6), *Collectio Avellana I* (CSEL 35 from 1895, see 2.7), Blakeney's *The Tome of Pope Leo the Great* (1923, see 2.8), Eduard
Schwartz's edition in ACO 2.4 (1932, see 2.9), Carlos Silva-Tarouca's edition (1932–1937, see 2.10), Hubert Wurm's edition of Leo,
Ep. 4 (1939, see 2.11), Benedikt Vollmann's edition of Leo, *Ep.* 15
(1965, see 2.12), and CFM Series Latina 1 (2001, see 2.13). The
chapter concludes in section 2.14 with the case for a new, complete
critical edition founded both on a broader survey of manuscripts
than hitherto and on scholarship's ongoing engagement with the
philology of Latin in Late Antiquity.

2.1 Giovanni Andrea Bussi (1470)

The first printed edition of Leo's works was by Giovanni Bussi in
1470.[1] Bussi's printing of the letters is worth little mention save
that it is the first. The letters contained in this edition are the
Tome which is placed just before the Christmas sermons, and then,
following the rest of the sermons (of which Bussi includes 95), four
letters, *Epp.* 119, 80, 145, and 165 with the *testimonia*. Bussi's primary consideration was clearly Leo's theology—he had access to
a comprehensive manuscript of the sermons, as his printing provided 95 of them for the reader. When Bussi provided this edition, he only gave the reader the final five Leonine letters of the
Collectio Dionysiana adaucta in order.[2] I can only assume that Bussi
had a defective manuscript of the *Dionysiana adaucta* since there
are three more dogmatic letters in that collection (and six decretals as well), all of them from the early stages of the Eutychian
controversy.

2.2 The Sixteenth Century

The 1500s saw multiple printed editions of Leo's letters, bringing
a growing number of Leo's letters available in print, although the
text remained what may be termed *vulgata*—the versions found in
the later mediaeval manuscripts, such as that of Ballerini Collec-

---

[1] NB: In older literature, Bussi tends to be called Johannes Aleriensis or
Johannes Andreae.

[2] On the *Dionysiana adaucta*, see below, Chapter 5.2.c.

tion 24, rather than a text based on the earliest, best manuscripts. However, the sciences of palaeography and codicology were as yet unborn, so the task of judging between different manuscripts was much more difficult for the sixteenth-century textual critic. In 1505, Bussi's text was reprinted by Bartolomeo de Zanis de Porte-sio, and again in Paris in 1511 with the addition of the tract, 'De Conflictu uirtutum et uitiorum'.[3] Jacobus Merlinus produced in 1524 an edition of Pseudo-Isidore that included 94 of Leo's letters. Our first real edition had to wait until the work of Peter Crabbe, who published a two-volume work on the councils in 1538 and his edition of Leo in 1551.

In September of 1546, Petrus Canisius published his own *Opera Omnia* of Leo's works in Cologne at the press of Melchior Nove-sianus. In this edition, Canisius included 103 of Leo's letters, counting all of them 'Epistolae Decretales'. His edition includes: *Epp.* 4, 7, 18 (addressed to Julianus, not Januarius), 16, 19, 20, 24, 23, 22, 26, 54, 28, 35, 29, 31, 32, 33, 36, 37, 30, 34 (addressed to Julian of Cos; sometimes this letter addressed to Juvenal of Jerusalem), 38, 39, 50, 59, 43, 44, 45, 49, 51, 47, 48, 60, 61, 69, 71, 70, 166 (dated to the consulate of Marcian, not Majorian), 78, 80, 81, 82, 90, 83, 84, 85, 93, 87, 89, 94, 95, 99, 102, 97, 106, 104, 105, 113, 112, 115, 116, 114, 119, 120, 3, 121, 122 (as to Eudocia, as in some mss), 123, 125, 127, 130, 134, 135, 139, 145, 148, 156, 155, 163, 162, 159, 168, 9, 118, 124, 14, 2, 1, 12 (in version miss-ing middle chapters, in **D–h**), JK † 551, 10, 41, 108, 167 (with **D** *capitula* listed at beginning), 15 (to 'Turbio'), 103, 138, a letter to the bishops of Thrace (from Leo, Victorius and Eustathius, 'Tanta seculi potestates'), 165 with *testimonia*, and 72. The letters run 87[r]–126[v]. Canisius gives almost no notes about variants from the manuscripts, and he frequently puts Leo in the salutation as 'Leo Romanae & vniuersalis Ecclesiae episcopus'. In 1561, the Carthu-sian Laurentius Surius produced another edition of Leo's works in Cologne, containing the same letters in the order of Canisius with the addition of *Ep.* 68 on the end, but emending the text (a minor example, 'Turibio' instead of 'Turbio'). He also distin-guished between what one would call 'decretals' and 'epistles'. In

---

[3] See P. Quesnel 1675, cited PL 54.33. This tract would later be attributed to Leo IX, PL 143.559–78.

1567, Leo's letters were once again printed in Cologne, this time a reprint of Surius' work in an edition of conciliar decrees.

1568 brought the edition of Joannes Sichardus, which was well regarded by Quesnel and cited often by him in his notes. Joannes Ulimmerius, prior of St Martin's at Leuven, produced an edition of letters from collations made by him and his monks, publishing it first at Leuven in 1575, again in 1577, then in Antwerp in 1583. A selection of Leo's letters was again included in an edition of conciliar decrees, this time the Venetian edition of Dominico Bolanus in 1585. In 1591, Antonio Carafa closed the century by publishing a monumental edition of all papal letters in Rome, right up to Innocent IX.[4]

2.3 The Seventeenth Century

In the 1600s the quantity of Leo's letters available in print continued to increase, beginning with Severinus Binius' edition of the Latin councils in 1606. He went to produce a bilingual Greek-Latin edition in 1618, and again in 1638. In both editions he included a collection of Leo's letters.[5] In 1614–1618, another *Opera Omnia* was published, this one joining Leo with Maximus of Turin and Peter Chrysologus. This collection was frequently reprinted, in Lyons in 1622, then in Paris in 1623, 1633, 1651, 1661, 1671, and 1672. Based upon the 1622 Lyons printing, Leo's letters run pp. 97–182. They begin with the run of Canisius, then add *Ep.* 68 as Surius did. The text seems not to be especially varied, still giving 'Julianum' with a note in the margin 'Januarium' for *Ep* 18, just as Canisius and Surius did. *Ep.* 166 is still dated to the consulship of Marcian, not Majorian. However, the *testimonia* of *Ep.* 165 have been subdivided into chapters. After *Ep.* 68, Binius' edition adds newly-found letters in the order of their collections. First come the five of the *Collectio Avellana* (*Epp.* 169–73), then *Ep.* 17 and 107 (both in Ballerini Collection 23), then *Epp.* 40, 42, 65, 66, and 67 from *Collectio Arelatensis*. The *Arelatensis* letters had originally been identified by Baronius in his *Annals*. This edition epitomises the seventeenth century—more letters are added, some problems

---

[4] For the editions before Canisius and after Surius, see Quesnel 1675, cited in PL 54.34–35.

[5] See Quesnel 1675, cited in PL 54.35.

are cleared up, and other problems persist. From Baronius' work, Vossius was working on producing an edition of Leo's letters at the time of his death. Jacques Sirmond continued the work of expanding and editing Leo using French manuscripts, giving Leo's letters as the fourth volume of his edition of the councils.[6]

2.4 Pasquier Quesnel (1675)

Quesnel produced an edition of Leo's letters on scientific principles, bringing together more letters than any previous editor. He provided an extensive introduction and thorough notes, making the basis of his readings and judgements much more transparent than most sixteenth- and seventeenth-century editions. He identified the *Collectio Quesnelliana* as being of great antiquity and, therefore, great worth. His introduction covers not only the life of Leo, as is usual for the day, but also the various editions available, giving Quesnel's judgements on each. He discusses the letters and their importance, as well as those manuscripts he accessed, as any good editor would do. His second volume discusses various issues related to the study of the life, work, and teaching of Leo. Quesnel makes progress in the scientific analysis of Leo's letters by attempting to date and rearrange the documents accordingly, not simply printing the order of earlier editions with new discoveries attached to the end. Quesnel is not merely a corrective to his predecessors but also to his successors, and is a critic worthy of dialogue.

2.5 Giacomo and Pietro Ballerini (1753–1755)

Although Quesnel's edition of Leo's works was very good, the papacy was not content to let the matter of the works of one of the great popes rest there. Since Quesnel was a Jansenist, Pope Benedict XIV recruited Giacomo and Pietro Ballerini to produce a new edition. This edition was to become the standard edition of Leo's letters, both because of its high quality and because Migne included it in *Patrologia Latina* 54–56. The first volume, reprinted as PL 54, provides the texts of Leo's sermons and letters with important introductory material. Both bodies of work are accompanied by introductions by the Ballerini discussing the

---

[6] For Baronius and Vossius, see Quesnel 1675, cited in PL 54.35–36.

origins and manuscripts of the texts. Throughout the letters, the Ballerini provide *Admonitiones* before the text of each individual letter that signal issues surrounding it. For some letters, the question surrounds its date. For *Ep.* 12, the concern is the existence of at least four different versions in the manuscripts and how to unravel them. These *Admonitiones* are very helpful to the interested reader. Where a letter exists in Greek, they provide Latin; however, see below for how this practice goes awry.

The second two volumes, reprinted as PL 55 and 56, are an ongoing conversation with Quesnel's work that the Ballerini had begun in PL 54. The second volume is an edition of the so-called 'Leonine Sacramentary' followed by other *spuria* attributed to Leo, and concluding with Quesnel's *dissertationes* on Leo's works. The third volume discusses ancient canonical collections, including their own edition of *Collectio Quesnelliana*, the collection called *Prisca*, the Nicene canons in Latin, a second Latin version of the Nicene canons with the canons of Serdica and Chalcedon as well, a compendium of other ancient documents of canon law, Quesnel's *dissertationes* on the *Codex canonum ecclesiasticorum*, and unedited sermons of Leo.

For many of their notes and much of the legwork, the Ballerini relied on Quesnel. This reliance on Quesnel is visible in the number of notes wherein they refer the reader Quesnel's edition. Furthermore, for some manuscripts they relied on Quesnel's work to gain access to their readings rather than travelling to the manuscripts themselves, an understandable choice in the eighteenth century. However, they also accessed more manuscripts than Quesnel had, manuscripts they described extensively in their introduction. Furthermore, they did not simply trust Quesnel's judgement, but reordered and re-dated some of the letters and diverged from his readings when they felt it was necessary. Finally, the Ballerini usually show good philological sense in the readings they chose. The resultant edition in 1753 of 173 letters was the largest, most authoritative edition of Leo's epistolary corpus ever put together.

However, this edition presents certain difficulties. First and foremost, even if every reading were true, the Ballerini gave us no *Conspectus Siglorum*. The footnotes are riddled with references to, 'Unus codex Vaticanus', 'Tres codices', and the like. Sometimes by cross-referencing these obscure references with the discussion of letter collections and manuscripts in the introduction, the reader can ascertain whence the variants came. Sometimes this is not possible. A second problem is that practical factors prevented the Ballerini from viewing every manuscript in person. They viewed certain manuscripts only through apographs, such as Paris lat. 3836, or others through the notes of Quesnel, such as *Collectio Grimanica*. Their text suffers because sometimes their apographs were wrong; through no fault of their own judgement, the Ballerini sometimes went astray in their documentation of the readings. Similarly, not every major variant was listed, as a simple comparison between my edition of *Ep.* 167 and theirs would prove. At times, the Ballerini give chapter headings and divisions without always clarifying their source—often headings and divisions not present in the whole manuscript tradition. Were these headings from one branch, from Quesnel, or from the editors themselves? Another problem that runs throughout the Ballerini edition of Leo's letters is the context of its compilation—the anti-Jansenist position of the editors and the pope. Rather than seeking only to assess Leo as a major figure of the fifth century, their notes at times engage in concerns of the eighteenth. For example, the 'Admonitio' to *Ep.* 1 discusses whether it and *Ep.* 2 are both genuine or if only one of them is. Amongst the arguments they discuss are questions of whether the contents of the different versions of *Ep.* 12 are *worthy* of the pope and the catholic faith. The scientific approach to this sort of question is, rather, whether the language and content are consistent with Leo, regardless of 'worthiness'.

There are two other problems with the Ballerini as editors. First, they included *Ep.* 11, which is actually Valentinian III, *Novella* XVII, only ever with Leo's letters in Oriel College MS 42. They include letters to and from the imperial family, but these are usually gathered together amongst Leo's letters and are easily forgiven. However, a more problematic practice was that the Ballerini also provided Latin translations for all Greek letters. In the case of *Epp.* 52 and 53 they provided their own, no Latin being extant. For *Ep.* 72 they provided a tidied-up version of an authentic mediaeval version. This practice can lead the reader astray, making him or her believe that the Latin is that of Leo's correspondents, whereas it is, in fact, that of Leo's editors. The usefulness of such translation in the 1700s when literacy in Latin amongst the educated was very high but in Greek less so, is understandable; however, the Ballerini's methods are ambiguous as to whether the

Latin is original or their own, a problem only compounded by the presence of original Latin documents, such as the *Tome*, alongside their Greek translations.

Finally, simple progress has rendered the Ballerini edition outdated. We have more manuscripts to compare than the Ballerini did, making the task more complex but also helping us determine the trends of transmission more clearly. Another example of progress is how the Pseudo-Isidorian Forgeries have gone through much assessment in recent years, sometimes affirming the Ballerini, as in dating Vat. lat. 630,[7] and sometimes going beyond not only them, but Hinschius, Pseudo-Isidore's nineteenth-century editor. Similar situations exist for many of the canonical collections used by the Ballerini in the preparation of their edition—scholarship has assessed the date, purpose, and location of their original compilation, all of which help us in classifying the manuscripts and judging the variants. Latin philology has not stood still since 1753, either. Many studies have delved into the use of both clausulae in classical and late antique Latin, the application of which to an author's corpus has helped editors choose between variants, as done by Silva-Tarouca in his edition.[8] For these reasons alone, a new edition of the entirety of Leo's epistolary corpus is long overdue—yet I cannot leave the Ballerini there, for they loom so very large in the study of Leo, and their judgement was so very good. Indeed, for most of the letters, even if an editor disagrees with them, the most important change a modern editor can hope to make is simply to provide a proper apparatus—and that is a worthy enough task.

2.6 *Epistolae Arelatenses genuinae* in MGH Epist. 3, ed. W. Gundlach (1892)

In 1892, *Monumenta Germaniae Historica* put out its third volume of *Epistolae, Merowingici et Karolini Aevi Tomus I*. This volume includes as its first item *Epistolae Arelatenses genuinae*, the epistles of the *Collectio Arelatensis*.[9] The six *Arelatensis* letters of Leo (items 9–14) are *Epp.* 40, 42, 41, 65, 66, and 67 (pp. 15–22). These six

[7] See below, Chapter 5.2.f.iii.

[8] See below, 2.10.

[9] MGH Epist. 3, 1–83. For a discussion of *Collectio Arelatensis* and its place in the transmission of Leo's letters, see below 3.2.n.

letters are a shining example in the history of Leonine epistolary textual criticism. For the first time since the Ballerini, an editor had himself consulted the manuscript tradition of a collection of Leo's letters, even providing a stemma with the resultant critical edition. Furthermore, unlike the Ballerini, Gundlach included a clear, easy-to-read critical apparatus for the reader. Finally, Leonine textual criticism was moving forward, even if for a mere six letters. Gundlach's introduction is almost entirely devoted to the manuscript tradition, with a small discussion of the collection's origins. Although MGH Epist. 3 is a step forward for Leonine epistolary textual criticism, it highlights for us the main problem besetting the modern editing of Leo's letters: its incomplete and fragmentary nature. All of the editors of Leo's letters from Gundlach onwards have been concerned only with certain collections or certain letters, not the corpus as a whole, as the totality of Leo's surviving correspondence. The most obvious gap, as we shall see, is the decretal material, left unedited since the Ballerini.

2.7 *Collectio Avellana I* (CSEL 35), ed. Günther

In 1895, Otto Günther produced, in two volumes, an edition of the ever-fascinating and interesting *Collectio Avellana* for Corpus Scriptorum Ecclesiasticorum Latinorum, volume 35, entitling it, *Epistulae imperatorum pontificum aliorum inde ab a. CCCLXVII usque ad a. DLIII datae Avellana quae dicitur collectio*. Here we meet the consistent refrain of editions from the nineteenth century onwards: Günther produced a scientific survey of the manuscripts and a proper critical edition of the *Collectio Avellana* as well as a series of studies, entitled *Avellana-Studien*. The *Avellana* is the only source for *Epp.* 169, 170, 171, 172, 173, and these are the only Leonine letters in the edition.

2.8 *The Tome of Pope Leo the Great*, by E. H. Blakeney (1923)

This text from SPCK's 'Texts for Students' series can be discussed very briefly. It is not meant as a critical edition, as the series title implies. Nonetheless, Blakeney here gives us the best text of the *Tome* between the Ballerini and Schwartz because he includes variants from Munich, Bayerische Staatsbibliothek, Clm 14540 in the notes at the suggestion of C. H. Turner. The main text is, nonetheless, that of the Ballerini. The book comes with a helpful but dated introduction, facing-page English translation, and explanatory notes.

2.9 Eduard Schwartz (1932)

In 1932, as part of the ambitious multivolume *Acta conciliorum oecumenicorum*, Eduard Schwartz published an edition of various of Leo's 'dogmatic' letters as the fourth part of his *Acta* of Chalcedon; this edition includes 115 letters, which is a sizeable portion of the corpus, amounting to approximately two thirds of Leo's epistolary output. The basis for Schwartz's edition is the ninth-century *Collectio Grimanica* of 104 Leonine letters;[10] to this, he has appended eleven items drawn from various epistolary collections with two more appended to the introduction: items 105–07 are Leo, *Epp.* 109, 144, 151, from *Collectio Ratisbonensis*; items 108 and 109 are *Ep.* 21, taken from *Collectio Casinensis* with two other items from *Casinensis* that are non-Leonine; item 112 is *Ep.* 103, as in *Corbeiensis*; item 113 is *Ep.* 124 as in *Quesnelliana*; and, in the Appendix, items 114 and 115 are *Epp.* 100 and 132 from *Thessalonicensis*. The introduction to ACO 2.4 is a thorough discussion of the manuscripts Schwartz used, that addresses the editions of Quesnel and the Ballerini, whose achievement is not downplayed by their twentieth-century successor. At the end of the introduction, Schwartz provides the reader with two letters he had meant to make available in the edition but overlooked; to the first of these he gives the number 116—it is *Ep.* 102; the second is a Greek version of part of *Ep.* 53. Beside the main collection of dogmatic letters in ACO 2.4, Schwartz has various other Leonine items scattered through ACO 2, located in their places within the different late antique and early mediaeval collections that make up the edition. Setting aside the Greek items in ACO 2.1, the *Tome* is thus not in 2.4 with the rest of Leo's letters, but is found in 2.2.1, pp. 24–33; other Leonine items in volume 2.2.1 (Schwartz's edition of *Collectio Novariensis*) are *Epp.* 22 (pp. 21–22), 26 (pp. 23–24), and 21 (pp. 33–34), as well as the final two items of *Novariensis* items 11 (pp. 77–79) and 12 (pp. 79–81), from Flavian of Constantinople and Eusebius of Dorylaeum respectively, both unknown to

---

[10] For a description of *Collectio Grimanica*, see below, Chapter 4.1.g.

the Ballerini.[11] In ACO 2.3, Schwartz gives references for those Leonine letters that would otherwise be repeated, directing the reader to their item numbers in ACO 2.4; the other Leonine letters are item 5, a different version of *Ep.* 22 from what is in ACO 2.2.1 (pp. 7–8); item 8, a different version of *Ep.* 26 from ACO 2.2.1 (pp. 9–11); items 18–24 (pp. 13–17), the letters from the imperial household to Theodosius with his responses (Leo, *Epp.* 58, 55–57, 62–64); item 27, *Ep.* 73 (p. 17); item 28, *Ep.* 76 (p. 18); and item 29, *Ep.* 77 (18–19). Of the seven letters, or thirteen if we count the ones amongst the imperial family, scattered throughout ACO 2.2.1 and 2.3, the only one repeated in 2.4 is *Ep.* 21. People who are interested in Leo *qua* Leo will wish that Schwartz had assembled all of his Leonine letters into one place, especially the *Tome* which is separated from the rest of the dogmatic letters. It is with his edition of the dogmatic letters in ACO 2.4 that we shall occupy ourselves for the rest of this analysis.

Schwartz makes a strong distinction in the introduction to this edition between *decretales* and *epistulae*, maintaining that decretals and epistles, by which one may assume he means dogmatic epistles, are not transmitted together in the collections up to the seventh century, or, if they are, they are in two separate parts of the same collection.[12] This observation of Schwartz's is usually true, but not always, as our fuller knowledge of mediaeval letter collections demonstrates. In *Collectiones Teatina* and *Remensis*, for example, the *Tome* is the only 'dogmatic' letter included, but is inserted in the middle of Leo's decretals. In the *Quesnelliana*, the decretals are scattered throughout the collection; rather than seeing this as a flaw in his argument, given that this collection may date as early as the fifth century, Schwartz sees it as a flaw in the collection.[13] Of the fifteen letters in *Collectio Pithouensis*, a few decretals at the beginning and end frame a series of non-decretal epistles. Nonetheless, we shall concede to Schwartz that most collections before the eighth century do not mingle decretals with the other letters; be that as it may, unlike Schwartz's edition, they are often still within the same collection, if separately.

---

[11] For more on *Collectio Novariensis*, see below, 4.1.e.

[12] ACO 2.4, i.

[13] In ibid., i, Schwartz calls it, 'congeries magis quam collectio epistularum decretaliumque Leonis'.

Schwartz uses this argument about the nature of early mediae-val letter collections to govern his editorial selection, effectively ruling out all decretals from inclusion. Had he simply produced an edition of *Collectio Grimanica*, the 104-letter collection that forms the edition's basis, all would have been well. Yet Schwartz aug-ments *Grimanica* with the abovementioned letters that he consid-ers either dogmatic or important enough for inclusion. Nonetheless, as full as Schwartz's edition is, this editorial choice meant that a number of Leo's letters, even ones related to the events following Chalcedon, were left out; for example, the letters that Leo sent to eastern bishops and the Emperor Marcian about the date of Eas-ter 455 are included by Schwartz because they are included with the 'dogmatic' letters in the manuscript tradition—this is because most of Leo's dogmatic letters were sent East and often, as he demonstrates, the collections derive from eastern archives.[14] How-ever, *Ep.* 133, a letter to Leo from Proterius of Alexandria on this very subject, is not included by Schwartz, presumably because it is included in a manuscript of the disdained, canonical *Collectio Quesnelliana*. Such is also the case for *Ep.* 138, where Leo informs the Spanish and Gallic bishops of the Easter date decided for that year; the exclusion of this letter is less surprising than the former, since it does not involve the East. However, the exclusion of both of these, while multitudinous other letters concerning the date of Easter 455 *are* included amongst the alleged 'dogmatic' letters, shows the weakness in Schwartz's system. A person wishing to do research on the question of dating Easter will be able to get the most up-to-date editions of most of the letters from Schwartz, yet will still be forced to rely on the older edition of the Ballerini.

In most areas related to the manuscript tradition, Schwartz's edition is a step forward from the Ballerini, as we shall see below. However, regarding Pseudo-Isidore, Schwartz takes on Hinschius' classification wholesale.[15] As a result, the only Pseudo-Isidorian manuscript Schwartz consulted for the production of this edi-tion is Vat. lat. 1340, a good witness of the thirteenth century, certainly, but neither as good nor as early as Vat. lat. 630 (saec.

---

[14] Ibid., xxi, xxxviiii–xxxx.

[15] Ibid., xxx–xxxii.

IX[med]), which Hinschius misdated and undervalued, as I shall demonstrate below.[16]

The ordering of the letters in Schwartz's edition is questionable. He has left the letters in the order of *Grimanica*, and then, when other letters that met his approval were found in other letter collections, he appended them to the end, telling the reader from whence in their original collections they came. The merit of this editorial style becomes clear to anyone seeking to study the mediaeval collections of Leo's dogmatic letters as collections—and, no doubt, such study is due, since the last was by C. H. Turner,[17] and the world of the ancient letter collection *as a collection* is now being explored, as we see, for example, in the work of Roy Gibson.[18] Nevertheless, this method means that Schwartz's edition, as an edition of Leo's letters, is as variable and anomalous as any number of mediaeval collections. The first 104 are an accurate representation of a systematised, mediaeval letter collection. But when one reaches the end of the Leonine material from *Grimanica* on page 131, one is confronted with letters from the *Collectio Ratisbonensis* not included in *Grimanica*, and in the order of *Ratisbonensis*, a technique continued for letters from *Collectiones Casinensis*, *Corbeiensis*, *Quesnelliana* and the two items from *Collectio Thessalonica*. Therefore, the whole collection of 113 letters is not, as a collection, systematised for the reader, but, rather, resembles the later mediaeval collections that Schwartz himself scorns in his introduction to the edition.[19] This method of compiling letters from different canonical collections is laudably transparent, then, but not without its problems. As no problem-free organisational method exists, we must leave Schwartz as he is. An online edition would alleviate some of the problems of ordering and text, since with the click of a mouse, one could see the letters in the order and wording of *Dionysiana*, and then with another, that of *Vaticana*. This, I believe, is the future of editing papal letters, but we cannot fault editors from the 1930s for not being able to do it!

---

[16] For the problems with Hinschius' classification and the dating of Pseudo-Isidorian mss, see below, 5.2.f.ii.

[17] Turner 1910.

[18] Gibson 2012.

[19] ACO 2.4, xxxv.

To leave the edition of Schwartz at a point of weakness would be to do a grave disservice to a work of high erudition that brought forward Leonine textual criticism from where it had stood for almost 200 years.[20] At the most basic level, Schwartz's edition is an improvement simply by giving the reader sigla and an apparatus. Unlike the Ballerini text, variants are clearly marked and easily identified; gone are the days of 'Unus codex Vaticanus'. More significantly, for those texts he edited in ACO 2.4, Schwartz used several early collections unknown to the Ballerini. These are *Collectiones Bobbiensis* and *Laudunensis*. Alongside these collections, Schwartz personally consulted manuscripts of which the Ballerini only had apographs or had not used in their edition, demonstrating some of the false readings provided by their second-hand knowledge. These collections are *Corbeiensis*,[21] *Rerum Chalcedonensium Collectio Vaticana*,[22] *Grimanica* itself,[23] and *Ratisbonensis* (which they knew through an apograph). Third, Schwartz drew connections between these various collections to demonstrate more clearly their filiation and origins, highlighting the vital importance of the Three Chapters Controversy for the preservation of Leo's dogmatic epistles.[24] This better understanding of the manuscript tradition and access to more manuscripts placed Schwartz in a better position for judging variants than the Ballerini, although their skill as Latinists must never be underestimated.

A further strength of Schwartz's edition is his production of a non-partisan edition of Leo's letters. As noted above, the Ballerini edition was commissioned to provide an alternative to Quesnel's because of Quesnel's Jansenist tendencies. The result is a text whose introductions and footnotes are riddled with discussions that are often not seeking to understand Leo and his text in the

---

[20] Indeed, it is part of the praise given the Ballerini by Turner that no one had been able to surpass their edition by 1910; Turner 1910, 701, calls their edition, 'perhaps the most remarkable achievement in the field of Patristic criticism down to Bishop Lightfoot's *Apostolic Fathers*'.

[21] See ACO 2.4, xiii.

[22] Described ibid., xv; PL 55.727 ff.

[23] As Schwartz observes (ACO 2.4, xxiiii), the Ballerini only accessed *Grimanica* through Quesnel's notes (PL 54.569–70).

[24] ACO 2.4, xxxv–xxxxi.

EDITING LEO'S LETTERS 85

fifth century, but, rather, safeguarding Catholic teaching in the eighteenth. Schwartz's text does away with these disputes and presents the reader with a text whose sole concern is Leo, what he meant, and what his manuscripts say. Such a text is an invaluable aid to those who wish to encounter this fifth-century author with as little taint from later times as possible.

2.10 Carlos Silva-Tarouca (1930s)

Carlos Silva-Tarouca also published a partial edition of Leo's letters in the 1930s.[25] In vol. 9 of *Textus et Documenta*, Silva-Tarouca provides his editions of *Epp.* 28 (the *Tome*) and 165 (the 'Second' *Tome*) with Leo's patristic *florilegium*, including critical discussion of the texts and manuscripts. Vols 15 and 20 represent his edition of the Leonine letters in the *Collectio Ratisbonensis*, and vol. 23 is an edition of *Collectio Thessalonicensis*, including both the Leonine and non-Leonine material without reproductions of Leonine letters that are in his previous volumes. These four volumes represent three different editorial programmes. Vol. 9 is the production of critical editions of Leo's most famous and influential dogmatic letters. Silva-Tarouca's introduction to these two letters discusses their importance and authority, including a discussion and vindication of Leo's theology, as well as their context and history, including the manuscript and print tradition. Having given a strong historical, philological, and theological introduction to Leo's two most famous letters, Silva-Tarouca gives us the texts themselves; first comes the *Tome*, divided *per cola et commata* into 205 sections; second come the *Testimonia* usually appended to the 'Second' *Tome*; third is the 'Second' *Tome*, subdivided into 174 sections. Certainly, Silva-Tarouca's arrangement makes it much easier to find a passage in either *Tome* than the Ballerini's or Schwartz's edition. However, this ease of use is diminished by Silva-Tarouca failing to include a *Conspectus Siglorum*; to discover what M and N mean in the *Tome* or what M, C, and Q signify in the 'Second' *Tome*, the reader must go through the introduction itself to find out. Aware of Schwartz's work, Silva-Tarouca chose to print the text of the *Tome* from Munich, Bayerische Staatsbibliothek, Clm

---

[25] C. Silva-Tarouca, *Textus et Documenta*, (Gregorian University) Series Theologica Vols 9, 15, 20, and 23 (1932, 1934, 1935, 1937).

14540, with references to Novara, Biblioteca Capitolare XXX
(66), referring the reader to Schwartz for more variants; he judged
these to be the best manuscripts available, and used them again
for the *Testimonia*, then *M* for *Ep.* 165 with notes from Paris, lat.
12097 (*C*) and Einsiedeln 191 (*Q*).[26]

The second two volumes of Silva-Tarouca's Leonine work, vols 15
and 20, represent a presentation of Leonine materials from a single epistolary collection. The introduction to these volumes, found
in vol. 15, covers the manuscript tradition with a chronological
table of the letters in that volume, and then prints F. Di Capua's
discussion of Leo's clausulae.[27] Di Capua's analysis of the clausulae is probably the most important part of the introduction, since
from it we gain insight into the editor's task as well as into Leo as
a stylist. Furthermore, Di Capua provides the reader with a table
of differences between *Ratisbonensis* and *Grimanica*, demonstrating
the superiority of the former as a faithful transmission of Leo's
text. This analysis of the quality of *Ratisbonensis* based entirely
upon internal, coherent evidence of the manuscript itself is an
important contribution to Leonine textual criticism. Hitherto, in
Schwartz's edition and the discussion of the dogmatic letters by
Turner, manuscripts were judged almost entirely by cross-analysis
and comparison of readings across the tradition. Yet when we do
not know what the truth is, we cannot judge the strengths and
weaknesses of two manuscripts simply by noting which gives a
reading we think better. Rather, coherent evidence from within
each manuscript, independent of the other, must be adduced. Di
Capua has done this for Silva-Tarouca's edition. Thus, although
his text is based on a collection that has 33 letters fewer than
Schwartz's choice, Silva-Tarouca's judgement of manuscripts is
more sophisticated and more reliable. In his text of *Ratisbonensis*,
he also gives variants in the apparatus from major manuscripts
of *Collectiones Grimanica*, *Quesnelliana*, *Coloniensis*, *Pithouensis*,
Hispana, *Vaticana*, *Chalcedonensis*, and *Novariensis*. The differences
between Silva-Tarouca and the Ballerini edition include the dating
of some letters and the names of some of the persons mentioned

---

[26] Silva-Tarouca 1932, 16–18.
[27] Di Capua 1934.

therein; the strengths of Silva-Tarouca's choices will be addressed in the course of this study.[28]

Silva-Tarouca's third programme was editing the *Collectio Thessalonicensis*; the production of an edition of an early mediaeval collection of canonical materials, an important source for canon law. The introduction provides the historical circumstances for the collecting of *Thessalonicensis* as well as its treatment in modern editions and the manuscript tradition. Thankfully, this edition includes a *Conspectus Siglorum*. Unlike his edition of *Collectio Ratisbonensis*, Silva-Tarouca's edition of *Thessalonicensis* includes the entire canonical collection as represented in the manuscript tradition. Thus, he provides us with a text that is eminently useful for the study of late antique and medieval canon law and the church in Thessalonica, not simply the study of Pope Leo. As a result, although he reproduces some of the idiosyncrasies of Schwartz's editions regarding selection and ordering, it seems to have been with more justification, since Silva-Tarouca is not providing us with every dogmatic letter he can find but giving us a clear window into certain traditions of ancient material in its mediaeval tradition. This editorial programme fits well with Silva-Tarouca's other work, such as his volume *Nuovi studi sulle antiche lettere dei Papi*,[29] in which he discusses the transmission of papal letters and the issues surrounding their study, and his work on thirteenth-century mediaeval manuscripts.[30]

2.11 Hubert Wurm, *Decretales Selectae*

In 1939, H. Wurm published an edition of two papal letters in *Apollinaris*.[31] Based upon collations of some of the earliest and reputable manuscripts—whose reliability will have been ascertained by his previous work, published the same year, *Studien und*

---

[28] For example, Silva-Tarouca re-evaluates the Ballerini dating of *Ep.* 59 (*Textus et Documenta* 15, 40 n. a) and replaces *Lucianus* with *Lucensius* in *Epp.* 104 and 107 *contra* the manuscript tradition (*Textus et Documenta* 20, 93–97, 105–06).

[29] Originally published in three parts in the journal *Gregorianum* 12 (1931): 1–56, 349–425, 547–98; repr. as *Nuovi Studi Sulle antiche lettere dei Papi*. Rome: Pontificia università gregoriana, 1932.

[30] *Codices Latini saeculi XIII*. Rome: Bibliotheca Vaticana, 1929.

[31] Wurm 1939*b*.

Texte zur Dekretalensammlung des Dionysius Exiguus, this is a good edition, even if very small. The first in this small edition is Innocent I to Exsuperius of Toulouse (JK 293), followed by Leo, *Ep.* 4. After introductory material about the manuscripts chosen (pages 79–82), the text of the epistle runs pages 82 through 93. The article itself begins with a discussion of the earliest collections and manuscripts, and the apparatus of both letters is extensive. One only wishes for more.

2.12 B. Vollmann, *Ep.* 15

In 1965, Benedikt Vollmann published *Studien zum Priszillianismus*, which considers the history and sources for the Priscillianist movement and includes an edition of Leo, *Ep.* 15 on pages 122–38, after an extensive introduction to the text and its manuscripts. This is a proper critical edition with a stemma on page 120 and uses forty-seven manuscripts throughout. This edition of a lone letter is the best edition of any of Leo's correspondence since the 1930s, and it is a welcome addition to the growing body of editions as well as to the study of Leo's letters and their transmission.

2.13 *Corpus Fontium Manichaeorum* Series Latina 1

The first volume of the Latin series of Brepols' CFM is *Sermones et Epistulae: Fragmenta Selecta* by Leo the Great, edited by G. H. Schipper and J. van Oort. This volume contains texts and translations of items from the Leonine corpus pertinent to the study of Manichaeism. Thus, we find here seven sermons and only two letters that are genuinely 'Leonine' based on their place in the tradition, *Epp.* 7 and 15, although *Ep.* 8, which is actually Valentinian's *Novella* XVIII 'De Manichaeis', is logically included, as is the letter of Turribius that the Ballerini appended to *Ep.* 15. As a sourcebook for understanding the position of Manichaeans in Rome during Leo's papacy, this is a helpful resource; however, the English is somewhat clunky. I would direct the reader to other translations instead; *Epp.* 7 and 15 have already been translated by C. L. Feltoe in the Victorian *Nicene and Post-Nicene Fathers*, Series 2, vol. 12, and all of the sermons more recently by J. P. Freeland and A. J. Conway for The Fathers of the Church, vol. 93. The Introduction, however, is useful as a guide to Manichaeism in the fifth century and Leo's response to it.

As an edition of Leo's letters, this text is by default almost useless since we have here only two genuine Leonine items. Not only
that, *Ep.* 7 is a reprint of the Ballerini version, including their
hard-to-follow footnotes for variants. *Ep.* 15 is based on the edition of B. Vollmann from 1965.[32] Nonetheless, making Vollmann's
edition of *Ep.* 15 more readily available while also taking into
account the Spanish version of the letter is helpful;[33] however,
once again we have a simple repetition of another's work. For the
so-called *Ep.* 8, however, the editors have only given us a reprint
of the Ballerini version, not even taking the time to provide us
the edition of Mommsen and Meyer instead.[34] CFM, Series Latina
1, serves only to highlight the pressing need for a new edition of
Leo's letters.

2.14 The Case for a New, Complete, Critical Edition

The above demonstrates quite clearly that a new, complete, critical edition is needed. Quesnel brought us near to a complete edition. The Ballerini came as close as anyone, barring the two items
discovered in the nineteenth century and edited by Schwartz
in ACO 2.2.1, 77–81. They, however, had a flawed and diffi-
cult-to-follow citation system. They also included items that did
not strictly belong with Leo's correspondence, although these documents are certainly helpful in contextualising the Leonine epistolary corpus. Since then, no one has even tried. MGH, *Epistulae*
3, gave us a good edition of the Leonine letters in *Collectio Arelatensis*; Schwartz provided a good edition of well over 100 items,
Silva-Tarouca of over 70. CFM, Series Latina 1, on the other hand,
reprinted editions of only two genuine Leo letters.

That is to say, the chief weakness of the twentieth-century editions is their incompleteness: the scholarly world needs a new edition of all of Leo's letters. Because Schwartz was only interested
in dogmatic epistles and Silva-Tarouca only in certain collections,
many letters remain without a sound, modern edition—especially,
but not only, the decretals. Our lack of a competent, critical edition of these decretals poses a serious problem to historians of

---

[32] Vollmann 1965, 87–138.
[33] For the Spanish version of *Ep.* 15, see Campos 1962.
[34] Mommsen and Meyer 1905, 103–05.

canon law, the papacy, and the development of church order. Leo left behind 17 decretals, a higher number than any of his predecessors, which, besides the *Tome*, were among the first Leonine letters to begin to be edited in the sixth century.[35] The exact nature of their transmission is shrouded in mist, and their text has not been improved since 1757.

[35] Jasper 2001, 49.

Chapter 3

Pre-Carolingian Canonical Collections

This chapter surveys and analyses the canonical collections that include collections of Leo's letters in the period before the middle of the eighth century. The organisational principle here is upon the date of the collections, not necessarily the manuscripts; many of these collections only exist in Carolingian manuscripts. Some of the collections that only exist in Carolingian manuscripts have had their pre-Carolingian existence challenged in recent scholarship; these collections are *Collectio Frisingensis prima* (**F**, section 3.2.a), *Collectio Vaticana* (**V**, section 3.2.d), *Collectio Teatina* (**Te**, section 3.2.i), and *Collectio Sancti Mauri* (**M**, section 3.2.r). Arguments for their inclusion in this chapter rather than the chapter on Carolingian collections are included in the study. As the analysis proceeds, relationships between manuscripts within the collections are analysed as well as relationships across collections.

Central to understanding these early canonical collections is the concept of the 'proto-collection', which is a collection of letters or documents that was used in the preparation of the existing canonical collections but which has no independent survival. Five proto-collections of Leo's letters have been identified in the survey and analysis of letter collections in this book; they are listed in summary form in the Appendix. By tracing the existence of the proto-collections, we are able to see the collection and dispersal of Leo's letters in those periods before our earliest collections such as the *Dionysiana* (**D**) and early manuscripts, such as that of *Collectio Corbeiensis* (**C**), filling in important parts of the transmission history.

The canonical collections analysed and surveyed in this chapter are *Frisingensis Prima* (**F**, see 3.2.a), *Diessensis* (**Di**, see 3.2.b), *Quesnelliana* (**Q**, see 3.2.c), *Vaticana* (**V**, see 3.2.d), *Sanblasiana* (**Sa**, see 3.2.e), *Dionysiana* (**D**, see 3.2.f), *Dionysiana Bobiensis* (**D–b**, see 3.2.g), Cresconius' *Concordia canonum* (no siglum, see 3.2.h), *Teatina* (**Te**, see 3.2.i), *Corbeiensis* (**C**, see 3.2.j), *Pithouensis* (**P**, see 3.2.k), *Thessalonicensis* (**Th**, see 3.2.l), *Avellana* (no siglum, see 3.2.m), *Arelatensis* (**Ar**, see 3.2.n), *Albigensis* (**Al**, see 3.2.o),

Remensis (**Re**, see 3.2.p), *Coloniensis* (**K**, see 3.2.q), *Sancti Mauri* (**M**, see 3.2.r), *Vetus Gallica* (no siglum, see 3.2.s), *Epitome Hispana* (no siglum, see 3.2.t), *Hispana* (**S**, see 3.2.u), *Hispana Systematica* (no siglum, see 3.2.v), Ragyndrudis Codex (no siglum, see 3.2.w).

3.1 The Earliest, Unknown Period of Transmission

The letters of Pope Leo I come down to us in fifty-eight collections, the earliest of which dates to the very late fifth century, around thirty years after Leo's death. The period before these collections is shrouded in a mist of uncertainty as with all papal letters before the sixth century.[1] These surviving collections have their origins in the previously mentioned proto-collections circulating in Italy and Gaul in the fifth century,[2] regional collections, and, potentially, the incipient papal archive. As noted above, the proto-collections are smaller collections that no longer have an existence independent from the collections that have come down to us. The contents of some such proto-collections can be postulated from the collation of the surviving canonical collections, which are collections of items pertinent to canon law: almost entirely canons and proceedings from church councils or papal letters although letters from local bishops are also included at times. The proto-collections that are found within them and that concern us tend to be small collections of papal material; we shall see examples of Leo's proto-collections throughout this chapter; others exist containing letters of his predecessors. As Jasper observes,[3] some of the proto-collections that contain his predecessors may be what Leo has in mind when he writes in *Ep.* 4, 'omnia decretalia constituta, tam beatae recordationis Innocentii, quam omnium decessorum nostrorum, quae de ecclesiasticis ordinibus et canonum promulgata sunt disciplinis'. Indeed, Dunn has recently argued that Leo has in mind the proto-collection of pre-Leo material embedded in *Collectio Corbeiensis* along with the Leo collection 4, 7, 15, and that the entire proto-collection of Leo and pre-Leo material was, in fact, of Leo's own creation.[4]

---

[1] Gaudemet 1985, 60.

[2] See the Appendix for a list and description of the proto-collections.

[3] Jasper 2001, 22, 26.

[4] Dunn 2015, 184–87. *Epp.* 4, 7, and 15, form my own proto-collection **proto-2**, discussed below at 3.2.j.i and with other relevant letter collections.

When these proto-collections are distilled from the larger collections that contain them, it becomes clear that most papal letters seem not to have circulated as individual units.[5] Instead, papal letters exist in small compilations from each pope, consciously gathered by their editors before being transmitted. Many of these proto-collections were circulating in Italy, making their way into the earliest Italian collections. However, Gallic collections also existed, such as those traceable in the sixth-century **C** and its related collections, or in the seventh-century **Ar** and **Al**. Proto-collections of Leo may have gained their contents from a variety of sources, possibly originating in the papal archive, possibly the epistolary recipients. They are not usually confined to documents pertaining to a specific area. For example, the earliest surviving Italian collections besides **D**—**Te**, **Sa**, and **V**— include letters sent by Leo to Constantinople, Gaul, Jerusalem, North Africa, Sicily, Spain, and Thessalonica. The early Gallic *Corbeiensis* likewise displays an international interest in the letters of Leo the Great, similarly drawing from letters to Constantinople, Gaul, Italy, Jerusalem, Spain, and Thessalonica. The presence of eastern letters implies that the proto-collections are, by and large, descendants of the papal archive, whether in Italy or Gaul. That said, the presence in **C**, a collection originating in Arles, of *Ep.* 10 concerning Hilary of Arles and *Ep.* 103 to all the bishops of Gaul, hints at the potentially local origins of some of the contents of these proto-collections. A further possibility, to return to the arguments of Dunn about **C**, is that Leo circulated his own letters to a wider circle than the original recipients, besides his own advice for recipients to circulate the letters.[6]

The purpose and origins of these proto-collections may be similar to those of the imperial *novellae* composed after the compilation of the Theodosian Code in 439, such as the collection composed during the reign of Majorian (457–61) and transmitted in Vat. lat. 7277;[7] however, the ecclesiastical equivalent of the collections and *breviaria* of imperial *novellae* may, in fact, be the fifth- and sixth-century canonical collections. Either way, the interest

---

[5] The exceptions are Siricius to Himerius of Tarragona and Innocent I to Decentius of Gubbio, as argued by Jasper 2001, 27–28.

[6] See, for one example of several, the close of *Ep.* 15.

[7] For this collection, see Mommsen and Meyer 1905, xiii.

in law, secular and sacred, was leading in the same period to collections of documents, even if the vast array of unofficial collections pertaining to canon law cannot be called codifications. These
proto-collections were no doubt put together by clerics wishing to
know the authoritative opinions of Roman bishops on certain subjects, and then circulated in the ensuing decades until they made
their way into the surviving collections. Perhaps they were copied
by their recipients to other bishops and clergy in their area; many
of our collections may be gathered from this sort of transmission.[8]

To move from the general to the particular: one of the proto-collections discussed by Jasper that has been postulated as having
been in circulation before Leo became pope in 440 is called the
Canones urbicani, including five letters: two from Innocent I (JK
293 and 303), one from Zosimus (JK 339), and one from Celestine I (JK 369 and 371).[9] Each proto-collection is very small and
illustrative of how papal documents were being transmitted before
the 490s. The diligent work of earlier scholars has also identified
a collection of seven of Leo's letters with other documents relating to the Eutychian crisis as an appendix to **C** and used by two
collections from shortly thereafter, *Coloniensis* (**K**) and **P**.[10] This
proto-collection contains Actio VII of the Home Synod of Constantinople of 448, Flavian's letter to Leo after the Home Synod
(Leo, *Ep.* 22), and Leo, *Epp.* 28, 103, 31, 35, 139, 59, and 165.[11]
Since this appendix to *Corbeiensis* seems to have been added early
in the collection's life, it can be dated to the mid-sixth century.[12]
That this particular collection was inserted wholesale into these
three collections is visible by the fact that they have its *incipit* in
common and close with 'finit' after *Ep.* 165.[13]

---

[8] This has been imagined by the Ballerini, PL 54.553–54, and Jalland
1941, 500, follows their lead. It seems an entirely likely, if unprovable, infer-
ence.

[9] Jasper 2001, 23–24. He also discusses (25–26) one proto-collection called
the *Epistolae decretales* and another that was a common source for **C** and **P**, on
which see below 3.2.k.iii.

[10] As discussed ibid.a, 44–45, with references to earlier literature. **K** and **P**
are discussed below at 3.2.q and 3.2.k respectively.

[11] Silva-Tarouca 1931 (1932), 413–14 (121–22), provides the description
from *Corbeiensis* in Paris, lat. 12097.

[12] See Jasper 2001, 45 n. 185, citing Turner 1929, 232.

[13] Jasper 2001, 45 n. 185, citing Wurm 1939, 171 n. 16.

Besides these proto-collections that later coalesced into the larger canonical collections of the sixth century and beyond, there were regional collections. The idea mentioned above of bishops circulating Leo's letters to their fellows possibly led to these regional collections; possibly they were born from the local archives of their respective bishoprics. Local circulation was recommended by Leo himself to a number of recipients,[14] and he addressed some letters to a number of bishops simultaneously.[15] Furthermore, letters in the ancient world were never a private affair. Gregory of Nyssa tells Libanius that when one of Libanius' letters arrived, everyone immediately acquired it for themselves, whether through memorisation or copying.[16] Gregory's brother, Basil of Caesarea, wrote to Libanius, and Libanius shared it aloud with those with him at the time.[17] We also have records of various bishoprics maintaining their own archives,[18] so a combination of the two forces probably produced these regional collections. Examples of such regional collections are the *Collectio Thessalonicensis* (**T**) from *c.* 531;[19] the mid-sixth-century *Collectio Arelatensis* (**Ar**) from the ecclesiastical archives of Arles;[20] and the seventh-century *Collectio Hispana* (**S**) that emerges from Spain and includes Leonine material related not only to Spain but to the concerns of the wider church as well.[21]

One source from which Leo's letters may have come to us is the fifth-century episcopal archive of the Church of Rome. The evidence for this archive is as follows. According to E. D. Roberts, our earliest reference to papal archives is from Julius I (337–52).[22] Presumably, the example Roberts had in mind was 'in sacro nos-

---

[14] e.g., *Epp.* 15, 108.

[15] e.g., *Epp.* 4, 5, 7, 10, 12, 13, 16, and 17.

[16] Gregory of Nyssa, *Ep.* 14.3–4 to Libanius; ed. P. Maraval, SC 363, 202–04.

[17] Basil of Caesarea, *Ep.* 338, ed. Courtonne, vol. 3, 205–06. For the references to Basil and Gregory as well as other instances of the non-private, even public, nature of personal correspondance in Late Antiquity, see Allen and Neil 2013, 19–20.

[18] e.g. *Acts* of Chalcedon, XIII.12, as evidence for archives at Nicaea.

[19] See below, 3.2.l.

[20] See below, 3.2.n.

[21] See below, 3.2.u.

[22] Roberts 1934, 191.

trae ecclesiae sedis scrinio'.[23] Liberius (pope, 352–66) also makes mention of a *scrinium*.[24] The most famous fourth-century reference, however, is from Damasus I (366–83). He is reputed to have converted his family home into the church of San Lorenzo in Damaso. Damasus' dedicatory inscription includes the lines (5–7):[25]

> Archiuis, fateor, uolui noua condere tecta,
>
> Addere praeterea dextra laeuaque columnas,
>
> Quae Damasi teneant proprium per saecula nomen.

It is assumed that the *archiua* here mentioned are the papal archives, being built a new home by Damasus. No archaeological evidence survives for archives at San Lorenzo, however.[26] Jerome mentions that anyone can go verify facts in the *chartarium Romanae ecclesiae*, in which important documents were stored.[27] Presumably Damasus' *archiua* at San Lorenzo are in Jerome's mind. Innocent I (401–17) writes, 'Omnem sane instructionem chartarum in causa archiuorum cum presbytero Senecione, uiro admodum maturo, fieri iussimus'.[28] According to E. D. Roberts,[29] Boniface I (418–22),[30] Celestine I (422–32),[31] Gelasius I (492–96),[32]

---

[23] *Ep.* 2.29 (PL 8.989).

[24] See his letter to Athanasius and the Egyptian bishops, 'de venerabili scrinio nostro' (PL 8.1408).

[25] Text ed. Ihm, no. 57; ed. Trout, 187–88.

[26] Smith 1990, 94. There is, however, evidence for a space that Krautheimer has identified as the episcopal *secretarium*, the hall of audience. See Krautheimer 2009, 274; Trout 2015, 189.

[27] *Apologia adu. libros Rufini*, 13.2. The text dates to 402–04, although probably drawing from memories of his own time in Rome 382–85. Cf. Gaudemet 1985, 60–61.

[28] *Ep.* 13 (PL 20.516–17).

[29] See Roberts 1934, 191–92, for this knowledge as well as for Hilarus' and Gelasius' involvement with libraries, albeit with no references.

[30] *Ep.* 4.2, 'scrinii nostri monimenta' (PL 20.760).

[31] *Ep.* 4.5, 'in nostris libelli scriniis continentur' (PL 50.433).

[32] In a synodal letter of Gelasius', the notarius Sixtus who wrote it includes in his *explicit*, 'jussu domini mei beatissimi papae Gelasii ex scrinio edidi' (*Ep.* 30, ed. Thiel, p. 447).

and Hormisdas (514–23)[33] all mention a 'scrinium sedis apostolae'. As my notes demonstrate, they actually use a variety of similar phrases, but the point is made. Leo's successor, Hilarus (461–68) built two libraries for pilgrims at San Lorenzo fuori le Mura,[34] but such libraries are clearly not an episcopal archive. Gelasius I's writings against Nestorius and Eutyches are said to be 'kept safe today in the archive of the church library', in a post-530 addition to the text of the *Liber Pontificalis*.[35] These are the traces of the papal archive in the fourth and fifth centuries. They are very scanty and tell us almost nothing about the *modus operandi* of this archive. One assumption that is typical about this early archive is that it included complete registers for all the papal letters such as we suspect existed by the episcopate of Gregory I. Poole contends that there is evidence in the *Collectio Britannica* of such a register existing for Gelasius I.[36] Even if a register for Gelasius were definitively demonstrated, it still says nothing about the operation of the episcopal archive at Rome in the pontificate of Leo I. Assumptions about the archive, then, are not safe to make, especially when we consider the state of early papal letters, including the collection of Leo's letters in the *Dionysiana* below.

If the primitive archive included any of Leo's letters, such survival may be known to us from the sixth-century editors at Rome, such as Dionysius Exiguus.[37] Dionysius likely used the papal archive,[38] and he himself says that he gathered together as many letters from Roman pontiffs as he could;[39] one would

[33] *Ep.* 26, 'documenta quoque de ecclesiae scriniis assumentes' (ed. Thiel, p. 793) and the statement, 'Bonifacius notarius sanctae ecclesiae Romanae ex scrinio edidit' (ed. Thiel, p. 795); *Ep.* 139 to the Synod of Constantinople closes, 'Gesta in causa Abundantii episcopi Trajanopolitani in scrinio habemus' (ed. Thiel, 967). Hormisdas also assumes that churches at large have *scrinia*, 'in scriniis ecclesiasticis', (*Ep.* 124, ed. Thiel, 930).

[34] *Liber Pontificalis*, 49.12.

[35] 'qui hodie biblioteca ecclesiae archivo reconditi tenentur', *Liber Pontificalis*, 51.6, trans. R. Davis.

[36] Poole 1915, 29–30.

[37] Jasper 2001, 49–50.

[38] Cf. Gaudemet 1985, 136.

[39] Praef. 1: 'ita dumtaxat, ut, singulorum pontificum quotquot a <me> praecepta reperta sunt, sub una numerorum serie terminarem, omnesque titulos huic praefationi subnecterem' (CCSL 85, 45).

assume, then, that he would have used the papal archive, such as it then was. And when we observe how scanty the Leonine pickings of Dionysius are—a mere seven letters—one cannot help asking how well-stocked the archive was. Given Dionysius' conciliar thoroughness, one would have expected far more than seven letters from an output of over 140. Indeed, when we take this fact into account in our observations about the early papal archive, it is difficult to imagine that in a short seventy years essentially the entire papal register of Leo the Great would have been destroyed, since Dionysius pre-dates the Gothic-Byzantine War. If the optimistic descriptions of the papal archive by Poole and Noble, for example,[40] that imagine the insertion of all papal letters into a papal register such as survives in part for Gregory the Great are true, then surely Leo's must have been severely damaged before the 510s. Perhaps the Laurentian-Symmachan schism of the years 498–506 resulted in damage to the archive.[41] Since papal letters were written on papyrus,[42] we admit to their fragility,[43] even in such registers as may have existed before Gregory I. In all probability, the archive never held the entire corpus of Leo's letters, nor those of any of the early bishops of Rome. Indeed, it does not even hold the entire corpus of Gregory VII, the first pope from whom we have the original copy of the register. Now it is time to turn from the unknown to what we do know and view the story of Leo's letters through the manuscripts of those canonical collections that *do* survive.

3.2 Pre–Carolingian Canonical Collections and the *renaissance gélasienne*

Various canonical collections served as the main sources for mediaeval canon law before the *Decretum Gratiani* of 1140.[44] Among

[40] Poole 1915, 13–17; Noble 1990, 86–90.

[41] Divisions and bitterness, however, persisted amongst the Roman clergy until Symmachus' death in 514. On this schism, see Reynolds 1979, 69–76.

[42] Poole 1915, 37.

[43] Nonetheless, the papyri of Ravenna have survived the ravages of time.

[44] For a description and discussion of the earliest sources of mediaeval canon law, see Gaudemet 1985 for the period ending in the seventh century; for the period from Pseudo-Isidore until Gratian, see Fournier and Le Bras 1931.

the most famous are the Pseudo-Isidorian forgeries, a collection both of genuine canonical material, which is at times manipulated to the forgers' ends, and of forged documents that are primarily papal decretals;[45] we shall discuss these in due course under Carolingian Collections.[46] Most canonical collections, however, do not deliberately contain inventions![47] Our investigation of the manuscripts begins, then, with the manuscripts of canonical collections compiled before the Carolingian era began in the eighth century. Questions concerning the compilation and ordering of the material included will be considered and the manuscripts, and their witness to Leo's letters discussed. This assessment will demonstrate the vital importance of a new edition as well as the problems facing the editor, especially when we behold the complexity of the textual tradition of the decretals found almost entirely in the canonical collections.

The most important pre-Carolingian moment in the history of western canon law is the period termed the *renaissance gélasienne*, running by G. Le Bras's reckoning from the accession of Pope Gelasius (492) to the death of Pope Hormisdas (523).[48] Following Le Bras's arguments, this was a time of compilation in western canon law.[49] Our earliest surviving canonical collections that include Leo—*Quesnelliana, Teatina, Vaticana, Sanblasiana, Dionysiana, Frisingensis Prima*—all date to this period. The western church had a growing awareness of its own canonical and legal legacy that could be promoted and regulated. Furthermore, thirty years after Leo's death, the power invested in the person of the pope now had theological foundations; the rulings of pope and council, then, were desired for the running of ecclesiastical life. Moreover, the consolidation of canon law manifest in the compila-

---

[45] Fuhrmann 2001 provides a detailed and useful introduction to the Pseudo-Isidorian forgeries and their study.

[46] Below 5.2.f.

[47] Some do, of course, contain forgeries; but these are not usually the work of the editors of the collections as with Pseudo-Isidore. Moreover, the mediaeval concept of forgery was not the same as ours. People invented documents on the grounds that, had the purported author written the text, he would have said the sort of things therein.

[48] See Le Bras 1930, 507.

[49] See Le Bras 1930, 506–11.

tion of large canonical collections meant the cessation of irregularities, such as canons forged in the names of apostles, and regularisation rather than localised canonical collections and penitentials.

While many of the above arguments from Le Bras's work are true, the parallel to the *Theodosian Code* or Justinian's work is not entirely apt.[50] The spirit of compilation in this age can certainly be adduced for both the *Theodosian Code* and the canonical collections, as well as for works such as Cassiodorus' *Institutions* or theological compilations. In fact, as Shane Bjornlie demonstrates in his discussion of Cassiodorus, the spirit of Late Antiquity was one of encyclopaedism, whether Cassiodorus' *Variae*, the manuscript containing the *Chronograph of 354*, the *Laterculus* of Polemius Silvius, or Isidore of Seville's *Etymologies*.[51] The spirit of codification, on the other hand, is harder to trace since none of these canonical collections dating from Le Bras's *renaissance gélasienne* are official works promulgated by the Roman episcopate. Furthermore, besides the fact that terming this possible *renaissance 'gélasienne'* may overemphasise the role of Gelasius—note again the unofficial character of these works as well as Gelasius' relative unimportance in the history of canon law[52]—the temporal boundaries also spill out beyond Le Bras's terminus. Six early collections come from this period, but eleven or twelve more come from the rest of the sixth or the early seventh century. Finally, if we are to term this period a renaissance, we will need evidence beyond canon law. It seems that, although there is some cultural flow-

---

[50] Ibid., 510. Moreover, the compilation of regional collections and penitentials continued well after this. The simplest example of the former is the fact that both *Collectio Arelatensis* and *Collectio Albigensis* post-date this period, and for the latter, consider the penitential material of Columbanus (*d.* 615) or the *Penitential* attributed to Theodore of Tarsus (*d.* 690).

[51] Bjornlie 2015.

[52] As emphasised by Firey 2008. Of course, we cannot ignore the vigorous correspondence Gelasius maintained during his four and a half years as pope. Nonetheless, in terms of impact in canon law, the *Decretum Gelasianum* is likely not authentically from Gelasius, leaving us with several letters on canonical issues, particularly *Ep.* 14—yet due to Gelasius' micromanaging, as Neil and Allen call it, few of his letters would have wider application due their very specificity, unlike the broader strokes taken by Leo; Neil and Allen 2014. On the authenticity of the *Decretum*, see Schwartz 1930.

ering in Ostrogothic Italy and early Merovingian Gaul,[53] there is no great break in literary and artistic production from the period before the 490s—no great increase in productivity or creativity. Furthermore, the *floruits* of the great literary figures of the Ostrogothic and Merovingian world overlap neither with each other nor with the canonical activity of this period. This so-called *renaissance* in canon law loses steam by the end of the sixth century, and the seventh is seen as a period of wider cultural decline in Merovingian lands and beyond,[54] visible in the enormous decrease of new canonical collections—the 600s produce a mere three canonical collections.

3.2.a. *Collectio Frisingensis Prima*[55] (**F**)

3.2.a.i. Dating and context

The *Collectio Frisingensis Prima* takes its name from a manuscript formerly in Freising, now in Munich, Bayerische Staatsbibliothek, Clm 6243. The manuscript has two collections in it, the second of which (*Frisingensis Secunda*, fols 192–96) is an early systematised canonical collection that contains none of Leo's letters.[56] **F** (fols 11–189), on the other hand, is a chronologically-organised canonical collection that was gathered in Italy after 495, the date of its most recent item.[57] Jasper proposes the idea that it came

---

[53] Look no further than Cassiodorus, Boethius, or Gregory of Tours.

[54] G. Brown 1994, 4. The decline of classical culture in southern Gaul begins in the sixth century after the close of the public schools, whereas it begins earlier in the north where there is a larger, ruling, warrior class of non-Roman origin; see Riché 1977, 206–10 for southern Gaul, and 210–18 for northern Gaul. Italy, having been ravaged by the Gothic War in the middle decades of the sixth century, was beset by new troubles in the form of high imperial taxation in the years immediately following and then the Lombardic invasions of the final decades. Cultural renaissances tend to require money to fund them—perhaps it is no surprise that it would be our first truly monastic pope, Gregory I, who would be the great light at the end of the century in an impoverished Italy, for the monastic impulse would be less affected by the economic travails of the age. The possible exception is Spain in the age of Isidore of Seville when we also witness the gathering of the *Collectio Hispana*.

[55] Not listed by Ballerini or Jalland. For a list of manuscripts and bibliography for this collection, see Kéry 1999, 2–3.

[56] Gaudemet 1985, 131. Edition in Mordek 1975, 618–33.

[57] Gaudemet 1985, 131–32.

from smaller, early collections dating to the era of Gelasius I,[58] while Schwartz argues that the original collection was, in fact, arranged in the 420s and later expanded.[59] The original nucleus of the collection would be from the canons through the documents pertaining to Apiarius of Sicca; the theory is that Celestine compiled this collection as a result of the embarrassment the Roman bishop faced in the case of Apiarius to prevent any similar occurrence in the future—thus, reliable copies of the canons were compiled along with important letters from Celestine's predecessors. As many canonical collections do, *Collectio Frisingensis Prima* begins with canons from fourth-century eastern councils, followed by letters of Popes Damasus, Siricius, Innocent I, and Zosimus. Next come documents pertinent to the business of the African presbyter Apiarius of Sicca Veneria, which are important for the history of canon law despite Apiarius being 'a very tiresome person',[60] and then letters from Popes Siricius, Leo, Gelasius, and Simplicius. The collection closes with documents relating to the Acacian Schism (484–519), a stage in Chalcedonian debate wherein Bishop Acacius of Constantinople (471–89) approved of Emperor Zeno's *Henotikon*, a document that attempted to bridge the gap between Chalcedon and its Miaphysite opponents.[61] Because of its lack of reference to Leo and Chalcedon, the western bishops opposed it, leading to the schism that only ended with the accession of the Chalcedonian Emperor Justin.[62]

---

[58] Jasper 2001, 49–50.

[59] Schwartz 1936, 61–83, arguing for a conciliar nucleus *c.* 420 at Rome largely on the basis of the forms of canons from Nicaea, Serdica, the acts of the 419 Council of Carthage, and how these relate to each other and fifth-century ecclesiastical history.

[60] Chadwick 1967, 231, n. 1. The case of Apiarius is discussed at length in Merdinger 1997, 111–35 and 183–99. The relevant primary sources are edited by Munier in CCSL 149, 78–172. See also *PCBE* 1, APIARIVS.

[61] The Acacian Schism is discussed more fully in Chaper 1 above.

[62] The text of the *Henotikon* can be found in ACO 2.2.3, 21–22; for discussions with a primarily eastern focus, see Gray 1979, 28–34 and Frend 1972, 143–83. For an analysis focussing on the popes, see Richards 1979, 57–68, 100–13, and now Moorhead 2015, 37–39, 59–64. However, Moorhead does not place a strong enough emphasis on the role the reception of Chalcedon truly played in this course of events. Blaudeau 2012 provides a reading that sees the Acacian Schism rooted in Rome's view of Constantinople's place in

F is thus divided into three very clear sub-collections, or even proto-collections. The question is whether we can be certain that this collection dates to the years following its latest item, a methodology of dating that has reasonably been cast into doubt by Rosamond McKitterick.[63] It is not unreasonable that someone in the Carolingian age had access to these three proto-collections and brought them together into a single codex for the first time in the eighth century. However, one of the questions we must keep in mind is to what end any of these collections was compiled. We have already seen how the first proto-collection makes sense as a compilation from the age of Celestine. The third of these proto-collections, that of material pertinent to the Acacian Schism, fits better in the late fifth or early sixth century than the eighth, when the Acacian Schism was no longer a live issue. What, then, of the second, the collection of Leo's letters? I believe that this collection, too, is fifth- or sixth-century by comparison with collections whose dates are not in doubt. For example, the *Collectio Dionysio-Hadriana* contains the canons of a Roman synod of Gregory II from the year 721. The *Collectio Hispana*, on the other hand, was added to at least once, possibly twice, as reflected in the manuscripts, which means that we can say that a version from after the Twelfth Council of Toledo in 681 was augmented after the Seventeenth Council of Toledo in 694 and also included letters sent to Spain by Pope Leo II. It seems, therefore, not unlikely that the second proto-collection that was compiled in **F** is from a date close to its final item, or at least not too many years distant. Unfortunately, we cannot say for sure whether the original compilation of these three proto-collections was in the late fifth/early sixth century or in the eighth. As sources for ecclesiastical regulation and reform, any of the documents in this collection could be useful at any particular time. Nevertheless, when we consider the Carolingian use of these collections as history as well as source-books for law, and when we recall the issues they faced, it seems

---

the hierarchy overall, not simply the *Henotikon* and the Chalcedonian Roman response whereas Grillmeier 1987, 288–326, provides a theological reading. No doubt both factors were at play.

[63] McKitterick 2004, 249–56. McKitterick does not deal with this collection specifically, but she does outline her methodology and her criticisms of this approach to dating.

more likely that this collection is a sixth-century compilation from the Acacian Schism or the period following the schism when Italians had reason to distrust Justinian than from the late eighth century under Charlemagne when it could easily have gained more material but did not.

If this canonical collection was compiled during the age of that schism, the inclusion of several of Leo's decretals should come as no surprise, since Leo was the hero of western Chalcedonian polemic. Furthermore, the organisation of this very early canonical collection into a clear division between the conciliar and papal material, and within the councils between east and west, with a further division into chronological order, is a method of organisation that will persist throughout the rest of the history of canonical collections.[64] **F** contains seven of Leo's letters, all so-called decretals: *Epp.* 14, 15, 159, 108, 4, 12, and 9.[65] *Ep.* 12 is in the *decurtata* recension.[66] **F** itself was used as a source for the *Collectio Diessensis*,[67] described below.[68]

3.2.a.ii. Manuscripts

The decretal portion of *Collectio Frisingensis Prima* can be found in two manuscripts:[69]

f: Munich, Bayerische Staatsbibliothek, Clm 6243 (saec. VIII[ex]), from the Lake Constance region.[70] Early Caroline minuscule. At Freising by the year 800; fols 200–16 and 233–38 saec. IX. Fol. 1 has Freising's library mark on it, and historical content

---

[64] See Gaudemet 1985, 132.

[65] For the contents, see Maassen 1870, 485–86.

[66] For the recensions of *Ep.* 12, see below, 5.2.d.iv, 5.2.e, and 7.12. The two original recensions, as argued by Hoskin 2018, are the *decurtata*, which the Ballerini print second (PL 54.656–63) and a version of the one they print first, lacking their chh. 6–8.

[67] As demonstrated by Gaudemet 1985, 148.

[68] 3.2.b.

[69] Kéry 1999, 2, lists a third manuscript for this collection (Würzburg, Universitätsbibliothek, M.p.th.f. 146 [saec. IX]), but the contents as described by Thurn 1984, 72–74, include no papal decretals.

[70] This manuscript is digitised: https://daten.digitale-sammlungen.de/~db/0005/bsb00054483/images/. Accessed 19 September 2021.

on 238^v confirms its Bavarian provenance.[71] Each item in the manuscript is given a rubricated uncial inscription of the type, 'INCP EPIST DECRETALIS AD ANATHOLIVM EPM THESSALONICENSIVM LEONIS PAPAE'. This manuscript gives the collection its name.

r: Munich, Bayerische Staatsbibliothek, Clm 5508, fol. 135 ff. (saec. IX), probably from Reichenau and likely a copy of *f*;[72] this manuscript has been digitised.[73] Early Caroline minuscule. *Frisingensis Prima* has here been appended to *Diessensis*.

There are also fragments of **F**'s conciliar canons in Würzburg, Universitätsbibliothek, M.p.th.f. 47 and 64a, from the second quarter of the ninth century and written in a late Hunbert script.[74] These are very similar to the *Frisingensis Prima* readings of the same passages;[75] while not useful for establishing the text of Leo's letters, knowledge of these fragments is useful in tracing the family tree and distribution of *Frisingensis Prima*.

3.2.a.iii. Manuscript relations

Research confirms that *r* is a copy of *f*. It follows the *f* text of Leo quite closely, including the uncommon spelling 'prumptum' in *Ep.* 14.1 as well as giving 'oboeditiae' for 'oboedientiae'. The majority of the differences are small errors on the part of *r*; a few examples from *Ep.* 14.1 are 'moderaminis diligari' instead of 'diligaui', 'curare' for 'curari', 'sint' for 'sit', the omission of 'et' in 'Vnde et beatus', 'moderatione' instead of 'moderatio', 'redda est' for 'reddenda est', 'pagines' for 'paginas', omitting 'in' from 'in litteris tuis', and omitting 'sponsione' following 'oboeditiae' [*sic*]. These are merely exemplary, but the point is made.

F's readings bear a very strong resemblance to **Q**. Out of the 58 **Q** variants for *Epp.* 14 and 159 in the table at 3.2.c.iii below,

---

[71] CLA 9, 1255; Bischoff 1998–2014, 2.3001. See also Mordek 1995, 321.

[72] Cf. Kéry 1999, 2. However, CLA 9, 1255, says Salzburg according to palaeography.

[73] Available at: https://daten.digitale-sammlungen.de/~db/0003/bsb00036890/images/. Accessed 19 September 2021.

[74] 'Hunbert script' is a script at Würzburg associated with the episcopacy of Hunbert (832–42); its history is discussed in Bischoff and Hofmann 1952, 15–17, with examples in Abb. 5 and 6.

[75] Ibid., 31 and 135.

F shares all but 8 of them. These eight are Variants 48, 50, 53, 62, 67, 74, 77, and 88. 48 and 62 are universal **Q** variants, both of which could have been easily emended to the **F** text or easily made in the **Q** text. 50 is only in two **Q** manuscripts (*p* and *b*), likewise 53 (*a* and *e*). **F**'s reading of 'recessit' against majority **Q** in 67 it shares with *v* and *w*—and its agreement with Variant 68 is also in alignment with *v* and *w*. Variant 74 is only a marginally majority reading of **Q** (MSS *a¹*, *e*, *v*, *w*). 77, on the other hand, is a significant minority reading in *a*, *p*, and *b*. Finally, 88 is a reading where the only **Q** manuscript with which **F** agrees is *p*; both could have been emended to produce the reading 'sanctificatio'. This close relationship with **Q** helps tie **F** down to an Italian origin.

3.2.b. *Collectio Diessensis*[76] (**Di**)

3.2.b.i. Dating and context

The first part of this seventh-century collection makes use of the *Collectio Dionysiana* (**D**) for its conciliar material, whereas the second part is from **F**, as discussed immediately above.[77] The earlier, **D** part of this canonical collection mingles conciliar canons, decretals, and secular documents with no discernable order, the latest of its pieces being from the Council of Clichy (626/27); the **F** material is taken entirely from the decretals.[78] Because the material added to the sixth-century sources is never later than the seventh century, this collection was most likely put together in the seventh century, since one would expect a Carolingian to include important Carolingian councils in a book of canon law. Perhaps all the Carolingians did was put both **Di** and **F** in the same codex. Not all of the non-**D** Leo material is drawn from **F**; in the first portion of **Di**'s manuscript, only three of the seven items are also in **D**, and at least one of these does not follow the text of **D**. **Di** contains two main collections of Leo's letters, all decretals: *Epp.* 15, 16, 159, 1, 2, and 12 (items XXXIIII–XXXVIIII);[79] item LIII is *Ep.* 167; and the other large selection, in which **Di** lacks numeration, is *Epp.* 14, 108, and 4, drawn directly from **F** and

---

[76] Unknown to the Ballerini and therefore Jalland. See Kéry 1999, 3–4.

[77] See Gaudemet 1985, 148.

[78] Ibid., 148.

[79] Maassen 1870, 627.

probably a copy of manuscript **F** *f*, as discussed above.[80] My eval-
uation, therefore, only concerns Leo's letters in the first section
of **Di**.

3.2.b.ii. Manuscript

It exists in one manuscript:

> Munich, Bayerische Staatsbibliothek, Clm 5508 (saec. VIII[ex]),
> written in Salzburg. It has been digitised.[81] Leo's letters are on
> fols 55[r]–68[r], 88a[r]-91[r], and 164[r]–170[v]. It is written in two columns
> of Caroline minuscule with uncial rubrication. Each major item—
> body of conciliar decrees, papal decretal, etc.—is given a *capitu-
> lum*. Many items end with 'EXPLICIT'.[82]

3.2.b.iii. Manuscript relations

Ep. 15 in **Di** shares its *incipit*, including the spelling of Turribius'
name, with **Te**, 'LEO THORIBIO EPISCOPO ASTORIENSI',
although **Di**'s scribe does better with the name of Turribius' city.
Beyond that, **Di**'s text of *Ep.* 15 stands out for being unlike that
in practically any other early collection—including **F**. Giving only
examples from the *Praefatio*, **Di** gives 'moueris' for 'mouearis';
'congrueagi deuotione' for 'dominico gregi deuotionem'; 'notitia
nostrae' for 'notitiae nostrae'; 'errorum moribus' for 'errorum morbus'; 'hereses qui' for 'hereses quae'; 'priscilianae' for 'Priscilliani';
'emersit' for 'immersit'; 'infecto sedorum' for 'in effectu siderum';
'offerri' for 'aufferri'; 'subuertisse' for 'suberti si'; 'recurrerunt' for
'recurrunt'; 'supplicio' for 'supplicium'; 'strinctim' for 'stricti'; and
'nec aliquid' for 'ne aliquid'. Finally, the phrase '-que rationem in
potestate daemonum' has been omitted. These are almost exclu-
sively errors of one sort or another, probably arising from carelessness and even weak Latinity on the part of the scribe. Beyond the
errors, it is worth noting that **Di** provides many non-**S** readings
in this letter as well as some contrary to **CP**: 'ab euangelio xpi

---

[80] Ibid., 634–35, where Maassen observes that **Di** leaves out those texts
from **F** that are doublets already included earlier in the manuscript when
drawing from **D**.

[81] For palaeographical grounds for dating and provenance, cf. CLA 9, 1247.
This is MS **F** *r* above. Available at: https://daten.digitale-sammlungen.
de/~db/0003/bsb00036890/images/. Accessed 19 September 2021.

[82] See CLA 9, 1247; Bischoff 1998–2014, 2.2987a.

nomine xpi deuiarunt' (**Te, C, P**; not **F**); 'tenebris etiam' (**Te, C, P**) *versus* 'tenebris se etiam' (**F, Q, S**); 'siderum conlocaret' (**F, Te**) *versus* 'siderum conlocarent' (**C, P, Q, S**); 'simulque diuinum ius humanumque' (**F, Te, Q, S**) *versus* 'simul diuinum humanumque' (**C, P**). In short, at different times **Di**'s text of *Ep.* 15 runs counter to **F, C, P, Q,** or **S**. Besides its unique errors, however, it is most consistently in accord with **Te**. Presumably, then, it owes its text of *Ep.* 15 to a source in common with **Te**. I maintain that *Epp.* 15, 16, 159, 1, and 2 are a proto-collection, designated **proto-3**; they come in that exact order in **Te** and **Re** as well. **Proto-3** is discussed more fully below at 3.2.p.[83]

The text of *Epp.* 16 and 159 is different enough from **D** to confirm a hypothesis that the compiler used a copy of **D** from its earlier, conciliar recension, not one with the decretals. Of the variants in the table at 3.2.f.iii for *Ep.* 16, **Di** shares variants 38, 40, and 48 with **D**. A few other **D** variants are shared, but not enough to signal a relationship. A few **Di** variants worth noting are in 16.1, 'accipitis' against 'accipistis' (Ballerini); it also gives 'beati petri apostoli sedes' (also Ballerini) rather than 'apostoli petri' (**Te, Re, D, V**); again in 16.1 'Ut licet uix' (also **Te, D** *a*) rather than 'Et' (Ballerini); in 16.2 'Quod in domo patris mei oportet' against 'quid in patris me oportet' (**D**) and 'quod in his quae patris mei sunt oportet' (Ballerini); 'sed aliter quaeque' against 'quoque' (**D** *c*) and 'quidque' (Ballerini); still in 16.2, **Di**[1] read, 'tempus quae tenere' before being scraped away and replaced with 'tempus potest pertinere' (also **D**) against Ballerini 'tempus posse pertinere'—this **Di**[1] reading is similar to **Te** and **V** omitting forms of 'posse' altogether. Further in 16.2 **Di** provides 'discretio' against 'districtio' (**D**; also **Te, V**) and 'distinctio' (Ballerini). In 16.3, **Di** agrees with **Te, D** *a* and **D–b** in giving 'quod' against Ballerini 'quidquid in illo'. One place where **Di** provides a text that concurs with the Ballerini is in 16.1 where **Di**[1] gives 'aestimat' (also Ballerini, **Te, V**) against **D** and **Di**[2] 'existimat'. In *Ep.* 16, it is clear that **Di** and **Te** do have some sort of relationship, possibly the shared proto-collection postulated above.

In *Ep.* 159, as is usual in the early collections regardless of letter, **Di** does not include 'episcopus' in the inscription. The inscrip-

---

[83] See the Appendix for a list and description of the proto-collections.

tion looks as though it has been modified from the original incipit: 'EPISTOLA LEO NICATE EPO AQVILIGENSE'.[84] Although 'EPISTOLA' has been thrust onto the front of this inscription, Leo's name has not been put into the genitive, presumably through *saut-du-même-au-même* from 'LEONISNICETE', possibly because 'LEONIC' looks a lot like 'LEONIS'. Indeed, one later hand seems to have assumed that 'ate' was not an especially apt name, and thus gave 'IANVARIO' as a suggestion, while another put parentheses around that name and rewrote 'NICETE' beside it. If we set aside 'EPISTOLA', had this incipit included 'salutem', it would have agreed with **Te**, **DD–b**, and **Q**. Like **Te**, **D**, and **Q**, **Di** omits 'a nobis' in the preface. In 159.1, **Di** agrees with **D** *c*, reading, 'quae uiros proprios' against 'qui' (**Te**, **Q**), 'quae cum uiros proprios' (**V**, Ballerini), and 'quae uiris propriis' (**D** *a*). Later in that chapter, **Di** provides 'liberandos et in aliorum' (also **Te**, **D**, **Q**) against 'ad aliorum' (Ballerini). At 159.5, **Di** provides 'consolatione' (similar to 'consulationis' in **D** *a*, **Te**, **V**) against 'consultationi' (**D** *c*, **Q**, Ballerini). Interestingly, at 159.6, **Di** writes 'ea esse custodienda moderatione'; while **D** provides the infinitive 'esse', no other manuscript gives 'moderatione' instead of 'moderatio'. Dates are often tricky for scribes; in *Ep* 159, **Di** closes with 'Data xv kl apr constantinop' against **D**, 'XIII kl april, cons marciani augusti' and Ballerini, 'Data xii …' XV is an easy enough corruption of XII, but the consular formula has been completely bungled. Overall, **Di** gives a mixture of readings in *Ep.* 159 that signify an Italian source; as we shall see at 3.2.p, it is the same source as **Re**.

In this manuscript, although *Epp.* 1, 2, and 12 come in the same order as in **Q**, they lack the protocols of that collection. Moreover, *Epp.* 1 and 2 are part of the postulated **proto–3**. Nonetheless, given how much attention has been paid to **Q** over the years, it is worth discussing how we can be sure that these three letters do not come from **Q** or another proto-collection shared with **Q**. The word 'CONTVLI' does not conclude the text of each letter, nor are the inscriptions the same. *Ep.* 1 is inscribed, 'EPISTOLA PAPAE LEONIS AD AQVILEGENSEM EPM' against, 'incip epla papae leonis ad aquilensem epm'; *Ep.* 2 has, 'INCIPIT EIVSDEM AD

---

[84] The original would likely have been 'EPISTOLA LEONIS NICETAE EPISCOPO AQUILIENSE', 'Nicetas' being the Aquileian bishop's proper name.

SEPTIMVM EPM' against, 'incipit epla papae leonis ad septi-
mum epm'; only *Ep.* 12 gives an exact correspondence between
the two collections with, 'INCIPIT EPISTOLA PAPAE LEONIS
AD MAUROS EPOS'. Like **Q**, however, **Di** produces the *decur-
lata* recension of *Ep.* 12, as do **F**, **V**, **Sa**, **Te**, and the **S** family of
collections.[85] **Di**'s text of *Epp.* 1 and 2 is close to that of **Sa** (see
table below at 3.2.e.iii). It shares variants 22, 23, 25, 26, 27, 28
(*l, c, k*), 29, 37, 39 (*sl, c*), and 41; that is to say, 10 out of 20 variants. When **Di** does not agree with **Sa**, it agrees with **Te** in 8 of
the remaining 10 variants. Of the 10 where **Di** agrees with **Sa**, it
shares 6 variants with **Te**. In all, then, **Di** is still here closer to
Te than to **Sa**, and the table at 3.2.p.iii shows us its similarly
close relationship to **Re**.

   Di provides the text of *Ep.* 167 with the *capitula* associated
with **Q** (and also, therefore, **Te**, **Re**, **Sa**, *Vetus Gallica*, etc.) rather
than those associated with **D**.[86] It also, however, inserts a chapter between 167.15 and 16 that builds on 167.15. The *capitulum*
for chapter 15 runs, 'De puellis quae aliquando in habitu religioso
fuerint non tamen consecrate si postea nupserint'. This new Chapter 16 (XVII in **Di**) is as follows:

> XVII De his qui [*sic*] iam consecrate sunt, si postea nupserunt,
> ambigi non potest magnum crimen admitti, ubi et propositum
> deseritur et consecratio uiolatur. Nam si humana pacta non pos-
> sunt inpone calcari, quid eas manebit quae corruperunt tanti foed-
> era sacramenti?

Di is the second appearance of this chapter, **Re** the first. A few
decades later, it also emerges in the *Collectio Hispana* (**S**)—a tradition that uses the **D** recension of *Ep.* 167's *capitula*. We will also
see it in **Q** *w*, added by a later hand that seems to be collating
the text against a manuscript from the wider **S** tradition (possibly
Pseudo-Isidore).

   Di, then, is a collection with diverse agreements and disagreements with the early Italian collections to which it seems to be
related. For *Epp.* 15 through 2, it is most closely similar to **Te**
and **Re**, yet even in those letters its divergences from **Te** are often

---

[85] For the recensions of *Ep.* 12, see 7.12 below.
[86] For the transmission of *Ep.* 167 and its *capitula*, see 7.167 below.

shared with other collections, demonstrating that it is descended not from **Te** but from a common source, **proto-3**.[87]

3.2.c. *Collectio Quesnelliana*[88] (**Q**)

3.2.c.i. Dating and context

This chronological collection of conciliar canons and decretals was compiled after 495.[89] Maassen gives strong arguments for the collection's origins in Gaul, which Duchesne narrows down to Arles;[90] however, his evidence is countered by Silva-Tarouca's demonstration of the Roman and Italo-Greek qualities of the Leonine portions in this collection,[91] as well as Le Bras's observation of a variety of items included here but not in contemporaneous Gallic collections.[92] Regarding Maassen's evidence, the fact that all of the manuscripts are Transalpine need not, in fact, give the collection a Gallic origin, as has been easily demonstrated by observing the possibility of the original Italian exemplar having been taken to Gaul.[93] When Maassen's Gallic elements are weighed up against Le Bras's and Silva-Tarouca's Italian evidence, an Italian origin seems more likely. Van der Speeten says it was used by Dionysius Exiguus for the canons of Nicaea and Serdica,[94] a fact which, if true, has little bearing on the relationship between the collections when Dionysius came to compiling the decretals. I do, however, doubt Van der Speeten's conclusion of direct transmission to **D** simply because of the vast differences between these collections in

---

[87] See the Appendix for a list and description of the proto-collections.

[88] Ballerini, Collection 5 (PL 54.556), Jalland 1941, Collection 1(v) (501). Because these two works are the most easily accessible discussions of the manuscripts, for each of the collections discussed henceforth, we shall reference them in the following manner: B5 (PL 54.556), J1(v) (501).

[89] The most recent item in the collection is a decretal of Pope Gelasius I, *Necessaria rerum*, from 494. See C. Silva-Tarouca 1931, 552.

[90] Maassen 1870, 492–94; Duchesne 1902, 159–62.

[91] Silva-Tarouca 1919, 661–62, and 1931, 552–59. My own research bears out the similarities between **Q** and the other early Italian collections in the text of Leo's letters.

[92] Le Bras 1930, 513.

[93] Silva-Tarouca 1919, 662.

[94] Van der Speeten 1985, 449–50.

Leo's letters;[95] if Dionysius used **Q** for the canons, he must no longer have had access to a copy when he compiled the decretals. The
Ballerini argue that **Q** is to be preferred to **D** for *Ep.* 167, since
it contains what looks to be the original text of Rusticus' queries rather than paraphrases.[96] However, it is unlikely that that
is actually the case, and probable that both the **Q** and **D** *capitula*
are scribal additions, as discussed below at 7.167. The collection is
named after Pasquier Quesnel and was foundational for his edition
of Leo's letters. The Ballerini themselves edited **Q** in the third
volume of their edition of Leo's letters under the belief that it was
a collection officially commissioned by the Roman episcopate;[97] no
evidence that **Q** is anything other than a private collection exists,
however.

Q contains 32 of Leo's letters, twelve of which are classed as
decretals in later tradition, and has thus been important for the
transmission of the letters through other collections: 165, 139, 28,
108, 15, 167, 14, 159, 18, 4, 7, 16, 31, 59, 124, 1, 2, 12, 33, 44, 45,
35, 29, 104, 106, 114, 155, 162, 163, 135, 93, 19. *a* and *p* add 97,
99, and 68 at the beginning of Leo's letters, although *p* begins
with the patristic *testimonia* of *Ep.* 165.[98] Schwartz maintains that
this is simply a disordered rabble of texts,[99] but closer investigation makes it plain that, instead, the editor had a number of
sources available to him that he did not dismember and reorganise
according to a single system; that is, rather than there being no
system at all, we have instead multiple systems working side by
side. The first three letters, *Epp.* 165, 139, and 28, all deal with

[95] When we consider, for example, the differences in readings between **Q**
and **D** in the Leo portion, such as the *capitula* of *Ep.* 167, as well as the vast
number of Leo's letters in **Q** *versus* the paucity in **D**, it seems very unlikely
that Dionysius made us of **Q** in producing his decretal collection. Perhaps the
similarities between the Nicene and Serdican canons derive from a source
common to both collections.

[96] PL 54.1198. Repeated by Jalland 1941, 501.

[97] Repr. PL 56.

[98] The Ballerini (PL 54.556) mention that some manuscripts add these
letters to the beginning, but fail to mention which ones. The rest of the **Q**
manuscripts include only *Ep.* 68 out of these three, despite the otherwise very
strong textual similarities in the rest of Leo's letters between *a* and *e* on the
one hand and *p* and *b* on the other.

[99] ACO 2.4, iii–iv.

the matter of Chalcedon—two are Leo's most famous dogmatic epistles. The next series, from 108 through 16, is of decretals, possibly drawn from more than one proto-collection—note the pairing of *Epp.* 4 and 7, just as in **D** and **proto-2**, a source of **C**, **P**, **Al** discussed below at 3.2.j-k;[100] *Ep.* 16 follows *Ep.* 7 in **D** as well. *Epp.* 31, 59, and 124 are another series of dogmatic letters—31 and 59 are also in **C** and **P** in that order, although with two other letters intervening. Nonetheless, these could be traces of similar proto-collections. *Epp.* 1, 2, and 12 form the next subcollection of **Q**, another of decretals;[101] 1 and 2 are often paired together as seen above in **Di**, as well as in **Sa**, **Te**, and other early collections. The next run of letters to *Ep.* 163 is a chronological selection of dogmatic letters, and then **Q** closes with *Epp.* 135, 93, and 19.[102]

3.2.c.ii. Manuscripts

The primary tradition of the *Quesnelliana* exists in the following manuscripts:[103]

> *a*: Arras, Bibliothèque municipale, 644 (572) (saec. VIII–IX).[104] It originates in Northeastern France and is likely from the same scriptorium as *e*. *a* begins Leo's letters at 124ᵛ with *Epp.* 97, 99, and 68, then provides the standard **Q** sequence, closing with *Ep.* 19 on 212ʳ. After 173ᵛ there is a lacuna of several folios; the text cuts off in *Ep.* 15 at 'mendax etiam resur[rectio' and resumes on 174ʳ with *Ep.* 167 towards the end of the *Praefatio* at 'seuerius castigare necesse est'. Another selection of missing folios occurs at the end of 180ᵛ, in the midst of *Ep.* 14.11 at,

---

[100] See the Appendix for a list and description of the proto-collections.

[101] Of interest is the fact that at the conclusion of these three letters in the **Q** manuscripts is found the word 'CONTVLI', meaning that the scribe has double-checked with his exemplar; its presence strengthens the identity of *Epp.* 1, 2, 12 as a discrete entity within **Q**. See Wurm 1939, 219–23, for the 'CONTVLI' protocol. Wurm sees this as evidence of a papal archive, but see the doubts of Schwartz ACO 2.4, iii, and Silva-Tarouca 1926, 38, and 1931, 132, n. 2.

[102] See similar conclusions of Wurm 1939, 210–19, against Schwartz. Jasper 2001, 50–52, generally agrees with Wurm.

[103] One further *Quesnelliana* MS exists, but it is incomplete and lacks Leo: Paris, lat. 3848A (saec. IX1/4). This manuscript is from the region around Metz; it made its way to the Bibliothèque Nationale from Troyes.

[104] CLA 6.713; Bischoff 1998–2014, 1.88.

'sicut in uno corpore multa membra'; the text resumes on 181^r midway through *Ep.* 159.2 at 'captiuitatem ducti sunt pertine-bant'. There is a third lacuna of missing folios at the end of 198^v, partway through *Ep.* 2 at 'constitutionem praecipimus custodiri ne[c\] ab his'. The text resumes on 199^r with *Ep.* 12 at 'tinetur nec putandus est honor ille legitimus'. Throughout this manuscript small errors of one or two letters have been corrected by a second hand of similar date; they have not been collated in the table below unless potentially significant.

e: Einsiedeln, Stiftsbibliothek, 191 (277), (saec. VIII–IX).[105] *e* includes a catalogue of popes (fol. V$_{11}$ through fol. 1^v) that closes during the papacy of Hadrian I (772–95), making a late eighth- or early ninth-century date for this manuscript likely. It is writ-ten in Caroline minuscule with rubricated *capitula*. 2^v is taken up entirely by an archway that resembles those of canon tables; the architecture is ornamented with knotwork in yellow, blue, purple and orange; this manuscript is more prestigious than many canon law codices. Bischoff argues that this decoration is from Charlemagne's court library, further securing the date of the manuscript and its prestigious origins.[106] Leo's letters run 161^r–162^r (*Ep.* 68) and 163^v–229^r; at 229^v a second hand takes over and a variety of *miscellanea* complete the manuscript. As well, the bottom four lines of 214^v are written in a different, smaller hand than the rest of the page and what follows. The collection of Leo's letters in this manuscript is the 'standard' version of **Q** with *Ep.* 68 two items beforehand; as in *b* below, the intervening item is Cyril's Second Letter to Nestorius. The main text of the manuscript is in Caroline minuscule with uncial rubrication. As usual for **Q**, Leo's letters are for the most part not divided into chapters with *tituli*.

p: Paris, lat. 3842A (saec. IX^{med}/3/4, Kéry).[107] Written in northern France in multiple hands with a selection of distinct palaeograph-ical features as noted by Bischoff. As noted above, Leo starts at 77^r with the *testimonia* of *Ep.* 165, and the sequence of letters is different from standard **Q**. They run 79^v–168^r, starting with *Epp.* 97, 99, 68, followed by the standard sequence to *Ep.* 19, then finishing 166^r–168^r with *Ep.* 120.

---

[105] CLA 7.874; Bischoff 1998–2014, 1.1116. This manuscript has been digitised: http://www.e-codices.unifr.ch/en/sbe/0191. Accessed 19 September 2021.

[106] Bischoff 1998–2014, 1.1116. There is a similar archway on folio V$_{10}$.

[107] Olim *Colbertinus* 932 as listed by the Ballerini and Jalland. For dating, see Kéry 1999, 27; Bischoff 1998–2014, 3.4281.

b: Paris, lat. 1454 (saec. IX3/4), from around Paris.[108] It made its
way into the Bibliothèque nationale via the cathedral chapter of Beauvais.[109] If the correct manuscript has been identified, this manuscript was one of those used by Quesnel in his
groundbreaking *Opera Omnia* of Leo in the seventeenth century.
Leo's **Q** letters run 162ᵛ–212ᵛ in the order described above, ending with *Ep.* 19; before the main series of letters, *Ep.* 68 runs
160ᵛ–161ʳ, followed by Cyril's Second Letter to Nestorius before
the rest of Leo's letters, as in *e*, *v*, and *w*. The rubrication comes
and goes for most of the collection: the *testimonia* of *Ep.* 165 are
rubricated only until 166ᵛ, 'SCI ATHANASII ALEXANDRINI
EPI ET CFESSORIS AD EPICTITU(M) EPM CORINTHIUM';
Ep. 124, which begins at the top of fol. 193ʳ, has no rubric or
inscription; from *Ep.* 144 (fol. 204ʳ) onward, there are no rubrics
or inscriptions to the letters (i.e. 'Leo eps Theodoro epo …')
although two lines have been left blank between each letter for
this purpose, and *Ep.* 155 is missing the D from 'Diligentiam'
that begins the letter. In *Ep.* 19, 212ʳ starts a new hand and
a new quire with 'pertinere ut s(an)c(t)arum constitutionum …'
In this new quire, after the *Damnatio Vigilii*, Leo *Ep.* 120 is on
214ʳ–216ʳ.

v: Vienna, Österreichische Nationalbibliothek, Cod. 2141 Han
(*c.* 780).[110] Leo's letters run fols 122ʳ–169ᵛ; the collection of letters is the 'standard' run of **Q** as described above, beginning
with *Ep.* 165 and closing with *Ep.* 19; as with *e*, *b*, and *w*, *Ep.* 68
is included after Pseudo-Clement to James and before Cyril's
second letter to Nestorius running 120ʳ⁻ᵛ. *v* is written in a Caroline minuscule with rubricated uncial headings in a single column.

w: Vienna, Österreichische Nationalbibliothek, Cod. 2147 Han.
(*c.* 780);[111] based on their scribal hands both Viennese manuscripts are from the area around Lorsch, written in pre-Caroline

---

[108] I believe this is the manuscript Jalland lists as Paris, lat. 1564, since
that manuscript is of the *Collectio Pithouensis* described at 3.2.k. It is digitised: https://gallica.bnf.fr/ark:/12148/btv1b8572237k. Accessed 19 September 2021. See Bischoff 1998–2014, 3.4014.

[109] Kéry 1999, 27.

[110] Ibid., 28. CLA 10.1505; Bischoff 1998–2014, 3.7218. This MS is http://
data.onb.ac.at/dtl/2942965. Accessed 19 September 2021.

[111] Kéry 1999, 28; Bischoff 1998–2014, 3.7219. *w* and *v* must be the old
'Caesarea Biblioteca' manuscripts in the Ballerini. This MS is digitised:
http://data.onb.ac.at/dtl/2942016. Accessed 19 September 2021.

and Caroline minuscule.[112] Leo's letters run in the **Q** sequence in fols 156^r–223^r; as with *e*, *b*, and *v*, *Ep*. 68 is included after Pseudo-Clement to James and before Cyril's Second Letter to Nestorius running 154^{r-v}.

This manuscript is atypical in two ways. First, in the middle of the collection a quire has been inserted, running 169^r–176^v. This quire comes after the end of *Ep*. 28 on 168^v and before the start of 108 on 177^r; the uncial incipit of this non-**Q** quire is, 'Incipiunt decreta papae Leonis aduersus Euticen Constantino-politanum abbatem, qui uerbi et carnis unam ausus est pro-nuntiare naturam, dum constet in Domino Iesu Christo unam personam nos confiteri in duabus naturis Dei atque hominis'. This incipit is that of *Collectio Hispana Gallica Augustodunensis* (**S–ga**), the ancestor of the Pseudo-Isidorian tradition (**I**) that incorporates the thirty-nine Leo letters of **S**. The addition con-sists of a series of **S** letters, *Epp*. 20, 23, 22, 115, 130, 134, 25, 60, 61, 69, 70, 71, and 79. The letters are taken in three selec-tions from **S**: *Epp*. 20, 23, 22; 130 and 134; 25; and 60 through 79. None of these letters is part of **Q**, and the quire has been added at a logical break in **Q** between the first run of dogmatic letters so-called decretals, not willy-nilly in the middle of a let-ter. Furthermore, the hand is similar enough to the surrounding quires that, taking all the evidence together, it was conceivably drawn up in the same scriptorium as a supplement to **Q**. The text of *Ep*. 79 ends three quarters of the way down 176^v at the bottom of which is written, 'EIUSDEM LEONIS AD THEO-DORUM FOROIULIENSEM EPM / Ut his qui in exitu sunt p(a)enitentia & communio non negetur'.

Second, after *Ep*. 19 ends on 223^r, a series of letters closes the manuscript, the first eight of which are Leo, *Epp*. 80, 82, 83, 85, 90, 168, 166, 9; *Epp*. 80–90 are from the sequence of Pseu-do-Isidore Class A1 (**I–a**), as are 166 and 9, *Ep*. 168 being the one out of order. These letters are written in a new hand imme-diately following *Ep*. 19 with 'Item Leonis ad Anatolium con-stantinopolitanum epm'. After Leo's letters come Popes Hilarus to Ascanius, 'Diuinae circa nos' (JK 561); Simplicius to Zeno, 'Plurimorum relatum' (JK 590); and Innocent I to Aurelius of Carthage 'Qua indignitate' (JK 312). Besides these two notable additions, a patristic *testimonium* has been slipped into *Ep*. 165 right after 160^v which closes 'in mea substantia loquebatur'; it is a small piece of parchment bound into the volume, about a quar-

[112] CLA 10.1506.

ter of a page, with a blank recto and the text on the verso, 'Item eiusdem ad sabinu(m) epm inter caetera. Vnde pulchre apostolus eiusde(m) uerbi …' which is a *testimonium* from Ambrose, *De Officiis*, that belongs on 161ʳ but had presumably been missed out by a scribe and added in this manner. Given these **S/I** additions to *w*, I believe that w^2 had a Pseudo-Isidorian Leo against which the text was collated. This explanation is bolstered by a number of small changes that bring the text of *w* into agreement with the **I** tradition; some of these are changes that also bring *w* into line with a vulgate tradition, so the Pseudo-Isidorian theory requires the other changes discussed above. However, *w* also includes Spanish *aeras* in the dates of some letters, such as *Ep.* 28, further increasing the Spanish-influenced passages within the text. Some examples of these small Pseudo-Isidorian changes are: 'carent culpam' (Var. 14 below) to 'carent culpa'; 'in paenitentiam' to 'paenitentia' (Var. 19); the addition of 'mortis' after 'metu' in 'aut metu, aut captiuitatis' (Var. 21); 'ad anatholium' to 'ad anastasium' (Var. 33); and 'siue ratione' to 'si uera ratione' (Var. 36).

There is one further manuscript of *Collectio Quesnelliana*, Oxford, Oriel College, 42 (saec. XII). This manuscript provides *Quesnelliana* up to Leo's letters, at which point a different, unique, collection of Leo's letters is included. Therefore, since this collection exists in but a sole twelfth-century manuscript and was likely compiled by the manuscript's scribe, William of Malmesbury, I have postponed discussion of Oriel College 42 until Chapter 6.2.a.

3.2.c.iii. Manuscript relations

The first table sets out those variants from the selected passages of the *Tome* (*Ep.* 28) where **Q** manuscripts are at variance with Schwartz's edition. They bear out the same findings in terms of manuscript relationships as the second, larger table on the disciplinary letters. The variant words are given in italics.

Var.	Q	Schwartz (control)	Significance
1	*epistulis* (a, e, p, b, v, w)	Lectis dilectionis tuae *litteris*	Common error **Q**
2	*credere* (a, e, p, b, v, w)	doctioribusque non *cedere*	Common variant **Q**
3	*hac insipientia* (a, e, v, w¹)	sed in *hanc insipientiam* (p, b, w²)	Common error a, e, v, w

Var.	Q	Schwartz (control)	Significance
4	*generandorum* (*w¹*)	omnium *regeneran-*dorum* uoce (*a, e, p, b, v, w²*)	Error *w¹*
5	*uerbo* (*p.¹, b*)	de *uerbi* dei incarnatione sentire (*a, e, p.², b, v, w*)	Common error *p.¹, b*
6	totam *separando* (*a¹, p.¹, b*)	sed totam *se reparando* (*a², e, p.², v, w*)	Common error *a, p, b*
7	*nos* possemus (*a, e, p, b, v, w*)	enim superare possemus	Common variant **Q**
8	*utinam* doctrinae (*b*)	propria tenebrarat, doctrinae (*a, e, p, v, w*)	Variant *b*
9	*interiori* (*a¹, p.¹*)	*interiore* adprehendisset auditu (*a², e, p.², b, v, w*)	Common error *a, p¹¹³*
10	*ademittit* ita (*b*)	forma non *adimit,* ita (*a, e, p, v, w*)	Error *b*
11	*utramque naturam* (*a², e, v, w¹*) *naturae* (*a¹*)	in *utraque natura* intellegendam (*p, b, w²*)	Common error *a²,* *e, v, w* Attraction
12	V ID (*p*) IUN (*p, b, w²*)	id ian (*a, e, v, w*)	Common error *p, b*
13	hera cccclxxxi contuli (*w*)	Om. (*a, e, p, b, v*)	Spanish influence

The following table contains a selection of readings drawn from certain of the **Q** letters on church discipline, namely *Epp.* 167, 14, 159, 18, 4, 7, 16, 1, and 2. Although not exhaustive for these letters, these variants are sufficient to make apparent the relationships among the six **Q** manuscripts.

---

[113] Given the frequency with which *e* and *i* are interchanged in mss, this shared variant alone is almost meaningless. However, since technically it is the difference between an ablative and a dative, if it occurs amidst other shared variants, then it is a minor piece of corroborating evidence. Therefore, it has been included in the table.

Var., *Ep.*	Quesnelliana	Ballerini (control)	Significance
1, 167 *Inscr.*	ad rustitium (*e, v, w*)		Agreement *e, v, w* *a* missing inscription
2, 167.Pr	Ecce inquit ego (*a, e, p, b, v, w*)	Ecce ego inquit	Common variant **Q**
3, 167.Pr	om. *de singulis* (*a, e, p, b, v¹, w*)	quaereretur *de singulis* si nobis (*v²*)	Common error **Q**
4, 167.Pr	*conspectus tui* (*a, e, p, b, v, w*)	si nobis *tui conspectus* copia	Common variant **Q**
4, 167 *Titulus* for q's	'Inquisitiones et responsiones' (*a, e, p, b, w*) 'Adinquisitiones eiusdem epi subiecta responsa' (*v*)		Agreement *a, e, p, b, w* *v* agreement with **D** Therefore, *a, e, p, b, w* = **Q**
5, 167.1	*qui* ad (*a, e, p, b, v, w*)	ordinati sunt *quae* ad proprios	Common error **Q** Attraction
6, 167.1	*est habenda* (*a, e, p, b, v, w*) *una* (*e, p, b, v¹, w*)	uana *habenda est* creatio	Common variant **Q** Common error **Q** (*a* easy correction)
7, 167.2	*hi* (*a, p, v*) *hii* (*b, e, w*)	consecrati *ii* pro	Common variant **Q**
8, 167.2	*orauit* (*a, e*) quis orabit *quis orabit* pro (*v*)	quis *orabit* pro illo (*p, b, w*)	Mere orthography *a, e* (i.e. insignificant) Dittography *v*
9, 167.3	*altaris ministris* (*a, e, p, b, v, w*)	eadem est *ministris altaris* quae	Common variant **Q**
10, 167.3	*cessent* (*a, e, p, b, v, w*)	connubiorum et *cesset* opera nuptiarum	Common error **Q** Attraction
11, 167.4 *Cap.*	*coniugio* (*a, e, v, w*)	uiro in *coniugium* dederit (*p, b*)	Common **error** *a, e, v, w*
12, 167.4	*uiro iuncta* (*a, e, p, b, v, w*)	mulier *iuncta uiro* uxor est	Common variant **Q**
13, 167.4	*heres est patris* (*a, e, p, b, v, w*)	heres est patris	**Q** agreement with Ballerini, unlike many other collections

Var., *Ep.*	Quesnelliana	Ballerini (control)	Significance
14, 167.5	*culpam* (*a, e, v, w¹*)	carent *culpa* si mulieres (*p, b, w²*)	Error *a, e, v, w* Scribe imagines *careo* + accusative
15, 167.5–6	Division of chh. 5 and 6 after 'aliud concubina', not after 'non fuerunt' (*a, e, p, b, v, w*)		This is where **D** divides chh. 4 and 5
16, 167.7	*expetiuerunt* (*a, e, v, w*)	necessarie *expetierunt* fideliter (*p, b*)	Common variant *a, e, v, w*
17, 167.8	*communicamus* (*a, e, v, w*)	non *communicauimus* mortuis (*p, b*)	Common error *a, e, v, w*
18, 167.10	*etiam a multis licitis* (*a, e, p, b*) oportet *etiam multis licitis* (*v, w*)	oportet *a multis etiam licitis* abstinere	Common variant *a, e, p, b* Common error *v, w*
19, 167.11 Cap	in *paenitentiam* uel (*a, e, v, w¹*)	in *poenitentia* uel post poenitentiam (*p, b, w²*)	Common error *a, e, v, w* due to attraction
20, 167.12	*omnino est* (*a, e, p, b, v, w*)	Contrarium *est omnino*	Common variant **Q**
21, 167.13	om. *mortis* (*a¹, e, p, b, v, w¹*)	aut metu *mortis*, aut captiutatis (*a², w²*)	Common error **Q**
22, 167.13	*iuuenalis* (*a, e, p, b, v, w*)	incontinentiae *iuuenilis*, copulam	Common variant **Q**; also **D, V**[114]
23, 167.13	Keeps *uenialem* (*a, b, v, w*) *ueniale* (*e*) *uenial* (*p*)	rem uidetur fecisse *uenialem*	NB: **Sa** gives *iuuenalem* here due to *iuuenalis* above, unlike **Q, D, V**, etc.
24, 167.14	innocens *sit* (*a, e, p, b, v, w*) *sit malititia* (*p*) *sit milicilia* (*w¹; w²* corr. *milicia*)	etsi innocens militia	Common variant **Q**

---

[114] Since this spelling affects variants in words around it, it is worth recording.

Var., *Ep.*	Quesnelliana	Ballerini (control)	Significance
25, 167.15 *Cap*	*post* (*a, e, b, v, w¹*) *potest* (*p*)	si *postea* nupserint (*w²*)	Common error *a, e, b, v, w* = **Q** Error *p*, from *post*
26, 167.15	non *parentum coactae* (*a, e, p, b, v, w*)	non *coactae parentum* imperio	Common variant **Q**
27, 167.15	si *nondum eis gratia* consecratio (*a², w²*)	si consecratio (*a¹, e, p, b, e, v, w¹*)	*a², w²* addition from **S**
28, 167.15/16	'INQ: De his qui iam consecrate sunt si ...' (*w²*)		Extra ch from **S** between 15 and 16
29, 167.16 *Cap*	Om. *et* (*a, e, p, b, v, w¹*)	sunt, *et* utrum (*w²*)	Common variant **Q**
30, 167.17	*etiam hoc* (*a, e, p, b, v, w*)	si *hoc etiam* ab ipsorum	Common variant **Q**
31, 167.19 *Cap*	*gentibus* (*a, e, p, b, v, w*)	a *gentilibus* capti sunt	Common variant **Q**
32, 167.19	*uisi* (*a*) immolaticiis *inter-fuisse* usi (*p*) immolatitiis *inter-fuisse uisi* (*b*)	immolatitiis *usi* sunt (*e, v, w*)	Error *a* Error *p*, probably from Variant *b*
33, 14 *Inscr*	'Incipit epistula decretalis ad *anastasium thessalonicensem* epm leonis pape' (*a*) *anatholium* for *anastasium* (*e, p, b, v, w¹*) *thessalonicensium* for *thessalonicensem* (*e, b, w*) epm *thess* (*p*)		Common error *e, p, b, v, w* (anatholium) Common variant *e, b, w* (thessalonicensium) Common variant *a, v* (thessalonicensem)[115]

[115] Scribes almost always write city-based adjectives in the accusative to agree with the addressee's name, so 'thessalonicensem' is more likely original to this *capitulum*. However, 'thessalonicensium', the genitive of the persons over whom Anastasius was bishop, is not impossible.

Var., *Ep.*	Quesnelliana	Ballerini (control)	Significance
34, 14.Pr	om. 'Leo … *Thessalonicensi*' (*a, e, p, b, v, w*)	*Leo episcopus urbis Romae, Anastasio episcopo Thessalonicensi.*	Common variant **Q** due to inscription above
35, 14.Pr	apostoli *sede* commissa (*a, e, p, b, v, w*)	apostoli *auctoritate sint* commissa	Common error **Q** Filling a gap where *auctoritate sint* had been
36, 14.Pr	*siue* ratione (*a, e, v, w'*)	*si uera* ratione (*p, b, w²*)	Common error *a, e, v, w*
37, 14.Pr	*perspicere* (*e*)	*perspiceres* et iusto (*a, p, b, v, w*)	Error *e*
38, 14.Pr	*seu* (*a, e, b, v, w*) *se* (*p*)	perspiceres *et* iusto	Common variant *a, e, b, v, w* Error *p* derived from variant, thus common to **Q**
39, 14.Pr	*iuncto* (*a, e, w*) *iuncta* (*p, b*)	de *iunctae* tibi sollicitudinis deuotione (*v*)	Common error *a, e, w* Common variant, probable error, *p, b*
40, 14.1	*qui ad* continenti (*a¹, a² e* pro *ad; e, w*) *si quid* (*v², v'* scraped away) *quo ad* (*p, b*)	impenderes: *siquidem* continenti	Common error *a, e, w* Error *v* Common error *p, b*
41, 14.1	*existunt* (*a, e, p, b, v, w*)	plerumque *existant* inter negligentes	Common variant **Q**
42, 14.1	*Paulus apostolus* (*a, e, p, b, v, w*)	Vnde et beatus *apostolus Paulus*	Common variant **Q**
43, 14.1	om. *nostris* (*a, e, v, w*)	fratribus et coepiscopis *nostris* sine offensione (*p, b*)	Common error *a, e, v, w*
44, 14.1	*sint* (*a, e, b, v, w*)	in sacerdotalibus *sunt* reprehendenda (*p*)	Common variant *a, e, b, v, w* *p* easy correction

Var., *Ep.*	Quesnelliana	Ballerini (control)	Significance
45, 14.1	*disciuisse* (*a, e, p, b, v, w*)	immodice *discessisse* cognosco	Common variant **Q**
46, 14.1	*ante* (*p.¹, v¹*)	quod *a te* (*a, e, p.², b, v², w*)	Simple error *p.¹* and *v¹*, probably independent
47, 14.1	*cognoui* (*a, e, p, b, v, w*)	quod a te *cognouimus* esse praesumptum	Common variant **Q**
48, 14.1	*diaconis* (*a, e, p, b, v, w*)	astantibus *diaconibus*[116] tuis	Common variant **Q**
49, 14.1	om. *tui* (*a, e, p, b, v, w*)	diaconi *tui* detulerunt	Common error **Q**
50, 14.1	*retulerunt* (*p, b*)	diaconi tui *detulerunt*	Common variant *p, b*
51, 14.1	*fuisset* (*a, e, b, v, w*)	deuotionis *fuisse*, quod (*p*)	Common error *a, e, b, v, w* *p* easy emendation
52, 14.1	*quid* (*a, e, p, b, v, w*)	doleo, *quod* in eum	Common variant **Q**
53, 14.1	*a* tua (*a, e*)	quid *ad* tua consulta (*p, b, v, w*)	Common error *a, e*
54, 14.1	*meis moribus* (*a, e, p, b, v, w*)	de *moribus meis* existimasti	Common variant **Q**
55, 14.1	*arguebat* (*a, e, b, v, w*) *argebat* (*p*)	criminis pondus *urgebat*?	Common variant **Q** Error *p* from majority **Q**
56, 14.1	om. *At* (*a, e, p, b, v, w*)	*urgebat*? *At* hoc quidem alienum ab	Common error **Q**
57, 14.3	bonae uitae *habeat testimonium habitus* non (*a, a² del. habitus*; *e, b, v, w*) *habeat testimonium* (*p*)	bonae uitae *testimonium habeat* non laicus	Common error *a, e, b, v, w* = **Q** Variant *p*, related to majority **Q**

[116] 'diaconibus' is a not uncommon spelling for what should, in fact, be 'diaconis' since it comes from the second declension Greek διάκονος. Nonetheless, a search of the Patrologia Latina database finds 1338 occurrences of this spelling but only 964 of 'diaconis'.

Var., *Ep.*	Quesnelliana	Ballerini (control)	Significance
58, 14.5	*uocata* (a^1, *e*, *v*, *w*)	partium se *uota* diuiserint (a^2, *p*, *b*)	Common error *a*, *e*, *v*, *w*
59, 14.6	om. *de* (*a*, *e*, *p*, *b*, *v*, *w*)	et *de* cleri plebisque consensu	Common error **Q**
60, 14.6	om. *ut* (*a*, *e*, *p*, *b*, *v*, *w*)	faciat *ut* ordinationem rite	Common error **Q**
61, 14.6	*ecclesiae eiusdem* (*a*, *e*, *p*, *b*, *v*, *w*)	ex presbyteris *eiusdem Ecclesiae*	Common variant **Q**
62, 14.7	*indicetur* (*a*, *e*, *p*, *b*, *v*, *w*)	assolent, *iudicetur.* Ac si	Common error **Q**, palaeographical
63, 14.7	om. *si* (*a*, *e*, *p*, *b*, *v*, *w*)	ut *si* coram positis partibus	Common error **Q**
64, 14.8	*occasione* (*a*, *e*, *p*, *b*, *v*, *w*)	quacumque *ratione* transtulerit	Common variant **Q**
65, 14.9	*agatur* (*a*, *e*, *p*, *b*, *v*, *w*)	res *agitur*, transfugam	Common variant **Q**
66, 14.9	*ecclesiam suam* (*a*, *e*, *p*, *b*, *v*, *w*)	ad *suam Ecclesiam* metropolitanus	Common variant **Q**
67, 14.9	*recesserit* (a^2) *precessit* (*p*) *processit* (*b*)	longius *recessit*, tui (a^1, *e* – *v*, *w* give *recessit*)	Common variant *p*, *b*
68, 14.9	*ui* (*v*, *w*) *ut* (*p*) *autui* (*b*)	recessit, *tui* praecepti (*a*, *e* give *tui*)	Related errors *p*, *b*, *v*, *w*
69, 14.9	*praeceptis* (*a*, *e*, *v*, *w*)	tui *praecepti* auctoritate (*p*, *b* give *praecepti*)	Common error *a*, *e*, *v*, *w*
70, 14.10	*iniuriis uidearis* (*a*, *e*, *b*, *v*, *w*) *iniuriis uideaturis* (*p*)	gloriari *uidearis iniuriis*	Common variant *a*, *e*, *b*, *v*, *w* Errror *p*
71, 14.11	*referentur* (*a*, *e*, *p*, *b*, *v*, *w*)	testificatione *referantur*, ut	Common variant **Q**
72, 14.11	*offendunt* (*a*, *e*, v^1, *w*)	de tuis *offenduntur* excessibus (*p*, *b*, v^2, *w*)	Common error *a*, *e*, *v*, *w*
73, 14.11	om. *que* (*a*, *e*, *v*, *w*)	salubriter*que* disposita (*p*, *b*)	Common error *a*, *e*, *v*, *w*
74, 14.11	*ad* dispositam nulla (a^1, *e*, *v*, *w*)	disposita nulla (a^2, *p*, *b*)	Common variant *a*, *e*, *v*, *w*

Var., *Ep.*	Quesnelliana	Ballerini (control)	Significance
75, 14.11	*ait apostolus* (*a, e, b, v, w*) om. *ait* (*p*)	sicut *Apostolus ait*: Vnusquisque	Common variant *a, e, b, v, w* Error *p*
76, 159.3	*est* quod (*a, e, b, v, w*)	restituendum quod fides (*p*)	Common variant *a, e, b, v, w*
77, 159.4	om. *sunt* (*a, p, b*)	impiae habendae *sunt* ita	Common error *a, p, b*
78, 159.4	*sunt habendae* (*e, v, w*)	impiae *habendae sunt* ita	Common variant *e, v, w*
79, 159.4	*laudabiles iudicandae* (*a, e, b, v, w*) *laudabiles* (*p*)	sunt *laudandae.*	Common variant *a, e, b, v, w* Variant *p* from above
80, 159.6	*similiter dilectio tua* (*a, e, p, b, v, w*)	de quibus *dilectio tua similiter* nos credidit	Common variant **Q**
81, 159.6	*est custodienda* (*a, e, p, b, v, w*)	ea *custodienda est* moderatio	Common variant **Q**
82, 159.6	*prospexeris* (*a, e, p, b, v, w*) *animo* (*w*)	animos *perspexeris* esse deuotos	Common variant **Q** Error *w*
83, 159.6	*habentes* (*a, e, p, b, v, w*)	etiam *habens* senilis aetatis	Common error **Q**[117]
84, 159.6	*respicientes* (*a, e, p, b, v, w*)	aegritudinum *respiciens* necessitates	Common error **Q**
85, 159.7	cum *baptizati ante* (*a, e, p, b, v, w*)	cum *antea baptizati* non	Common error **Q**
86, 159.7	*sola spiritus sancti inuocatione* (*a, e, b, v, w*)	*sola inuocatione spiritus sancti* per impositionem (*p*)	Common variant *a, e, b, v, w*
87, 159.7	Vnus *d(eu)s* (*a, e, b, v, w*)	Vnus *dominus,* una fides (*p*)	Common error **Q**; easily emended by *p*
88, 159.7	*sanctificationem* (*a¹, e, w*) *sanctificatione* (*a², b, v*)	sola *sanctificatio* Spiritus sancti (*p*)	Common error *a, e, w* Common error *b, v*

[117] Both here and in 84, the participle is modifying 'tu', and is therefore singular.

Var., *Ep.*	Quesnelliana	Ballerini (control)	Significance
89, 159.7	om. *et* (*a*, *e*, *b*, *v*, *w*)	ad omnes fratres *et* comprouinciales (*p*)	Common variant *a*, *e*, *b*, *v*, *w*
90, 159.7	Maioriano Aug primum cons (*a*, *e*, *p*, *b*, *v*, *w*)	consulatu Maioriani Augusti	The inclusion of 'primum' hints at the compiler of **Q** having access to knowledge of consuls, although normally 'primum' would be omitted since Majorian was consul only once.
91, 18 *Inscr.*	'ITEM INCIPIT EPISTVLA PAPAE LEONIS AD IANVARIVM DE HERETICIS ET SCISMATICIS' (*a*, *e*, *p*, *b*, *v*, *w*)	N/A	Agreement **Q**
92, 18	Om. *urbis Romae* (*a*, *e*, *p*, *b*, *v*, *w*)	Leo episcopus *urbis Romae*, Ianuario episcopo	Common variant **Q**
93, 18	*cognouimus* (*a*, *e*, *p*, *b*, *v*, *w*)	noueramus, *agnouimus*, congratulantes	Common variant **Q**
94, 18	*gregum* (*a*, *e*, *p*, *b*, *v*, *w*)	ad custodiam *gregis* Christi	Common variant **Q**
95, 18	enim *est* et … plenissimum ut (*a*, *e*, *b*, *v*, *w*) Om. *est* (*p*)	Saluberrimum enim et … plenissimum *est* ut	Common variant **Q**
96, 18	diaconi subdiaconi *uel* cuiuslibet (*a*, *e*, *p*, *b*, *v*, *w¹*) *w²* add. *'siue'* ante *'subdiaconi'*	diaconi, *uel* subdiaconi, *aut* cuiuslibet	Common variants **Q**
97, 18	*ad hanc* rursum (*a*, *e*, *p*, *b*, *v*, *w*)	amiserant, rursum reuerti	Common variant **Q**

Var., *Ep.*	Quesnelliana	Ballerini (control)	Significance
98, 18	*errorem suum* (*a, b, e, v*) *errorem suam* (*p*)	prius *errores suos* et	Common variant *a, e, b, v* Error *p*
99, 18	ipsos *erroris* auctores errorum (*a, p*) ipsos *erroris auctores* damnari (*e, b, v, w*) – *om.* errorum	ipsos *auctores errorum* damnari	Common error *a, p* Common variant *e, b, v, w*
100, 18	prauis *et dudum* peremptis (*b, v, w*)	prauis *etiam* peremptis (*a, e, p*)	Common variant *b, v, w*
101, 18	*inuenietur* (*a¹, e, b, v, w*)	in quo *inueniuntur* ordine (*a², p*)	Common error *a, e, b, v, w*
102, 18	*perpetua stabilitate permaneant* (*a, e², v*) *perpetua stabilitate permaneat* (*e¹, p, b, w*)	*stabilitate perpetua maneant*	Common variant *a, v* Common error *e, p, b, w*
103, 18	*iteratae tinctionis sacrilegio* non (*a, e, v, w*) *iterate intentionis sacrilegio* non (*p, b*)	si tamen *iterata tinctione* non	Common variant *a, e, v, w* Common error *p, b* derived from above
104, 18	*Dm* (*a, e, b, v, w*)	apud *Dominum* noxam (*p*)	Common variant *a, e, b, v, w*
105, 18	*debeat* (*a, e, v, w*) Om. *debet* (*p*)	non *debet* licere suspectis. (*b*)	Common error *a, e, v, w* Error *p*
106, 18	*ac* (*a*)	circumspecte *atque* uelociter (*e, p, b, v, w*)	Variant *a*
107, 18	Data III k *Iulias* (*a*) Data *IIII* kl *iul* (*e, p, b, w*) Data *IIII* no ian (*v*)	Data *III* kalend. *Ianuarii*	Common variant *a, e, p, b, w* Common variant *e, p, b, v, w*

Var., *Ep.*	Quesnelliana	Ballerini (control)	Significance
108, 4.Pr.	Om. *episcopus urbis Romae* (*a, e, p, b, v, w*)	Leo *episcopus urbis Romae*	Common variant **Q**
109, 4.Pr.	*uniuersis* episcopis (*a, e, p, b, v, w*)	*omnibus* episcopis per	Common variant **Q**
110, 4.Pr.	canonum *et* ecclesiasticam disciplinam (*a, e, p, b, v, w*)	canonum ecclesiasticam*que* disciplinam	Common variant **Q**
111, 4.1	*uestrae prouinciae* (*a, e, p, b, v, w*)	omnes *prouinciae uestrae* abstineant	Common variant **Q** Agreement with **D**
112, 4.1	*substrahatur* (*a, e¹, p, b, v, w*) *substratur* (*e²*)	uinculis *abstrahatur*	Common variant **Q** **Q** agreement with **D** *a*
113, 4.1	*munerosa* (*e*)	*numerosa* coniugia (*a, p, b, v, w*)	Error *e*
115, 4.5	Maximo *ii* et Paterio *cons* (*a, e, p, b, v, w*)	Maximo *iterum* et Paterio *uiris clarissimis consulibus*	Common variant **Q**
116, 7 *Inscr.*	per *diuersas* prouincias (*a, e, p, b, v, w¹*)	per *Italiae* prouincias (*w²*)	Common variant **Q**
117, 7.2	*XIII* (*a, e, p, b, v, w*)	Theodosio *XVIII* et Albino	Common error **Q**
118, 16.Pr.	Om. *episcopus* (*a, e, p, b, v, w*)	Leo *episcopus* uniuersis	Common variant **Q**
119, 16.1	Om. *observantiae ... esset* (*p*)	inde legem totius *observantiae sumeretis: ... dignitatis, esset* ecclesiasticae magistra rationis	Error *p*
120, 16.1	Om. *petri* (*a, e, b, v¹, w*)	et beati *Petri* apostoli sedes (*v²*)	Common variant *a, e, b, v, w*
121, 16.1	*Vt* (*a, e, p, b, v, w*)	*Et* licet uix	Common error **Q**
122, 16.2	*mortuo persecutore* (*a, e, p, b, v, w*)	in Galilaeam, *persecutore mortuo* reuocatus	Common variant **Q**

Var., *Ep.*	Quesnelliana	Ballerini (control)	Significance
123, 16.2	*quaerebatis me* (*a, e, p, b, v, w*)	quod *me quaerebatis*?	Common variant **Q**
124, 16.2	Om. *his quae* (*a¹, e, v, w*) in *domo* patris (*a²*) Om. *in* (*p*)	quod *in his quae* Patris mei sunt oportet me esse? (*b*)	Common error *a, e, v, w* Error *p*
125, 16.2	*quaeque* (*a, e, b, v, w*) *quemque* (*p*)	sed aliter *quidque*	Common error *a, e, b, v, w* Error *p*, likely descendent from source of above
126, 16.2	Om. *posse* (*a, e, p, b, v, w*)	ad tempus *posse* pertinere	Common error **Q**
127, 16.2, 1 Cor. 1:10	*scientia* (*a, e, p, b, v, w*; some Vulgate and Vetus Latina mss[118])	et in eadem *sententia* (some Vulgate and Vetus Latina mss)	Common variant **Q** Agreement with **V**
128, 16.3	*quod* (*a, e, p, b, w*) *et* (*v¹*)	totumque *quidquid* in illo (*v²*)	Common variant *a, e, p, b, w* Error *v*
129, 16.3	*Pentecosten* (*a, e, p, b, v¹, w*)	*Pentecostes* ex aduentu (*v²*)	Common error **Q**
130, 16.3	*sancti spiritus* (*a, e, p, b, v, w*)	aduentu *Spiritus Sancti*	Common variant **Q**
131, 16.3, Jn 14:26	Pater *meus* (*a, e, p, b, v, w*; one Vetus Latina MS)[119]	mittet Pater in nomine meo (Vulgate)	Common variant **Q**
132, 16.3	*utriusque* (*a², e*) Om. *que* off *nomen* (*e, p, b, v¹, w*)	nomen*que* Paracleti *utrique* sit (*a¹*)	Common error *a², e* Common error *e, p, v, w*
133, 16.4	*promissum* (*e, v¹, w*) *promisso* (*p, b*)	*promissus* Spiritus sancti (*a, v²*)	Common error *e, v, w* Common error *p, b*

[118] For the text and MSS of the Vetus Latina of 1 Corinthians 1:10, see Houghton et al., 2019, 176.

[119] Codex Sangermanensis secundus: Paris, Bibliothèque Nationale de France, lat. 13169 (saec. X). See H. A. G. Houghton's online edition of the Vetus Latina of John: http://www.iohannes.com/vetuslatina/edition/index.html. Accessed 19 September 2021.

Var., *Ep.*	Quesnelliana	Ballerini (control)	Significance
134, 16.4	*sancti Spiritus* (*a, e, p, b, v, w*)	promissus *Spiritus sancti* repleuit	Common variant **Q**
135, 16.7	*cura* (*a, e, p, b, v, w*) *Petro apostolo* (*a¹, e, p, b, v, w*) *Petri apostoli* (*a²*)	coram *beatissimo apostolo Petro*	Common error **Q** Common variant **Q** Attempted emendation *a²*
136, 16.7	quae, inspirante Domino, *uobis* (*a, e, p, b, v, w*) inspirante *deo* (*p, b*)	quae *uobis*, inspirante Domino, insinuanda	Common variant **Q** Common variant *p, b*; probably an error due to *nomina sacra*
137, 16.7	*et* (*a, e, p, b, v, w*)	Bacillum *atque* Paschasinum	Common variant **Q**
138, 1.1	*ceditur* (*a, e¹, p, b, v, w*)	quidem *conceditur* usurpasse (*e²*)	Common variant **Q**
139, 1.2	*hoc* (*a, e¹, v, w*)	*hac* nostri auctoritate (*p, b, e²*)	Common error *a, e, v, w*
140, 1.2	diaconi, *uel cuiusque* (*a, e, p, b, v, w*)	diaconi, *siue cuiuscumque* ordinis	Common variant **Q**
141, 1.2	*quod* (*a, e, p, b, v, w*)	*quidquid* in doctrina	Common variant **Q**
142, 1.2	*eorum* (*a, e, p, b, v, w*) *uersutia* (*p*)	*istorum* esse uersutiam	Common variant **Q** Error *p*
143, 1.4	Om. *in* (*a, e, p, b, v, w*)	huiusmodi *in* homines exstincta	Common error **Q**
144, 1.5	*ordine* (*a, e, p, b, v, w*)	nec in subsequenti *officio* clericorum	Common variant **Q**
145, 2.1	diaconi, *uel* cuiuslibet (*a, e, p, b, v, w*)	diaconi, *siue alii* cuiuslibet	Common variant **Q**

What we see in the above chart is a vast array of variants common to all of **Q**, very frequently places where the Ballerini text is an inversion of what **Q** provides. A number of these are also common errors. Besides those things shared by all of **Q**, the next fact that stands out is the near-independence of *p* from the wider **Q** tradition. The **Q** manuscript whose readings it most closely resembles is *b*, but it also shows a number of cases where it provides an error that is a descendent of the wider **Q** readings. In some instances, *p* also gives us readings that agree with the Ballerini text where **Q** disagrees, whether **Q** is in error or not. This demonstrates that, while *p* and *b* are closer to each other than they are to the other four **Q** manuscripts, they are not twins and probably not copies of each other. On the other hand, *a*, *e*, *v* and *w* all stand in the same tradition, given how frequently they agree against *p* and *b*. *a* and *e* are both from the Lorsch region and of a similar time; Bischoff says that they are sister manuscripts,[120] and their extreme similarity bears out his assessment. *v* and *w* are from another branch of the same tree as *a* and *e*, probably twins as well, for the same reasons. The various modifications of *w* would make one question this; however, its text is too similar to that of *v* for any other interpretation. They are born from the same exemplar, but *w* has been modified in very specific ways by its copyist-editor, explaining its difference. What the table does not show us is the great number of places where **Q** agrees with the Ballerini against other traditions. This is especially true for *Ep.* 167, despite the variant concerning 167.5–6; the Ballerini clearly valued **Q** above the other collections for their text of this letter.

Before moving on from **Q**, it is worth mentioning its protocols. Throughout this body of manuscripts, the inscriptions for letters are united, as are their incipits. For example, *Ep.* 18 has the inscription, 'ITEM INCIPIT EPISTVLA PAPAE LEONIS AD IANVARIVM DE HERETICIS ET SCISMATICIS' in every manuscript. Very few of the letters are subdivided into chapters. Only in *Ep.* 167 can they be considered to have chapter headings. However, a few of them have been thus divided. For the sake of example, *Ep.* 14—a notably long letter—has been divided into six chapters, marked out by Roman numerals that are sometimes in the margin and sometimes in the midst of the text itself, depending on the manuscript. They are, ch I at, 'In ciuitatibus quarum rectores obierint'; II at, 'Prouinciales episcopi ad ciuitatem metropoli conuenire'; III at, 'De conciliis autem episcopalibus non aliud indicimus'; IIII at, 'Si quis episcopus ciuitatis suae mediocri-

---

[120] Bischoff 1998–2014, 1.1116.

tate despecta'; V at, 'Alienum clerum inuito episcopo'; and VI at, 'In euocandis autem ad te episcopis moderatissimam esse'. These divisions do not correspond with the Ballerini chapter divisions, reminding us that there is more than one way to skin a cat. These features show us that at the very beginning of the tradition of canonical collections, there was a desire to organise the texts in some fashion to make them easier to use. While we ought not to read the history of canon law teleologically, in a fashion that makes Gratian's *Decretum* and the rest of the *Corpus Iuris Canonici* the necessary and natural end-points of mediaeval canon law,[121] we should be aware that the tendency that produces Gratian's *Decretum* is the same tendency that subdivides longer texts into chapters and that will move on to the addition of *capitula*, or *tituli* as the canonists themselves call them.

3.2.d. *Collectio Vaticana*[122] (**V**)

3.2.d.i. Dating and context

This collection was compiled in the first quarter of the sixth century in Rome,[123] making use of **D** for the canons;[124] it arguably pre-dates the **D** recension with decretals. It has long been recognised as one of the oldest canonical collections, designated by the Ballerini as 'vetustissima',[125] and used by them in their investigations of early Roman recensions of councils. The sixth-cen-

[121] As some articles do, such as Flechner 2009, a very illuminating article about Insular canon law.

[122] B3 (PL 54.555), J1(iii) (501). Throughout, I have attempted to follow pre-existing *sigla* for the collections where possible, preferably those of Schwartz in ACO 2.4. However, Schwartz's *siglum* L is not useable in this case because of the need to provide a *siglum* to *Collectio Laureshamensis*, which Wurm 1939 designates as L. Therefore, since V is Wurm's choice and is not otherwise used by Schwartz, I have adopted it.

[123] Fournier and Le Bras 1931, 25–26, argue for a Roman origin for *Vaticana*, not only for an Italian one as argued for this collection, *Sanblasiana*, and *Teatina*, by Maassen 1870, 500–04. They cite the presence of the Symmachan Forgeries in a collection compiled during Symmachus' pontificate and the fact that all three collections utilise the canonical collection termed the *Prisca*.

[124] For the contents and sources of the collection, see Maassen 1870, 514–22.

[125] PL 56.20C.

tury date of the collection has been doubted by McKitterick, who argues that, based on the two manuscripts *a* and *b*, the contents of the manuscripts are too disparate to conclude that they transmit an older, sixth-century collection.[126] Rather, she argues, *a* and *b* transmit to us two separate Carolingian collections. Such an argument has strength in that it takes into account the entire contents of each manuscript, both Carolingian and late antique, and provides an answer. Nevertheless, when all three manuscripts are considered together, and the texts are collated, the evidence weighs in favour of these three manuscripts using an earlier canonical collection that they amplified with more recent material in different ways. Therefore, although scholars of the development of canon law and of Carolingian history should take into account McKitterick's argument against seeing these manuscripts as a united triad, I argue that those of us who are examining the manuscripts in the other direction must account for the similarities in contents and textual variation in some way. The most plausible way is to posit a common source, in this case **V**. **V**, therefore, predates its Carolingian manuscripts. The argument for it being as early as the sixth century lies once again in the fact that its Carolingian copyists added newer material, but there is no intervening material. Furthermore, the inclusion of the Symmachan Forgeries alongside the various other authentic canonical material pinpoints the moment of interest for this compilation in the sixth century when the Symmachan Forgeries were documents of interest.

V contains 16 of Leo's letters, the first seven of which are so-called decretals: 14, 167, 16, 1, 12 (in the *decurtata* version), 159, 9, 139, 145, 119, 23, 22, 20, 28, 165, 80. These are items XVIII and LIIII–LXVIIII. As discussed in greater detail below,[127] **V** shares a common source with the *Collectio Dionysiana adaucta* (**D-a**), which I term **proto-4**.[128] This source consists of **V**'s dogmatic letters, from *Ep.* 145 to *Ep.* 80. Finally, the Ballerini description of **V** is misleading and fails to note that *Ep.* 14 is separated from the rest of the letters by a significant portion of this collection.

---

[126] McKitterick 2005, 962–69.

[127] 5.2.c.i.

[128] See the Appendix for a list and description of the proto-collections.

3.2.d.ii. Manuscripts

It exists complete in three manuscripts.[129] Chronologically, these are:

a: Vat. lat. 1342 (saec. VIII or earlier), from central Italy.[130] The Ballerini say that *a* is believed to be one of those which was in the old Lateran Library.[131] It is written in an eighth-century uncial of Roman style. The main collection of Leo's letters begins fol. 131[r]. This manuscript and *b* are described by the Ballerini as 'pervetusti', 'antiquissimi', and 'perantiqui'.[132] The analysis of *a*'s readings is based upon the apparatus of Schwartz in ACO 2.4.

b: Vat. Barb. lat. 679 (olim XIV. 52; 2888), fol. 1–295[r] (saec. VIII[ex]-IX[in]), from northern Italy, 'perhaps Aquileia'.[133] *b* has been arranged *per cola et commata* in a single column, written mainly in uncials with uncial rubrics with some pre-Caroline minuscule text.[134] It belonged to San Salvatore, Monte Amiata, near Siena in the eleventh century.[135] *Ep.* 14, item XXVIII, is on fols 103[r]–107[v]; the main body of Leo's letters begins with Ep. 167 (using *capitula* associated with **Q**) at fol. 193[r]; 199[r–v] contain canons from a Council of Braga; then follow *Epp.* 16, 1, 12, 159, 15, 9, 139, 145, 119, 80, 23, 22, 20, 28, and 165. While this last run of letters includes everything in *Collectio Vaticana*, we note that *Ep.* 15 is added and the order of letters is modified slightly. The addition of this particular letter to Spain along with the inclusion of the Council of Braga make me wonder if some of the material travelled through Spain before coming to Aquileia.[136] *b*

[129] The fourth manuscript is Düsseldorf, Universitätsbibliothek, E.1 (saec. IX[2]), fol. 3ra-44ra; the **V** fragment does not reach Leo. However, the *Dionysio-Hadriana* portion to which **V** is joined does. See below, 5.2.a.

[130] Dating and location on palaeographic grounds, CLA 1.9.

[131] 'Vaticanus codex 1342 ... unus ex his esse creditur qui ad veterem bibliothecam Lateranensem spectabat', PL 56.135.

[132] e·g. PL 56.1072, 135, and PL 54.555.

[133] Kéry 1999, 25, and Bischoff 1998–2014, 3.6426. However, CLA 1.65, places it in central Italy because of its time spent near Siena, noted below.

[134] CLA 1.65.

[135] From a record added on fol. 133[r].

[136] However, none of the potentially 'Spanish' spellings herein are definitive ('bacatione' for 'uacatione' [*Ep.* 167, *Praef.*, fol. 194[r]], 'captibi' for 'captiui' in the margin at the start of *Ep.* 159, fol. 210[r]. Another example is 'guuernator' for 'gubernator' [*Ep.* 167, *Praef.*, fol. 194[r]]). If *b* has any relationship to Spain, it is more likely through its exemplar or another MS with Spanish material influencing it. Adams 2007 details the fact that the interchangeabil-

also distinctively adds Hs to the beginning of certain words, e.g. 'hubi' and 'heutices' (fol. 2ᵛ).

c: Florence, Biblioteca Medicea Laurenziana, Aedil. 82 (saec. IX3/4), with a northern Italian origin.[137] Leo's letters run fols 70ʳ–73ʳ, 116ʳ–146ᵛ. As with Vat. Barb. lat. 679, this manuscript does not follow the 'official' order described by the Ballerini; instead, after the gap between *Epp.* 14 and 167, where non-Leonine items are found, it runs from fol. 116ʳ as follows: *Epp.* 167, 16, 1, 12, 159, 15, 9, 139, 145, 119, 80, 23, 22, 20, 28, and 165 with *Testimonia.*[138]

3.2.d.iii. Manuscript relations

In *Ep.* 167, *b* and *c* both include the phrase 'subditis responsionibus et ad eiusdem consulta respondentibus' between the salutation 'LEO EPISCOPVS RVSTICO NARBONENSI'[139] and the Ballerini start of the body, 'Epistolas fraternitatis tuae'. This is a trait shared with a significant body of other collections, including *Collectiones Dionysio-Hadriana* (**D–h**), *Sanblasiana* (**Sa**), and the Oriel MS of **Q**. In most **Q** manuscripts, this phrase follows the inscription for the letter, in a manner similar to the Ballerini text which writes, 'EPISTOLA CLXVII. AD RVSTICVM NARBONENSEM EPISCOPVM. *Subditis responsionibus ad eiusdem consulta rescriptis*'. (PL 54.1196) The difference seems to be whether the inscription is such as 'Incp epl ci leonis ad rusticu epm narbonense' (**Q** *p*) or whether the salutation is used as the inscription; in **V** *c* the salutation is rubricated, and in *b* it is written in uncials. The *capitulum* 'LVII INCIPIVNT AD INQVISITIONES EIVSDEM / pape leonis subiecta responsa'[140] precedes the series of questions which Leo answers in this letter. Before providing the table for *Ep.* 167 in **V**, one of the most significant other **V** variants in this letter

ity between V and B is common across the entire Roman Empire, not just Spain, in Chapter X.

[137] Although this MS is also listed in the literature as including the *Collectio Vetus Gallica*, it is to be noted that none of the *Vetus Gallica* Leo material is present in it. Bischoff 1998–2014, 1.1207.

[138] This variation in order is the main reason why McKitterick doubts a late antique origin for **V**; see McKitterick 2004, 253–54.

[139] As *b*, *c¹*; *c²* *add.* 'episcopo' *post* 'rustico'.

[140] **V** *b*; *c*: 'Quod INCIPIT AD ...'

is towards the very end; 167.19 is divided in two, and a twenti-
eth chapter is subdivided with the *capitulum*, 'XX DE HIS QVI
IDOLA ADORAVERVNT AVT HOMICIDIIS VEL FORNICA-
TIONIBVS IN QVI NATI SVNT',[141] between 'esse participes' and
'Si autem aut idola'.

Var.	**V** text	Ballerini (control)	Significance
1, 167.Pr	*conspectu tui* (*b*)	tui conspectus (*c*)	*b* variant **Sa, D, D–b** 'conspectus tui'
2, 167.4	De presbytero *et* diacono (*c*)	De presbytero *uel* diacono qui filiam suam (*b*)	*c* variant Agreement with **Sa**
3, 167.7	*expetiuerunt* (*c*) *expetuerunt* (*b*)	*expetierunt*	*c* variant *b* error derived from *c* variant *c* agreement with **Sa, D, D–b**
4, 167.8	*paenitentiam iam deficientes* (*b*, *c*)	de his qui *iam defi-cientes poeniten-tiam* accipiunt	**V** variant Agreement with **Sa**
5, 167.10	*postulante* (*b*) oportet *etiam multo* (*c¹*; *c² multis*)	ueniam *postulan-tem* oportet *a mul-tis* etiam licitis	Error *b* Error *c*
6, 167.10	omnia licent (*b*, 1 Cor. 10:23)	omnia *mihi* licent (*c*, 1 Cor. 6:12; **Q B** Oriel MS 42)	Variant *b*; agree-ment with **D**; **D–b**; **D–h** *v m a r d*; **Sa** *l r c k*; **Te**; **Di**; **Re**; **S** *o*; **S–ga**
7, 167.13	om. *mortis* (*b*, *c¹*)	si urguente aut metu *mortis* aut captiuitatis peri-culo (*c²*)	Common error **V** Agreement with **Sa**
8, 167.13	*iuuenalis* (*b*, *c*)	lapsum inconti-nentiae *iuuenilis*	As with **D, Q**, etc., in contrast to **Sa**, orthography does not lead to *iuuen-alem* for *uenialem* in this case

---

[141] **V** *b*; *c* 'CAP XX De his qui idola adhorauerunt aut homicidiis uel forni-
cationibus in qui \contami/nati sunt'.

Var.	**V** text	Ballerini (control)	Significance
9, 167.18	impositionem *uocata* (*b*) per manus *impositione uocata* (*c¹*; *c²* *impositionis*)	sed per manus *impositionem inuo- cata* uirtute	Variant **V** Error *c*
10, 167.19 *cap.*	om. *adhuc iuuenes* (*c*) *Cap.* in *b* different: 'DE GENTILI- BUS QUE ESCIS IMMOLATICIIS USI SUNT'	cum ad Roma- niam adhuc iuuenes uenerint	Error *c*; agrees with **Sa**

Ep. 167 closes with:

EXPLICIT LEONIS PAPE AD RVSTICVM NARBONENSEM EPISCOPVM DE ORDINATIONIBVS SACERDOTIVM ET LAPSVS ET REBAPTIZANDIS CAPTVLI H XX[142]

In *b* the rest of the folio is blank, and the next folio adds material from a synod of Braga, after which it again joins *c* for *Ep.* 16. The **V** inscription reads, 'Incipit eiusdem episcopis Siculis de non baptizandum Theophaniorum et duo per annum episcopi Romae proficiscantur'.[143] The results for *Ep.* 16 are as follows:

Var.	**V** text (*b*, *c*)	Ballerini text (control)	Significance
1, 16.Pr	om. *episcopus* (*b*, *c*)	Leo *episcopus* uni- uersis	Common variant **V** Agreement with **D, D–b**
2, 16.Pr.	om. *in domino salutem* (*b*, *c¹*)	constitutis *in dom- ino salutem.* (*c²*)	Common variant **V**
3, 16.Pr	*inueniat* (*c¹*)	si quid usquam reprehensioni *inu- enitur* (*b*, *c²*)	Error *c¹*
4, 16.Pr	*Monente* (*b*, *c*)	*Manente* enim Dominicae uocis	Error **V**

[142] As *b*; *c* closes the rubric with 'capitula numero XX'.

[143] As *b*; *c* has errors: 'eiusdem opusculi ... duo eandum epi ...'

Var.	**V** text (*b, c*)	Ballerini text (control)	Significance
5, 16.Pr	*negligens totiens* (*b*)	quia *negligenter pascens* totiens (*c*)	Error *b*
6, 16.1	*apostoli petri* (*b, c*)	et beati *Petri apostoli* sedes	Common variant **V** Agreement **D**, **D–b**
7, 16.2	*generandum* (*c¹*)	temporaliter *gerendarum* in Incarnatione (*b, c²*)	Error *c¹*
8, 16.2	*obligationem* (*b*)	adoratum paruulum mystica munerum *oblatione* uenerantur. (*c*)	Error *b*
9, 16.2	om. *baptizato Domino Iesu* (*b, c¹*)	quando *baptizato Domino Iesu* Spiritus Sanctus (*c²*)	Error **V**
10, 16.2	om. *posse* (*b, c*)	ad tempus *posse* pertinere baptismatis	Error **V** **D, D–b** *v* give *potest*
11, 16.2	*rationalis* seruanda *districtio* (*b, c¹*; *c²* mod. *rationa\bi/lis*)	*rationabilis* seruanda *distinctio*	Variant **V** *districtio* agreement **D, D–b** *c²* agrees with control text
12, 16.2 1 Cor. 1:10	*scientia* (*b, c*)	et in eadem *sententia*	Common variant **V** Agreement with **D** *c*
13, 16.3	indigens *remissionem* peccati (*b*) *remissione* peccati indigens (*c*)	indigens *remissione* peccati	Error *b* Variant *c*
14, 16.3	om. *in se* (*b, c¹*)	baptismi autem sui *in se* condidit (*c²*)	Error **V**

Although 'quia' in 5 agrees with **D** and **D–b**, it is an easy enough error that it signals no relationship. In 8, although *b* gives us an error, the section of this passage that, as seen below, has given other Italian copyists difficulty is here written out meaningfully and, presumably, correctly. The omission of 'posse' in 10 is of note because most of the **D** tradition provides us with a variant reading for the verb, 'potest', raising the question as to whether perhaps the Italian tradition lacks the verb and **D** was emending to make up for it. In 12, 'scientia' is a reading in some of the Vulgate manuscripts according to the fifth edition of the *Biblia Sacra iuxta Vulgatam Versionem* by Weber and Gryson. In 13, the movement of 'indigens' to the end of the clause in *c* is possibly a case of missing and then re-inserting a word; furthermore, the word order of *c* and the Ballerini produces a cretic spondee, and this phrase is at the end of the phrase, 'Dominus enim nullius indigens remissione peccati', followed by, 'nec quaerens remedium renascendi'. Elsewhere, the variants are notable for agreements with the **D** tradition, signalling a wider Italian transmission of this document. The variants of c^2 are often enough at variance with *b* that I can make a cautious affirmation that *c* was later collated against a different tradition.

The above should be illustrative of the **V** tradition for the disciplinary letters. The 'dogmatic' letters close the collection. The following table covers variants from *Epp.* 139 and 145.

Var.	**V** text (*a, b, c*)	Silva-Tarouca (control)	Significance
1, 139	Leo *episcopus* (*a, b, c*)	Leo Iuuenali episcopo	Shared variant **V** Agreement with **Q**, **C**, **P**, **Cl**, Laon 122, **D–adaucta**, Ps-Is
2, 139	*constantia* (*b*) *perdidisset* (*c*)	haereticis *constantiam perdidisse*, quia (*a*)	Errors *b, c*
3, 139	om. *enim* (*a, b, c*)	beatae *enim* memoriae Flauiani	Shared variant **V**
4, 139	*etanden ossis* e(ss) e (*c*)	*tanden possis* esse (*a, b*)	Error *c*
5, 139	*locorum ipsorum testimonii* (*a, c*)	sed *ipsorum locorum testimoniis* eruditur (*b*)	Shared word-order variant *a, c*; **D–a** Shared error *a, c*
6, 139	*de his* (*a, c¹*)	in quibus *degis*, testificatione (*b, c²*)	Shared error *a, c¹*
7, 139	*instruatur* (*c*) *unde* (*a, c*)	auctoritatibus *instruantur, ut de* (*b*)	Error *c* Shared error *a, c*

Var.	**V** text (a, b, c)	Silva-Tarouca (control)	Significance
8, 145	LEO LEONI AVG IIII (a, b, c)	Gloriosissimo et clementissimo filio Leoni augusto, Leo episcopus	Shared variant **V**
9, 145	diuinitus *paratum laboris* (c)	diuinitus *praepara- tum fauoris* (a, b)	Errors c
10, 145	uniuersum (a, b, c)	in *uniuersa* fidei	Variant **V** Agrees with **G**
11, 145	*ante* (a, b, c)	quae *antea* catholi- cis fuit	Variant **V** Agrees with **G**
12, 145	*sanctum spiritum* (a, b, c) om. *per* (c)	concilio *per spiri- tum sanctum* con- gregato	Variant **V**; **G** Error c
13, 145	om. *in* (a, b, c) *fide* perfectione (c)	et *in fidei* perfec- tione	Error **V** Error c
14, 145	*Constante* (a, b, c)	*Constantino* et Rufo <uu cc> conss.	Error **V**; **D–a**, Ps-Is

It is evident that *a* and *c* have a closer connection than either of them to *b*. The possibility that *c* is a descendant of *a* cannot be ruled out. If it is not a descendent, however, they likely share a common ancestry different from *b*. Based only on these select collations of the Leo contents of this collection, we can postulate either of the following scenarios:

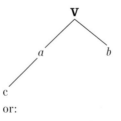

or:

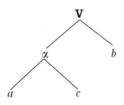

3.2.e. *Collectio Sanblasiana (Italica)* (**Sa**)[144]

3.2.e.i. Dating and context

This collection was compiled in the early sixth century. Since its compiler seems to have made use of **D** for the conciliar portions but not for the papal letters,[145] we can postulate a date *c.* 500–20. Our earliest manuscripts, as will be seen below, originate in Italy; thus, we can postulate an Italian origin for the collection.[146] It consists of conciliar canons and then papal letters, all arranged chronologically and ending with Pope Gelasius I (d. 496).[147] The Chalcedonian decree against Eutyches and its *Definitio fidei* may seem to run contrary to this otherwise ordered collection; however, they immediately follow the letters of Pope Leo, thus being absorbed into his *oeuvre*. Moreover, their inclusion alongside material from Gelasius may reflect the context of Chalcedon under dispute, such as the Acacian Schism or the Three Chapters Controversy. **Sa** contains 4 letters of Leo, all of which are letters on church discipline: 167, 12, 1, and 2. Its *capitula* for *Ep.* 167 follow the **Q** format, and its text of *Ep.* 12 is in the version called *decurtata* by the Ballerini. It is worth observing that, like the other very early collections, **Te** and **Q**, **Sa** gives us *Epp.* 1 and 2 together. Because of their close similarities, *Epp.* 1, 2, and 18 have been scrutinised and the possibility of forgery postulated.[148] However, since *Epp.* 1 and 2 are attested together in our earliest collections, the evidence of the manuscripts and early collections suggests that they are probably both genuine. The first two of Leo's letters are simply variants copied out to different recipients, possibly even on the same day.

3.2.e.ii. Manuscripts

In chronological order, the five manuscripts of **Sa** with Leo material are:[149]

---

[144] B4 (PL 54.556), J1(iv) (501).

[145] Maassen 1870, 509–10 gives us the compiler's sources.

[146] As Turner 1929, 9–11.

[147] For a description of the contents, see Maassen 1870, 505–08.

[148] As outlined in PL 54.582–84.

[149] There is one further manuscript, Paris, lat. 4279 (saec. IX[med]) from western France, which was brought to Paris by Colbert. This manuscript

s: Sankt Paul im Lavanttal, Stiftsbibliothek, MS 7/1 (olim XXIX Kassette 1; XXV a. 7). Based on the palaeographyof its uncial and minuscule scripts,[150] s has an Italian origin but was on the island of Reichenau in Germany by the end of the eighth century. The abbey of Sankt Blasien which gave the collection its name acquired it between 1768 and 1781; it came to its current home in 1807.[151] Leo runs fols CXXI^v–CXXXIV^v.

k: Cologne, Erzbischöfliche Diözesan- und Dombibliothek, 213 (olim Darmstadt 2336),[152] dates from the beginning of the eighth century and originates either in Northumbria or a part of the continent with Northumbrian missionaries; since it was in Cologne during the eighth century,[153] one imagines it to have been produced by Northumbrian missionaries in that region, although CLA 8 maintains that it was 'doubtless' written in Northumbria.[154] Recently, Michael Elliot has argued that it was from England on both palaeographical and codicological grounds;[155] nevertheless, given the early date of k, these arguments still seem inconclusive, if enticing. With the rest of the holdings of Cologne's Dombibliothek, this manuscript was taken to Arnsberg in 1794, then to Darmstadt, and was returned to Cologne Cathedral in 1867.[156] k is written in an Insular half-uncial, hence its connection with Northumbria. It includes Insular-style illuminated *litterae notabiliores*, begins with a full-leaf illumination, and is rubricated for new items and numbers but not for individual canons. Leo runs 123^v–134^v; by the Leo stage of the manuscript, the *litterae notabiliores* have dissipated.

c: Paris, lat. 3836 (olim Colbert 784, Regius 3887 3.3) originated in Corbie or the surrounding area, from the second half of the eighth century,[157] and written in Corbie a-b.[158] Leo runs 79^v–87^r.

---

contains only the beginning of the *Collectio Sanblasiana* and therefore none of the Leonine material.

[150] CLA 10.1457.

[151] CLA 10.1457.

[152] This manuscript has been digitised with the following URN: urn:nbn:de:hbz:kn28-3-2304 Accessed 20 September 2021.

[153] Kéry 1999, 30.

[154] CLA 8.1163.

[155] Elliot 2013, 250–53.

[156] See CLA 8.1146; this applies to all of the Dombibliothek MSS with a Darmstadt number.

[157] CLA 5.554; Kéry 1999, 30.

[158] Bischoff 1998–2014, 3.4277a.

The opening line of each *capitulum* is in large uncials, and the text of each of the letters begins with a *littera notabilior*.

l: Lucca, Biblioteca Capitolare Feliniana, 490, fols 236ʳ–271ᵛ, is written in uncials and pre-Caroline minuscules; it originated in Lucca and bridges the eighth and ninth centuries.[159] Lucca 490 is composed of three manuscripts bound together; **Sa** is in the second part of the third of these (fols 212–354), written on different parchment with different hands.[160] It is worth noting that in the second part of this manuscript, opening with **Sa**, we also encounter the *Decretum Gelasianum*, *Dicta Gelasii papae*, and *capitula* of the Second Council of Orange. When we look backward to the first part and ahead to the end of the third in Lucca 490, we find a variety of other regulatory texts, including texts on computus and the date of Easter. Leo runs fols 260ᵛ–265ᵛ.

r: Paris, lat. 1455, 3ʳ–79ᵛ (saec. IX3/4), likely from the area around Reims.[161] This manuscript combines **Sa** and **Q** elements; Leo runs 33ʳ–76ʳ. The sequence of the letters is *Epp.* 16, 165, 31, 59, 28, 35, 139, a synodal letter, 104, and 106. Leo reappears in the manuscript on 57ʳ partway through *Ep.* 15 in a different hand, fol. 56ᵛ having ended midway through a letter of Gelasius I. *Ep.* 15 is followed by *Epp.* 18 and 4, then another series of non-Leo items, taking up Leo again on 71ʳ with *Epp.* 97, 99, the *acta* of the African *Concilium Thelense* of 418 that includes a letter from Siricius to the Africans,[162] and then *Ep.* 68. These letters look at times like groups of two or three taken from **Q**, such as *Epp.* 16, 31, and 59 (with *Ep.* 165 dropped in the middle); 104 and 106; 18 and 4; and, most interesting, 97, 99, and 68. As noted above, these final three letters are appended to the front of **Q** in certain manuscripts. When all of the **Q** texts are accounted for, this manuscript still has two of Leo's letters not included there. Finally, its order is as idiosyncratic as that of **Q**—the letters on church discipline are mingled with the dogmatic letters and no chronology of letters is attempted. Foll. 1–2 give some canonical excerpts, including one from Leo on fol. 1ᵛ:

---

[159] See CLA 3.303b; Bischoff 1998–2014, 2.2524, *c.* 800.

[160] Schiaparelli 1924, 15; the full description of the third manuscript runs 14–19.

[161] Kéry 1999, 30; Bischoff 1998–2014, 3.4015, suspects a point of origin at Sens. This manuscript is digitised: https://gallica.bnf.fr/ark:/12148/btv1b100337527 Accessed 20 September 2021.

[162] Ed. CCSL 149:59.19–63.113. This council is the only source of this letter of Siricius; see Jasper 2001, 34.

Ex dec pp Leonis metropolitano defuncto cum in loco ei(us) alius
fuerit subrogando conprouinciales epi ad ciuitate(m) metropolitani
conuenire debebunt ut omnium clericorum adque omnium ciui-
u(m) uolu(n)tate discussa ex presbiteris ei(us)dem aeccl(esi)ae uel
ex diaconis optim(us) eligatur.[163]

3.2.e.iii. Manuscript relations

Four of the five manuscripts display many similarities in orthography and variants; *k* is at variance with the other manuscripts
in the following except where noted. They give 'adque' for 'atque'
and 'scribtum' with related words, such as 'conscribtas', for 'scriptum'; in *Ep.* 167.5, *l* gives 'nubserint' for 'nupserint'. Excepting *r*,
these four tend to give '-ūs' for '-os', and *c* gives '-ci' for '-ti', as
in 'iusticia'. **Sa**, including *k*, prefers the spelling 'paenitentia' and
tends not to assimilate prefixes, giving 'conmercium', 'inlustris',
'inplicat', and sometimes even 'obportunius'—although in the latter case *k* gives 'oportunius'. For the most part, these orthographic
commonalities are uninteresting and amongst the many 'standard'
choices used by mediaeval scribes, with the exception of 'obportunius'. Primarily, they show us the depth of unity these manuscripts share.

Sa variants of note are:

Var., *Ep.*	**Sa** text	Ballerini text (control)	Significance
1, 167 *Praef.*	Om. *de singulis* (*s, l, r, k*)	opportunius quae-reretur *de singulis* si nobis tui conspectus copia proueniret. (*c*)	Error *s, l, r, k*
2, 167 *Praef.*	*conspectus tui* (*s, l, r, c, k*)	*tui conspectus*	Common variant **Sa**
3, 167.1	sunt *qui* ad proprios (*s, l, c, k*) ... sunt *quia* ad proprios ... (*r*)	ordinati sunt *quae* ad proprios episcopos pertinebant	Common error **Sa**
4, 167.4	De presbytero *et* diacono (*s, l, r, c, k*)	De presbytero *uel* diacono qui ... dederit	Common variant **Sa**

---

[163] *Ep.* 14.6.

Var., *Ep.*	**Sa** text	Ballerini text (control)	Significance
5, 167.4	*patri* (*s, l, k*)	nec omnis filius haeres est *patris* (*r, c*)	Variant *s, l, k*
6, 167.7	*expetiuerunt* (*s, l, r, c*)	*expetierunt* (*k*)	Variant *s, l, r, c*
7, 167.8 *cap.*	qui *paenitentiam iam deficientes* (*s, l, r, c, k*)	de his qui *iam deficientes poenitentiam* accipiunt	Common variant **Sa**
8, 167.10	Om. *a* (*s, l, r, c, k*) Om. *postulantem* (*k¹, add. k²*)	Sed illicitorum ueniam *postulantem* oportet *a* multis etiam licitis abstinere	Common error **Sa**
9, 167.10 (1 Cor. 6:12 & 10:23)	omnia licent (*l, r, c, k*, 1 Cor. 10:23)	omnia *mihi* licent (*s*; 1 Cor. 6:12; **Q B** Oriel MS 42)	Common* variant **Sa**
10, 167.13	Om. mortis (*s, l, r, c, k*)	si urguente aut metu *mortis* aut captiuitatis periculo	Common error **Sa**
11, 167.13	et postea timens lapsum incontinentiae *iuuenalis* (*s, l, r, c, k*)	... *iuuenilis*	Common variant **Sa**
12, 167.13	rem uidetur fecisse *iuuenalem* (*s, l, r, k*)	rem uidetur fecisse *uenialem* (*c*)	Error *s, l, r, k*
13, *Ep.* 167.18 *cap.*	*Maritania* (*s, l, c*) *auritani* (*k*)	*Mauritania* (*r*)	Error *s, l, c*
14, 167.18	sed manus *inpositione* uirtute spiritus sancti(*s, l, r, c*; *k* does not om. per)	sed *per* manus *impositionem inuocata* uirtute spiritus sancti	Common error **Sa** and error *s, l, r, c*; *per* likely dropped to make sense of ablative *inpositione*
15, 167.19 *cap.*	om. *adhuc iuuenes* (*s, l, r¹, c, k*)	cum ad Romaniam *adhuc iuuenes* uenerint (*r²*)	Common error **Sa**

Var., *Ep.*	**Sa** text	Ballerini text (control)	Significance
16, 12.4	Om. *priuilegia, sed etiam laborum* (*s, l*)	matrimoniorum *priuilegia, sed etiam laborum* merita (*r, c, k*)	Error *s, l*
17, 12.2	in el*e*gendo (*s, l, r¹, c, k*)	in el*i*gendo sacerdotem (*r²*)	Common variant **Sa** – Not stemmatically significant in isolation, since *e* and *i* frequently switch in MSS. However, since these are two different words, this variant is worth noting.
18, 12.2	*affecit* (*s, l, r¹, c, k*)	semetipsum *afficit* damno (*r²*)	Common variant **Sa** – See 17.
19, 12.2	Om. *de* (*s, l, r¹, c, k*)	fuerit *de* praeuaricatione (*r²*)	Common error **Sa**
20, 12.4	*emeritis? exinde* quidem (*s, l, r¹, c*) *emeriti? exinde ...* (*k*)	*emeritis? et in domo* quidem (*r²*)	Common variant **Sa** and unique error *k*
21, 12.4	*praedictus* (*s¹, l*)	quis bonis moribus *praeditus* (*s², r, c, k*)	Error *s, l*
22, 1.1	Om. *ne* (*s, l, r, c, k*)	nostrorum *ne* insontibus	Common error **Sa**
23, 1.1	*ceditur* usurpasse (*s, l, r, c*) *... creditur ...* (*k*)	quidem *conceditur* usurpasse	Common error **Sa** and unique *k*
24, 1.1	domu*s sedeant* et per falsi (*s¹, l, r¹, c*) domo*s sedeant ...* (*k*)	domu*s adeant* et (*s², r²*)	Common variant **Sa** and unique error *k*
25, 1.1	*receptionem* (*s, l, c*)	in talium *receptione* seruassent (*r, k*)	Error *s, l, c*
26, 1.2	*hoc* (*s, l, r, k*)	*hac* nostri auctoritate (*c*)	Error *s, l, r, k*

Var., *Ep.*	**Sa** text	Ballerini text (control)	Significance
27, 1.2	diaconi, *uel* cuiuscumque (*s, l, r, c, k*)	siue presbiteri, siue diaconi, *siue* cuiuscumque ordinis	Common variant **Sa**
28, 1.2	*possint* (*l, c, k*) *possent* (*r*)	nullis *possit* (*s*)	
29, 1.2	*quod* in doctrina (*s, l, r, c, k*)	*quidquid* in doctrina	Common variant **Sa**
30, 1.2	Om. *esse* (*s, l, r, c, k*)	istorum *esse* uersutiam	Common variant (error?) **Sa**
31, 1.2	istorum uersutiam (*r, c, k*) stolarum ... (*l*) itholarum ... (*s*)	As above	Agreement *r, c, k*, but sim. error *s, l*
32, 1.4	Om. *per ... dudum* (*s¹, l, r, c, k*)	ne *per huiusmodi in homines exstincta dudum scandala* (*s²*)	Common error **Sa**
33, 1.5	Om. *nec ... officio* (*s, l, r, c, k*)	diaconatus ordine *nec in subsequenti officio* clericorum (*s², r²*: paraphrase omission)	Common error **Sa**
34, 1.5	deprauátus *ubi ubi* ordinatus (*s, l, c*)	deprauatus *ubi* ordinatus (*r, k*)	Variant *s, l, c*
35, 2.1	Om. *pertinere* (*s, l, r, c, k*)	periculum cognosceret *pertinere* si quisquam	Common error **Sa**
36, 2.1	*cognoscere* (*l*), *cognoscerit* (*r*), *cognusciret* (*c*)	periculum *cognosceret* (*s, k*)	These variants can easily all come from the same archetype.
37, 2.1	*uel* (*s, l, r, c, k*)	diaconi, *siue* alii cuiuslibet ordinis clerici	Common variant **Sa**
38, 2.2	*illa* (*s, l, r, c*)	*illam* canonum constitutionem (*k*)	Error *s, l, r, c*; *k* conjecturable – common **Sa**

Var., *Ep.*	**Sa** text	Ballerini text (control)	Significance
39, 2.2	*cum quo* recte (*s, l, c*) ... *cum quod* ... (*k*; *k¹* om. recte, *k²* add. recta)	transire. *quod cum* recte (*r*)	Error *s, l, c, k*
40, 2.2	*sponsionibus* (*s¹, l, r¹, c*)	curam suam *dispo-sitionibus* (*s², r², k*)	Variant *s, l, r, c*
41, 2.2	*incolumitate* (*s, l, c, k*)	ad totius ecclesiae *incolumitatem*, et (*r*)	Error *s, l, c, k*; *r* conjecturable – common **Sa**

r also had the following errors at variance from the rest of **Sa** in *Ep.* 12:

	r	*s, l, c, k*
Ep. 12.1	Om. *necessarium fuit*	relatione patefecit *necessarium fuit* ut
Ep. 12.3	*ipsam* suo	et aliam praeter *missam* suo
Ep. 12.3	Om. *releuata iam*	sub *releuata iam* gratia

The majority of the common variants serve simply to reinforce **Sa** as a collection in more than simply contents; these manuscripts all derive from the same source. The following are common errors in *s, l, r, k*: 1, 12, and 26. Var. 12 is a case of attraction due to the spelling 'iuuenali's (Var. 11) above; it is a liminal case of being a common error, as it would be easily emendable by the scribe of *c* if the exemplar contained 'iuuenalem'. The following are common variants in *s, l, r, c*: 6 and 40; Var. 6 is a trivial difference, largely dependent on the scribe's choice of spelling. However, 'expeti-uérunt' scans _u_/_ _ while 'expetiérunt' _uu/_ _; the first is one of Leo's favoured metrical clausulae to match the accentual *cursus planus*.[164] Of the common errors in *s, l, r, c*, Variant 14 is curious because *k* includes 'per' but then ungrammatically agrees with the other manuscripts in giving 'inpositione' rather than 'inpositionem'. The common variant in *s, l, c* is: 34, while the common errors are: 13 and 25. 13 could have been emended by the scribe

---

[164] See the results of Di Capua 1937, 37–39. Parallels are easily found: *Ep.* 167.6 closes, 'est honestatis'; *Ep.* 165, explicit: 'regnare cum Christo'; *Ep.* 9.1, opening, 'impendamus affectum'.

of *r* and 25 by those of *r* and *k*, just as 12 could have been by the
scribe of *c*. The following are the common errors in *s*, *l*: 16, 21.
In variant 31, *s* and *l* differ between each other while the rest of
the manuscripts agree with the Ballerini. The only other time *s*
and *l* are at variance is variant 36, where *s* and *k* agree with the
Ballerini but *l*, *r*, and *c* give their own divergent readings. *s* and
l, therefore, are more closely united than any other two manuscripts of **Sa**; they are from a common branch of the *Sanblasiana*
tree, possibly twins, possibly *l* descended from *s*—these two manuscripts are both Italian. *k* has a few unique readings, such as
secondary variants in 20 and 24 as well as divergences from the
rest of **Sa** for 23 and 14; it is also the manuscript from farthest
afield, whether Northumbria or the area of Reichenau. *r* also displays some unique readings in *Ep.* 12 due to carelessness. At first
glance, *r* and *c* seem to be closely related, but they are at variance
with each other more often than *s* and *l* are. *c* is thus separate
from the wider **Sa** tradition. One test to further these arguments
would be to check for contamination of *c*'s parent against manuscripts of other traditions.

3.2.f. *Collectio Dionysiana*[165] (**D**)

3.2.f.i. Dating and context

Unlike with our other early canonical collections, the compiler
of the *Collectio Dionysiana* is known—Dionysius Exiguus (*c.* 470–
c. 540), a monk most famous for his Easter computation that the
Roman church was to adopt and thereby set our current dating of Christ's birth.[166] Dionysius came from 'Scythia', noted as
'Scytha natione' by Cassiodorus, to Rome shortly after the death
of Pope Gelasius I (d. 496);[167] as Firey argues, Dionysius' origin
is most significant for the fact that Scythia was long Latinised

---

[165] B6 (PL 54.557–58), J1(vi) (501–02).

[166] Dionysius' texts on the dating of Easter are in Krusch 1938, 63–87.

[167] Besides Dionysius' own work and his introductions to it, we derive information about him from Cassiodorus, *Institutiones divinarum et humanarum
lectionum*, 1.23; 1.23.2 includes the important information: 'fuit enim nostris
temporibus et Dionisius monachus, Scytha natione sed *moribus omnino Roma-
nus, in utraque lingua valde doctissimus*, reddens actionibus suis quam in libris
Domini legerat aequitatem'. (Emphasis added). The only other person of this
era whom I have found to be described explicitly as *scytha natione* is John

and its monks often involved in doctrinal quarrels—thus, Dionysius was well-positioned to translate Greek texts for the use of
Latin churchmen.[168] The first version of *Collectio Dionysiana* was
a translation of Greek canons into Latin during the pontificate of
Symmachus; Dionysius' collection of papal letters followed shortly
thereafter.[169] Since we know who compiled this collection, we can
also safely say where it was compiled with no conjecture: Rome.
Furthermore, Dionysius seems to have used the incipient papal
archive, as mentioned above.[170]

Gaudemet judges that **D** is the most important canonical collection of this era.[171] Part of its importance lies in its use by later
canonists, as visible below. For example, Cresconius' *Concordia
Canonum*, which is one of our first systematic collections, is based
on Dionysius' work, as are the *Collectiones Dionysio-Hadriana*
(**D-h**) and *Dionysiana Bobiensis* (**D-b**), the other canonical collections descended from the *Dionysiana* containing these decretals.[172]
The *Dionysiana* also exerts influence upon the *Collectio Hispana*
and its text of these letters, thereby also the later collections
related to the *Hispana*, such as *Hispana Gallica Augustodunensis*,
Pseudo-Isidore, and Ballerini collections 21 and 22. **D** contains
seven Leonine epistles, all of which are later designated decretals:
4, 7, 16, 18, 167, 14, 159.

Cassian; both are bilingual monks who brought Greek learning to the Latin
West.

[168] See Firey 2008. The best brief description of Dionysius' life and work
within their historical context is still Duchesne 1925, 134–37.

[169] For dates of the compiling of *Collectio Dionysiana*, see Gaudemet 1985,
134; Fournier and Le Bras 1931, vol. 1, 24. That the decretals were added
shortly after the original collection highlighted in the italicised phrase from
his own introduction to the decretal collection: 'ita dumtaxat ut singulorum pontificum, quotquot a me praecepta reperta sunt, sub una numerorum
serie terminarem, omnesque titulos huic praefationi subnecterem, *eo modo,
quo dudum*, de graeco sermone patrum transferens Canones, ordinaram, quod
vobis nimium placuisse cognoueram'. (CCSL 87: 45).

[170] At 3.1. See also Gaudemet 1985, 136.

[171] Ibid., 134.

[172] The *Collectio Dionysiana adaucta* (**D-a**) is also descended from Dionysius' collection, but it is an amplification appended to **D**, and thus is a separate collection that occurs in **D** or **D-h** manuscripts.

3.2.f.ii. Manuscripts

As the existence of the independent introduction implies, Diony-sius' decretal collection was originally a discrete entity from that of the canons.[173] However, in the manuscript tradition, it always comes with the conciliar material. The manuscripts are:[174]

a: Paris, lat. 3837 (saec. IX; before 829), from Angers, scriptorium of Saint-Maurice cathedral;[175] the table of contents includes Leo at fols 96^v–98^v; his letters run 140rb-158ra. Written in two columns, it is a minuscule manuscript with rubricated capitals and uncials for the *tituli*. This manuscript and *c* also include the preface to the decretals.

c: Vat. lat. 5845 (*c.* 915 and 934), from Capua; written in two columns of 27 lines each. The hand is Beneventan script.[176] It was written by monks of Montecassino in exile at Capua when they had fled the Saracens, first to Teano in 883, then to Capua from 896–949.[177] The contents list Leo 73^r–74^r, and his letters in the **D** portion run from 112^v–126^v. The first hand of the Leo portion runs until 118^v, the second beginning at 119^r; since 118–24 are a single quire, the change of hands is due to a change of scribe at time of writing, not later damage to the manuscript. The first hand is larger, clearer, and darker. The rubrics throughout are very pale and almost illegible.[178] This manuscript also includes the *Collectio Dionysiana adaucta* (**D–a**), for which see below at 5.2.c.

---

[173] The introductions are edited in CCSL 87:31–51.

[174] See the helpful table of the *Dionysiana* manuscripts in Firey 2008. Kéry 1999, 10, also lists Paris, lat. 3845 under the Second Recension with the note 'also decretals'. However, this manuscript does not contain the decretals, and is not listed on page 11 with the other decretal manuscripts. Firey 2008 reproduces this.

[175] Bischoff 1998–2014, 3.4278. The manuscript gives a catalogue of the Bishops of Angers ending with Benedict (d. 828/29). See *Catalogue géné-ral*, Bibliothèque nationale de France. https://archivesetmanuscrits.bnf.fr/ark:/12148/cc61802r Accessed 20 September 2021.

[176] Lowe 1980, vol. 1, 69. Costantino Gaetano classified the script as Lombard in the 1600s according to the old methodology of assigning scripts to people groups; he also wrote, 'il piu quasi antico codice di Concilij, che habbia la Libraria Vaticana'. See his letter to Urban VIII inscribed in Vat. Barb. lat. 3150, fols 356 and 358; full text in Ruysschaert 1964, 268–71, quotation from p. 270.

[177] Lowe 1980, vol. 2, 53–54.

[178] Kéry lists Vat. lat. 5845 as both *Dionysiana adaucta* and *Dionysiana*; however, since its contents for Leo are those of the *Dionysiana*, I have classed it here for our purposes.

The decretal collection also exists in two manuscripts that excerpt decretals from the *Dionysiana*; however, these manuscripts do not contain Leo's letters.[179] Finally, the decretals were edited by Christophe Justel;[180] however, as Gaudemet has observed, Justel's edition of the *Dionysiana* decretals is actually a reprint of either the 1525 edition of **D–h** by Johannes Wendelstinus (Cochlaeus) or that of Pithou from 1609.[181]

3.2.f.iii. Manuscript relations

Before setting forth the many *Dionysiana* variants, it is worth observing that these two manuscripts are orthographically distinct. For example, *a* frequently uses '-us' for '-os', and gives '-tium' where *c* gives '-cium', as in 'officium'. Throughout, *a* has a tendency to interchange *i* and *e*, giving each where the control text provides the other; such a difference is due not to error, nor even to a variant in the copyist's mind, but, rather, to the sound of Latin to the copyist's ear.[182] Both manuscripts, however, prefer 'inp-' to 'imp-', and 'inr-' to 'irr-', as in 'inperitia' and 'inrationabilis'. Besides the variations in spelling, *a* demonstrates greater carelessness in copying. Although both texts demonstrate numerous variants from the control text, those in *a* that are not shared with *c* are more frequently demonstrable errors than in *c*, as the following table will show. In total, out of the 238 **D** variants analysed, 95 of them are definitive errors unique to *a*, while only 34 are definitive errors unique to *c*. On those grounds, *c* seems to be the more reliable manuscript—although not free of error. However, *c* tends to omit 'uc' or 'uu cc' from the consular formulae at the ends of letters, an omission not present in *a*. One of the notable errors in *c* is the failure of the first scribe to finish column 2 of fol. 118ᵛ, missing out the last chapter of *Ep.* 16 and all of *Ep.* 18. A much later, possibly early modern, hand, and not the scribe who

---

[179] These manuscripts are Paris, lat. 10399, fol. 20–25, and Paris, lat. 3847 of the twelfth century.

[180] C. Justel 1628 and 1643, decretals in 183–248; and PL 67.137–316, decretals in 230–316.

[181] Gaudemet 1985, 136, n. 19. Justel has certainly produced a **D–h** text, since PL 67.298B–302C prints for us *Ep.* 12, the one addition to Leo's letters in that version.

[182] The interchange between *i* and *e* in select circumstances is discussed at great length in Chapter X of Adams 2007.

took over on 119ʳ, thus wrote the *incipit* of *Ep.* 167 at the bottom of 118ᵛ, col. 2:

Leo epus Rustico Narbonensi epo. Eplas sncitatis tuae, quas Hermes archidiaconus suus detulit, libenter accepi diuersarum quidem causarum connexione

119ʳ begins 'connexione multiplices'. This lacuna seems not to have affected the later manuscripts of the **D** tradition, so we can assume *c* has no descendents.

In the following table, all of the variants from *Ep.* 4, which begins the collection, have been included, and select other readings—all of the errors unique to *a* after *Ep.* 4 have been excluded for the sake of space. Despite these readings being a fraction of those investigated, the quantity of variants in the table below is still extensive; this extensive laying out of relationships is important for the *Dionysiana* because of its early date and wide influence. The better we understand **D**, the better we understand the later collections and their textual development. The results for the *Collectio Dionysiana* are as follows:

Var., *Ep.*	**D** text	Ballerini text (control)	Significance
1, 4, *Praef.*	et *per* uniuersas (*c*)	Tusciam et uniuersas prouincias (*a*)	Variant *c*
2, 4, *Praef.*	*errore* (*a*)	nos *maerore* contristat (*c*)	Error *a*
3, 4, *Praef.*	*et* ecclesiasticam disciplinam (*a*, *c*)	constituta canonum ecclesiasticam*que* disciplinam	Variant **D**
4, 4, *Praef.*	om. *esse* (*a*)	speculatores *esse* uoluit (*c*)	Variant *a*
5, 4, *Praef.*	*quis* corpus (*a*) *sincere* (*c*)	permittentes *sincerum* corpus	
6, 4, *Praef.*	*purum macula* (*a*, *c*)	quod ab omni *macula purum*	Variant **D**
7, 4, *Praef.*	dissimulationem (*a*)	dissimilationem (*c*)	Variant *a*; very common variant spelling, of no consequence

Var., *Ep.*	**D** text	Ballerini text (control)	Significance
8, 4.1	*atque* (*a*)	Duplex *itaque* in hac (*c*)	Error *a*
9, 4.1	*uestrae prouinciae* (*a, c*)	omnes *prouinciae uestrae*	Variant **D**
10, 4.1	*temerari* (*a*)	uolumus *temperari*: nisi (*c*)	Error *a*
11, 4.1	*nulla necessitate saeculi subtrahatur* (*c*)	*nullis necessitatis uinculis abstrahatur* (*a*)	Error *c*
12, 4.2	*constituet* (*a*)	unicuique *constiterit* (*c*)	Error *a*
13, 4.2	om. *quibus* (*a*)	quosdam etiam *quibus* (*c*)	Error *a*
14, 4.2	om. *licentiam* (*a*)	et ad omnem *licentiam* uita (*c*)	Error *a*
15, 4.2	*adyticum* (*a*)	patefactis *aditibus* fuisse (*c*)	Error *a*
16, 4.2	*quia* (*a*)	uocem, *qua* talibus (*c*)	Variant *a*
17, 4.2	*quod* (*a*)	praeceptum, *quo* dicitur et (*c*)	Error *a*
18, 4.2	huius discussion*es* (*a*)	huius discussion*is* (*c*)	Orthographic variant – *e* and *i* often interchangeable in *a*.
19, 4.2	*liceat* (*a*)	*licuerit* sacerdotem (*c*)	Error *a*
20, 4.2	*regulis canonum* (*a, c*)	*canonum regulis* fuerit	Variant **D**
21, 4.2	*consuerunt* (*a*)	enecare *consueuerunt* (*c*)	Variant *a*
22, 4.3	om. *turpis* (*a*)	quosdam lucri *turpis* cupiditate (*c*)	Error? *a*
23, 4.3	*constitutos* (*a*)	officio *constituti* (*c*)	Error *a*
24, 4.4, Cap.	fenus *exerceant* (*a*) *exerceat* (*c*)	N/A	

Var., *Ep.*	**D** text	Ballerini text (control)	Significance
25, 4.4	*non* (*a*, *c*)	ita *nec* alieno nomine	Error **D**
26, 4.4	*indecus* (*a*)	*indecens* enim est (*c*)	Error *a*
27, 4.5	a suo *scianit se* officio (*c*)	a suo *se nouerit* officio (*a*)	Error *c*
28, 4.5	*custodire* (*a*)	a uestra dilectione *custodiri* (*c*)	Error *a*
29, 4.5	maximo et paterio uu cc conss (*a*) om. *uu cc* (*c*)	Maximo iterum et Paterio uiris clarissimis consulibus	Variant *c*
30, 7.1	*ne* (*a*, *c*)	inueniat latebrarum *ut* quod a nobis	Error **D**
31, 7.1	*uigilanti ad uulgauit* (*c*)	reperit *uigilantia diuulgauit* auctoritas (*a*)	Error *c*
32, 7.1	*que* (*c*)	*quid* refugeret aut uitaret (*a*)	Error *c*
33, 7.2	quos ne absoluerent (*a*, *c*)	quos *hic*, ne *se* absoluerent	Error **D**
34, 7.2	om. *per acolythum nostrum* (*a*, *c*)	misimus *per acolythum nostrum*; ut	Variant **D**
35, 7.2	Dat III kl Febr Theodosio XVIII et Albino uc cons (*a*) Dat III kl Feb theodosio XVIII et Albino conss (*c*)	Data tertio kalendas Februarii, Theodosio Augusto XVIII et Albino uiris clarissimis consulibus	
36, 16, *Praef.*	om. *episcopus* (*a*, *c*)	Leo *episcopus* uniuersis	Variant **D**
37, 16, *Praef.*	*cleri* (*a*, *c*) om. *sollicitudine* (*a*)	obnoxium *celeri sollicitudine*	Error **D** Error *a*
39, 16.1	*apostoli petri* (*a*, *c*)	et beati *Petri apostoli* sedes	Variant **D**

Var., *Ep.*	**D** text	Ballerini text (control)	Significance
40, 16.2	*mistico munerum oblato* (*a, c*)	paruulum *mystica munerum oblatione* uenerantur	Error **D**
41, 16.2	*mortuo persecutore* (*a, c*)	in Galilaeam, *persecutore mortuo* reuocatus est	Variant **D**
42, 16.2	*esse se*; om. *et* (*a*) om. *se* (*c*)	significans eius *se esse* filium cuius esset *et* templum	Variants *a* Error *c*
43, 16.2	... *districtio* ... (*a, c*)	seruanda *distinctio* quia	Error **D**
44, 16.2	dicit (*a*)	apostolus docet (*c*)	Variant *a*
45, 16.2	in eodem *sententiendam* sententia (*a*) *scientia* (*c*)	in eodem *sensu et in eadem sententia*	Error *a* Variant *c*
46, 16.3 (Jn 14:26)	... Pater *meus* in ... (*c*)	quem mittet Pater in nomine meo (*a*, Vulgate)	Variant *c*
47, 16.5 (VI)	Quia *si* sunt (*a, c*)	Quia *etsi* sunt alia quoque festa	Variant **D**
48, 16.6	ob hoc *existimat* (*a, c*)	ob hoc *aestimat* priuilegium	Variant **D**
49, 16.6	om. *implendo finire* (*c*)	sed implere et *implendo finire* (*a*)	Error *c*
50, 16.6	*primatum* (*a, c*)	in omnibus *primatus* tenens	Variant **D**
51,[183] 16.7	quae, inspirante Domino, *uobis* (*a*)	quae *uobis*, inspirante Domino, insinuanda	Variant *a*
52, 16.7	*Vacillum et Paschasium* (*a*)	coepiscopos nostros *Bacillum atque Paschasinum*	Variant *a*
53, 16.7	*a* gives no date in *explicit*		Error *a*

[183] Variants 53–58 are where *c* has a lacuna.

Var., *Ep.*	**D** text	Ballerini text (control)	Significance
54, 18	*gregum* (*a*)	ad custodiam *gregis* Christi	Variant *a*
55, 18	*Deum* (*a*)	Non leuem apud *Dominum* noxam	Variant *a*
56, 18	Data III kl iul alipio et ardabure conss (*a*)	Data III Kalend. Ianuarii Calepio et Ardabure uiris clarissimis consulibus	
57, 167, *Praef.*	*debeas adhibere* (*a, c*)	spiritalem *adhibere debeas* medicinam	Variant **D**
58, 167, *Praef.*	*conflictatione* (*c*) nulla *perfectorum portio a conflictione* (*a*)	nulla *piorum portio a tentatione* sit libera	Variant *a, c* Variant *a*
59, 167, *Praef.*	*pastorum* (*a*)	Si *pastoris* cura non uigilet?	Variant *a*
60, 167, *Praef.* (Jn 16:33)	*confidite* (*a, c*; Vulgate)	habebitis; sed *bono animo estote,* quia	Variant **D**
61, 167, *Praef.*	om. *de singulis* (*a, c*)	quaereretur *de singulis* si nobis conspectus	Error **D**
62, 167, *Praef.*	*conspectus tui* ... (*a, c*)	nobis *tui conspectus* copia	Variant **D**
63, 167, *Praef.*	om. *patrum* (*a, c*)	decretis sanctorum *patrum* inueniatur	Error **D**
64, 167.1	*doceatur* (*a, c*)	quod non docetur fuisse collatum?	Error **D**
65, 167.1	*qui* (*a*) *quia* (*c*)	in eis ecclesiis ordinati sunt *quae* ad	Error *a* Error *c*
66, 167.1	*consecratio* (*a*)	habenda est *creatio* quae (*c*)	Variant *a*
67, 167.7 (Bal.)	*sit* poenitus *desperanda* (*c, a*)	Culpanda *est* talium negligentia, sed non *poenitus deseranda*	Variant **D**

Var., *Ep.*	**D** text	Ballerini text (control)	Significance
68, 167.10 (1 Cor. 10:23 & 6:12)	omnia licent (*a, c*; 1 Cor. 10:23)	omnia *mihi* licent (1 Cor. 6:12)	Variant **D**; **Sa**
69, 167.18	impositionem, *uir-tutem* (*a, c*)	sed per manus impositionem, *inuocata uirtute* Spiritus Sancti	Variant **D** **Sa** also om. *inuo-cata*
70, 14 *Inscr.*	Quod semper thesalonicenses antistites uices apostolicae sedis *impleuerint* (*c*) ... *impleuerit* (*a*)		Error *a*
71, 14, *Praef.*	... Petri auctori-tate *commissa sunt* (*a*) *patris* auctoritate *commisa sunt* (*c*)	a beatissimi Petri *apostoli* auctori-tate *sint commissa*	Error *c* Shared variant *a, c* This comes at the end of a clause, and '–tate com-missa sunt' scans _u_/_u_, prefera-ble to '–tate sint commissa': _u_/_ _u.
72, 14, *Praef.*	*siue ratione* (*a, c*)	*si uera ratione*	Error **D**; haplog-raphy
73, 14.1	uniuersis *et* eccle-siis (*c*) om. *ecclesiis* (*a*)	quam uniuersis *Ecclesiis*	Variant *c* Error *a*
74, 14.1	*impenderis et* continenti (*c*) *impenderes et con-tinet* (*a*)	*impenderes siq-uidem* continenti	Variant *c* Error *a*
75, 14.1	*audientiae* (*a, c*)	salubritatem *oboedientiae* prouocares	Error **D**
76, 14.1	*seniores* (*c*)	*seniorem* ne (*a*)	Variant *c*
77, 14.1 (1 Tim. 5:1)	*obsecraris* (*c*)	Sed *obsecra* (*a*, Vulgate)	Variant *c*; likely wrong

Var., *Ep.*	**D** text	Ballerini text (control)	Significance
78, 14.1	*credenda* (*c*)	*reddenda* est (*a*)	Error *c*
79, 14.1 (Phil. 2:21)	*Christi Iesu* (*a*, *c*, Vulgate)	quae *Iesu Christi* facile	Variant **D**
80, 14.1	*trahi* in culpam sentio (*a*, *c*)	in culpam *trahi* sentio	Variant **D**
81, 14.1	*concessum* (*c*)	quodque *consensum* suum etiam (*a*)	Error *c*
82, 14.1	de *meis moribus aestimasti* (*a*, *c*)	bene de *moribus meis existimasti*	Variant **D**
83, 14.1	om. *sunt* (*a*, *c*)	quae perperam *sunt* gesta	Error **D**
84, 14.1	*commendamus* (*a*) *commendabimus* (*c*)	tibi *commendauimus*	Variant *a* Variant *c*; orthography[184]
85, 14.3	*testimonio fulceatur* (*a*) *testimonio fulciatur* (*c*)	etiamsi bonae uitae *testimonium habeat*	Variant **D**; viable possibility as correct reading
86, 14.4	*uel* secundo tercio *uersandum* (*a*) *aut* secundo, tertio seruandum (*c*)	*aut* secundo *uel* tertio *seruandum*	Error & variant *a* Variant **D**
87, 14.5	... *praeponatur* ... (*a*, *c*)	is alteri *praeferatur* qui	Variant **D**
88, 14.8	Si quis *autem* episcopus (*a*)	om. *autem* (*c*)	Variant *a*
89, 14.11	om. *Nemo ... Apostolus ait* (*a*, *c*)	turbentur. *Nemo quod suum est quaerat, sed quod alterius, sicut Apostolus ait:* Unusquisque	Error **D**
90, 14.11 (Ro. 15:2)	om. *uestrum* (*a*, *c*)	Unusquisque *uestrum* proximo (Vulgate)	Variant **D**

[184] The orthography of *c* is inconsequential, but the reading is, however, of note, whether with a *b* or a *v*, since it differs from *a*.

Var., *Ep.*	**D** text	Ballerini text (control)	Significance
91, 14.11	et haec *quidem* connexio (*a, c*)	haec connexio totius quidem corporis	Variant **D**
92, 159.1	liberandos, *et in* aliorum … (*a, c*)	liberandos, *ad* aliorum coniugium	Variant **D**
93, 159.1 (Pr. 19:14)	scriptum 'a *dom-ino* … (*a, c*)	scriptum, *quod* 'a *Deo* iungitur'	Neither is Vulgate, which follows Heb.; Latin trans. of LXX. Variant **D**
94, 159.2	om. *habeatur* (*a, c*), thus allowing 'iudicetur' to govern 'peruasor' peruasor *per perso-nam* (*a*)	peruasor *habeatur* qui	Variant **D** Error *a*
95, 159.2	*sit* (*a, c*)	quanto magis … faciendum *est*	Variant **D**
96, 159.7	sola *spiritus sancti inuocatione* (*c*) *sancti spiritus inuocatione* (*a*)	sola *inuocatione Spiritus Sancti*	Variant *a* Variant *c*
97, 159.7, *Explicit*	om. date (*a*) Dat XIII kl April, cons. marciani Augusti (*c*)	Data XII kalendorum Aprilium, consulatu Maioriani Augusti	Error *a* Variant or error *c*

This table shows us that, while *a* may be a somewhat corrupt text, it is certainly not irredeemable. **D** has a number of notable common variants from the control text: 43 out of these 97, of which 12 are errors and 30 neutral variants with one that is debatable. *c* introduces fewer errors as well as its own variants. Overall, with *c* and *a* frequently correcting each other, these two manuscripts could help produce an ur-**D** of Leo's letters that would be in the running for the urtext itself—but we have a third witness, **D–b**, which makes that task even easier. **D** is a good text, and we are fortunate it was so influential for the transmission of these seven letters through the Middle Ages. The transmission of these letters in traditions indebted to **D** runs through **D–h**, **S** and its children, thus also **I** and its children—spreading, that is, into canon law collections from Italy into Spain and Gaul, thence to Germany and Britain as well as back again into Italy.

3.2.g. *Collectio Dionysiana Bobiensis*[185] (**D–b**)

3.2.g.i. Dating and context

This collection is a seventh-century augmentation of the *Collectio Dionysiana*. Later material was added to the original *Dionysiana*, and then at an even later date were added canons from Roman councils of Pope Zacharias in 743 and Pope Eugenius II in 826.[186] Nonetheless, according to Wurm's research on the text, **D–b** is descended from a more or less 'pure' *Dionysiana*.[187] The Leonine material bears this out, being the same as in *Collectio Dionysiana* and following readings that may be considered 'typical' of that collection, as I shall demonstrate. As discussed below, **D–b** is important as a third witness to the text of **D**, but drawn from a source independent of our two **D** manuscripts.

3.2.g.ii. Manuscripts

D–b survives in two manuscripts:

> *m*: Milan, Biblioteca Ambrosiana S. 33 sup. (saec. IX), caroline minuscule with capitalis *tituli*,[188] originating in Bobbio during the abbacy of Agilulf (887–96); Leo's letters run 224^r–245^r. *m* has a single column of text. There are two hands in the writing of this manuscript, and for Leo's letters the second hand is an obsessive corrector, who even corrects orthography such as 'quicumque' to 'quicunque'. Besides interlinear glosses that are typically simple synonyms, such as 'letitiam' for 'gratulationem' or 'ordinatus' for 'compositus' (see fol. 224^r), *m*^{2} also provides marginal glosses, especially on fols 227^v, 229^v, and 230^r. Pantarotto persuasively argues that *m*^{2} is also responsible as the primary scribe for several other quires.[189] My own examination of

---

[185] Unknown to Ballerini and therefore to Jalland.

[186] See Fowler-Magerl 2005, 42, and Kéry 1999, 13.

[187] Wurm 1938, 32–33.

[188] Bischoff 1998–2014, 2.2655.

[189] Pantarotto 2007 demonstrates that many of the additions to the *Dionysiana* that make it *Bobiensis* are done by *m*^{2} on new quires added at a later date than the transcription of the rest of the manuscript. Based upon style of writing as well as use of abbreviations, *m*^{2} went on to correct and gloss the text of *m*^{1} in the rest of the manuscript.

the manuscript bears out the essentially contemporary nature of these two hands in the Leo portion of the manuscript.

v: Vercelli, Biblioteca Capitolare, CXI (saec. X).[190] *v* is written in a Caroline minuscule with uncial *capitula* that alternate between red and same ink as text. Leo's letters run fols 162ᵛ–180ᵛ.

3.2.g.iii. Manuscript relations

Of minor importance yet still worth noting is the fact that *m* and *v* differ orthographically. For example, *m* gives 'praesumat' but *v* 'presumat'; others are *m* 'tanquam', *v* 'tamquam'; *m* 'aggregandus', *v* 'adgregandus'; *m* 'paenitus', *v* 'poenitus'; and *m* 'quae', *v* 'que'. At first glance such orthographic differences make one suspect that *v* is not a copy of *m*. However, as Wurm has already argued,[191] *v* is a descendant of *m*—and likely a direct copy. My own collation of the two manuscripts demonstrates that *v* takes on too many of *m*'s non-**D** variants to be independent of the *m* tradition. The following table gives a brief selection of some of these readings to demonstrate this dependency:

Ep.	**D–b** (*m* and *v*)	**D** and Ballerini (control)
4.2	*obstiterant*	quod *obstiterat*, non fuerunt
7.1	om. *suis*	in occultis traditionibus suis habent
7.2	om. *fratres karissimi*	sanctitas uestra, *fratres karissimi*, sollicitius
16, *Praef.*	*Monente*	*Manente* enim dominicae uocis
16.2	in templum *in* Ierusalem	in templum Ierusalem
16.2	*recolamus*	honore *colamus*, omnia tempora
16.3	*Pentecosten*	*Pentecostes* ex aduentu
16.3	*magister latius*	quae *latius magister* gentium
167, *Praef.*	*castigare*	*castigari* necesse est Although *e* and *i* can be interchangeable in mss, here this is the difference between passive and active.
167.1	*in* iudicio	consensu et iudicio praesidentium
14.1	*profectu*	opportunoque prospectu
14.1	*nostrae*	*nostra* erat expectanda

---

[190] Bischoff 1998–2014, 3.6999.

[191] Wurm 1939, 32–33.

These errors common to **D–b** but distinct from **D** help show us the independence of **D–b** from both **D** a and c, as does the fact that at times it agrees with **D** a, at times with **D** c. Very frequently, v follows m^2 in deviating from **D**-Ballerini; however, at times v follows m^1. The question thus arises whether m^2 is a single hand, as previously argued, or more than one hand. By the appearance of the manuscript, m^2 looks to be a single hand of similar date to m^1, as discussed above. However, since m is late ninth-century and v early tenth-century, a third m hand in the same script could be postulated to account for cases where v deviates from m^2 and follows the m^1 reading although it had already been corrected; this postulated m^3, however, runs against the current of most scholarship on the manuscript, and I, myself, have observed no palaeographical reason to believe in a third hand. A likely cause of v choosing m^1 over m^2 is the fact that m^2 both obsessively corrects and glosses; for someone making a copy, an interlinear correction could be mistaken for an interlinear gloss. An important piece of evidence for v dependency on m is in 16.7 where a marginal gloss from m has been added to the main text of v.[192] Furthermore, as the table below will demonstrate, v introduces many corruptions into the text that m lacks, pointing to a later stage of transmission within the same family. Finally, in those few instances where v provides a better reading than m, these are moments where the text could easily have been emended by the scribe. These instances are in *Ep.* 7.1, where v agrees with the Ballerini in giving 'dispergat ecclesias', but m gives the corrupt reading 'ecclesiis'; in 18 v gives 'spiritalis medicinae' but m provides 'spiritali'; in 167, *Praef.*, v gives 'recensitis', while m gives two variants, 'recensiti' (m^1) and 'recensentes' (m^2); in 14.1, v provides 'temperantia frequenter instruximus' against m's 'frequentia'; in 14.1 v also writes 'nostro uiderentur gesta' rather than either 'uideantur' (m^1) or 'uidearentur' (m^2); again in 14.1, v has 'euocatus adesse differret' but m 'adesset'; later in the same chapter, v has 'noui apud Te criminis' rather than m 'apud se'; in 14.11, v gives 'exigit concordiam sacerdotum' instead of the m corruption 'concordia'; in 159.3, v provides 'in captiuitatem reuersi', but m 'in

---

[192] The text is, 'Quod itaque laboriosum non est si uicissim inter uos haec consuetudo seruetur' (m fol. 231^v; v fol. 169^r).

captiuitatem persereuersi'. This accounts for the total number of instances where *v* provides a sound reading against an *m* corruption; it is obvious that a good scribe could have corrected the text before in each of the above rather than requiring either a different exemplar or a second text to bring in contaminations.

A selection of other **D–b** variants is described below. The purpose of this table is to demonstrate the dependency of *v* upon *m* as well as the textual derivation of **D–b** from the work of Dionysius. My collations of these manuscripts found 236 variants of one sort or another from the Ballerini control text. Therefore, I present only a selection of the findings to demonstrate and illustrate my argument; the variants provided are drawn from *Ep.* 4 as well as some of the significant other variants of the collection.

Variant: *Ep.*	**D–b** (*m, v*) **D** (*a, c*)	Ballerini text (control)	Significance
1, 4, *Praef.*	Tusciam et *per* uniuersas prouincias (*v; c*)	om. *per* (*m; a*)	Variant *v; c*
2, 4, *Praef.*	praesumpta uel *contempta* (*m¹, v*)	*commissa* (*m²; a, c*)	Error *m¹, v*
3, 4, *Praef.*	debemus *ambigendo* improba (*v*)	*ambientium* (*m; a, c*)	Error *v*
4, 4.1	honorem *accipiat* (*m¹, v*)	*capiat* (*m²; a, c*)	Variant *m¹, v*
5, 4.1	om. ad (*v*)	*ad* illicitae usurpationis (*m; a, c*)	Error *v*
6, 4.1	om. *uestrae* (*m*) *uestrae prouiniciae* (*v; a, c*)	omnes *prouinciae uestrae* abstineant	Variant *m* Variant *v*
7, 4.1	*tamen* (*v*)	non *tantum* ab his, sed ab aliis (*m; a, c*)	Variant *v*
8, 4.1	*ordinationi* (*v*)	aut alicui *conditioni* obligati (*m; a, c*)	Variant *v*
9, 4.1	*necessitatis calculis* (*v*) *necessitatibus calculis* (*m¹*)	nullis *necessitatis uinculis* abstrahatur (*m²; a*)	Variant *v* Error *m¹* by assimilation

Variant: Ep.	**D–b** (*m, v*) **D** (*a, c*)	Ballerini text (control)	Significance
10, 4.2 Cap.	*uim* (*m*) sacerdotum *uel* uiduarum (*v; a, c*)		Error *m*
11, 4.2	om. *constiterit* (*m², v*)	uniquique *con-stiterit natalium* (*m¹; c*) *constituet* (*a*)	Error *m², v*
12, 4.2	*protectione* (*v*)	diuina *praeceptione* didicimus (*m; a, c*)	Error *v*
13, 4.2	*quod* (*v; a*)	legis praeceptum, *quo* dicitur (*m, c*)	Error *v; a*
14, 4.2	*auellantur* (*m², v*)	radicitus *euellan-tur* (*m¹*)	Variant *m², v*
15, 4.2	*qua nata segetem et necare consuerunt* (*v*) *consuerunt* (*m; a*)	si ea *quae natam segetem enecare consueuerunt* (*m; c*)	Error *v*
16, 4.3	*decreuimus* (*m¹, v*)	confutati *decerni-mus* (*m²; a, c*)	Variant *m¹, v*
17, 4.3	*adimitatur* (*v*)	opportunitas *adi-matur* (*m; a, c*)	Error *v*
18, 4.4	*mensuram* (*m*) *tribuet* (*v*)	in perpetuum *mansura retribuet* (*a, c*)	Error *m* Variant *v*
19, 4.5	*statuta* (*m², v*)	contra haec con-*stituta* uenire (*m¹; a, c*)	Variant *m², v*
20, 4.5	om. *forte* (*m¹*)	a nobis *forte* creda-tur (*m², v; a, c*)	Error *m¹*
21, 4.5	*nostra* (*v*) *custodire* (*m; a*)	ita a *uestra* dilectione *custodiri* (*c*)	Error *v* Error *m; a*

Finally, **D–b** shares the following common **D** variants from the table at 3.2.f.iii: 3, 6, 30, 34, 38, 39, 41, 43, 50, 57, 62, 69, 75, 79, 80, 82, 87, 90, 92, 93, 94, 95; *m¹* and *v* share 60, 61, and 89 with the table; *m²* and *v* share 85. *m* also shares 48, 68, 69, and 91; *m¹* shares 63 and 67, while *m²* shares 64, and *v* shares 9. Furthermore, the **D–b** reading of 40 is a variation on the **D** variant from that printed by the Ballerini; **D** provides 'mistico munerum oblato', and **D–b** gives 'mystico munere oblato'. Given the occasions where m^1 alone of the **D–b** hands follows the consensus of **D**, while at times in the same place m^2 gives a reading that matches the Ballerini control text, it is my contention that the second hand of m is not collating against the exemplar. Of the agreements between the four manuscripts, the most apparent convergences between **D–b** and **D** are those inversions of the Ballerini's choice of word order, such as the frequent 'Sancti Spiritus' instead of 'Spiritus Sancti' or 'debeas adhibere' for 'adhibere debeas' (*Ep.* 167, *Praef.*).

Furthermore, while m has a certain number of its own peculiarities, as does the **D–b** tradition *in toto*, c and m nevertheless have fewer errors than **D** a, further bearing out Wurm's thesis mentioned above that **D–b** is simply an expansion of a 'pure' **D**. When we consider the age of these manuscripts—each is as old as either of the two surviving **D** manuscripts—their witness to the urtext of **D** is not to be discounted. Thus, if anyone were to seek to replace Justel's edition of the papal letters—based as it is on **D–h**—**D–b** as well as **D** a, c would be an important source.

3.2.h. Cresconius, *Concordia canonum*[193]

3.2.h.i. Dating and context

Cresconius compiled this collection around the middle of the seventh century using Dionysius' work, as mentioned above.[194] Although chronologically precedent to **D–b**, I have placed Cresconius after that collection because of the textual closeness of **D–b** to **D**. Like Dionysius he refers to himself as 'Exiguus' as a mark of humility: 'Cresconius Christi famulorum exiguus';[195] Cresconius made the *Concordia* for a Bishop named Liberinus, writing that the purpose of church sanctions was to help the faithful live correctly in contrast to secular law which primarily constrains the wayward, and to that end:

> you enjoin that I collect together for you all of the canonical ordinances which from the very beginnings of the Christian service

---

[193] This collection is a subsection of both of B6 and J1(vi).

[194] See 3.2.f.i.

[195] *Praef. ll.* 1–2.

both the holy apostles and apostolic men laid down through the
succession of time; and setting down their agreement (*concordia*)
and placing preceding *tituli* amongst them, we publish them more
clearly.[196]

Unlike the handbook of Ferrandus of Carthage, writes Cresconius,
his own work did not summarise the canons but anthologised them
in their original wording and entirety, although the editor left out
selections not suited to his task. The purpose of the *Concordia* is
to help those judging ecclesiastical cases in a manner similar to
the *Theodosian Code*, as Cresconius says:

> when an extremely fair judge has examined for himself that each
> and every canonical ruling of a decree concerning which a question
> has been stirred up at some time has been set in order in many
> ways, he may learn by proveable examination whether he ought
> to guide his judgement through severity or through leniency.[197]

Cresconius here prefigures Ivo of Chartres, whose own canonical
collection would place conflicting canons side by side in order for
a judge to decide whether to apply justice or mercy, maintaining
that the canons are remedies for the sick.[198]

The *Concordia canonum* exists complete in very many manuscripts as well as in excerpts and fragments.[199] Cresconius included
excerpts from the same seven of Leo's letters as the *Dionysiana*:
4, 7, 16, 18, 167, 14, 159. The *Concordia* is our earliest systematic canonical collection that includes Leo, one that rearranges the
conciliar canons and rulings of popes according to subject matter. As a result, Cresconius does not transmit to us entire letters
but, rather, a selection of excerpts. The usefulness of individual
readings can be compared from these excerpts, which can show us

---

[196] 'praecipis ut cuncta canonica constituta quae ab ipsis exordiis militiae
Christianae tam sancti apostoli quam apostolici uiri per successiones tem-
porum protulere uobis colligamus in unum, eorumque concordiam facientes
ac titulorum praenotationem interponentes ea lucidius declaremus'. *Praef.
ll.* 14–18.

[197] 'aequissimus iudex coram perspexerit multimode esse digestum, proba-
bili examinatione condiscat utrum ex seueritate an ex lenitate suum animum
debeat moderari'. *Praef. ll.* 50–52.

[198] Ed. Brasington 2004, 116.

[199] Kéry 1999, 35–36, lists the excerpts and fragments.

something about the mid-sixth century and the early decades of the *Dionysiana*.

The following table sets out those chapters of Cresconius extracted from Leo's letters.

Cresconius, chh.	Leo, *Epp.*
4,4	14.3
17,6	14.8
18,5	14.9
19,8	4.2
27,6	167.2
39,5	14.7
39,6	14.11 (rubric)
44,4	4.3
44,5	4.4
61	18
62,1	167.16–17
63	167.18
64	159.6
65	159.7
74	159.5
87,2	167.19
101,3	167.14
101,4	167.15
109,2	167.3
195,2	4.1
212,2	16.1
212,3	16.2
212,5	16.4
212,6	16.5–6
218,3	14.2
220,3	167.10
226,2	159.1
226,3	159.2
226,4	159.3

Cresconius, chh.	Leo, *Epp.*
226,5	159.4
228,3	167.1
228,4	14.5
230	167.4–6
231	167.6
232	167.8
233	167.10
234	167.11
235	167.12
236	167.13
237	14.4

Cresconius includes excerpts from six of **D**'s seven Leo letters. The missing letter is *Ep.* 7, which is Leo's anti-Manichaean letter. All but the final chapter of *Ep.* 4 have been excerpted in various places throughout the collection; that chapter is of a very general nature and does not lend itself to a topically arranged collection such as this. Most of *Ep.* 14 is included in various chapters of Cresconius as well, excluding chh. 1, 6, 10, and the body of 11, although Cresconius uses Dionysius' rubric for 14.11 at 39,6. In this case, 14.1 includes no general precepts but concerns itself with the matters of the case at hand and the relationship of Rome and Thessalonica's bishops; 14.6 includes explicit references to Thessalonica but has some general information about the election of a bishop that one could have imagined would have secured its inclusion, and the other excluded chapters are of a similar nature. *Ep.* 16, except its final chapter, has been excerpted in a string of chapters by Cresconius; the final chapter of this letter contains explicit instructions for the Sicilian bishops. The entirety of *Ep.* 18 has been excerpted by Cresconius as a single chapter. *Ep.* 159 is lacking only its introductory paragraph. *Ep.* 167 is missing the prefatory letter and chh. 7 and 9 of Leo's responses to Rusticus' queries. That is to say, the vast bulk of **D**'s Leo letters are included with only a few exceptions, these exceptions being due to Cresconius' interest in creating a universally applicable handbook of canon law.

3.2.h.ii. Manuscripts

Klaus Zechiel-Eckes has divided the manuscripts of Cresconius into two categories, rubricated and unrubricated, with further groupings within those as listed below.[200]

Rubricated manuscripts

Group I:

O: Oxford, Bodleian Library, Laud. misc. 436 (saec. IX1/3), from Würzburg.[201]

K: Cologne, Erzbischöflliche Diözesan- und Dombibliothek, 120 (saec. X^{in}), from eastern France/Belgium.[202]

S: Salzburg, Bibliothek der Erzabtei St Peter, a. IX. 32 (saec. XI[1]), from around Cologne.[203]

E: Einsiedeln, Stiftsbibliothek, 197 (saec. X2/3), from Einsiedeln.[204]

Group II:

Ve: Verona, Biblioteca Capitolare, LXII (60), fols 4^r–103^r (saec. VIII–IX), pre-caroline minuscule from northern Italy, likely Verona.[205]

V$_5$: Vat. lat. 5748 (saec. IX/X) from Bobbio.[206]

M: Munich, Bayerische Staatsbibliothek, Clm 6288 + Clm 29390/1 (saec. X3/3), written by hands from Freising and northern Italy.[207]

Group III:

V$_3$: Vat. Reg. lat. 849, fols 118^r–216^r (saec. X^{in}), from eastern France.[208]

---

[200] Zechiel-Eckes 1992, vol. 2, 415–16. The Ballerini list five manuscripts of Cresconius: Ve, V$_1$, V$_4$, V$_3$, and R. The sigla throughout are those of Zechiel-Eckes.

[201] Bischoff 1998–2014, 2.3862; Zechiel-Eckes 1992, vol. 2, 332–34.

[202] Bischoff 1998–2014, 1.1930; Zechiel-Eckes 1992, vol. 2, 319–21.

[203] Zechiel-Eckes 1992, vol. 2, 337–38.

[204] Zechiel-Eckes 1992, vol. 2, 318–19.

[205] CLA 4.512; Bischoff 1998–2014, 3.7048b; Zechiel-Eckes 1992, vol. 2, 349–51.

[206] Bischoff 1998–2014, 3.6906; Zechiel-Eckes 1992, vol. 2, 346–47.

[207] Zechiel-Eckes 1992, vol. 2, 327–30.

[208] Bischoff 1998–2014, 3.6741; Zechiel-Eckes 1992, vol. 2, 341–44.

Group IV:

R: Rome, Biblioteca Vallicelliana, T.XVIII (saec. Xex-XIin), from central Italy.[209]

Group V (fragments):

Ve$_1$: Verona, Biblioteca Capitolare, LXI (saec. VIII), from around Verona.[210]

P$_1$: Paris, lat. 3851 (saec. IX[1]), from Lorsch.[211]

B$_3$: Berlin, Deutsches Historisches Museum, unnumbered fragment (saec. X[1]), from southern Germany.[212]

P$_2$: Paris lat. 3851A (saec. X), from southwestern France.[213]

W$_1$: Wolfenbüttel, Herzog August Bibliothek, 404.7 (25 a) Novi (saec. X).[214]

V$_6$: Vat. lat. 15204 (saec. X).[215]

Manuscripts without rubrication

Group I:

B$_1$: Berlin, Deutsche Staatsbibliothek, Phill. 1748 (saec. VIII/IX), from southern Burgundy.[216]

Mo: Montpellier, Bibiothèque interuniversitaire (méd.), H 233 (saec. IX1/3), Rhaetian.[217]

N: Novara, Biblioteca Capitolare, LXXI (saec. IX[med]-3/4), from Novara.[218]

---

[209] Zechiel-Eckes 1992, vol. 2, 336–37.

[210] CLA 4.511; also contains *Epitome Hispana*. Zechiel-Eckes 1992, vol. 2, 348–49.

[211] Bischoff 1998–2014, 3.4290; Zechiel-Eckes 1992, vol. 2, 334–35.

[212] Zechiel-Eckes 1992, vol. 2, 317–18.

[213] Zechiel-Eckes 1992, vol. 2, 335–36.

[214] Zechiel-Eckes 1992, vol. 2, 354.

[215] Zechiel-Eckes 1992, vol. 2, 347–48.

[216] CLA 8.1062; Bischoff 1998–2014, 1.420; Zechiel-Eckes 1992, vol. 2, 313–14.

[217] Bischoff 1998–2014, 2.2848; Zechiel-Eckes 1992, vol. 2, 325–27.

[218] Bischoff 1998–2014, 2.3632; Zechiel-Eckes 1992, vol. 2, 331–32.

Group II:

W: Wolfenbüttel, Herzog August Bibliothek, Helmst. 842 (saec. IX2/4), written in Fulda *c.* 840 by one Ercanbertus.[219]

W$_2$: Wolfenbüttel, Herzog August Bibliothek, Helmst. 219 (saec. XVI). A copy of W made for Lutheran theologian M. Flacius Illyricus (1520–1575).[220]

V$_4$: Vat. lat. 1347, fols 1^r–63^v (saec. IX^{med-ex}), from Reims.[221]

Mc: Monte Cassino, Archivio dell'Abbazia, 541 (saec. XI).[222]

V$_2$: Vat. Reg. lat. 423 (saec. IX^2), from Weissenburg in Bavaria.[223]

V$_1$: Vat. Pal. lat. 579, fol. 1ra-94ra (saec. IX2/4), from western Germany.[224]

Group III:

Kr: Krakow, Biblioteka Jagiellońska, Inv.-Nr. 1894 (saec. IX2/3), from northeastern France.[225]

B$_2$: Berlin, Staatsbibliothek Preussischer Kulturbezitz, lat. fol. 626 (saec. XII).[226]

Group IV:

Mi: Milan, Biblioteca Ambrosiana, S. P. 6/14 no. 131 (saec. XI).[227]

Cresconius' *Concordia* exists complete in 20 manuscripts listed by Kéry. When I considered the relatively minor significance of Cresconius for Leo's text as well as the very good edition of K. Zechiel-Eckes,[228] I decided to forego investigating all 20 manuscripts. Therefore, only partial collations of one Cresconius manuscript were made for comparison with **D** manuscripts and to

---

[219] Bischoff 1998–2014, 3.7342; Zechiel-Eckes 1992, vol. 2, 352–54.

[220] Zechiel-Eckes 1992, vol. 2, 351–52.

[221] Bischoff 1998–2014, 3.6856; Zechiel-Eckes 1992, vol. 2, 344–46.

[222] Zechiel-Eckes 1992, vol. 2, 323–24.

[223] Bischoff 1998–2014, 3.6675, saec. IX^{med}/3/4; Zechiel-Eckes 1992, vol. 2, 339–41. It also includes fragments of Leo, *Epp.* 14 and 7 on fols 62^v–63^v. This MS is digitised: https://digi.vatlib.it/view/MSS_Reg.lat.423. Accessed 20 September 2021.

[224] Bischoff 1998–2014, 3.6547; Zechiel-Eckes 1992, vol. 2, 338–39.

[225] Zechiel-Eckes 1992, vol. 2, 321–22.

[226] Zechiel-Eckes 1992, vol. 2, 314–17.

[227] Zechiel-Eckes 1992, vol. 2, 322–23.

[228] Zechiel-Eckes 1992, vol. 2, 419–798.

confirm the quality of Zechiel-Eckes' readings. Alongside Zechiel-Eckes' edition, then, I made use of manuscript W.

When we consider Cresconius, we realise just how important his predecessor, Dionysius, was, for we have over twenty manuscripts that contain Cresconius' work that range all the way into the sixteenth century. For Leo, these manuscripts contain the same material with the same or similar readings as **D**. Thus Dionysius Exiguus, though called 'the short', has a millennium-long reach. Three printed editions of this work exist. First is the 1661 edition of G. Voellius and H. Justellus. Second is Turner's edition in EOMIA. Last comes the aforementioned 1992 edition of Zechiel-Eckes. In an edition of Leo's work, Cresconius would serve as a further witness to **D**, especially in cases where his readings would add weight to a minority **D** reading.

3.2.h.iii. Manuscript relations

The readings of Cresconius against **D** are generally unremark-able—the text is basically Dionysian. Nonetheless, a few interest-ing points emerge through comparing the table above at 3.2.f.iii to the edition of Zechiel-Eckes. While most Cresconius manuscripts agree with a at Variant 11, V_2 gives '*nullus* necessitatis', while V_5 and M give, 'necessitatibus calculis'. At Variant 12, where **D** a gives 'constituet' against c 'constiterit', a series of Cresconius man-uscripts ($WV_4V_2V_1$) gives 'consisterit'. At Variant 16, instead of either 'qua' (**D** c) or 'quia' (**D** a), V_3 and Kr give 'qui', while at 17 Kr agrees with **D** a in giving 'quod'. At 20, no Cresconius manu-script agrees with **D** a and c in the wording 'regulis canonum', but N reads, 'canonum fuerit regulis'. At 23, we have a case of Cresco-nius agreeing with **D** a against c wholesale. Variant 40 is notori-ous for giving scribes trouble. The majority of Cresconius read, 'mystico munerum oblato' with **D** a, c, but several ($KSEWV_4V_1$) read, 'mystica munerum', and all but E have 'oblatione' instead of 'oblato'. At Variant 42, the majority agree with **D** c in omitting 'se' from 'eius se esse', but three (WV_4V_1) write 'se' before 'eius'. Variant 43 brings with it much division; B_1MoNV_4 read 'discre-tio', while K and S read 'distinctio', and the rest agree with **D** in reading 'districtio'. Variant 45 sees for the first time the whole range of options for 'eadem sententia'; R concords with the Baller-ini, while $KSEV_5M$ read 'scientia' with **D** c, and the rest provide 'sapientia', which is the **D–h** reading (see table below at 5.2.a.iii). At 56, the majority of Cresconius manuscripts write the date as 'IIII kalendas' against **D** a and the Ballerini who write 'III' (**D** c has a lacuna here), along with V_3EWV_4. In the quotation from 1 Corinthians 6:12, most write 'omnia licent' in agreement with **D** and the Vulgate, but Kr and P_2 write 'omnia mihi licent' at 220,2; when the chapter is repeated at 233, only P_2 writes 'mihi'. At 86 we encounter another **D–h** reading when E and R write 'tertioue' against the majority Cresconius reading, 'tertioque', the Ballerini 'uel tertio', and **D** which has no conjunction for 'secundo' and 'tertio' at all. In Variant 93, the majority of the Cresconius manuscripts write 'scriptum a domino' in agreement with **D**, but several write 'scriptum quod' ($KSEWV_4V_1$), and E writes 'deo' for 'domino'. Various other divergences from **D** a and c are found throughout the Cresconius text, but these are the most significant. They serve as a reminder that the two 'pure' **D** manuscripts are not enough, and they also look ahead to **D–h** suggesting that some of the **D–h** readings may be genuine Dionysius readings and not corruptions.

3.2.i. *Collectio Teatina*[229] (**Te**)

3.2.i.i. Dating and context

The *Collectio Teatina*, also known as the *Collectio Ingilramni*[230] or the Collection of Chieti,[231] is from Italy and dates from around 525, certainly after the death of Pope Hormisdas in 523 and possibly before that of John I in 526.[232] The precision of this date comes from the papal catalogue in **Te**, but it can also be corroborated by a consideration of the manuscript's contents, for it makes sense as a collection compiled in the later years of Theoderic when, as the account in *Anonymus Valesianus II* describes it, he was becoming increasingly paranoid about the loyalty of his catholic subjects. After the councils and papal letters, we have the *acta* of a

---

[229] B1 (PL 54.554), J1(i) 500.

[230] Kéry 1999, 24.

[231] As in, e.g. Le Bras 1930, 507.

[232] This dating is based on the inclusion of a catalogue of popes in the MS that ends with Pope Hormisdas, a method of dating defended above. McKitterick 2005, 969, states that this collection should be considered Carolingian.

local Roman council of 499 (fols 116^v–121^v), the catalogue of popes (121^v–122^r), another Roman council, this time from 6 November 502 dealing with the Symmachan-Laurentian schism, and thus moving us into the relationship between the Roman Church and King Theoderic (122^r–137^r). This change of focus to the relationship between church and monarch—and a monarch they would have called 'Arian' at that—is a likely cause for the inclusion of a commentary on the Nicene Creed attested only here (137^{r}ff). The concerns of the collection as a whole are wide-ranging over the whole of Roman canon law—canons concerning eligibility for the episcopacy and the priesthood and clerical orders at large, clerical continence, marriage both clerical and lay, admission of penitent heretics into communion, penitents more generally, various aspects of monastic life in relation to the wider church, and more.

However, the Roman councils of 499 and 502 signal this collection's real interest. It is about the relationship of the Roman/western church to the secular authorities that is the author's real concern. Having been compiled during the episcopate of Hormisdas, the Roman Church will have recently re-entered communion with that of Constantinople; if compiled before Pope John I's death, the relationship with Theoderic would still have been good,[233] but in the time around John's death, it was deteriorating. The Emperor Justinian had a renewed relationship with the Roman Bishop and Latin Christianity that had been severed during the Acacian Schism. How are bishops meant to relate to the secular authorities—especially when the secular authorities are catholic and orthodox on the one hand, but, from their perspective, heretical Arians on the other? This is the new question facing the western church in the episcopate of John, one that would force itself into sharp relief in the years immediately following his death in Theoderic's prisons. The fact that John's death date is not listed is also, then, a contributing factor to the date of the collection given the significance of his demise. That said, Ingilramnus will have had it copied in the Carolingian era because of the ongoing interest in authoritative texts from the past. But it was not made in his episcopate, for in that case we would expect inclusion of

---

[233] For the argument that relations were still good, see Moreau 2015, 182–86, with further bibliography in n. 14, 182.

some newer documents, exclusion of some older documents, and an updated papal catalogue.

This collection of canons and papal letters was not gathered with an eye either to system or to chronology,[234] although a perusal of its contents shows that it was likely compiled from several of the proto-collections that lie at the root of many of the canonical collections;[235] it is broadly divided between canons and decretals, but even these overlap, and the contents within the divisions are not chronological. The collection contains eight of Leo's letters in two divisions of six and two: *Epp.* 167, 12, 28, 15, 16, 159 (fols 57^v–82^r) and 1 and 2 (fols 114^r–116^v); all but *Ep.* 28 (*Tomus ad Flavianum*) will come to be designated decretals. Its text of *Ep.* 167 shares its *capitula* with **Q**, **Sa**, and **V** against **D**. It is thus close in date to, but independent of, **D**, with which it differs on this and several points. Furthermore, it gives the *decurtata* version of *Ep.* 12, which it shares in common with **Q**, **Di**, **F**, **Sa**, and **S**. Although likely compiled in Italy, its variations from **D** make it unlikely that this collection originates in the papal archive. Alongside **Q**, **D**, **Sa**, and **V**, **Te** is one of our important early canonical collections from the so-called *renaissance gélasienne*.[236]

3.2.i.ii. Manuscript

It exists in one manuscript:

> Vat. Reg. lat. 1997 (VIII–IX or IX^{med}), from Chieti[237] and written in an Italian Pre-Caroline Minuscule with rubricated uncial *capitula*.[238] Each letter begins with a *littera notabilior*, many of which are illuminated. Foll. 73^v, Column B, and 74^r, are written entirely in uncial, and then the hand switches back to the same pre-Caroline minscule as before. Within the Leo portions, the scribe has shown off by writing in Greek characters on two occasions: first, on fol. 62^r, at the top of Column A, 'ΕΞΠΛΙΧΙΤ ΕΠΥΣ/ΘΥΛΑ SCI LEONIS'; the second time on fol. 78^r, Column B, 'ΕΞΠΛΙΧΙΘ'.

---

[234] Kéry 1999, 24.

[235] The contents are described by Reifferscheid 1976, 333–36.

[236] Discussed above at 3.1.

[237] Kéry 1999, 24; the provenance was determined from the colophon on fol. 153, pictured in CLA 1.113.

[238] This MS is digitised: https://digi.vatlib.it/view/MSS_Reg.lat.1997 Accessed 20 September 2021. See Bischoff 1998–2014, 3.6804.

The archetype of this manuscript or the manuscript itself was written by a certain Sicipertus for Ingilramnus, Bishop of Metz (768–91), whence comes its alternate name.[239]

3.2.i.iii. Manuscript relations

Teatina's text of Leo demonstrates several important features. Of great significance is its lack of *capitula* throughout most of the text—*Ep.* 167 is the only letter herein with proper *capitula*—albeit lacking for chh. 17–19, and the initial words of each chapter of *Ep.* 15 are rubricated uncials;[240] no other letter has been thus subdivided. That early collections such as this and **Q** lack *capitula* indicates that the chapter headings are more likely to have been added by later users who were reading Leo's letters as sources for canon law or theology than being added by Leo and his *notarii* who made no such use of them. **Te** further demonstrates a close affinity with **Sa**. The following variants are shared by the two collections, referencing the table at 3.2.e.iii: 1, 2, 3, 5, 8, 9, 10, 11, 12, 'inpositione' of 14 but keeps 'per', 24, 25, 26, 27, 29, 34, 37, and 39. **Te** also includes the second of the unique errors from the **Sa** *r* version of *Ep.* 12, 'aliam praeter ipsam'. Of the **Sa** variants **Te** lacks, the majority come from *Ep.* 12, and on several occasions **Te** is still in agreement with one or more **Sa** manuscripts when they, too, agree with the control; finally, some of the **Sa** variants are in the *capitula* not included in **Te**. It seems most likely that for these four letters, *Epp.* 167, 12, 1, and 2, *Teatina* and *Sanblasiana* employed a common source, thus accounting both for similarities and for differences between their readings.

In *Ep.* 28, for the majority of the 26 diagnostic readings from across the tradition, **Te** displays a majority reading; only on seven occasions does this collection diverge. It shares a few of its divergent readings with **D–a**, in particular numbers 4 and 5,[241] although Variant 5 is also shared with **Q** *t* and **V** *c*.[242] Variant 6, 'qui cum agnoscendam ueritatem', is very close to the **D–a** read-

---

[239] CLA 1.113.

[240] e.g. '**I PRIMO ITAQUE CAPITULO DEMONSTRATUR QUAM IMPIAE SENTIANT D**e Trinitate divina'.

[241] Variant 4, **Te**: 'sapientioribus doctoribusque non recedere'. Majority: 'doctioribusque'.

[242] See 3.2.c and 3.2.d respectively.

ing which gives 'ad agnoscendam'. **Te** Reading 10 is, 'qua fidelium
uniuersitas', which it shares with **Q**, including *o*. In Reading 12
it agrees with **V**, but in 14 it is alone in giving, 'legens epistolas'
rather than '*in* epistola'. Reading 23 is a unique error, 'in utraque
naturae intellegenda'. Finally, for the *explicit* of *Ep.* 28, **Te** provides, 'DAT ID IUN asturio et protogene uc conss'.

Te is one of the earliest attestations of *Ep.* 15, along with **C**
and **Q**; the next collection to include this letter is **P**. **Te** spells
Turribius 'Thoribius'. Like **P** and **C**, **Te** does not give *capitula* for
the various chapters of this letter, simply writing the first line or
two in rubricated uncials.[243] For our purposes, it is sufficient to
discuss only the first ten of the 30 readings collated from *Ep.* 15.
Amongst these, **Te** presents a variant for Reading 4 (*Ep.* 15.
Praef.), giving, 'ab euangelio xpi nomine xpi deviarunt', in contrast to the Ballerini 'ab Euangelio *sub* Christi nomine deviarunt',
and **Q** 'ab Euangelio Christi nomine deuiarunt'. In the phrase
immediately following, **Te** omits 'se' after 'tenebris'. In Reading 5
(*Ep.* 15.*Praef.*), **Te** writes, 'usquam uiueret', rather than Ballerini
and **Q** 'uiuere'. Reading 6 (*Ep.* 15.*Praef.*) gives, 'ad spiritale(m)'
rather than 'ad spiritale' and agrees with **P** and the Ballerini in
giving 'corporale supplicium' against **Q** 'corporale iudicium'.[244]
Reading 7 (*Ep.* 15.*Praef.*) provides 'stricti omnia' in place of 'stric-
tim omnia', as does **P**—an easy error to make. In Reading 9
(*Ep.* 15.1), it omits 'nunc filius' from 'Deus nunc pater, nunc filius,
nunc spiritus sanctus', an error shared with **P** and **C**. In Reading
10 (*Ep.* 15.1), at variance with the Ballerini and **Q**, which omit
the word 'ea', **Te** provides 'contrarium est, ea quae'; this variant
is likely traceable back to a common ancestor with the **P** and **C**
reading 'contrarium est, et que'. Although **Te**, **P**, and **C** share a
few variants within the first 10 readings, many of the most significant **P** and **C** variants are unattested in **Te**. The relationship
between the text of *Ep.* 15 in the Italian **Te** and the Gallic **P** and
C is, therefore, tenuous, given the lack of any other similarities
between the collections and lack of important variants from these
two in **Te**. Thus, it is more significant that, although **P** and **C**

---

[243] **P**, on the other hand, gives, e.g. 'explicit. Incipit secunda'.

[244] **C**, however, gives 'corporali supplicium'—nonetheless, given that *I* and
E are often interchangeable in this manuscript, the reading is essentially the
same as **P** and **Te**.

happen to have some of the same variants as **Te**, our purportedly earliest Italian collection, **Q**, does not. This suggests independence from **Q** in the compilation of **Te**.

In *Ep.* 16's *incipit*, like **D** and **V**, **Te** does not include 'episcopus' after Leo's name, as the Ballerini do. At 16.1, although it agrees with the Ballerini in giving 'Quam', **Te** provides the variant 'Quam culpa nullo'. In 16.1, it agrees with **D** and **V** in giving 'beati ap(osto)li Petri sedis', rather than 'Petri apostoli'. One of **D**'s *a* variants proves in this letter to be of note, as **Te** agrees in giving 'Ut' rather than 'Et licet uix ferendum'—probably a simple shared error. 16.2 gives an oft-corrupted passage, here as 'mystico munerum oblatione(m) venerantur' against Ballerini 'mystica munerum oblatione uenerantur'.[245] One of the many frequent word reversals of the manuscripts against the Ballerini also comes shortly in 16.2, giving 'mortuo persecutore' rather than 'persecutore mortuo' (as, e.g., **D**, **V**). **Te** also gives 'quod quaerebatis me' in place of 'quod me quaerebatis', as in **D** and **V**. Later in that chapter, in the phrase, 'ad tempus posse pertinere', **Te** omits 'posse' like **V**. **Te** once again agrees with **D** in giving 'rationabilis servanda districtio quia' against Ballerini 'distinctio'; **V** likewise provides 'districtio', although with the adjective 'rationalis'. In 16.3, **Te** agrees with **D** *a* and **D–b** in giving 'totumque quod in illo' rather than Ballerini 'quidquid', whereas **D** *c* provides 'quid'. From this brief selection of variants for *Ep.* 16, **Te** and **V** may be related, since they frequently agree, at times against both **D** and the Ballerini. Let it be noted, however, that each of these early traditions at times agrees with the Ballerini control text against the other two.

The final letter to be considered, and the last from **Te**'s initial group of 6, is *Ep.* 159. Like the other **Te** letters, this epistle is found in some of the earliest collections—**Q**, **V**, and **D** besides **Te**. As frequently elsewhere, so also here **Te** omits 'episcopus' after 'Leo' in the incipit.[246] In the *praefatio*, **Te** omits 'a nobis', like **D** and **Q**. In 159.1, **Te** provides 'qui uiros proprios' in agreement with **Q** against Ballerini and **V**, 'quae cum uiros proprios', **D** *c* 'quae uiros proprios', and **D** *a* 'quae uiris propriis'. Again in

---

[245] On many occasions we have seen manuscripts give corrupted readings of this phrase. Besides its basic comprehensibility, the Ballerini version gains weight from the fact that it produces a clausula of the 'esse uideatur' type.

[246] As also **D**, **D–b**, and **Q**.

159.1, **Te** provides 'liberandos. Et in aliorum', agreeing with **D** and **Q**, whereas the Ballerini give 'ad aliorum', and **V** omits the preposition altogether. In 159.4, **Te** has 'mulieres, quae reuertit ad' rather than Ballerini 'reuerti'. Like **D**, at 159.4, **Te** gives 'impiae sunt habendae', unlike Ballerini 'habendae sunt'; **Q** and **V** both omit 'sunt'. At 159.5 in agreement with **V**, **Te** gives the unsurprising reading of 'esse polluti, *consolationis* caritatis' for Ballerni, **D** *c*, and **Q** 'consultationi'—this manuscript often gives *consol-* for *consult-* readings. At 159.6 with **D**, **V**, and **Q**, **Te** gives 'similiter dilectio tua' *versus* Ballerini 'dilectio tua similiter'. Also in 159.6, **Te** agrees with **Q** and writes, 'ea est custodienda moderatio' against the Ballerini and **V** 'ea custodienda est moderatio', and **D** 'ea esse custodienda'. **Te** agrees with **D** in 159.6, providing 'aegritudinum respicientes necessitates' against Ballerini 'aegritudinis respiciens necessitates', and **V** 'egritudinum. Respiciens necessitates'; **Q** *p* comes close, 'aegritudinum respicienti sunt necessitates'. In 159.7, **Te** provides 'cum baptizati ante' with **V** and **Q** against Ballerini 'cum antea baptizati'; **D** *a* and **D–b** 'cum baptizati antea'; and **D** *c* omitting *ante/antea* altogether. **Te** gives 'sola sci sps inuocatione' with **D** *a* and **V** against Ballerini and **Q** 'sola inuocatione Spiritus Sancti' and **D** *c* 'sola spiritus sancti inuocatione'. In 159.7, the quotation from Ephesians 4:5 shares the error 'Vnus deus' with **D** *c* and **D–b** against the Ballerini, Vulgate, **D** *a*, **V**, and **Q** 'Vnus Dominus', most likely caused by the similarity between the *nomina sacra* 'ds' and 'dns'; 'dominus' must be correct because it translates the Greek. The letter closes with '**DAT XV KL APRL CONSTAN GLP MAIVRIANO AVG**', in contrast to **D** *c* giving the date as 'XIII kl April, cons. marciani augusti' and **D–b** 'XII kl aprl maioriano aug primum cons', which basically agrees with the control text and **Q** *p*.

From the above discussion, various conclusions can be drawn. First, in terms of contents, **Te** is most similar to **Sa**, all of whose contents are also included herein. Furthermore, the text of **Te** is also similar to that of **Sa**, and they likely share a common source. One theory that presents itself is that **Sa** is based on a damaged copy of **Te**, but given the spread of the eight letters throughout **Te**, it is more likely either that they derive the four letters from a similar source, some lost proto-collection, or that **Sa** sampled letters from **Te**, the compiler not being interested in the other selections of Leo. After **Sa**, **Te** demonstrates a close affinity with **Q** in its variants, although the two have their share of disagreements, visible in the various moments when **Te** agrees with **D**, or even **P** and **C** against **Q**. It is, however, highly significant that all of **Te**'s letters are included in **Q**. They are not in the same order, and other letters often intervene. It is more likely, then, that **Q** and **Te** drew upon a common source, rather than **Te** being derivative of **Q**. **Te** also shows a number of agreements with **C** and **P**; however, they share only *Epp.* 15 and 28 in common, so their similarities are likely to stem from a point further back in the transmission of the letters or from errors easily made. **Te** shares many readings with **D** against the Ballerini, but rarely with **D** alone. In sum, then, based upon its text, **Te** is definitively part of the group of early Italian collections that trace themselves to a common core of proto-collections, and it is most similar to, yet independent of, **Q** and **D** but at variance with **V**; since it shares only two letters with **C** and **P**, it is unlikely to have used the proto-collection shared by those collections and **Al**—indeed, **C**, **P**, and **Al** are all Gallic and are likely common descendents of a Gallic proto-collection, not the Italian source of **Te**. As the examination of **Re** will show (3.2.p), one of **Te**'s sources was **proto-3**.[247]

3.2.j. *Collectio Corbeiensis*[248] (**C**)

3.2.j.i. Dating and context

Jasper dates **C** as a whole to after 524,[249] while Kéry dates its compilation more precisely to the pontificate of Vigilius (537–55) in Gaul, likely at Arles.[250] Vigilius' pontificate is most likely, given that the catalogue of popes included in the collection ends with him. It contains both conciliar canons and decretals, and is arranged chronologically.[251] *Collectio Corbeiensis* exists in one manuscript and contains 14 Leonine epistles, the first five of which are decretals, and grouped into three batches: 4, 7, 15 (fols 34^r–44^v); 10 (82^r–86^v); 22, 28, 103, 31, 35, 139, 59, 165, 138, 108, 15 (fols 97^{r}ff.). As discussed above,[252] **C** includes elements of two of

---

[247] See the Appendix for a list and description of the proto-collections.

[248] B2 (PL 54.554–55), J1(ii) (500).

[249] Jasper 2001, 44–45.

[250] Kéry 1999, 47.

[251] For a description of its contents, see Maassen 1870, 556–74.

[252] 3.1.

the oldest proto-collections of Leo's letters, both shared with *Collectio Pithouensis* (**P**).[253] One of them (**proto-1**), shared with **P** and *Coloniensis* (**K**), includes: *Epp.* 28, 103, 31, 35, 139, 59, and 165, although **K** misses out *Ep.* 139. As with **P** below,[254] **C** appends *Ep.* 22 to the beginning of this proto-collection. To the end of **proto-1**, **C** and **P** append four more of Leo's letters, 165, 138, 108, and 15. Silva-Tarouca refers to **proto-1** as 'the oldest level of the tradition of Leo's letters'.[255] Elsewhere in the collection are *Epp.* 4, 7, and 15 (chh. X–XII), and *Ep.* 10 (ch. XXXIIII)—this is **proto-2** listed in the Appendix. **Proto-2** is not simply dropped randomly into the collection but rather grouped with other items of similar interest to the reader, whether of canon law or theological controversy.[256] **Proto-2** is used by **Al** as well as **C** and **P**.[257] These three traditions all originate from southern and western Gaul in the same period; all also introduce their decretals with the same heading 'Incipiunt decreta papae Leonis', and *Epp.* 7 and 15 begin in each of these collections with the phrase, 'Incipiunt eiusdem papae Leonis de Manichaeis'. These collections also all bear a resemblance to **D** (see above at 3.2.f) which begins with the same decretals, *Epp.* 4 and 7, and with the same heading, 'Incipiunt decreta papae Leonis'. Finally, **Q** may also have added *Epp.* 4 and 7 from **proto-2**, given that it also pairs them together (see above, 3.2.c).[258]

3.2.j.ii. Manuscript

Collectio Corbeiensis exists in one manuscript:[259]

---

[253] **C**'s connection with **P** is well-known, as discussed by Kéry 1999, 48; Jasper 2001, 44–45, 52–53; Dunn 2015.

[254] 3.2.l.

[255] Silva-Tarouca 1926, 37, 'die älteste Überlieferungsschicht der Leo-Briefe'. On 41–42, he says that **C** was sent directly from Rome to Gaul. As usual in these arguments, the analysis is based upon the rubrics.

[256] For a full description, see Maassen 1870, 556–74; for both **C** and **P**, see Dunn 2015, Tables II.1 and II.2.

[257] Jasper 2001, 53–53. For **Al**, see below 3.2.o.

[258] See Appendix 3 for a list and description of the proto-collections.

[259] In ACO 2.4, 1, among the manuscripts of this canonical collection, Schwartz lists Cologne, Erzbischöfliche Diözesan- und Dombibliothek 213 and Paris, lat. 1564; the former of these manuscripts is of **Sa** and the latter is **P**. It is most likely that 213 here is a typographical error for 212, given that

Paris, lat. 12097, fols 1ʳ–232ᵛ, which dates from the second quarter of the sixth century.[260] CLA 5 dates fols 1–139ᵛ to *c.* 523 and 139ᵛ–224 to saec. VI–VII. Part of the dating comes from the fact that its papal catalogue originally ended with Hormisdas (*d.* 523) on fol. 1ᵛ. It was written in southern France, possibly at Arles.[261] It made its way to the Bibliothèque nationale from Corbie, whence comes its name, via St-Germain-des-Prés.[262] Leo's letters begin on fol. 34ʳ. This manuscript contains annotations in bookhands from Corbie that demonstrate its use in forming monasatic theology there.[263]

The relationship between this manuscript and the other collections that make use of the same proto-collection will be discussed presently, in the treatment of *Collectio Pithouensis* (3.2.k.iii).

3.2.k. *Collectio Pithouensis*[264] (**P**)

3.2.k.i. Dating and context

This canonical collection contains the following 14 of Leo's letters, of which the first three and the last are decretals: 4, 7, 15, 2 non-Leo items, 10, 22, 28, 103 (with the *exemplar sententiae* as a separate item), 31, 35, 139, 59, 165, 138, and 108. It draws upon the same proto-collection of Leo's letters as **C** and **Al** (**proto-2**), mentioned by Jasper and discussed more thoroughly above at 3.2.j;[265] it also uses **proto-1**,[266] as do **C** and **K**. The relationship with **C** is so striking and similar that the Leo portion of the manuscript is cited in the online catalogue of the Bibliothèque natio-

Cologne 212 contains *Collectio Coloniensis* (**K**), one of the collections that utilises the same proto-collection as **C** and **P**, whereas these collections have no relationship with **Sa**. On **Sa** and **P**, see 3.2.e and 3.2.k respectively.

[260] CLA 5.619; Ganz 1990, 127. This MS is digitised: https://gallica.bnf.fr/ark:/12148/btv1b525030636.r = 12097.langEN. Accessed 20 September 2021.

[261] Kéry 1999, 47.

[262] See the online catalogue of the Bibliothèque nationale de France: https://archivesetmanuscrits.bnf.fr/ark:/12148/cc73447g. Accessed 20 September 2021. See also fol. 2ʳ.

[263] Ganz 1990, 40, 69.

[264] Not listed by Ballerini or Jalland. Cf. Kéry 1999, 38–49, for bibliographical information on this collection. Also called *Collectio canonica Pithoeana*, as on the BnF website.

[265] See Jasper 2001, 44–45.

[266] See the Appendix for a list and description of the proto-collections.

nale de France as *Collectio Corbeiensis*.[267] **P** dates from the end
of the sixth or the beginning of the seventh century. A further
aspect of this collection's significance in the history of canon law
is the fact that it was also used as a source for the early systematic collection, *Collectio Vetus Gallica*, a collection discussed below
at 3.2.s. In fact, marginalia on Leo, *Ep.* 28, are part of Mordek's
argument to that end.[268]

3.2.k.ii. Manuscript

It exists in one manuscript:

> Paris, lat. 1564 (*c.* 785–810), from Northern France; Leo's letters
> run fols 41ᵛ–48ᵛ (*Epp.* 4, 7, 15), 65ᵛ–68ᵛ (*Ep.* 10), and 83ʳ–100ᵛ
> (the rest of the letters as described above).[269] Its bookhand is a
> Caroline minuscule written in a single column.

3.2.k.iii. Manuscript Relations

Collectio Pithouensis has the same collection of Leo's letters as *Corbeiensis*, whatever other differences the two collections may have
in contents. Not only does *Pithouensis* contain the same letters,
they are in the same groupings, drawn presumably from the same
proto-collections. **Proto-2** consists of *Epp.* 4, 7, and 15; it displays
great textual similarities between **C** and **P**. Out of 64 **P** variants
for *Epp.* 4 and 7, **C** shares 42 and provides other similar readings, such as 'f k' where **P** gives 'fratres karissimi'. Many of the
variants the two collections do not share are errors on the part
of **P**, such as omitting 'talis' from 'ministerium talis consortii' in
4.1, or largely orthographical, such as giving 'propari' for 'pro-
bare', also in 4.1.[270] Throughout *Ep.* 15, which they do not share
with **A1**, these two manuscripts also demonstrate a strong textual

---

[267] See https://archivesetmanuscrits.bnf.fr/ark:/12148/cc59512f. Accessed
20 September 2021.

[268] Mordek 1975, 86.

[269] CLA 5.529; Bischoff 1998–2014, 3.4027. This MS is digitised: https://
gallica.bnf.fr/ark:/12148/btv1b9066891d.r = latin+1564.langEN. Accessed 20
September 2021. The Bibliothèque nationale's catalogue misses out some
folios of Leo's letters, only giving '41ᵛ–48, 65ᵛ, 84–100ᵛ'; see https://archive-
setmanuscrits.bnf.fr/ark:/12148/cc59512f. Accessed 20 September 2021.

[270] On the other hand, **A1**, as I discuss below (3.2.o), is probably not derived
from **C** but from a common source.

relationship. For example, in the salutation **C** calls the recipient, Bishop Turribius of Astorga, 'chorebio', and **P** 'Choribio' (in the dative); the former is evidently an orthographical variation of the latter. In Reading 2, **C**[1] and **P** write 'eorum morbus exarserit', although **C** gives 'reliquiis' and **P** 'regulae quis'. In Reading 4, both provide 'qui ab Euangelio xpi nomine xpi diuiarunt, tenebris etiam' against Ballerini 'qui ab Euangelio sub Christi nomine deuiarunt, tenebris se etiam ...'. The rest of *Ep.* 15 is much the same, pointing to the shared inheritance of these two collections running deeper than shared contents and confirming the postulation of common sources.

Once again, in *Ep.* 10, these two manuscripts demonstrate a close textual similarity. I collated a sample of 76 **P** variants from this very long letter, which had 122 variants from the Ballerini control; 31 of its variants are shared by both **P** and **C**. This not as high a ratio as in **proto-2**. However, alongside these 31 are a few examples where a corrupted **C** reading could be seen as the ancestor of the **P** reading. For example, in 10.3, where the Ballerini text reads, 'ad sacram militiam', **C** gives 'ad sacram militia', and **P** corrects in the wrong direction, giving, 'ad sacra militia'. Later in 10.3, for Ballerini 'cognitionem', **C**[1] gives 'cogitationem', but an early correcting hand makes it a hard-to-read 'cognitionem'. If **P**'s scribe was confronted with this same text, the hard-to-read word was easily transposed into 'cognitione'. A shining example of a corrupted text in **C** is at 10.4, Ballerini, 'Esto ut breuis'. **C** gives, 'esto o[...]tus', and **P**, 'Est obretus'. Many of the **P** variants not shared by **C** are simple errors, such as 'iudicio' for 'iudicium' in 'Remotum est ergo iudicium'; 'suicessit' for 'successit'; 'tradetatum' for 'tarditatem'; 'uideatur gloria' instead of 'gloriam'; *et cetera*. Finally, the shared variants between **P** and **C** tend to include significant variations from the Ballerini text. Almost every **C** omission is also omitted in **P**, including the omission of 'Romae episcopus' from the inscription; and 'uoluit' from 'pertinere uoluit, ut' (10.1). They also both write 'id' for 'in' at 10.1, 'ut *in* beatissimo Petro'.

However, the tempting theory that these two Gallic manuscripts are directly related, with **C** as the archetype for the original of **P**, takes a serious blow when we see that **P** does not omit the phrase 'concordiam custodiri cupimus sacerdotum, ad unitatem uos uinculo charitatis hortantes' as **C** does. **P** does not appear to be collated against another manuscript of Leo's letters anywhere else. Since **C** is likely the original manuscript of its collection, dating as it does to the time and place of the compilation, how does **P** retain the phrase? This manuscript is not the original if *Collectio Pithouensis* was compiled in the later sixth century, whereas manuscript **P** is written in a Caroline minuscule. One hypothesis is a Gallic text of *Ep.* 10 was available to a copyist of *Pithouensis* at some stage of its transmission, and either when the collection was compiled or copied between **C** and **P**, this omission was corrected; given the size of the omission, it would be much more easily noticed by someone with a knowledge of the text or a second version to compare than the many little words here and there, scattered throughout the text. This is only a hypothesis, but it has the beauty of maintaining a line of descent between **C** and **P**, something like **C**-P—**P**, but with a dotted line for the postulated alternate version of *Ep.* 10 to account for the difference in the texts at this point. I shall delay the *stemma* until the end of this section.

In the dogmatic proto-collection that they share with **K**, we see this similarity again. To make this demonstration easier, I give a table for *Epp.* 22 and 28, using Schwartz as a control text:

Var., *Ep.*	**C, P, K**	Schwartz, ACO 2.2.1, 21–22 (*Ep.* 22); 24–33 (*Ep.* 28)
1, 22	*adque deursum* (**C, K**)	sursum enim *atque deorsum* peruolans (**P**) This is an almost meaningless variant without others.
2, 22	*posset* (**P**)	quos *possit* deuorare (**C**)
3, 22	*ut* fatuas (**C, P, K**)	est *et* fatuas
4, 22	*uitari det sequia* (**C**) uitare *de id* sequi (**P**) uitare *dit* (**K**)	*uitare decet, sequi* **C P K** all attempts to emend the same text.
5, 22	*clericos* (**C**) *clerecus* (**P** simple orthography)	sub me *clericus* degens
6, 22	om. *resiliit* (**C, P, K**)	exiliit *resiliit* a proposito diuino
7, 22	sunt *quidem* (**C, P, K** illeg. from mildew after 'sunt')	narrare sunt *enim*

Var., *Ep.*	**C, P, K**	Schwartz, ACO 2.2.1, 21–22 (*Ep.* 22); 24–33 (*Ep.* 28)
8, 22	enim *essent* (**C, P, K**)	si enim de nostro numero
9, 22	*infirmi* (**P**)	autem *infirmae* fidei (**C**)
10, 22	*perdicione* (**P**) *peredicatione* (**K**)	in *perditionem* praecipitant (**C**)
11, 22	*lingua sua* (**P**)	enim *linguam suam* quasi (**C**)
12, 22	*secta* (**C, P**) *sectaip* (**K**)	*sectam* sapiebat
13, 22	*uiri* (**P**)	praeceptum *ueri* dei dicentis (**C**)
14, 22	*legetur* (**P**)	asinaria *ligetur* (**C**)
15, 22	om. *omnem* (**P, K**)	autem *omnem* abiecit (**C**)
16, 22	*adseuerebat* (**C**) *adseuerauit* (**P**) *adsuerabat* (**K**)	synodo *adserabat*
17, 22	*coessentiam* nobis *subsistere* (**C**) *quoessentiam* nobis esse (**P**)	*coessentiuam* nobis esse (**K**)
18, 22	*esset* ex uirgine (**C**) *esset si essit* ex *uirginem* (**P**) esse *etsi essit* ex (**K**)	*esse quod est* ex uirgine
19, 28	om. *gestorum* (**C¹, P**)	seras, et *gestorum* episcopalium ordine
20, 28	*recensitas* (**P**)	ordine *recensito* (**C**)
21, 28	*ipsum* (**P** attraction)	etiam de *ipso* dictum (**C**)
22, 28	*doctoribusque* non *credere* (**C, K**) *doctoribus quae* non *credire* (**P**)	sapientioribus *doctoribusque* non *cedere*
23, 28	*insipientia* (**P**)	sed in hanc *insipientiam* (**C, K**)
24, 28	*agnuscendam* (**P**) *agnoscendam* (**K**)	cum ad *cognoscendam* ueritatem (**C**) **P K** variant word choice
25, 28	*reparandum* (**P**) om. *se* (**K**)	sed totam *se reparando* (**C**)
26, 28	*possimus* (**C**), *possumus* (**P, K**)	enim superare *possemus*
27, 28	*propriae tenebrabat* (**P**)	*propria tenebrarat* doctrinae (**C, K**)
28, 28	*tenit* (**C**) *sene* (**P**)	homo; *tenet* enim *sine* (**K**)

Var., Ep.	C, P, K	Schwartz, ACO 2.2.1, 21–22 (Ep. 22); 24–33 (Ep. 28)
29, 28	*humilitatem* (**P**) *humitate* (**K**)	*humilitate* cunarum, magnitudo (**C**)
30, 28	*utramque naturam* intellegandam (**C** attraction) utraque *quae* natura intellegendam (**P**) utraque natura *intellegendum* (**K**)	in *utraque natura intelligendam*

Ep. 22 maintains the trend whereby **P** follows **C** very closely, the majority of the differences between the two being errors on the part of **P**. However, *Ep.* 28 is, like *Ep.* 10 above, divergent. Once again, there is likely to be another source influencing the text of **P**. After all, *Ep.* 28 is the most commonly copied of all of Leo's letters. It is the most read and the best-known. As a result, it is also the most likely to be contaminated. That is to say, *Ep.* 22, being somewhat less common, can account for the majority of **P**'s variations from **C** through scribal error, whereas *Ep.* 28 compounds scribal error with a text or texts— viewed or remembered—from a different tradition. Therefore, although the case for **P** as a direct descendent of **C** for the Leo material is weakened and not airtight, it is still worth upholding.

When all of these variants are considered together, and given the relative ages of the manuscripts and their collections, it is my contention that **P**, as far as its Leo contents are concerned, is, in fact, a descendant of **C**, at least for Leo's letters. They have the exact same letters, drawn from two different proto-collections, each of which is shared with only one other collection, and they have very similar contents. Furthermore, **P** tends to add errors of omission and includes all of the variants of addition included in **C**, as well as most of **C**'s omissions. This is more likely caused by dependence rather than the manuscripts being twins. Finally, **P** very frequently uses rare spellings for words such as 'negliendo' that **C** also uses. Therefore, it is my contention that the **C** manuscript is, in fact, the ancestor of **P**, and the *stemma* would thus be as follows:

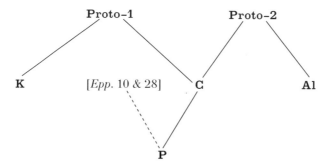

However, the matter cannot rest there. Geoffrey D. Dunn has recently argued that **P** is not dependent on **C** but that they share a common source for their Leo material, one that may also include the material in the collections just before Leo, including both **proto-1** and **proto-2**.[271] The arguments against **P** being a copy of **C** are concerned with its copying of the protocols, as well as where the collection of documents comes in the manuscript. If **P** is a copy of **C**, it seems that the copyist rearranged some of the material and changed the protocols. Considering the kind of differences between the manuscripts and how few they are, this seems more likely than **P** using a now-lost third manuscript with the same contents as **C** and **P** that was then rearranged, which requires an unnecessary complication. Even if **P** did not copy **C** for much of its material, it seems to me that it did for Leo. Dunn is also concerned, however, as to why *Epp.* 7 and 15 follow *Ep.* 4, because *Ep.* 4 matches the non-Leo collection of papal decretals that immediately precedes it in terms of content.[272] However, if we see *Epp.* 4, 7, and 15 as the unit **proto-2** then the sudden inclusion of *Ep.* 7 about Manichaeans in the midst of letters about episcopal rights and ordinations is not a surprise. The collector liked *Ep.* 4 because of its confluence with the other material, and *Ep.* 4 comes with *Ep.* 7, which he added for good measure.

3.2.1. *Collectio (ecclesiae) Thessalonicensis*[273] (**T**)

3.2.1.i. Dating and context

This collection includes 24 letters from Popes Damasus (366–84) through Hilarus (461–68), including Leo I; letters between the

---

[271] Dunn 2015.
[272] Dunn 2015, 185–86.
[273] B16 (PL 54.566), J2(iii) 505–06).

Emperors Honorius and Theodosius II from after 421; and two letters to Pope Leo I from the Emperor Marcian in 450 and to Anatolius of Constantinople in 454. The collection was arranged to demonstrate that the Bishop of Rome had ecclesiastical jurisdiction over Eastern Illyricum, even after the division of the Prefecture of Illyricum meant that the eastern half was administered politically by the Eastern Empire following the death of Theodosius I in 395 rather than by the Western Empire. Frequently, the divisions of the ecclesiastical administration followed those of the imperial administration; therefore, if Eastern Illyricum had fallen under the political administration of the Eastern Empire, some felt that its ecclesiastical administration ought to have followed as well. This perspective on ecclesiastical administration, as we have seen, runs counter to that in Rome; Leo's resistance to allowing political jurisdiction to coincide with ecclesiastical jurisdiction appears in his correspondence with Arles and resistance to 'Canon 28' of Chalcedon. Furthermore, he makes clear the principle of apostolic foundation and resultant hierarchy in *Epp.* 9 to Dioscorus of Alexandria and 119 to Maximus of Antioch. With this perspective in mind, the Bishops of Rome were loath to surrender their power and authority in Illyricum, as is visible in Leo, *Ep.* 14, to Anastasius, Bishop of Thessalonica, where he emphasises very strongly Anastasius' role as papal *vicarius*.

Collectio Thessalonicensis seems to have been compiled when Stephen, Metropolitan of Larissa in Thessaly, was deposed by the Bishop of Constantinople and made appeal to a Roman Synod of 7 and 9 December 531.[274] The clear argument in the collecting of these documents is not only that Eastern Illyricum is under the jurisdiction of Rome, but also that the Bishop of Thessalonica is papal *vicarius*. **T** includes ten of Leo's letters as items XVII–XXVI: 100, 104, 106, 136, 132, 135, 6, 5, 13, and the first half of *Credebamus post* (JK 351)—a letter to which we shall return. Of these letters, nos 100, 136, 132, 6, 5, 13 were unknown to modern readers of Leo prior to Holstenius' use of them in his edition of 1662. These previously unknown letters are particular rarities; *Epp.* 100, 132, 6, 5, 13, and *Credebamus post* exist only in **T**; *Ep.* 136 exists only in **T**, *Ratisbonensis* (**E**), and *Grimanica* (**G**).

---

[274] See Jasper 2001, 81–82.

Of these rarities, the most difficulty lies in Item XXVI, *Credebamus post*. It has the inscription, 'DILECTISSIMO FRATRI ANASTASIO LEO', yet it is dated, 'Data XIV kal. octubr. Monaxio uc cons.'—to 419 in the pontificate of Boniface I. Furthermore, in the second half there is reference to one Perigenes, and it is known from item VII in **T** (Boniface, *Ep.* 4 [JK 350]) that Perigenes was involved in a disputed episcopal election in Corinth, and his opponents had appealed to Pope Boniface in the issue. Prior to Silva-Tarouca, editors had assumed that item XXVI was falsely attributed to Leo and simply changed the inscription to make the whole text match. Silva-Tarouca, however, following arguments put forward by Schwartz,[275] chose to divide the text in two. The first half was a fragmentary letter of Leo I to Anastasius of Thessalonica from *c.* 446, the second half a fragmentary letter from Boniface I to Rufus from 419.[276] Geoffrey D. Dunn has recently upheld this theory,[277] arguing thoroughly from internal and external evidence that the second half is most assuredly from Boniface to Rufus; since it goes over much the same ground as item VII, Dunn argues that it was sent shortly thereafter when Boniface had gained more information in the case of Perigenes. Item XXVI(b) cannot be a different transmission of item VII since the contents are too different. Dunn then argues that Schwartz and Silva-Tarouca are essentially right concerning the first half of *Credebamus post*, that it was a letter from Leo to Anastasius that became damaged and spliced together with the letter from Boniface. The general content of the first half of *Credebamus post* could point to either Anastasius or Rufus as recipient. However, when taken with the Leo letters immediately preceding it—*Ep.* 6 in which Leo declares Anastasius his *vicarius*, and *Ep.* 13 to all the bishops of Illyricum complaining about lack of discipline—this letter, sent 'post epistulas nostras pro ecclesiasticae disciplinae observacione [*sic*] transmissas', fits well. Here the author commends the recipient for his industrious vigilance and encourages him to maintain strong discipline.

[275] Schwartz 1931, 151–59.
[276] Silva-Tarouca 1937, 62.
[277] Dunn 2014.

Added to these arguments are those of style—although this is not hard and fast, given the stylistic similarities amongst the writings of popes of all ages. Nonetheless, certain phrases strike the reader as especially Leonine. The opening sentence includes the phrase 'post epistulas nostras pro ecclesiasticae disciplinae obseruatione transmissas', wherein the separation of the noun 'epistulas' from the participle 'transmissas' is not unlike Leo, as in a most common incipit, 'Leo episcopus uniuersis episcopis per Siciliam constitutis' (*Ep.* 16).[278] Elsewhere in *Credebamus post*, we see the *genitivus identitatis*: 'Vigilantiae tuae laudamus industriam'. Such usage is frequently found in Leo, as in *Ep.* 10.1, 'hanc petrae istius sacratissimam firmitatem'. Divorcing 'hunc' from 'timorem' is also the style of Leo: 'hunc te Dei nostri habere professus timorem'. Examples abound on almost every page of his letters; a few are, 'a suo se nouerit officio submouendum' in *Ep.* 4.5; 'per uestras se dispergat ecclesias' and 'suarum furtim cuniculos inueniat latebrarum' in *Ep.* 7.1. Towards the close we find a partitive genitive, 'plurimi sacerdotum', rather than simply 'plurimi sacerdotes'; I provide two examples of Leo using it with persons: 'aliquis clericorum' (*Ep.* 4.3); and 'quis fratrum' (*Ep.* 4.5). Far less compelling are this letter's use of terminology, as most of it could easily be termed either papal or ecclesiastical.

The strongest stylistic test for authorship is scansion; I include it for thoroughness, but it will help us little because of how short the sample text is. *Credebamus post* contains only 9 long sentences, the final clausulation of which is as follows:

Sentence ending	Clausula
ecclesiástica éxigit disciplína	*cursus velox* with a resolved cretic-double-trochee
inefficácem cognóuimus fuísse	*cursus trispondaicus* with a double-iamb-trochee
lítteris sentiámus	*cursus velox* with a cretic-double-trochee
ecclésiis fuerímus expérti	*cursus planus* with a cretic-spondee
rectóris utáris offício	*cursus tardus* with a double-trochee-iamb or cretic-tribrach

[278] Cf. e.g. *Epp.* 4, 7, 10, 12, 16, *et cetera*.

Sentence ending	Clausula
légimus fundaméntum	*cursus velox* with a cretic-double-spondee
et prudénter utáris	*cursus planus* with a cretic-trochee
pertulisse dixísti	*cursus planus* with a cretic-spondee
mémores, sunt proféssi	*cursus velox* with an anapest-double-trochee

What we see here is a united system, a *cursus mixtus* that includes both the accentual *cursus* as well as the metrical clausulae of Cicero. As has been thoroughly demonstrated by F. Di Capua, Leo uses such a system. 5/9 of the accentual rhythms are the *cursus velox* and 3/9 (1/3) the *cursus planus*—these two accentual clausulae are often favoured by Leo, as Di Capua's conclusions show.[279] Furthermore, following again Di Capua's conclusions,[280] our three forms of the *cursus planus* herein follow the metrical clausulae most favoured by Leo with this combination: _u_ _x. The *cursus veloces* do likewise, with 4 out of 5 being xux_u_u. Due to the brevity of the text under examination, the question of authorship cannot be closed decisively, but we may be fairly safe in saying that the first portion of item XXVI in **T** may be by Leo I, not Boniface I.

3.2.1.ii. Manuscripts

It exists in three manuscripts:

Vat. lat. 5751, fols 55^r–75^r (saec. IX–X) from northern Italy, Bobbio or Verona.[281] This manuscript is the best,[282] but it is incomplete and muddled, perhaps due to a mixed-up exemplar with misplaced folios.[283] The state of the manuscript explains the state of item XXVI. In 1618, it came from Bobbio to the Vatican with a number of other Bobbio manuscripts under the watch of Paul V (1605–1621), and is known to have been in the city in 1648.[284]

---

[279] See Di Capua 1937, 37–40, 54.

[280] Ibid., 20.

[281] Kéry 1999, 41; Bischoff 1998–2014, 3.6909.

[282] Silva-Tarouca 1937, viii; Jasper 2001, 82.

[283] Ibid., 82.

[284] Silva-Tarouca 1937, viii. Collura 1943, 133–34, identified the MS as no. 57 in the Bobbio inventory of 1461. (Cited in Dunn 2014, 478, n. 10).

Vat. lat. 6339 (saec. XVI); an apograph of Vat. lat. 5751. Foll. 12–62ᵛ contains emendations and notes in the seventeenth-century hand of Lucas Holste.[285]

Vat. Barb. lat. 650 (*olim* 3386 saec. XVII), another copy of Vat. lat. 5751.

Two modern editions are worth mentioning, the *editio princeps* under the name of Lucas Holstenius in 1662 and Silva-Tarouca's in 1937.[286] The earlier edition comes under severe fire by Silva-Tarouca due to the many unnecessary emendations it included as well as what the twentieth-century editor considered an increase of corruptions.[287] Due to inaccessibility of the manuscripts, Silva-Tarouca's 1937 edition was the first since 'Holstenius' to view the ancient volumes themselves. Due to the soundness of Silva-Tarouca's edition as well as the paucity of manuscripts worth investigating, his work has been used in the comparison of variant readings in the course of this project.

3.2.1.iii. Manuscript relations

Since two of our three manuscripts are, in fact, apographs of the first, the relationships amongst manuscripts of **T** need not be investigated. Nevertheless, the relationship of **T** to the wider tradition is worth observing. Since *Epp.* 100, 132, 6, 5, and 13 only exist in **T**, they obviously have no relationship to the wider manuscript tradition. *Epp.* 104, 106, and 136 edited by Silva-Tarouca in *Textus et Documenta* 20 as items 37, 38, and 57, include no notable variants in **T**. *Ep.* 135, given its inclusion in more collections, bears slightly more fruit. First, it alone bears the inscription, 'DILECTISSIMO FRATRI ANATHOLIO LEO', vs Schwartz, 'Leo Anatolio episcopo'; **Q**, **G**, 'Leo Anatolio episcopo per Nec-

---

[285] Silva-Tarouca 1937, viii.

[286] L. Holstenius, *Collectio Romana bipartita a veterum aliquot historiae ecclesiasticae monumentorum*, Pars 1 (Rome 1662), 1–163; and C. Silva-Tarouca, *Epistularum Romanorum pontificum ad vicarios per Illyricum aliosque episcopos collectio Thessalonicensis* (Rome 1937). Silva-Tarouca observes that the Holstenius edition post-dates Holste, and writes that it was published 'a nescio quibus ignaris compilatoribus' (viii).

[287] Silva-Tarouca 1937, viii–ix. He writes, 'Textus erroribus et ineptis emendationibus scatens', and that 'series epistularum ita ineptis et arbitrariis mutationibus turbata appareat' (viii).

tarium agentem in rebus'; and Ballerini Collection 13, 'Leo urbis romae episcopus Anatholio episcopo in domino salutem'. At **G**, 'sanctis praecessoribus tuis', **T** gives the false reading 'processoribus' against **Q** and Ballerini Collection 13 (**m**) 'praecursoribus'. At Schwartz, 'uidebatur, cum et haereticorum', **T** joins **G** and **Q** in omitting 'et'. At no other point within my diagnostic passages does **T** diverge from Schwartz's text in *Ep.* 135. Very briefly, then, we see that **T**, while a largely independent source of Leo's letters, offers us no great changes wrought in the *scrinia* of Illyricum.

3.2.m. *Collectio Avellana*[288]

3.2.m.i. Dating and context

This collection dates from the time of Pope Vigilius (pope, 537–55). It contains five of Leo's letters, numbers 51–55 of the collection, not found elsewhere; by the Ballerini numbering, they are *Epp.* 169, 170, 171, 172, 173. The collection as a whole contains 244 items dating 367–553, thereby giving us the likely date of its gathering—the latest item is from Vigilius himself. Included are not only letters from popes but also from emperors and magistrates of both the eastern and western Roman Empires as well as from other bishops, priests, and synods.[289] Leo's five letters, along with over 200 other documents in the collection, are unique.[290] The collector of the *Avellana* put together the text from five distinct parts, of which the Leonine component is the third;[291] given the high number of rarities exhibited in the collection, its collector seems to have been seeking to edit items hitherto little or never published.

The *Collectio Avellana*, besides gathering together letters not in circulation elsewhere, is very frequently concerned with episcopal-imperial relations, helping to further tie down its origins in the sixth century. As discussed in relation to the Three Chapters Controversy, Pope Vigilius was at different times an opponent and a supporter of Justinian's measures against the Three Chapters.

---

[288] B14 (PL 54.564–65), J2(i) (505).
[289] Günther puts it much the same, CSEL 35.1, ii.
[290] Ibid.
[291] Ibid., iii.

His tergiversations were based not only theological considerations but on the political outcomes of his actions. In a climate where the emperor was legislating in matters of religion with recourse to bishops and councils after the fact, and where he was forcing the recalcitrant to accept his position, a collection of documents from emperors and popes about their respective spheres would be supremely timely. Moreover, the vision of the two spheres produced here could be read as supporting the so-called Gelasian doctrine, spelled out in his *Ep.* 12, that the emperor's main sphere of influence was the temporal and that in the spiritual realm he was under the authority of the bishops. Viezure argues further that the *Avellana* was compiled with the intent of showing the independence of the popes from Ostrogothic policy.[292]

3.2.m.ii. Manuscripts

The *Collectio Avellana* exists in two medieval manuscripts:

Vat. lat. 3787 (saec. XI).[293] This manuscript is of 163 fols, written in two columns. Nine scribes were involved in the composition of this manuscript, and Günther argues that its exemplar was written in minuscule. Leo's letters run 26^v–27^v.

Vat. lat. 4961 (Günther, saec. X^{ex}-XI^{in}, Dolezalek, saec. XI^{in}) from Santa Croce, Avella; hence the collection's name.[294] This is a manuscript of 109 fols, also written in two columns and of the same form as Vat. lat. 3787. Four scribes wrote it besides more recent correctors. Leo's letters run 19^r–20^r. The existence of this manuscript at Santa Croce, Avella, is of great interest, for the eleventh-century reformer Peter Damian (*d.* 1072/3) was abbot of Santa Croce. Given his association with Leo IX and the growth of reform in Italy, it is tempting to see this collection with its emphasis on the proper spheres of influence of secular and ecclesiastical authority appealing to Damian.

---

[292] Viezure 2015.

[293] This manuscript is digitised: https://digi.vatlib.it/view/MSS_Vat.lat.3787 Accessed 20 September 2021. See Günther, CSEL 35.1, iii–xvii, and Dolezalek 2008.

[294] This manuscript is digitsed: https://digi.vatlib.it/view/MSS_Vat.lat.4961 Accessed 20 September 2021. See Günther, CSEL 35.1, xvii–xviii, and Dolezalek 2008.

Several early modern copies of this collection exist, none of which is very useful for establishing the text of Leo, all being either descendants of the two manuscripts listed above or corrupted and damaged:

Venice, Biblioteca Nazionale Marciana, Iur. can. 13 (171) from 1469; possibly a copy of either Vat. lat. 4961 or another copy thereof.[295]

Vat. lat. 3786 (XVI saec.), possibly a copy of Vat. lat. 3787 or another copy thereof.[296]

Vat. lat. 4903 (XVI saec.); listed by Kéry as a probable copy of Vat. lat. 4961 as well,[297] but Günther demonstrates a number of parallels with Vat. Ott. lat. 1105, despite a seventeenth-century hand claiming its descent from Vat. lat. 4961.[298]

Vat. lat. 5617 (XVI saec.); this manuscript's version of *Avellana* is impure, with some letters added and others omitted.[299]

Vat. Ott. lat. 1105 (XVI saec.); Günther argues for a lost exemplar dependent upon Vat. lat. 4961.[300]

Venice, Biblioteca Nazionale Marciana, Iur. can. 14 (172) (XVI saec.); this manuscript is a copy of the other Venetian codex.[301]

Rome, Biblioteca Angelica, 292 (XVI/XVII saec.); this manuscript is a copy of Vat. lat. 5617 that is missing its beginning.[302]

Rome, Biblioteca dell'Accademia Nazionale dei Lincei, Corsin. 817 (XVI–XVII saec.); this manuscript admits to being a copy of Vat. lat. 4961, and scholars agree.[303]

El Escorial, Real Biblioteca de San Lorenzo, C.II.21 (XVII saec.), a copy of Vat. lat. 4961.[304]

This canonical collection has a modern edition by O. Günther in the *Corpus Scriptorum Ecclesiasticorum Latinorum*.[305] Günther's edi-

---

[295] Günther, CSEL 35.1, xxvi.

[296] Ibid., xxvii.

[297] Kéry 1999, 37.

[298] CSEL 35.1, xxxii–xxxiii.

[299] Ibid., xxx.

[300] Ibid., xxvii–xxviiii.

[301] Ibid., xxvi.

[302] Ibid., xxxi.

[303] See ibid., xxxiii.

[304] Ibid., xxxiii.

[305] CSEL 35.1–2; Vienna, 1895–1898.

tion is very good, and we need not detain ourselves with this collection any longer, since it is independent of the rest of the Leo tradition.

3.2.n. *Collectio Arelatensis*[306] (**Ar**)

3.2.n.i. Dating and context

This collection, known on the catalogue of the Bibliothèque nationale de France as *Collectio canonum ecclesiae Arelatensis* and by Jasper as the *Liber auctoritatum ecclesiae Arelatensis*,[307] contains six of Leo's letters: *Epp.* 40, 42, 41, 45, 66, and 67; between *Epp.* 66 and 67 is interposed a letter of Pope Hilarus (JK 557). Four of these letters are not found in any earlier collection: 40, 42, 66, and 67; of these, 42 and 67 are unique to **Ar**, while 40 and 66 are shared with **Al**. **Al** has used **Ar** as a source and also includes *Epp.* 41 and 65. **Ar** was probably compiled around the time of its latest portion, which is Pope Pelagius I's confession of faith (JK 938) from April 557 or early 558.[308] W. Gundlach produced an edition for *Monumenta Germaniae Historica* in 1892.[309] This collection is important for the study of Leo principally because it is our earliest attestation for the four previously mentioned letters. It also demonstrates for us aspects of the archive at Arles whence these documents come. Clearly Leo's letters to the bishops of Gaul were important to the see of Arles in the sixth century, a reminder to us that this pope's importance, preservation, and influence throughout the centuries is no mere accident and rides on more than the Chalcedonian settlement.

3.2.n.ii. Manuscripts

The manuscripts are:[310]

> *1*: Paris, lat. 2777 (olim Colbert 5024, Regius 3989[3.3]), fol. 20–42[v] (saec. IX1/2), from Lérins (Gundlach) or Lyons (Bischoff).[311] This

[306] B15 (PL 54.565), J2(ii) (505).

[307] For the BnF, see https://archivesetmanuscrits.bnf.fr/ark:/12148/cc60559t. Accessed 20 September 2021. See Jasper 2001, 85–87.

[308] Ibid., 87.

[309] MGH Epist. 3, 1–83. See above, 2.6.

[310] For consistency, I used Gundlach's *sigla* with these MSS.

[311] Bischoff 1998–2014, 3.4228.

manuscript contains Leo's letters from the *ante gesta Chalcedon-ensia* of Rusticus' edition of the *Acta Chalcedonensia*,[312] which are followed by the *Collectio Arelatensis* with summaries of contents and marginal commentaries.[313] Leo's **Ar** letters run fols 20ᵛ–25ᵛ.

2: Paris, lat. 3849 (olim Mazarin 316, Regius 3989) (saec. IX) from eastern Gaul (Gundlach) or Italy (Bischoff);[314] fols 4ʳ–6ʳ include Leo's *Epp.* 40, 41, and 42. Fol. 6ᵛ is blank, and folio 7ʳ begins with a letter from Pope Zosimus to Hilarius of Narbo (JK 332); the manuscript moves on to Pope Hilarus at fol. 9ᵛ after Zosimus is finished. This is the only fragmentary **Ar** version of Leo's letters.

3: Paris, lat. 5537 (XI/XII saec.), from Colbert's library; Leo's letters run fols 5ᵛ–19ʳ. According to Jasper, this is the most complete version of the *Collectio Arelatensis*.[315]

4: Paris, lat. 3880, fol. 70–91ᵛ, (saec. XII); the table of contents runs 70ʳ–71ʳ, and Leo's letters in this manuscript run 72ᵛ–76ᵛ.

3.2.n.iii. Manuscript relations

Of these manuscripts, *3* and *4* are descendants of *1*, according to Gundlach.[316] They demonstrate enough similarities to assume them to be twins, and are different enough from *1* that *1* is not their exemplar but still an ancestor, and there is an intervening manuscript, now lost. *2*, on the other hand, stands alone. *1* and *2* are both descended from the now lost archetype of **Ar**. Gundlach's edition is very thorough, and is not based solely on *1* and *2*, but also includes readings from **Al** *l*; readings from *3* and *4* are included in his apparatus. Doing this helps demonstrate their dependence on *1*, making the edition a window into the manuscripts, even though they themselves are not of great assistance in establishing the original text of **Ar**. My own readings of these four manuscripts confirm what Gundlach has written, seen in my *stemma* at 3.2.o.iii.

[312] For which, see below, 3.c.

[313] See Jasper 2001, 86.

[314] See ibid., 86; Bischoff 1998–2014, 3.4289.

[315] Jasper 2001, 86. There are two early modern copies of this manuscript that, following Jasper, I consider 'of no editorial value' (Ibid., 86 n. 378): Rome, Biblioteca Vallicelliana, G.99; Carpentras, Bibliothèque muncipale, 1856, fol. 50–96.

[316] Gundlach 1892, 2.

3.2.o. *Collectio Albigensis*[317] (**Al**)

3.2.o.i. Dating and context

This canonical collection contains several groupings of Leo's letters: *Epp.* 4 and 7 (items 34 and 35; presumably from **proto-2**, shared with **C** and **P**: see 3.2.k.iii);[318] *Ep.* 10 (item 47); *Epp.* 40, 41, 65, and 66 (items 62–65, taken from **Ar**).[319] The Toulouse manuscript also includes a fragment of *Ep.* 165. Three of these letters, 4, 7, and 10, are defined as decretals, although the canonical matter of items 62–65 makes one wonder about how we designate a letter 'decretal' or otherwise. The date of the collection is contested, as noted in Kéry, with estimates ranging from 549 to after 604.[320]

3.2.o.ii. Manuscripts

It exists in two manuscripts. The first is in two parts:

t: Toulouse, Bibliothèque municipale, 364 (I.63) + Paris, lat. 8901 (before 666/67), fols 88ᵛff. of the Toulouse portion of the manuscript contain Leo. This manuscript was written by a scribe named Perpetuus in Albi at the command of Bishop Dido of Albi,[321] as learnt not from this manuscript itself since it is damaged, but from the tenth-century copy of it in Albi which we shall describe below.[322] The subscription as preserved in Albi

---

[317] Not included by the Ballerini or Jasper; for a list of manuscripts and bibliography, see Kéry 1999, 46–47.

[318] See the Appendix for a list and description of the proto-collections.

[319] For a full description of its decretal collection, see Wurm 1939, 279–83.

[320] Kéry 1999, 46.

[321] Duchesne 1910, 43, argues that Dido was Bishop of Albi at the time of Pope Gregory I based upon the contents of this manuscript: the canons stop at 549, and the Bishops of Rome end with Gregory, giving his name but no dates—although perhaps the contents determine the date of its exemplar, not its copying by Perpetuus. I have found no other reference to Dido of Albi to help secure the date of either the collection or its copying, a situation that has persisted since the time of Traube 1909, 36, 'The Toulouse MS was accordingly written by a presbyter Perpetuus at the command of Bishop Dido of Albi, of whom we unfortunately know nothing further'.

[322] See CLA 6.836, which gives the lost subscription: Explicit liber canonum. Amen. Ego Perpetuus quamuis indignus presbyter iussus a domino meo Didone urbis Albigensium episcopum hunc librum canonum scripsi. Post incendium ciuitatis ipsius hic liber recuperatus fuit Deo auxiliante sub die VIII Kal. augustas anno IIII regnante domni nostri Childerici regis.

cites the manuscript as having been saved from a fire in July of the fourth year of the reign of King Childeric, which, assuming Childeric II, is either 666 or 667.[323] This manuscript was in the Augustinian monastery in Toulouse in 1715, and the portion now in Paris was stolen by the book thief Libri (Guglielmo Libri Carucci dalla Sommaja, 1803–1869).[324] Both the Toulouse and Paris portions of this manuscript are digitised.[325] Like other early Gallic canonical manuscripts, it is written in an uncial hand in a single column of text with few *tituli*—none break up the monotony of text in the individual letters of Leo, although each item is given an initial rubricated *titulus*. Leo is found in the Toulouse portion of the manuscript at fols 45^r–46^r, 67^v–72^r, 88^v–92^r, and the fragment of *Ep.* 165 is at 104^r–106^v. 45^{r-v} contain the beginning of *Ep.* 4, and 46^r the close of *Ep.* 7.

a: Albi, Bibliothèque municipale, 2 (147) (saec. IX–X).[326] This manuscript, as noted, is a copy of the bipartite one above. It is written in a Caroline minuscule in a single column with rubricated *tituli* for the begining of letters, but not for internal divisions. Leo's letters are at 63^v–66^r, 95^r–100^r, and 121^v–125^r. The missing portions of *Epp.* 4 and 7 have been added by the scribe; that these are additions and not the state of *t* when it was copied is demonstrated by the fact that 65^v stops about one third of the way down the page, and the top of 66^r is the same as the top of *t*. 46^r, where *Ep.* 7 begins. The *a* text of the missing sections of *Epp.* 4 and 7 is textually similar to the **C P** text, so it likely came from another Leo manuscript of the Gallic type, probably one of those in the Albi scriptorium.

---

[323] I cite the century as the seventh and thus the King as Childeric II out of deference to earlier scholarship, but I find no reason that there could not have been a Bishop Dido in Albi at the time of Childeric III in the 700s.

[324] See CLA 6.836.

[325] Toulouse: https://rosalis.bibliotheque.toulouse.fr/ark:/12148/ btv1b10560139j.r = 364?rk = 21459;2. Accessed 20 September 2021. Paris: https://gallica.bnf.fr/ark:/12148/btv1b9077669g.r = Latin+8901.langFR. Accessed 20 September 2021.

[326] Kéry 1999, 47, dates it to the second half of the ninth century, whereas CLA 6.836 claims it is tenth-century, and the Médiathèque at Albi, comparing it with other Albigeois manuscripts, dates it 880–90 (see https://cecilia. mediatheques.grand-albigeois.fr/idurl/1/104. Accessed 20 September 2021). The palaeography fairly surely dates it ninth-tenth century, even if we cannot be more precise than that. See also Bischoff 1998–2014, 1.16. This manuscript is digitised https://cecilia.mediatheques.grand-albigeois.fr/viewer/104/ ?offset = Accessed 20 September 2021.

3.2.o.iii. Manuscript relations

Epp. 4 and 7 are introduced with the same incipit as in **C** and **P**, 'INCIPIUNT DECRETA PAPAE LEONIS', pointing immediately to **proto-2** (*Epp.* 4, 7, 15 in **C** and **P**; see above, 3.2.j-k).[327] Of the first 25 **P** variants in *Ep.* 4, which are all that *l* contains, **Al** has 12 of 16 common **C**, **P** variants and one **P** variant. In 4.2, **Al** gives 'exiuerant' whereas **C** and **P** give 'exteterant' against Ballerini 'quod illis obstiterat'. The most significant disagreements amongst **C**, **P**, and **Al** are that **Al** gives 'Picenam' rather than 'Ticinam' in the inscription and omits 'Pauli' from 'beati Pauli Apostoli uocem' in 4.2. The similarities point towards a common source for all three—the postulated proto-collection—but independence from **C** on the part of **Al**. *Ep.* 7 bears this out. Even in the added portions, *a* provides the same incipit as **C** and **P** for *Ep.* 7, 'INCIPIT EIVSDEM PAPAE LEONIS DE MANICHEIS', and agrees with those two collections for 8 of the first 9 variants; if, as the codicological evidence suggests, *a* did not get its text for the lacuna in *Ep.* 7 from *l*, it used a source from the same family as **proto-2**. Of the remaining 15 **P** variants for *Ep.* 7, **Al** contains 8 of the 12 common **C**, **P** variants, its variations from **C** once more demonstrating its independence from that collection yet a common source for all three. Since I have already demonstrated **P**'s dependence upon **C**, it is worth noting that, since *Ep.* 15 is lacking from **Al**, **proto-2** may not have had all three letters, since **C** could have acquired *Ep.* 15 from another source, and **P** got it from **C**. Furthermore, **D** also begins with *Epp.* 4 and 7 with the same incipit. However, it could alternatively be posited that *Ep.* 15, a letter to a Spanish bishop about Priscillianism which is very long, may have been dropped from the proto-collection by the compilers of **A1** and **D** because of a lack of interest—why take the time and money to make a copy of something so large in which one has little interest? By the mid- to late-sixth century, when **Al** was compiled, Priscillianism was likely not an issue in southern Gaul. *Ep.* 10 proves to be from a shared ancestry as well. **Al** shares 18 of the first 21 common **C**, **P** variants of this letter with those two collections. This collection also agrees with **C** at 10.3 in omitting 'se' from 'quamuis ipse se suis', whereas **P** omits

---

[327] See the Appendix for a list and description of the proto-collections.

'ipse se suis' entirely in a case of *saut-du-même-au-même*. At 10.2, **C** gives 'ita se uos cupiens', **P** 'ita saeuus cupiens', and **Al** gives 'ita se cupiens'. These three readings could all be descended from the same damaged text. Furthermore, they all use the spelling 'Helarius' for 'Hilarius'.

The final batch of Leo letters in **Al** is the selection from **Ar**, for which *l* is the earliest manuscript, predating by over a century by the earliest **Ar** manuscript. Although Gundlach has chosen to print **Al** variants as his text, in many cases these variants are not preferable readings. For example, in *Ep.* 40 **Al** reads, 'Quod ergo in Arelatensium ciuitatem', against **Ar** 'ciuitate', which is better; later, we read, 'Quia electione pacificam atque concordem', where 'electionem', the **Ar** reading, is correct. This letter closes in **Al** with 'uiris clarissimis consoles', rather than 'consulibus'. In *Ep.* 41 **Al** gives 'habetur antestis' rather than **Ar** 'antistes'; immediately following this orthographical error comes 'cuius primi et adiuuentur', for which **Ar** gives 'plurimi'—again, a reading that is clearly right. Another error from **Al** is 'quid de sinceritatem' for **Ar** 'sinceritate', as is 'constantia mansuetudo conmendet' instead of **Ar** 'constantiam'. Likewise we see 'iustitia lenitas temperet' in **Al** where **Ar** gives the correct 'iustitiam'. Passing over the other errors in *Ep.* 41, we move on to *Ep.* 65, which in fact lacks its inscription in **Al**. Here, **Al** has a tendency to agree with **Ar** *2* when it is at variance with the rest of the **Ar** tradition. In this letter, **Al** provides a good reading at 'Rauennius in ciuitate', agreeing with **Ar** *2* (as well as *3* and *4*) against **Ar** *1* 'ciuitatem'. However, its next agreement with **Ar** *2* against **Ar** *1* (here with *3* and *4*) is less fortunate, giving the dative 'caritati' in 'tanta dignatione et caritati fuisse responsum' rather than 'caritate'. We see another shared error with **Ar** *2* against **Ar** *1* at 'maximam coronae uestrae' instead of 'maxime'—a phrase from which **Al** omits 'uestrae'. Yet another agreement with **Ar** *2* against **Ar** *1* is 'gratia morum suorum mansuetudine et sanctitate meruisse', where **Ar** *1* (*3*, *4*) give 'manusetudinem' and 'sanctitatem'; the latter reading makes more sense in the sentence as a whole, providing an accusative direct object for 'meruisse'. The rest of *Ep.* 65 is much the same, with shared variants between **Al** and **Ar** *2* that are sometimes good readings, sometimes not. Finally, *Ep.* 66 includes some names more fortuitously spelt in **Al** than **Ar** *2*, such as 'stefano' over 'sthefano' and 'theodoro' over 'theudoro'. In the phrase 'siquidem postuletis, ut ei, quod' (as **Ar** *1*), **Al** gives 'postuletes', preferable to **Ar** *2*, 'postholetis'. An interesting variant in this letter is 'adhiberetur iusta moderatio' (**Al, Ar** *2*) in opposition to 'iustitiae moderatio' (**Ar** *1* [*3, 4*]). Both of these readings make sense, but I am inclined towards the *genitivus identitatis* of 'iustitiae moderatio' as being more typically Leo's style than a simple 'iusta moderatio'. **Al** alone contains the good reading, 'Considerantes enim ...', a *lectio difficilior* in what is a long sentence that undoubtedly caused an early **Ar** scribe to write 'Consideratis enim ...' When the sentence is parsed, it is clear that 'ita ... repperimus' contains the main verb, and it is not like Leo to produce a run-on sentence. Therefore, *nos* should be inferred earlier, and the syntactically preferable participial phrase of **Al** accepted over the second person plural of the **Ar** tradition. Finally, **Al** closes this letter at 'augusto VII et Abieno', omitting the rest of the consular date, 'uiris clarissimis consulibus', and the **Ar** sentence saying that Pope Symmachus confirmed Leo's ruling in the consulate of Probus. We can now postulate the following **Al-Ar** stemma:

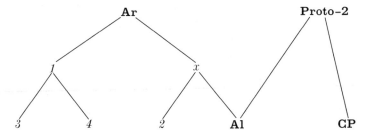

3.2.p. *Collectio Remensis*[328] (**Re**)

3.2.p.i. Dating and context

This canonical collection from the second half of the sixth century includes eight decretals of Leo as well as the *Tome*: *Epp.* 14, 12, 28, 15, 16, 159, 1, 2, 167.[329] As an early witness to Leo's let-

---

[328] Not included by the Ballerini or Jasper; for a list of manuscripts and bibliography, see Kéry 1999, 50.

[329] For a description of the whole collection, see Wurm 1939, 287–92.

ters that was not investigated by the Ballerini, *Remensis* is an important corpus of documents. The collection is chronologically arranged and divided by conciliar canons and decretals. Its place of origin seems to be Gaul, although the collection of Leo's letters came there from Italy. Nonetheless, there is no reason to doubt its Gallic origin, borne out by various Gallic items included therein, such as the letter 'TEMP(O)R(E) SIGISMUNDI REGIS / Ab epis in urbe lugdunum [*sic*]' from a synod in Lyons during the reign of the Burgundian King Sigismund (*d.* 524).

3.2.p.ii. Manuscript

It is in the following manuscript:

> Berlin, Staatsbibliothek Preußischer Kulturbesitz, Phill. 1743 (VIII2/2), written at Bourges according to Kéry or Reims according to CLA 8.[330] The manuscript is disordered; Leo's letters are the twelfth through twentieth items in the contents, following the order listed above; in that order, they are in the following fols: 257[r]–265[r] (*Epp.* 14 and part of 12), 208[v]–239[r] (the rest of *Ep.* 12 to the end). This single-column manuscript is written in Luxeuil script, which, according to Bischoff, was in use 'until the time of Boniface',[331] who died in 754; its rubrics are uncials. This is a manuscript where the scribe writes 'with an accent', if you will; we see such spellings as 'nubi' for 'noui', as well as various other switches of *u* for *o* and *o* for *u*. On many occasions, *i* and *e* are also switched.

3.2.p.iii. Manuscript relations

The primary relationship **Re** shares is with **Te** and **Di**, the former older than it, the latter younger. *Epp.* 15, 16, 159, 1, and 2 are shared in the same order by all three of these collections; this is the aforementioned **proto-3**.[332] **Re** adds 14, 12, and 28 to the beginning, while **Te** adds 167, 12, and 28. *Epp.* 12 and 28 are not included in this proto-collection because they are two letters that

---

[330] Kéry 1999, 50; CLA 8.1060; Bischoff 1998–2014, 1.419a. It was written at the same centre as Hague 10 B 4; Paris, lat. 2034; and Cassel MS Theol. 4° 10 81141, according to CLA 8.1060.

[331] Bischoff 1990, 104.

[332] See the Appendix for a list and description of the proto-collections.

very frequently circulate independently of the rest of the corpus. Furthermore, if they were part of the original question, we would need to postulate that **Di** has somehow lost *Ep.* 28 and ask why it moves *Ep.* 12. Ockham's rasor thus cuts these two off the beginning of **proto-3**, although perhaps they were originally part of it in an earlier recension available to the collectors of **Te** and **Re**, but not of **Di**; perhaps the compiler of **Di** had no interest in *Ep.* 28 and found himself moving *Ep.* 12, anyway. At the end of **proto-3**, **Re** has appended *Ep.* 167 with **Q** *capitula*. **Di**, on the other hand, adds *Ep.* 12 at the end of **proto-3**, but 167 at a later point in the manuscript. Variants suggest, however, that **Di** and **Re** have a common source for *Ep* 167. The table below sets out selected variants for *Epp.* 16, 159, 1, and 2.

Var., *Ep.*	*Collectio Remensis*	Ballerini text (control)	Significance
1, 16. Pr.	om. *episcopus* in incipit	Leo *episcopus*	Shared variant **Re, Te, Di, D, V**
3, 16.1	*accepistis*	*accipitis*	Error **Di**
4, 16.1	beati *apostoli petri* sedes	beati *petri apostoli* (**Di**)	Shared variant **Re, Te, D, V**
5, 16.1	*Vt*	*Et* licet uix	Shared variant **Re, Te, Di, D** *a*
6, 16.2	om. *uenerantur*	mystica munerum oblatione *ueneran-tur* (**Di**)	Omission aside, agreement **Re** and **Di** against **Te**
7, 16.2	gallileam *ortuo persecutore*	galilaeam *persecutore mortuo*	Missing *m* aside, shared variant **R** and **Te** (**Di** om. *mortuo*) with **D, V**
8, 16.2	quod *quaerebatis me*	quod *me quaerebatis*	Shared variant **Re, Te, Di, D, V**
9, 16.2	om. *his quae* and *sunt*	quod in *his quae* patris mei *sunt* oportet (**Te?**)	Shared variant **Re, D** against **Di** ('in *domo* patris')
10, 16.2	*quicquid*	sed aliter *quidque*	Variant against **Di** (quaeque), **D** *c* (quoque)
11, 16.2	om. *posse*	ad tempus *posse* pertinere	Shared variant **Re, Te, V**

Var., *Ep.*	*Collectio Remensis*	Ballerini text (control)	Significance
12, 16.2	*discritio*	rationabilis seruanda *distinctio*	Shared variant **Re, Di**, similar to **D, Te, V** (*districtio*)
13, 16.3	*quod*	totumque *quidquid* in illo	Shared variant **Re, Te, Di, D** *a*, **D–b**
14, 159. Pr.	om. *episcopus*	Leo *episcopus* Nicetae	Shared variant **Re, Te, Di, D, D–b**
15, 159. Pr.	om. *salutem*	episcopo Aquiliensi *salutem*	Shared variant **Re, Di**
16, 159. Pr.	Includes 'a nobis'	de his *a nobis* auctoritatem	Omission of *a nobis* in **Di, Te, D, Q**
17, 159.1	*quae uerus proprius*	*quae cum uiros proprios*	Shared variant **Re, Di** against **Te**
18, 159.1	*Et in* aliorum	liberandos. *Ad* aliorum	Shared variant **Re, Di, D, Q**
19, 159.5	*consultacioni* (this reading in agreement with Ballerini, but not certain other collections)	*consultationi* (**D** *c*, **Q**)	Against **Di** ('consolatione'); **Te, D** *a*, **V** ('consulationis')
20, 159.6	similiter dilectio tua	dilectio tua similiter	Shared variant **Re, Te, D, V, Q**
21, 159.6	ea *est* custodienda	ea custodienda *est*	Shared variant **Re, Te, Q**
22, 159.6	*aegritudinum respicientes*	*aegritudinis respiciens* necessitates	Shared variant **Re, Te, D**
23, 159.7	cum baptizati *ante*	cum *antea* baptizati	Shared variant **Re, Te, V, Q**
24, 159.7	*sancti spiritus* inuocatione	sola inuocatione *Spiritus Sancti* (**Q**)	Shared variant **Re, Te, D** *a*, **V**
25, 159.7 (Eph. 4:5)	*deus*	Unus *Dominus*, una fides (Vulgate, **D** *a*, **V, Q**)	Shared error Re, Te, D c, D-b, S-ga h due to nomina sacra ('ds' and 'dns'); Vulgate and Greek give 'Dominus'/ 'κύριος'

Var., *Ep.*	*Collectio Remensis*	Ballerini text (control)	Significance
26, 159.7	DAT XV kal	Data *xii* kal (**D–b**, **Q** *p*)	Shared variant, probably error **R**, **Te**, **Di**
27 (**Sa** 22), 1.1	*pie*	nostrorum *ne* insontibus	Error **Re**
28 (**Sa** 23), 1.1	*cedeturus*	quidem *conceditur* usurpasse	Errors Re: 'ceditur' for 'conceditur' and dittography
29 (**Sa** 25), 1.1	*receptionem*	in talium *receptione* seruassent	Shared error **Re**, **Sa** *sl c*
30 (**Sa** 26), 1.2	*hoc*	*hac* nostri auctoritate	Shared error **Re**, **Sa** *sl r k*
31 (**Sa** 27), 1.2	*uel*	siue diaconi *siue* cuiuscumque	Common variant **Re, Sa**
32 (**Sa** 29), 1.2	*quod*	*quidquid* in doctrina	Common variant **Re, Sa**
33 (**Sa** 33), 1.5	om. *nec*	diaconatus ordine *nec* in subsequenti	Error **Re**
34 (**Sa** 34), 1.5	*ubi ubi*	deprauatus *ubi* ordinatus	Common variant **Re, Sa** *sl c*
35 (**Sa** 37), 2.1	*uel* cuiuslibet ordinis	*siue alii* cuiuslibet	Shared variant **Re, Sa**
36 (**Sa** 38), 2.2	*illa*	*illam* canonum constitutionem	Shared error **Re**, **Sa** *sl r c*
37 (**Sa** 39), 2.2	*cum quod*	*quod cum* recte	Shared error **R**, **Sa** *k*
38 (**Sa** 41), 2.2	*incolumitate*	ad totius ecclesiae *incolumitatem*	Shared error **Re**, **Sa** *sl c k*

What the table shows is that, while **Re**, **Te**, and **Di** are certainly related, none seems to be descended from any of the others. **Re** frequently agrees with both of the others, but sometimes only **Te**, sometimes only **Di**. Therefore, an agreement between two of them can be assumed to be the reading of **proto-3**. Furthermore, the Italian nature of the text of Leo letters is confirmed by the frequent agreements with other collections such as **D**, **Sa**, and **V**.

Ep. 167 is not part of that proto-collection, so it is treated separately. The most important feature of this letter, besides using the **Q** *capitula*, is the presence of chapter XVI, 'De his qui <i>am consegrate sunt si postea nupserint', a logical continuation of XV, 'De puellis qui alequandio in habito religioso fuerint non tamen consegrate si post nupserint'. This chapter is not present in the earliest collections, **Q, D, Te, V, Sa**, but it is present in **S**, dating to the 680s and **Di** from the 630s. Thus, its appearance in **Re**, assuming it is original to the manuscript's exemplar and therefore the collection, is its earliest attestation. Furthermore, its presence here but not in **Te** bolsters my argument that **Te** is not the source for **Re**, especially combined with the different placement of this letter in the collection. Moreover, **Re** is not likely to be the source for **Di** even though they both share this extra chapter, because **Di** separates it from the rest of the letters with a number of intervening items. All three of these collections contain *Epp.* 12, 28, and 167 at some point. Yet the texts as they provide them do not always line up, nor are the letters always included in the same place in the collection. These are three of Leo's longest letters, and each of them has something important to say to the wider community—*Ep.* 12 about the ordination of bishops, *Ep.* 28 about Christology, and *Ep.* 167 about various matters of canon law. Given their length and usefulness, it is not unlikely that they were circulating independently in the fifth through sixth centuries and even into the seventh. As a result, we gain the differing versions of the letters, especially *Epp.* 12 and 167—and amongst the versions of the letters thus gained we acquire a version of *Ep.* 167 with 21 chapters, the sixteenth of which is not original to Leo but likely a marginal annotation added to a copy to aid the curious reader. The rest of **Re**'s variants for *Ep.* 167 are laid out in the following table with numeration continuing from the above; variants resulting from **Re**'s orthography are omitted. Variants 39–80 are an exhaustive tabulation of the *Praefatio*, whereas 81 to the end are comparisons with variants from **Sa** and **Q**.

Var., *Ep.*	*Collectio Remensis*	Ballerini text (control)	Significance
39, 167	HAEC EPI-STOLA PAPAE LIONIS AD RVSTI\C/IO EPO NARBONENSE DIRECTA		

Var., *Ep.*	*Collectio Remensis*	Ballerini text (control)	Significance
40, 167. Pr.	om. inscription		
41, 167. Pr.	*spacia*	ita *patientiae* legentes	Error **Re**
42, 167. Pr.	*conpetra*	allegatione *con-cepta*	Error **Re**
43, 167. Pr.	*auctionis suae*	presbyteris *actionis tuae*	Errors **Re**
44, 167. Pr.	*esse* quaerimu-niam	iustam *superesse* querimoniam	Error **Re**
45, 167. Pr.	*ora statim*	charitatis *hortatu*, ut	Error **Re**
46, 167. Pr.	*tandem egresi*	ut *sanandis aegris* spiritalem	Error **Re**
47, 167. Pr.	*stodeas* adhibere; om. *debeas*	spiritalem adhibere *debeas*	Error **Re**, corruption of *debeas*, which would have preceded 'adhibere' in the original
48, 167. Pr.	*scripturam*	dicente *Scriptura*:	Error **Re**
49, 167. Pr.	*zelo pudicitiam*	qui *pudicitiae zelo*	Variant **Re** with an error
50, 167.Pr.	*uacatione*	ut *uacationem* ab episcopatus	Error **Re**
51, 167. Pr.	*optare*	laboribus *praeoptare* te dicas	Error **Re**
52, 167. Pr.	om. *atque otio*	silentio *atque otio* uitam	Error **Re**
53, 167. Pr.	*agire*	uitam *degere*, quam	Variant **Re** (assuming 'agire' misspelled 'agere', otherwise error)
54, 167. Pr.	om. *Nam ... praed-icationem*	patientiae? *Nam secundum apostolicam praedicationem*, omnes	Error **Re**

Var., *Ep.*	*Collectio Remensis*	Ballerini text (control)	Significance
55, 167. Pr. (2 Tim. 3:12)	*persecutione*	uiuere *persecutionem* patientur (Vulgate)	Error **Re** (elsewhere **Re** gives ablative for accusative ending in -*em*)
56, 167. Pr.	*tanto*	in eo *tantum* computanda	Error **Re**
57, 167. Pr.	om. *contra*	quod *contra* Christianam	Error **Re**
58, 167. Pr.	*negutia*	periculis *nec otia* careant	Error **Re**
59, 167. Pr.	*custodiet ouis*	luporum *oves custodiet*	Variant **Re**
60, 167. Pr.	*quieretis*	amor *quietis* abducat?	Error **Re**
61, 167. Pr.	tenenda *iustitiae* benigne	tenenda *est iustitia, et* benigne	Errors **Re**
62, 167. Pr.	*haberentur*	Odio *habeantur* peccata	Variant **Re**
63, 167. Pr.	*tolerint*	tumidi, *tolerentur* infirmi	Error **Re**
64, 167. Pr.	om. *in peccatis*	quod *in peccatis* seuerius	Error **Re**
65, 167. Pr.	*seuenienter*	non *saeuientis* plectatur	Error **Re**
66, 167. Pr.	*animus*	plectatur *animo*, sed medentis	Error **Re**
67, 167. Pr.	*sit* uirebus *resistendum*	propriis *sit* uiribus *resistendo*	Variant **Re**
68, 167. Pr.	om. *inquit*	Ecce ego, *inquit*, uobiscum	Error **Re**
69, 167. Pr.	*dubitacione*	sine *dubio*	Variant **Re**
70, 167. Pr.	om. *nullis ... electioni*	sunt, *nullis debemus scandalis infirmari, ne electioni* Dei uideamur	Error **Re**
71, 167. Pr.	sunt *deo* uedeamur	As above	Error resulting from Var. 70

Var., *Ep.*	*Collectio Remensis*	Ballerini text (control)	Significance
72, 167. Pr.	om. *de singulis*	quaereretur *de singulis*, si nobis	Error **Re**
73, 167. Pr.	*conspectu tui*	nobis *tui conspectus* copia	Error **Re**, derived from word-order variant
74, 167. Pr.	*quadam*	cum *quaedam* interrogationes	Error **Re**
75, 167. Pr.	si *quod*	Quia si*cut* quaedam	Error **Re**
76, 167. Pr.	*possit*	nulla *possunt* ratione conuelli	Variant **Re**
77, 167. Pr.	*ha* multa	*ita* multa sunt	Error **Re**
78, 167. Pr.	*ut*	quae *aut* pro consideratione	Error **Re**
79, 167. Pr.	*necessitatem*	pro *necessitate* rerum	Error **Re**
80, 167. Pr.	incipiunt risponsa secundum communiturium consolencis		
81, 167.2	*hii*	consecrati, *ii* pro	Common variant **Re, Q**
82, 167.3	*orauit* pro *illum*	quis *orabit* pro *illo*	Common variant **Re, Q** Error **Re**
83, 167.2	om. *altaris*	eadem est ministris *altaris* quae	Error **Re**
84, 167.3	*cessint*	connubiorum, et *cesset* opera	Common error **Re, Q**
85, 167.4	*uiro coniuncta*	mulier *iuncta uiro*	Variant **Re**, similar to **Q** (*uiro iuncta*)
86, 167.5–6	Division of chh. 5 and 6 after 'aliud concubina', not after 'non fuerunt'		Agreement **Re, Q**
87, 167.10	om. *a*	oportet *a* multis etiam licitis	Common error **Re, Sa**

Var., *Ep.*	*Collectio Remensis*	Ballerini text (control)	Significance
88, 167.10 (1 Cor. 6:12 & 10:23)	om. *mihi* (1 Cor. 10:23)	omnia *mihi* licent (1 Cor. 6:12)	Common variant **Re, Sa**
89, 167.11 *Cap.*	*paenitenciam*	in *poenitentia* uel	Common variant (accusative vs ablative) **Re, Q**
90, 167.12	*omnino est*	Contarium *est omnino*	Common variant **Re, Q**
91, 167.13	om. *mortis*	aut metu *mortis*, aut	Common error **Re, Q, Sa**
92, 167.15 *Cap.*	*post*	si *postea* nupserint	Common error **Re, Q**
93, 167.17	si *eam hoc*	si *hoc etiam*	Error **Re**, based on variant **Q**
94, 167.19 *Cap.*	*gentibus*	a *gentilibus* capti sunt	Common variant **Re, Q**

The significance of this table is twofold. First, it is evident that **Re** contributes a great many of its own errors. Second, here as elsewhere, it contains many variants common to other Italian collections. However, its lack of many of the variants of **Sa** and **Q** against which it was collated, demonstrate that its text of *Ep.* 167 is independent of theirs.

3.2.q. *Collectio Coloniensis*[333] (**K**)

3.2.q.i. Dating and context

Dating from around 600, **K** includes seven of Leo's letters, none of which are decretals: 66 [followed by 12 non-Leo items], 22, 28, 103, 31, 35, 59, and 165. This collection includes the set of the letters found in **C** and **P** which I termed **proto–1** above at 3.2.j.i,

---

[333] This collection not listed by the Ballerini or Jalland. See Jasper 2001, 44–45, and Kéry 1999, 44–45. A description of the earlier portion (items 15–52) of the decretal collection is in Wurm 1939, 276–78.

missing out *Ep.* 139.[334] **K** was most likely compiled in Gaul, not only because of its relationship with other Gallic collections but also because of the presence of canonical material from Gaul in the collection beyond Leo.

3.2.q.ii. Manuscript

It exists in one manuscript:

> Cologne, Erzbischöfliche Diözesan- und Dombibliothek, 212 (olim Darmstadt 2326) (*c.* 600), provenance in Cologne since eighth/ninth centuries.[335] In agreement with CLA 8.1162, A. von Euw's description of the manuscript on the digitisation's website argues that it must be before 604 because it cites no pope later than Gregory I. He also argues, based on the decoration and bookhand, that it was probably produced in southern Gaul before reaching Cologne. Given its relationship with **Ar** and **Al** in the Leonine corpus, this point of origin makes sense. It is written in a single column in half-uncials and uncials with red *capitula* for letter headings but no chapter divisions. Much of the rubrication is flaking off, making decipherment difficult; infrared would undoubtedly help with this.

The table of contents which is written in paired colonnaded arches on two of the unnumbered folios that start the volume, listed in the digitisation as V_4-V_5, include as item XL<I> 'It epist papae leonis', which is followed by the 12 non-Leonine items, and on V_6 we read:

> LIII definitionis synodi aduersus eutichen
>
> LIIII epist flauiani epi constantinopolitani ad leonem urbis romae epm
>
> LV epist leonis epi ad flauianum epm
>
> LVI epist papae leonis ad epis p(ro) gallia constitutis
>
> LVII epist papae leonis ad leonem imp contra eutichen
>
> LVIII regulae siue definitionis expositae ab epis cl
>
> LVIIII epist papae leonis ad pulche agost
>
> [col. 2]
>
> LX eiusd ad iulianum epm

---

[334] See the Appendix for a list and description of the proto-collections.

[335] CLA 8.1162; Bischoff 1998–2014, 1.1946a. This manuscript is urn:nbn:de:hbz:kn28-3-937. Accessed 21 September 2021.

LXI eiusd papae leonis ad constantinopolitanus ciues

LXII can(on) anquiritani

LXIII can(on) caesariensis

LXIIII can(on) grangensis

Items LV through LXX have rubricated numbers but no items written opposite. *Ep.* 66 is on 122^v–123^v, and the later block of letters on 136^r–159^r.

3.2.q.iii. Manuscript relations

Ep. 66 is shared by **K** only with **Ar** and **Al**. In the list of recipients, **K** gives 'sthefano' and 'theudoro' in agreement with **Ar** *2* against 'stefano'/'stephano' and 'theodoro' of **Ar** *1* and **Al**. It also agrees with **Ar** *2* in the spelling 'regolinus' against **Ar** *1* and **Al** 'regulinus'. It further agrees with **Ar** *2* in 'Vasensis antistetis' against **Ar** *1* and **Al** 'antestitis'; and in 'uero ciuitatis' against their 'ciuitates'. **K** gives 'temperantiam ita' with **Ar** *2* and **Al** against **Ar** *1* 'temperantia'—**Al** could easily have emended the text. Another **Ar** *2* spelling in **K** is 'stodiosum caritatis' against **Ar** *1* and **Al** 'studiosum'. Although small, these variants demonstrate that **K** drew its text of *Ep.* 66 from a copy of **Ar** that is related to *2*, not to *1-3-4* or **Al**.

The main body of Leo's letters herein begins at fol. 136^r with the same incipit for *Ep.* 22 as **C** and **P**: 'INCP EPISTVLA FLA-VIANI EPI / CONSTANTINOPOLITANI AD LEONEM / urbis romae episcupum'. Unfortunately, the salutation is rubricated, and the aforementioned flaking has made it illegible, so we cannot say whether **K** writes, 'amabili' with **CP** against 'amacissimo' in the Ballerini. Besides those in the table at 3.2.k, **K** and **C** demonstrate the following shared variants:

Var., *Ep.*	**C** and **K**	Schwartz (control)	Significance
1, 28.2	om. *se* (**K**)	totam *se* reparando (**C**)	Error **K** haplography?
2, 28.2	*possumus* (**K**) *possimus* (**C**)	enim superare *possemus*	Variants **C**, **K**
3, 28.2 (Is. 9:6)	angelus *dei* (**K**) angelus *admirabilis* deus (**C**^{2})	angelus *deus* (**C**^{1}, Vulgate)	Error **K**

Var., *Ep.*	C and K	Schwartz (control)	Significance
4, 28.4	*desinentibus* (K)	non *desidentibus* ambulare (C)	Error K
5, 28.5	*utramque naturam* (C)	in *utraque natura* (K)	Error C
6, 28.6	Dat in dieb iuniis (K) om. date (C¹) d e in die id iuniis (C²)	DAT ID IVN	Error K Error C²
7, 28.6	asterio et proto-gene uucc conss (K) astorgo et pro-tagene uc conssb (C²)	ASTVURIO ET PROTOGENE VV CC CONSS	Variant spelling K Completely differ-ent name C²

What we see from the *Epp.* 22 and 28 variants from these two tables is that **K** contains most of the **C** variants. When **K** intro-duces an error, however, the error is not derived from a **C** variant. Furthermore, **K** does not persist in all of **C**'s errors. Combining these facts concerning the variants with the differences in letter selection, it can now be said with certainty that **K** and **C** have a common descendent for *Epp.* 22, 28, 103, 31, 35, 59, and 165, but that neither is the other's descendent.

A proposed stemma for **K**, then, would be:

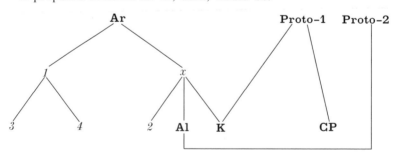

3.2.r. Collectio Sancti Mauri (M)

3.2.r.i. Dating and Context

The origin of this collection is the later sixth century, based upon the fact that its original papal catalogue was compiled in two parts, up to Felix IV (*d.* 530) and then up Pelagius II (*d.* 590), although, since its earliest manuscript is from the eighth century, it has initially been extended to Hadrian I (*d.* 795) with later additions up to Leo III (*d.* 816).[336] Its collection of papal letters, not only those of Leo, seems idiosyncratic, in terms both of the selection and of the order.[337] After canons of synods, the collection of papal letters begins with Leo, *Epp.* 168 and 159, then Celestine I to the bishops of Apulia and Calabria (JK 371); Zosimus to Hesychius of Salona (JK 339); Symmachus to Caesarius of Arles (JK 764); Innocent I to bishops gathered at Toulouse (JK 292); Innocent I to Exsuperius of Toulouse (JK 293); Siricius to Himerius of Tarragona (JK 255); and Celestine I to the bishops of Viennensis and Narbonnensis (JK 369). Although some of the pre-Leo letters are included in the *Epistulae decretales* and *Canones Urbicani*, the order and selection, when considered alongside other inclusions, such as the two Leo letters and the letter of Symmachus, point away from a connection with those collections, although, like them, it probably originated in Gaul. Moreover, its textual similarities run closer to **Q** and **Sa** than any other collection.[338] Older scholarship tried the impossible, arguing different locations for its compilation;[339] we shall never know. At a certain level, we should take very seriously Rosamond McKitterick's arguments about dating these, even if we think they are pre-Carolingian, at least in terms of the importance of them in their actual manuscripts, which makes this a collection from the Carolingian age worthy of consideration in that context, not only sixth-century Gaul.

3.2.r.ii. Manuscripts

This collection exists in three manuscripts:

> *h* = The Hague, Museum Meermanno, 9 (MS 10 B 4) (saec. VIII).[340]
> Caroline minuscule, from northern France; palaeographically

---

[336] Cf. Maassen 1870, 614.

[337] For a full description of the papal letter collection, See Wurm 1939, 292–93; cf. Maassen 1870, 613–24, for a description of the whole collection.

[338] Wurm 1939, 98. The online catalogue of Medieval Manuscripts in Dutch Collections claims it is an abbreviation of **D**, but I have seen no evidence for this. See http://www.mmdc.nl/static/site/search/detail.html?recordId = 10463 Accessed 21 September 2021.

[339] The argument for Narbonne is in Duchesne 1907, 144, and for Arles in Turner 1916, 238.

[340] CLA 10.1572a.

related to Berlin, Staatsbibliothek Preußischer Kulturbesitz, Phill. 1743; Paris, lat. 2034; and Cassel MS Theol. 4° 10 81141.

e = Vat. Reg. lat. 1127 (saec. IX).[341] The manuscript is written in two columns in Caroline minuscule. After a table of kindred and affinity, the canonical collection begins on 4^v. Leo's letters are on fols 131^r–133^r, followed by a series of letters by earlier popes.

f = Paris lat. 1451 (saec. IX).[342] Caroline minuscule from 800–16; from the region of Tours. As with *e*, *f* begins with a table of kindred and affinity, the collection beginning on fol. 2^r. Leo's letters are on fols 95^r–96^v. The papal catalogue ends with Pelagius II (16^r), thus tightening the origins of the collection to the sixth century.

3.2.r.iii. Manuscript Relations

Both **M** *e* and *f* are descendants of *h*. For example, they include the interlinear 'nestorius eps', written above 'nectarius eps' in *h*, alongside 'nectarius eps' in the account of the 381 Council of Constantinople.[343] Moreover, the later two manuscripts both demonstrate confusion at the same point of *h* where several folios are added and damage done to the original text.[344]

3.2.s. *Collectio Vetus Gallica*[345]

3.2.s.i. Dating and context

This canonical collection was compiled in Lyon at some point between 585 and 626–27. It is transmitted through a few different classes of manuscript: the Northern French Subclass and Southern French Subclass, both parts of the wider French Class as well as a Southern German Class.[346] Typically, the *Vetus Gallica* includes the following excerpts from Leo: *Ep.* 14, ch. 3 (ch. XLI, 30g in

---

[341] Bischoff 1998–2014, 3.6764. This manuscript is digitised: https://digi.vatlib.it/view/MSS_Reg.lat.1127 Accessed 21 September 2021.

[342] CLA 5.528; Bischoff 1998–2014, 3.4011. This manuscript is digitised: https://gallica.bnf.fr/ark:/12148/btv1b9066901b Accessed 21 September 2021.

[343] Turner 1930, 3.

[344] Turner 1930, 4–7.

[345] Not listed by Ballerini or Jalland. For a list of manuscripts and bibliography, cf. Kéry 1999, 50–53.

[346] The manuscripts are listed by Kéry 1999, 51–52.

Mordek), *Ep.* 15, and *Ep.* 167, ch. 2 (following **D**, ch. XLI, 30f in Mordek) as well as chh. VIIff. of *Ep.* 167 which follow **Q** for the *capitula* (ch. LXV, unedited by Mordek).

3.2.s.ii. Manuscripts

Given how little Leo material is found in the collection and the vast range of manuscripts, combined with Mordek's edition in *Kirchenrecht und Reform im Frankreich*,[347] prudence led me to examine only two manuscripts of the *Vetus Gallica* myself:[348]

> Paris, lat. 1603 (saec. VIII/IX), and early Caroline minuscule from northeastern France and provenance of Saint-Amand;[349] of the Northern French Subclass. *Ep.* 167, beginning at *Cap.* VII, 'De his qui in egritudine penitentiam accipiunt, et cum revaluerint, agere eam nolunt', runs fols 71ᵛ–74ᵛ.

> Stuttgart, Württembergische Landesbibliothek, HB.VI.109 (IX1/4 saec.) from southwestern Germany, with provenance of Constance, cathedral chapter, then Weingarten; of the Northern French Subclass.[350] This manuscript includes the same selection from *Ep.* 167, fols 90ᵛ–94ᵛ.

Because of the multiplicity of versions of *Vetus Gallica*, I consulted a transcription of a third manuscript that represents a completely different redaction from that of the two manuscripts listed above,[351] called S₁ by Mordek and relying heavily upon **D**.[352] It is worth a brief mention if only because of the varying contents of this collection and the difficulties it would present to a reconstruction of Leo's text if not for the various other manuscripts and collections. This manuscript is:

> Stuttgart, Württembergische Landesbibliothek, HB.VI.113 (saec. VIIIᵉˣ), fols 92ᵛ–195ᵛ; it is writtten in Rhaetian minuscule.[353]

---

[347] Mordek 1975, 343–617.

[348] MSS as described in Kéry 1999, 51–52.

[349] CLA 5.531; Bischoff 1998–2014, 3.4035.

[350] Bischoff 1998–2014, 3.6073.

[351] The transcription was made by Michael D. Elliot for the Carolingian Canon Law Project and formerly available online. This MS is digitised: http://digital.wlb-stuttgart.de/purl/bsz343517760. Accessed 21 September 2021.

[352] Mordek 1975, 229.

[353] For a description of this manuscript's contents, see ibid., 229–37. See also CLA 9.1360; Bischoff 1998–2014, 3.6074.

Leo appears in this redaction of the collection at fols 184^r–185^r (*Ep.* 9, chh. 1, 2), 185^r–186^r (*Ep.* 159, chh. 1–4), and 189^v–190^r (*Ep.* 167, chh. 4–6).

As with other systematic collections, such as that of Cresconius, the *Vetus Gallica* is a collection to be aware of, but will not be taken into account in the edition since it is not a letter collection proper and since so many manuscripts and collections of such early date exist that *do* contain proper letter collections. The traces of Leo's letters in collections such as *Vetus Gallica* tend to be few, and the likelihood of one of these collections maintaining a true original reading or true conjecture not found elsewhere is extremely slim.

3.2.t. *Epitome Hispana* (*Hispanico*)[354]

3.2.t.i. Dating and Context

The *Epitome Hispana* is a chronological collection of excerpts made in the early 600s, its most recent text from the Council of Huesca of 598. After canons drawn from earlier collections, such as the *Capitula Martini*, and from conciliar collections, the *Epitome Hispana* gives a series of excerpts from papal letters from Clement, Siricius, Innocent I, Zosimus, Boniface I, Celestine I, Leo I, Gelasius I, Felix III, and Vigilius, ending with a letter from Jerome to Patroclus. It contains portions of the following eleven of Leo's letters: 14, 12, 167, 16, 159, 4, 108, 166, 168, 9, 15. In addition, Canon 2.32.1 is a letter of Leo III to Alcuin ('Ternam mersionem'), misinscribed as 'Ex epistola leonis pp ad balconium', that is, to Balconius who was Bishop of Braga during Leo the Great's tenure as Bishop of Rome, and who was involved in anti-Priscillianist activity. This collection was used from an early time in Gaul, northern and central Italy, and southern Germany as evidenced by the manuscripts listed below.

Martínez Díez produced an edition in 1962,[355] the goal of which, as he wrote in his historical and critical discussion of 1961, was to

---

[354] Fowler-Magerl 2005, 34–36; Kéry 1999, 57–60.

[355] Martínez Díez, 'El Epítome Hispánico. Una colección canónica Española del siglo VII', in *Miscelanea Comillas* 37.2 (1962), 322–466.

provide evidence for the *Epitome* as one of the sources for the *Collectio Hispana*, the national collection of Spain; for him, the value of the *Epitome* was found in the *Collectio*.[356] For the text critic of the *Epitome*'s sources, on the other hand, its main value lies in precisely the opposite direction. It provides us with a Spanish collection from the turn of the seventh century that is an important textual witness to its sources; it is several decades after the earliest collections, but a century or more before the major collections of the Carolingian era. For these reasons, it is worth examining as a witness to the text of Leo's letters.

3.2.t.ii. Manuscripts

The *Epitome Hispana* exists in the following manuscripts, many of them fragmentary:[357]

Verona, Biblioteca Capitolare LXI (59) (saec. VII/VIII).[358]

Lucca, Biblioteca Capitolare Feliniana, 490 (*c.* 800), fols 288^r–309.[359]

Copenhagen, Kongelike Bibliothek, Ny Kgl. Saml. 58 8° (shortly after 731), fols 52^r–69^v, from Gaul in a book hand with Spanish influence, called Visigothic by CLA 10, with provenance in Regensburg.[360]

Munich, Bayerische Staatsbibliothek, Clm 14468. This manuscript was written in 821 under Abbot Baturich in Regensburg; it is a copy of the Copenhagen manuscript.[361]

Paris, Bibliothèque nationale, Collection Baluze 270 (saec. IX), fols 177^r–178^v + Lyon Bibliothèque de la ville, 788, fols 100^r–101^v (saec. IX).[362]

Vat. Lat. 5751 (saec. X), fols 31^r–41^v, from northern Italy, once a possession of monastery of Bobbio, is an excerpt of the *Epitome*.

---

[356] Martínez Díez 1961, 14.

[357] See Kéry 1999, 58–59.

[358] CLA 4.511.

[359] CLA 3.303d. Discussed above at 3.2.e.ii, MS **Sa** 1.

[360] CLA 10.1568.

[361] As demonstrated by Fowler-Magerl 2005, 35. See Bischoff 1998–2014, 2.3208.

[362] Bischoff 1998–2014, 3.3944 + 2.2588.

3.2.u. *Collectio Hispana*[363] (**S**)

3.2.u.i. Dating and context

The *Collectio Hispana* is an important source for both the wider ecclesiastical and secular history and the history of canon law in Visigothic Spain. No post-Roman kingdom left behind as extensive a body of canonical documents as this. At its broadest extent, this canonical collection combines the canons of Greek councils, African councils, 'ecumenical' councils, Spanish councils, and more alongside an extensive body of papal letters. We are thus given insight into what sorts of documents were considered authorities for discerning canon law in early mediaeval Spain. We can also see the canonical activity of the Spanish church as its bishops gathered together in council. Furthermore, since they were so assiduous in taking *acta* and maintaining them in this collection, the *Collectio Hispana* is a major source for the secular events of Visigothic Spain under Catholic rule, since we have a paucity of narrative sources.[364] The *Collectio Hispana* stands in stark opposition to the catastrophist position on the post-Roman world. While we can certainly agree that fifth- through eighth-century Spain was not a time of perfect rest and quietness, it is a testament to the stability developed by the Visigothic kingdom in the late sixth and seventh centuries that so many church councils were able to meet within its borders—especially since its power was, in many ways and especially at the beginning, decentralised due to the realities of Iberian history and topography.[365] The bulk of the major Visigothic councils begin in 589 with the Third Council of Toledo, when Reccared—the first Nicene-Catholic Visigothic king—officially brought his kingdom into the Catholic Church, after his father Leovigild (*r.* 569–86) had united the vast major-

---

[363] This collection not listed by the Ballerini or Jalland. See ACO 2.3.1 S, p. 2; Martínez Díez 1966, vol. 1; and Kéry 1999, 61–67 for descriptions. Note, however, that ACO 2.3.1 only lists the dogmatic letters and adds *Ep.* 25 between *Epp.* 20 and 23.

[364] See Wickham 2005, 38–39, on the Spanish councils as major historical sources.

[365] For the tension between economic localisation and political centralisation in Visigothic Spain, see ibid., 93–97. A good overview of the Visigothic kingdom in Spain can be found in Wickham 2009, 130–49.

ity of the peninsula. These two unifying events help explain the extraordinary number of synods to follow, up to the 'Eighteenth Council' of Toledo in the early 700s (for which no *acta* or canons exist),[366] under a decade before the Islamic conquest.

S may originally have been edited by Isidore of Seville, according to Martínez Díez.[367] Its oldest recension dates from after the Fourth Council of Toledo in 633, and the form contained in most of the manuscripts, the *Vulgata*, covers the Seventeenth Council of Toledo in 694. It was used in the formation of the collections known as the *Hispana Gallica* and *Hispana Gallica Augustodunensis*.[368] It includes the following 39 Leonine letters: 20, 23, 22, 28, 25, 33, 44, 45, 60, 61, 69, 70, 71, 79, 80, 82, 83, 85, 90, 93, 104, 106, 115, 130, 134, 165, 15, 7, 16, 4, 18, 167, 14, 159, 12, 108, 166, 9, and 168.[369] The decretal collection that closes this selection of Leo's letters, from *Ep.* 15 onwards, draws *Epp.* 7–159 from **D**, including many of the **D/D-b** variants throughout, as shall be seen, including the **D** *capitula* in *Ep.* 167 and elsewhere. Their order is almost identical to that of **D**, simply transposing *Ep.* 4 to after 16 instead of before 7. *Ep.* 12 exists here in the *decurtata* version.

The earliest recension, that of *c.* 633 which is possibly edited by Isidore, is known as the Primitive *Hispana* or the *Isidoriana*. This recension does not exist in any manuscripts but can be reconstituted from the lost *Codex Rachionis*, from manuscript W of the Galician tradition of the *Vulgata*,[370] and from Gallic manuscripts that rely on the *Hispana*.[371] This original recension consisted of a preface, index, Greek councils, African councils from a source only

---

[366] The Seventeenth Council of Toledo in 694 is the last for which we have proceedings. See Wickham 2005, 38.

[367] Martínez Díez 1966, 257–70; Munier 1966, 240–41, expresses misgivings on the identification of the compiler as Isidore because Isidore elsewhere seems ignorant of some of its contents. For other scholars who disagree, see Kéry 1999, 61. Part of the argument for Isidore's authorship is the similarity between the introduction to the collection and Isidore, *Etymologiae* 6.16. However, a later author could easily have borrowed from Isidore on this point.

[368] See Jasper 2001, 53–55. Discussed below at 5.2.d-e.

[369] Martínez Díez 1966, 214.

[370] Kéry 1999, 62.

[371] Fournier and Le Bras 1931, vol. 1, 68.

used by the *Hispana*, canons of ten Gallic councils, and fourteen Spanish councils, ending at the Fourth Council of Toledo, which is followed by the *Capitula Martini*, the *Sententiae* attributed to the Council of Agde, and 104 decretals.[372]

The second known recension of the *Hispana* is the *Juliana* recension from after 681. This recension adds eight more Toledan councils from the Fifth Council of Toledo (636) to the Twelfth (681). It falls into two subcategories, the Gallican and Toletanian. The Gallican subcategory omits the signatures of the bishops from the councils of Agde, Orléans, and Toledo III–XI and reorders the papal letters. This subcategory exists in at least three manuscripts.[373] The second subcategory of the *Juliana* is the Toletanian. This subcategory has varying additions of the Twelfth Council of Toledo and was written before 775.[374]

The third recension—the second which survives—is the *Vulgata*, compiled between 694 and 702; this recension represents the bulk of the manuscripts. It builds on the *Juliana*, adding fourteen councils ending at the Seventeenth Council of Toledo in 694[375] as well as the *Definitio Fidei* of the Sixth Ecumenical Council which took place in Constantinople 680–81; the *Definitio* is the version sent to Spain by Pope Leo II and is followed by five papal letters.[376] The *Vulgata* exists in two subcategories. The first is the Común, which represents most of the manuscripts, including two now lost from Lugo, Carrión de los Condes and San Juan de Peña.[377] The second is the Catalan subcategory.

---

[372] Ibid.

[373] Rome, Biblioteca Vallicelliana, D.18 (saec. X) which is also classified as of the *Collectio Hispana Gallica* (see Kéry 1999, 67); Vat. Pal. lat. 575 (saec. IX–X) of unknown provenance, but formerly at the library of the church St Martin at Mainz according to fol. 3ʳ (MS V in Martínez Díez), which does not include Leo; and Vienna, Österreichische Nationalbibliothek, lat. 411 (iur. can. 41) (saec. VIII–IX), also categorised under *Hispana Gallica* (MS W in Martínez Díez). For full lists of all manuscripts of all recensions, see Kéry 1999, 62–64; Martínez Díez 1966, 11–15.

[374] Kéry 1999, 62.

[375] Kéry 1999, 62.

[376] Fournier and Le Bras 1931, vol. 1, 68.

[377] Kéry 1999, 62.

3.2.u.ii. Manuscripts

3.2.u.ii-a. Vulgata

Manuscripts of the Común recenions of the *Vulgata* that include decretals are:[378]

R = Madrid, Biblioteca Nacional de España, MSS/1872 (olim P.21, Vitrina 14.4), fols 2^r–345^v (XI saec.), known as *Codex of the Biblioteca Regia.*[379]

T = Madrid, Biblioteca Nacional de España, MSS/10041 (olim Toledo XV,16), fols 1^v–237^v, of 1034–1072, with provenance of Cordoba, residing at Toledo since 1455, and known as *Codex Toledanus.*[380]

S = El Escorial, Real Biblioteca de San Lorenzo, e-I-13, fols 1^r–103^v (X–XI saec.), provenance of Cordoba and very fragmentary, known as *Codex Soriensis.*

C = Toledo, Archivo y Biblioteca Capitular, 15–17 (olim Tol. 31,5), fol. 1va-348rb, written 16 May, 1095 ('Iulianus indignus presbiter scripsit; a. 1095, IIII feria, XVII K. Iunius era ICXXXIII'),[381] with provenance of Alcatá de Henares, the purest complete *Vulgata* known as *Codex Complutensis.*

There are also two manuscripts of the Catalan subcategory:

G = Gerona, Archivo de la Santa Iglesia Catedral Basilica, Códice Conciliar, fol. I^r-XXIII^r and 1^r–365^v, known as *Codex Gerundensis.*

U = Seo de Urgel, Biblioteca Capitular, 2005, fols 1^r–290vb (XI^{ex} saec.), with provenance probably from Seo de Urgel, known as *Codex Urgelensis.*

---

[378] The sigla are those of Martínez Díez. Schwartz used R and T in his edition of Leo, ACO 2.3.1, 2; note, however, that the information on these two manuscripts is taken from Kéry 1999, 63.

[379] This manuscript is digitised: http://bdh-rd.bne.es/viewer.vm?id = 0000015460&page = 1 Accessed 21 September 2021.

[380] This manuscript is digitised: http://bdh-rd.bne.es/viewer.vm?id = 0000064759&page = 1 Accessed 21 September 2021.

[381] As transcribed in Kéry 1999, 63.

3.2.u.ii-b. Juliana

The following three *Juliana* manuscripts are those which were consulted in the course of this project:[382]

  e: El Escorial, Real Biblioteca de San Lorenzo, d-I-1, fols 19ᵛ–316ᵛ, written 992–94 with provenance of San Millán de la Cogolla, known as *Codex Emilianus*.[383] According to Guilmain, based on the illuminations, this manuscript is a copy of El Escorial d-I-2, below.[384] However, the illustrations in the Leo portion of the manuscript are not at all the same as in d-I-2; Guilmain says that the illuminator set himself free from slavish copying. This seems correct, since most of the illuminations in this portion of the manuscript are of animals, mermaids, and other fantastic beasts.[385] The question of the illuminations matters as part of the transmission of the manuscript and its copying. The contents of the manuscript nevertheless beginning with excerpts from Isidore of Seville's *Etymologiae*, are the same as d-I-2, confirming that both images and text are copied.

  v: El Escorial, Real Biblioteca de San Lorenzo, d-I-2, fols 20ʳ–238ᵛ and 248–341ʳ, written between 974–76, with provenance of San Martin de Alveda, known as *Codex Albeldensis* or *Vigilanus*— after the first of its scribes, Vigila.[386] This prestige manuscript is written in two columns of 40 lines each in Visigothic minuscule. The chapter numbers are always in the margin, and there are stylistically unique images throughout,[387] most especially of Leo at 277ʳ where he is rebuking Eutyches, 286ᵛ where he addresses Marcian, and 300ᵛ where he stands holding a scroll; 277ᵛ also

---

[382] Schwartz, ACO 2.3.1, 2, lists these manuscripts indiscriminately beside two manuscripts of the *Vulgata*, not making a distinction between the two recensions.

[383] For a description of the manuscript, see Guillermo 1910, 320–68.

[384] Guilmain 1965, 36–37. Guillermo 1916, 534, also notes that the miniatures are copies from d-I-2.

[385] For images of illuminations, see Domínguez Bordona 1930, plates 27, 28, 29b (black and white); and Mentré 1996, plate 37.

[386] A minutely detailed description is available Guillermo 1910, 368–404.

[387] The illumination is not typically Mozarabic in style but exhibits more 'classicism', according to Domínguez Bordona 1930, 19. For examples, see Domínguez Bordona 1930, plates 23–26, 29a (black and white); and Mentré 1996, plate 56 (colour). They are, nonetheless, drawn in a disarming Iberian style.

includes an image of Flavian. Leo's letters begin with an interlace A of Mozarabic style rather than a simple *littera notabilior*.[388]

o: El Escorial, Real Biblioteca de San Lorenzo, e-I-12, fols 1ʳ–323ᵛ
(saec. IX, although Schwartz and the *Catalogo* say X),[389] known
as *Codex Oxomensis*. This is a two-column manuscript of 39 lines
per page in Visigothic minuscule with rubricated majuscule *tituli*. Leo's letters run 240ᵛ–296ʳ, the decretals (*Epp.* 15 to the end)
beginning at fol. 273ᵛ.[390] *Ep.* 16 cuts off partway through at 281ᵛ,
'per fratres et quoepiscopos uestros' and picks up on 282ʳ towards
the end of *Ep.* 4 at, 'Hoc itaque admonitio nostra denuntiat'.

3.2.u.ii-c. Other Hispana manuscripts

Four more Hispana manuscripts are known, the first a collection
of decretals, the other three of uncertain recension:

K = El Escorial, Real Biblioteca de San Lorenzo, o-I-13, fols 1ʳ–136ᵛ
(saec. XV), of unknown provenance.

Florence, Biblioteca Medicea Laurenziana, Ashburnham 1554,
fols 99ᵛ–119ᵛ (saec. XII¹). The *Hispana* portion of this manuscript does not include Leo's letters, although a selection is
included later in the codex, discussed below at 5.3.g.

Oxford, Bodleian Library, Holkham misc. 19 (XIIⁱⁿ saec.), from
Tuscany, probably Pistoia.

Paris, lat. 4280 (XII saec.).[391] On fol. 2ʳᵇ, this manuscript includes
a fragment from Leo, *Ep.* 167.

3.2.u.iii. Manuscript relations

Since *e* is a copy of *v*, the relationship to be assessed is that
between *v* and *o*. My assessment is of selected passages from the
letters at the end of **S**, *Epp.* 15, 7, 16, 4, 18, 167, 14, 159, 12,
108, 166, 9, and 168. First, we immediately encounter some ste-
reotypical Iberian spellings in **S**: 'mobearis' for 'mouearis', 'debo-
tionem' for 'deuotionem', 'uibere' for 'uiuere', 'fabentia' for 'fauen-
tia', etc.; *o* also provides 'habitabit' where *v* and our control text

---

[388] For interlace in *Codex Vigilanus*, see Guilmain 1960, 211–18; at 215, its
interlace is characterised as 'Franco-Insular'.

[389] ACO 2.3.1, 2; Guillermo 1911, 17.

[390] For a minute description of this manuscript, ibid., 17–28.

[391] This manuscript is digitised: https://gallica.bnf.fr/ark:/12148/
btv1b9068478s Accessed 21 September 2021.

give 'habitauit'; and *v* gives 'solba' where *o* and the control give
'solua'. Another **S** orthography but one that is not necessarily Iberian is 'blasfemia' for 'blasphemia'. *v* and *o* tend not to assimilate
prefixes, giving 'inpietas' (*v*), 'conlocarent' (*v*, *o*), conprehendi (*v*,
o), adserunt (*o*), inmersit (*v*, *o*) and so forth—although the rarely
assimilated 'eandem' (*v*, *o*) appears, not 'eamdem'. These variants
are not stemmatically significant, however. Indeed, many are
common enough outside Iberia as to not even signal Spain as the
point of origin.

Turning to the variants, one of the most important differences
between these two manuscripts that emerges from the start is the
addition of proper *capitula* in *v* Ep. 15, whereas *o* uses the first
line of each chapter as a heading as in **Te**, but, since the lines
fall differently, the phrases that serve as *capitula* are not exactly
the same. Unlike a number of other collections, **S** spells Turribius' name 'Turibius' rather than a variant on 'Thoribius'. **S** provides 'per diacoconum tuum' against Ballerini 'diacoconem' and
Te 'diacoonum'. **S** reads 'impietas *ipsa* contagium' *versus* Ballerini
'*ista*'. In a reading that many manuscripts discussed above have
seemingly faltered on, **S** provides, 'qui ab euangelio xpi sub xpi
nomine deuiarunt' against the control's 'qui ab Evangelio sub
Christi nomine deuiarunt'; this is also in contrast to **Te**, **C**, **P**,
'euangelio xpi nomine xpi', with their omission of 'sub' and **Q**,
'euangelio xpi nomine deuiarunt' omitting 'sub' and the second
'xpi'. As the evidence weighs up, it seems that the Ballerini omission of 'Christi' following 'euangelio' in this passage of *Ep.* 15,
Praef., is an error, but their inclusion of 'sub' is not. Also in 15,
Praef., **S** reads 'sequeris tamen xpianorum principum constitu-
tionibus' against 'seueris' (**Q**, **Te**, **C**, **P**, Ballerini). Later in the
same sentence, **S** gives 'ad spiritalem' with **Q** *a p*, **Te**, **C**, and
P, against Ballerini 'spiritale'; this common error is so easily
made that it tells us nothing. In 15.1, *saut-du-même-au-même* does
not cause **S** to omit 'nunc filius' as in a number of other collections. In 15.1, we have two important variants that run counter
to the Ballerini methodology, where *v* gives 'homousione' and *o*
'homo[h\]usyon' against their definitely false Greek 'ὁμοούσιον'.
Although the spellings for this word are many and varied in the
manuscripts,[392] every single one of them makes use of the Latin

---

[392] A few examples: 'homousion' (**Q** *p*, **Te**, **24** *f.*), 'homohosion' (**C**), and
'omohosion' (**P**).

alphabet, not the Greek, according to a common practice of Latin scribes as observed by Aaron Pelttari.[393] Against the Ballerini and the majority early tradition in 15.3, **S** gives 'sermone' at 'Tertii uero capituli sermo designat' robbing 'designat' of its subject. At 15.5, **S** reads 'anima' against Ballerini 'quod animam hominis divinae asserant esse substantiae' (**Te**, **C**); this is an error, since 'asserant' introduces *oratio obliqua*, 'that the soul of a man is of the divine substance'. In case the common heritage of these two manuscripts were not becoming clear already, they concur with **C** in giving the spelling 'subolis' at 15.9 where the Ballerini text provides 'ne illa soboles quae de carnis semine nascitur'.[394] This is a reading based on pronunciation, as could be done by any scribe at any time but is not irrelevant. In 15.10, **S** gives 'in corpore' along with **Te**, **C**, and **P**, against Ballerini 'sine corpore'. The sentence, given as in *v* reads, 'animas que humanis corporibus inseruntur fuisse in corpore'; it makes much better sense to read 'sine' than 'in'—'spirits that had been *without* a body which were inserted in human bodies' is the logical formulation Leo gives here. **S** reads 'est dicere eosdem quod' (**C**, **P**)[395] in 15.13, an inversion against 'eosdem dicere' (Ballerini). In 15.14, **S** gives 'creatur' against 'pro terrena qualitate teneatur' (**Te**, **C**, **P**, Ballerini). At the start of 15.15, **S** writes 'quinto decimi' against 'quinti decimi' (**Te**, **C**, **P**, Ballerini). In 15.17, against the Ballerini and **C**, 'Si autem aliquid, quod absit, obstiterit', **S** gives 'obstiterint' in error.

The independent variants of *v* are as follows. Further in 15, *Praef.*, *v* omits 'que' in 'omnemque coniugiorum copulam solui' (*o*; Ballerini). In 15.1, *v* writes, 'quia patris, et filii' rather than 'qui' (*o*; **Te**, **C**, **P**, Ballerini); *v* also gives 'procedit' for 'processit' (*o*; **Q**, **Te**, **C**, **P**, Ballerini), a simple but clear error. A variant that is most likely wrong is the use of 'at' by *v* against the majority 'sed'

---

[393] Pelttari 2011 observes that Augustine wrote Greek in Latin script, visible in contemporary and near-contemporary manuscripts (464–68); based on the manuscript evidence Macrobius, who wrote Greek phrases in Greek script, seems to have been inconsistent as to which alphabet he used for individual words (471–76); and Ausonius similarly sometimes wrote individual Greek words in Latin, sometimes in Greek script (476–80). Modern editors such as the Ballerini, on the other hand, have usually printed Greek words in Greek script, even when the entire manuscript tradition is against them.

[394] Cf. **Te**, **P** 'sobolis'.

[395] **Te** *om.* 'dicere'.

(*o*; **Q**, **Te**, **C**, **P**, Ballerini) in 'sed non in tribus sit accipienda'. A purely orthographical variant in *v* is 'katholice' in 'catholicae fidei' (*o*, etc.) in the final sentence of 15.1 and again in 15.4. Also orthographical but, or so it seems to this writer, difficult to pronounce is 'ueruum' in 15.4 in place of 'uerbum' (*o*, etc.); this is a spelling likely not to live long. A clear error is in 15.12, 'animas' instead of the partitive genitive 'partes animae' (*o*; **Te**, **C**, **P**, Ballerini). Another error comes in 15.14, with *v* giving 'propter' for 'pro' in 'pro terrena qualitate' (*o*, etc.), but leaving the case after the preposition unchanged. In 15.17, *v* writes, 'die tertia' against 'tertio' (*o*; **Te**, **C**, **P**, Ballerini). Here either could be correct, the feminine following the classical usage for a set day, while the masculine is the natural gender of the word. The Vulgate text of Jesus' predictions of his resurrection and St Paul's reference in 1 Corinthians, however, use the feminine.[396] The question is whether the scribe of *v* emended on the basis of a remembered phraseology from the Vulgate, or if the scribes of the other manuscripts made an error using the natural gender of the word 'die'. The *v* reading is very tempting, for it seems that Leo would use the feminine, given its use in classical Latin. Towards the end of 15.17, *v* writes 'stantia tua' instead of 'instantia tua' (*o*, etc.).

The following are the *o* variants for *Ep.* 15. In the final sentence of 15, *Praef.*, *o* gives 'dilectio tua fidei' against 'fideli' (*v*; **Q**, **Te**, **C**, **P**, Ballerini). An interesting *o* variant is 'hominis' for 'humanis' (*v*; **Te**, **C**, **P**, Ballerini) in the phrase 'quae humanis corporibus inseruntur' (15.10); 'hominis corporibus', 'bodies of man', makes for a striking English translation, but the phraseology does not feel like Leo, nor is it normal Latin. Leo would, rather, have written, 'hominum corporibus'. The early majority is more likely correct here. Later in 15.10, *o* makes the common error of replacing 'ob' (*v*; **Te**, **C**, **P**, Ballerini) with 'ab' in 'ob hoc a sublimibus ad inferiora delapsas' (*v*). In 15.14, *o* erroneously omits 'uero' from 'decimo uero capitulo' (*v*, etc.), presumably a case of *saut du même au même*. A simple error in *o* is 'iuxta' for 'iusta' in 15.15 (*v*, etc.). *o* omits 'est' from 15.17, 'mortua est et sepulta' (*v*, etc.). In 15.17, *o* writes 'possint' instead of 'quo minus possit celebrari' (*v*, etc.).

---

[396] Mt. 17:22, 'die tertio' in Weber-Gryson, however 'tertia' in many mss; Mk 10:34, 'tertia die'; Lk.'18:33 'die tertia'. See also 1 Cor. 15:4, 'tertia die'.

The scribe of *o* did not know what to do with 'Ceponius', giving the garbled, 'quoaeponius' in 15.17.

What we learn from this discussion is that *v* and *o* seldom disagree, and when they do disagree, it is usually because one of them has made a clear error. While many of their shared variants are readings that could be correct, most of their independent variants are errors. From *Ep.* 15 alone we have seen that **S** has a strong, united text type. To demonstrate this fact even more fully, the table that follows will give select variants from other decretal letters but in lower frequency than for *Ep.* 15. First, a few notes before the table to assist the reader are in order. *v* tends to divide letters into chapters throughout; the *capitula v* uses are the same as those of **D/D–b**; similarly, the inscriptions at the heads of letters, used by both *v* and *o* are those of **D/D–b**. A sample of twenty-two variants from *Epp.* 7, 16, and 4 can give us an idea of the behaviour of **S** in the letters it has clearly taken from **D**:

Var., *Ep.*	*Collectio Hispana* (**S** *v*, *o*)	Ballerini (control)	Significance
1, 7	*Cap.*: 'LXIII **Item eiusdem leonis ad episcopos per Italiam constitutos** De eo quod plurimi maniceorum uigilantia papae leonis in urbe roma delecti sunt'. (*v*; *o* no significant variants)		Unity
2, 7.1	sub legibus (*v*)	subditi legibus (*o*)	Error *v*
3, 7.2	quos ne absoluerentur (*o*; **D–b** *v*) absolberentur (*v*)	quos *hic*, ne *se* absolueret	Om. *hic* and *se* shared variant **D**, **D–b** *v* Om. *hic* only **D–b** *m* Error **S**
4, 7.2	om. *fratres charissimi* (*v*, *o*)	uestra, *fratres charissimi*, sollicitius	Error **S**
5, 7.2	*pestibus* (*v*, *o*)	mentibus, ne *pestis* haec	Error **S**

Var., *Ep.*	*Collectio Hispana* (**S** *v, o*)	Ballerini (control)	Significance
6, 7.2	*diligens* (*o, v*)	a Deo *dignae* remunerationis praemium	Error **S**
7, 7.2	*suae* (*v, o*)	de reatu negligentiae *se* non poterit	Variant **S**
8, 7.2	*sacrileges* (*v*) *sacrilegms* (*o*)	contra *sacrilegae* persuasionis auctores	Error **S**
9, 7.2	Datum tertio kl fbrs theodosio XVIII et Albino vc cns (*v*) Datum iii kls fbas teudosio XVIII et Albino viris clarissimis consulibus (*o*)	Data tertio kalendas Februarii, Theodosio Augusto XVIII et Albino uiris clarissimis consulibus	
10, 16 *Cap.*	LXII eiusdem leonis ad episcopos per siciliam cum capitibus suis (*o; v* om. 'cum capitibus suis'—*o* lists chapters, *v* straight into text)		
11, 16 Pr.	om. *episcopus* (*v, o*)	Leo *episcopus* uniuersis	Variant **S** Agrees with **D**, **D–b**
12, 16 Pr.	reprehensionem (*v, o*)	si quid usquam *reprehensioni* inuenitur	Error **S**
13, 16 Pr.	quo *beatissimus Petrus* apostolus (*o*)	quo *beatissimus apostolus* Petrus (*v*)	Variant *o*
15, 16.1	*accipitis* (*o*) *accip*[... (*v*)	consecrationem honoris *accipitis*	Variant **S** Agrees with **D**, **D–b**
16, 16.1	*apostoli petri* (*v, o*)	et beati *Petri apostoli* sedes	Variant **S** Agrees with **D**, **D–b**

Var., *Ep.*	*Collectio Hispana* (**S** *v*, *o*)	Ballerini (control)	Significance
17, 16.2	*mistico* munerum *oblatio veneratur* (*v*) *mistico* munerum *oblato* venerantur (*o*)	paruulum *mystica* munerum *oblatione uenerantur*	*o* agrees with **D**, **D–b**
18, 4 Pr.	*per* uniuersas (*v*; lacuna *o*)	Tusciam et uniuersas prouincias	Variant *v* Agrees with **D** *c*, **D–b**
19, 4 Pr.	constituta kanonum *et* ecclesiasticam disciplinam (*v*; lacuna *o*)	canonum ecclesiasticam*que*	Variant *v* Agees with **D**, **D–b**
20, 4 Pr.	*puram macula* (*v*; lacuna *o*)	quod ab omni *macula purum*	Variant *v* Word order agrees with **D**, **D–b**
21, 18,	*secta* delapsus et (*v*, *o*)	schismaticorum *sectam delapsus est*, et	Variant **S** Agrees with **D** *a*
22, 18	*deum* (*v*, *o*)	leuem apud *Dominum* noxam	Variant **S** Agrees with **D** *a*
23, 18	Datum iii kl lls alipio et ardabure cns (*v*) \Datum/ iii kls lhas alipio et ardabure consulibus (*o*)	Data III Kalend. Ianuarii Calepio et Ardabure uiris clarissimis consulibus	'alipio' agrees with **D**, **D–b**

Next, as mentioned above, we have *Ep.* 12. After this come letters likely drawn from the *Epitome Hispana*, although their order differs; however, the order of the **D** letters in **S** also differs, so that may simply be due to editorial choice. From this final section of four letters I present a table of the variants from *Ep.* 9:

Var.	*Collectio Hispana* (*v*, *o*)	Ballerini (control)	Significance
1	**LXVIIII eiusdem leonis ad dioscorum alexandrinum epm** (*v*, *o*)	N/A	Agreement **S**
2	I De ordinatione prsbri uel diaconi ut subbato sco celebretur id est die dominico	N/A	Divergence **S**

Var.	Collectio Hispana (v, o)	Ballerini (control)	Significance
	II De festiuitatibus si una augenda pplis non sufficerit nulla sit dubitatio iterare sacrificium (o; om. v)		
3	dioscoro alexandrino salutem (v) dioscoro alexandrino epsco salutem (o)	Dioscoro *episcopo Alexandrino* salutem	Divergent variants, v, o
4	*effectum* (v, o)	impendamus *affectum*	Error **S**
5	*festinemus* (v, o)	fundare *desideramus*	Variant **S**
6	*ipsius* (v, o)	discipulus *eius* Marcus	Variant **S**
7	et *ad eandem* (v) et *ad eam* (o)	et ea fidelium multitudo conuenerit	Errors **S**
8	*processoribus* (o)	nostris *processionibus* atque ordinationibus frequenter interfuit (v)	Error o
9	*sedis* auctoritatis (v add.)	in omnibus apostolicae auctoritatis teneremus (o)	Variant v; false

This table definitively demonstrates first, that *v* and *o* are descended from the same ancestors, but the ways in which they diverge from one another mean that *v* is neither copy nor descendent of *o*, and they are not twins. Their ancestor is the earlier **S** tradition and those of its sources. Second, some of the variants are possibly true. Third, the **S** *capitula* help us see how early mediaeval readers were using and reading Leo's letters.

3.2.v. *Collectio Hispana systematica*

Between 675 and 681, the *Collectio Hispana* was reorganised into a systematic collection, the *Collectio Hispana systematica*.[397] Bas-

---

[397] Martinez Díez 1976, 247–50. A complete and thorough summary of its contents are in vol. 2.1, 279–426.

ing my identifications on Martínez Díez's synopses of the canons, those which have been extracted from Leo are:

Hispana Systematica	Leo, Epistula
1.1.22	4.2
1.1.38	4.1
1.13.1	4.4
1.16.1	167.2
1.26.7	9.1
1.26.8*	not from known Leo, nor from *Collectio Hispana*; source unknown
1.31.10	9.1
1.34.9	12.1
1.34.10	167.1
1.34.14	4.2
1.34.16	12.3
1.34.19*	Letter from Celestine, misattributed to Leo, as observed by Martínez Díez
1.34.21	14.4
1.38.6	83 (most likely)
1.38.7	85 (most likely)
1.47.7	9.1
1.49.4	14.2
1.51.5	14.1
1.55.10	167.3
1.58.36	14.8
1.58.40	83 (again)
1.58.41	85 (again)
1.60.25	4.1
1.60.28	14.9
2.6.2	167.14
2.7.6	12.4
2.7.8	167.13
2.12.7	167.12
2.15.1	108.4
2.16.1	108.3
2.16.4	108.4
2.17.3	167.7
2.18.13	4.2

Hispana Systematica	Leo, *Epistula*
2.18.14	108.1
2.18.15	108.5
2.19.9	167.8
2.19.10	167.9
2.19.11	167.10
2.23.14	167.11
3.1.1	167, *Praef.*
3.1.2	12.1
3.26.21	16.7
3.26.22	14.7
3.26.24	14.10
3.26.25	14.11
3.30.2	167.6
3.40.1	28.1
3.41.5	93
3.41.7	12.3
3.41.9	130.1–2
3.41.10	130.3
3.41.20	12.5
3.41.23	4.5
4.11.1	9.2
4.24.1	16.3
4.26.5–10	16.1–6
4.26.7	168.1
4.30.2	167.15
4.30.3	166.1
4.35.9	166.2
4.35.10	159.7
4.35.12	167.16
4.35.14	159.6
5.1.12	159.1
5.1.13	159.12
5.1.14–15	159.3–4
5.1.16–17	167.4–5
6.3.13	4.3
8.2.6	15.1
8.3.8	15.3

Hispana Systematica	Leo, Epistula
8.4.1	15.2
8.4.2–3	165.2–3
8.4.4–7*	Flavian to Leo, Ep. 22.1–4
8.4.8–12	28.2–6
8.4.15	134
8.6.5–17	15.4–16
8.8.2	7
9.8.1	79
9.8.2	78
9.8.3	82
9.8.4	83 (again)
9.9.6	90?
10.4.14	167.17
10.4.25	159.5
10.4.27	14.2
10.4.30	12.2
*10.4.31**	Letter from Innocent I misattributed to Leo and not caught by Martínez Díez
10.4.32	106 to Anatolius
10.5.1	106.3
10.6.6	106.4 concerning Julian
10.6.7	106.1 'De gratulatione fidei missis'

Since we are blessed with such an abundance of *Hispana* manuscripts and other descendants, such as *Hispana Gallica Augustodunensis* and Pseudo-Isidore, that maintain the letter collections intact, the *Hispana systematica* will not figure in the editing of Leo's letters.

3.2.w. Ragyndrudis Codex

3.2.w.i. Dating and Context

The collection of documents in this codex is itself unique, although the book is most famous for its connection with Boniface. It is, thus, a transitional codex for us, as perhaps the last pre-Carolingian collection we shall consider, or the first of the Carolingian collections. A later tradition claims that this is the book with which Boniface protected himself while being martyred; this claim

is, inevitably, unverifiable. It is not implausible for this book to
have been in Boniface's possession—I would argue that its contents about the catholic faith would make it useful not only for
evangelistic missionary work such as Boniface is popularly considered to have undertaken, but also for the reform work in which he
engaged, albeit less famously. Simply containing anti-Arian tracts
does not make the main focus of a collection actual controversy
with known 'Arians'—the full divinity of Christ is a main tenet of
catholic Christianity, and therefore we cannot rule out the usefulness of these works in the context evangelism and reform.[398] If it
was one of Boniface's books, it was an acquisition from his time on
the continent, given that it is written in a script related to Luxeuil script; this is the argument of Schülung.[399] Once again, it is not
implausible for Boniface to have acquired the book during or for
his missionary work, given how long he was on the continent and
how important existing monastic centres were to the success of his
mission. Ultimately, proving any relation to Boniface in his own
lifetime is as difficult as proving that this is book with which he
defended himself. The more certain link of the volume, however, is
not with Boniface but with the titular Ragyndrudis, a laywoman
who had it written. A few noblewomen of this name are possible
candidates for its commissioner, and McKitterick thinks that the
Ragyndrudis married to Waldbertus is the most likely of these.[400]
The lay connection of the book is itself interesting, pointing to
interests of lay piety not simply to Isidore's *Synonyma*, which are
what gain attention from McKitterick,[401] but its doctrinal content.
Piety and theology can easily go hand in hand. That said, the volume does end up in clerical hands, and it is likely that Ragyndrudis commissioned it for monastic use. Nevertheless, the question
of the ownership of the volume, while interesting, is, perhaps, less
important than the codex itself.

The actual collection of documents in Codex Ragyndrudis is
worth considering, for here we have a unique collection of doc-

---

[398] While I am not explicitly arguing for Boniface's ownership, it is worth
keeping these factors in mind, *contra* the assertion that anti-Arian tracts
require an Arian context in Aaij 2007, § § 13–14.

[399] Schülung 1961, 302–03.

[400] See McKitterick 1989, 259.

[401] Ibid., 267–68.

uments in this volume from the very early Carolingian period, and the codex itself is worth considering in that light, regardless of whether any famous person ever owned it. Codex Ragyndrudis is named after the scribe, editor, or commissioner whose name is included on fol. 2ᵛ: *in honore dni nostri ihu xpi ego ragyndrudis ordinaui librum istum*. The collection begins with two of Leo's letters, *Ep.* 28 (2ᵛ–11ᵛ) and *Ep.* 159 (11ᵛ–14ᵛ). The rest of the collection is varied and seems not to be concerned with any single topic, including several anti-Arian tracts as well as the *Decretum Gelasianum*, *De locis apostolorum*, and Isidore of Seville's *Synonyma*. It is, perhaps, better seen as a general collection of texts useful for early medieval education in the catholic faith, including, therefore, the divinity of Christ and the Trinity alongside Leo's teaching on Christ's two natures and the list of works in the *Decretum Gelasianum*. Leo in this manuscript is a touchstone of orthodoxy.

3.2.w.ii. Manuscript

Fulda Cathedral, Domschatz, Codex Bonifatianus II (saec. VIII), Luxeuil minuscule.[402]

3.3 Conclusion

This chapter has covered the transmission of Leo's letters from the fifth century to the eighth as used in collections of canon law documents. Although these collections are largely collections for the use of canon law, those letters of Leo's included in them are not always what the later tradition would consider 'decretals'. This simple fact of transmission is actually one of the first conclusions worthy of consideration, given how the term 'decretal' or 'epistula decretalis' is frequently retrojected into discussions of late antique papal letters. While the full argument against dividing Leo's letters between 'decretals' and other letters cannot be made here, the treatment of his letters by copyists is, nevertheless, part of the argument. The copyists do not treat the so-called 'decretals' with great distinction from the others, such as the so-called 'dogmatic letters'. They are often all headed with a common rubric 'Epistulae decretales leonis papae', in fact. This was argued in part during the analysis of *Collectio Quesnelliana* (**Q**, see 3.2.c).

---

[402] CLA 8.1197.

Emerging from the analysis of the collections are the proto-collections that fill in the gaps between Leo and the earliest manuscripts and collections. Four proto-collections were discovered through this study; a fifth that was used by both *Vaticana* (**V**) *and Dionysiana adaucta* **D–a** will be discussed in Chapter 5.2.c. These four proto-collections are:

Proto-1	*Epp.* 28, 103, 31, 35, 139, 59, 165	*Corbeiensis* (**C**), *Pithouensis* (**P**), *Coloniensis* (**K**)
Proto-2	*Epp.* 4, 7, 15	*Corbeiensis* (**C**), *Pithouensis* (**P**), and *Albigensis* (**Al**); *Quesnelliana* (**Q**) and *Dionysiana* (**D**) may have used it, but the evidence is inconclusive.
Proto-3	*Epp.* 15, 16, 159, 1, 2	*Teatina* (**Te**), *Diessensis* (**Di**), and *Remensis* (**Re**)
Proto-4	*Epp.* 20, 23, 22, 28	*Vaticana* (**V**), *Hispana* (**S**), *Dionysiana adaucta* (**D–a**)

In considering these sources, it is also worth observing that, for Leo's letters at any rate, *Collectio Pithouensis* is a copy of *Collectio Corbeiensis*. Furthermore, while many collections exist only in later manuscripts, *Collectio Corbeiensis* survives solely in one of our earliest manuscripts of Latin canon law, Paris lat. 12097 from the second half of the sixth century, *Coloniensis* in a sole manuscript of the seventh (Cologne 212 [Darmstadt 2326]) and *Albigensis* in a seventh-century manuscript (Toulouse 364[I.63]). Thus, the emergence of these proto-collections is very soon after the time of Leo, if not in his own lifetime. Moreover, these manuscripts bring us to the very substratum of Latin canon law in the Early Middle Ages, being the very books used in the pre-Carolingian era and not simply the same texts in later copies.

Many of these early manuscripts are of significance in terms of tracing the early use and presence of Leo's works in both the period under consideration and the Carolingian era, whether in known copies or the presence of earlier manuscripts in Carolingian scriptoria. In terms of the ongoing story of the transmission of Leo's letters, a few collections stand out more boldly. First, the *Collectio Dionysiana* (**D**, see 3.2.f) is a foundational collection for later canon law. Likely compiled at the papal archive, there are only two manuscripts of a 'pure' *Dionysiana* letter collection:

Paris, lat. 3837 (saec. IX) and Vat. lat. 5845 (*c.* 915–34), but the *Dionysiana Bobiensis* (**D–b**, see 3.2.g) has proven a reliable witness to the *Dionysiana* text of Leo's letters. Furthermore, the first systematic canonical collection was compiled from *Dionysiana* material in Cresconius' *Concordia canonum* in the seventh century (see 3.2.h). The best manuscripts of this foundational **D** tradition are **D** *c* and **D–b** *m*; that said, **D** *a* is not irredeemable, and **D–b** *v* is a copy of **D–b** *m*. **D** would go on to have a Carolingian afterlife, including some degree of incorporation into the Pseudo-Isidorian tradition.

The second-most famous of these collections is the *Collectio Quesnelliana* (**Q**, see 3.2.c). Long thought to be a child of the papal chancery, this collection is still of major significance whether or not it is from Rome, elsewhere in Italy, or even southern Gaul. A few important conclusions from the analysis of the six major **Q** manuscripts are as follows. First, the independence of manuscript *p* (Paris, lat. 3842A) has been demonstrated. Second, the two Viennese manuscripts, *v* and *w*, have been shown to be sisters from Lorsch. However, *w* (Vienna Cod. 2147 Han.) has had an entire quire of the *Collectio Hispana Gallica Augustodunensis* (**S–ga**, see 5.2.e) inserted, no doubt explaining the later relationship between **Q** and the Pseudo-Isidorian tradition of which **S–ga** is the foundation. Finally, I wish to remind the reader that the **Q** manuscript much lauded by later tradition, Oxford, Oriel College 42, does not contain the **Q** collection of Leo's letters and is thus dealt with at chapter 6.2.c.

Chapter 4

Chalcedonian Collections and the Greek
Transmission of Leo's Letters

Beginning with the first, official Greek *acta* published by Marcian
in the 450s, when *acta* of the Council of Chalcedon were put together
and circulated, the compilers usually, but not always,[1] included a
selection of other documents with them. Usually, amongst these
documents would be a selection of Leo's letters pertinent to inter-
preting the council. Other documents might include Marcian's letters summoning and enforcing the council and pre-Chalcedonian
documents such as Cyril's anti-Nestorian letters or the letter of
Athanasius to Epictetus of Corinth about Christology. These documents, sitting alongside Leo's letters and the conciliar *acta*, would
serve to bolster the position of the council as in line with Alexandria and not Nestorius. As we saw in Chapter One, Chalcedon was
almost immediately imprinted in Latin Christianity's conscious-
ness as the great standard of orthodoxy, and any challenge to its
authority or theology or to that of Leo was courting heresy in
western eyes. Therefore, when challenges arose, such as the *Henotikon*, the Three Chapters, and Monotheletism, the circulation and
ongoing translation of the council documents with their related
dossiers was assured. These collections then provided the material
for western resistance to imperial policy in ecclesiastical affairs.

One example of a supporter of the Three Chapters with access
to Leo's letters is Facundus, Bishop of Hermiane in Africa, in the
540s. Facundus had access to the library of the *Acoimetae* in Constantinople in 546–48, the same library Rusticus would later use
to make his own collection, discussed below. In the course of his
Pro Defensione Trium Capitulorum, Facundus cites Leo, *Epp.* 28,
106, 119, 139, 164, 162, 156, 160, and 161. Not only is *Collectio
Grimanica* (**G**) the only collection that includes all of these letters,

---

[1] Consider, for example, Vat. lat. 1321 (saec. XV), a manuscript of the *Acta
Chalcedonensia* that does not include a dossier of letters but does, after the
conciliar acts, include works of Facundus of Hermiane. This MS is digitised:
https://digi.vatlib.it/view/MSS_Vat.lat.1321 Accessed 21 September 2021.

it is the only source for *Epp.* 160 and 161. Having taken this fact into consideration, along with **G**'s origins in Verona, the region of Italy that went into schism with Rome over the Three Chapters, and the fact that **G** is devoted to Leo's so-called 'dogmatic' letters, **G** will be considered alongside the Chalcedonian collections below. Besides these specific letters from **G**, Facundus' work is filled with allusions and references to Leo.

On the other hand, Liberatus of Carthage only cites two of Leo's letters, *Epp.* 28 and 33, in his *Breviarium*, thus not signalling to us which dossier of Leo's letters he had. Certainly, Liberatus had access to a library with many of the sources detailing the Christological controversy, but his work is much shorter than that of Facundus, although he does cover a broad scope of theological history in the *Breviarium*. Similarly, Pelagius the deacon, future bishop of Rome, demonstrates knowledge of several of Leo's letters in his *Pro Defensione trium capitulorum*, including *Epp.* 108, 162, and 167.[2]

Some of the Chalcedonian collections are back-translations from Greek, others a combination of translated texts and Latin originals. Greek translations of Leo's letters as well as copies of letters originally composed in Greek have also been transmitted to us, although they are not the main focus of this study. While the Latin transmission of Leo is concerned with both theology and church discipline, the Greek transmission concerns itself only with theology, the letters surrounding Chalcedon, and therefore serves as part of this same category of letter collection. The Ballerini observe that these Greek translations are not always that good, just like their Latin counterparts.[3] Forty-one letters edited by the Ballerini exist in the Greek transmission of Leo the Great: *Epp.* 20, 22, 23, 25, 26, 28, 29, 30, 32, 33, 35, 43, 44, 45, 46, 50, 51, 52, 53, 55, 56, 57, 58, 62, 63, 64, 72, 73, 76, 77, 93, 98, 100, 101, 104, 106, 110, 114, 115, 139, and 165.

Among the Chalcedonian collections, six Latin collections of Leo's letters exist, at times overlapping. At the same time as these collections appended to *acta* were compiled, defenders of Chalce-

---

[2] Ed. Devreesse 13–14; 53–54; and 14–15.

[3] 'Sicut enim hac aetate apud Latinos rari erant qui Graecam linguam probe callerent, et exactam versionem e Graeco redderent; ita apud Graecos rari qui perfecte tenerent linguam Latinam, accuratamque interpretationem ex Latino producerent'. PL 54.576.

don also put together other anti-Eutychian and pro-Chalcedonian dossiers, of which two are discussed below, *Collectio Novariensis* and *Collectio Casinensis*. Next we shall consider the *Codex
Encyclius* and its relationship to the transmission of Leo's letters
and legacy. Finally, we shall analyse the Greek transmission of
Leo's letters. One final word is that canon law manuscripts are so
abundant in the Latin Middle Ages that the task of investigating
all of the manuscripts containing the *acta* of Chalcedon and the
associated letter collections is far from complete. Thus, before discussing the known collections, I would like to signal that further
research remains to be done on the following manuscript and its
letter collection:

> Vat. Ott. lat. 744 (saec. XV–XVI). Foll. 121^r–136^v contain a letter
> collection whose contents have yet to be ascertained by me, but
> which likely contains material from Leo, based upon the descrip-
> tion on the Vatican Library website, citing P. Crabbe, *Concilio-
> rum omnium*, ed. Coliniae 1551, t. 1, 726–36, a description the
> catalogue uses for both **Ru** and **Ca**, described below.

This chapter analyses the following Latin collections: Early Latin
Acta numbered 17 by Ballerini (**Ac**, see 4.1.a), the collection of
Vat. lat. 1322 (**A**, see 4.1.b), Rusticus' *Acta* (**Ru**, see 4.1.c), the
Versio Gestorum Chalcedonensium antiqua correcta (**Ch**, see 4.1.d),
Novariensis (**N**, see 4.1.e), *Casinensis* (**Ca**, see 4.1.f), *Grimanica*
(**G**, see 4.1.g), *Codex Encyclius* (no siglum, see 4.1.h), manuscript
Verona LIX (57) (no siglum, see 4.1.i), and a Carolingian frag-
ment of the *Tome* (no siglum, 4.1.j). The Greek collections are cat-
egorised by Schwartz's *sigla*: Collection M (see 4.2.a), Collection B
(see 4.2.b), and Collection H (see 4.2.c).

4.1 The Latin Chalcedonian Collections

4.1.a. Ballerini Collection 17, an Early Edition of the Latin *Acta*[4] (**Ac**)

4.1.a.i. Description of collection

These *Acta* include two Leonine letters, 28 and 98. *Ep.* 28 is
included within the *acta* of the council in the 'tertia cognitio'
('cognitio' being the term these *Acta* use of the sessions), while
Ep. 98 comes in its place after the council. Worth noting is the

---

[4] PL 54.569 § 36, J2(iv) b (506).

fact that these *Acta* do not include 'Canon 28'[5] within their list of the canons of the Council of Chalcedon. Maassen argues that the collection was compiled in the early 500s before the *Dionysiana*, and believes that the similarities between the two are a later contamination from the *Dionysiana*.[6]

4.1.a.ii. Manuscripts

The collection exists in three manuscripts:

> *p*: Paris, lat. 16832 (olim F1: D2; Notre-Dame 88) (saec. VIII2/2 or IX), formerly in Colbert's Library, with provenance of Notre-Dame.[7] Baluze consulted this manuscript and left a note on fol. 124[r], 'Contuli. Absolvi VI. Kalend. April. MDCLXXXIII. Stephanus Baluzius'. This manuscript is written in a Caroline minuscule in two columns with uncial rubrication. It was most likely written by a team of scribes because the text of several quires ends partway through the final folio, and often a visibly different hand has written the following quire.

> *v*: Vat. Reg. lat. 1045 (saec. IX3/4), from Reims.[8] Leo is found on fols 107[r]–110[r] (*Ep*. 29) and fols 173[r]–174[r] (*Ep*. 98).

> Vat. Barb. XIV: 53. This manuscript was listed by the Ballerini, although not by Maassen,[9] and I cannot determine what manuscript it is today.

4.1.a.iii. Manuscript Relations

Since the events at Chalcedon were transacted in Greek, the original and official *Acta* were promulgated in that language. Therefore, it is reasonable to wonder if *Ep*. 28 would be back-translated from the Greek into Latin. Such seems not to be the case. The text of *Ep*. 28 shows no signs of having been translated out of Greek, such as synonyms for Latin words varying from the original text. The *incipit*, a rubricated uncial in both manuscripts, reads, 'INCIPIT EPISTOLA LEONIS PAPAE VRBIS AD FLA-

---

[5] That is, the granting of jurisdiction to Constantinople over Pontus, Asiana, and Thracia, with its concurrent equality of honour with Rome.

[6] Maassen 1870, 743–44.

[7] Bischoff 1998–2014, 3.4988. This MS is digitised: https://gallica.bnf.fr/ark:/12148/btv1b8577525z. Accessed 21 September 2021.

[8] Bischoff 1998–2014, 3.6759. This manuscript is digitised: https://digi.vatlib.it/view/MSS_Reg.lat.1045 Accessed 21 September 2021.

[9] Maassen 1870, 739.

VIANVM EPISCOPVM DE HERESE EVTYCHIANORVM PROPRIAE DE IPSO EVTYCHAE'. *p* varies from that in giving 'EVTICHIANORVM' and *v* in giving, 'EVTYCHE'. As the table below sets out, *p* has a better text than *v*, but this is not to say that *v* has an especially bad text.

Var., Silva-Tarouca §	Ac	Silva-Tarouca text (control)	Significance
1, 5	de *eo* (*p*) *deo* (*v*)	etiam de *ipso* dictum	Variant *p* Error *v* derived from variant *p*, thus variant **Ac**
2, 6	*doctoribusque* (*p*)	sapientioribus doctioribusque (*v*)	Error *p*; very common shared with S-T *M*
3, 7	*agnoscendam* (*p*) *ignosdam* (*v*)	qui cum ad *cognoscendam*	Variant *p* Error *v*
4, 14	*quam* (*p*, *v*)	*qua* fidelium	Shared error **Ac**
5, 27	*superare possemus* (*p*) *superare possimus* (*v*)	Non enim *possemus superare* peccati et mortis auctorem, nisi	Common variant **Ac**; since Silva-Tarouca does *not* give us a good clausula, but *p* and *v* do, yet because this is not the end of a colon, his text is to be preferred
6, 41 (Is. 9:6)	om. *princeps pacis* (*p*, *v*)	Deus fortis *princeps pacis* pater futuri (Vulgate)	Common error **Ac**
7, 75	*admittit* (*v*)	forma non *adimit* (*p*)	Error *v*
8, 202	*ab domnem* (*v*)	*ad omnem* uero causam (*p*)	Error *v*
9, 202	*fidelium* (*v*)	sed et *filium* meum hilarum (*p*)	Error *v*
10, 202	*uoce* nostra *diximus* (*p*) *diximus* (*v*)	*uice* nostra *direximus*	Error and variant *p* Error *v* derived from variant *p*
11, 204	*diuinita* (*v¹*) *diuinitati* (*v²*)	*diuinitatis* auxilium (*p*)	Errors *v*

Ep. 28 ends with the explicit, 'EXPLICIT EPLA LEONIS PAPAE VRBIS AD FLAVIANUM EPISCOPVM'. Of the **Ac** variants, 1, 3, and 5 could possibly be the result of back-translating out of Greek. Var. 1, 'Vt etiam de eo dictum sit a propheta' for 'ipso' is, 'ὡς περὶ αὐτοῦ καὶ τὸ τοῦ προφήτου εἰρῆσθαι';[10] given the wide variance between the Latin and Greek word order, although 'eo' could possibly have come from αὐτοῦ, it is not likely that the entire phrase was translated from Greek. In Var. 3, 'cognoscendam' in Silva-Tarouca is given as a near-synonym 'agnoscendam'; this is the sort of variant one may expect in a back-translation from the Greek verb 'γνῶναι'.[11] However, this variant is shared with the sixth-century Italian *Collectio Teatina* (**Te**, 3.2.i) and the eleventh-century *Dionysiana adaucta* (**D-a**, 5.2.c). Var. 5 is a word inversion that would only point to a Greek origin if the Greek copy had the words in that order, and even then would be a weak argument since such simple inversions occur frequently in Latin texts; and according to Schwartz's text, the Greek is, 'ἠδυνήθημεν νικῆσαι'.[12] Furthermore, the **Ac** text is in agreement here with *Collectio Novariensis de Re Eutychis* (**N**, 4.1.e), *Collectio Vaticana* (**V**, 3.2.d), **Te**, *Collectio Quesnelliana* (**Q**, 3.2.c; not including manuscript *o*), and **D-a**, albeit lacking 'nos' between 'superare' and 'possemus' as the other collections do. Therefore, it is obvious that this version of *Ep.* 28 was not translated from Greek. On the contrary, it was added from a Latin source.

Ep. 98 exists in two recensions, and the version represented here is the older of the two. The other is the translation from Rusticus' *Acta* of Chalcedon (**Ru**, 4.1.c). It begins with the inscription:

> EXEMPLAR RELATIONIS ARCHETYPAE SANCTAE MAG-
> NAE ET VNIVERSALIS SYNODI QVAE IN CALCHEDONIAE
> METROPOLI CONGREGATA EST AD SCAE MEMORIAE
> PAPAM LEONEM

The text of *Ep.* 98 is inevitably a translation, since the council fathers will have drafted the original in Greek, even if there is an 'official' Latin version. The later recension is but a different translation of the same Greek text. Here are the variants of this version, collated against the Ballerini as a control:

[10] ACO 2.1, 11 *l.* 5.
[11] Ibid., 11 *l.* 8.
[12] Ibid., 11 *l.* 30.

Var.	**Ac** text	Ballerini text (control)	Significance
1	*quaem* (*p*)	synodus *quae* secundum Dei (*v*)	Error *p*
2	amatorum *nostrorum* (*p*, *v*)	amatorum principum	Variant **Ac**
3	*quae de* mandaui (*v*)	*quaecumque* mandaui (*p*)	Error *v*
4	*abiectam* (*p*, *v*)	infructuosam autem et *derelictam*	Variant **Ac**
5	*denudantes* (*p*)	pelle *nudantes*, quo (*v*)	Variant *p*
6	*natu* (*p*, *v*) *gubernanti* (*p*)	sed *nutu* diuino *gubernati*	Error **Ac** Error *p*
7	om. *uim* (*v*) *insinuamus* (*v*) *insiniauimus* (*p*)	gestorum *uim* insinuauimus	Error *v* Variants **Ac**
8	om. *ad* (*v*)	et *ad* eorum quae (*p*)	Error *v*
9	*depositionem* (*p*, *v*)	confirmationem et *dispositionem*	Variant **Ac**
10	*uos* (*p*) *nos* (*v*)	ualere *me* in Domino	Error *p* descended from variant *v*
11	*deum* (*p*, *v*)	*Deo* amantissime pater	Variant **Ac**
12	*urbis* (*p*, *v*)	magnae *ciuitatis* Antiochiae	Variant **Ac**

The text of *Ep.* 98 closes with Juvenal of Jerusalem's subscription, followed by 'EXPLICVIT FILICITER' (*v* om. 'FILICITER'). Juvenal's is only the third out of 65 subscriptions included by the Ballerini[13] and **A** *a* (below, 4.1.b). *Ep.* 98 is the last item in this version of the *Acta Chalcedonensia*.

4.1.b. Collection of Vat. lat. 1322[14] (**A**)

4.1.b.i. Description of collection

This collection of documents related to Chalcedon—not, as Schwartz observes,[15] *acta*—contains several of Leo's letters at the

---

[13] PL 54.963–65.

[14] PL 54.570 § 37; ACO 2.2.2, v–xx.

[15] ACO 2.4, xv.

beginning of the collection, including Leo, *Epp.* 114, 87, 89, 93, and 94. In manuscript *a*, *Epp.* 28 and 98 follow in their locations within the context of the council. The contents of *o* differ on this point. The abbreviated *Acta* of *a* are similar in age to those of Rusticus below; their use of the older translation of *Ep.* 98, discussed above, is evidence of the collection's antiquity.

4.1.b.ii. Manuscripts

The letter collection exists in two manuscripts that otherwise differ in certain respects:

> *a*: Vat. lat. 1322 (saec. VI[ex]), half-uncial.[16] Foll. 1–24 of this manuscript, where the initial letter collection is found, are from the eighth or ninth century; in this collection, Leo's letters run 18[v]–22[r]. The text frequently runs into the margins in this section. The *Acta* themselves, where *Epp.* 28 (37[v]–46[v]) and 98 (fols 273[v]–278[r]) are to be found, are from the end of the sixth century.[17] Schwartz, however, argues that *Ep.* 98, 'nisi oculi me fallunt', was written by the same hand as the letter collection at the start of the manuscript.[18] My own judgement coincides with that of Schwartz. The whole manuscript, including both the sixth- and eighth-century portions, was written at Verona.

> *o*: Novara, Biblioteca Capitolare XXX (66) (saec. IX/X).[19] Written at Novara in a Caroline minuscule, with 37 lines in two columns per page. The protocols are in brown capitals. This is also *Collectio Novariensis*.

4.1.b.iii. Manuscript relations

First, our examination will consider the letter collection unique to *a*. The incipits of the letters included here are of the type, 'LEO PAPA AD SYNODVM CALCEDONENSEM', (*Ep.* 114) at variance with Silva-Tarouca's editorial decision to write the much wordier

---

[16] CLA 1.8, written in a hand related to Verona LIII (51), which contains Facundus, thereby highlighting the place of Verona and the Istrian Schism in transmitting documents relevant to Chalcedon. For Verona LIII (51), see Marchi 1996, 104–05. See also Kuttner 1986, 51–52, and Bischoff 1998–2014, 3.6852. This manuscript is digitised: https://digi.vatlib.it/view/MSS_Vat.lat.1322 Accessed 21 September 2021.

[17] CLA 1.8.

[18] ACO 2.2.2, v.

[19] Bischoff 1998–2014, 2.3627.

formula, 'Leo episcopus sanctae synodo apud Calchedonam habitae, dilectissimis fratribus, in Domino salutem'. The table below sets out some of the notable variants of **A**:

Var., Ep.	*Ante Gesta Epistularum Collectio*, MSS *a* and *o*	Silva-Tarouca (control for *Ep.* 114); Schwartz (for *Epp.* 89, 93, 94)	Significance
1, 114	*definitionem* (*a, o*)	non ambigo *definitiones*	Error **A**
2, 114	*dubita de* (*a*) *dubitale* (*o*)	interpretes *dubitabile* uideatur	Error *a* derived from variant found in *o*
3, 114	perfidiam *ueri* uel (*a*) perfidiam *tueri* uel (*o*)	*tueri* perfidiam, uel Eutyches	Error *a* derived from variant *o*
4, 114	*et* (*a, o*)	elatio, *ut* adpetitus	Variant **A**
5, 114	...]ra *dilectione* (*a*)	uestra *lectione* cognoscere (*o*)	Error *a*; 'uestra' goes with sanctitas; the scribe has misread as the typical address 'uestra dilectione'
6, 89	*uoluisti* (*a*)	nunc fieri *uoluistis* (*o*)	Error *a*
7, 89	om. *GL* (*a, o*)	errorem, *GL.* si	Variant **A**
8, 89	*murmurat* (*a*) *murmurum* (*o*)	quid ergo *morborum*, si	Error *a* derived from variant *o*
9, 89	*turbidinis* (*a*) *turbinis* (*o*)	contra *turbines* falsitatis	Error *a* Variant *o*; orthographical
10, 89	om. *enim sum* (*a, o*)	certus *enim sum* quod	Error **A**
11, 89	viii kl *iun* (*a*) *ianuario et* adelfio uc cons (*a, o*)	viii kl iul adelphio uc cons	Variant **A**
12, 93	*sanctitas* (*a, o*)	uestra *fraternitas* aestimet	Variant **A**
13, 93	*Efese* (*a*)	prioris autem *Ephesenae* synodi (*o*)	Error *a* derived from Efesi

Var., Ep.	Ante Gesta Epistularum Collectio, MSS a and o	Silva-Tarouca (control for Ep. 114); Schwartz (for Epp. 89, 93, 94)	Significance
14, 93	Data (a, o) iii kl iulias adelfio cu consulae (a)	dat vi kl iul adelfio uc cons	Variant **A** Variant a, probable error of iii from ui
15, 94	iungerentur, *gloriae* (a, o)	praesentiae iungerentur, *GL.*	Error **A**, expansion of GL should be 'gloriosissime' or 'gloriosissime imperator'
16, 94	*ea* (a, o)	si in *eam* fidem	Error **A**
17, 94	*fratres* (a, o)	per sanctos *patres* nostros	Error **A**

The above table of 17 variants seems, at first glance, to be a powerful indictment against *a*'s text of these letters. Most of its variations from Schwartz's or Silva-Tarouca's edition are errors. However, this is but an illusion. The data set from which these 17 variants are drawn is a selection of 38 passages from the entirety of *a*'s letter collection. At only 17 places from the 38 does it provide us with a different reading from the editors (who, even if not always correct, provide at least *good* texts)—that is to say, less than one half. Of these 17, 12 are definitively errors, while of the remaining five, some might be—Var. 14 almost certainly is. On the other hand, the omission of one 'GL' (Var. 7) and its wrong expansion another time (Var. 15), done by both *a* and *o*, makes it likely that, like **G**, **A** is descended from a version that made use of that abbreviation. Moreover, given that *a* has errors derived from the text found in *o*, but *o* is a later manuscript, it is evident that *o* makes use of a better text of **A** than *a*.

As discussed above, *a* also includes *Epp.* 28 and 98 within its conciliar portion; *Ep.* 98 seems to have been written by the same hand as the letter collection just discussed, whereas *Ep.* 28 comes within the sixth-century section of *a*. Of the two, the ensuing discussion will only cover *Ep.* 28 as being the more important of the two letters. The incipit from *a* is: 'INC EPISTVLA LEONIS PAPE AD FLAVIANUM EPI DE HERESE EVTHICI', similar

but probably unrelated to *o*, 'INCIPIT EPISOLA PAPAE LEO-
NIS AD FLAVIANVM EPM CONSTANTINOPOLITANVM
DE EVTYCHEM'. The following table shows the selected variants in *Ep.* 28 from *a* as well as those of *o*, although they are not
descended from the same tradition. The control text, as with **Ac**,
is that of Silva-Tarouca.

Var., Silva-Tarouca §	**A** *a* and MS *o*	Silva-Tarouca text (control)	
1	Dilectissimo fratri flauiano leo (*a*; om. *o*)	Included in <>	
1, 1	*lectionis* (*a*)	lectis *dilectionis* tuae litteris (*o*)	Error *a*
2, 2	*ordinem* (*a*)	*ordine* recensito (*o*)	Error *a*
3, 5	*de eo praedictum* (*a*)	etiam *de ipso dictum* sit (*o*)	Variant *a*
4, 6	*doctoribusque* non (*a*)	sapientioribus *doctioribusque* non *cedere* (*o*)	Error *a*
5, 6	*credere* (*a*)	As above	Error *a*
6, 7	*agnoscendam* (*a*)	ad *cognoscendam* (*o*)	Error *a*
7, 12	*incarnationem* (*a*)	de Verbi dei *incarnatione* sentire (*o*)	Error *a*
8, 14	*quam* (*a*)	*qua* fidelium (*o*)	Error *a*
9, 25	Sed totum se *homini reparando* (*a*) Sed *totam separando* homini (*o*)	Sed *totum se reparando homini*	Variant *a* Error *o*
10, 27	*superare possumus* (*a*) *superare possimus* (*o*)	enim *possemus superare*	Error *a* Orthography *o*
11, 34	*inueniret* (*a*)	*inueniens* promissionem	Error *a*
12, 41 (Is. 9:6)	*dei* (*a*)	angelus *Deus* fortis (*o*; Vulgate)	Error *a*

Var., Silva-Tarouca §	**A** *a* and MS *o*	Silva-Tarouca text (control)	
13, 115	*desinenter* (*a*)	non *desidentibus* ambulare (*o*)	Error *a*
14, 126	*naturae intellegendae* (*a*)	in utraque *natura intelligendam*	Error *a*
15, 154	apostoli *praedicantem quod sanctificatio spiritus per aspersionem fiat sanguis Iesu Christi nec transitoriae legat eiusdem apostoli uerba* (*a*)	beati apostoli *et euangelistae Iohannis expauit dicentis*: Omnis (*o*)	Variant *a*
16, 200	*fidei* (*a*)	fructuosissime *fides* uera defenditur (*o*)	Error *a*
17, 202	*iulianum* (*a*)	*Iulium* episcopum (*o*)	Error *a*
18, 203	nobis *probita est fides* (*a*)	cuius nobis *fides esset probata* (*o*)	Error *a*
19, 204	*diuini causa qualium* (*a*)	adfuturum *diuinitatis auxilium* (*o*)	Error *a*
20, 205	*damnetur* (*a*)	sui prauitate *saluetur* (*o*)	Error *a*

The explicit to *Ep.* 28 is, 'EXP EPISTVLA LEONIS PAPE VRBIS AD FLAVIANUM EPISCOPVM'. Immediately, it becomes evident from the foregoing table that *a* and *o* are unrelated in their transmission of *Ep.* 28. This comes as no surprise, since in *a* it comes within the Chalcedonian documents, whereas in *o* it comes amidst a different collection of documents pertaining to the matter of Eutyches (collection **N**, 4.1.e below). The majority of these variants are errors. However, of note is Var. 15, an uncommon variation on the introduction of 1 John 4:2–3 that helps us place *a*'s text in the wider transmission of *Ep.* 28.

4.1.c. Rusticus' *Acta Chalcedonensia*[20] (**Ru**)

4.1.c.i. Dating and Context

Rusticus, fraternal nephew of Pope Vigilius, was a Roman deacon at Constantinople who was enmeshed in the Three Chapters Controversy. He was originally a strong supporter of Justinian's condemnation of the Three Chapters, going so far as to circulate the edict without official permission, but he changed sides in the debate when he saw how strong the support of the Latin West was for the Three Chapters. He took actions against Vigilius' support of Justinian's edict, going so far as to join a number of excommunicated clerics in submitting a *commonitorium* to Justinian against Vigilius' *Judicatum*, a text supporting the condemnation of the Three Chapters. Rusticus was accordingly excommunicated by his uncle in 550, and, later, when he published a tract attacking the Second Council of Constantinople of 553, was banished to the Thebaid by Justinian to silence him.[21]

In 565 Rusticus returned from exile to Constantinople where he found a good hideout in the monastery of the *Acoemetae*.[22] There, he published his own edition of the Latin *Acta* of the Council of Chalcedon,[23] part of his *Synodicon* that also contained *acta* of First Ephesus. His source was a codex containing the recension called Φ^c in Schwartz's *sigla* of the *Acta*, which he collated with other Greek and Latin collections of the *Acta* and to which he then added various letter collections—using the Latin where

---

[20] PL 54.566–67 § 33, J2(iv) c (506–07), ACO 2.3.1, 2, Φ^r; ACO 2.4, 1, Φ. Schwartz has edited both **Ru**'s and **Ch**'s letter collections together, since they seem to derive from a common source, in ACO 2.3.1.

[21] For an account of Rusticus and Justinian's various actions against him and other western clerics who had the temerity to oppose the imperial will in matters within ecclesiastical jurisdiction, see Richards 1979, 145–47, 153. He is a figure awaiting 'a major study', as noted by Moorhead 2015, n. 11, 141.

[22] The *Acoemetae*, or Sleepless Monks, were staunch supporters of Chalcedon and were, I imagine, the leading eastern monastic opposition to Justinian's condemnation of the Three Chapters, as they had been opposed to the *Henotikon* from the accession of Pope Felix III (483–92) until the reconciliation of 519 as well as to Theopaschism starting in the 530s (see Allen 2000, 819, 823). Rusticus' refuge amongst them would point to a resistance to the condemnation of the Three Chapters as well.

[23] Cf. ACO 2.3.1, XI–XII.

available, according to Jalland.[24] My own research bears this out, as the discussion below demonstrates. Rusticus' *Acta* include the following Leonine letters with the *Ante Gesta Chalcedonensia*: 20, 25, 23, 22, 72, 26, 35, 32, 29, 30, 33, 43, 44, 45, 46, 58, 55, 56, 57, 62, 63, 64, 50, 51, 73, 76, 77; and with the *Gesta* themselves: 28, 98, and 114. As well, the collection begins with the epistle from Flavian to Theodosius II, 'Nihil ita convenit',[25] followed by the sequence of Leo's letters. Following Leo's letters are several other items before the *Acta* proper begin. Clearly, Rusticus did not see these items as entities separate from the Leonine collection— indeed, it is he who includes the letters sent among the members of the imperial family with Leo's letters, *Epp.* 55–58 and 62–64.

4.1.c.ii. Manuscripts

These *Acta* exist in nine manuscripts:

l: Paris, lat. 2777, fol. 1–19[v] (saec. IX1/2) from Lérins.[26]

c: Paris, lat. 11611 (saec. IX),[27] written at St-Denis with provenance at Corbie; it moved to St Germain in the seventeenth century before going to the Bibliothèque nationale in Paris. It is written in a single-column Caroline minuscule. Leo's letters run fols 1[r]–14[r].

Vat. lat. 1319, (saec. XII[ex]),[28] includes a transcription of *c* after *Collectio Casinensis*.[29]

p: Paris, lat. 1458 (olim Colbert 2576; Regius 3887[1]) (saec. X),[30] which Schwartz says is not as important as Paris, lat. 11611,[31] and Jalland calls *Codex Colbertinus*.[32]

---

[24] Jalland 1941, 506–07.

[25] ACO 2.3.1, 5.

[26] This MS was discussed above at 3.2.n. ii in relation to the *Collectio Arelatensis* (**Ar**) which it also contains.

[27] Bischoff 1998–2014, 3.4692. This manuscript is digitised, https://gallica.bnf.fr/ark:/12148/btv1b90683096. Accessed 20 September 2021.

[28] Kuttner 1986, 45, with full description of MS, 45–48.

[29] ACO 2.3.1, XII. Jalland 1941, 507, lists this manuscript as *Codex Corbeiensis*. For a description of the MS and its contents from *Collectio Casinensis*, see below, 4.1.f.

[30] Bischoff 1998–2014, 3.4017.

[31] ACO 2.3.1, XII.

[32] Jalland 1941, 507.

d: Montpellier H 58 (saec. X),[33] possibly from the Loire region. *d* includes variant readings between the lines and in the margins, some of which are useful and noted by Schwartz.[34] It is written in a minuscule hand with capitalis rubrics throughout. Leo's letters run fols 1^r–10^v. *m* is damaged and at times illegible, including the bulk of *Ep.* 20; the last eleven lines of the outer column of fol. 1 are missing the outer half. Such trimming persists through the manuscript, creating a series of lacunae throughout the text.

y: Verona, Biblioteca Capitolare LVIII (56) (saec. X) from Italy,[35] which may have crossed paths with Codex Casinensis 2. The manuscript has undergone extensive damage from moisture at some point; some pages have rotten through along the edges and have holes in them. In other places, the text has flaked away. Leo's letters run 4^r–22^v; the contents of the manuscript are listed on fols 2^v–3^v.

Vat. lat. 1323 (saec. XV), from Rome, which is based on *v*.[36]

Vat. lat. 4166 (saec. XV).[37]

Vat. Chig. C.VII.212 (saec. XVI).[38]

4.1.c.iii. Manuscript Relations

Select passages from *Epp.* 20, 25, 23, and 22 from the *Ante Gesta* have been chosen to examine the relationship between the manuscripts. The first table consists of the letters from the *Ante Gesta*. *Ep.* 22 is not in the version printed in ACO 2.4 ('Nulla res diaboli'), but a different translation from Flavian's original Greek, 'Nihil est quod stare faciat'. The Ballerini print both translations, giving this one first.[39]

---

[33] Bischoff 1998–2014, 2.2824. This is Jalland's MS *Divionensis*.

[34] ACO 2.3.1, XII–XIII.

[35] Bischoff 1998–2014, 3.7047.

[36] See Kuttner 1986, 53. This manuscript is digitised: https://digi.vatlib.it/view/MSS_Vat.lat.1323 Accessed 21 September 2021.

[37] This manuscript is digitised: https://digi.vatlib.it/view/MSS_Vat.lat.4166 Accessed 21 September 2021.

[38] Presumably this is the manuscript listed by Ballerini as Chig. 483.

[39] PL 54.723–27.

Var., Ep.	Rusticus' *Ante Gesta Epistularum Collectio*	Schwartz's text (*Epp.* 20, 25, 23) or Ballerini text (*Ep.* 22) (controls)	Significance
1, 20 *Incip.*	EPISTOLA LEONIS ARCHIEPI ROMAE AD EVTYCHEN SCRIPTA (*l* om. *ad*; *c* om. *scripta*; *p*; *d* illeg.; *y* om. *epi*)		Small variations, but general agreement on *incipit*
2, 20	*Desiderantissimo filio euthyci leo eps* (*l, c, p, d, y*)	*Leo Eutychi presbytero*	Common variant **Ru**
3, 20	*litteris* (*l, c, p, d, y*)	*epistulis* rettulisti	Common variant **Ru**, and unless Leo received more than one letter from Eutyches, likely correct
4, 20	*saluum costodiat* (*l, c, p, d, y*)	Deus te *custodiat incolumem*	Common variant **Ru**
5, 25	INCIPIT EPISTOLA PETRI EPI RAVENNIENSIS AD EVTYCHEN PRBM SCRIPTA (*l rauennatis*; *c* om. *epistola*; *p*; *d*; *y* om. *scripta*)		As with Var. 1
6, 25	Dilectissimo *et honore digno filio eutychi* (*l, c, p, d, y*)	Dilectissimo *filio et merito honorabili* Eutychi	Common variant **Ru**
7, 25	Om. *Tristis ... per* (*c*)	*Tristis legi tristes litteras tuas et scripta maesta merore debito percurri* (*l, p, d, y*)	One line of *c* skipped; rewritten in bottom margin
8, 25	g[lacuna of 4–5 letters] *uerbum aut caelestis* (*d*)	*gloria in excelsis deo, caelestis* (*l, c, p, y*)	Error *d*
9, 25	*rescripturas* (*c, y*)	Haec breuiter respondi, frater, litteris tuis, plura *rescripturus, si* (*l, p, d*)	Shared error *c, y*

Var., Ep.	Rusticus' *Ante Gesta Epistularum Collectio*	Schwartz's text (*Epp.* 20, 25, 23) or Ballerini text (*Ep.* 22) (controls)	Significance
10, 23	INCIPIT EPISTOLA SANCTISSIMI ARCHIEPI VRBIS ROMAE LEONIS AD FLAVIANUM ARCHIEPM CONSTANTINOPOLITANVM (*c*) om. VRBIS (*l, p, d, y*)		Variant *c*
11, 23	*Dilectissimo fratri flauiano episcopo leo eps* (*l, c, p, d, y*)	*Leo Flauiano episcopo Constantinopolitano*	Common variant **Ru**
12, 23	*incedentibus* (*l, c, d, y*)	quibus rebus *intercedentibus* (*p*)	Shared variant *l, c, d, y*
13, 23	fuerit *in se* (*c, d*)	*in se* fuerit (*l, p, y*)	Shared variant *c, d*
14, 22.Pr.	*amicissimo* (*d*) om. *Sanctissimo ... salutem.* (*l*)	Sanctissimo et Deo *amantissimo* patri et consacerdoti Leoni Flauianus in Domino salutem. (*c, p, y*)	Variant *d* Error *l*
15, 22.1	*nequitia* (*l, d*)	diaboli *nequitiam* (*c, p, y*)	Error *l, d*
16, 22.1	quem (*l, c, p, d*)	Quos conturbet *quos* deuoret (*y*)	Shared variant *l, c, p, d*
17, 22.1	*Deponentes* (*l, y*) itaque *timorem* tumorem (*timorem* om. *subpunc., y*)	*Deponens* itaque tumorem luctus (*c, p, d*)	Shared error *l, y*
18, 22.1	om. *unus* (*l, c, p, d, y*)	quoniam *unus* eorum qui	Common variant **Ru**
19, 22.4	*uestram beatitudinem* (*l*)	cum *uestra beatitudine* (*c, p, d, y*)	Error *l*
20, 22.4	om. *doneris nobis* (*l*)	pro nobis *doneris nobis* amantissime pater (*c, d, y*)	Error *l*

Rusticus' text stands out for providing rubricated inscriptions at the start of each letter as well as keeping the salutations. The fact that his salutations differ from our controls in all four of the above occasions could be taken as evidence that these letters were all translated from Greek copies in Constantinople and are not based on Latin originals. The use of synonyms by Rusticus in Variants 3, 4, and 6 of *Epp.* 20, 25, and 23, supports this theory; *Ep.* 22 is definitively a translation from Greek. Rusticus presumably has made his own for *Epp.* 20 and 25, since these will have had Greek originals, whereas *Ep.* 23 would be a back-translation into Latin. There is no overwhelming pair or trio of manuscripts here—none of them agrees more frequently with any other than it does with the rest. The convergences are as follows: *l, p, d* = 9; *l, c, d, y* = 12; *c, d* = 13; *l, d* = 15; *l, c, p, d* = 16; *l, y* = 17. Although *l* and *d* have but one occurrence of agreement against the other manuscripts (Var. 15), they also agree on three more variants that include others. *c* and *d* show a similar trend, but only on two other variants, both of which happen to also include *l* as well. Therefore, based on this data, the two most similar manuscripts are *l* and *d* which also bear a resemblance to *c*. Having said that, *l* also includes a number of independent errors of omission, thus setting it apart from *d*.

4.1.d. *Versio Gestorum Chalcedonensium antiqua correcta*[40] (**Ch**)

4.1.d.i. Dating and Context

This version of the *Acta* contains the following letters from the Leonine corpus in the *Ante Gesta*: 20, 25, 23, 22, 72, 26, 35, 32, 29, 30, 33, 43, 44, 45, 46, (up to here, the same as **Ru**) 50, 51, 73, 76, 77 (these are the same as the final five of **Ru**), and 118. *Ep.* 118 is the only letter included herein that is not also in **Ru**; this collection lacks seven of **Ru**'s letters.

4.1.d.ii. Manuscripts

It exists in three manuscripts:

> *p*: Vat. lat. 5750 (saec. VII), from Bobbio, taken to Rome by Paul V in 1618.[41] *p* was written by three scribes in Bobbio's scriptorium.

---

[40] Not in Ballerini or Jalland. Cf. ACO 2.3.1 Φᶜ, p. 2.

[41] CLA 1.26a. This was number 135 in Bobbio's 1461 inventory. This manuscript is digitised: https://digi.vatlib.it/view/MSS_Vat.lat.5750 Accessed 21 September 2021.

It is the basis for this collection as a discrete entity from **Ru**, especially considering *d* below.

d: Montpellier H 58 (saec. X), from the Loire region.[42] This manuscript has been discussed above with **Ru** because it contains the first 15 letters of **Ru** in the text of **Ch**, then, after *Ep.* 46, takes up **Ru**'s text beginning at *Ep.* 55. Given its frequency of agreement with **Ru** *l* for the first four letters of these two collections, let alone **Ru** as a whole, it is evident that **Ru** and **Ch** do not differ extensively in those letters for which they share a common source.

m: Montecassino 2 (saec. XII), written in many hands. Due to textual similarities between *m* and **Ru** *c*, Schwartz argues that they come from the same place, so this manuscript does not originate in Montecassino.[43]

4.1.d.iii. Manuscript Relations

These three manuscripts are not necessarily related to each other directly. *p* provides the 'original' collection, but *d* modifies the collection to make something essentially **Ru**, and *m* also shares many variants with **Ru** against *p* and *d*. Their ancestor is a collection of letters related to Chalcedon, but always bound up in manuscripts with a variety of other material. This same collection was the basis of **Ru**, given the fact that **Ch** and **Ru** share all of the common **Ru** variants; occasionally *m* strays from **Ch Ru** but simply by giving a variant/error that derives from this tradition. Thus, in Var. 1 **Ch** *m* omits 'ROMAE'; in 2, it gives 'eutyche pbro' when the rest do not give 'pbro'; in 11, it omits 'episcopo'. The disparate nature of these manuscripts is borne out by **Ch** *p* alone giving, 'ROMANI' in Var. 1. The idiosyncratic nature of many **Ru** variants is also attested by **Ch**, as Variants 7–9, 12, and 20 are not attested in it. As well, in 10, **Ch** agrees with the majority of **Ru** against **Ru** *c* and does not give 'VRBIS'. At Var. 13, **Ch** *p*, *m* give 'in se fuerit' in agreement with **Ru** *l*, *p*, *y*—and not, therefore, with **Ch/Ru** *d*. They also agree with **Ru** against *d* in giving 'amantissimo', not 'amicissimo' in Var. 14. Var. 15 is in neither *p* nor *m*. At Var. 16, **Ch** gives 'quem' in agreement with most of **Ru** against *y*; at 17, **Ch** gives 'deponens', not 'deponentes' and at 19

---

[42] Bischoff 1998–2014, 2.2824.
[43] ACO 2.3.1, x.

Ch *p* and *m*, 'cum uestra beatitudinem'. The long and short of it is that Schwartz's decision to classify **Ru** and **Ch** as two different recensions of the same letter collection (*Φ*, as *Φ^r* and *Φ^c* respectively) makes perfect sense, since **Ru** does seem simply to be an amplified **Ch**—or **Ch** a truncated **Ru**.

4.1.e. *Collectio Novariensis de Re Eutychis*[44] (**N**)

4.1.e.i. Dating and Context

Schwartz argues that this collection could have been put together by none other than Leo himself.[45] First, it seems to have been compiled within the lifetimes both of Theodosius II and Flavian, since it knows of the deaths of neither, yet includes material from Leo as well as from events in Constantinople in 448. Second, the *Tome* ends with the subscription, 'ET ALIA MANV: TIBVRTIVS NOTARIVS IVSSV DOMINI MEI VENERABILIS PAPAE LEONIS EDIDI'. This, Schwartz maintains, is evidence that *Ep.* 28 is here in the copy Leo circulated in the period after Dioscorus refused to have it read at Second Ephesus. Third, the acts of the 448 Home Synod of Constantinople lack the sessions where Cyril's letters are read out; this, argues Schwartz, is evidence for Leo's editorial hand because Leo wanted his *Tome* to be the sole standard for orthodoxy. I doubt this argument because Leo elsewhere, as in the *Testimonia* he would later append to *Ep.* 165, upholds his orthodoxy precisely through Cyril. Schwartz's fourth argument is the poor translation out of Greek into Latin in some of the documents, pointing to a mid-fifth-century origin for the collection because there were few high-quality Greek interpreters in Rome at the time. The first two arguments are the strongest and certainly seem to point to someone with access to Roman archival material; whether Leo or not, it is ultimately impossible to say. But Leo is an attractive choice. **N** includes Leo *Epp.* 22, 26, 28, and 21 as a collection; at the end of **N** come two texts sent to Leo and first edited by Amelli in *S. Leone Magno e l'Oriente*, 1882, and again by Mommsen in 1886,[46] before being edited by Schwartz in ACO 2.2.1, 77–81. These are the *libelli appellationis* to Leo from

---

[44] In neither Ballerini nor Jalland. Ed. with introduction, ACO 2.2.1.

[45] ACO 2.2.1, vi–viii.

[46] Mommsen 1886, 362–68.

Flavian of Constantinople on the one hand and Eusebius of Dorylaeum on the other. **N** is the only known source for these texts.

4.1.e.ii. Manuscript

This collection exists in only one manuscript, described as **A** *o*
above (4.1.b), Novara, Biblioteca Capitolare XXX (saec. IX/X).[47]
Its relationship with **A** *a* has also been discussed already.

4.1.f. *Collectio Casinensis*[48] (**Ca**)

4.1.f.i. Dating and context

The wider contents of this collection seem to have been copied
from Rusticus' *Synodicon*. It contains the following Leonine letters: 24, 37, 54, 89, 94, 78, 111, 156, 164, 148, 145, 105, 84, 116,
38, 36, 39, 49, 87, 47, 74, 85, and 21. **Ca** shares none of its Leo
material with Rusticus. Of interest, as Schwartz pointed out in
his introduction, is the editorial choice to group letters by recipient, a relatively uncommon act. They are in five groups: three
to Theodosius, four to Marcian, four to Emperor Leo I, three to
Pulcheria, four to Flavian, and the final items individually to
Anatolius, Anastasius of Thessalonica, Martinus Presbyter, and
Anatolius again. This collection of letters was probably drawn
together somewhere in central Italy, given the origins of its two
manuscripts.

4.1.f.ii. Manuscripts

It exists in the following two manuscripts:

 m: Montecassino 2 (saec. XIII), whence comes its name.

 v: Vat. lat. 1319 (saec. XII–XIII);[49] **Ca** collection of Leo runs
 fols 93^r–98^v. 93^r is the beginning of a new quire, so something
 has evidently fallen out, as 92^v ends mid-sentence, and 93^r
 begins in the middle of *Ep.* 89 in a different hand. The order

---

[47] Bischoff 1998–2014, § 3627.

[48] Not listed by the Ballerini or Jalland. For what follows, see ACO 2.4,
x–xiii, 143.

[49] See above 4.1.c.ii; Kuttner 1986, 45–48, Leo is on page 46. This manuscript is digitised: https://digi.vatlib.it/view/MSS_Vat.lat.1319 Accessed 21
September 2021.

264 CHALCEDONIAN COLLECTIONS AND THE GREEK TRANSMISSION

of letters differs from above, adding *Ep.* 21 after 85. After the
Leonine letters of **Ca** end on fol. 98ᵛ, this manuscript provides a
transcription of Paris, lat. 11611, of Rusticus' collection of Leo's
letters.[50]

4.1.f.iii. Manuscript Relations

m and *v* are frequently united in their readings and probably
come from a common ancestor; neither is a copy of the other. Of
more interest is their relationship to other collections, especially
since so many items in **Ca** are rarities. A rare Leo item, *Ep.* 24,
which starts this collection is also found in Pseudo-Isidore C (**I–c**),
Ratisbonensis (**E**), *Grimanica* (**G**), *Bobbiensis* (**B**) and Ballerini Collection 24 (**24**). For this letter, the collated variants are:

Var.	**Ca** *m*	Schwartz	Significance
1	religionis *habens*	religionis *habetis* (**G**, **E, 24**)	Error **Ca**
2	*agreement*	Constantinopolitana ecclesia (**Ca, E, 24**) **G** *constantiniana*	Error **G**
3	*per turbationes*	ecclesia *perturbatio-nis* acciderit quod (**G, 24**) **E** ecclesia turbationis	Error **Ca**
4	*nicine*	asserens se *Nicaenae* synodi constituta **G, 24** niceni **E** Nichaenae	Variant **Ca**
5	misit, *deo unum*	presbyter misit, *de obiectionum* euiden-tia (**G, E**) **B, 24** *de obiectionis* **E, B** euidentiam	Error **Ca**
6	Between *tamen* and *in eo*, **Ca** adds a fragment of a dis-putation concerning Eutyches *urgueret* (**I–c**)	tamen in eo sensum *argueret*, non eui-denter expressit (**G**) **E, B24** *arguerit* **B, E** sensu	Error **Ca**

---

[50] See above 4.1.c.iii.

Var.	Ca *m*	Schwartz	Significance
7	*agreement*	quibus eum aestiment arguendum (**Ca**, **E**) estimet (**G**) estimat (**B**, **I–c**, **24**)	---
8	om. *nobis*	primitus *nobis* cuncta reserare (**E**, **24**) **G**, **B** reseruare	Error **Ca**
9	*reductis*	ut in lucem *deductis* his (**E**) *ductis* (**G**, **B**, **24**)	Variant **Ca**

For *Ep.* 24, at least, we can see from the table that **Ca** is largely independent of the wider transmission. To test this theory, we skip ahead to *Ep.* 94, the first full letter which both *m* and *v* share. As the table below demonstrates, *Ep.* 94 further demonstrates this independence. No single other collection predominates in the sharing of errors and variants.

Var.	Ca *m*, *v*	Schwartz	Significance
1	item ad marcianum aug per bonephatium pbrm	Leo Marciano augusto.	Inscriptions often vary
2	*quo* ad (*m*, *v*; **A** *a* [Vat. lat. 1322], **I–c**)	studium *quod* ad reparationem (**G**, **B**, **E**, **O**)	Shared error **Ca**, **A** *a*, **I–c**
3	*agreement*	aptius expectari tempus optassem (**G**, **B**, **A** *a*, **O**) **E** spectari **I–c** expectare	Wide agreement
4	*agreement*	etiam de longinquioribus prouinciis euocari (**G**, **B**, **E**, **A** *a*, **O**) Ps-Is C longinquis	Wide agreement
5	*Bonefatium* (*m*, *v*)	tradita, et *Bonifatium* de conpresbyteris meis (**G**, **E**, **A** *a*, **I–c**, **O**) **B** bonifatio	Shared variant **Ca**; minor

Var.	Ca *m, v*	Schwartz	Significance
6	partis *meae praesentia* iungerent\ur/, GL. (*m, v*)	implendas partes meae praesentiae iungerentur, GL. (**G, B**) gloriae (**A** *a*, **O**) GL om. **E, I-c**	Shared variant **Ca**
7	*erit* (*m, v*)	dies synodo fuerit constitutus (**G, B, E, I, O**) fuerint (**A** *a*)	Shared variant **Ca**
8	*adsensum* (*m*; **B**)	sanctae fraternitatis assensu quae uniuersali (*v*; **G, E, I-c, A** *a*) ascensu (**O**)	Shared variant *m*, **B**
9	*agreement*	probanda concordia, si in eam fidem quam euangelicis (**G, E**) concordiam, si in ea (**A** *a*) in ea (**O**) in eandem (**I-c**) quae euangelicis (**B**)	Agreement **Ca**, **G, E**
10	om. *omnium* (*m*)	declaratam per sanctos patres nostros accepimus et tenemus, *omnium* corda (*v*; **E, A** *a*) declarat tam per sanctos fratres (**O**) per quos patres (**B**) per antiquos patres (**I-c**) accipimus (**G**)	Error *m*
11	Data (*m, v*; **A** *a*, **O**, **I-c**) xiiii (*m, v*; **B**, **I-c**) kl adelfio aug consule (*v*)	DAT XIII KL AUG ADELFIO VC CONS (**G**) **E** om. VC	

Besides the independence of **Ca** from much of the wider tradition, the above two tables also demonstrate that it seems fairly reliable for the items it contains.

4.1.g. *Collectio Grimanica*[51] (**G**)

4.1.g.i. Dating and Context

A copy of *Collectio Grimanica*, as discussed above, was a probable source for Facundus of Hermiane in the sixth century. Schwartz argues that **G** was transcribed in the ninth century from a sixth-century codex in Verona, related to Verona's other Chalcedonian manuscripts, according to Turner's investigations: the second part of Vat. lat. 1322 of Latin *Acta Chalcedonensia*;[52] Verona LIII (51) of Facundus' *Defense of the Three Chapters*; Verona XXII (20) which includes documents related to the Acacian Schism; and Verona LIX (57) which includes writings on the Trinity and Incarnation, the *Acta* of Ephesus and Chalcedon, and Leo, *Epp.* 28 and 167.[53] These manuscripts would be good company for a collection such as **G**. **G** is the most extensive collection of Leo's letters,[54] consisting of 104 of them arranged chronologically; it served as the basis for Schwartz's edition, but Jasper rightly doubts the textual value of this collection when compared with *Collectio Ratisbonensis* (**E**).[55] It includes: 20, 24, 23, 72, 35, 27, 29, 30, 54, 32, 31, 33, 34, 36, 37, 38, 39, 44, 50, 47, 49, 48, 45, 51, 43, 46, 61, 60, 70, 69, 71, 74, 75, 59, 79, 78, 37, 81, 82, 86, 83, 84, 85, 87, 88, 89, 90, 91, 92, 94, 95, 93, 102, 104, 105, 106, 107, 111, 112, 113, 115, 116, 117, 114, 118, 119, 121, 122, 123, 125, 120, 126, 127, 130, 129, 128, 131, 134, 135, 137, 136, 139, 140, 143, 141, 142, 145, 146, 147, 149, 150, 148, 152, 153, 155, 154, 156, 158, 162, 160, 161, 157, 164, 165. The letters found herein for the first time are: 27, 75, 86, 92, 117, 131, 140, 141, 147, 152, 88, 91, 143, 146, 157, 126, 128, 137, 142, 129, 153, 149, 150, 154, 158, 160, 161, 164. Its value, therefore, is great, even if its variants, when held up against those of **E**, may not be of the highest quality.

---

[51] B18, J3(i) (507).

[52] See above 4.1.b.

[53] ACO 2.4, xxiiii, citing EOMIA 2.1, viii.

[54] Jasper 2001, 46.

[55] As discussed above, 2.9.

4.1.g.ii. Manuscript

It exists in the following manuscript:

> Paris, Bibliothèque Mazarine, 1645 (saec. IX/X [Schwartz] or IX1/3 [Bischoff]),[56] from the region of Friuli whence also comes its first known owner, Petrus Passerinus in the sixteenth century. Passerinus gave it to Antonius Bellonus, through whom it came to Cardinal Grimani, after whom the collection is named. Upon the dissolution of Grimani's library, the manuscript was purchased by André Hurault Mersy, then on a diplomatic mission to the Republic of Venice. It passed through Mersy's family to the Parisian Oratory of St-Michel, whence it came to the Bibliothèque Mazarine upon the suppression of the Oratory in the eighteenth century. Quesnel's edition of the manuscript was based on the apograph in the Vatican Library. We shall consider this manuscript further in Chapter 4 in our investigation of *Collectio Ratisbonensis* (**E**).[57]

4.1.h. *Codex encyclius*[58]

4.1.h.i. Dating and Context

This collection contains letters sent to Emperor Leo I and was translated from Greek into Latin in the sixth century at Cassiodorus' command.[59] The Greek original has been lost. It contains letters from bishops to Emperor Leo affirming their support for Chalcedon, including Pope Leo, *Ep.* 156 (Item XII). As discussed in Chapter One, the bishops are almost all in support of Chalcedon, even if not completely enthusiastic. Given that the Leo extract herein is back-translated from Greek, it is of little use in

---

[56] Bischoff 1998–2014, 3.3938. This manuscript is available on microfilm, Mf 1069 from the Bibliothèque Mazarine. There is also an apograph made for Quesnel, Vat. Reg. lat. 1116.

[57] See below, 5.3.b.

[58] See Mansi, *Concilia* vol. 7, col. 785–92, for incipits; J2(iv) d (507); ACO 2.4, L. Ed. Schwartz, ACO 2.5, 1–98.

[59] Cf. Jalland 1941, 507; see Cassiodorus, *Institutions* 1.XI.2, 'The Codex Encyclius bears witness to the Council of Chalcedon and praises the reverence of that council so highly that it judges that the council ought to be compared to sacred authority. I have had the complete collection of letters translated by the erudite scholar Epiphanius from Greek into Latin'. (trans. J. W. Halporn).

establishing a text of Leo's letter, so the manuscripts have not
been consulted in the course of this project.

4.1.h.ii. Manuscripts

It exists in the following manuscripts:

> Paris, lat. 12098 (saec. IX), from Corbie via St Germain before
> arriving at the Bibliothèque nationale.[60] Charlemagne's copy was
> the exemplar of this codex,[61] heralding to us the importance of
> the discussion of Charlemagne's reign and book production that
> follows in Chapter 4.

Vienna, Österreichische Nationalbibliothek 397 (saec. X).[62]

4.1.i. Verona LIX (57)

As noted above,[63] this manuscript includes writings on the Trinity and Incarnation, the *Acta* of Ephesus and Chalcedon, and Leo,
Epp. 28 and 167.

> Verona, Biblioteca Capitolare, MS LIX (57) (saec. VI–VII).[64] *Ep.* 28
> is on fols 152^v–162^v; *Ep.* 167 is on fols 210^r–215^v.

4.1.j. A Carolingian Fragment of the *Tome*

> Verona, Biblioteca Capitolare, MS I (appendice), Fragm. V (saec.
> VIII). This is a fragment from the *Acta* containing *Actio II* and
> chapter 6 of *Ep.* 28.[65]

4.2 The Greek Transmission of Leo's Letters

The Greek letter collections identified by Schwartz have been
given the letters M, B, and H. They date to the fifth century
when the *Acta Chalcedonensia* were being compiled. As seen above,
these collections are variously related to the Latin collections
already discussed.

---

[60] Bischoff 1998–2014, 3.4729; Ganz 1990, 148.

[61] Ganz 1990, 64.

[62] Bischoff 1998–2014, 3.7115.

[63] 4.1.g.

[64] CLA 4.509; Bischoff 1998–2014, 3.7047a.

[65] Marchi 1996, 50.

4.2.a. Collection M

4.2.a.i. Description of Collection

Collection M consists of Leo, *Epp.* 43, 55, 56, 57, 62, 63, 64, 76, 77, 73, 28, Leo's patristic florilegium (usually appended to *Ep.* 165), 44, two letters from Valentinian III and Marcian from before the council,[66] a letter from Pulcheria to Strategios the governor of Bithynia,[67] another letter from the emperors,[68] and Leo *Ep.* 93 in the *ante Gesta*; after *Actio II* in the *Acta*, it consists of Leo *Epp.* 20, 25, 23, 22, 72, 35, 32, 29, 30, and 33.

4.2.a.ii. Manuscripts

  M: Venice, Biblioteca nazionale Marciana, Gr. Z 555 (saec. XI). This is the only complete manuscript of collection M, and the only manuscript of Collection M that includes the letter collection after *Actio II*.

  P: Paris, gr. 415 (saec. XII).[69] P bears some relationship to Collection M, because it contains *Ep.* 28 with the florilegia beginning at κοινωνίας θείας, which is exactly where p, copied from P, cuts off.

  p: Venice, Biblioteca nazionale Marciana, Gr. Z 165 (saec. XV), a copy of P containing material now missing from P, in particular Collection M, Leo, *Epp.* 43–28.

  S: Monastery of St Catherine, Mount Sinai, 1690 (saec. XIII). S begins with the first eleven letters of Collection M, including Leo's florilegium after *Ep.* 28. Schwartz consulted a facsimile of fols 228ᵛ–400ᵛ, beginning in *Ep.* 76 at ὥστε θείοις γράμμασιν.

---

[66] 'Omnibus negotiis' / 'Τῶν πραγμάτων' (ed. ACO 2.1, 27–28; Latin: Maier 2012, 107); 'Et quidem per sacras litteras' / 'Σπεύδοντας ἡμᾶς' (ed. ACO 2.1, 28–29).

[67] 'Intentio nostrae tranquillitatis' / 'Σκοπὸς τῆι ἡμετέραι' (ed. ACO 2.1, 29; Latin: Maier 2012, 108).

[68] 'Dudum quidem at per alias diuinas' / '῞Ηδη μὲν καὶ δι᾽ ετέρων' (ed. ACO 2.1, 30; Latin: Maier 2012, 109).

[69] This manuscript is digitised: https://gallica.bnf.fr/ark:/12148/btv1b1072 2081n Accessed 21 September 2021.

4.2.b. Collection B

4.2.b.i. Description of Collection

Collection B overlaps with Collection M. In the *ante gesta*, B provides the same five items that close M: the four imperial letters and Leo, *Ep.* 93. After the condemnation of Dioscorus in *Actio II* B consists of a letter of Flavian to Theodosius II, Leo *Epp.* 20, 25, 23, 22, 72, 35, 32, 29, 30, 33, 43, 44, Theodoret *Ep.* 82, Leo, *Epp.* 101, 100, 106, 104, 110, 114, 115, and 139.

4.2.b.ii. Manuscripts

B: Vienna, Österreicheische Nationalbibliothek, hist. gr. 27 (saec. XII).

V: Vat. gr. 1455 (saec. XV).

In preparing his edition for Collection B, Schwartz also consulted Vat. gr. 720 (saec. XI), a *varia* volume of canonical material, which includes Leo, *Ep.* 139, and was the source for the fragment attributed to Leo published by the Ballerini as a second appendix to Leo's works.[70] It does not include Collection B, however.

4.2.c. Collection H

4.2.c.i. Description of Collection

Collection H consists of the same letter of Flavian to Theodosius II that B places first after *Actio II*, the libellus of Eusebius of Dorylaeum,[71] Leo *Epp.* 22, 72, 26, 35, 32, 33, 44, 29, 30, 45, 46, 58, 50, 51, the first of the imperial letters in Collection M,[72] the letter of Pulcheria to Strategios,[73] two further imperial letters,[74] and Leo, *Ep.* 93.

---

[70] PL 54.1258–1260.

[71] See *Actio I*, 225 and 230, ACO 2.1, 100–01.

[72] 'Omnibus negotiis' / 'Τῶν πραγμάτων' (ed. ACO 2.1, 27–28; Latin: Maier 2012, 107).

[73] 'Intentio nostrae tranquillitatis' / 'Σκοπὸς τῆι ἡμετέραι' (ed. ACO 2.1, 29; Latin: Maier 2012, 108).

[74] 'Et quidem per sacras litteras' / 'Σπεύδοντας ἡμᾶς' (ed. ACO 2.1, 28–29); and 'Dudum quidem at per alias diuinas' / '῍Ηδη μὲν καὶ δι᾿ ετέρων' (ed. ACO 2.1, 30; Latin: Maier 2012, 109).

4.2.c.ii. Manuscripts

> H: London, British Library, Arundel 529 (written 7 June 1111). Collection H runs fols 32ʳ–71ʳ.[75]
>
> X: Paris, gr. 1115 (from 1276).[76]

4.3 Conclusion

In this chapter we have seen the transmission of the collections of Leo's letters that are most helpful for understanding his theology and the events surrounding the Council of Chalcedon. These collections all take us back to the fifth century when they were compiled and the sixth century when debate surrounding the reception of the council and Justinian's 'Three Chapters' raged, with northern Italy proving a particularly fertile land for Chalcedonian opposition to Justinian. Of note first, then, is the provenance of these manuscripts. Those dating to the time of the Three Chapters Controversy as well as several later copies come from Verona; we also have manuscripts from Novara, Bobbio, the Friuli region, Rome, Montecassino, and various places in France. Here we see how controversy influenced textual transmission.

Although the council acts and *Ep.* 98 were translated out of Greek, the letter collections appended to the *acta* were not. Where a Greek translation of one of Leo's letters survives, the Chalcedonian collections of his correspondence present us with a copy of the original Latin text. This even includes Rusticus' collection, which he compiled in Constantinople at the same time he was translating the conciliar *acta* into Latin. Related to the question of translation, it has also been shown that *Ep.* 98 exists in two different Latin translations, one from before the 550s and preserved in the early *acta* of Ballerini Collection 17 (**Ac**) and the collection of Vat. lat. 1322 (**A**), and the other made by Rusticus for his *acta* (**Ru**).

While the text of the *Tome* in these collections bears resemblance to the text in some canonical collections, such is not the case for the other letters which have here an independent transmission, although elsewhere there are similarities between Bal-

---

[75] This manuscript is digitised: http://www.bl.uk/manuscripts/FullDisplay. aspx?ref = Arundel_MS_529 Accessed 21 September 2021.

[76] This manuscript is digitised: https://gallica.bnf.fr/ark:/12148/ btv1b10723555f Accessed 21 September 2021.

lerini Collection 17 (**Ac**) and *Collectio Dionysiana* (**D**). These were probably contamination from the more popular collection into this one; moreover, this contamination cannot touch the Leo letters since none of them are held in common between the two.

Finally, the Greek collections of Leo's letters are few in number, as are the manuscripts. We have only three collections to consider, all of them dating to the era of the compilation of the *acta*. The Greek manuscripts themselves range in dates from the eleventh to the fifteenth century. Greek Collection M is the probable source for Rusticus' collection (**Ru**), given the fact that its two collections of Leo's letters are almost identical to his, maintaining the same order when M misses something that is in **Ru**, and because M's first collection of letters is not reproduced in B or H.

Chapter 5

The Carolingian Tradition of Manuscripts

5.1 The Carolingian Context

As discussed above, the early to mid-sixth century, with its so-called *renaissance gélasienne*,[1] is a crucial period for the assembly of epistolary collections that include Leo's letters, whether canonical collections or more theologically-oriented collections gathered in response to Chalcedon and the Three Chapters. The Carolingian Age, on the other hand, is primarily important for the proliferation of manuscripts that contain Leo's letters. The Carolingian superabundance of manuscripts is well-known, often accompanied by such figures as these: from before 800 we have in total 2000 Latin manuscripts; from the ninth century alone we have 7000.[2] With almost all Latin texts, even when our earliest manuscript pre-dates the Carolingians, we usually have a Carolingian copy or copies. This alone merits the appellation 'Carolingian explosion', which I use here to refer to the proliferation of manuscripts in that age and its effect upon the transmission of patristic documents. First, I will display how the numbers of Leo's manuscripts amply demonstrate this explosion, then I shall discuss the causes of this explosion. Having introduced this significant era, I shall discuss those collections of Leo's letters compiled during it.

First, I shall illustrate the Carolingian explosion. In the table below, I present the pre-Carolingian collections, how many manuscripts each has, and the relationship of these manuscripts to the Carolingian era. The *Collectio Hispana* (**S**) is not included because it and its manuscripts are all Spanish, and the Spanish centres whence these manuscripts come, were not part of the Carolingian world.[3] Numbers in parentheses represent manuscripts that could be either pre-/post- or Carolingian.

---

[1] See 3.2.

[2] G. Brown 1994, 34.

[3] See 3.2.u above for **S**. Catalonia, however, was conquered by Charlemagne.

Collection	Date	Total mss	Pre-Carol. mss	Carol. mss	Post-Carol. mss
Frisingensis Prima	Post-495	3		3	
Dionysiana	*c.* 500	2 complete		1	1
Teatina	*c.* 525	1		1	
Vaticana	VII/4	4	(1)	3 + (1)	
Sanblasiana	VI^{in}	6	1	5	
Quesnelliana	VI^{in}	5		4 + (1)	(1)
Thessalonicensis	531	3		1	2[4]
Corbeiensis	537–55	1	1		
Avellana	537–55	2			2
Cresconius	VI^{med}	20+1 Rev. Car.		11+1	9
Arelatensis	557–58	4		2	2
Remensis	VI2/2	1		1	
Pithouensis	VI^{ex}-VII^{in}	1		1	
Albigensis	549–604	2	1	1	
Coloniensis	VImed	1	1		
Rusticus' *Acta*	VImed	7		2	5
Casinensis	VImed	2			2
Codex Encyclius	pre-583	2		1	1
Vetus Gallica	585–627	13 complete		12	1
Diessensis	VII	1		1	
Dio-Bobiensis	VII	2		1	1
Totals		84	5 (4)	52 (54)	27 (26)

Out of the twenty-one collections of Leo's letters gathered before the Carolingian era presented above, two exist only in pre-Carolingian manuscripts, two only in post-Carolingian manuscripts, and the remaining seventeen collections include Carolingian manuscripts. Of those seventeen, six collections have only Carolingian manuscripts, as well as two that include manuscripts that may or may not be Carolingian (*Vaticana* and *Quesnelliana*), making the potential number of collections existent only in Carolingian man-

---

[4] It is worth noting that one of these manuscripts is a direct copy of the existing Carolingian manuscript.

uscripts eight. Of the remaining nine collections, eight have a Carolingian manuscript as their earliest. Finally, to repeat the results in the final row of the table, these twenty-one collections represent eighty-four manuscripts: fifty-two are Carolingian (61%), five are pre-Carolingian (5.9%), and twenty-seven are post-Carolingian (32%).

To strengthen the case that the Carolingian era, alongside the sixth century, is the most significant period for the transmission of Leo's letters, we have only to look at the Carolingian collections themselves. The most widely distributed of these is the *Dionysio-Hadriana*, with ninety-one manuscripts, sixty-two of which are Carolingian. In second place comes Pseudo-Isidore,[5] all major recensions of which include Leo, including Pseudo-Isidore C, recently dated to the ninth century, as discussed below. When those later recensions are taken into account, the number of Pseudo-Isidorian manuscripts known to contain Leo is forty-five with an additional thirty manuscripts listed by Kéry that have not been given a Hinschius classification, and whose Leo contents are as yet unknown to me.[6]

Collection	Date	Total mss	Carol. mss	Post-Carol. mss
Ratisbonensis	VIII	2	1	1 (copy of Car.)
Dio-Hadriana	Pre-774	91	62	28 (+1 date?)
His-G-August.	840s	2	2	
Dio-adaucta	850–72	6	2	4
Grimanica	pre-840s	1	(1)	(1)
Ps-Isidore A1	840s	25	1	24
Ps-Isidore A/B	840s	5	2	3
Ps-Isidore C	IX	7	0	7
Cluny Ps-Is	840s	12	1	11
Bobbiensis	IX	1	1	
Totals		152	72 (73)	79 (78)

The *Collectio Dionysio-Hadriana* (**D–h**) alone has more manuscripts than all pre-Carolingian collections of Leo's letters combined. These are 152 manuscripts who trace their descent to the copy-

---

[5] See 5.2.f below.
[6] See Kéry 1999, 100–08.

ists and compilers of the Carolingian Renaissance. Furthermore, unlike the pre-Carolingian collections, all of the Carolingian collections save Pseudo-Isidore C have manuscripts of their own era, that is, within a century or a century and a half of compilation.

To take both eras together, we have a total of 236 manuscripts representing twenty-nine collections. 124 (52.5%) of these 236 are Carolingian and 106 (44.9%) are post-Carolingian; of the post-Carolingian manuscripts, only the *Collectiones Avellana* and *Casinensis* lack any Carolingian precedents. For the transmission and history of Leo's letters, no age compares to the Carolingian in numbers alone. Without these manuscripts, a great many of Leo's letters and letter collections would have been lost to us or preserved only in a handful of witnesses—the fate of many classical authors even with Carolingian manuscripts, such as Lucretius or Ammianus, as well as of Greek Fathers such as Justin Martyr. Leo's wide popularity in the West assured his survival.

Accompanying this explosion in manuscripts is a revolution in the size of Leo's letter collections compiled by the Carolingians. The largest pre-Carolingian collections of Leo's letters are the *Hispana* with 39, the *Quesnelliana* with 32, Rusticus' collection with 29, the *Chalcedonensis correcta* with 29, the *Thessalonicensis* with 24, the *Vaticana* with 16, and the *Pithouensis* and *Corbeiensis* with 14 letters. The other collections are closer in size to the seven-letter *Collectio Dionysiana* or the four-letter *Sanblasiana*. The largest Leonine collection of them all, the 104-letter *Collectio Grimanica*, may pre-date the Carolingians, yet even it exists only in a Carolingian manuscript. We have already discussed this collection in the previous chapter on the assumption that the surviving manuscript's archetype was compiled much earlier than the manuscript itself. Yet is it not striking that, even if that dating is true, nothing before the Carolingians rivals it for size? The next contender is firmly Carolingian, Pseudo-Isidore C, with 102 letters. Finally, in third place we have another Carolingian collection, the *Collectio Ratisbonensis* with 72 letters, which in terms of numbers ties some post-Carolingian collections.[7] Besides the two great Carolingian collections, we also have the 55 letters of Pseudo-Isidore A1. *Collectio Bobbiensis* holds 26 letters, and the *Dionysiana adaucta*

---

[7] That is, those collections identified by the Ballerini as numbers 23 and 24; see below at 6.3.d-e.

contains 15 of Leo's letters while the *Dionysio-Hadriana* has only eight letters, adding one to the original seven of the *Dionysiana*. The impact upon the transmission of Leo's letters should be obvious—to have so many letters being gathered together is a likely way to ensure the survival of larger numbers, a fact borne out by that very survival. Furthermore, many letters that do not exist elsewhere, such as in *Collectio Grimanica*, are preserved in these massive Carolingian endeavours, frequently based on now-lost exemplars.

How is it, then, that the Carolingian scriptoria were able to produce not only so many manuscripts, but collections of such size—not only of Leo's letters, but canonical collections more broadly? The *Collectio Dionysiana* has only 39 papal letters in total, yet the Carolingians a little over two hundred years later are able to gather together over one hundred of Leo alone. That is to say, what drove the Carolingian Renaissance that drove manuscript production and canonical activity? First comes the mindset of Carolingian kings, most fully realised in Charlemagne, that the king is to be involved in the reform of the kingdom, not only in secular law and politics but also in ecclesiastical affairs; the word for this reform is *correctio*,[8] which seems to trace itself back to Isidore of Seville's etymology of *rego* from *corrigo*.[9] Charlemagne uses cognates of the word *correctio* in his capitularies, as do the reform efforts of his father, Pippin the Short.[10] For example, in Charlemagne's *Epistola Generalis*, *c.* 786–800, to the 'religiosi lectores' of his dominion, he states that it is his care to promote the improved state of the churches and thus the liberal arts to that end:

> Amongst these [goals] we have already precisely corrected all the books of the Old and New Testaments, corrupted by the ignorance of scribes, with God helping us in all things.[11]

---

[8] As used by G. Brown 1994, 45, and Costambeys et al. 2011, 144. It is also the title of the final chapter in McKitterick 2008, 292–380.

[9] *Etym.* 9.3.4. This is certainly one of the earliest and most explicit uses of *correctio* cognates in this way, one which is part of the common heritage of the Carolingian intellectual world.

[10] See the cited purpose of Council of Verium (755), 'correctum quo aeclessiae Dei ualde cognoscit esse contrarium'. The term is used again in ch. 3. Ed. Boretius 1883, MGH Leges III, *Capitularia* I, 33, *ll.* 27–28, 41–43.

[11] 'Inter quae iam pridem uniuersos ueteris ac noui instrumenti libros, librariorum imperitia deprauatos, Deo nos in omnibus adiuuante, examussim correximus'. Ed. Boretius 1883, 80 ll. 28–30.

This is merely exemplary of a wider use of such cognates from from the sources of the Carolingian reform,[12] setting aside instances where Charlemagne and others use synonyms for correction, such as *emendatio*. Explicit instances of *correctio* cognates cover everything from correcting biblical texts, to clerical *correctio*, to the *correctio* of *comites*, and even when the terms are lacking, this spirit of correction persists throughout all levels of the Carolingian reform.

The mindset of royal *correctio* of church and society itself is not new, however, being present in the Anglo-Saxons and Visigoths,[13] even the Merovingians,[14] and tracing its heritage back to the late Roman world.[15] However, as Giles Brown makes clear, the

[12] See, *inter alia*, references in the following passages edited by Boretius 1883: 47 *l.* 28; 53 *l.* 41; 54 *ll.* 1, 3; 60 *l.* 32; 94 *l.* 14; 98 *l.* 20; 204, *l.* 2; 159 *l.* 1. As well, see these in Louis the Pious, ed. Boretius 1883: 274 *l.* 47; 278 *l.* 11; 279 *l.* 36; 303 *l.* 18; 304 *l.* 37; 305 *ll.* 25–26; 309, *l.* 14; 342, col. 1. *l.* 23 and col. 2, *l.* 22 (this is two versions of the same text). These examples plus many more not only from Charlemagne and Louis the Pious but their successors as well attest to the widespread use of terminology of *correctio* in Carolingian capitularies, whether the *correctio* of texts, behaviour, liturgy, and whether *correctio* by an individual of himself, or by laws and the church of the community and its behaviour or its texts.

[13] Brief references are as follows: For the Anglo-Saxons, Bede preserves views on kingship throughout his *Ecclesiastical History of the English People*; see, e.g., the reign of King Oswald and his desire to convert/reform Deira and Bernicia, 3.3–7. Post-Carolingian, see King Alfred's 'greed' for learning in Asser, *Life of King Alfred*, 76–79. For Spain, Isidore of Seville writes, amongst other things, the play on words 'he who does not correct (*corrigit*) does not rule (*regit*)' (*Etym.* 9.3.4); quoted by Brown 1994, 2. Visigothic Spain epitomises the desire for reform by holding seventeen church councils in Toledo alone before the year 702.

[14] The Merovingian kings in the early seventh century display their concern for *iustitia* and *pietas* more effectively than later Merovingians, as discussed by Wallace-Hadrill 1971, 47–53. See also Gregory of Tours, *Historiae*, e.g., the speech of Avitus of Vienne to Gundobad upon the latter's conversion to Catholicism that the king should be both religious reformer and public example (2.34). Terminology cognate to *correctio* in Merovingian capitularies is sparser than in Carolingian ones—however, fewer Merovingian capitularies exist. E.g. edict of Guntram of 10 November, 585, to all priests and bishops ed. Boretius 1883, 11 *ll.* 41–43, and 12 *ll.* 6 and 8; the royal precept of Childebert I, ed. Boretius 1883, 2 *l.* 31.

[15] G. Brown 1994, 1–3. For the later Roman Empire, recall the various imperial laws directed against heretics, pagans, and Jews, as well as Jus-

Merovingians whom the Carolingians succeeded did not achieve the *correctio* of their people and realms overall, despite certain centres that continued to flourish culturally.[16] One result of this failure at *correctio* is the extreme paucity of manuscripts from the Merovingian world. The Merovingian age, both within their realms as well as in Italy, is when many classical authors were palimpsested, and very few copied.[17] Of the 2000 Latin manuscripts that survive from anywhere before the year 800, 300 of them, including both whole manuscripts and fragments, are from Merovingian lands; McKitterick observes that this is a considerable number, given how difficult it is for any manuscript to survive from such early times;[18] many more would have been copied, now lost to us. However, given that 7000 come from the ninth century alone,[19] and that we know many classical authors survived into the Merovingian world, it seems evident that during the later Merovingian period, even if book production continued, its pace had slackened, and many texts were lost in the sixth and seventh centuries. The later seventh century for the Merovingian and Italian worlds has been argued to have been a time of cultural decline;[20] to cite one example, besides the scarcity of manuscripts mentioned above, few Gallic and Italian canonical collections can be dated to this period and few church councils met, while church properties were often taken over by secular powers.

Part of why the later Merovingians failed at *correctio* is their lack of effective power. In the final decades of Merovingian rule, power was not in the hands of the monarchs, who were often child kings, as Patrick Wormald reminds us,[21] but in those of the

tinian's prime example of this coalescence of administrative force, including church architecture, church councils, edicts on theology, etc., alongside projects such as the codification of Roman law.

[16] Ibid., 7–11.

[17] Reynolds and Wilson 1991, 85.

[18] McKitterick 1994, 235.

[19] G. Brown 1994, 34.

[20] See G. Brown 1994, 4–8. Reynolds and Wilson 1991, 85, characterise the period thus, 'Although few ages are so dark that they are not penetrated by a few shafts of light, the period from roughly 550 to 750 was one of almost unrelieved gloom for the Latin classics on the continent'.

[21] Wormald 2005, 573. Regencies make for the rise of new powers at court, and the Merovingians had their share of them, visible as early as Gregory's *Historiae*.

majordomos, the ancestors of the Carolingians. Furthermore, there was much political unrest in this age, in part due to the Frankish practice of dividing monarchical inheritance between sons who would inevitably compete for complete power, in part due to the vying for power at court during a king's minority, in part due to the fall of Visigothic Spain and the need to protect Frankish land from the Islamic invaders—a feat achieved by Charles 'the Hammer' (Martel) at the Battle of Tours in 732. Political instability meant that the powers who would have funded *correctio* and its correlated cultural products were not in a position to do so, not having the necessary real power and authority. Furthermore, the wealth to do so would be lacking as well—wars of defence are costly with none of the booty that comes with wars of conquest. And, as the stories of Merovingian civil strife demonstrate, sources of internal wealth or potential cultural production, such as towns and monasteries, often suffered heavily in this period. Political stability, strong leaders, and wealth to fund the desired changes are the necessary corollaries to a 'successful' *correctio* that leads to cultural flourishing. The Carolingians, unlike their predecessors, were more often powerful than not, patronising monasteries and courtiers and philosophers—they had the political wherewithal to make Merovingian dreams of *correctio* possible.[22] Second, they had wealth. Under Charlemagne, they expanded their territory to include Italy and expanded, subdued, and 'tamed', if you will, more lands across the Rhine for the Franks. An example of wealth through expansion is the subjection and conquest of the Avars (790–803), whose own sacred treasury, the Ring of the Avars, was raided.[23] This expansion brought wealth through both plunder and tribute, and manuscript production and the other aspects of cul-

---

[22] Carolingian power is visible in the ability of Carloman and Pippin III 'the Short' even as *majordomos* to call the reform councils over which Boniface presided, between 742 and 747 (e.g., see Boniface, *Epp.* XL/50 to Pope Zacharias and XLV/57 from Zacharias to Boniface).

[23] Einhard on the Avars: 'All the wealth and treasure they had assembled over many years was seized. Human memory cannot record any war against the Franks that left them richer and more enriched. Until that time they had seemed almost paupers but they found so much gold and silver in the palace and so much valuable booty was taken in the battles that the Franks might be thought to have justly taken from the Avars what the Avars had unjustly taken from other peoples'. *Life of Charlemagne* 13, trans. Ganz.

tural and artistic renaissance require wealth for the procuring of materials as well as of manpower.[24]

The Carolingians, then, were able to achieve *correctio* because of their material wealth and secular dominion. What were the results of *correctio* for our purposes? First, people demanded correct copies of foundational texts—the Bible, liturgy (usually the so-called *Gregorian Sacramentary*),[25] St Benedict's *Rule*, and canon law texts—this last being provided at the beginning by the *Collectio Dionysio-Hadriana*. The *Dionysio-Hadriana*, as we shall see below,[26] was sent from Pope Hadrian I to Charlemagne and thus seen by the latter as authoritative. However authoritative Charlemagne may have considered the *Collectio Dionysio-Hadriana*, it is also the case that a number of other canon law books have been associated with his court library. We have already met his copies of *Collectio Quesnelliana*, Einsiedeln, Stiftsbibliothek, 191 (277), in Chapter 2, and of the *Codex Encyclius*, Paris, lat. 12098, in Chapter 3. Obviously, copies of *Dionysio-Hadriana* are all descended at one stage or another from a manuscript of Charlemagne's court library; moreover, manuscript *h* of the *Collectio Hispana Gallica Augustodunensis* (**S–ga**), includes an Anti-adoptionist treatise composed at his court—this Corbie manuscript had an encounter with Charlemagne's court activity as well.[27] Outside of Charlemagne's immediate vicinity, the drive for *correctio* meant that the earlier canonical collections continued to be copied and corrected in this period, as the table above displays, for *correctio* included not only the dissemination of the approved texts but the correction of the existing ones. Carolingian scriptoria were, as a result, centres of

[24] Manuscript production was not an inexpensive thing when one considers the materials and labour involved. McKitterick 1989, 135–64, devotes a chapter to the economic realities of book production and possession. She cites various Carolingian examples of book theft and book sale that show how much a book could be worth then assesses the cost of production, including the number of animal skins per manuscript, the cost of materials for the ink both for writing and illuminating, as well as the cost of the binding. Books are shown to be indisputably items of luxury, and McKitterick moves on to discuss the social world of books as wealth and gifts.

[25] See the letter from Pope Hadrian I to Charlemagne concerning the reform of the liturgy, MGH Epist. 1, p. 626. See also Wilson 1915, xxi–xxiii.

[26] 5.2.a.

[27] Ganz 1990, 52.

text editing as well as copying, and the existence of pre-Carolingian collections was secured. We must keep Carolingian textual *correctio* in mind when reading any Latin text that passed under their quills, for a reading that seems legitimate on the basis of Latinity and content may be a Carolingian conjecture; it may be true; it may be both. Finally, regardless of royal policy, we should keep in mind that manuscript production was also favoured simply by the relative stability and wealth of the period. Other ages might have acted similarly could they have been able to. Furthermore, Leo himself is copied profusely because of his enduring relevance to canon law, whether kings fund *correctio* or not.

This chapter analyses the following collections in section 5.2: *Dionysio-Hadriana* (**D–h**, see 5.2.a), *Hadriano-Hispanica* (**H–s**, see 5.2.b), *Dionysiana adaucta* (**D–a**, see 5.2.c), *Hispana Gallica* (**S–g**, see 5.2.d), *Hispana Gallica Augustodunensis* (**S–ga**, see 5.2.e), Pseudo-Isidore (**I**, see 5.2.f) including Hinschius A/B and B (**I–b**, see 5.2.f.iii), Hinschius A1 (**I–a**, see 5.2.f.iv), the Cluny/Yale Pseudo-Isidore (**Y**, see 5.2.f.v), and Hinschius C (**I–c**, see 5.f.vi), and then Vat. Reg. lat. 423 (no siglum, see 5.2.g) and systematic as well as unorganised collections of extracted canons at 5.2.h, covering thirteen such collections. In section 5.3 the following collections are analysed: *Bobbiensis* (**B**, see 5.3.a), *Ratisbonensis* (**E**, see 5.3.b), the Roman Homiliary (no siglum, see 5.3.c), and the Homiliary of Agimond (no siglum, see 5.3.d).

5.2 Carolingian Canonical Collections

5.2.a. *Collectio Dionysio-Hadriana*[28] (**D–h**)

5.2.a.i. Dating and Context

As noted above,[29] Pope Hadrian I had the *Collectio Dionysio-Hadriana* compiled and sent to Charlemagne around 774.[30] It includes the same seven letters of Leo as the *Dionysiana* (**D**) with the addition of letter 12.[31] *Ep.* 12 is included in the truncated version edited

---

[28] B7 (PL 54.557–58), J1(vii) (502).

[29] In my discussion of the *Collectio Dionysiana* at 3.2.f.

[30] See Gaudemet 1985, 134.

[31] Therefore *Epp.* 4, 7, 16, 18, 167, 14, 159, and 12.

by the Ballerini first,[32] that is, it does not include Ballerini chh. 6–8 but includes 9-end. I term this letter *Ep.* 12a. This collection was highly influential due to its connection with Charlemagne— together with Cresconius, **D–h** is the main disseminator of Dio- nysius Exiguus' work. In 789 Charlemagne provided a summary of some of **D–h** in the *Admonitio Generalis*, and in 802 he again promulgated this collection as the official stance of the Frankish empire on canon law.[33] The *Admonitio Generalis* references Leo at chh. 5 (*Ep.* 4.3–4), 23 (*Ep.* 4.1, 3–4), 56 (*Ep.* 1), 57 (*Ep.* 4.1), and 58 (*Ep.* 4.5).[34] For the age of Charlemagne, this was the source for canon law *par excellence*, which was sought precisely as a defini- tive guide to aid in the task of reform that required texts both authentic and authoritative.[35] Before discussing its manuscripts, it is necessary to observe the influence of **D–h** as visible in the *Collectio Hadriano-Hispanica*, a composite collection drawing upon both this and the *Collectio Hispana* (**S**).[36] The main manuscript of the *Hadriano-Hispanica*, Vat. lat. 1338 (saec. XI), shares a colo- phon with the fragmentary **D–h** manuscript, Würzburg, Universi- tätsbibliothek, M.p.th.f.72 (saec. IX2/4 or 3/4). The colophon runs:

> Iste codex est scriptus de illo authentico, quem domnus Adrianus apostolicus dedit gloriosissimo regi Francorum et Langobardorum ac patricio Romano, quando fuit Romae.[37]

We feel like we are almost able to touch Charlemagne with this colophon—yet its presence is not only in the ninth-century Würz- burg codex but again in the much later eleventh-century Vatican codex. Therefore, even the earlier *Dionysio-Hadriana* manuscript

---

[32] PL 54.645–56.

[33] See McKitterick 1977, 3–10.

[34] Ed. A. Boretius, MGH, *Capitularia regum Francorum*, vol. 1, 53–62.

[35] As McKitterick 1994, 242, notes, 'There is … a preoccupation with authority, orthodoxy and correctness which is also a prevailing characteristic of Carolingian scholarship'. For Charlemagne's need of a definitive source of canon law, see also McKitterick 1977, 3.

[36] See Fournier and Le Bras 1931, 103, working from Hinschius 1884.

[37] See Traube 1898, 77, who refers to these two MSS and 'Frankfurt 64' as of simply the same collection, leading to repetitions that some MSS of the *Dionysio-Hadriana* contain this colophon by Lietzmann 1921, XVI, and McKitterick 1992, 119. However, we have two different collections here, one of which is a fragment of only the beginning of the collection.

may not be a direct copy of Pope Hadrian's. Nonetheless, this colophon reminds us of the weighty importance **D–h** held in Carolingian times, and the influence it extended.

5.2.a.ii. Manuscripts

The importance and influence of **D–h** is displayed by the vast array of manuscripts containing it. Kéry lists ninety-one **D–h** manuscripts.[38] The Ballerini consulted only the following ninth- and tenth-century manuscripts:

v: Vat. lat. 4979 (saec. IX1/4), from Verona in the time of Archdeacon Pacificus.[39] Leo is found at fols 88ᵛ–108ᵛ. Written in a half uncial, this manuscript has large pages divided into two columns of 30 lines each. In the bottom margin of 92ʳ, a note keenly observes, 'multa desunt'; the text ends that side of the folio at 16.1, 'mysterio nullam', and starts 92ᵛ at the beginning of 16.4, 'Hoc nos autem'. *v* starts with a list of the *tituli*, rather than giving the *tituli* before each author.

m: Vat. Pal. lat. 578 (saec. IX), from Mainz.[40] Leo's letters run fols 46ᵛ–72ᵛ; 46ᵛ–48ʳ is a list of their *tituli*, and the corpus of letters begins on 48ʳ. It is written in a single-column Caroline minuscule hand with half-uncial rubrication. 46ᵛ starts the *tituli* with the inscription, 'TIT DECRETORVM PAPAE LEONIS: NVM XLVIII'.

a: Vat. Reg. lat. 1021 (saec. IX1/4, 828 at latest), from Saint-Amand; Leo is found at fols 155ʳ–174ᵛ.[41] This manuscript is written in a Caroline minuscule hand. The *tituli* are given in a table of contents at the beginning.

b: Vat. Reg. lat. 1043 (saec. IX), probably from the Rhône region of Burgundy;[42] Leo runs fols 116ʳ–132ʳ. *b* is written in Caroline minuscule with half-uncial rubrication; in the contents, the *tituli* are black letters with yellow and orange colouring. In the main

---

[38] Kéry 1999, 13–20 gives a list of the manuscripts of the *Dionysio-Hadriana*.

[39] Cf. Ibid., 17; Bischoff 1998–2014, 3.6901. The Ballerini misprinted its catalogue number as 4969, in their own edition at 520, not just in PL 54.

[40] Bischoff 1998–2014, 3.6546. This MS digitised: https://digi.vatlib.it/view/bav_pal_lat_578. Accessed 21 September 2021.

[41] Bischoff 1998–2014, 3.6753. This MS is digitised: https://digi.vatlib.it/view/MSS_Reg.lat.1021. Accessed 21 September 2021.

[42] Cf. Kéry 1999, 17; Bischoff 1998–2014, 3.6758. This MS is digitised: https://digi.vatlib.it/view/MSS_Reg.lat.1043 Accessed 21 September 2021.

text, the rubrics look to have been red but have largely oxidised to being black/blue with a few spatterings of red. Unlike *m*, which gives the *tituli* immediately before Leo's letters, *b* gives the *tituli* for the whole collection at the very beginning; those for Leo are at fol. 11ʳff. The manuscript has 20 lines per page in a single column.

r: Vat. lat. 1337 (saec. IX^in), from the Upper Rhine; Leo is found in fols 120ʳ–139ʳ.[43] As in *m*, the text of Leo begins at 120ʳ–121ᵛ with the *tituli* of Leo's decretals. This manuscript was written in an elegant Caroline minuscule in two columns of 29 lines each. *Capitula* are rubricated whilst the first line of each author is given in orange, yellow, and green. Leo's letters begin, 'INCI PAPAE LEONIS DECRETA'.

g: Rome, Biblioteca Vallicelliana, A.5 (saec. IX), from central Italy.[44] As with *v* above, the Ballerini misprinted its shelfmark, this time as A S. *g* also includes Cresconius, *Concordia canonum*, and the *Collectio Dionysiana adaucta* (**D–a**). Leo's epistles in the **D–h** portion of this manuscript run 152ʳ–171ᵛ. The *tituli* are listed at the beginning of the Leo portion of the manuscript.

p: Paris, lat. 1458, a manuscript made of various different fragments, ranging from the ninth through seventeenth centuries. The second part of this manuscript is **D–h**, from the ninth through tenth centuries.[45] The text begins at ch. 7 of *Ep.* 16, covering fols 33ʳ–46ᵛ.

d: Düsseldorf, Universitätsbibliothek, E.1, (saec. IX2/2) originating from Italy, likely in Rome.[46] *d* contains a partial version of *Collectio Vaticana* (**V**) that has been combined with material from the tradition of **D–h**. The Leo contents are all **D–h**, running fols 104ᵛ–120ʳ, with *tituli* running from 103ᵛ–104ᵛ. *d* is written in a neat Caroline minuscule in two columns with uncial rubrication; at fol. 114ᵛ, the rubrication disappears, although it reappears for the second letter of Pope Hilarus who immediately fol-

---

[43] Bischoff 1998–2014, 3.6854; Kuttner 1986, 67–69. This MS is digitised: https://digi.vatlib.it/view/MSS_Vat.lat.1337. Accessed 21 September 2021.

[44] Kéry 1999, 20, however, only lists this MS for the *Dionysiana adaucta*. Bischoff 1998–2014, 3.5349, says it is from Rome.

[45] Cf. 'Bibliothèque nationale de France, Archives et manuscrits – Latin 1458', accessed 21 September 2021, http://archivesetmanuscrits.bnf.fr/ead.html?id = FRBNFEAD000059426&qid = sdx_q0#FRBNFEAD000059426_e0000165. See also Bischoff 1998–2014, 3.4018. Listed by neither the Ballerini nor Kéry 1999.

[46] Bischoff 1998–2014, 1.1070. This manuscript is digitised: http://digital.ub.uni-duesseldorf.de/man/content/titleinfo/3870845. Accessed 21 September 2021.

lows Leo. Fol. 107^r has a brief lacuna in *Ep.* 16.2, missing the words, 'uel quibus ab Aegypto in Galilaeam, persecutore mortuo, reuocatus est'. At 114^r, the second half of line two is scraped away, along with the seven lines following. A new hand takes over, and the text jumps ahead from *Ep.* 14.1 to 14.10. Finally, 115^r begins with a new hand and changes twice in column 2.

The Ballerini make mention of one further manuscript which they cite as Vallicelliana XVIII. If this is T.XVIII, (saec. X), from central Italy, it is not **D–h**. This manuscript begins with Cresconius, *Concordia canonum*, fols 1–58^v. Foll. 207^r–208^r include a fragment from Leo, *Ep.* 16, and 246^r–252^v have a variety of Leo excerpts. First comes Leo, *Ep.* 167.7-end, then an item, '**De coniuratis ex concilio calcedonensem /** Apud extrinsecas leges penitus amputatur'. Leo, *Ep.* 106, covers fols 251^r–252^r, followed by an excerpt from *Ep.* 162.1:

> **Ex epistula eiusdem sci leonis ad leonem augustum:**
>
> **A**pud niceam mysticus ille patrum numerus definiuit ne catholicorum confessio aut unigenitum dei filium in aliquo crederet patribus im patrem aut eundem cum facuts est filius hominis non ueram carnis nostre atque anime habuisse naturam; Qui numerus ideo misticus esse dicitur qui a trinitatem significat reuera enim si trecentos decem et octo patres diuidas nihil omnino remanebit;

Ep. 93 closes the Leo section of this manuscript. T.XVIII, as it turns out, is not **D–h**, but the *Collectio LXXII capitulorum*, a systematic collection discussed below at 5.2.h.

Besides the manuscripts consulted by the Ballerini, around which the following survey is based, other early **D–h** manuscripts that include the papal letters are:

> Paris, lat. 8921 (saec. VIII).[47] Corbie a-b script with Corbie decoration; presumably from the Corbie scriptorium. Turner and the *Catalogue générale* of the Bibliothèque nationale says that it is the earliest copy of **D–h**.[48] Any future work into the text of **D–h**, whether for Leo or for the other contents, must take this codex into account. Leo's letters run 103^v–120^v. Ganz notes that, although Corbie a-b manuscripts have previously been dated

---

[47] This MS is digitised: https://gallica.bnf.fr/ark:/12148/btv1b90670308. Accessed 21 September 2021.

[48] Turner, EOMIA I.2, 1, p. xii, and II.1, p. 35. *Catalogue générale* available online: https://archivesetmanuscrits.bnf.fr/ark:/12148/cc62450r. Accessed 21 September 2021. Wurm 1939, 34, cites Turner.

earlier than Maurdramnus manuscripts, such as Paris lat. 11711 below, many were, in fact, produced at the same time. He gives a range for datable a-b manuscripts of 790–830,[49] overlapping the use of Maurdramnus script, for the Maurdramnus Bible is from *c.* 771–83. Therefore, Paris, lat. 8921 and 11711 may, in fact, be contemporaries. Whether they are contemporary or not, they are probably related.

Paris, lat. 11711 (saec. VIII–IX).[50] Written at Corbie in Maurdramnus script; provenance of St-Germain-des-Prés (MS 365). Ganz dates to after 789,[51] but it could be earlier, since **D–h** came north in the 770s, at a simliar time to Maurdramnus' abbacy. However, it is also highly likely that most copies of **D–h** are post-789 because of the *Admonitio Generalis* and its influence upon canon law in the Frankish kingdom. Leo's letters run fols 87ʳ–104ᵛ. On fol. 87ʳ, after the introductory paragraph of *Ep.* 4, the *tituli* for all of Leo's letters are given. These *tituli* are not included in the text of the letters. Such a drastic difference between the two manuscripts makes it unlikely that the two Corbie copies of **D–h** are twins or parent and child. Textually speaking, these manuscripts share the common **D–h** readings. 11711 is more likely to be a copy of 8921 than the other way around, because readings it shares with 8921 are often corrected by a contemporary hand. Furthermore, although this argument is not airtight, it seems that it would be easier to go through 8921 and copy out all of the *tituli* at the beginning of the text as in 11711 than to flip back and forth in 11711 and add them to 8921.

Paris, lat. 11710 (written in 805).[52] This manuscript was written in Burgundy and has a provenance of St-Germain-des-Prés (MS 367). It includes all the *tituli* in a table of contents at the start of the manuscript.

Reims, Bibliothèque municipale, 671 (saec. IXⁱⁿ).[53] From Reims.

Munich, Bayerische Staatsbibliothek, Clm 14517 (saec. VIII–IX) + Clm 14567 (saec. Xᵐᵉᵈ).[54] Clm 14517 comes from the region of Southwestern Germany, Switzerland, or Northern Italy, and Clm 14567 comes from Regensburg.

---

[49] Ganz 1990, 49–51.

[50] Ganz 1990, 136. See also Kéry 1999, 16. This MS is digitised: https://gallica.bnf.fr/ark:/12148/btv1b10038458h. Accessed 21 September 2021.

[51] Ganz 1990, 46.

[52] Wurm 1939, 34; Kéry 1999, 16. This MS is digitised: https://gallica.bnf.fr/ark:/12148/btv1b10032734z. Accessed 21 September 2021.

[53] Kéry 1999, 17.

[54] Kéry 1999, 16.

5.2.a.iii. Manuscript Relations

The first fact that we can observe is the treatment of *tituli* in different **D–h** manuscripts. **D–h** *v a b g*, Paris, lat. 11711 and 11710 all begin with a list of *tituli* before the main text of the *Dionysio-Hadriana*. On the other hand, *m r g*, and Paris, lat. 8921 all list the *tituli* at the beginning of the author. Manuscripts *d* and *p* are too fragmentary for us to know this feature. Nevertheless, here are two broad categories for beginning to trace a lineage. Of note is the fact that antiquity tells us nothing in this case, since two of our oldest manuscripts, both from Corbie, Paris, lat. 8921 and 11711, differ in this regard.

Of the 97 **D** variants in the table above at 3.2.f.iii, 44 are common to **D** *a c*. Of these 44, all of **D–h** agree with **D** in 23 cases;[55] in eight cases, all collated **D–h** manuscripts agree with **D** except for **D–h** *m*;[56] in three cases, they all agree with **D** except *v*;[57] twice they all agree with **D** except *v* and *m*;[58] once they all agree with **D** except *v* and *a*;[59] and once, all but *p* agree with **D**. Moreover, of the variants where *c* has a lacuna, **D–h** agrees with **D** *a* at Variant 53. With these data should be included Variant 60, for which all **D–h** manuscripts agree with **D** *c* in giving 'conflictatione' against Ballerini 'tentatione', except for *p*, which agrees with **D** *a*, 'conflictione', a variant well within the **D** family of readings. As well, **D–h** agrees with **D** in Variant 84, except for *m*, which provides 'meis moribus exaestimasti' against **D**, 'meis moribus aestimasti'. Given that 'aestimo' and 'extimo' are often interchangeable (visible throughout the variants discussed in this project), this variant is not significant. These many correspondences alone demonstrate that **D–h** is descended from a strand of the **D** tradition similar to **D** *a c*. Variant 73, *Ep.* 14.Pr., has multiple variants: first, the order of the words, 'sint commissa', and the mood of the verb. **D** gives 'commissa sunt', with which all but **D–h** *p*

---

[55] Varr. 6 (but see **D–h** *g* 'homine' for 'omni'); 9, 28; 32; 35; 36; 41; 43; 49; 50; 52; 59; 62; 63; 64; 65; 69; 71; 82; 85 (although **D–h** *m* slightly different from others); 87 (all agree with **D** *c*); 93 and 94.

[56] Varr. 38; 40 (**D–h** *m¹*—*m²* modifies text to rest of **D–h**); 77; 84; 88; 91; 92; and 95.

[57] Varr. 3; 26; and 81.

[58] Varr. 96 and 97.

[59] Var. 66.

give; *p* follows the word order but gives the subjunctive 'sint'. As well, Variant 73 is an omission of 'apostoli' before 'auctoritate'. *m* includes 'apostoli'—*m* is the most like the Ballerini variants of the **D-h** manuscripts, as seen in the cross-references to **D**. Here again is a major convergence between **D** and **D-h**. These major convergences are not the whole story, however. **D** gives 'regulis canonum' in Variant 21, but all of **D-h** agrees with the Ballerini order, 'canonum regulis'.

Of variants/errors unique to **D** *c*, all but **D-h** *d* agree with Variant 1; here, *d* gives, 'per diuersas prouincias' against the others, 'per uniuersas' and the Ballerini who do not put 'per' between 'et' and 'uniuersas'. Another example is Variant 48, where all but **D-h** *a* give, 'Pater meus in nomine meo' against the Ballerini— and Vulgate—omission of 'meus'. In Variant 76, **D-h** agrees with **D** *a*, 'impenderes et', but with **D** *c* and the Ballerini in keeping, 'continenti', against *a*'s error. In Variant 83, all but *v* and *m* agree with **D** *c*, 'concessum', although *p* changes 'quodque' to 'quodcumque'. With these data in mind, we can start to separate out *v* and *m* from the rest of **D-h**, and move along in our investigation to questions other than how closely are **D** and **D-h** related. The following table provides the variants where there is greater diversity amongst the **D-h** readings, agreement with **D** *a* against **D** *c*, or **D-h** is at variance from **D**. Where no reading is given for *v*, *p*, or *d*, this is because there is a gap in the text. Where no reading is given for *g*, on the other hand, this is because of time restraints upon access to the manuscript, of which only partial collation was possible. The variants are simply listed with their numbers from **D**.

Var.	*Collectiones Diony-sio-Hadriana* (**D-h**) and *Dionysiana* (**D**)	Ballerini text (control)	Significance
5	*quis* (**D** *a*) *sincere* (**D** *c*) *sinceram* (**D-h** *d*) *sincer* (**D-h** *b'*)	permittentes *since-rum* corpus (**D-h** *v*, *m*, *a*, *b²*, *r*, *g*)	Errors *d* and *b'*
7	*dissimulationem* (**D** *a*; **D-h** *m*, *a*, *b*)	*dissimilationem* (**D** *c*; **D-h** *v*, *g*)	Shared variant **D** *a*; **D-h** *m*, *a*, *b*
11	*nulla necessitate saeculi substrahatur* (**D** *c*) *nullus* (**D-h** *a*)	*nullis necessitatis uinculis abstrahatur* (**D** *a*; **D-h** *v*, *m*, *a*, *b*, *r*, *g*, *d*)	Error **D-h** *a*

Var.	*Collectiones Diony-sio-Hadriana* (**D–h**) and *Dionysiana* (**D**)	Ballerini text (control)	Significance
13	*constituet* (**D** *a*) *constituerit* (**D–h** *a*, *b¹*, *r*, *g*, *d*)	unicuique *constiterit* natalium (**D** *c*; **D–h** *v*, *m*, *b²*)	Shared variant **D–h** *a*, *b¹*, *r*, *g*, *d*
19	*liceat* (**D** *a*; **D–h** *v*, *m*, *a*, *b*)	*licuerit* sacerdotem (**D** *c*; **D–h** *r*, *d*)	Shared error **D** *a*; **D–h** *v*, *m*, *a*, *b*
20	*regulis canonum* (**D** *a*, *c*)	*canonum regulis* (**D–h** *v*, *m*, *a*, *b*, *r*, *d*)	**D–h** differs from **D**
21	*consuerunt* (**D** *a*; **D–h** *m*, *r²*, *g*, *d*) *consuluerunt* (**D–h** *r¹*)	*consueuerunt* (**D** *c*; **D–h** *v*, *a*)	Common variant (error?) **D** *a*; **D–h** *m*, *r²*, *g*, *d*
23	*constitutos* (**D** *a*; **D–h** *v*, *m*, *a*, *b*, *r*, *g*, *d*)	*constituti* (**D** *c*)	Shared error **D** *a*; **D–h**
24	*exerceant* (**D** *a*) *exerceat* (**D** *c*; **D–h** *v*, *m*, *a*, *b*, *r*, *g*, *d*)	N/A	Common reading **D** *c*; **D–h**
28	*a* uestra dilectione *custodire* (**D** *c*) *ut* uestra dilectione *custodiri* (**D–h** *v*, *m*, *a*, *b*, *r*, *d*)	*a* uestra dilectione *custodiri* (**D** *a*)	Common error **D–h**
29	maximo et paterio uu cc conss (*a*) om. *uu cc* (**D** *c*) Maximo iterum et paterno conss (**D–h** *m*, *a*, *b*, *r*, *g*, *d*) **D–h** *v* as above, but 'uua consulibus'	Maximo iterum et Paterio uiris clarissimis consulibus	Common variant on names **D–h** Error in abbrev. **D–h** *v*
32	*que* (**D** *c*) *qui* (**D–h** *a*, *b*)	*quid* refugeret (**D** *a*; **D–h** *v*, *m*, *r*, *d*)	Common error **D–h** *a*, *b*
35	Dat III kl Febr Theodosio XVIII et Albino uc cons (**D** *a*) Dat III kl Feb theodosio XVIII et Albino conss (**D** *c*) Data III Febr Theodosio Augusto XVIII et	Data tertio kalendas Februarii, Theodosio Augusto XVIII et Albino uiris clarissimis consulibus	Agreement in content, diversity in abbrev.

Var.	Collectiones Diony-sio-Hadriana (**D-h**) and Dionysiana (**D**)	Ballerini text (control)	Significance
	Albino uiris claris-simis consulibus (**D-h** v) Data Feb \kl/ Theodosio XVIII et Albina uua cons (**D-h** a) Dat iii k Feb Theodosio XVIII et Albino uucc cons (**D-h** r) Data iii kl feb Theodosio XVIII et Albino conss (**D-h** g) DAT III kl febr theodosio XVIII et albino conss (**D-h** d)		
37	cleri (**D** a, c; **D-h** b¹, d)	obnoxium celeri sollicitudine (**D-h** v, m, a, b², r, g)	Common error **D**; **D-h** b¹, d
40	mistico munerum oblato (**D** a, c; **D-h** d) mystico munerum oblatio (**D-h** a, b¹, r)	mystica munerum oblatione (**D-h** m, b²)	Common error **D**; **D-h** d Common error **D-h** a, b¹, r
43	districtio (**D** a, c; **D-h** m, b, r) discrectio (**D-h** a) destrictio (**D-h** d = districtio)	distinctio	Common variant **D**; **D-h** m, b, r
45 1 Cor. 1:10	in eodem sentendien-dam sententia (**D** a) et in eadem scientia (**D** c; many Vulgate mss) et in eadem sapien-tia (**D-h** b, r, d) in eodem sensum et in eadem sententiam (**D-h** g)	in eodem sensu et in eadem sententia (**D-h** a; some Vulgate mss)	Common variant **D-h** b, r, d Error **D-h** g based on same text as **D-h** a

Var.	*Collectiones Diony-sio-Hadriana* (**D–h**) and *Dionysiana* (**D**)	Ballerini text (control)	Significance
52	*Vacillum et Pascha-sium* (**D** *a*) *Vacchillum atque Pascasinum* (**D–h** *v*) *Vaccillum et Pas-chasinum* (**D–h** *m, a, r, g*) *Vacillum et Pas-chasinum* (**D–h** *b, d*) *Vacillum* atque (**D–h** *p*)	*Bacillum atque Pas-chasinum*	Various spellings derived from 'Vac-illum et Paschasi-num' For 'et/atque', agreement **D** *a*; **D–h** *m, a, b, r, g* against **D–h** *v, p* and Bal-lerini
54	*gregum* (**D** *a*) *gregem* (**D–h** *a, b, r, g, p, d*)	*gregis* (**D–h** *v, m*)	Shared error **D–h** *a, b, r, g, p, d* derived from variant **D** *a*; **D–h** *v, m* variant a possible emendation of error
55	*Deum* (**D** *a*; **D–h** *r, d*)	apud *Dominum* (**D–h** *v, m, a, b, p*)	Shared variant **D** *a*; **D–h** *r, d*
56	Data III kl iul alipio et ardabure conss (**D** *a*; **D–h** *p*) Data III kl Ianu-arias alypio et ard-abure consulibus (**D–h** *v*; abbrevv. vary, but also: *m, a, b, r*) Data III kl Ian Olympio et Ard-abure consulibus (**D–h** *g, d*)	Data III Kalend. Ianuarii Calepio et Ardabure uiris clar-issimis consulibus	**D–h** *v, m, a, b, r* in essential agreement with Ballerini save 'alipio' for 'Calepio' Shared variant **D** *a*; **D–h** *p* Shared error **D–h** *g, d* derived from rest of **D–h**
59	*pastorum* (**D** *a*; **D–h** *v, m, a, b, r, g, p, d*)	*pastoris* cura	Shared variant **D** *a*; **D–h**
65	*qui* (**D** *a*; **D–h** *v, m, a, b, r, p, d*) *quia* (**D** *c*)	in eis ecclesiis ... *quae*	Shared error **D** *a*; **D–h** Error **D** *c* an attempt to correct above error
66	*consecratio* (**D** *a*; **D–h** *v²*, *m, r*) *con creatio* (**D–h** *v¹*) *creato* (**D–h** *b*)	*creatio* (**D** *c*; **D–h** *a, p, d*)	Shared variant **D** *a*; **D–h** *v²*, *m, r* Error **D–h** *v¹* derived therefrom Error **D–h** *b* derived from **D** *a*; **D–h** *a, p, d*

Var.	Collectiones Diony-sio-Hadriana (D–h) and Dionysiana (D)	Ballerini text (con-trol)	Significance
70	apostolicae sedis *impleuerit* (**D** *a*; **D–h** *m, b, r, d*) *impleuerint* (**D** *c*; **D–h** *a*) *impleuerunt* (**D–h** *v*) *apostolica si impleu-erint* (**D–h** *p*)	N/A	Shared error **D** *a*; **D–h** *m, b, r, d* Error **D–h** *v* derived from **D** *c*; **D–h** *a, p* verb number Error **D–h** *p*
72	*siue ratione* (**D** *a, c*; **D–h** *g, p*)	*si uera ratione* (**D–h** *v, m, a, b, r, d*)	Shared error **D**; **D–h** *g, p*
86	*uel* secundo tercio *uersandum* (**D** *a*) *aut* secundo, tertio seruandum (**D** *c*) *aut* secundo tertio*ue* (**D–h** *v, p*) *uel* secundo tertio*ue* (**D–h** *m, a, b*) *uel* secundo tertio seruandum (**D–h** *r*)	*aut* secundo *uel* ter-tio seruandum	Shared variant **D–h** *v, p* Shared variant (**D–h** *m, a, b* with familial trait of above Variant **D–h** *r* **D–h** *-ue* common to this branch of wider D family
88	Si quis *autem* epis-copus (**D** *a*; **D–h** *v, m, a, b, r, g, p*)	Si quis episcopus (**D** *c*)	Shared variant **D** *a*; **D–h**
96	*spiritus sancti inuo-catione* (**D** *c*) *sancti spiritus inuo-catione* (**D** *a*; **D–h** *v, m, b², r, d*) *sancti spiritus inuo-cationem* (**D–h** *a, b¹, g*)	*inuocatione Spiritus Sancti*	Shared variant **D** *a*; **D–h** *v, m, b², r, d* Shared error **D–h** *a, b¹, g* based on vari-ant above
97	Omission of date (**D** *a*) Dat XIII kl April, cons. marciani Augusti (**D** *c*) Data XII kal April consulatu maioriani augusti (**D–h** *v*; abbrevv. vary, but also *m, a, b, r, p, d*) Dat kl April consuli martiano (**D–h** *g*)	Data XII kalen-darum Aprilium, consulatu Maioriani Augusti	Basic agreement with Ballerini **D–h** *v, m, a, b, r, p, d* Error **D–h** *g*

This table sets forth many elements of **D–h** to us. First of all, some errors or variants that seemed isolated to either *a* or *c* of **D** are now seen in a wider context of agreement with **D–h**, while some that seemed to be definitively **D** are seen not to exist in **D–h**. Second, two manuscripts that stand out as related are *b* and *r*, which also very often agree with *m* and occasionally *d*. *b* and *r* are from the Rhône region of Burgundy and the Upper Rhine, respectively—there is a slim possibility that they have a common descent. Highly significant is their shared variant of 'sapientia' in Variant 45, a variant no other **D–h** manuscript has and which is not cited by Weber-Gryson for manuscripts of the Vulgate Bible. Its significance increases when we recall its presence in some Cresconius manuscripts. *m*, despite its similarities to *b* and *r*, stands out as the manuscript that most frequently provides a reading in agreement with the Ballerini against the rest of **D–h**; those instances where *b* agrees with *m* in such readings, it is *b*'s correcting hand, not the original. Thus, *b* and *r* still stand united, and *m* stands to one side, sometimes with *v*. However, *m* and *v*, unlike *b* and *r*, are further removed from each other in origin, from Mainz and Verona respectively. They furthermore agree less frequently than *b* and *r*, and some of their agreements against **D–h** could be independent conjectures, such as 'gregis' against the obviously corrupt and ungrammatical 'gregem'. *g* and *d* are related in providing 'Olympio' against the reading 'Alypio' of the rest of **D–h**, although the consul's real name was 'Calypius', given by the majority of Leo manuscripts. Since *g* is alone amongst the manuscripts of **D–h** in mistaking 'Marciano' for 'Maioriano', it is probably an error independent of **D** *c*, especially since *g* omits the number of the date before 'k April'. For a copyist of Leo's letters, Majorian would be a less common sight than Marcian, so it is no surprise that Marcian occasionally appears in consular formulae instead of Majorian; it is highly unlikely to have gone the other way.

Now that we have seen the latest of the **D** family of Leo's letters (I class **D–a** separately), the following stemma can be put forward:

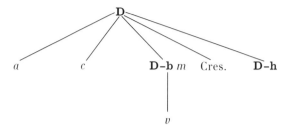

5.2.b. Collectio Hadriano-Hispanica[60] (**H–s**)

5.2.b.i. Dating and Context

This collection is a modified version of the *Collectio Dionysio-Hadriana* with material from the *Collectio Hispana Gallica*. It contains the same collection of Leo's letters as **D–h**: *Epp.* 4, 7, 16, 18, 167, and 14. It was formed in the first half of the ninth century, presumably as an attempt to make material from **D–h** and **S–g** more readily available.

5.2.b.ii. Manuscripts

The *Hadiano-Hispanica* exists in four manuscripts, of which I have collated *g* and *v*:

Mantua, Biblioteca Comunale, C.II.23 (saec. XII2/2).

g = St Gallen, Stiftsbibliothek, 671 (saec. IX^in), from Swabia, probably St Gallen itself.[61] Pages 2–82 are written in an Allemannian hand, and 83 onwards in Caroline minuscule. The collection of Leo's letters is that of **D–h/H–s**, found on pp. 290–358.

v = Vat. lat. 1338 (saec. XI), from France.[62] Leo's letters end partway through *Ep.* 14 at fol. 268ᵛ with the words, 'Quae moderatio si quibuscumque inferioribus membris'. The catchphrase for the next quire, 'ex apostolica institutione', is at the bottom of the page, and here the manuscript ends.

Venice, Biblioteca Nazionale Marciana, lat. IV.48 (2301) (saec. XV1/2), from Italy.

---

[60] Kéry 1999, 69.

[61] Bischoff 1998–2014, 3.5828. This manuscript is digitised: https://www.e-codices.unifr.ch/en/list/one/csg/0671 Accessed 21 September 2021. See also Autenrieth 1956, 81.

[62] Kuttner 1986, 70–71. This manuscript is digitised: https://digi.vatlib.it/view/MSS_Vat.lat.1338. Accessed 21 September 2021.

5.2.b.iii. Manuscript Relations

Textually, this collection is another witness to **D-h**. The Sankt Gall manuscript provides us with yet another ninth-century **D-h** alongside those discussed above.

5.2.c. *Collectio Dionysiana adaucta*[63] (**D-a**)

5.2.c.i. Dating and Context

This canonical collection was gathered between 850 and 872, mostly likely in Ravenna, but possibly in Rome.[64] Massigli provides strong evidence for an origin in Ravenna based on the following: the northern Italian origin of *v* and *p*; a Ravenna origin for *g*, itself based on its presence in Ravenna within a century and a half and certain textual variants leaning to a non-Roman origin; and the Greek Italian origins of **D-a** *c*.[65] Chavasse also points to northern Italy, citing the presence of an anti-Arian dossier in **D-a** that would make sense if its source had been those parts of Italy in the close neighbourhood of the supposedly Arian Lombards;[66] if the Lombards were more pagan than Arian, as argued by Fanning,[67] Northern Italy would still be the Italian region most likely to produce anti-Arian tractates and compendia, given the existence of at least some Lombard Arians as well as the possible legacy of the previous Arian invaders, the Gepids and Ostrogoths. Indeed, Thomas S. Brown has taken Fanning's article to task and argued that there was a significant element of Arianism within the Lombard kingdom and élite, citing various examples from the 600s which Fanning had failed to mention as well as the aforementioned populations of Ostrogoths and Gepids amongst the

---

[63] B8 (PL 54.557–58), J1(viii) (502).

[64] Landau 1999, 429–30, n. 19, argues for Rome.

[65] Massigli 1912, 369–77; Wurm 1939, 35, agrees with Massigli.

[66] Chavasse 1964, 162.

[67] Fanning 1981 argues from the documentary evidence that the Lombards were primarily pagan upon entering Italy in 568 but with Catholic and Arian minorities that persisted into the 600s when the Catholic conversion of the Lombards took place. Brown 2009 takes issue with Fanning concerning Arianism, however—see below. Either way, some of the archaeology points towards the ongoing life of pre-Christian practices within the Lombard community, as visible in the artifacts on display at the Civico Museo Archeologico di Milano.

Lombards.[68] Furthermore, regardless of how many Arians were amongst the Lombards as a people, Paul the Deacon—who sees them as primarily pagan in the 500s—says that there were many Arian bishops in the Lombard kingdom.[69] That is to say, Chavasse's argument for an anti-Arian compendium likely originating in northern Italy still holds in the face of any continued Lombard paganism and the catholic elements in Lombard society.

The collection is either an augmented *Dionysiana*, according to Wurm, or *Dionysio-Hadriana*, according to Maassen; Wurm's arguments that the additions to the original collection come from the *Vaticana* (**V**) as well as being present in the otherwise 'pure' *Collectio Dionysiana* manuscript, Vat. lat. 5845 (*c*), make a compelling case that, in fact, we have here an augmented *Dionysiana*, not *Dionysio-Hadriana*.[70] However, Bibliotheca Vallicelliana A.5 (*g*), on the other hand, is a manuscript of the *Dionysio-Hadriana*, not the *Dionysiana*. Chavasse sidesteps the issue of which Dionysian collection has been augmented by simply addressing the augmentation itself through the lens of its two earliest manuscripts, *c* (*Dionysiana*) and *g* (*Dionysio-Hadriana*). The additions he refers to as S, looking to their source.[71]

Since **D–a** is an augmentation that compilers felt compelled to append to both the *Dionysiana* and *Dionysio-Hadriana*, it comes as no surprise that the characteristic letters of the collection are not those of **D**. **D–a** contains fifteen of Leo's letters, the first six of which are so-called decretals: 9, 15, 1, 2, 108, 17, 20, 23, 22, 28, 139, 119, 80, 145, and 165. Chavasse argues that the source of **D–a** made use of some of the same sources as other collections, thereby explaining the common groupings of letters found herein. The selection of dogmatic letters, which we shall analyse shortly, consists of two proto-collections related to **V**, whereas the body of six 'decretals' is hitherto unattested in any other canonical collection,[72] although we have frequently seen *Epp.* 1 and 2 attached together.

---

[68] On Arianism, see T. S. Brown 2009, 293–95.

[69] *Historia Langobardorum* 4.42: 'Huius temporibus pene per omnes ciuitates regni eius duo episcopi erant, unus catholicus et alter Arrianus'.

[70] Maassen 1870, 454; Wurm 1939, 35.

[71] Chavasse 1964.

[72] See the chart ibid., 169.

More significant is the body of 'dogmatic' letters in **D-a**. As Chavasse demonstrates, there are two selections of Leo's dogmatic letters included in both **D-a** and **V**: *Epp.* 20, 23, 22, and 28; and *Epp.* 139, 119, 80, 145, and 165.[73] In **D-a**, they run as items 111–23 (*g*) or 46–58 (*c*); in **V** they are items 61–70 and 82–89. Between the two collections, they are in a different order. In the **D-a** order, they appear to be documents with two distinct concerns. The first selection of four letters is about the issue of Eutyches, consisting of *Ep.* 20, Leo's anti-Nestorian letter to Eutyches; the account of the trial of Eutyches at the Home Synod of 448; then *Ep.* 23 to Flavian of Constantinople where Leo expresses his shock that he'd not heard about Eutyches' heresy sooner; *Ep.* 22, in which Flavian initially tells Leo about Eutyches, but given here as though a reply to *Ep.* 23; then Leo's *Tome* (*Ep.* 28), presented as the final judgement on the issue. In **V**, the Home Synod is delayed until later in the collection. This selection of letters is also apparent in *Collectio Hispana* (**S**), where these four (*Epp.* 20, 23, 22, and 28)—omitting the Home Synod—are also edited together.[74] These come together as **proto-4**,[75] a fairly straightforward anti-Eutychian collection.

The second selection of five letters is about the relationships amongst the highest-ranking episcopates; *Ep.* 139 is addressed to Juvenal of Jerusalem, where Leo both congratulates Juvenal on being restored to his see and reprimands him as the likely source of the problem of his forced exclusion from the city and the uncanonical enthronement of a rival bishop, the monk Theodosius; *Ep.* 119 is to Maximus of Antioch, whose Nicene episcopal privileges Leo sees as threatened by both Anatolius of Constantinople and Juvenal of Jerusalem; in *Ep.* 80 to Anatolius of Constantinople, Leo urges him to remove Dioscorus of Alexandria, Juvenal of Jerusalem, and Eustathius of Berytus from the diptychs;[76] *Ep.* 145 is addressed to Emperor Leo I and concerns itself with the establishment of an orthodox episcopacy in Alexandria; and *Ep.* 165 is

---

[73] See ibid., 158.

[74] Ibid., 169–70.

[75] See the Appendix for a list and description of the proto-collections.

[76] The diptychs were lists of major bishops with whom an episcopal see was in communion that were read out as part of the intercessions in the celebration of the Eucharist.

Leo's famous 'second' *Tome* to Emperor Leo I. This collection is **proto-5**, *Epp.* 139, 119, 80, 145, and 165.[77] Chavasse argues that **proto-5** would have been considered important during the Acacian Schism, when bishops' names were being erased from diptychs, and when Bishops of Rome were involved in wrangling with emperors over the definition of orthodoxy.[78] The two collections have been split up and rearranged in **V**, but they are still clearly evident in the selection of Leo's letters. Chavasse has thus discovered two more proto-collections for us. It is time to consdier how these relationships hold out in the realm of textual variation.

5.2.c.ii. Manuscripts

D-a exists in six manuscripts, all listed below, but only five consulted for this project:

   c: Vat. lat. 5845 (915–34).[79] For palaeography and origins, see **D** *c* above at 3.2.f.ii. Leo's letters are items 40–58.[80] In *c*, **D-a** has been appended to the *Collectio Dionysiana*, not the *Dionysio-Hadriana*.

   m: Munich, Bayerische Staatsbibliothek, Clm 14008 (saec. IX2/2), originating in Rome with provenance of St Emmeram, Regensburg.[81] It is written in a Caroline minuscule with capitals as rubrication. *m* like *g* and *v*, contains both **D-h** and **D-a**; a damaged selection from **D-h** can be found at fols 111^v–120^v, where the text of *Ep.* 14.11 ends somewhere shortly after 'conflueret'; fol. 121^r is mostly flaked away and illegible, and when legible text resumes on 121^v, we are in the letters of Pope Hilarus. Leo's **D-a** letters run fols 203^v–235^v; after *Ep.* 20 ends on 213^v, before moving on to *Ep.* 23, we have 'EXEMPLA GESTORUM VBI IN CONSTANTINOPOLITANA SYNODO A SCO FLAVIANO CONFESSORE EVTICHES HERETICVS AVDITVS ATQVE DAMNATVS EST', running 213^v–216^v.

---

[77] See the Appendix for a list and description of the proto-collections.

[78] Ibid., 172–75.

[79] This manuscript is digitised: https://digi.vatlib.it/view/MSS_Vat.lat.5845. Accessed 21 September 2021.

[80] If the number seems too large, this is because *Ep.* 165 is items 55–58.

[81] Bischoff 1998–2014, 2.3125. This manuscript is digitised: https://daten.digitale-sammlungen.de/~db/0003/bsb00032665/images/. Accessed 21 September 2021.

g: Rome, Biblioteca Vallicelliana, A.5, from the third quarter of the ninth century, from central Italy; for more information, see **D–h** *g* above (5.2.a).[82] The **D–a** Leo runs 270rb-298^v. The text is minuscule while the rubrics are capitals. If this manuscript comes from Ravenna, as argued by Massigli, then the arguments for a Ravennate origin for this collection are bolstered; acts of Ravennate councils are inscribed on fol. 16 in a tenth-century hand. The correcting hand (*g²*) looks to be contemporary, if not the original scribe.

v: Vercelli, Biblioteca Capitolare, LXXVI (saec. X), originating in Vercelli itself. The entire text, including rubrics, is in a minuscule hand. *v*, like *g*, contains Cresconius and **D–h** as well as **D–a**; in fact, it contains the same material as *g*, excepting where *g* is damages, such as the table of contents. It seems very likely that *v* is copied, if not from *g*, from a sibling of *g* or another descendant of *g*. Outside of commonalities in Leo's letters, in the *tituli* at the beginning, besides having the same wording, at times even the line breaks are the same. At the end of the manuscript, *v*, like *g*, contains a letter of Pope Zacharias and then part of Augustine's *De Trinitate*. Howevr, in the **D–h** portion of these manuscripts, *g* and *v* seem not to agree with each other more frequently than other **D–h** manuscripts, based on collations of Innocent I to Decentius of Gubbio (JK 311). That is to say, the main commonalities of these two manuscripts lie in their contents; their readings do not speak very strongly of a closer relationship between *v* and *g* than between them and other **D–a** manuscripts.

p: Vat. lat. 1343 (saec. X^{ex}-XI^{in}) from Pavia, Italy.[83] This manuscript only contains parts of **D–a** and is a merging of material from both this collection and Pseudo-Isidore.[84] From the **D–a** collection of Leo's letters I was able to find only *Ep.* 9 on fol. 148^{r-v}. The text of *Ep.* 9 cuts off short at 'multitudo conuenerit', and a letter of Pope Zacharias suddenly takes its place.

b: Vat. lat. 1353 (from 1460) which was copied from a manuscript from Bergamo, according to Johannes Barozzi.[85] Massigli says of this manuscript, 'le texte ne présente pas d'autre particularité

---

[82] Bischoff 1998–2014, 3.5349.

[83] See Kuttner 1986, 86–94, for a full description. This manuscript is digitised: https://digi.vatlib.it/view/MSS_Vat.lat.1343. Accessed 21 September 2021.

[84] Kéry 1999, 21.

[85] For this and other information on the MS, see Kuttner 1986, 116–18.

notable que de donner un grand nombre de mauvaises lectures et aucun détail extérieur ne nous renseigne sur la patrie de l'arché-type'.[86] It has thus been excluded from my analysis.

5.2.c.iii. Manuscript Relations

The following table is based upon select readings from *Epp.* 9, 15, 1, and 2.

Var., *Ep.*	*Collectio Dionysiana adaucta* (**D-a**)	Ballerini text (control)	Significance
1, 9 *Inscr.*	**LEO EPIS- COPVS DIO- SCORO ALEX- ANDRINAE ECCLESIAE DE SACERDOTVM VEL LEVITA- RVM ORDINA- TIONE** (*m, g, p*) … **ordinationem** (*v*) … **alexandriae** … (*c*)	N/A	Error *v* Variant *c*
2, 9	*probetur* (*p*)	*comprobetur.* Cum enim (*m, g, v, c*)	Variant *p*
3, 9	*nefas est* quod sanctus discipulus *ipsius* Marcus (*m, g, v, p, c*)	*credere* quod sanc- tus discipulus *eius* Marcus	Common variant **D-a**
4, 9	*apostolis* (*m, g, v, c*)	quod cum *Apostoli* (*p*)	Common error *m, g, v, c*; *p* possible emendation
5, 9	*aeternum princip- ium* (*m, g, v, p, c*) hac *capituli* (*p*)	et uita accepit *initium.* In hac *apostoli*	Common variant **D-a**
6, 9	*iunias* (*m, c*) *iun* (*g, v*)	Data XI kalendas *Iulias*	Common variant *g, v* The abbrevia- tions in *m g v* are not counted here as variants.

[86] Massigli 1912, 368–69.

Var., *Ep.*	*Collectio Dionysiana adaucta* (**D-a**)	Ballerini text (control)	Significance
7, 15 *Inscr.*	**CVI ITEM STATVTA LEONIS AD TOROBIVM EPM ASTVRICENSEM PROVINCIE HISPANIE** (*v*; *m*, *c* om. 'cui' and 'prouincie hispanie'; *g* om. 'prouincie hispanie')	Leo episcopus Turribio episcopo salutem	
8, 15.Pr.	om. *ab* and *sub* (*m*, *c*) ab euangelio *xpi* sub xpi nomine deuiarunt (*g²*, *v*) om. *sub xpi* (*g¹*)	qui *ab* Evangelio *sub* Christi nomine deviarunt	Errors *m* Common variant *g*, *v*
9, 15.Pr.	om. *se* (*m*, *g*, *v*, *c*)	tenebris *se* etiam	Common error **D-a**
10, 15.Pr.	*immersa* (*m*, *g*, *v*, *c*)	paganitatis *immersit*, ut	Common error **D-a**
11, 15.Pr.	in *effectum* (*m*, *c*) *collocaret* (*g*, *v*)	in *effectu* siderum *collocarent*	Error *m*, *c* Common error *g*, *v* Not stemmatically significant, simple error from assuming suspension of letter m in a predecessor.
12, 15.Pr.	*qui* etsi *sacerdotalis* (*m*, *c*) *et* (*v*)	*quae* etsi *sacerdotali* (*g*)	Error *m*, *c* Variant (likely error) *v*
13, 15.Pr.	*christianissimorum* (*v*)	tamen *Christianorum* principum (*m*, *g*, *c*)	Variant *v*
14, 15.Pr.	*spiritalem* (*g*, *v*)	ad *spiritale* ... remedium (*m*, *c*)	Common error *g*, *v*; easily emended by *m* and *c*
15, 15.Pr.	*xvii* (*m*, *c*) *xvi* (*g*) *xvimi capitulit* (*v*)	opiniones *sedecim capitulis*	Error *m* Error *v*

Var., *Ep.*	*Collectio Dionysiana adaucta* (**D–a**)	Ballerini text (control)	Significance
16, 15.17	*cuiusdam* (*m, g, v, c*)	miror *cujusquam* catholici	Common variant **D–a**
17, 15.17	*laborem* (*m*) *labo\ra\re* (*g*) *labore* (*c*)	intelligentiam *laborare* (*v*)	Errors *m, g, c*
18, 15.17	sit *ascendente* (*v*)	sit *an descendente* ad inferna (*m, g, c*)	Error *v*
19, 15.17	om. *est* (*m, g, v*)	et mortua *est* et sepulta	Common variant **D–a**
20, 15.17	*tertia resuscitata* (*g, v*) tertio *resuscitata* (*m*) tertio *resurrectio resuscitata* (*c*)	die tertio suscitata	Common variant **D–a** Common variant *g, v*
21, 15.17	*ydacianus* (*m, c*) *datius* (*g*) *dacius* (*v*)	fratres nostri *Idatius* et	Errors *m, g, v, c; g, v* clearly related
22, 15.17	*substantia* (*g*)	cum eis *instantia* tua (*m, v, c*)	Error *g*
23, 15.17	No date given (*m, g, v*) data xii k aug callipio et ardabore conss (c^2)		Common variant **D–a**
24, 15.17	EXPLICIT (*g*) EXPLIC (*v*) om. 'explicit' (*m, c*)	N/A	
25, 1 *Inscr.*	**INCIPIT PAPE LEONIS AD AQVILENSEM EPISCOPVM** (*m*; g^2, *v add.* 'ianuarium' *post* 'ad') … ad alense(m) epm (*c*)	N/A	
26, 1.1	om. ne (*m, g, v, c*)	nostrorum *ne* insontibus	Common error **D–a; Sa**

Var., *Ep.*	*Collectio Dionysiana adaucta* (**D–a**)	Ballerini text (control)	Significance
27, 1.1	dom*os sedeant* ... (*m, g, v, c*)	plures dom*us adeant* et per falsi	Common variant **D–a**; **Sa**
28, 1.1	in talium *receptio-nem* seruassent (*m*)	*receptione* (*g, v, c*)	Error *m*; agreement with **Sa** *s, l, c* coincidental
29, 1.2	*hoc* nostri auctoritate (*m, g, v, c*)	*hac*	Common error **D–a**; **Sa** *s, l, r, k*
30, 1.2	diaconi, *uel* cuiuscumque ordinis (*m, g, v, c*)	diaconi, *sive* cuiuscumque	Common variant **D–a**; **Sa**
31, 1.2	*possint* (*m, g, v, c*)	nullis *possit* (*s*)	Common error **D–a**; **Sa** *l, c, k*
32, 1.2	*quod* in doctrina (*m, g, v, c*)	*quidquid* in doctrina	Common variant **D–a**; **Sa**
33, 1.2	om. *esse* (*m, g, v, c*)	istorum *esse* versutiam	Common variant (error?) **D–a**; **Sa**
34, 1.2	hanc iustorum versutiam (*m, g, v, c*)	As above	Common error **D–a**
35, 1.4	om. *per ... dudum* (*m, g, v, c*)	ne *per huiusmodi in homines exstincta dudum scandala suscitentur* (*s²*)	Common error **D–a**; **Sa**
36, 1.5	om. *nec ... officio* (*m, g, v, c*)	diaconatus ordine *nec in subsequenti officio* clericorum (*s², r²*: paraphrase omission)	Common error **D–a**; **Sa**
37, 2 *Inscr.*	**EXPLICIT AD AQVILENSEM EPM INCIPIT PAPAE LEONIS AD SEPTIMVM EPM ALTINEN-SEM** (*m, g, v*; *g* 'ad quilensem'; *m, g,* 'expl'; *om. c*)	N/A	

Var., *Ep.*	*Collectio Dionysiana adaucta* (**D–a**)	Ballerini text (control)	Significance
38, 2.1	cognoscere (*m, g, v, c*)	periculum cognosceret …	**D–a** agreement with **Sa** *l*
39, 2.1	*uel* cuiuslibet (*m, g, v, c*)	*siue* cuiuslibet	Common variant **D–a**; **Sa**
40, 2.2	*cum quod* (*m, g, v, c*)	transire *quod cum* recte	Common variant **D–a**
41, 2.2	*sponsionibus* (*m, g, v, c*)	curam suam *dispositionibus* nostris	Common variant **D–a**; **Sa** *s, l, r, c*

Throughout these four letters, *m, g, v,* and *c* are strongly united in what seem to be the most characteristic variants of this collection—indeed, in *Ep.* 9, *p* follows suit. On several occasions (Variants 6, 8, 11, 14, 20, 21, and 25 where *v* includes an addition by g^2 [of approximate date to g^1] that *m* lacks), *g* and *v* agree against the rest of the collection. *v* also introduces a number of errors that *m* and *g* lack (Variants 1, 12, 13, 15, and 18). From the foregoing table, it looks as though *v* is possibly a descendant of *g*. However, *g* gives the reading *instantia* where *v* and the majority tradition give *substantia*. It is relatively unlikely that *v* would introduce a correct reading in place of such an error, thus making it more likely that *g* and *v* are relatives but do not stand in a direct line of transmission from *g* to *v*. Manuscripts *m* and *c*, on the other hand, demonstrate themselves as a pair in contrast to *g* and *v*. They are more likely a second branch of the family tree (they only agree with *g* against *v*, besides *v*'s errors, twice, Variants 7 and 17). Thus, from our point of origin, we have two known branches of the tree, *g—v* or *gv* and *mc*. Manuscript *p* lacks too much Leo material to classify. Finally, the resemblance between **Sa** and **D–a** in *Epp.* 1 and 2—including significant omissions the Ballerini print—speaks of some relationship between their texts, probably a common Italian source.

The following table sets forth the relationships for *Epp.* 20 and 22, adding *c*'s readings as collated by Schwartz in ACO 2.4; Schwartz does not list all of the **D–a** variants I found—these are the variants in the table that do not list *c*. For an edition, the entirety of *c* will have to be collated.

Var., Ep.	Collectio Dionysiana adaucta (**D–a**)	Schwartz (control)	Significance
1, 20 Inscr.	INCIPIT EPIS-TOLA LEONIS EPI VRBIS ROMAE AD EVTYCHETEM PBRM ATQVE HERETICVM (c, m, g) ... PAPAE VRBIS ROME ... (v)	N/A	Agreement c, m, g; variant v
2, 20	epistola (c, m, g, v)	tuae dilectionis epistulis rettulisti	Common variant **D–a**
3, 20	pullaret (g, v)	studiis pullularet (m)	Common error g, v
4, 20	ambigas (c, m, g, v)	non ambigis auctorem	Common variant **D–a**
5	INCIPIVNT EXEMPLA GESTORUM VBI IN CON-STANTINO-POLITANA SYNODO A SCO FLAVIANO CONFESSORE EVTICHES HERETICVS AVDITVS ATQVE DAM-NATVS EST (m, g) ... GESTORUM URBI IN ... (v)	N/A	Agreement m, g Error v
6, 23 Inscr.	INCP EPIS-TOLA LEONIS PAPAE VRBIS ROMAE AD FLAVIANVM EPM CON-STANTINO-POLITANAE VRBIS (g) INCIPIT EPLA ... (m, v)	N/A	c gives this inscription, but whether it abbrev. 'incipit' or not unspecified by Schwartz Agreement **D–a**

Var., Ep.	Collectio Dionysiana adaucta (**D–a**)	Schwartz (control)	Significance
7, 23	*Dilectissimo fratri flauiano Leo.* (*c, m, g, v*)	Leo Flauiano episcopo Constantinopolitano.	Common variant **D–a**
8, 23	*scae laudabilis fidei* (*c, m, g, v*)	sancta et laudabili fide pro	Common variant **D–a**
9, 23	*eccla catholica pacis* (*c, m, g, v*)	pro *ecclesiae catholicae pace* sollicitus	Common variant **D–a**
10, 23	*necdum* (*c, m, g, v*)	intercedentibus *nondum* agnoscimus	Common variant **D–a**
11, 23	*seuiore* (*g*)	quod *seueriore* sententia (*c, m, v*)	Error *g*
12, 23	ab errore reuocatis nostra quorum *auctoritate* fides (*g*) nostra *auctoritate* quorum (*c, m, v*)	ab errore reuocatis *auctoritate* nostra quorum fides	Error *g* Common variant *c, m, v*
13, 23	quid in se fuerit *inuentum* (*c, m, g, v*)	quid *inuentum* in se fuerit	Common variant **D–a**
14, 23	*dei inspiratione* (*c, m, g, v*)	ea obseruantia *deo inspirante*	Common variant **D–a**
15, 22	**INCIP RESCRIPTA FLAVIANI** (*c, m*) **... FLAVIANA** (*g, v*)	N/A	Agreement **D–a** Common error *g, v*

Although its version of **D–a** is appended to **D**, not **D–h**, we can now say that *c* is definitively within the family of manuscripts of **D–a** based both on its readings as well as its contents. It provides the same rubrication and the same variants. It also becomes apparent that *g* is not, as hypothesised, the ancestor of *v*, since Variants 11 and 12 are clear errors on the part of *g* that *v* does not repeat; in the former case *v* and all other **D–a** manuscripts concur with Schwartz's text, whereas in the latter *v* agrees with the other **D–a** manuscripts against Schwartz. The relationshp between *g* and *v*, then, is less clear than had been anticipated. Perhaps, instead, *g* and *v* share a now-lost ancestor from Ravenna, *R*.

With the above information, we can create the following stemmata for **D–a**. *c* is treated separately because of its inclusion in a

D manuscript, not a **D–h** manuscript, so the intervening manuscript *I* between it and the original **D–a** must differ from that
between the other manuscripts and **D–a**, *X*.

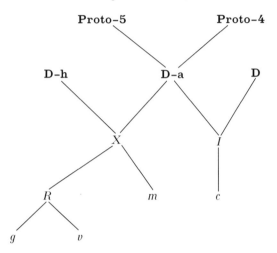

and:

5.2.d. *Collectio Hispana Gallica* (**S–g**)

5.2.d.i. Dating and Context

This a version of the *Collectio Hispana* (**S**) from the Frankish part
of Gaul. This ancestor of **S–ga** is no earlier than the later seventh century, based on its inclusion of Toledo XIII from 683. Its
earlier manuscript is from the eighth century. Most of its variations from **S** lie outside the collection of Leo's letters, as seen in
Maassen's description of the collection, and the damage done to
Leo here persists into **S–ga** which will be discussed more fully
presently.[87] The *Hispana Gallica* is the intermediate step between

---

[87] Maassen 1870, 710–16.

the pure *Hispana* and **S–ga**. During the eighth-century Islamic invasion of Spain, the *Hispana* crossed the Pyrenees into the area of Narbonne and spread along the lands of the Rhine by the end of the century. In this process of transmission, however, the text was itself transformed. A version of this *Hispana* from across the Pyrenees written in Strasbourg in 787 was lost in a fire of 1870; however, a copy of the 787 version survives in Vienna, Österreichische Nationalbibliothek, lat. 411 from *c*. 800. The Viennese manuscript shows us the birth of the *Hispana Gallica*. The *Hispana Gallica* is missing the later Visigothic councils and the *Sententiae* of Agde, and adds various items besides changing the order of the decretals. Fournier and Le Bras consider it 'corrompu, barbare'.[88] This collection survives in three manuscripts.

5.2.d.ii. Manuscripts

Rome, Biblioteca Vallicelliana D.18, fols 1–168. (saec. X).[89] Provenance unknown.

Vat. Pal. lat. 575 (saec. IX–X).[90] Provenance unknown.

Vienna, Österreichische Nationalbibliothek, lat. 411 (saec. VIII–IX), from eastern France or western Germany.[91] Written in Caroline minuscle.

5.2.e. *Collectio Hispana Gallica Augustodunensis*[92] (**S–ga**)

5.2.e.i. Dating and context

S–ga was likely compiled after the mid-840s in Gaul. Not only is it the base text for most of the genuine material in the Pseudo-Isidorian Decretals (**I**): it is itself a product of this group of forgers, evident from certain Pseudo-Isidorian readings and additions.

---

[88] For the above, see Fournier and Le Bras 1931, 100–02.

[89] This manuscript is misprinted by the Ballerini, PL 54.559–60, as Caesareum Vindebonense 41 (olim 281); they record it as of their 'Hispana', which is **S–ga** soon to be described; note, however, that the *Hispana*, *Hispana Gallica*, and **S–ga** all have the same selection of Leo's letters, and they all trace themselves back to the same Iberian source.

[90] This manuscript is digitised: https://digi.vatlib.it/view/MSS_Pal.lat.575. Accessed 21 September 2021.

[91] CLA 10.1477; Bischoff 1998–2014, 3.7116.

[92] B9 (PL 54.559–60), J1(ix) (502).

Using the *Collectio Hispana Gallica* as a base, the forgers added other genuine items as well as three forgeries and tweaked their material slightly.[93] They were thereby able to produce a collection of documents with a strong aura of authority that supported their objectives. The objectives of these skilful forgers and editors was primarily to influence the working out of canon law in favour of local bishops against their metropolitans; to this end, they invested greater power in the office of the primate and limited the ability of the metropolitan to intervene in a bishop's diocese.[94] If we consider this preliminary stage of their operations, the Pseudo-Isidorian forgers were mostly being selective in their material, using known canonical sources that would sway the opinion of their readers towards their position, with an ambitious range of concern throughout the entire ecclesiastical hierarchy.

S–ga includes the same thirty-nine of Leo's letters as **S**; the 'dogmatic' letters are in roughly chronological order,[95] and twelve so-called decretals are included. Although the manuscripts mention forty letters, including three to Marcian, items 51, 52, and 53, only two to Marcian are in the collection at this point, *Epp.* 82 and 83. Since the collection matches **S**, the error lies with the table of contents, not with the contents themselves. The Leonine epistles included are thus *Epp.* 20, 23, 22, 28, 25, 33, 44, 45, 60, 61, 69, 70, 71, 79, 80, 82, 83, 85, 90, 93, 104, 106, 115, 130, 134, 165, 15, 7, 16, 4, 18, 167, 14, 159, 12 (*decurtata* recension), 108, 166, 9, and 168. However, neither of our two **S–ga** manuscripts contains Leo's letters in this order; furthermore, neither of them preserves them in the same order. **S–ga** has been edited online through Monumenta Germaniae Historica by A. Grabowsky and D. Lorenz;[96] I have checked this edition against *a* and found it to be sound.

---

[93] For the publication of the *Hispana Gallica Augustodunensis* and its relationship to Pseudo-Isidore as described herein, cf. Fuhrmann 2001, 144–49. The three forged items are a letter from Archbishop Stephen to Pope Damasus, Damasus' response to said letter, and one more item by Damasus, 'De vana superstitione chorepiscoporum vitanda'.

[94] For the purpose behind the Pseudo-Isidorian forgeries, cf. Fuhrmann 2001, 140–44.

[95] Jalland 1941, 502.

[96] http://www.benedictus.mgh.de/quellen/chga/ Accessed 21 September 2021.

5.2.e.ii. Manuscripts

The *Hispana Gallica Augustodunensis* exists in two manuscripts:

   h: Berlin, Staatsbibliothek Preussischer Kulturbesitz, Hamilton
132, fol. 1ra-128va (saec. VIII^{ex} or IX$^{in\text{-}med}$), with provenance in
Corbie.[97] This manuscript is damaged, rearranged, and somewhat
of a mess. Leo is to be found in fols $47bis^r$, 76^r–95^v, $98^{r\text{-}v}$, and
$103^{r\text{-}v}$. The text of Leo is Caroline minuscule except the following
folios of Corbie a-b: 85^r, col. 2, to 86^v; and 88^r, col. 2, to 94^v.[98]
$47bis^r$ contains the fragmentary end of *Ep.* 106, beginning at the
same point as the collection does in *a*, 'nulla sibimet'. 76^r begins
with *Epp.* 20, 23, 22 without merging with the end of *Ep.* 7 as
does *a* below, then the sequence from 28 through to the end of
106 on 84^v. 85^r begins with *Ep.* 7 in its entirety without merging with *Ep.* 22 as does *a* below, then *h* gives *Epp.* 16, 4, 18,
167, 14, 159, 12, and JK † 551 up to 95^v. Leo resumes again on
$98^{r\text{-}v}$, where we encounter *Epp.* 108, 166, and 9 up to 'aliis regulis
traditionu(m) e(st)'. Finally, $103^{r\text{-}v}$ begins with the conclusion of
Ep. 9 from 'suarum decreta formauerit', where 98^v had ended;
then follows *Ep.* 168, which runs from column 2 of 103^r to a third
of the way down column 2 of 103^v, where the text of 103^v ends.
This sequence of letters is **S/S-ga** as described above; however,
we have here the interpolation of JK † 551 and a gap covering
Epp. 106–15. It looks as though *h* was written in the expected
order and then dismembered.[99]

---

[97] CLA 8.1047; Bischoff 1998–2014, 1.353. My transcription of the Leo portion of this manuscript is now available online: https://ccl.rch.uky.edu/corpus/
by-title-and-shelfmark/BerHam132. Accessed 21 September 2021.

[98] Firey 2015 has evaluated the composition of this manuscript, which has
many more sections of Corbie a-b than those mentioned here, and makes a
compelling case that two scriptoria wrote the text, one using Caroline minuscule, the other Corbie a-b. Her contention is that the Corbie a-b portions are
the product of a nunnery scriptorium, the rest a monastic scriptorium. Certainly, as I have observed, the fact that the Corbie a-b text contains many
more corrections, and all of them in a Caroline minuscule hand, than the Caroline minuscule text points to the Caroline minuscule portions of the manuscript being from some sort of head of the manuscript's production, while the
quires and folios in Corbie a-b were written elsewhere and then incorporated.
I would like to thank Dr Firey for providing me with proofs of her article
before it went to print.

[99] When the contents of Vienna 411, *Hispana Gallica*, (cf. Chavasse 1975,
29–30) are compared with *h*, we see that *h* lacks the damage done to the
collection in that MS. If *h* truly is **S-ga**, it is descended not from Vienna 411

a: Vat. lat. 1341 (saec. IX),[100] with provenance in Autun, although
it may have been written in Corbie.[101] In *a*, we have Leo's letters
in the following order, matching that of Vienna, MS 411 of the
Hispana Gallica, including errors:[102] the end of *Ep.* 106, then 115,
130, 134, 165, 15, the beginning of *Ep.* 7 which is cut off partway through, then the end of *Ep.* 22, followed by the sequence of
Leo's letters as noted above from *Epp.* 28, through the beginning
of *Ep.* 106. *a* then gives us letters from Popes Innocent I through
Celestine I, then resumes the collection of Leo's letters with
Epp. 20, 23, and the start of *Ep.* 22. *Ep.* 22 then merges with
the latter part of *Ep.* 7, then provides the rest of the collection
as described above, ending with *Ep.* 168. When the **S-ga** is used
to created the various collections associated with Pseudo-Isidore
(**I**), the transposition between *Epp.* 7 and 22 is maintained. In
Ep. 22, the cut off is at 'ualentini et apollonaris reparans sectum:
hos enim diuulgauit', running into *Ep.* 7 at 'diuulgauit auctoritas
et censura coercuit' and running through to its end. In *Ep.* 7 the
text cuts off at 'uigilantia diuulgauit, qui non' and provides the
missing text of *Ep.* 22 beginning with 'qui non timebant prae-
ceptum ueri dei dicentis' and continuing to the end. The transposed section of *Ep.* 7 is 287 words consisting of 1837 characters; the transposed section of *Ep.* 22 is 206 words consisting of
1282 characters. In **I-a** and **I-b** the 39 letters of Leo are placed
back together in the right order; someone likely observed that
the actual contents differed from that in the table of contents.
However, this error of the merged letters was maintained. This
explains why the two transposed sections are of differing lengths,
for it was not simply two letters switching endings but the entire
corpus of Leo's letters being moved around. It is not only their
use of the same collection of letters but this shared error that
makes **I** and **S-ga** worth consideration as a single family. **I** is
also, thus, descended from *a* and its branch of the family tree,
not the branch of *h*.

5.2.e.iii. Manuscript relations

S-ga is clearly descended from **S**, albeit not from either *v* or *o*,
both of which it pre-dates. Nonetheless, the following table, using

but something else, whereas *a* is descended either from Vienna 411 or another
MS with the same errors, as discussed below.

[100] Wurm 1939, argues X[ex]. See Kéry 1999, 70.

[101] Kéry 1999, 70; Bischoff 1998–2014, 3.6855 argues Corbie, as does Kuttner 1986, 80; Kuttner's full entry for this MS runs 78–81.

[102] Discussed and described by Chavasse 1975, 29–30.

the variant numbers from the two tables at 3.2.u.iii demonstrates this descent:

Var., Ep.	S (*v, o*) S-ga (*a, h*)	Ballerini (control)	Significance
1, 7	*Cap.*: '**LXIII Item eiusdem leonis ad episcopos per Italiam consti-tutos** De eo quod plurimi maniceorum uigi-lantia papae leonis in urbe roma delecti sunt'. (*v*; *o* no signi-ficant variants) om. *h* LXIII. EIVSDEM LEONIS AD EPISCOPOS PER ITALIAM QVOD PLVRIMI MANI-CHEORVM VIGI-LANTIA PAPAE LEONIS IN VRBE ROMA DETECTI SVNT' (*a*)	N/A	Unity **S**, **S-ga** *a*
2, 7.1	sub legibus (*v*) subditi legimus (*a*)	subditi legibus (*o; h*)	Error *v*
3, 7.2	quos ne absolueren-tur (*o; a;* **D-b** *v*) absolberentur (*v*) *nos* ne absolueren-tur (*h*)	quos *hic*, ne *se* abso-lueret	Om. *hic* and *se* shared variant **D**, **D-b** *v* Om. *hic* only **D-b** *m* Error **S**, **S-ga** Error **S-ga** *h*
4, 7.2	om. *fratres charis-simi* (*v, o; h, a*)	uestra, *fratres cha-rissimi*, sollicitius	Variant **S**, **S-ga**
5, 7.2	*pestibus* (*v, o*)	mentibus, ne *pestis* haec (*h, a*)	Error **S**
6, 7.2	*diligens* (*v, o*)	a Deo *dignae* remu-nerationis prae-mium (*h, a*)	Error **S**

Var., Ep.	**S** (*v*, *o*) **S-ga** (*a*, *h*)	Ballerini (control)	Significance
7, 7.2	*suae* (*v*, *o*)	de reatu negligen-tiae *se* non poterit (*h*, *a*)	Variant **S**
8, 7.2	*sacrileges* (*v*) *sacrilegms* (*o*)	contra *sacrilegae* persuasionis aucto-res (*h*, *a*)	Error **S**
9, 7.2	Datum tertio kl fbrs theodosio XVIII et Albino vc cns (*v*) Datum iii kls fbas teudosio XVIII et Albino viris claris-simis consulibus (*o*) Data III kl FEBR Theodosio VIII et Albino uucc cons (*h*, *a*)	Data tertio kal-endas Februa-rii, Theodosio Augusto XVIII et Albino uiris claris-simis consulibus	
10, 16 Cap.	LXII eiusdem leo-nis ad episcopos per siciliam cum capitibus suis (*o*; *v* om. 'cum capitibus suis'—*o* lists chh, *v* straight into text) *h* '... siciliam con-stitutos'; does not mention chh but lists them *a* 'cum capitul(is) suis', lists chh		Unity **S**, **S-ga**
11, 16 Pr.	om. *episcopus* (*v*, *o*; *h*, *a*)	Leo *episcopus* uni-uersis	Variant **S**, **S-ga** Agrees with **D**, **D-b**
12, 16 Pr.	*reprehensionem* (*v*, *o*) *a reprehensione* (*h*) *reprehensione* (*a*)	si quid usquam *rep-rehensioni* inuenitur	Error **S** Error **S-ga**
13, 16 Pr.	quo *beatissimus Petrus* apostolus (*o*) *beatissimi apostolus* Petrus (*h*)	quo *beatissimus apostolus* Petrus (*v*; *a*)	Variant *o* Error *h*

Var., *Ep.*	**S** (*v, o*) **S-ga** (*a, h*)	Ballerini (control)	Significance
15, 16.1	*accipitis* (*o; h, a*) *accip*[... (*v*)	consecrationem honoris *accipistis*	Variant **S, S-ga** Agrees with **D, D-b**
16, 16.1	*apostoli petri* (*v, o; h, a*)	et beati *Petri apostoli* sedes	Variant **S, S-ga** Agrees with **D, D-b**
17, 16.2	*mistico* munerum *oblatio veneratur* (*v*) *mistico* munerum *oblato* venerantur (*o*) *mistico mi\u/nero\ um/ o\b/lato ueneran-tur* (*h*)	paruulum *mystica* munerum *oblatione uenerantur* (*a*)	*o* agrees with **D, D-b**
18, 4 Pr.	*per* uniuersas (*v; h, a;* lacuna *o*)	Tusciam et uniuersas prouincias	Variant *v*, **S-ga** Agrees with **D** *c*, **D-b**
19, 4 Pr.	constituta kanonum *et* ecclesiasticam disciplinam (*v*; 'canonum' *h, a;* lacuna *o*)	canonum ecclesiasticam*que*	Variant *v*, **S-ga** Agees with **D, D-b**
20, 4 Pr.	*puram macula* (*v;* lacuna *o*) *purum macula* (*h, a*)	quod ab omni *macula purum*	Variant *v*, **S-ga** Word order agrees with **D, D-b**
21, 18,	*secta* delapsus et (*v, o; h, a*)	schismaticorum *sectam delapsus est*, et	Variant **S, S-ga** Agrees with **D** *a*
22, 18	*deum* (*v, o*)	leuem apud *Dominum* noxam (*h, a*)	Variant **S** Agrees with **D** *a*
23, 18	Datum iii kl lls alipio et ardabure cns (*v*) \Datum/ iii kls lhas alipio et ardabure consulibus (*o*) DATVM III KL IANVARIAS ALIPIO ET ARD-ABVRE CONS-VLIBVS (*h*) Data III kl ian Alapio et Ardabure consulibus (*a*)	Data III Kalend. Ianuarii Calepio et Ardabure uiris clarissimis consulibus	'alipio' agrees with **D, D-b** **S-ga** *a* 'Alapio' descended from 'alipio'

Var., Ep.	**S** (*v*, *o*) **S-ga** (*a*, *h*)	Ballerini (control)	Significance
Table Two (*Ep.* 9)			
1	**LXVIIII eiusdem leonis ad diosco-rum alexandri-num epm** (*v*, *o*; *h*) LXXIIII ... epis-copum (*a*)	N/A	Agreement **S**, **S-ga**
2	I De ordinatione prsbri uel diaconi ut subbato sco cele-bretur id est die dominico II De festiuitatibus si una augenda pplis non sufficerit nulla sit dubitatio iterare sacrificium (*o*; om. *v*) *aut* diaconi (*h*, *a*) sp. 'sabbato', 'agenda', 'iterari' (*h*, *a*) *a* expands abbrev.	N/A	Divergence **S** Agreement **S** *o*; **S-ga**
3	dioscoro alexan-drino salutem (*v*; *a*) dioscoro alexan-drino epsco salutem (*o*)	Dioscoro *episcopo Alexandrino* salu-tem (*h*)	Divergent variants, *v*, *o* Agreement **S** *v* and **S-ga** *a*
4	*effectum* (*v*, *o*)	impendamus *affec-tum* (*h*, *a*)	Error **S**
5	*festinemus* (*v*, *o*; *a*, *h*)	fundare *desider-amus*	Variant **S**, **S-ga**
6	*ipsius* (*v*, *o*; *a*, *h*)	discipulus *eius* Marcus	Variant **S**, **S-ga**
7	et *ad eandem* (*v*; *h*, *a*) et *ad eam* (*o*)	et *ea* fidelium mul-titudo conuenerit	Errors **S**, **S-ga**
8	*processoribus* (*o*)	nostris *procession-ibus* atque ordina-tionibus frequenter interfuit (*v*; *h*, *a*)	Error *o*

Var., Ep.	S (*v*, *o*) S–ga (*a*, *h*)	Ballerini (control)	Significance
9	*sedis* auctoritatis (*v*, *a add.*) *sedis auctoritatibus* (*h*)	in omnibus apostolicae auctoritatis teneremus (*o*)	Variant *v*, S–ga *a*; false

S–ga is clearly not a descendent of the same **S** tradition as *v* and *o*. Nonetheless, its close similarity to these manuscripts on a number of points, especially rubrication, demonstrates that it is firmly a member of the wider **S** family. We see also that, at several points where **S–ga** diverges from **S** that *h* and *a* are united, drawing them closer together as a unit, despite the differing damage done to the collection in its manuscripts.

5.2.f. Pseudo-Isidorus Mercator, *Decretales* ('Pseudo-Isidore'; 'False Decretals'; I)

5.2.f.i. Dating and Context

The next collection to consider is the tradition associated with the name 'Isidorus Mercator'. This family of manuscripts is a compilation of forgeries, manipulated conciliar canons and decretals, and unmodified canons and decretals. The Pseudo-Isidorian forgery scheme includes five projects identified thus far.[103] The first project comprises the Capitularies of Benedictus Levita, himself fictional, completed 847–57;[104] the second stage is **S–ga**,[105] which is followed by the third stage, those canonical collections published under the name of Isidorus Mercator. For a long time, these collections were thought to be the product of Isidore of Seville, but, as we shall see below, research has demonstrated that they are the product of a clever group of ninth-century forgers.[106] Two smaller projects were also carried out by the Pseudo-Isidorian forgers, the

[103] Unless otherwise stated, the information about the history of the Pseudo-Isidorian workshop comes from Fuhrmann 2001.

[104] This stage of the Pseudo-Isidorian forgeries does not involve Leo.

[105] Discussed immediately above at 5.2.e.

[106] Martínez-Díez 1965, 265, in his brief survey of the modern study of the *Collectio Hispana*, cites Antonio Agustin (1516–1586) as 'the first to distinguish between the genuine *Hispana* and the False Decretals'.

Capitula Angilramni and the *Collectio Danieliana*, which have both been edited by K.-G. Schon. The former is a forged piece of royal legislation and need not concern us. The latter is a canonical collection, identified by Schon as Pseudo-Isidorian,[107] that includes a single Leonine quotation from the rubrics of **D-h**.[108]

These forgeries are a product of the secular and ecclesiastical politics of the Carolingian age. The organisation of the Carolingian court as crafted and fine-tuned by Charlemagne involved the conjunction of the Church, the royal family, and the nobility to run the Empire. Throughout the reign of his son Louis the Pious (r. 814–40) moments of calm were scattered amidst various rebellions—his nephew Bernard rebelled, then his younger son Pippin. At a later point, there were rebellious counts in Aquitaine; then both of Louis' sons rebelled, and then his elder son Lothar alone rebelled. All of these rebellions involved clergy, as when Lothar used the aid of Pope Gregory IV to depose his father in 831 and had himself crowned king of Francia; following this deposition, when Louis was released from captivity by his son Pippin, bishops loyal to Louis reinstated him as sole ruler of the Frankish realms. Upon Louis' death, his younger sons Louis the German and Charles the Bald fought against Lothar and Louis' grandson Pippin II for rule of the empire. Despite a treaty in 843, hostilities resumed in 844 and lasted until 848.[109] Time and again, bishops were deposed, exiled, and imprisoned for having supported the losing side in one of these conflicts; it is only natural that they would take an interest in canon law to protect themselves.[110] Something about Leo and his geo-ecclesiology was attractive to

---

[107] Schon 2006*b*.

[108] 'Ut non amplius ab statuto concilii tempore quam diebus XV remorentur episcopi'. From *Ep.* 14. See *Collectio Danieliana*, 36, ll. 6–8.

[109] See Nelson 1995, 110–25.

[110] Of course, as the case of Praetextatus in Gregory of Tours reminds us, canon law and forgeries thereof can also harm bishops. In order to have his way in the case against Praetextatus, Chilperic forged a document: 'King Chilperic went home to his lodging. He sent to us a book of the canons, with a newly-copied four-page insert, which contained what appeared to be apostolic canons, including the following words: "A bishop convicted of murder, adultery or perjury shall be expelled from his bishopric"'. *Historiae* 5.18, trans. Thorpe.

these Carolingian churchmen, for they gather and copy his letters in abundance.

In this milieu arose a group of forgers in the diocese of Reims, very likely at the monastery of Corbie.[111] They compiled a notable amount of canonical information about the rights of bishops which they proceeded to modify when they felt it necessary. And if modification alone was not enough, they forged canonical items—especially decretals. These forgeries fooled people for a long time, but one clue that a decretal is a forgery is if a pope from before Gregory the Great uses the formula, 'seruus seruorum Dei'—for this was an introduction of his. And the forged decretals purporting to be of the third and fourth centuries do just that. In the imaginary Benedictus Levita and the *Capitula Angilramni*, they also produced secular legislation that favoured bishops. Through their projects of forgery and publication, the Pseudo-Isidorian forgers protected the rights of bishops from metropolitans and the secular authorities, frequently through either investing power at the diocesan level or turning the papacy into the protector of the bishops. They invested greater power in the position of primate, and proceeded to delineate the treatment of clergy throughout the entire ecclesiastical hierarchy.[112] After they are first wielded in ecclesiastical politics by Hincmar of Reims and his nephew Hincmar of Laon in 868,[113] the Pseudo-Isidorian forgeries become widely disseminated, in Cologne by 887, Mainz by 888, Metz by 893, Tribur by 895, but Rome even earlier, being attested during the papacy of Nicholas I (pope, 858–67), and in Milan by 882 or 896.[114] In time, Pseudo-Isidore was disseminated throughout the entire former Frankish Empire, and even into England, becoming the most widely disseminated piece of canonical literature before Gratian—

---

[111] Note that **S–ga** *h* comes from Corbie, and *a* may have as well.

[112] For the purpose behind the Pseudo-Isidorian forgeries, see Fuhrmann 2001, 140–44.

[113] Although we have a citation of Pseudo-Isidore as early as 852, the False Decretals really explode into the scene with the Hincmars. See Wallace-Hadrill 1983, 275–78, 292–303, for a very lucid account of the Hincmars and their use of Pseudo-Isidore. However, for the textual origins of Pseudo-Isidore, Furhmann 2001 is to be preferred.

[114] See Fuhrmann 2001, 181–83.

as the many manuscripts from across Europe demonstrate.[115] And, as we shall see in Chapter 6, when codices devoted to Leo were compiled with both sermons and letters, **I** formed the basis of more than one letter collection.

Being the most widespread pre-Gratian canonical collections alone makes the collections **I** of interest to the student of Leo; they represent a major force for the transmission of Leo's letters and their use in canon law before the *Decretum* of Gratian in the 1140s. Furthermore, the Pseudo-Isidorian collections have an extensive selection of Leonine letters, some of which, while not always occurring here for the first or only time, are rare. Thus, for such letters, Pseudo-Isidore is an important witness. However, for the 39 **S/S-ga** letters, **I** is of less interest, especially since the repetition of the confused texts of *Epp.* 7 and 22 throughout the manuscripts makes their descent from **S-ga** *a* likely.

Although edited by Paul Hinschius in 1863,[116] Pseudo-Isidore has never been fully collated. Happily, a critical edition is currently underway under the auspices of Monumenta Germaniae Historica at *Projekt Pseudoisidor*.[117] For the authentic decretals, Hinschius simply reused the current editions of these texts. As a result, scholars of mediaeval canon law lack a suitable tool for fully investigating how the Pseudo-Isidorian forgers modified their texts. The interpolations and purposeful modifications make collating Pseudo-Isidore tricky, especially in the face of the rare letters. If a reading occurs in a letter attested only in Pseudo-Isidore and *Collectio Ratisbonensis* that differs between the two traditions, is the difference due to Pseudo-Isidorian modification or due to the usual errors of scribal transmission? If the latter is the case, one should ask whether the *Ratisbonensis* reading is necessarily the better. Since *Ratisbonensis* pre-dates Pseudo-Isidore, its readings might be preferred, *ceteris paribus*, but a Pseudo-Isidorian variant need not necessarily be an interpolation or error. It may even preserve an older, 'better' tradition. Part of this evaluative task is considering *how* the variant affects the text. If it is clear that a

---

[115] Ibid., 153.

[116] P. Hinschius, ed., *Decretales Pseudo-Isidorianae et Capitula Ingilramni*, Leipzig: Tauchnitz, 1863.

[117] K.-G. Schon, K. Zechiel-Eckes, and W. Hartmann, edd., *Projekt Pseudo-isidor*, http://www.pseudoisidor.mgh.de/, accessed 21 September 2021.

Pseudo-Isidorian reading is both a minority reading and promotes the Pseudo-Isidorian agenda, it may be cautiously assumed to be an interpolation, especially if the other variant fits better with Leo's style and content of the Leonine corpus.

Having said that, my collations of Leo's letters do not demonstrate any serious deviation from the pre-**I** tradition save the frequent inclusion of the *spurium* JK † 551. The variants that I have found in the **I** manuscripts are the sorts of corruptions/emendations one would expect within any body of manuscripts where there was no suspicion of intentional modification of the text to suit any particular party.

5.2.f.ii. Hinschius' Classification System

The Ballerini identified four different collections of Leo's letters within the Pseudo-Isidorian manuscript tradition, covering their Collections 10–13.[118] Hinschius identified five classes of Pseudo-Isidorian material: A1, A2, A/B, B, and C; of these, current research points to A1, A2 and A/B as coming from the Pseudo-Isidorian workshop,[119] although C is not far behind, as the following discussion will show. Hinschius considered A1 the oldest and best class,[120] and it contains all three strands of the Pseudo-Isidorian tradition as he perceived it:

1. Decretals from Popes Clement I (d. *c.* 97) to Miltiades (d. 314);[121]

2. Councils from Nicaea I in 325 to Seville II in 618, although there is also material from Toledo XIII of 683 that precedes Seville II in the manuscripts;

3. Decretals from Silvester I (d. 335) to Gregory II (715–31).[122]

This class bears a significant resemblance to **S–ga**; strand two is the same as the first portion of the earlier collection, and the decretals of strand three are largely the same as therein. Fuhrmann judges Pseudo-Isidore as represented by Class A1 to be 'a *Hispana* expanded by adding false papal letters', not forgetting

---

[118] PL 54.560–64.

[119] Fuhrmann 2001, 155–59.

[120] Hinschius 1863, xviii–xix.

[121] Hinschius refers to this latter bishop of Rome as 'Melchiades'.

[122] Fuhrmann 2001, 155.

the inclusion of material from the *Dionysio-Hadriana*.[123] The main expansion of Class A1, the early decretals, only includes pre-Constantinian material; the canonists have forged letters to cover the period before **S–ga** and placed them at the beginning, maintaining the chronological nature of most early mediaeval canonical collections.

Class A2 only contains decretals from Clement I to Damasus (336–84);[124] therefore, it does not concern us. Class A/B was judged by Hinschius to be inferior to both A1 and A2; it is the source whence Hinschius believed Classes B and C derive, hence its resemblance to them and its label 'A/B'. Hinschius considered this class inferior due to his dating of Vat. lat. 630, which the Ballerini judged to be one of our oldest Pseudo-Isidorian manuscripts.[125] Contemporary scholarship as represented by Fuhrmann follows the Ballerini in dating this manuscript, not Hinschius. Having examined the manuscript myself, I, too, follow the Ballerini dating of Vat. lat. 630 on palaeographical grounds. This dating is corroborated by the early dating of the other A/B manuscripts. The result is that A/B's closer resemblance to the *Hispana* manuscripts, especially to **S–ga**, can be ascribed to its proximity to the original forgers, not to later modification as proposed by Hinschius,[126] who imagined Class A/B to be a later, eleventh-century blending of material from A1 and B, not a product of the original forgers' workshop.[127] Classes B and C, derived from A/B, are of later origin than the other strands of the Pseudo-Isidorian tradition, and therefore come last in the classification of Pseudo-Isidorian manuscripts. After these classes comes the recently identified Yale or Cluny recension, itself dated to the ninth century. Finally, as discussed below, Ballerini Collection 13, which I name *Collectio Florentina*, seems related to Pseudo-Isidore.

Our discussion of the manuscripts themselves, now that we have set forth the Pseudo-Isidorian playing field, will be organised around the Ballerini collections, not only because of how pre-

---

[123] Ibid., 155.
[124] Ibid., 155.
[125] See ibid., 156, citing Hinschius 1863, xvii, and Ballerini, PL 56.251 ff.
[126] Fuhrmann 2001, 156.
[127] See Hinschius 1863, lx–lxvii, esp. lx–lxi.

dominant their study remains for Leo—especially for Anglophones since Jalland simply gave an English version of it in his work—but also because it is broadly chronological and easily maps onto the other widely-used system of Pseudo-Isidorian classification, that of P. Hinschius. Neither system is perfect, as my discussion below demonstrates. Nevertheless, in using them, it is hoped that my study and analysis can easily be compared with the work of earlier scholars. Ballerini Collection 10 corresponds with Hinschius A/B and B; Ballerini 11 with Hinschius A1; and Ballerini 12 with Hinschius C.[128] Each classification of Pseudo-Isidorian decretals begins with the manuscripts listed by the Ballerini, then moves on in a subsection to the others that share Hinschius' classification.

5.2.f.iii. Ballerini Collection 10;[129] Hinschius A/B and B (I–b)

Ballerini Collection 10 (I–b) generally contains the same 39 letters of Pope Leo as S/S–ga, with the same *decurtata* form of *Ep.* 12, which I term *Ep.* 12b, cutting off midway through chapter 9. Although classed distinctly by Hinschius among the wider Pseudo-Isidorian collections, both A/B and B are the same collection of Leo's letters, which is why I give them a single *siglum* as a collection. Furthermore, all of the manuscripts of A/B and B are from northern France or Flanders with the exception of the Montecassino manuscript. If Hinschius' system still holds any merit, this fact is worth keeping in mind. And if the theory of the forgers working in Corbie is also of worth, then this geographical spread of manuscripts makes sense, assuming they all descend from the Corbie scriptorium; indeed, this centre provides us with one ninth-century manuscript (*c*), and possibly a second (*l*), both approximately contemporary with the forgers. Given the ages of the manuscripts, it is likely that Hinschius' Class B is a descendant of A/B that was modified. Because I–b is so clearly dependent upon S/S–ga, I have not taken the time to produce detailed tables for these letters. The most important manuscripts are *c* and *l*.

The I–b manuscripts that were assessed by the Ballerini, are, in chronological order:

---

[128] Cf. Kéry 1999, 100–08.
[129] PL 54.559–60, Jalland 1(x) (503).

c: Vat. lat. 630 (saec. IX[med]),[130] from Corbie via Arras.[131] Hinschius classed this manuscript as A/B, as seen above, and dated it much later than the Ballerini, to the end of the eleventh or beginning of the twelfth century, basing his arguments upon palaeographical data and the contents of the manuscript itself.[132] However, as noted above, my own assessment of *c* on palaeographical grounds reaffirms the Ballerini dating. Leo's letters run fols 228[r]–252[r]. Leo's letters begin with a magnificent *littera notabilior* D with intricate knot designs forming the letter itself. The rubrics are in an uncial hand, as is the first line of each epistle. The collection of Leo's letters begins:

Incipiunt decreta papae leonis aduersus euticen constantinopolitanum abbatem. Qui uerbi et carnis unum ausus est pronuntiare naturam dum constat in domino ihu xpo unam personam nos confiteri in duabus naturis dei scilicet atque hominis. Scriptum leonis episcopi urbis romae ad euticen constantinopolitanum abbatem aduersus nestorianam heresem.

f: Vat. lat. 631 (saec. XIII), from Flanders via France, classed as B by Hinschius.[133] *f* is bound in two volumes, and Leo's letters are in Part 2 of the manuscript, running 242[r]–268[v].

5.2.f.iii-a. Hinschius Class A/B[134]

Four other manuscripts are listed as being Class A/B:

l: Leipzig, Universitätsbibliothek Leipzig, Rep. II 7 (Leihgabe Leipziger Stadtbibliothek) (saec. IX); this manuscript may have originated in Corbie; its provenance is Leipzig. Leo's letters run fols 52[v]–end, beginning with the same programmatic incipit as *c*. Sadly the manuscript is water-damaged in several places, tops of some pages are missing, and occasional mending covers some of the text. Its damaged state is further visible in its incomple-

---

[130] Access to the MGH collation of this MS is available at: http://www.pseudoisidor.mgh.de/html/handschriftenbeschreibung_vat_lat_630.html. Accessed 21 September 2021.

[131] Jasper 2001, 54–55; Kuttner 1986, 20–22; Bischoff 1998–2014, 3.6844; Ganz 1990, 144–45.

[132] Hinschius 1863, xvii–xviii.

[133] This MS is digitised: https://digi.vatlib.it/view/MSS_Vat.lat.631.pt.2. Accessed 21 September 2021.

[134] There is one further A/B MS: Leipzig, Universitätsbibliothek, II.8 (olim Stadtbibliothek, Naumann CCXL) (saec. XII), of unknown origin. This manuscript is fragmentary, consisting of a mere seven folios, and contains no Leo material.

tion, cutting off at *Ep.* 4.2 'quicumque tales admissi sunt, ab ecclesiasticis'. That we have a ninth-century Class A/B manuscript that was possibly written in Corbie is of significance when one considers Zechiel-Eckes' contention that the entire project originated in Corbie.[135]

m: Monte Cassino, Archivio e Biblioteca dell'Abbazia, 1 (saec. XI), originating in Monte Cassino itself.

o: Saint-Omer, Bibliothèque municipale, 189 (saec. XI), from northern France with provenance of the chapter library of Notre-Dame at Saint-Omer.

5.2.f.iii-b. Hinschius Class B

Hinschius Class B contains six more manuscripts, none earlier than the 1100s, one of which lacks Leo:[136]

b: Boulogne, Bibliothèque municipale 115 (saec. XII), from Flanders with provenance in Boulogne.

g: Boulogne, Bibliothèque municipale 116 (saec. XII), also from Flanders with provenance in Boulogne.

p: Paris, lat. 14314 (olim Saint-Victor 184), of 1138–1143, from Flanders but with provenance in Paris.[137] This manuscript has its contents laid out in a late mediaeval or early modern hand. The original contents of the twelfth century are on fol. 4ᵛ and simply say, 'Decreta Leonis p(a)p(ae) c(um) ep(istu)la flauiani constantinopolitani ep(iscop)i ad eu(n)de(m) (et) ep(istu)la pet(ri) rauennensis ep(iscop)i ad euticen hereticu(m)'.

a: Paris, lat. 3853 (1154–1159), from Saint-Amand in Pévèle, Flanders (modern France). This is a very large manuscript, measuring 500 × 320 mm. It is written in a minuscule hand in two columns with red and green rubrication. The *litterae notabiliores*

---

[135] See Zechiel-Eckes 2002, 1–26.

[136] Vat. Reg. lat. 976 (saec. XIII), from northern France or Flanders, seems to be missing a quire at the end of Celestine on fol. 116ᵛ, and picks up the text on 117ʳ with Hilarus. The manuscript is written in two columns of Proto-Gothic script. Space was left by the first scribe for rubrication and *litterae notabiliores*, but these decorative features were not added. One could speculate that the missing quire may never have existed, or at least was never bound into the rest of the codex, since 116ᵛ leaves an entire column blank. This MS is digitised: https://digi.vatlib.it/view/MSS_Reg.lat.976. Accessed 21 September 2021.

[137] This MS is digitised: https://gallica.bnf.fr/ark:/12148/btv1b10035229x. Accessed 21 September 2021.

that commence each letter alternate amongst blue, green, and red; the *incipit* of each letter receives a large *littera notabilior* and then the content receives a small, rubricated letter at its start. In terms of presentation, this manuscript and Paris, lat. 14314, were produced on basically the same template.

y: York, Minster Library, Add. 8, from 1469, with the 39 Leonine letters in fols 309ᵛ–345, which was written in France for Simon Radin (*d.* 1510), who was *consiliarius* of the French king and a senator of the order of 'Parrisi';[138] an anthology of *opuscula* from various church fathers was dedicated to him in 1500 by Cipriano Beneto.[139] This manuscript was acquired by one Thomas Jessop in 1826 and bequeathed to York Minster upon his death in 1864.[140]

Prague, Národní Muzeum, XII.D.2 (saec. XIV), with provenance in Prague itself.[141]

Prague, Národní Muzeum, I.G.15 (saec. XV), identical to Prague XII.D.2.

5.2.f.iv. Ballerini Collection 11;[142] Hinschius Class A1 (I-a)

This collection contains the following Leonine letters: 120, 97, 99, 139, 28, 31, 59, 124, 1, 35, 29, 114, 155, 162, 135, then the 39 of **S/S-ga**, with *Ep.* 19 added as described by the Ballerini. However, what the Ballerini fail to mention is the fact that the 39 letters from **S** are not in the same order, and that there are further variations found in the many Pseudo-Isidorian manuscripts. My collations confirm the following order for the **S** letters that follow *Ep.* 135 as described by Hinschius:[143] 20, 23, 22 (as in other Pseu-

[138] Radin is listed in Blanchard 1647, 33–34, in the 'Catalogue de tous les conseillers'.

[139] A digitised version of this *incunabulum* is online: https://daten.dig-itale-sammlungen.de/~db/0003/bsb00036947/images/index.html?seite = 00005&l = en&viewmode = 1. Accessed 21 September 2021. More about Radin I have not been able to ascertain. The spelling 'Parrisi' above comes from this text.

[140] On this MS, see Ker and Piper 1992, 795–97.

[141] Although Hinschius classed this MS as C (Kéry 1999, 103), it has been securely identified as B by Williams 1971, 50, and Fuhrmann 1972, 169, n. 61; see also the correction of Fuhrmann in Mordek 1978, 475, n. 19. For bibliography on this MS, see Kéry 1999, 104.

[142] PL 54.559–62, J1(xi) (503).

[143] Hinschius 1863, xxvi–xxviii.

do-Isidorian manuscripts), 115, 130, 134, 165, 15, 7, 28, 25, 33, 44, 45, 60, 61, 69, 70, 71, 79, 80, 82, 83, 85, 90, 93, 104, 106, 16, 4, 18, 167, 14, 159, 12, 108, 166, 9, JK † 551, *Damnatio Vigilii*, 168, and 108 in the same form as its earlier appearance. *Ep.* 106 cuts off at: 'in aliqua unquam sit parte solubilis', then adds: 'quos uidet dignatio tua non posse reprobari eligere debebis quos clericos facias'. Hinschius does not identify the interpolation; it is a passage from Innocent I, *Ep.* 37.4.[144] *o* adds *Ep.* 19 after *Ep.* 16, while *v* adds it before. The whole collection of Leo's letters in this recension begins, 'FINIVNT EPISTOLAE DECRETORVM CELESTINI ET SIXTI; DEHINC SEQVVNTUR DECRETA PAPAE LEONIS'. The text of *Ep.* 28 is said to come from the ancient homilaries, many of which contain this epistle (as discussed below), and thus differs in certain regards from the text of **S** without changing the order.[145] The letters added to Pseudo-Isidore in **I-a** are all in **Q** save *Ep.* 35. Jasper observes that the **Q** and **S-ga** texts found here have 'melded together into a single body of texts', most notably in *y*—their manuscripts crossed paths as medieval editors made new collections.[146] As discussed above, **I-a** was favoured by Hinschius.

Before we discuss the manuscripts, it is worth taking note that this collection contains the third form of *Ep.* 12 as identified by the Ballerini; it is a conflation of two other partial versions of the text—12b, described as *decurtata* by the Ballerini, which cuts off in chapter 9 (in **I-b** and **S/S-ga**), and 12a, the form used in the *Dionysio-Hadriana* (**D-h**), which lacks Ballerini chapters 6–8. This conflated form takes the second form and adds the *decurtata* chapters 6 through 8 to the end. The other collections that share this reading of *Ep.* 12 with **I-a** are Ballerini Collections 20, 21, and 23, as well as their Collection 22,[147] whence comes the only manuscript that actually alerts the reader to the conflation's existence.[148] It is my contention, since Ballerini Collections 20 through 23 date from the twelfth through fifteenth centuries, that the original conflation

---

[144] PL 20.604.

[145] Jalland 1941, 503.

[146] Jasper 2001, 55.

[147] See below at 6.3.a-d.

[148] Venice, Biblioteca Nazionale Marciana, Lat. Z. 79 (= 1665). For this information, see PL 54.640.

of the two forms of this letter was done by the Pseudo-Isidorian workshop itself. As we have seen, form two is favoured by **D–h**, which itself has left traces in the Pseudo-Isidorian collection. We know that the group associated with **I** had access to **D–h** from the aforementioned *capitulum* in *Collectio Danieliana*. Therefore, when they prepared this stage of the task of forgery, they had become aware of the discrepancy between the **S–ga** form of *Ep.* 12 and the **D–h** form. Accordingly, they sought to create a form of this letter that included all of the material available to them.

Finally, a note about the geographic spread of **I–a** is in order, as with **I–b**. 26 manuscripts are listed below. Our earliest come from France/northern France or the Rhine-Moselle region of Germany, which shared close political and cultural ties in the Early Middle Ages. Of the manuscripts below, two are classified incorrectly, and another is a copy of one of those, reducing our manuscripts to 23. The table below demonstrates the spread of Pseudo-Isidore from northern France, although **I–a** is copied primarily in that country, with only a couple from Rhenish Germany and northern Italy.

	Saec. IX	Saec. XI	Saec. XII	Saec. XIII+
France	2 (or 3; 1: IX–XI)	5 (or 6; 1: IX–XI)	4	2 (XV)
Northern Italy				2
Rhine-Moselle		3		
England				2
Unknown			3	

All of this is to reinforce the geographical centre of the Pseudo-Isidorian forgers upon northern France. Furthermore, when we glance at the dates of the **I–a** manuscripts versus those of **I–b**, we see that **I–a** is not to be preferred on grounds of dating as Hinschius put forward, since there are more **I–b** manuscripts of the ninth century than **I–a** ones. The most important **I–a** manuscripts are *o* (because of its age) along with *v* and *p*, our other early **I–a** manuscripts but with fewer corruptions than *o*, despite being later—as noted below, these latter two manuscripts are clearly related in their treatment of Leo's letters.

The Ballerini mention five manuscripts that include this collection, in chronological order:

y: New Haven, Yale University, Beinecke Library 442 (saec. IX[med]), probably from Reims.[149] In terms of dating this manuscript, Kéry observes, *contra* Williams,[150] that it was not written in the decade after 850, but in John VIII's pontificate (872–82);[151] this argument is based on the pope list found in *y*, a reliable means of obtaining a *terminus post quem*. However, as Bischoff notes, this manuscript has many hands, and the papal catalogue is the first item; thus, Willliams could be right for the dating of the rest of the contents. The Yale manuscript itself causes us some problems, because Schon has used it to identify another strand of original Pseudo-Isidore, which he calls the 'Cluny' recension, the name based on his identifying the manuscript as having a provenance of Cluny.[152] This means that when we turn our attention to all other A1 manuscripts, we should keep in mind that further research may reveal to us that these are, in fact, manuscripts of the proposed Cluny recension, not Class A1. Furthermore, the Yale Pseudo-Isidore and its related manuscripts do not contain the collection of **I–a** but the same one as Ballerini, Collection 21. It will be discussed more fully below.

o: Vat. Ott. lat. 93 (saec. IX[med]), originating and with provenance in northern France, possibly Chartres according to Bischoff.[153] This manuscript is mutilated at its conclusion, and since Leo concludes the volume, running 129[v]–149[v], this has an effect upon his text. Fol. 149[r] closes with the increasingly illegible *capitula* to *Ep.* 14, and 149[v] proved unreadable. The final folios, 150–51, are neither Pseudo-Isidore nor original to the manuscript. Due to the illegibility, we are effectively missing all of *Ep.* 14 as well as what followed. As mentioned above, this manuscript adds *Ep.* 19 after *Ep.* 16 in Hinschius' order.

v: Vat. lat. 3791 (saec. XI), from northern France as well. Leo's letters run fols 88[r]–166[v]. In general, the readings herein are better than in *o*. Unlike *o*, it adds *Ep.* 19 before *Ep.* 16, as noted above. The synopsis of *Ep.* 44 at fol. CXXXVI[v] is incorporated into the text of the letter, as with Paris, lat. 9629.

Vat. Barb. lat. 57 is mentioned by the Ballerini for this category as well. This manuscript is a copy of the *Ad Herennium* attributed to Cicero.

[149] Bischoff 1998–2014, 2.3486. This MS is digitised: https://brbl-dl.library.yale.edu/vufind/Record/3528435. Accessed 21 September 2021.

[150] Williams 1971.

[151] Kéry 1999, 102–03.

[152] See Schon 1978.

[153] Kéry 1999, 105; Bischoff 1998–2014, 3.6433. This MS is digitised: https://digi.vatlib.it/view/MSS_Ott.lat.93. Accessed 21 September 2021.

5.2.f.iv-a. Hinschius Class A1

Hinschius Class A1 as listed by Kéry is enormous. Since one of the listed A1 manuscripts in Milan (Biblioteca Ambrosiana A.87 inf.) does not include Leo, not every manuscript that Hinschius identified as A1—and he did view the Milanese manuscript, as attested by the list of consulters—contains Leo's letters. Below I list all of the known manuscripts classified as A1 to give a picture of the magnitude of Pseudo-Isidore. However, I only consulted select manuscripts from the list below, namely *p*, *m*, and *f*. I begin with the manuscripts assessed before listing the others.

> *p*: Paris, lat. 9629 (Reg. 3887.8.A) (saec. IX–X) from France.[154] Leo's letters run 102^v–142^r. This manuscript adds *Ep.* 19 after *Ep.* 16. The *capitula* are rubricated uncials for which the scribe of the text failed to leave enough room; as a result, entire words and phrases frequently spill over into the margins. The synopsis at the start of *Ep.* 44, fol. 122^r, col. 2, is incorporated into the main text of the letter, as with *v*, with which it also shares the spelling 'capud' in *Ep.* 12.

> *m*: Florence, Biblioteca Nazionale Centrale, Conv. soppr. J.III.18 (saec. X–XI) from northern Italy with Florentine provenance. I believe that this is the manuscript the Ballerini identify as being San Marco 182. When the Florentine priory of San Marco was suppressed under Napoleon, the vast majority of its manuscripts were dispersed, ending up in the Biblioteca Nazionale Centrale di Firenze today; before reaching San Marco, this manuscript spent time in the library of the Florentine humanist Niccolò Niccoli whose library was only surpassed in Florence by that of Cosimo de' Medici.[155] According to the catalogue of the Biblioteca Nazionale Centrale di Firenze, this manuscript was formerly San Marco 675. Following the *Inventario dei codici di San Marco ricevuti nel 1883*, San Marco 182 is now Conv. soppr. J.IV.20; however, according to the *Inventario* of 1768, San Marco 182 is not canonical; having viewed Conv. soppr. J.IV.20, I confirm that this manuscript does not contain Pseudo-Isidore. Conv. soppr. J.III.18 is, however, from San Marco, for the front-page, verso, reads, 'Iste liber est conuentus S. Marci de flò ordinis predic / Ex hereditate uiri doctissimi Nicolai de Nicolis Florentini'. Finally, the contents of *m* match those of Ballerini, San

---

[154] Bischoff 1998–2014, 3.4619. This MS is digitised: https://gallica.bnf.fr/ark:/12148/btv1b100342551/f1.item. Accessed 21 September 2021.

[155] See *The Encyclopaedia Britannica*.

Marco 182, a manuscript classified as Collection 13 by the Ballerini, not Collection 11 which would have made the manuscript Class A1. It is most likely, then, that the shelfmark recorded by the Ballerini was no longer correct at the time of the dissolution of the priory over fifty years later. Since the Leo contents of *m* are clearly not **I–a**, it will be dealt with amongst the other high medieval descendants of Pseudo-Isidore at 6.3.f.

f: Florence, Biblioteca Nazionale Centrale, Panciatichi 135 (saec. XV); this manuscript comes from a form lacking the conciliar portions,[156] as I saw myself. Leo runs fols 142^r–188^v. It does not follow the order established for Class A1 by Hinschius as described above, but, rather, the order of Ballerini Collection 21; I shall therefore discuss it more fully in its place.[157] Nevertheless, the rest of the manuscript appears to be Pseudo-Isidore A1.

Bernkastel-Kues, Bibliothek des St.-Nikolaus Hospitals, 52 (olim 37; C. 14) (saec. XI), provenance of Bernkastel-Kues 'from monastery of S. Eucharius-Matthias at Trier'.[158]

Rouen, Bibliothèque municipale, 702 (E.27) (saec. XI) from Angers with provenance of Rouen.

Vat. Reg. lat. 1054 (saec. XI) from France.[159]

Vendôme, Bibliothèque municipale, 91 (saec. XI) from Angers, provenance of Vendôme.

Cologne, Historisches Archiv, W 50 (saec. XI–XII); this and the Cologne manuscript below include the A1 decretals in an abridged form.[160]

Cologne, Historisches Archiv, W 101 (saec. XII).

Avranches, Bibliothèque municipale, 146 (saec. XII), from Northern France, provenance of Avranches.

Eton, College Library, B.1.I.6 (saec. XII), likely written in Normandy with provenance of the cathedral chapter of Exeter, written in a Norman hand, with papal decretals on fol. 88–232.[161]

---

[156] Mordek 1978, 474.

[157] See below 6.3.b.

[158] See Kéry 1999, 101.

[159] This MS is digitised: https://digi.vatlib.it/view/MSS_Reg.lat.1054. Accessed 21 September 2021.

[160] Kéry 1999, 102.

[161] Ker 1977, 708–11. Although Hinschius did not classify said manuscript, we can thus safely assume that the Eton Pseudo-Isidore is Class A1 along with London, British Library, Royal 11.D.IV which is a copy of it; be aware,

London, British Library, Cotton Claudius E.V. (saec. XII), written in Normandy with provenance in England.

[Vat. lat. 1344 (saec. XII) from France.[162] This manuscript is actually a copy of the Yale or Cluny Pseudo-Isidore.]

Rome, Biblioteca Casanatense 496 (olim A. V. 40) (saec. XII).

Vat. Reg. lat. 978 (saec. XII).

Vienna, Österreichische Nationalbibliothek, lat. 2133 (saec. XII), with both place of writing and provenance uncertain.

Cambridge, University Library, Dd.I.10–11 (saec. XIV), a copy of British Library, Cotton Claudius E.V. written in England, with provenance of Cambridge.

Florence, Biblioteca Medicea Laurenziana, Plut. 16.18, fol. (saec. XV), from Florence, which is an incomplete copy of Florence, Biblioteca Nazionale Centrale, Conv. soppr. J.III.18 (*m*).

London, British Library, Royal 11.D.IV (saec. XV) from England, 'either directly or indirectly copied from Eton, College Library, B.1.I.6',[163] above.

Paris, lat. 3855 (saec. XV) from Paris.

Paris. lat. 15391 (olim Sorbonne 729) (saec. XV), from France, provenance of Paris.

Rome, Biblioteca Casanatense 221 (D.III.16; olim A.II.14) (saec. XV) from Italy.

Venice, Biblioteca Nazionale Marciana, lat. IV.47 (= 2126) (saec. XV) with provenance of Northern Italy.

5.2.f.v. The Cluny Recension, or Yale Pseudo-Isidore (**Y**)

As discussed above (at 5.2.f.iv), in 1978, K.-G. Schon identified the Yale manuscript of Pseudo-Isidore as yet another recension of the collection from the ninth century; this recension is called the

---

however, that it also has some relationship with Saint-Omer 189, which Hinschius classed as A/B (Kéry 1999, 101, 104). Somerville 1972, 305–06, summarises arguments for/against its French/English origins, noting that, either way, it was in Exeter well before the fourteenth century, possibly as early as the mid-twelfth. Ker 1977, 711, thinks that MSS written in such a script as this have provenance of Exeter, but acknowledges that they may be French.

[162] See Kuttner 1986, 94–98 for a full description. This manuscript is digitised: https://digi.vatlib.it/view/MSS_Vat.lat.1344 Accessed 21 September 2021.

[163] Kéry 1999, 102.

Cluny Recension because of its use in Cluny at a later date. The Yale Pseudo-Isidore is not, strictly speaking, **I–a** as it was previously classed. Indeed, we need look no further than its collection of Leo's letters to demonstrate this fact: *Epp.* 20, 23, 22, 28, 25, 35, 29, 31, 33, 59, 44, 45, 60, 61, 69, 70, 71, 79, 80, 82, 83, 85, 90, 93, 104, 106, 120, 97, 99, 139, 115, 114, 134, 135, 130, 124, 163, 162, 155, 165, 15, 7, 1, 19, 16, 4, 18, 167, 14, 159, 12, 108, 166, 9, JK † 551, and 168. This collection of letters corresponds to that of Ballerini Collection 21 (see below at 6.3.b). E. Knibbs has argued that *y*'s edition of Leo's letters originally contained just the 39 letters of **S/S–ga**, and that the sixteen other letters, known from the other manuscripts of **I–a**, were added. The evidence for the addition of new letters into a manuscript that already existed with the 39 is found in the fact that new folios have been added into the manuscript, and text has been erased and recopied, the modifications producing the collection as described above.[164]

Schon lists twelve manuscripts of the Cluny Recension:[165]

1. New Haven, Beinecke Library 442 (saec. IX; **I–a** *y*)[166]

2. Cologne, Erzbischöfliche Diözesan- und Dombibliothek 113 (saec. X/XI)

3. Paris, Bibliothèque nationale, nouv. acq. lat. 2253 (saec. X/XI)

4. Venice, Biblioteca Nazionale Marciana, lat. IV. 47 (saec. XV)

5. Paris, lat. 15391 (saec. XV)

6. Vat. lat. 1344 (saec. XII)

7. Paris, lat. 16897 (saec. XIII)

8. Oxford, Bodleian Library, Hatton 6 (saec. XIII)

9. Toulouse, Bibliothèque municipale, I.9 (saec. XIII)

10. Paris, Bibliothèque de l'Arsenal 679 (saec. XIV)

11. Paris, lat. 5141 (saec. XIV)

12. Grenoble, Bibliothèque municipale 473 (saec. XII)

Part of the proof that these manuscripts are descendants of MS *y* is found, in fact, in the letters of Leo the Great. In *y*, Leo's letter

---

[164] See Knibbs 2013.

[165] For the following discussion, see Schon 1978.

[166] See 5.2.f.iv above.

to Theodoret of Cyrrhus, *Ep.* 120, has been corrected; in MS 2, these corrections are repeated:

MS 1/*y* before corrections	1/*y* after corrections	MS 2
sede	*fide* sede	fide sede
comple*us*	comple*t*	complet
memoriae	tamen et	tamen et
inui*n*cibilis	inuisibilis	inuisibilis

These corrections are not enough, of course—2 could have been the manuscript from which *y* was corrected. However, Schon also observes that *y* includes a number of gaps in it—due, no doubt, to the insertions identified by Knibbs. 2 does not include these gaps. Manuscripts 3–5 have been grouped together by Schon; they have the same content as *y*, but lack the characteristic gaps of *y*; they are thus descended from that manuscript as well. MS 6 includes the contents and text type of *y*, but it presents them in a different order. MSS 7–11 are also derived from *y*, including the corrections of *y* in *Ep.* 120. MS 12 does not include everything from 7–11, but there is still a selection from Leo's letters; it is, thus, a truncated version of the collection of *y*. Thus we see the groups of the Cluny Recension of Pseudo-Isidore, descending from manuscript *y*: 2, 3–5, 6, 7–11, and 12.

5.2.f.vi. Ballerini Collection 12;[167] Hinschius Class C[168] (I–c)

This collection of 102 of Leo's letters, the second-largest in existence,[169] is made of 39 letters from **S**, textually similar to **I–b** *c*, then 62 letters in the order of their sources, drawing on the *Quesnelliana* (**Q**), *Grimanica* (**G**), and *Bobbiensis* (**B**)—which is to say, the collections, not necessarily any of the surviving manuscripts.[170] The Ballerini's description of this collection's contents has proven to be disordered, while Hinschius' and Chavasse's are more accurate. First, *Ep.* 24 has been added as the second let-

---

[167] PL 54.562–63, J1(xii) (503).

[168] Hinschius 1863, lxix–lxx; see also Chavasse 1975, 37–38.

[169] The largest is the *Collectio Grimanica*, discussed above at 4.1.g.

[170] Jasper 2001, 55–56.

ter in the **S/S-ga** series. Having compared my collations with Hinschius, after these forty letters, the following series of Leo's epistles is found: 102, 121, 122, 162, 2, 1, 19, JK † 551, 10, 41, 35, 29, 31, 59, 95, 32, 94, 155, 105, 113, 111, 112, 118, 123, 125, 124, 120, 127, 163, 135, 114, 139, 99, 68, Cyril's Second Letter to Nestorius, 168, a letter from a different Leo,[171] 103, 138, 54, 34, 36, 37, 38, 39, 50, 47, 49, 48, 51, 74, 78, 81, 84, 87, 89, 116, 119, 145, 148, 156, and 30. As Jalland notes, from *Ep.* 54 onwards this collection corresponds to the collection of Leo's letters in **G**;[172] however, **G** contains many more letters at this stage in the manuscript, so it is difficult to affirm a common source for both **I-c** and **G** based solely upon these grounds. Furthermore, **G** does not include *Ep.* 30 in the position that **I-c** does. **I-c**'s *Ep.* 12 is from the shorter, *decurtata*, form of that letter (*Ep.* 12b), derived from **S-ga**. Finally, yet again we see northern French origins for the manuscripts of a Pseudo-Isidorian collection.

Pseudo-Isidore C has generally hitherto been regarded as a late expansion to Pseudo-Isidore, given the lateness of its manuscripts. However, it has recently been re-dated to the ninth century by Steffen Patzold,[173] who bases his argument on knowledge of letters known only in Pseudo-Isidore C by ninth-century figures, such as Hincmar of Reims and Hincmar of Laon. In particular, Patzold focusses on certain letters of Pope Vitalian, as well as other letters, including rare Leo letters, in what seems to be class C's text type.[174] Moreover, as Patzold observes, Mordek has already observed that the ninth-century *Collectio Dacheriana* A/B demonstrates knowledge of Pseudo-Isidore C.[175] Furthermore, Pseudo-Isidore C includes texts attributed to Gregory I that are germane to the marriage and incest debates of the Carolingian world, found also in the Cluny Pseudo-Isidore; not only are these texts in circulation in the ninth century, they would be of less relevance in the eleventh or twelfth.[176] Patzold also demonstrates the familiarity of Hincmar of Rheims with several rare items from Pseu-

---

[171] Ed. Ballerini, PL 54.1239–1240.
[172] Jalland 1941, 504.
[173] The arguments for a later date are set out by Patzold 2015, 14–27.
[174] Patzold 2015, 43–45.
[175] Mordek 1967, 591, cited in Patzold 2015, 43.
[176] Ibid., 45–47.

do-Isidore C, rarely attested all together in the same collection; however, Hincmar is not designated as the compiler himself.[177] Based upon the intersection of these traces of Pseudo-Isidore C in the ninth century, Patzold dates the collection no earlier than the 840s, likely the 850s.[178] Not only the original manuscript but another twelfth-century copy that added later material are lost,[179] making the textual study of Pseudo-Isidore C increasingly difficult. Nonetheless, as the second-largest collection of Leo's letters, and almost as early as many other collections and the earliest manuscripts of many earlier collections, the importance of Pseudo-Isidore C as a transmitter of Leo's letters is increased, and we gain yet another window into the Carolingian interest in the correspondence of Leo the Great.

Antoine Chavasse provides what is still the most logical lineage of the evolution of **I-c**.[180] First, the thirty-nine letters from **S** with the addition of *Ep.* 24 (**I-b**), which evolves into **Y**, thence to the letters of **73** (see 6.3.g below). To **73** are added selections from **Q**, and then further letters taken from **G** and **B**. As Knibbs has pointed out, this evolution is discernible in the way the collection can be broken down—he thus questions whether it could all have taken place so quickly in the 840s as argued by Patzold.[181] That said, the only stage that has not been previously argued to have a pre-Carolingian existence is **73**. All the other material in **I-c** is drawn from either Carolingian or pre-Carolingian collections—**Q**, **G**, **B**, **I-b**, and **Y**. It is plausible, then, that a scriptorium with access to a well-stocked library could have had access to all of these materials, especially given the relationship amongst **Q**, **I-b**, and **Y**.

However, in further analysis, drawing on the work of Jean Devisse, Knibbs argues against Patzold's use of Hincmar for dating on the grounds that Hincmar was a known hunter for Leo's letters;[182] he would not have needed a single source for the letters. Besides the four **I-c** rarities in Hincmar's *Opusculum LV capitulo-*

---

[177] Ibid., 47–53.

[178] Ibid., 53–54.

[179] Ibid., 55–56.

[180] Chavasse 1975, 37–39.

[181] Knibbs 2016a.

[182] Knibbs 2016b; Devisse 1975–1976, vols 1–3.

rum, which are the basis for Patzold's argument, Knibbs identifies a further nine Leo rarities known from Pseudo-Isidore C as identified by Devisse, used by Hincmar in works from 856/7 through 875, albeit rarely.[183] Knibbs' final shot is the idea that perhaps Hincmar was the inspiration for **I-c**, rather than **I-c** being the source for Hincmar. Nevertheless, if **S-ga** can become **I-b** and **Y** in this period, and if Pseudo-Isidore can reach Rome during the papacy of Nicholas I, why should not a further expansion with rare material lead from **Y** to **I-c** in the ninth century? In fact, I would argue that Knibb's argument against Hincmar based on further use of **I-c** rarities by the Bishop of Reims serves only strengthen Patzold's argument, not weaken it.

When we consider the vast number of much earlier manuscripts of Leo's letters than any of this collection—none earlier than the twelfth century—collating the entirety of all six manuscripts of such a large collection seemed a futile, time-consuming task. Therefore, I selected only the rare letters of **I-c** for collation: *Epp.* 102, 121, 122, 105, 123, 127, 36, 39, 47, 48, 74, and 156. I also chose to examine earlier rather than later manuscripts: *f* and *m*. The Ballerini list the two following **I-c** manuscripts:

> *f*: Vat. lat. 1340 (saec. XIII), from Flanders, provenance in France.[184] This illuminated manuscript with gold leaf is written in a beautiful proto-Gothic hand. Leo begins with a *capitula* list on 197^r, the text of the letters running 200^r–248^r.

> *v*: Venice, Biblioteca Nazionale Marciana, lat. Z. 169 (also 168) (= 1615, 1616) (saec. XV), with provenance of Venice, based on a late twelfth-century northern French manuscript.[185]

5.2.f.vi-a. Hinschius Class C

I-c exists in four other manuscripts:

> *r*: Reims, Bibliothèque municipale, 672 (G. 166), fol. 7–191^v, from between 1154–1159, originating in Reims itself.

> *m*: Montpellier, Bibliothèque Interuniversitaire, H 013 (saec. XIII), from northern France with provenance in Pontigny. This manu-

---

[183] See Devisse 1975–1976, vol. 3, 1439–1448.

[184] Kuttner 1986, 74–78. This manuscript is digitised: https://digi.vatlib.it/view/MSS_Vat.lat.1340 Accessed 21 September 2021.

[185] See Kéry 1999, 105.

script's Gothic hand gives away its century of origin. Each letter begins with a large, intricate *littera notabilior.*

Paris, Bibliothèque de l'Assemblée nationale 27 (B.19, olim 681) (saec. XII[ex]) which bears a 'striking correspondance to Reims, Bibliothèque municipale, 672 and Venezia, Zenetti lat. 168 and 169';[186] it was penned in northern France, and its provenance is from Paris.

Prague, Národní Knihovna Ceské Republiky, IV.B.12 (saec. XV), which is based on a late twelfth-century source from Reims, and has provenance in Prague.

The differences between *f* and *m* are slight, such as 'ignota' (*f*) vs. 'incognita' (*m*), as well as *m* including 'epc' after 'Leo' in the inscription, as the sole differences between their texts for *Ep.* 102. In *Ep.* 121, the differences are of similar but slightly greater magnitude. First we have 'septuagesima et quartus est annus' (*f*) vs. 'septuagesimus et quartus est agnus' (*m*); *m* provides a better reading until—amusingly—placing 'agnus' for 'annus'. Anyone who has spent a long time copying out texts longhand knows how easily a tired mind and hand could have produced that slip! Next there is 'leui' (*f*) vs. 'leuiter' (*m*)—*m* is preferred; and 'mearum diem' (*f*) vs. 'in eam diem' (*m*)—again, *m* wins. Significantly, they are united in the rubrics, giving, for example, 'Leo eudochiae augustae de pascha' as the heading for *Ep.* 122; this attribution is striking, given that *Ep.* 122 is cited elsewhere as to Julian of Cos.[187] In that letter, *f* gives 'institutionis' against *m*, 'instructionis'—each is a credible reading, although 'instructionis' has the weight of **G**, **E**, and **B** behind it; 'diligentius inuestigare' against 'diligentior inuestigare'—in this case, each has a major collection on its side,[188] although both of them add 'inuestigare' at variance with those collections. Finally, we have *f* 'tua petitur' against *m* 'tua poterit', both against **E** and **B** 'reppererit' and **G** 'repperit'. The sentence runs, 'quicquid autem de hac re *diligentior* inuestigare sollicitudo tua *poterit*' (*m*), and I believe that *m* 'poterit' makes better sense than *f*. Not to overburden us with more evidence, *m* gives a better text of **I–c** than *f*.

---

[186] Ibid., 103.

[187] i·e. **G**, **E**, and **B**. Ballerini Collection 24, however, maintains this attribution, demonstrating its dependence upon the tradition of **I** for its contents.

[188] diligentius: **G**, **B**; diligentior: **E**.

Before leaving Pseudo-Isidore, it remains to mention a host of manuscripts listed by Kéry but not included by the Ballerini and not, apparently, classified by Hinschius or later scholars.[189] As a result, we cannot be sure which—if any—collections of Leo's letters are gathered in these manuscripts. Investigating these manuscripts, of which we know thirty, and classifying them would be a research project in itself. Besides these many Pseudo-Isidorian manuscripts that, if not complete, are fragments from presumably complete manuscripts, Kéry lists a large number of manuscripts containing excerpts from the Pseudo-Isidorian tradition.[190]

5.2.g. The Canon Law Manuscript Vat. Reg. lat. 423

5.2.g.i. Description of collection

This is a ninth-century collection of various canonical materials. It begins with Gallic councils (fols 1^v–25^v), followed by Cresconius (26^r–61^v), after which come Leo, *Epp.* 14 and 7 (62^v–63^r), then a letter from Damian of Pavia to Constantine IV (64^v), closing with fragments of Priscian's *Institutio de arte grammatica* (65^r–68^v). The behaviour of the compiler in including only two of Leo's letters is the sort of behaviour that we will see more frequently in the High Middle Ages, although we also saw it on the cusp of the Carolingian age with the Ragyndrudis Codex.

5.2.g.ii. Manuscript

> Vat. Reg. lat. 423 (saec. IX).[191] Leo's letters are on fols 62^v–63^r. The manuscript is a single-column Caroline minuscule.

5.2.h. Systematic as well as Unorganised Collections of Extracted Canons

Besides these canonical collections that include letter collections of Leo's work, there also exists a large number of systematic and unorganised canonical collections. These collections have taken passages from councils and decretals out of their original context

---

[189] See Kéry 1999, 100–05.
[190] See ibid., 106–08.
[191] This MS is digitised: https://digi.vatlib.it/view/MSS_Reg.lat.423. Accessed 21 September 2021.

and rearranged them; in the systematic ones, they are placed in an order according to topic, as with Cresconius, *Concordia cano-num*.[192] They are not, as a result, very useful for determining the text of Leo's letters. Nonetheless, they represent an important mode whereby his thought was transmitted through the Middle Ages, for systematic collections become by far the favoured form of compilation in the Central Middle Ages. Thus, although these collections are not to be consulted for the purposes of textual crit-icism, I list them to demonstrate their importance for the trans-mission of Leo the Great, who, it proves, was one of the more important Bishops of Rome, given the diversity and spread of col-lections containing his letters. The following 14 collections contain excerpts from Leo's letters. Much of this material was gathered from Linda Fowler-Magerl, *Clavis Canonum: Selected Canon Law Collections Before 1140*; to streamline references, this work will be cited as *Clavis* throughout.

- The *Collectio Herovalliana* (saec. VIII2/2), which is an extension of the *Collectio Vetus Gallica*;[193]

- The *Collectio LXXII capitulorum*, in Rome, Biblioteca Vallicelli-ana T.XVIII, which is descended from the ninth-century *Hero-valliana* manuscript, Bamberg, StB Patr. 101.[194]

- *Collectio Bonavallensis prima*, (saec. IX[in]).[195]

- *Collectio Capitularium* of Ansegis, by the end of January 827.[196] As listed in the *Clavis Canonum* CD-ROM, this collection con-tains only one paraphrase of Leo, *Ep.* 167.14, at 1.22.

- *Collectio capitularium* of Benedictus Levita, c. 847–52.[197]

- The *Collectio Dacheriana*, early ninth-century; this collection used the *Collectio Hispana systematica* as a source and originates in Gaul.[198]

---

[192] See above 3.2.h.

[193] *Clavis*, 37. On the *Vetus Gallica*, see above 3.2.s.

[194] *Clavis*, 49. Discussed above at 5.2.a.

[195] *Clavis*, 37–38. Fowler-Magerl provides divergent names for this collec-tion. On 37–38 of the book, it is called *Collectio Bonavellensis prima*, the name I adopt here as correct; on p. 37, this collection is giving the Key **BA** for the CD-ROM, which in the index of the *Clavis* Keys as well as in the software is named *Collectio Bonavellensis secunda*.

[196] *Clavis*, 51–52.

[197] *Clavis*, 51–52. Mentioned in relation to **I**, 5.2.f.

[198] *Clavis*, 55–56.

- The *Quadripartitus* (saec. IX2–3/4) which is dependant on the *Dacheriana*.[199]

- The *Pittaciolus* of Hincmar of Laon, which he presented to his uncle Hincmar of Reims at the assembly called by Charles the Bald in November 869 at Gondreville.[200] This collection has but one canon from Leo, *Ep.* 4.5.

- From around the same time as Hincmar's *Pittaciolus* and associated with him are five collections in Berlin, SBPK Phillipps 1764;[201] of these Subcollection 1 contains several canons from Leo's letters.

- The *Collectio canonum Anselmo dedicata*, dedicated to Anselm II of Milan (882–96).[202]

- All three collections of canons in Milan, Biblioteca Ambrosiana, A. 46 inf. (saec. IX[ex]), from Reims.[203]

- The *Collectio CCCXLII capitulorum* (saec. IX).[204]

- The Council of Aachen of 816–19 in Rome, Biblioteca nazionale centrale Vittorio Emanuele II, Vittorio Emanuele, Vitt.Em.1348 (*c.* 816–50; formerly Phillipps 6546).[205] A considerable portion of the codex is taken up with excerpts from the church fathers. Chh. 62 and 63 are excerpts from Leo, *Epp.* 14 and 1.

5.3 Other Carolingian Collections

5.3.a. *Collectio Bobbiensis*[206] (**B**)

5.3.a.i. Dating and context

Following a selection of Pope Gregory I's letters, this collection contains twenty-six of Leo's letters. The title page lists 50 letters; those which survive are: *Epp.* 9 & 14 of Leo, then an anti-Pelagian letter of Aurelius, Bishop of Carthage (d. 430), following which are the *acta* of a North African council against Pelagians;

---

[199] *Clavis*, 59–60.

[200] *Clavis*, 64–65.

[201] *Clavis*, 65.

[202] *Clavis*, 70–74.

[203] *Clavis*, 66–67.

[204] *Clavis*, 61–63.

[205] See Schenkl 1891, § 1630, and the catalogue entry of the Istituto Centrale per il Catalogo Unico delle Biblioteche Italiane e per le informazioni bibliografiche, https://manus.iccu.sbn.it/opac_SchedaScheda.php?ID = 68921 Accessed 21 September 2021.

[206] Not listed by Ballerini or Jalland.

five so-called decretals of Leo, *Epp.* 12, 167, 16, 159, 15, and then *Epp.* 24, 31, 94, 95, 93, 102, 104, 105, 113, 111, 112, 118, 121, 122, 123, 125, 128, 127, 130. The text breaks off partway through *Ep.* 130. *Ep.* 167 has the **D** *capitula*, and *Ep.* 12 is in the *decurtata* recension, *Ep.* 12b. These same five decretals are shared by **Te**, but with *Ep.* 28 added into the mix and a different order; *Epp.* 15, 16, and 159 are also in the proto-collection common to **Te**, **Di**, and **Re, proto-3**.[207] The difference in order and the *capitula* of *Ep.* 167 makes it unlikely that they are directly related, however. One could just as easily postulate a relationship with **D** due to the presence of *Ep.* 167 with **D** *capitula* and *Epp.* 16 and 159. However, the text of **B** does not correspond very closely to any of the above collections. It seems to be heterogeneous as a type of text. Yet whatever other sources it may have had, it seems likely that **B** used either **G** (if not its sole manuscript, then a common exemplar) or a common source with **G**, given that its letters from 24 onwards are in almost the same order as they appear in **G**, although, obviously, missing out many items and with an occasional difference in order. Nonetheless, some of the letters do appear in matching batches between the two collections, such as *Epp.* 94, 95, 93, 102, 104, 105. Throughout these letters, **B** shares a great many readings with **G**. This close relationship with **G** should be unsurprising, since both **B** and **G** have a northern Italian origin.

5.3.a.ii. Manuscript

It exists in one manuscript:

> Milan, Biblioteca Ambrosiana C.238 inf., (saec. IX2/2) with provenance of San Colombano, Bobbio.[208] Written in a minuscule with more than one hand, as identified by Bischoff. Leo's letters run fols 141^r–172^v.

5.3.b. *Collectio Ratisbonensis*[209] (**E**)

5.3.b.i. Dating and Context

This collection of letters was the basis for Silva-Tarouca's edition.[210] It includes 72 letters, as Jasper says, 'compiled hierarchi-

---

[207] See the Appendix for a list and description of the proto-collections.

[208] Bischoff 1998–2014, 2.2611.

[209] B19 (PL 54.572), J3(ii) 507).

[210] Jasper 2001, 41, n. 173.

cally according to their recipients, and frequently according to their date of dispatch, thus betraying an editor's orderly hand'.[211] The Ballerini and Jasper prefer *Ratisbonensis* over *Grimanica*.[212] It includes the following letters of the Leonine corpus: 24, 23, 29, 30, 28, 35, 34, 33, 32, 37, 38, 44, 45, 51, 50, 54, 60, 61, 69, 70, 75, 78, 79, 80, 81, 83, 84, 85, 86, 88, 90, 91, 92, 93, 94, 95, 104, 105, 106, 107, 114, 119, 109, 102, 115, 116, 117, 121, 122, 123, 126, 127, 139, 130, 129, 131, 136, 142, 143, 144, 145, 146, 147, 148, 149, 150, 151, 152, 153, 164, 165, 162. Silva-Tarouca observes that **E** is one of those rare collections organised by recipient and argues that this collection is a direct descendent of the papal archive.[213] He argues this on the basis that the painstaking order of the documents, by recipient and by date, bespeaks of archival access, given how difficult organising them would be if they came from elsewhere. The strongest argument is that **E**'s compiler knew that *Epp.* 149 and 150 were two different redactions of the same letter. The beginning of the letter was sent to Basilius of Antioch (edited as *Ep.* 149 by the Ballerini), and thus, after 'commonemus', **E** writes, 'Vsque hic Basilio', then continues the rest of the text; the longer version is edited as *Ep.* 150 by the Ballerini. **G**, on the other hand, keeps these as two letters, with no acknowledgement of their relationship. We know from the evidence in our earliest surviving original copy of a papal register, that of Gregory VII (*c.* 1088),[214] that letters sent to multiple people in the same words or different redactions were noted down as having been thus sent by the scribes.

5.3.b.ii. Manuscripts

E exists in the following two manuscripts:

> *m*: Munich, Bayerische Staatsbibliothek, Clm 14540 (VIII/IX saec.), from the Benedictine Abbey of St Emmeram, Regensburg.[215] Leo runs fols 1ᵛ–157ᵛ; 158–245 are *Excerpta ex patribus*, identified by Bischoff as also being from St Emmeram. It is written in a very

[211] Ibid., 48, cf. also n. 197.

[212] PL 54.572, Jasper 2001, 47–48.

[213] For **E**, see Silva-Tarouca 1926, 25–31.

[214] Ed. E. Caspar 1920–1923, MGH Epistolae Selectae 2, 2 vols. The MS is Vatican City, Archivio Apostolico Vaticano, Registra Vaticana, t. II (saec. XI).

[215] CLA 9.1305; Bischoff 1998–2014 2.3231.

attractive and fluid Caroline minuscule; it is unrubricated with uncial explicits and incipits. As noted above in Chapter 2, Silva-Tarouca used *m* as the basis for his edition of *Ep.* 28, and, as noted at Chapter 2.8, Blakeney collated it against the Ballerini text at C. H. Turner's recommendation.

Vienna, Österreichische Nationalbibliothek 829 (XII saec.), which is a transcript of the above. Di Capua has demonstrated seventy-nine variants where this manuscript differs from the above; in all seventy-nine, the Munich manuscript demonstrates clausulae more in line with Leo's style.[216]

5.3.b.iii. Manuscript Relations

E and **G** are the foundations of the two largest editions of Leo's letters in the twentieth century. Schwartz, in choosing **G** in 1932, selected a text whose greatest virtue was comprehensiveness and size, not quality. When Silva-Tarouca prepared his text which was published two years later in 1934, then, he chose with greater perspicacity. His introduction to the collection, in *Textus et Documenta: Series Theologica* 15, includes a discussion of Leo's clausulae by F. Di Capua who would go on to write *Il ritmo prosaico nelle lettere dei papi e nei documenti della Cancelleria Romana dal IV al XIV secolo*, the first volume of which (1937) also deals with Leo's prose rhythm. Drawing from this discussion of the clausulae, Silva-Tarouca gives a sample of eight places where the **E** variants demonstrate better clausulae than **G**.[217] This sampling is as follows (numbering is that of the letters in **E**, with line numbers of Silva-Tarouca's edition):

Epistle	*Collectio Ratisbon-ensis* (**E**)	*Collectio Grimanica* (**G**)	Clausulae (my scansion)
I *l.* 8	religionis habeatis _uuu/_u	religionis habetis	**E**: Trispondaicus, both metrical and accentual **G**: Cursus planus
I *l.* 27	pietatis exegit	pietatis exigit	**E**: Planus cretic/spondee **G**: Nothing

---

[216] Di Capua 1934, xxix–xxxi.

[217] Silva-Tarouca 1934, ix. He goes so far as to say that this codex preserves clausulae 'melius quam omnes ceteri codices'.

Epistle	Collectio Ratisbon-ensis (**E**)	Collectio Grimanica (**G**)	Clausulae (my scansion)
III *ll.* 22–23	ueniam reseruauit	ueniam reseru-auerit	**E**: Velox (pre-ferred, cretic spondee) **G**: Velox 2 or octo-syllabicus (double cretic)
III *l.* 23	se esse promitteret	se expromitteret	**E**: Tardus (pre-ferred) **G**: Tardus (with hiatus)
IV *l.* 27	audet astruere	audeat astruere	**E**: Tardus **G**: Nothing
IV l. 54	melius consuletur	melius consulitur	**E**: Velox **G**: Nothing
VII l. 35	credimus sacerdo-tum	credidimus sacer-dotum	**E**: Velox (cretic spondee) **G**: Velox (cretic spondee)
X l. 20	fuisset abstentum	fuisset abstinen-dum	**E**: Planus, both metrical and accentual **G**: Trispondaicus

Given the regularity of Leo's prose rhythm and his clear system-atisation thereof, one need look no further than Di Capua's work to demonstrate the clear superiority of **E** over **G**.

5.3.c. *Ep.* 28 in the Roman Homiliary

5.3.c.i. Description

Ep. 28 not infrequently appears as one of a handful of Leo's letters or the sole representative of Leo's letters in several manuscripts, including those of the homiliaries. Most homiliaries, including the Carolingian ones discussed here, were composed for monastic use, following the *Rule* of St Benedict 9.8, to be used during the night office. The homiliary of Alan of Farfa (*d.* 769) includes *Ep.* 28 in the course of homilies for Summer; it is part 2, number 89 in Grégoire's edition and description.[218] The various homiliaries are

---

[218] Grégoire 1966, 67.

often contaminated, and the transmission of the Roman homiliary is no exception. In Grégoire's edition of Alan of Farfa's homiliary, he cites the homiliary of St Peter's as a separate entity from Alan's, having a sixth-century core,[219] but he later uses the same manuscripts that contain the homiliary of Alan of Farfa alongside the manuscript of the homiliary of St Peter's in his analysis of the 'Roman Homiliary'.[220] Regardless of the spider's web of relations between homiliaries, which present the same challenges to editors as letter collections, the manuscripts will be listed below based on Grégoire's two analyses. First, those of the Roman homiliary of St Peter's, given the siglum *S* in Chavasse's edition of Leo's sermons,[221] then those used by Grégoire in 1966 to edit Alan of Farfa. The literature is not always clear which manuscripts contain which part of the homiliary. If it is unclear whether a manuscript includes *Ep.* 28, an asterisk (*) will mark its entry. In this way, some clarity may be gained.

5.3.c.ii. Manuscripts of the homiliary of St Peter's (Chavasse, Homiliary *S*)

Vatican, Arch. Cap. S. Pietro C.105 (saec. X^ex).[222] This manuscript is the basis of the homiliary of St Peter's as described by Grégoire as a different entry from the Roman homiliary.[223]

Vatican, Arch. Cap. S. Pietro C.107 (saec. XII).

5.3.c.iii. Manuscripts used to edit Alan of Farfa's homiliary (Grégoire 1966)

Troyes, Médiathèque de l'Agglomération Troyenne, MS 853 (saec. VIII/IX).[224]

Munich, Bayerische Staatsbibliothek, Clm 4547 (saec. VIII/IX). Provenance of Benediktbeuern.[225]

---

[219] Grégoire 1966, 8.

[220] Grégoire 1980, 135.

[221] Chavasse 1973, xlvii.

[222] This manuscript is digitised: https://digi.vatlib.it/view/MSS_Arch.Cap.S.Pietro.C.105 Accessed 21 September 2021.

[223] Grégoire 1980, 223–44.

[224] CLA 6.840. The basis of Grégoire's analysis, described in Grégoire 1966, 18–21.

[225] The seven Munich manuscripts are cited by Grégoire 1966, 21, and part of the description of the homiliary of Hosp 1936 and 1937.

Munich, Bayerische Staatsbibliothek, Clm 4564 (saec. VIII/IX). Provenance of Benediktbeuern.*

Munich, Bayerische Staatsbibliothek, Clm 18092 (saec. VIII2/2). Provenance of Tegernsee.*

Munich, Bayerische Staatsbibliothek, Clm 14368 (saec. IX). Provenance of St Emmeram.

Munich, Bayerische Staatsbibliothek, Clm 17194 (saec. IX). Provenance of Schäftlarn.*

Munich, Bayerische Staatsbibliothek, Clm 18091 (saec. XI). Provenance of Tegernsee.*

Munich, Bayerische Staatsbibliothek, Clm 7953 (saec. XII). Provenance of Kaisheim. This manuscript is a copy of Alan of Farfa rearranged by Eginon of Verona. *Ep.* 28 is item 191 in this collection.[226]

5.3.d. *Ep.* 28 in the Homiliary of Agimond

5.3.d.i. Description

Another homiliary that includes *Ep.* 28 is the Homiliary of Agimond. Leo is in part 3 of this homiliary, item 45.[227]

5.3.d.ii. Manuscript

Vat. lat. 3836 (saec. VIII).[228] This is the second surviving volume of the homiliary, that which contains *Ep.* 28.

5.4 Conclusion

The Carolingian era has transmitted to us more Leo manuscripts than any other, even though fewer new collections were assembled in this age than the prior. Besides its significance for transmitting earlier collections, the Carolingian era saw the creation of the new collections analysed in this chapter. A central moment of the Carolingian Renaissance and its relationship to canon law was the assembly of the Pseudo-Isidorian collections (**I**, see 5.2.f). In and of themselves, there are four Pseudo-Isidorian collections

---

[226] Grégoire 1966, 67.

[227] Grégoire 1980, 382.

[228] CLA 1.1934.

that contain Leo the Great, covering a total of 55 manuscripts. All four collections have been shown to be Carolingian in origin, including Pseudo-Isidore C (**I-c**, see 5.2.g.vi), formerly dated to the twelfth century. Moreover, this project influenced letter collections in the High Middle Ages, as we shall see in the next chapter, including *Collectio Lanfranci* (no siglum, see 6.2.a), Ballerini Collection 21 (**Y-a**, see 6.3.b), Ballerini Collection 22 (**22**, see 6.3.c), the *Collectio Florentina* (Ballerini Collection 13, **m**, see 6.3.f), Ballerini Collection 23 (**23**, see 6.3.d), Ballerini Collection 24 (**24**, see 6.3.e), and the collection of Pope Eugenius IV (no siglum, see 6.3.n) amongst other, less well-distributed collections, accounting for a further 65 manuscripts. The pre-history of this collection is also part of the Carolingian world, for the Pseudo-Isidorian collection takes as its foundation the *Collectio Hispana Gallica Augustodunensis* (**S-ga**, see 5.2.e), itself an adaptation of a Gallic version of the *Collectio Hispana* (**S**, discussed above at 3.2.u) called the *Hispana Gallica* (**S-g**, see 5.2.d). The texts of *Epp.* 7 and 22 are damaged and confused in **S-ga** manuscript *a* (Vat. lat. 1341, saec. IX) and this damage is repeated throughout the Pseudo-Isidorian tradition, rendering **S-ga**, for its thirty-nine letters, perhaps more useful than Pseudo-Isidore, especially given the opportunities for contamination in Carolingian scriptoria. Nevertheless, the ongoing expansion of **S-ga** by the Pseudo-Isidorian forger-compilers means that, for the rest of the letters, Pseudo-Isidore is still very much worthy of consideration.

In the Carolingian era, the journey of the *Dionysiana* (**D**) comes effectively to a close as far as Leo is concerned; the ongoing transmission of his letters in the High and Late Middle Ages will be the fruit of Pseudo-Isidore's popularity, not that of Dionysius Exiguus. In Chapter 3.2.g, we saw how the *Dionysiana Bobiensis* (**D-b**) was simply an expansion of the *Dionysiana* that did not affect Leo's letters at all, and the text seems to be a fairly reliable text. The *Dionysiana* had continuing popularity at Rome that resulted in a version we know as the *Collectio Dionysio-Hadriana* (**D-h**, see 5.2.a) being sent to Charlemagne by Pope Hadrian I in 774; **D-h** adds one Leo letter to **D**. This collection would be further amplified into the *Hadriano-Hispanica* (**H-s**, see 5.2.b) with material from the *Collectio Hispana Gallica* (**S-g**), albeit with no further additions to Leo. However, an entirely new canonical collection was added to the *Dionysiana* tradition in the mid-ninth century, the *Collectio Dionysiana adaucta* (**D-a**, see 5.2.c), sometimes being added to manuscripts of the *Dionysiana*, sometimes to the *Dionysio-Hadriana*. The latest manuscript of this wider *Dionysiana* tradition is a **D-a** manuscript of 1460, Vat. lat. 1353, showing the enduring popularity of this tradition in canon law.

We also have two important manuscripts that must be considered with one of the manuscripts from Chapter 4, the *Collectio Grimanica* (**G**, see 4.1.g), and those are *Bobbiensis* (**B**, see 5.3.a) and *Ratisbonensis* (**E**, see 5.3.b). *Bobbiensis* is a north-Italian collection that seems to have used either *Grimanica* or a relative of *Grimanica* as a source when the selection of letters is considered; given the differences in readings, it is more likely from a relative of *Grimanica*, or at least not the surviving **G** manuscript. *Ratisbonensis*, on the other hand, may not even be a Carolingian collection but may pre-date this era by quite a bit. Either way, its relationship with *Grimanica* is not an organic, relational one but, rather, one created by the desire for editors to have a foundational text for their work. *Grimanica*, as the largest collection, formed the basis for Schwartz's work, but *Ratisbonensis* formed the basis for Silva-Tarouca's. My research bears out Silva-Tarouca's conclusions that *Ratisbonensis* transmits a better text of Leo than *Grimanica* for the letters they hold in common.

Finally, for the first time in the Carolingian era we see the transmission of Leo's *Tome* (*Ep.* 28) independent of his other letters, as analysed in the transmission of homiliaries at 5.3.c and 5.3.d. Prior to this, the closest we came to such bald transmission was the Ragyndrudis Codex (see 3.2.w), itself almost Carolingian, and a further Carolingian fragment of the *Tome* in Chapter 4 at 4.1.j. In this independent transmission of the *Tome*, we see a further way in which the Carolingians were themselves the consolidators and foundation-layers for the rest of the Middle Ages at least in terms of its engagement with Leo the Great.

Chapter 6

Post-Carolingian Collections

The Age of Reform and Scholasticism

6.1 Introduction to High and Late Medieval Contexts

After the Carolingians, the next occasion when manuscripts of
Leo's letters peak is the era of reform and Renaissance in the eleventh and twelfth centuries. To reduce to a short compass on the
page a large, multifaceted current of events, trends, and personalities such as the reform movement is fraught with peril. Nonetheless, we must venture it here as we did with the Carolingians. The
discussion will begin with a consideration of the reform movement
and its relation to Leo the Great's letters followed by a look at its
impact on manuscripts before moving on to the twelfth-century
Renaissance and Scholasticism.

What we today perceive as the 'reform' movement was a multifaceted series of events and personalities acting in the central
Middle Ages to curb ecclesiastical abuses and seeking to bring
vitality to ecclesiastical life. It had manifestations in monastic
life, liturgy, ecclesiastical buildings, and canon law; one could
even posit that its theological manifestations emerge in a greater
concern for orthodoxy and heresy in this age. One result of this
concern, for example, is the controversy surrounding Berengar of
Tours, whose teaching on the Eucharist was condemned by the
reform-minded Lanfranc of Bec. And, while the largest evidence
for the transmission of Leo's letters comes in the context of canon
law in this period, Lanfranc does, in fact, quote one of Leo's letters in his *De Corpore et Sanguine Domini*.[1] In the generation after
Lanfranc, the cultural currents that we perceive today as reform

---

[1] For Lanfranc against Berengar, see Cowdrey 2003, 59–74. A fine study of
Lanfranc's eucharistic theology can be found in Vaillancourt 2009, 3–11. The
quotation of Leo is *Ep.* 80 (PL 54.914A-B), in *De Corpore et Sanguine Domini*,
19, PL 150.435A-B: Aliter enim in Ecclesia Dei, quae corpus est Christi, nec
rata sunt sacerdotia, nec vera sacrificia, nisi in nostrae proprietate naturae
verus nos Pontifex reconciliet, verus immaculati Agni sanguis emundet. Qui

and renaissance would lead to the rise of a theologian of the stature of Anselm of Canterbury, who also has citations and allusions to Leo in his work. Moreover, both Anselm and Lanfranc are part of the story of the rise of scholasticism and the twelfth-century Renaissance that would follow them, to be discussed shortly. What matter for us the most now are the currents of canon law in the age of reform—Leo's letters in the era of reform are transmitted to us largely in canonical collections although the twelfth-century Renaissance also sees the emergence of codices dedicated to Leo alone. From the perspective of canon law, then, perhaps it can be stated that the age of reform is an era when high-ranking prelates sought to enforce what they saw as the purity of ancient canon law in a uniform way through Latin Europe against what they perceived to be abuses and neglect of good church order. Throughout, the most prevalent concerns are simony and married clergy. From Gregory VII onwards, lay investiture becomes a major part of the reforming agenda as well.

For our purposes and as part of a wider understanding of the history of church authority and canon law, the reform movement is not to be associated with the name of Pope Gregory VII (pope, 1073–1085), for it pre-dates him, and some of those unsympathetic to certain of his causes (in particular on the question of lay investiture) are themselves a part of this movement.[2] Gregory VII is certainly a mover and shaker in ecclesiastical reform, but the impulse within canon law is not restricted to his orbit. The pope widely considered the first reforming pope, Leo IX, pre-dates Gregory VII, and Lanfranc of Bec (Archbishop of Canterbury 1070–1089), while certainly a reformer, was no promoter of papal power in England.[3] Indeed, if we set aside the issue of investiture, Anglo-Norman bishops are part of the wider movement of reform,

---

licet in Patris sit dextera constitutus, in eadem tamen carne quam sumpsit ex Virgine sacramentum propitiationis exsequitur.

[2] For the argument against calling this the Gregorian Reform, see Gilchrist 1970, 1–10. For the origins of the term 'Gregorian Reform' and its lack of usefulness, see Cushing 2005, 33–37.

[3] For Lanfranc's efforts at reform of the English church, see Cowdrey 2003, 120–43, although various aspects of reform emerge in the surrounding chapters. For an older discussion of reform in England under Lanfranc and William the Conqueror, see Brooke 1989, 117–46. For Alexander II and reform in England at this time, see Cushing 2005, 77–78.

acting against simony and married clergy, for example—the two sole issues highlighted in Symeon of Durham's account of Gregory VII's synod of 1074.[4] In fact, throughout Symeon's *Historia regum* of around 1128–1129, these issues and investiture arise as being among the gravest issues facing the post-Conquest church. Some examples are that a main event of 1099 is Urban II's council against lay investiture; in 1102 he discusses King Henry I of England's opposition to simony and married clergy; in 1103 he deals with Henry's clash with Anselm over investiture; in 1106 Symeon deals further with investiture; in 1107 he gives the resolution of Henry against Anselm in favour of the archbishop; in 1108 he includes a reform-minded statement by Anselm, the Archbishop of York, and others against simony and married clergy. Although the case of Anselm is more nuanced than a simplified concept of lay investiture would imply, Symeon makes the reforming concern with lay investiture clear. Elsewhere, in his *Libellus de exordio* about the history of the church of Durham, Symeon also demonstrates the reform's concern with married clergy, including one priest who has intercourse with his wife meeting divine punishment and being unable to celebrate the Eucharist and a vision of priests' wives in hell.[5] Symeon is one among many figures we could have chosen to highlight the concerns of individuals associated with reform in the eleventh and twelfth centuries, such as his contemporary English historians William of Malmesbury and Eadmer of Canterbury, the latter of whom makes the issue of lay investiture the theme of his *Historia Novorum*.[6] For the question of how and why Leo was so popular in these centuries, Symeon may be more important than popes and high prelates because he represents reform 'on the ground', if you will, as the librarian and chronicler of Durham Cathedral Priory. As a pope of the patristic age, Leo's statements in favour of celibate clergy would find support in the climate of eleventh-century reform.

In fact, the movement for reform in ecclesiastical hierarchy, canon law, monasticism, and liturgy pre-dates not only Gre-

---

[4] Symeon of Durham, *Historia regum Anglorum et Danicorum*, ch. 160, ed. Arnold 200.

[5] Symeon of Durham, *Liber de exordio*, XLV (3.10) and LXVIII (4.10), ed. Rollason 172–73 and 250–51.

[6] Eadmer, *Historia Novorum*, Praef.

gory VII, but Leo IX as well, and Kathleen G. Cushing has shown its origins in the social world and related canonical activity of the Peace of God movement in the later tenth century.[7] However, the early boundaries of reform are not the only ones that need fluidity. The Investiture Controversy, for example, does not end with the Concordat of Worms in 1122, and it persists in different places and with different manifestations for the rest of the twelfth century. Pope Innocent III's interdict on England during the reign of King John (r. 1199–1216), for example, is part of a larger struggle between royal and papal power in ecclesiastical appointments. Furthermore, when we consider the increase of manuscripts of Leo the Great in this era, the reform movement is not the only cultural force at play, although there is a strong likelihood that the so-called 'Twelfth-Century Renaissance' was, like the Carolingian Renaissance discussed in Chapter 4, related to the movement for reform. Besides these movements within Europe, the boundaries of a united western European Christendom, Latin Christendom, were themselves expanding in these centuries,[8] with the result that more centres of manuscript production and preservation came to exist. To make a comparison with Carolingians, just as our first German manuscripts of Leo begin appearing in the eighth century, so now do we see Scandinavian manuscripts of Leo. Finally, although Anglo-Saxon England was rich in its own manuscripts, Anglo-Norman England is richer, at least in terms of survival; at this time, we get our first Leo manuscripts from England.[9] It is now time to consider Leo's place in the reform movement.

Leo has great weight and importance in this age of reform in the High Middle Ages. Immediately what should spring to anyone's mind is Bruno's name change when he became Pope— Leo IX (pope, 1049–1054) was not a random choice,[10] especially

---

[7] See Cushing 2005, 39–54.

[8] Bartlett 1993; the idea of this expansion of Latin Christendom is succinctly encapsulated through the expansion of bishoprics described in pages 5–23.

[9] Acknowledging, however, Michael D. Elliot's argument that one **Sa** MS, *k*, is English (Elliot 2013, 250–53; see 3.2.e.ii above); the Ragyndrudis Codex, even if it was the property of Boniface, does not count as English.

[10] Leo IX in PL 143.559–800, Mansi vol. 19; *Acta et scripta quae de controversiis ecclesiae Graecae et Latinae*, ed. C. Will, 1861.

in his letters to the East wherein he always pairs Leo and Marcian alongside Chalcedon; he is using the former cooperation of pope and emperor to further bolster his own position, as well as arguing forcibly, at times, for the papal reading of Matthew 16.[11] Leo is similarly used a few decades later by Gregory VII (pope, 1073–1085). In the *Register* of Gregory VII, there are five allusions to the letters of Pope Leo the Great; the only patristic pope with more allusions is Gregory the Great. Moreover, Leo is explicitly cited in Gregory VII's *Register* as a source on three occasions. The first is in 7.14*a*, chapter 6; 7.14*a* is a record of the Lenten synod for 1080. Here the papal curia writes, 'For if he to whom consecration rightly belongs by not correctly consecrating (as blessed Leo testifies) forfeits grace to confer blessing, it follows that he who shall descend to a corrupt election is deprived of the power of electing'.[12] Cowdrey posits that Gregory here has in mind Leo, *Ep.* 12.2–3, where Leo warns the Mauretanian bishops against consecrating people rashly and unduly. The second occasion is not a citation of Leo's writings but simply a statement that Leo confirmed 'the faith of the four councils' (*Register* 8.1).[13] The third is another citation of *Ep.* 12, this time chapter 5, where Leo warns of consecrating hastily. Here, Leo's example is being used to call for moderation. In *Epistola vagans* 9, Gregory refers to Leo, *Ep.* 14.4, as evidence that subdeacons should not marry. In *Ep. vag.* 45, he quotes *Ep.* 167, 'Let him not be numbered among the bishops who is not elected by the clergy and desired by the people'.[14]

This time of the movements of reform included many bishops, of course, and they, too, made use of Leo. Between 1012 and 1023, Burchard of Worms compiled his *Decretum*, a handbook on church

---

[11] For his use of Leo I, see PL 143.749, 772, 774. For his interpretation of Matthew 16, see PL 143.747–48, 774–75.

[12] Trans. Cowdrey.

[13] References to the 'four councils' throughout the Middle Ages are interesting, and go back as early as Gregory the Great, who explicitly lists only Nicaea I through Chalcedon, although elsewhere testifies to his acceptance of Constantinople II. Some lists give Eight Ecumenical Councils (Constantinople IV, 869, is the eighth), a number that will also fall awkwardly on a modern ear, used to discussing the Seven Ecumenical Councils.

[14] Trans. Cowdrey.

law for the clergy of his diocese being its admitted purpose.[15] In the *Decretum* of Burchard, Leo is cited thirty-five times out of ten of his letters.[16] Ivo of Chartres' *Decretum* of the early 1100s cites Leo's letters sixty-one times, making use of sixteen of his letters, including the spurious item JK † 551.[17] The anonymous *Collectio in LXXIV titulos* cites Leo's letters thirty-two times, drawing from seventeen epistles.[18] These citations and uses of Leo as an authority by reforming figures are evidence that Leo was being read in some form. However, of those collections that have been studied, it is clear that, even if the letters and sermons of Leo the Great are their *material* sources, their *formal* sources, that is, the immediate sources of the texts, are other systematic collections of excerpted canons. For example, Burchard used Regino of Prüm's *Libri duo*, and Ivo, in turn, used Burchard's *Decretum*.[19] Moreover, even Gratian and his expanders rarely used collections of letters directly—only a few instances can be detected of his unmediated use of Pseudo-Isidore or of the *Register* of Gregory the Great.[20] All of the above shows us the enduring importance of Leo the Great, but we should not make it seem greater than it was. In Gratian, Augustine was more prominent.[21] Overall, Gregory the Great is the most prominent. Gregory the Great's clearer, firmer influence in the age of reform is only to be expected, for Gregory also has many more surviving writings from his own vigorous incumbency of the see of Rome. Moreover, Gregory is revered not only as a pope but as a Church Father, listed by name as a major

[15] For its date, see Austin 2009, 20. For its educational purpose, ibid., 76–83.

[16] See Hoffmann and Pokorny 1991, 268.

[17] See Bruce Brasington and Martin Brett, 'Inscription Index', 59–60. Available online at: https://ivo-of-chartres.github.io/decretum/idsource.pdf. Accessed 21 September 2021. Date / revision stamp: 2015–2009-23 / 898fb.

[18] As cited in the Index of Gilchrist 1980, 263–64.

[19] For a full listing of the sources of Burchard's *Decretum*, see Hoffmann and Pokorny 1991, 173–244. For Ivo's use of Burchard, see Rolker 2010, 107–12.

[20] Gratian, as research makes clear, compiled the *Decretum* in the 1130s in a shorter form than the one more widely diffused from the 1140s on, as demonstrated by Winroth 2000. For the sources, see Landau 2008, 34.

[21] See the Prolegomena to Friedberg's edition of Gratian, cols xxxiv–xxxvi.

authority by Burchard, for example.[22] Gregory the Great is possibly the most popular patristic writer of the Latin Middle Ages, whether we are considering canon law, theology, or asceticism,[23] with even the traditional Roman liturgy in his name. Therefore, his greatness should not diminish the enduring importance of Leo, but simply be accepted as a more prevalent reality. Nevertheless, Leo the Great was important to the eleventh- and twelfth-century reformers because of his status as a father of the ancient church, as a *papa magnus*, as a source cited in the books of canon law, in the homiliaries, in the sources for the church's dogma.

Besides his presence in the writings and compilations of the reformers, Leo the Great is transmitted to us in the manuscripts of the reform. Alongside the letter collections that are the subject of this chapter, we see that pre-reform collections of Leo are being copied in this era. One important example is the *Collectio Avellana*. Much attention has been given to this collection, in part due to the rarities it contains, in part due to the interest of the documents whether rare or not, not only because it is readily and easily available in a high-quality critical edition but because it is a rare collection of both papal and imperial correspondence from Late Antiquity. Most of this attention has reflected upon the era of the collection's compilation and what purposes it would serve then.[24] However, what most of these studies do not highlight or emphasise are the origins of the manuscripts. The *Collectio Avellana*'s namesake manuscript was written in the monastery at Fonte Avellana in the age of reform. Fonte Avellana is significant because its reforming abbot, Peter Damian, was a major figure in wider reform. If we read the *Collectio Avellana* in an eleventh-century context, our vision of this collection takes on a new hue. Documents such as *Ep.* 38, for example, are significant for helping set precedent for the division of the two spheres of influence, secular and sacred, emperor and bishops. This epistle is a letter from the Emperor Honorius to his brother Arcadius, lamenting, amongst other things, the removal from office of John Chrysostom and the

---

[22] Austin 2009, 103.

[23] For Gregory's influence on exegesis, see de Lubac 1998, 132–34. That Gregory was the most popular Latin father in the Middle Ages, see Pelikan 1978, 16.

[24] See the discussion of *Collectio Avellana* above, 3.2.n.

ensuing violence; Honorius argues that his brother, as a secular leader, had no right to interfere in the church's business. In an age when lay investiture of bishops and abbots was the root of literal war, the copying of an ancient collection of letters that would serve the purposes of dividing the two spheres and thus stopping lay investiture points towards the quest for an ancient, authoritative precedent for the reformers on Gregory VII's side of the Investiture Controversy. Likewise, although new arguments have demonstrated that Pseudo-Isidore C belongs to the ninth century, its only manuscripts were written in this era. At a time when it seems that the systematic collections—Burchard's, Ivo's, Anselm of Lucca's, etc.—are gaining ground, we should not let it go unnoticed that the largest Pseudo-Isidorian collection was copied multiple times in many places, and this collection is itself chronological and transmits the second-largest collection of Leo's letters, the largest being *Collectio Grimanica*. Thus, in their writings, their systematic collections, and the texts they choose to copy, we see Leo invoked throughout the age of reform. It comes, then, as no surprise that so many manuscripts of his letter collections date to this era.

The Age of Reform overlaps with the twelfth-century Renaissance and the birth of scholasticism. Here we can see Leo again. An important sign of the transmission and use of Leo the Great by the figures of these cultural movements is the **Q** manuscript Oriel College 42, which we have already seen.[25] This manuscript's Leo collection is not **Q**. Oriel 42 was written by the hand of William of Malmesbury (1080–1143). William is possibly the foremost English historian of the twelfth century, most famous for *Gesta Regum Anglorum*, but he also wrote *Gesta Pontificum Anglorum*, *Historia novella*, and a commentary on Lamentations. The new rise in education and learning that scholars consider the twelfth-century Renaissance brought to William's hands not only **Q** but also a collection of Leo's letters that closely resembles **I-c** and survivals of late antique Roman law: this is the only Leo letter collection that includes the two *Leges novellae* of Valentinian III, edited by the Ballerini as *Epp.* 8 and 11. This renaissance, then, meant the transmission of more of Leo's letters than before, and

---

[25] 3.2.c. See below, 6.2.c, also.

in greater quantities. It led to Leo being read in more countries than hitherto as well.

Part of this renaissance, coupled also with reform, is the monastic spirituality of the Cistercians and others, as much in line with Anselm's legacy as the scholastics, whom we shall consider shortly, would be.[26] Again, we see the impact and presence of Leo in the abbeys. In fact, we have already considered his presence in the abbeys in *Collectio Avellana* and William of Malmesbury. The worlds of renaissance, reform, monasticism, and scholasticism are intextricably bound together. With a closer regard to the abbeys, to the Cistercians in particular, two tantalising manuscripts are worth mentioning. They are the twelfth-century manuscripts **24** *l.* now in Troyes (discussed below), and Florence, Biblioteca Medicea Laurenziana, Ashburnham 1554, both with provenance of Clairvaux. Could the great monastic theologian Bernard have read these manuscripts?

In these same centuries, as part of the wider cultural milieu of western Europe, we also see the rise of scholasticism. Scholasticism is associated with the medieval schools, ultimately and especially the universities and their establishment, and the use of dialectic and Aristotle in educational methodology as well as in the development of philosophy (including natural philosophy, or what we call 'science' today) and theology. A simple yet significant moment showing Leo's presence amongst the scholastics is the pre-scholastic monastic theology of Anselm of Canterbury. In Anselm's *Monologion* 28, we encounter an almost verbatim quotation from Leo's *Tome*: 'mirabiliter singulari et singulariter mirabili', alluding to 'singulariter mirabilis et mirabiliter singularis' in Leo.[27] The passage quoted was, of course, originally in the context of Christology. Yet when Anselm redeploys it, it comes amidst pneumatology. This allusion reminds us of the monastic schools, so elegantly discussed by Jean Leclercq, where the vast bulk of educational material was classical and patristic.[28] Anselm had so

[26] For the cultural and spiritual world of the Cistercians, see Melville 2016, 136–57.

[27] Anselm, *Monologion* 28, ed. Schmitt, vol. 1, 45, l. 25; Leo, *Ep.* 28, the *Tome*, ed. ACO 2.2.1, 26 *l.* 24.

[28] See Leclercq 1982, 51–150, for a study of the sources of monastic culture.

deeply drunk from the well of patristics, that a quotation from Leo the Great simply spilled forth from his pen unbidden.

When education moves from monastic schools more and more to cathedral schools and ultimately universities, the memory of Leo may operate differently from the Anselmian monastic allusion, which at once calls forth Leo and transforms him, but still it endures. To consider but a single yet indispensable author, his letters are cited by Peter Lombard's *Sententiae* twelve times in book 4.[29] I have already discussed his use by Gratian; Gratian represents both the canonical tradition of the Age of Reform and scholastic tradition of the early universities.

The age under consideration here, like the other bursts of manuscript activity seen in this book, is one of quests for authority and quests for truth. In order to reform the church, the reformers needed canonical collections and other material and formal sources of canon law. Outside of the pentitentials, Leo is almost always there, whether in a letter collection proper or in a systematic collection of excerpts. When historians like William of Malmesbury were seeking out sources for their own new knowledge, they felt the inadequacy of what they had, and at least one new collection of Leo's letters was created. When the scholastics sought to systematise and articulate philosophy, theology, and canon law using Aristotelian dialectical methods, they sought out the ancient authorities to argue with, for, or against in their quest for truth. Leo is one of those authorities.

The final moment of Leo's letters in the manuscript codices is the fifteenth century. The twelfth century is the last great moment of new collections of Leo's letters. While a few new collections and manuscripts appear in the thirteenth and fourteenth centuries, more new manuscripts appear in the fifteenth. Twenty-nine fifteenth-century manuscripts are discussed in the analysis below. These many fifteenth-century manuscripts of Leo tend to be copies of manuscripts devoted to Leo alone—copies of **Y-a** or **24** with a sermon collection, often with extracts about Leo's life. The owners of the fifteenth-century manuscripts include Eugenius IV, Bessar-

---

[29] *Ep.* 16.5–6, 4.40.3; *Ep.* 80.2, 4.150.5; *Ep.* 108.2, 4.94.3; *Ep.* 108.4–5, 4.113.1; *Ep.* 156.5, 4.150.5; *Ep.* 159.1–4, 4.216.2; *Ep.* 159.6, 4.112.2; *Ep.* 167.3, 4.212.3; *Ep.* 167.4, 4.162.2; *Ep.* 167.7, 4.109.1; *Ep.* 167.16–17, 4.39.2; *Ep.* 168.2, 4.94.7. Leo *Ep.* 35.3 is also mis-cited as Augustine at 3.6.2.

ion, Juan de Torquemada, Nicholas of Cusa, Domenico Capraneca, Angelo Capraneca, and Nicholas V. Malatesta Novello included one his public library. Alongside cloistered orders, the Lateran Canons also had copies of Leo's letters. The fifteenth century is one of the humanist centuries, and these manuscripts remind us that the pagans were not the only ancient authors finding a new audience in this era. The fifteenth century is also an era of reform, with attempts to end papal schism and curtail curial and papal abuses found in the Conciliarist Movement and its opponents; these currents would produce a natural readership in Leo, and several of the known owners of Leo's letters were, in fact, at the Council of Ferrara-Florence.

The Council of Ferrara-Florence began in 1438 in Ferrara as a continuation/rival council to the Council of Basel that had begun in 1431 but had already been dissolved by Pope Eugenius IV. In 1439 it moved to Florence to avoid plague at Ferrara. Although dissolved in 1437, the Council of Basel continued, deposing Eugenius and raising its own rival pope, Felix V. The fifteenth-century Conciliar Movement flexed its muscles most forcefully at the Council of Basel and found itself defeated by papal supremacy at the Council of Ferrara-Florence. However, the struggle for power in which these manuscripts were born was not limited to the western church but also involved a wide-ranging movement for reunion with the eastern churches—not only those in communion with Constantinople, but Copts and Armenians as well.

Leo the Great's letters speak directly to the situation of this council, just as they did to Nicholas of Cusa, himself originally a conciliarist and who would be deeply invested in East-West reunion, Bessarion, also involved in East-West geo-ecclesiology, Giordano Orsini who opened the Council of Basel in 1431 and was present at its continuation at Ferrara and Florence where he presided over some of the sessions, and Juan de Torquemada who supported Eugenius IV at Basel and was present at the Council of Florence, all of whom also owned manuscripts of Leo's letters. On the one hand, Leo represents one of the first systematic representatives of articulate papal theology. On the other hand, he also represents a pope not only forcible in his relations with the Eastern Church and Empire, but friendly. It comes as no surprise that men involved in these fifteenth-century movements owned codices of Leo's works.

Did these intellectual currents produce an interest in Leo, or did reading Leo fuel these movements? Both are true—it is as much the case that readers of Leo and others like him became the producers of these currents. One cannot help but note that Nicholas of Cusa went from conciliarist to papal supporter, owned at least two Leo manuscripts, and has writings replete with references to and quotations from this patristic pope. Indeed, Nicholas perhaps represents every stream of the fifteenth century, Renaissance, Reform, Council, Pope. Having set the stage, this study now turns to the manuscripts that were produced and used in the ages of these cultural currents of reform, renaissance, and schoolroom.

This chapter analyses the following canonical collections in section 6.2: *Lanfranci* (no siglum, see 6.2.a), *Britannica* (no siglum, see 6.2.b), the collection of William of Malmesbury (**o**, see 6.2.c), pre-Gratian systematic and unorganised collections of extracted canons at 6.2.d which covers sixty-two such collections, and Gratian's so-called *Decretum* at 6.2.e. Section 6.3 covers the following collections: Ballerini Collection 20 (no siglum, see 6.3.a), Ballerini Collection 21 (**Y–a**, see 6.3.b), Ballerini Collection 22 (**22**, see 6.3.c), Ballerini Collection 23 (**23**, see 6.3.d), Ballerini Collection 24 (**24**, see 6.3.e), *Florentina* (**m**, see 6.3.f), the Collection of 73 Letters (**73**, see 6.3.g), Ashburnham 1554 (no siglum, see 6.3.h), Vat. Reg. lat. 293 (no siglum, see 6.3.i), an eleventh-century pair of Leo's letters (no siglum, see 6.3.j), Milanese sermon collection *D* (no other siglum, see 6.3.k), Ambrosiana C.50.inf. (no siglum, see 6.3.l), Vat. Ross. 159 (no siglum, see 6.3.m), Eugenius IV's collection (no siglum, see 6.3.n), later manuscripts of the *Tome* (see 6.3.o), and other high and late medieval manuscripts with only one Leo letter (see 6.3.p).

6.2 Post-Carolingian Canonical Collections

6.2.a. *Collectio Lanfranci*[30]

6.2.a.i. Dating and Context

This collection is a shortened form of Pseudo-Isidore named after Lanfranc of Bec, who was Archbishop of Canterbury from 1070

---

[30] For description of collection, see Fowler-Magerl 2005, 181–82; for manuscripts, see Kéry 1999, 239–43.

to 1089. The collection is named after Lanfranc due to his possession of the copy that is now Cambridge, Trinity College B. 16. 44, which he had acquired while abbot of Saint-Étienne at Caen (1066–1070). The collection dates to after 1059. Besides his citation of Leo, *Ep.* 80, in *De Corpore* around 1062, Lanfranc also cites Leo, *Ep.* 104.3, in his *Ep.* 24.[31] Both of these letters are part of the collection. In global structure, this collection differs from Pseudo-Isidore by grouping together the decretals up to Gregory II at the beginning and then the conciliar canons from Nicaea to Seville as the second portion, as opposed to the Pseudo-Isidorian order of ante-Nicene decretals, conciliar canons, then post-Nicene decretals. The decretals exist occasionally in shortened forms. *Collectio Lanfranci* contains the following 27 of Leo's letters: *Epp.* 124.1–2, 1, 163, 165.1–3, 15, 44, 45, 61, 69, 70, 79, 80, 104, 106, 16, 19, 4, 18, 167, 14, 159, 12, 108, 166, 9, JK † 551, and 168. Álvarez de las Asturias argues that *Collectio Lanfranci*, based on the Leonine letters, is based upon either **I–b** (Pseudo-Isidore as in Vat. lat. 630, see above 5.2.f.iii) or the Yale/Cluny recension (**Y**, see 5.2.f.v).[32] Neither of the two contains all the letters of Leo in Lanfranc's collection. Moving on from those collections and drawing upon a wider spread of evidence amongst manuscripts, Álvarez de las Asturias goes on to argue for a relationship between *Collectio Lanfranci* and the Eton Pseudo-Isidore (Eton College, MS 97).[33] When this manuscript was discussed above, I observed that it likely had origins in Normandy; since Lanfranc brought his canon law manuscript with him from France, these origins remain likely.

Lanfranc was a vigorous reformer in canon law, in monastic life,[34] in building projects. Before becoming Archbishop of Canterbury, he was involved in the eucharist controversy surrounding Berengar of Tours. This collection was part of his reforming programme, and we have copies of it from multiple English cathedrals. As a result, *Collectio Lanfranci* became the touchstone

---

[31] Lanfranc of Canterbury, *Epistle* 24.8–9, ed. Clover and Gibson, 108. Leo, *Ep.* 104, PL 54.995A.

[32] Álvarez de las Asturias 2008, 23.

[33] Ibid., 24–30.

[34] See his *Consuetudines* ed. Knowles 2002. The oldest copy is in the Durham Cantor's Book, Durham Cathedral Library B.IV.24, fols 47^r–71^v, written by Eadmer and dating before 1096, according to Knowles 2002, xliv.

of English canon law before Gratian's arrival after 1140, even if other canonical collections were certainly in use and circulation the whole time as well. The deletions and abridgements of the *Collecto Lanfranci* are, for the most part, repetitions or not matters of canonical discipline. As a result, the *Collectio Lanfranci* transmits the same views on hierarchy and discipline as Pseudo-Isidore.[35] Therefore, English canon law moves on the same tracks as continental canon law from the Conquest onwards, if not earlier.[36]

6.2.a.ii. Manuscripts[37]

The *Collectio Lanfranci* exists in many English manuscripts because Lanfranc had it copied for the use of English bishops when he came over from Normandy. Therefore, of the complete manuscripts of *Collectio Lanfranci*, only Lanfranc's archetype seems fruitful for consideration, especially in a project of such enormous scope as this. Nevertheless, to give an idea of how Leo's letters in this collection and recension were distributed, the complete manuscripts of *Collectio Lanfranci* are listed below. In chronological order, these manuscripts are:

> Cambridge, Library of Trinity College, B.16.44 (405) (saec. XI), provenance either of Bec, according to Kéry 1999, or Caen, according to Fowler-Magerl 2005. Leo's letters run pages 115–57. We can confirm that this is Lanfranc's own copy because it contains his notice of purchase.

> Cambridge, Peterhouse 74 (saec. XI), provenance Durham Cathedral Priory. This manuscript is of great interest because it was the property of William of St-Calais (Bishop of Durham 1080–1093), who was himself a reforming bishop, refounding the religious community at his cathedral as a Benedictine Priory and starting the magnificent Romanesque structure still there today. In 1088, he was in dispute with King William II 'Rufus', and brought before the king's court at Old Sarum. Throughout the trial, as described by Symeon of Durham, *De Vexacione*, he referred to the canons. As Mark Philpott has shown, each time William referred

---

[35] Philpott 1993.

[36] The implications of the narratives of Eadmer and Symeon are that, because of external threat and internal chaos, much of church life had fallen into ruin by 1066. See Eadmer, *Historia Novorum*, 1.4–5, and Symeon, *Historia regum* s.a. 1074.

[37] See Kéry 1999, 240, and Brooks 1989, 231.

to the canons, we find a relevant canon in this manuscript that has been noted in the margin.[38]

Cambridge, Library of Corpus Christi College, 130 (saec. XI–XII).

Hereford, Cathedral Library O. 8. viii (saec. XI–XII).

Hereford, Cathedral Library O. 4. v + P. II. viii (saec. xii), a copy of O. 8. viii above.[39]

London, British Library, Cotton Claudius D.IX (saec. XI–XII).

Salisbury, Cathedral Library 78 (saec. XI–XII).

London, British Library, Royal 9.B.XII (saec. XII[1]), prov. Worcester.

Lincoln, Cathedral Chapter Library 161 (saec. XII[in]), made at Lincoln.[40]

London, British Library, Royal 11.D.VIII (saec. XII), prov. Gloucester Abbey.

London, British Library, Cotton Claudius E.V (saec. XII).

Chartres, Bibliothèque municipale, 409 (saec. XIV), destroyed 1944.

London, British Library, Royal 11.D.IV (saec. XV).

Paris lat. 1563 (saec. XV).

Besides these copies of the complete collection, there are four manuscripts that contain just the decretals. Significant is the fact that all of these manuscripts come from Normandy in the period of Anglo-Norman political and cultural union, save the earliest, which is from Exeter. These are probably also descendants from Lanfranc's copy. They are:

Exeter, Cathedral Library, 3512 (saec. XII[in]), from Exeter.

Paris, lat. 3856 (saec. XII), from Normandy.

Rouen, Bibliothèque municipale, 701 (E.78) (saec. XII), from Abbey of Jumièges.

Rouen, Bibliothèque municipale 703 (E.23) (saec. XII), from Abbey of Jumièges, possibly written elsewhere.

Because *Collectio Lanfranci* is yet another reworking of **I**, and a late one that adds nothing (unlike **I–c**), it has not been consulted in the course of this project. The 27 letters of **I** that Lanfranc

---

[38] See Philpott 1994.
[39] See Mynors and Thomson 1993, 57.
[40] Thomson 1989, 130.

included are very well attested in the early manuscripts of **S**, **S–ga**, and **I**, especially **I–b**, with the result that even without this collection we would have more than enough material to compose a critical text that sheds light on Leo's own words.

6.2.a.iii. Abridgements

To highlight the enduring significance of Leo the Great in the medieval world, it is also worth observing that a few abridgements of or collections of excerpts from *Collectio Lanfranci* exist, as discussed by Martin Brett.[41] These are idiosyncratic collections made for and by particular persons in their own circumstances, and they are not always discernibly useable by a modern scholar. Nonetheless, these include:

> Oxford, Bodleian Library, MS Bodley 561 (saec. XII), fols 1–60ᵛ, derived largely from the *Tripartita* and *Lanfranci*.[42]

> Durham Cathedral Library B.IV.18 (saec. XII), which includes the so-called Canterbury Abridgement.

> Lambeth Palace 351 (saec. XII), which includes the so-called Canterbury Abridgement.

> Rochester Cathedral Library, MS A.3.5. *Textus Roffiensis* (c. 1125).

To consider only the Canterbury Abridgement, my own analysis of the Durham manuscript shows it lacking in rubrication and any apparent organisational feature beyond chronology. Clearly the canons were copied directly from a codex of *Lanfranci* as it lay open before the scribe as he went. The extracts treat a wide variety of topics, such as who is fit to be clergy or what to do with people who have been living as captives amongst pagans, from a wide array of popes up to Gregory II in seventeen folios before moving into conciliar canons.

6.2.b. *Collectio Britannica*[43]

6.2.b.i. Description of Collection

This collection was compiled some time after 1090, possibly soon after 1108 in northern France with an association with Ivo of

---

[41] Brett 1992 for the discussion that follows.

[42] Ibid., 159–61.

[43] For description, see Fowler-Magerl 2005, 184–87.

Chartres,[44] and exists in a sole manuscript. It is most notable not for the decretals of Leo but, rather, for those items herein not found elsewhere, especially letters of popes Gelasius I, Alexander II, John VIII, Urban II, Stephen V, and Leo IV. However, Leo the Great does make an appearance in the section of the manuscript scholars entitle *Varia I* (fols 52^r–120^r), which is a mixture of papal decretals, patristic texts, and Roman law. It includes *Epp.* 42 (without its incipit) and 66 (without its incipit or explicit). As mentioned in my analysis above, these two letters are amongst those found in *Collectio Arelatensis* (**Ar**) for the first time; *Britannica* is known to have made use of the *Arelatensis* in other portions of the collection, and the compiler seems to have been looking for some items not in wide circulation.

6.2.b.ii. Manuscript

London, British Library, Add. 8873 (saec. XII^{in}). Caroline minuscule.

6.2.c. The Collection of William of Malmesbury

This collection was first introduced in our discussion of **Q** (3.2c). The manuscript that transmits it is a **Q** manuscript—indeed, considered *Quesnelliana*'s 'most reliable manuscript'.[45] The collection is found in Oxford, Oriel College, 42 (saec. XII; *o*), originating in Malmesbury—written by William of Malmesbury himself. The hand is a minuscule hand; each page has 36 lines of text in 2 columns. New items have rubricated minuscule *tituli*, and the first initial of each text is an uncial *littera notabilior*; these *litterae notabiliores* alternate blue and red, and the rest of the opening word is typically uncial as well, but of the same size as the minuscule text. The ruling is by hardpoint. This manuscript was the starting basis for Quesnel's edition of Leo's letters and contains a different selection of Leonine material from the rest of **Q**, a collection of forty-five letters, of which fifteen are decretals: *Epp.* 28, 68, 99, 97, 29, 31, 33, 44, 45, 69, 70, 93, 114, 104, 106, 79, 80, 135, 163, 155, 61, 59, 162, 165 (without the *testimonia* which are at 53^r–56^v), *gesta* from the Constantinopolitan Home Synod of 448 condemn-

---

[44] For the 1108 date and Ivo, see Rolker 2009.
[45] Kéry 1999, 27.

ing Eutyches,[46] 124, 139, 35, 108, 15, 7, 8, 167, 159, 18, 1, 2, 166, 19, 14, 9, JK † 551, 138, 168, 4, 16, 12, Valentinian III's *Nov.* XVII,[47] followed by a series of sermons, a brief life of Leo in a different hand, and ending with *Epp.* 133 and 3.[48] The main collection of letters, including Valentinian's *novella*, runs 91^r–140^v, with the final two letters at 213^r–216^r.

This manuscript is demonstrably not a **Q** manuscript as far as its Leo portion is concerned. First, the selection and order of the letters is different from **Q**, as noted above. Furthermore, the readings in *o* are not **Q** readings. When a **Q** variant tends to be an inversion of what the Ballerini chose, *o* usually agrees; however, as the cross-references in the table above at 3.2.c.iii show, many such variants are common among the diverse traditions of Leo's letter collections. For example, in Var. 10, *o* alone provides the singular 'cesset' as well as the variant 'coniugiorum' for 'connubiorum'. In 21, *o* provides 'mortis'; in 22, the spelling given is 'iuuenilis'; in 167.14, *o* reads 'ducere' for 'accipere'; *o* omits 'sit' in 24; in 25, *o* gives 'postea'; in 34, *o* provides the incipit; in 42, *o* gives the Ballerini order; in 44, *o* follows the minority **Q** *p* reading; *o* does not omit 'tui' in 49; *o*^{1} writes 'urgebat' in 55 instead 'arguebat', although *o*^{2} changes it to 'arguebat'. Many more examples could be provided where *o* does not accord with the rest of the **Q** tradition. Few of its variants that do agree are especially significant for the establishing of the ur-**Q**. This heterogeneous collection of Leo's letters drawn from the disparate sources at William's disposal, including a possible form of Pseudo-Isidore C, with which it shares some rarities, and a source with the two *leges novellae* of Valentinian III. Another option is that this is a much older collection that William found at Malmesbury—itself a centuries-old seat of learning since the days of Aldhelm—and used to replace **Q**'s Leo collection given what to many eyes have seemed the collection's defects.

---

[46] 'Gesta dampnationis Euticetis in sinodo constantinopolitana praesente sancto flauiano confessore eiusdem urbis episcopo'.

[47] Leo, *Ep.* 11.

[48] Both the Ballerini, PL 54. 556, and Jalland 1941, 501, are misleading on this manuscript as they fail to mention the separation of the *testimonia* from *Ep.* 165, the inclusion of *gesta* from the Home Synod of 448, and Valentinian III, *Nov.* XVII, and make the sermons seem to be simply appended to *Epp.* 133 and 3.

6.2.d. Systematic as well as Unorganised Collections of Extracted Canons Before Gratian

The Carolingian era did not see the end of the ongoing work of forming and re-forming canonical collections. However, after that age the trend emerged for a greater number of systematic collections like the earlier *Concordia* of Cresconius. The most important of these was the *Decretum Gratiani*. As above at 5.2.h, using the *Clavis canonum* software by Linda Fowler-Magerl (abbreviated as *Clavis*), I have identified the following 61 collections of canons. Some of these are unsystematised, while others are systematic. Sometimes all they contain is a sentence from one of Leo's letters. Sometimes they will contain extended passages, but none of them contains a letter collection, and their disparate parts, when pieced back together, do not give us extensive re-formed letters of Leo, unlike Cresconius. Therefore, as with the Carolingian collections of canons, these collections will not be used in the assessment of readings and editing of texts. A further reason for their limited usefulness is the fact that we have an extensive corpus of much earlier manuscripts that contain the collections from which the following are derived. Nonetheless, an awareness of their diversity and existence is important for observing and tracing the long voyage of Leo's letters from the moment of his dictation to the first printing by Giovanni Bussi.

- The *Collectio IV librorum* in Cologne, Erzbischöfliche Diözesan- und Dombibliothek 124, of no earlier than the beginning of the tenth century.[49]

- The *Libri duo de synodalibus causis et disciplinis ecclesiasticis* of Regino of Prüm, from around 906.[50]

- The *Collectio IX librorum* of the MS Vat. lat. 1349 from the tenth century.[51]

- The *Liber decretorum* of Burchard of Worms, between 1012 and 1022.[52]

---

[49] *Clavis*, 68–70.

[50] *Clavis*, 77–79. The *Clavis* Key for this collection is **RP**; however the index to the Keys lists its name incorrectly as the *Collectio canonum* of Regino of Prüm.

[51] *Clavis*, 79–82.

[52] *Clavis*, 85–90.

- Both the first and amplified versions of the *Collectio XII partium*, from the early eleventh century and two or three decades later, respectively.[53]

- The *Collectio V librorum* from shortly after 1014.[54]

- A derivative of the *Collectio V librorum* is a canonical collection in Rome, Biblioteca Vallicelliana, Tome XXI, fols 284^r–302^v; it includes one canon attributed to Leo on fol. 290^v, but the material given in the *Clavis* is insufficient to determine which Leo it is.[55]

- The *Collectio canonum* of the MS Celle, Bibliothek Oberlandesgericht C.8, which contains excerpts from the *Collectio IV librorum* and Burchard of Worms' *Liber decretorum*.[56]

- The *Collectio canonum Barberiniana*, sections from mid-eleventh-century and later eleventh-century.[57]

- The *Collectio canonum Ashburnhamensis* in Florence, BML Ashburnham 1554, and Paris lat. 3858C, both from the second half of the eleventh century.[58]

- The *Liber canonum diversorum sanctorum patrum*, also known as the *Collectio CLXXXIII titulorum* or the collection of Santa Maria Novella, from the decade after 1063, possibly compiled in Lucca;[59]

- the 'reduced version' of this collection, a *Collectio V librorum* in Vat. lat. 1348, also compiled in Tuscany (probably in Florence), contains Leo as well and dates to the later eleventh century.

- The *Collectio canonum* of the canonry of Saint-Hilaire-le-Grand, compiled during or soon after the papacy of Alexander II (1061–1073).[60]

- *Collectio Sinemuriensis*.[61] This collection dates from after 1067; as described by Fowler-Magerl, it is a pastiche of selections from different canonical sources, neither chronologically nor system-

---

[53] *Clavis*, 91–93.

[54] *Clavis*, 82–85.

[55] *Clavis*, 94–95.

[56] *Clavis*, 121–22.

[57] *Clavis*, 95–96.

[58] *Clavis*, 148–50.

[59] *Clavis*, 100–02.

[60] *Clavis*, 126–29.

[61] *Clavis*, 104–10. Cf. Kéry 1999, 203–04. This collection is also called *Remensis* but should not be confused with the one discussed above at 3.2.p.

atically arranged.[62] Due to the lateness of its gathering as well as its format as selections of dismembered canons, this canonical collection is less important than those listed above; therefore, its manuscripts were not collated. As represented by the *Semur* manuscript, it contains selections from the following of Leo's letters: *Epp.* 162, 22, 15, 104, 106, 4, 167, 14, 108, 119, 9, 16, and 168.

- The *Diversorum patrum sentenie* or *Collectio LXXIV titulorum*,[63] first attested use by Bernold of Constance in 1073/74; the rearrangement of this collection in Paris, Bibliothèque nationale, n. a. lat. 326 also contains Leo, as does the form in Paris lat. 13658,[64] and the first part of Vat. lat. 4977.[65]

- The *Collectio IV librorum*, compiled not long after the *Collectio LXXIV titulorum*.[66]

- The *Collectio canonum* of Munich, Clm 12612, related to the circle of Bernold of Constance.[67]

- The *Collectio canonum Ambrosiana II* in Milan, Biblioteca I. 145 inf., whose latest item is a letter of Alexander II.[68]

- The *Breviarium canonum* of Atto of San Marco, shortly after 1073.[69]

- The *Collectio Burdegalensis*, possibly 1079–1080.[70]

- The *Collectio canonum* in the MS Madrid, BN lat. 11548, from after 1080.[71]

- The first version of the *Collectio Tarraconensis* from after 1080, including the version in MS Tarragona 26.[72]

- The *Collectio canonum* of Anselm of Lucca, before 1086.[73]

---

[62] *Clavis*, 104–10.
[63] Alternately, *Collectio in LXXIV titulos*.
[64] On these three collections, see *Clavis*, 110–18.
[65] *Clavis*, 204.
[66] *Clavis*, 119–20.
[67] *Clavis*, 168–69.
[68] *Clavis*, 124–25.
[69] *Clavis*, 138–39.
[70] *Clavis*, 129–30.
[71] *Clavis*, 167–68.
[72] *Clavis*, 133–36.
[73] *Clavis*, 139 ff.

- The *Collectio canonum* of Deusdedit, compiled while he was cardinal priest of Santi Apostoli in Eudoxia (today San Pietro in Vincoli) before his election as pope in 1087.[74]

- The *Collectio II librorum* or *VIII partium*, which exists in two manuscripts; in two books, it dates to around 1100, and was later divided into eight parts.[75]

- The *Collectio XIII librorum* of Berlin, SBPK Savigny 3, *c.* 1089, which, besides including genuine Leo material, mistakenly labels Canon 1.122, which is from a letter of Innocent I to Felix of Nocera, as of Leo I.[76]

- The *Collectio VII librorum* in Turin, BNU D. IV. 33 from the late eleventh century.[77]

- The *Collectio canonum* of Rome, Vallicelliana B. 89, drawn from several eleventh-century collections.[78]

- *Liber de vita christiana* of Bonizo of Sutri late 1080s or early 1090s.[79]

- The *Collectio Sangermanensis IX voluminorum* of around the time of the Council of Clermont (1095).[80]

- The *Collectio canonum* in Munich, Clm 16086; the manuscript is from the late eleventh or early twelfth century.[81]

- From the twelfth century comes the *Collectio Brugensis* as found in London, BL Cleopatra C. VIII and Bruges, Bibliothèque de la Ville 99;[82] the canons of the Bruges manuscript that the London

---

[74] *Clavis*, 160–63.

[75] The book for the *Clavis canonum*, 150, lists this as 'The *Collectio canonum* in the MSS Vat. lat. 3832 and Assisi, BCom 227 (2L/8P)', whereas the index to the Key for its beginning (**VA**) and end (**VB**) names the collection as in the text here. In Kéry 1999, 227–28, they are listed as two separate collections of one manuscript each, *Collectio 2 Librorum* as the Vatican manuscript, and *Collectio 8 Partium* as the Assisi manuscript.

[76] *Clavis*, 155 ff.

[77] *Clavis*, 163–66.

[78] *Clavis*, 171–72.

[79] *Clavis*, 174–75. This collection, **BO** in the *Clavis canonum* software, is incorrectly labelled *Collectio canonum* of Bonizo of Sutri in the index to the *Clavis* Keys.

[80] *Clavis*, 207–09. Confusingly, the index to its *Clavis* Key **WO** lists the collection as *Collectio IX voluminorum Sangermanensis*.

[81] *Clavis*, 179.

[82] *Clavis*, 183–84.

manuscript lacks do not contain Leo, but those in the London manuscript lacking in Bruges do contain him.

- *Collectio Atrebatensis*, c. 1093.[83]

- The *Collectio canonum Ambrosiana I* in Milan, Archivio Capitolare di S. Ambrogio M. 11, from the last decade of the eleventh century.

- The *Collectio Farfensis* c. 1099.[84]

- The *Collectio canonum* in Paris, lat. 13368, from the 1090s.[85]

- The *Decretum* of Ivo of Chartres (bishop of Chartres, 1090–1115), from after 1093.[86]

- The *Panormia*, which is a shortened version of Ivo's *Decretum*.[87] Compiled around 1118, this was formerly attributed to Ivo, with the *Decretum* seen as a preparatory text in advance, but Christof Rolker has demonstrated the fact that the *Panormia* is not by Ivo.[88]

- The *Collectio Tripartita* draws on three main sources (hence its name), one of which is Ivo's *Decretum*.[89]

- From shortly after Ivo's *Decretum* is the *Collectio X partium* of Cologne, Historisches Archiv W.Kl. fol. 199.[90]

- From after 1097, the second version of the *Collectio Tarraconensis*.[91]

- The canonical collection in the second part of Vat. lat. 4977.[92]

- The *Collectio canonum Sancte Genoveve*, beginning of the twelfth century.[93]

- The *Polycarpus* by Gregory, cardinal priest of San Crisogono in Rome, from as early as 1104 (amongst its canons it mistakenly

---

[83] *Clavis*, 206–07.
[84] *Clavis*, 122–23.
[85] *Clavis*, 136.
[86] *Clavis*, 193–98.
[87] *Clavis*, 198–202.
[88] Rolker 2010, 248–89.
[89] Rolker 2010, 101–06; *Clavis*, 187–90.
[90] *Clavis*, 191–92.
[91] *Clavis*, 166–67.
[92] *Clavis*, 204–05.
[93] *Clavis*, 205.

lists passages from *Ep.* 16 as being by Leo Quintus); the additions to the *Polycarpus* also include Leo material.[94]

- The *Collectio canonum* of Paris, Bibliothèque de l'Arsenal 713, from after 1108.

- The *Collectio X partium* from sometime before 1110.[95]

- The *Collectio Gaddiana*, early twelfth century.[96]

- The *Collectio XIII librorum* found in Vat. lat. 1361, which used the A' version of Anselm of Lucca, Ivo of Chartres' *Panormia*, and the *Polycarpus*; it dates to the early twelfth century.[97]

- The *Collectio VII librorum* in Vienna, Österreichische National-bibliothek, Codex 2186, from during or soon after the papacy of Paschal II (1099–1118).[98]

- The *Collectio Catalaunensis I*, possibly from 1100–1113.[99]

- The *Collectio canonum* of the MS Paris, Bibliothèque de l'Arsenal 721, after 1110.[100]

- The *Collectio III librorum*, from after 1111, was one of Gratian's major sources.[101]

- Based upon the *Collectio III librorum* is the *Collectio IX librorum* of MS Vatican, Archivio di San Pietro C. 118, from after 1123.[102]

- The *Collectio canonum* of Codex 203 of the Biblioteca Civica Guarneriana in San Daniele del Friuli, from before 1119.[103]

- The *Collectio Beneventana*, after 1119.[104]

- The *Collectio canonum* of the MS Paris, lat. 4283 from after 1119.[105]

---

[94] *Clavis*, 229–32.

[95] *Clavis*, 209–10.

[96] *Clavis*, 214–15.

[97] *Clavis*, 225.

[98] *Clavis*, 232–34.

[99] *Clavis*, 238.

[100] *Clavis*, 237–38.

[101] *Clavis*, 234–35.

[102] *Clavis*, 235–36. This collection also exists in the MS Berlin, Staatsbibliothek Preussischer Kulturbesitz, lat. fol. 522.

[103] *Clavis*, 228–29.

[104] *Clavis*, 227–28.

[105] *Clavis*, 203.

- The *Collectio Caesaraugustana*, first version, *c.* 1120, which, alongside some original Leo material, includes the forgery *Quali pertinacia* (JK † 446).[106]

- The *Collectio canonum* in the MS Turin, BNU 903 (E. V. 44), fols 71ᵛ–86ᵛ, likely dating to the papacy of Paschal II (1099–1118) or shortly thereafter.[107]

- The abbreviation of Anselm of Lucca's *Collectio canonum* that is found in Pisa, Seminario Santa Catarina 59, dating after 1123;[108] this collection may include Leo canons from Anselm of Lucca, and also includes one excerpted canon amongst its additions on fol. 127ʳ from *Ep.* 14.

- The second version of the *Collectio Caesaraugustana*, compiled around 1143/44, also contains Leo material.[109]

- The *Collectio canonum Pragensis I*, also known as the *Collectio CCXCIV capitulorum*, from shortly after 1140.[110]

- A Veronese of chronologically-arranged extracts from councils and papal letters, Verona, Biblioteca Capitolare LXIII (61) (saec. X–XI). Extracts from Leo, *Ep.* 167 on fol. 27ᵛ and further extracts on fols 32ᵛ–33ʳ.[111]

6.2.e. The *Concordia discordantium canonum (Decretum)* of Gratian

Around 1140, the most significant canon law collection of the High Middle Ages was compiled by a Master of the University of Bologna, Gratian. Originally titled *Concordia discordantium canonum*, it has circulated under the title *Decretum* for most of its existence; I shall call it thus. Gratian's *Decretum* is a massive systematic collection that not only brings together the discordant canons, as in Cresconius or Ivo, but also provides Gratian's own resolutions in his *Dicta*. The *Decretum* is a work designed for the schoolroom, and as such was so popular because it was suited to the growing world of medieval cathedral schools and universities. Anders Winroth has shown us that it was originally written in a shorter form than the most popular version of the text; he and a team of scholars

---

[106] *Clavis*, 239–42.

[107] *Clavis*, 172–73.

[108] *Clavis*, 221–24.

[109] *Clavis*, 242–43.

[110] *Clavis*, 244–46.

[111] See Marchi 1996, 123 for Leo, 121–24 for complete MS.

have prepared an edition of this first recension, destined for Monumenta Iuris Canonici, and available online through the Stephan Kuttner Institute for Medieval Canon Law in the meantime.[112] In this first recension, Winroth has identified the following nine citations from Leo's epistles:[113]

Ep. 12: C. 1 q. 7 c. 18; C. 1 q. 1 c. 43.

Ep. 18: C. 1 q. 1 c. 42; C. 1 q. 1 c. 112.

Ep. 80: C. 1 q. 1 c. 68

Ep. 159: C. 34 q. 1&2 c. 1

Ep. 167: C. 1 q. 1 c. 40; C. 24 q. 2 c. 1; C. 33 q. 2 c. 14.

The second and most popular recension of Gratian was last edited by Emil Friedberg in 1879. In this recension, Leo appears 75 times as well as three citations from spuria.[114] The first recension exists in four manuscripts, the second in countless manuscripts from across western Europe. Six glossed copies of Gratian survive from Durham Cathedral Priory alone.[115] From one angle, Gratian may be the most significant dispersal of Leo's canonical thought. Yet from another, it is clear that Leo's legacy must exist independently of the systematic collections, regardless of how large the collections are or how widely dispersed. The Scholastics prove Leo was being read, but the above citations in Gratian and only twelve in Lombard, *Sentences* 4, as discussed above, are scant evidence of the ongoing life of Leo the Great in the High and Late Middle Ages.

Gratian's *Decretum* may very quickly have held the field, but this did not stop new configurations and systemisations being made. Indeed, as papal decretals expanded the body of law to be drawn upon, new systematic collections were put together, extracting material from both the older collections and the new decretals. Leo occasionally turns up in these as well; one English case is symptomatic. In the *Collectio Dunelmensis Prima*, a collection

---

[112] https://gratian.org/ Accessed 22 September 2021.

[113] See the 'Fontes Materiales' document at gratian.org.

[114] See the Prolegomena to the edition of Friedberg, xxvii.

[115] These MSS are: Cambridge, Sidney Sussex College 101; Durham Cathedral Library (DCL) C.IV.1; DCL C.III.1; DCL C.I.7; DCL C.II.1; and DCL C.I.8.

largely of late twelfth-century decretals that starts with canons drawn from the *Decretum* of Burchard of Worms (*c.* 1012),[116] one of the canons is an extract from Leo, *Ep.* 12. A complete and systematic study of the later systematic collections would undoubtedly find other such references. However, they are increasingly few due to the popularity of Gratian. The later systematic collections instead tend to be derived from collections of the new decretal law coming from the papal chancery while older law is accessed via Gratian.

6.3 Other Post-Carolingian Collections

6.3.a. Ballerini Collection 20[117]

This collection contains 27 of Leo's letters, the last 11 of which are in what the Ballerini consider an expected order, the first 16 of which are 28, 35, 31, 59, 124, 1, 163, 165, etc.[118] It contains *Ep.* 12 with appendices, presumably, then, the form of *Ep.* 12 from Pseudo-Isidore. A few non-Leonine items are amongst Leo's letters. It exists in one manuscript, which the Ballerini accessed in Rome at the Biblioteca della Basilica di Santa Croce in Gerusalemme 237 (saec. XI). At the dispersal of Santa Croce's library in 1873, this was one of the manuscripts that went to the Biblioteca nazionale di Roma and subsequently went missing in the spring of 1940.[119]

6.3.b. Ballerini Collection 21[120] (**Y–a**)

6.3.b.i. Description of the Collection

The Ballerini say that this collection resembles **I–a** but with different readings. However, some **I–a** readings are still intact, such as rubrication for *Ep.* 7 and other similarities. The differences in the text probably come from the corruptions independent of **I–a**

---

[116] In Durham Cathedral Library, C.III.1, fols 1–18. See Duggan 2008, 256–57. For a description, see Holtzmann 1979, 75–99. See also Duggan 1965, 179–85.

[117] PL 54.573, J3(iii) 1 (508).

[118] Ballerini: 'epist. 165 ad Leonem Augustum, etc.'

[119] Jemolo and Palma 1984, 29–30.

[120] PL 54.573, J3(iii) 2 (508).

or contamination from other collections in the Leonine tradition, since even **I** traditions did not go unchanged in their passage through the Carolingian scriptoria of Europe and on into the Central Middle Ages. Unmentioned by the Ballerini is the fact that not only are the readings of the letters different from **I-a**, so is the order. The letters of this collection, based on v, are in the order: 20, 23, 22, 28, 25, 35, 29, 31, 33, 59, 44, 45, 60, 61, 69, 70, 71, 79, 80, 82, 83, 85, 90, 93, 104, 106, 120, 97, 99, 139, 115, 114, 134, 135, 130, 124, 163, 162, 155, 165, 15, 7, 1, 19, 16, 4, 18, 167, 14, 159, 12, 108, 166, 9, JK † 551, and 168. This, as it turns out, is the same collection of letters as the Cluny or Yale Recension of Pseudo-Isidore (**Y**) discussed above at 5.2.f.v. The connection of this collection to the Pseudo-Isidorian tradition is highlighted by the fact that some of its manuscripts include their numeration from Pseudo-Isidore; that is, not only the texts but the paratexts have been carried over. Its earliest manuscript is twelfth-century, making this set of manuscripts considerably later than that discussed above, for the earliest manuscript of this particular collection as a whole is, of course, $1/y$, of the ninth century. I count it as a separate collection from the Cluny Recension because it has been disassociated from Pseudo-Isidore and transmitted alone. As a result, the character of the letters has changed, from sources for canon law to patristic authorities worthy in and of themselves. In fact, in some of these manuscripts, as noted below, the letters follow the sermons, changing Leo from a pope to be mined for canons to a church father. Here we see the emergence of a new trend in the transmission of Leo's works, of manuscripts solely devoted to him, perhaps associated with the twelfth-century Renaissance. Finally, although this collection's earliest manuscripts are twelfth-century, many of them are from the fifteenth, signalling an interest in Leo by humanists and reformers yet again.

6.3.b.ii. Manuscripts

Of the manuscripts listed below, given the lateness of the collection as well as of many of its manuscripts, I consulted only v, r, m, p, and o. Some of the manuscripts of this collection contain collection B of Leo's sermons while others do not.[121]

---

[121] Collection B is described in Chavasse 1973, cxxv–vi.

v: Venice, Biblioteca Nazionale Marciana, Lat. Z. 170 (= 1569), fol. 2–100 (saec. XII). Its text includes letters dated in Spanish *aerae*, recalling the connection with Spain and **S–ga** shared with **I**. It is written in a clear minuscule hand with rubrication in a single column per page. The contents run 1ᵛ–2ʳ, and Leo's letters cover 2ᵛ–100ᵛ.

Vat. lat. 542 (saec. XV).[122] Written in a humanist hand. This codex belonged to Paul II (pope, 1464–1471). Leo's letters run to folio 105ᵛ, and the manuscript closes with Leo, *Serm.* 96; Hilarus, *Ep.* 1; and two more sermons of Leo, 51 and 95. This manuscript does not contain the sermon collection.

r: Vat. lat. 543 (saec. XII).[123] Provenance of Esrom, Cistercian Monastery of St Mary. Written in a late Carolingian hand, and, according Kuttner, 'probably in a German Cistercian house if not in Esrom itself'.[124] This manuscript is written in two columns of 30 lines each. Foll. 1ᵛ–2ʳ list the contents, and Leo runs 2ʳ–82ʳ. The scribe was careful in certain respects, such as marking out numbers from the rest of text in the format ·v·. The influence of the centuries and some lack of knowledge of context are visible in providing 'Theodericus Cypri' for 'Theodoritus Cyri'. After Leo's letters, it contains Alcuin, *De fide S. Trinitatis*, books 1–3, fols 86ʳ–111ᵛ.

Munich, Bayerische Staatsbibliothek, Clm 21248 (saec. XI/XII). This is the oldest copy of **Y–a**. This manuscript begins with Leo's letters, and then moves on to Anselm of Canterbury, beginning with the *Monologion* on fol. 58. Based upon contents and readings, this is the exemplar for the letters in Vat. lat. 548. Note that this manuscript does not include the sermons.

Vat. lat. 548 (saec. XV).[125] This manuscript was written in a single column with a humanistic hand. It includes sermon collection *B*, and the letters begin 196ʳ with typical fifteenth-century foliage. After the letters comes Anselm of Canterbury, *Monologion* 1–6. Leo's letters derive from Munich, Clm 21248.

---

[122] Kuttner 1986, 2–4. This MS is digitised: https://digi.vatlib.it/view/ MSS_Vat.lat.542. Accessed 22 September 2021.

[123] Kuttner 1986, 4–5. This MS is digitised: https://digi.vatlib.it/view/ MSS_Vat.lat.543. Accessed 22 September 2021.

[124] Kuttner 1986, 4.

[125] Kuttner 1986, 9–10. This MS is digitised: https://digi.vatlib.it/view/ MSS_Vat.lat.548. Accessed 22 September 2021.

Vat. lat. 547 (saec. XV).[126] Copy of Vat. lat. 548. Belonged to Marco Barbo (card., 1467–1491).

Vat. Ross. 158 (saec. XV[in]).[127] Leo's letters run fols 131–211; this manuscript includes sermon collection *B*. It clearly has a relationship with Vat. lat. 548, since it also includes the beginning of Anselm's *Monologion*.

Vat. lat. 546 (saec. XV).[128] Former property of Teodoro de Lelli, Bishop of Treviso (1464–1466). This manuscript begins with collection *B* of Leo's sermons, fols 1[r]–142[r].[129] The letters follow, 144[r]–228[v]. It closes, 232[r–v], with excerpts from the *Liber Pontificalis* on the life of Leo.

Vat. Urb. lat. 65 (saec. XV). This manuscript begins with collection *B* of Leo's sermons, to fol. 120[r].[130] After an intervening text from Augustine's *Sermones ineditae* (120[r]–121[v]), the letter collection follows, 122[r]–191[r]. It repeats *Ep.* 22 twice and omits *Ep.* 25.

Florence, Biblioteca Medicea Laurenziana, Plut. 21.11 (saec. XV[ex]).[131] This manuscript begins with sermon collection *B*; the letters run fols 140[r]–223[v]. They include their numeration as in Pseudo-Isidore.

Florence, Biblioteca Medicea Laurenziana, Plut. 21.13 (saec. XV).[132] This manuscript has the same contents as Plut. 21.11 above.

p: Florence, Biblioteca Medicea Laurenziana, Plut. 21.14 (saec. XV, after 1470).[133] As discussed by Chavasse, fols 1–174 contain a copy of Bussi's 1470 edition of the sermons and of four letters.[134] On fol. 174, at the of the *testimonia* of *Ep.* 165 are five blank lines, followed by a version of **21** that adds *Epp.* 119 and 145 but omits *Epp.* 4 and 18 with doublets of *Epp.* 14, 12, 166, and 9.

---

[126] Kuttner 1986, 8–9. This MS is digitised: https://digi.vatlib.it/view/ MSS_Vat.lat.547. Accessed 22 September 2021.

[127] Collection *B*, MS *B 14*, ibid., cxxxi.

[128] Kuttner 1986, 6–7. This MS is digitised: https://digi.vatlib.it/view/ MSS_Vat.lat.546. Accessed 22 September 2021.

[129] Chavasse 1973, cxxxi

[130] Ibid., cxxxvi. This MS is digitised: https://digi.vatlib.it/view/MSS_Urb. lat.65. Accessed 22 September 2021.

[131] This MS is digitised and can be found by searching its shelfmark at: http://mss.bmlonline.it/ Accessed 22 September 2021.

[132] Sermon MS *B 25*, Chavasse 1973, cxxxv.

[133] This MS is digitised and can be found by searching its shelfmark at: http://mss.bmlonline.it/. Accessed 22 September 2021.

[134] Chavasse 1973, cxliv.

Florence, Biblioteca Medicea Laurenziana, Plut. 21.23 (saec. XV).[135]

Florence, Biblioteca Medicea Laurenziana, Plut. 23 dex.10 (saec. XIII).[136] This manuscript contains a selection of twenty-six letters taken from **Y–a** after sermon collection *F*.

Carpentras, Bibliothèque municipale, 31 (L 32) (saec. XIV).[137] On fols 65–66, this manuscript includes the same two of Leo's letters (*Epp.* 124 and 1) that begin the letter collection in Florence, Biblioteca Medicea Laurenzia, Plut. 23 dex.10 above.

Florence, Biblioteca Medicea Laurenziana, Strozzi 16 (saec. XV).[138] After sermon collection *B*, the letters run 137^r–219^v, starting in the middle of *Ep.* 23. Forty-one of them include their numeration as in Pseudo-Isidore.

m: Florence, Biblioteca Medicea Laurenziana, Fiesol. 48 (saec. XV^{med}).[139] I based the dating of this manuscript upon the palaeographical features as well as the style of illumination on the first page; the decoration and book hand are very similar to Fiesol. 46, which includes a date of 1461 by the scribe. The nearest to a date we find is on the last folio of the MS, 'an(n)o LXIIII'. *Litterae notabiliores* persist throughout starting *libri*, but not *capitula*, and only the first of Leo's letters. It contains a variety of items, compiled into this manuscript at the same time. From fol. 190 to the end there is a circular hole eaten through the manuscript by woodworm, three-quarters of the way down the inner column of the page. A few other holes are present in the margins and do not affect the text. Leo runs 260^r–303^v.

p: Florence, Biblioteca Nazionale Centrale, Panciatichi 135 (saec. XV).[140] Leo runs fols 142^r–188^v. The manuscript is written in a very fine, clear humanist hand mimicking Caroline minuscule. The original contents do not list Leo, although a later hand added a complete index by canon rather than by letter at the back of the manuscript. It has been described as a Pseu-

---

[135] This MS is digitised: http://opac.bmlonline.it/Record.htm?record = 555012437329. Accessed 28 January 2020.

[136] This MS is digitised: http://mss.bmlonline.it/s.aspx?Id = AWOMrrHDI-1A4r7GxMYcn&c = S.%20Leonis%20papae%20Sermones%20et%20Epistolae#/book. Accessed 22 September 2021.

[137] Sermon MS *F 5*; see Chavasse 1973, lxxix.

[138] Sermon MS *B 24*, ibid., cxxxiv.

[139] At the time of the Ballerini's work, this manuscript was at the Augustinian abbey in Fiesole and is listed therefore as 'Faesulanus can. Lateran. 7'. They date it saec. XV as well.

[140] See Mordek 1978, 474.

do-Isidorian manuscript of Class A1,[141] but this description is inaccurate as far as the Leo contents are concerned—although the other contents appear to be Pseudo-Isidorian.

Madrid, Biblioteca Nacional de España, 7126 (saec. XV).[142] This manuscript belonged to Cardinal Juan de Torquemada (d. 1468). After sermon collection B, fols 1–145, comes letter collection **Y-a**, 146–247ᵛ.

Milan, Biblioteca Ambrosiana, A.142.sup. (saec. XV).[143] This manuscript was written for Archbishop Pigolpassi (d. 1443). Leo's letters run fols 1ᵛ–85ᵛ; this manuscript also includes collection B of the sermons.

Milan, Biblioteca Ambrosiana, B.11.inf. (29 October 1456, from Convent of Santa Maria Coronata, Milan, according to 4ᵛ and 228ᵛ).[144] Leo's letters run fols 5–85ᵛ. This manuscript also includes sermon collection B.

Milan, Biblioteca Nazionale Braidense, AD.XIV.10.3 (completed 12 August 1462 at S. Pauli de Gradi Mediolanen, cf. 207ᵛ).[145] This manuscript is a copy of Milan, Biblioteca Ambrosiana, A.142. sup. Leo's letters run fols 127–205.

Rome, Biblioteca Angelica, 5.10.

Vat. lat. 541, written in the year 1452 at Rome for Nicholas V (pope, 1447–1455, successor to Eugenius IV);[146] this manuscript has 12 more letters following the 56 above, 11 of which are from Ballerini Collection 24.[147] It also includes collection B of the sermons.[148]

Turin, Biblioteca Nazionale, E.III.28 (saec. XV).[149] Leo's letters run fols 1–77ᵛ. Contains sermon collection B.

El Escorial, Real Biblioteca de San Lorenzo, Q.II.11 (saec. XV).[150] This paper manuscript omits the last ten letters of the collection, which runs fols 1–68. Sermon collection F follows the letters.

---

[141] See above, 5.2.f.iv.

[142] MS *B 18* of sermons, Chavasse 1973, cxxxii.

[143] MS *B 9* of sermons, ibid., cxxviii–cxxix.

[144] MS *B 10* of sermons, ibid., cxxix.

[145] MS *B11* of sermons, ibid.

[146] Kuttner 1986, 1–2. This MS is digitised: https://digi.vatlib.it/view/ MSS_Vat.lat.541. Accessed 22 September 2021.

[147] See PL 54.574.

[148] Chavasse 1973, cxxviii.

[149] Collection *B*, MS *B 5*, ibid., cxxvii.

[150] Sermon MS *F 6*; for a description, see ibid., lxxix.

El Escorial, Real Biblioteca de San Lorenzo, T.I.7 (saec. XV).[151] **Y–a** runs fols 1–35^v, followed by three items of Hilarus that normally accompany the collection, 35^v–36^v. Foll. 37–42 include a selection of other Leo letters: *Epp.* 102, 121, 122, 10, 41, 113, 112, 118, 123, 125, 127. After sermon collection *B* (fols 47–106ra), this collection is followed by an excerpt from Leo, *Ep.* 119 (106rb-106vb).

Wroclaw, Biblioteka Uniwersytecka, I F 141 (from 1472). This paper manuscript includes **Y–a** before sermon collection *B*, fols 1–121. The collection's order is modified. After *Ep.* 106, the final twelve letters of the collection have been interposed, and *Ep.* 120 is omitted.

The Ballerini note that to this collection can be added two other manuscripts that contain the same 56 letters.[152] Although eleven of the letters taken from the end of this collection are inserted after *Ep.* 26 in these manuscripts, nevertheless, they otherwise preserve the same order and readings as the rest of the collection. These two manuscripts are:

Vat. lat. 3137 (saec. XV^{ex}).[153] This humanist manuscript was the property of Francesco Patrizi of Siena, Bishop of Gaeta who died in 1494, an identification based upon the coat of arms on fol. 9^r.[154]

o: Vat. Ott. lat. 332. This single-column manuscript is written in a late Gothic hand with lovely illuminated *litterae notabiliores*; its use of capital letters is reminiscent of modern usage, starting sentences and for proper nouns. It tends not to abbreviate, not even for *nomina sacra*. Those abbreviations it does use point to a date of saec. XIV–XV: 'epus' for 'episcopus', 'lris' for 'litteris', 'pplus' for 'populus', and others. The folios have their original numbering in gold leaf and blue in Roman numerals; the first folio is II. The text begins partway through *Ep.* 23 and closes at *Ep.* 19; Leo runs fols II^{r}ff.

An idiosyncratic version of **Y–a** was made for Nicholas of Cusa:

Bernkastel-Kues, Bibliothek de St Nikolaus-Hospitals, 39.[155] This paper manuscript was written for Nicholas de Cusa, completed

---

[151] Collection *B*, MS *B 6*, ibid., cxxvii–cxxviii.

[152] PL 54.574.

[153] This MS is digitised: https://digi.vatlib.it/view/MSS_Vat.lat.541. Accessed 22 September 2021.

[154] See Dolezalek 2008.

[155] MS *B 12*, Chavasse 1973, cxxix–cxxx.

on 5 December 1459 during his stay at Mantua. Its collection of Leo's letters runs 148–210^v after an idiosyncratic version of sermon collection *B*. The collection begins with the Leo letters from *Dionysiana adaucta* (**D-a**) with *Ep.* 22 added in this order: *Epp.* 9, 15, 1, 2, 108, 17, 20, 23, 22, 28, 139, 119, 80, 145, 165. Between *Ep.* 165 and the patristic *testimonia* come Innocent I to Decentius of Gubbio (JK 311), the letter of Boniface to Honorius, the emperor's response, and Celestine to Venerius and Marinus. After these pre-Leo papal interpolations, the remaining forty-five letters of **Y-a** follow, keeping their own order. The pre-Leo inclusions and their position in the manuscript present the likelihood of a connection with **23**, which exists in a sole manuscript pre-dating the Kues MS. However, **23** gives a larger letter collection after the intrusions, and its manuscript includes no sermons.

Holkham Hall, MS 142 (saec. XV3/4, *c.* 1464), written in Florence.[156] This manuscript, as with the Kues manuscript and **23**, begins with the rearranged series of **D-a** letters and the pre-Leonine papal letters. However, between Leo, *Ep.* 165, and Innocent to Decentius, Holkham 142 includes Nicene anathemas. Unlike the Kues manuscript and **23**, it only includes forty-two items from **Y-a**: *Epp.* 7, 25, 35, 29, 31, 33, 50, 44, 45, 60, 61, 69, 70, 71, 79, 97, 82, 83, 85, 90, 104, 106, 42, 99, 103, 135, 130, 124, 163, 162, 155, 19, 16, 4, 18, 167, 14, 159, 12, 166, 2, 168. The first selection of letters runs fols 1^r–49^r, the second 53^v–137^v. *Ep.* 25 ends in the middle of a quire at 'nos frater' in chapter 1, leaving twenty blank lines on fol. 55^r.[157] This manuscript includes sermon collection *B*.

Finally, two of the manuscripts of sermon collection *B* include five letters from **Y-a**, of which three are shortened:

Oxford, Bodleian Library, MS New College 130 (saec. XII^{ex}).[158] Leo's letters are on fols 240–43: *Epp.* 35 (shortened), 31, 33, 59 (shortened), and 165 (shortened).

Oxford, Bodleian Library, MS Bodl. 252 (S.C. 2504) (saec. XIII 1/2 or XII/XIII).[159] Leo's letters are on 225^v–228^v. Leo's letters are *Ep.* 35 (shortened), 31, 33, 59 (shortened), and 165 (shortened).

---

[156] Reynolds 2015, 111–13.

[157] Reynolds 2015, 112.

[158] MS *B 1*, ibid., cxxvi.

[159] MS *B 2*, ibid.

6.3.c. Ballerini Collection 22[160] (22)

6.3.c.i. Description of Collection

This collection contains letters from Ballerini Collection 21 (**Y–a**) and 17 from Rusticus' *Acta* (**Ru**):[161] first come the first 26 letters of **Y–a** (up to *Ep.* 106), in the same order, followed by those of Rusticus in their order, save those that would have been repeated, and then the rest of the letters from **Y–a** with three of them (97, 99, 168) missing, the order unchanged, and the readings basically the same. Included with the letters from **Ru**, and unmentioned by the Ballerini, is a series of imperial letters pertinent to Chalcedon. Taking all of this into account, from *Ep.* 106 onwards the order of the letters is as follows: *Epp.* 106, a letter from Flavian of Constantinople to Theodosius II 'Nihil ita conuenit', 22, 72, 26, 32, 30, 43, 46, 58, 55, 62, 63, 64, 50, 51, 73, 76, 77, Valentinian III and Marcian 'Omnia ad ueram', Valentinian III and Marcian 'Omnibus rebus oportet', 'Studii nostri est congruenter', Pulcheria 'Intencio nostre tranquillitatis', Valentinian III and Marcian 'Festinantes ad sanctum', Valentinian III and Marcian 'Dudum quidem per alias', 120, 139, 124, 1, 114, 155, 162, 163, 135, 115, 130, 134, 165, 15, 7, 16, 19, excerpts from *Ep.* 16, 4, 18, 167, 14, 159, 12, 108, 166, 9, and JK † 551. This concludes the letter collection which is followed by sermon collection *B*.[162] The collection as a whole is very likely of an age with the manuscript that includes it, compiled at a time with interest in Leo as an author all together, rather than the earlier canonical interests.

6.3.c.ii. Manuscript

This collection exists in Venice, Biblioteca Nazionale Marciana, Lat. Z. 79 (= 1665), fols 1^r–102^v (saec. XV).[163] There is a page attached to the front of this manuscript declaring:

CODEX LXXIX

in 4. membranaceus foliorum 270.

saeculi XV

---

[160] PL 54.574, J3(iii) 3 (509).

[161] See above, 6.3.b and 4.1.c respectively.

[162] Sermon MS *B 28*, Chavasse 1973, cxxxiii–iv.

[163] Valentinelli 1868, vol. 2, 274. This manuscript also contains Chavasse's sermon collection *B* as described in Chavasse 1973, cxxxiii.

S. LEONIS Papae Epistolae omnes & aliorum ad Leonem. Nota Epistolam missam Doro Episcopo in Codice ad Cap. IV. tantum extendi.

This page then lists the sermons, but not the letters. The first folio begins with the words, 'In nomine domini incipiunt epistole Leonis pape urbis Rome quas pro defensione fidei catholice in diuersas mundi partes direxit'. The manuscript is written in a humanist hand in a single column, 29 lines to a page. There is decoration on the first folio in the bottom margin as well as lovely *litterae notabiliores*; the images are primarily floral motifs, although the marginal illustration on fol. 1^v includes a cardinal's hat, that of Bessarion, corroborated by the Ballerini saying that this manuscript's provenance is 'Bessarione'. Every letter also begins with an intricate *littera notabilior* wherein the letter itself is gold leaf in a rectangle with floral designs that are primarily blue but with green and red as well. The rubrication ceases at fol. 34^v, although the *litterae notabiliores* remain throughout.

6.3.d. Ballerini Collection 23[164] (23)

6.3.d.i. Description of Collection

This collection begins with the fifteen letters of the *Dionysiana adaucta* (**D–a**), up to *Ep.* 165. Then four papal documents of pre-Leonine date are inserted: Innocent I to Decentius, Boniface I to Emperor Honorius, the response of Honorius to Boniface, and Celestine to Venerius. After these four letters come the *Testimonia patrum* from *Ep.* 165, then the 56 letters of **Y–a**, omitting those already in appearance and a few changes in order. The collection then adds Leo, *Epp.* 107, 50, 49, 51. Based on this information, this collection includes the following letters: 9, 15, 1, 2, 108, 17, 20, 23, 22, 28, 139, 119, 80, 145, 165, 4 non-Leonine texts, *Testimonia patrum*, the 56 letters of Collection 21, 107, 50, 49, 51. Gerardus Vossius published two letters from this manuscript, nos 17 and 107, as the Ballerini brothers learned from the 1604 edition of Gregorius Thaum.[165]

---

[164] PL 54.574, J3(iii) 4 (509).
[165] PL 54.575.

6.3.d.ii. Manuscript

23 exists in one manuscript:

> Vat. Ott. lat. 2324 (*olim* 297, as in the Ballerini).[166] It is a paper man-
> uscript, placing it no earlier than the thirteenth century although
> the Ballerini date it to the twelfth, and it uses the abbreviation
> 'fc3' for 'scilicet' that Cappelli says is fourteenth-century.[167] This
> manuscript was produced with care, evident in the writing of a
> catchword from the start of the next folio at the bottom of each
> folio's *verso*; each letter begins with a rubricated *capitulum* such
> as, 'leo papa dioscoro alexandrie ecclie epo de sacerdotum uel
> leuitarum ordi(n)atio(n)e et celebrande imisarum' (fol. 1ʳ). Leo's
> letters fill this 129-folio manuscript.

6.3.e. Ballerini Collection 24[168] ('La Collection léonine des 71 lettres'[169] **24**)

6.3.e.i. Description of Collection

This collection contains 71 of Leo's letters, consisting of 54 from
Y-a—missing *Epp.* 25 and 97—with 17 rare letters shared with
I-c interspersed throughout:[170] *Epp.* 2, 10, 24, 41, 94, 95, 102, 105,
111, 112, 113, 118, 121, 122, 123, 125, 127. Most of these are also
shared with **B/G** and follow the **B** order, except for *Epp.* 10 and
41; furthermore, *Epp.* 18 and 20 come in the opposite order in **B**.[171]
The collection is grouped into three selections. The first, items
1–53, consists of letters from **Y/Y-a** in order with some additions.
The second, 54–71, consists of **Y/Y-a** letters with additions, all
rearranged by geographical designation. The third is an anti-Pelagian dossier, not Leonine.[172] This letter collection often accom-
panies sermon collection *A*. Based upon the geographic spread of
its earliest manuscripts, **Y-a** was born in northern France in the
twelfth-century, and, like **21** above, it is transmitted in manuscripts solely devoted to Leo, possibly as a result in the shifting

---

[166] The current Vat. Ott. lat. 297 is a Bible.
[167] Cappelli 2011, 343.
[168] PL 54.575, J3(iii) 5 (509).
[169] Chavasse 1975, 35.
[170] Ballerini Collection 12.
[171] See the extraordinarily helpful table in Chavasse 1975, 34.
[172] Cf. ibid., 35–37.

intellectual culture we associate with the so-called twelfth-century Renaissance. Certainly this collection is associated with one of the most famous intersections of twelfth-century Renaissance and reform—the Cistercians. The earliest manuscripts of this collection all come from Cistercian monasteries, including Cîteaux and Clairvaux.

6.3.e.ii. Manuscripts

24 exists in the following manuscripts:

t: Troyes, Médiathèque de l'Agglomération Troyenne, MS 225 (saec. XII), from Clairvaux, MS I 20. This manuscript also includes sermon collection *A*.[173] The inscription on the last page reads, 'Liber iste sce marie clareuallis qui abstulerit anathema sit'. It is written in a neat Gothic hand in two columns of 31 lines each. *t* was unknown to the Ballerini, but it is definitely a manuscript of **24**; its contents of sermons and letters are the same, and its table of contents is identical to that of *n*, including the incipits of the letters. Furthermore, after Leo's letters it includes the same anti-Pelagian dossier as *n*, then ends, 'Expliciunt eple beati leonis pp que in hoc uolumine continentur'. Another similarity it shares with *n* includes the use of Spanish aerae in letters such as *Ep.* 33 on fol. 122^r. The table of contents runs 114^v–115^r, and then the letters themselves run 115^r–183^v, ending with *Ep.* 15 before the anti-Pelagian dossier takes over. One significant difference between *t* and *n* is the inclusion in *t* of 'Ad iulianum epm aquileiensem' at the end of the table of contents which was then struck out, whereas *n* includes 'Ad ianuarium epm aquiliensem' in the margin of the contents.

n: Vat. lat. 544 (saec. XII).[174] On the final folio of this codex is an ex libris note, 'Liber Sancte Marie de Fonte Neto', signalling its origin at the Cistercian abbey of Fontenay. The *capitula* are rubricated in a half-uncial hand, while the body of the texts is in minuscule; *n* is written in two columns of 40 lines each. It begins with Leo's sermons in collection *A*;[175] the letters run fols 115^r–191^v; they begin with a table of contents to which modern numerals were added at a later date (fols 115^r–116^r). The contents include in the margin 'Ad ianuarium epm aquiliensem',

---

[173] Sermon MS *A 1*, Chavasse 1973, cxiv.

[174] Kuttner 1986, 5–6. This MS is digitised: https://digi.vatlib.it/view/MSS_Vat.lat.544. Accessed 22 September 2021.

[175] Sermon MS *A 5*.

which has been crossed out in *t*. On fol. 125^v, *Ep.* 33 is dated 'era qua supra'—however, this is the first of the letters to include aerae. The letters of **Y-a** must derive, if not from **Y-a** itself (as the Ballerini claim they do not), from another source related to **S** and other Spanish sources. An idiosyncrasy of this manuscript is the spelling 'Martinianum' for 'Martianum' in the rubrics and contents, while the text provides the latter form.

Paris, Bibliothèque Mazarine, 586 (351) (saec. XII).[176] Leo's letters run fols 115^v–196^v. This manuscript also contains sermon collection *A*. There is a lacuna of six folios between 149^v and 150, cutting the end of *Ep.* 123 and *Epp.* 125, 124, and the beginning of 120. There is a second lacuna at the end, cutting *Ep.* 15 short.

Dijon, Bibliothèque municipale, MS 167 (134) (saec. XII).[177] From Cîteaux. Leo's letters run fols 112^v–187^v after sermon collection *A*.

El Escorial, Real Biblioteca de San Lorenzo, &.I.6 (saec. XII^{ex}).[178] This manuscript of Cistercian origins includes Leo's letters on fols 106^v–177.

Charleville, Bibliothèque municipale, 223 (saec. XII), from the Cistercian abbey of Signy (E. XXXIII).[179] After sermon collection *A* comes the table of contents of letters on fol. 87^{r-v}, followed by the letter collection on 97^v–145. After the letters come the anti-Pelagian dossier, a letter of Gregory the Great signalling the 'Fides Leonis pape' with a Leonine *spurium* (*Sermo I* of the *Sermones attributi ad Leonem Papam*, PL 54.477–87) and canons against Eutyches, and then the short recension of the canons of the Council of Reims, 1148.

Worcester, Chapter Library of Worcester Cathedral, Q. 7 (saec. XII).[180] Leo's letters run to fol. 123, followed by anti-Pelagian documents from Aurelius of Carthage.

v: Vat. Reg. lat. 139 (saec. XIII), from France.[181] After sermon collection *A*,[182] Leo's letters run fols 80va–158vb. *Epp.* 59 and 44 are missing here but added at the end. After Leo's letters come the

---

[176] Sermon MS *A 3*; for a description see Chavasse 1973, cxv.

[177] Sermon MS *A 4*; for a description see ibid.

[178] Sermon MS *A 6*; for a description see ibid., cxvi.

[179] Sermon MS *A 7*; for a description see ibid.

[180] See Kestell and Hamilton 1906, 110–11.

[181] This MS is digitised: https://digi.vatlib.it/view/MSS_Reg.lat.139. Accessed 22 September 2021.

[182] Sermon MS *A 8*, Chavasse 1973, cxvi–cxvii.

same documents as in the Charleville and Reims manuscripts (see below), followed by complementary sermons, and then, on fols 207va–210vb, *Epp.* 59 and 44. The manuscript ends partway through Ep. 44: 'decreta testantur quae a totius mundi sunt sacerdotibus consti'.

Reims, Bibliothèque municipale, 412 (E 292) (saec. XII^{ex}), from Reims, as seen on fol. 3^{a}, 'Liber sancti Remigii francorum apostoli'. After sermon collection *A*,[183] Leo's letters run 85^{v}–138^{v}. Like *v* and the Charleville manuscript, this manuscript has the selection of documents pertaining to Leo and Eutyches but not the canons of Reims 1148.

Paris, lat. 14488 (saec. XII), from the abbey of Saint-Victor, Paris, as seen on fols 1 and 176: 'Iste liber est sancti Victoris parisiensis'.[184] This manuscript served as the basis of Quesnel's edition, as identified by Chavasse.[185] Given both the abbey's and Quesnel's connection with the Jansenist movement, this is no great surprise. After sermon collection *A*, Leo's letters run 103^{v}–174. *Ep.* 45 has been written twice and crossed out the second time.

Paris, lat. 16866 (Saint-Martin 88) (saec. XII), from the Cistercian abbey of Chaalis.[186] After sermon collection *A*, Leo's letters run fols 104vb–175^{v}, starting with the table of contents.

Saint-Omer, Bibliothèque municipale, 209 (saec. XII), from the Cistercian abbey of Clairmarais.[187] After sermon collection *A*, Leo's letters run 89^{r}–153, starting with the table of contents.

Bruges, Bibliothèque de la Ville, MS 279 (saec. XIII), from the Cistercian abbey of Ter Doest, either a descendant or close relative of the Saint-Omer manuscript above.[188] Leo's letters run 102^{v}–175^{v}, starting with the table of contents.

Avranches, Bibliothèque municipale, 96 (saec. XII), from Mont St-Michel.[189] This manuscript is written in a single column

---

[183] Sermon MS *A 9*; for a description, see ibid., cxvii.

[184] Sermon MS *A 10*; for a description, see ibid., cxvii–cxviii. This MS is digitised: https://gallica.bnf.fr/ark:/12148/btv1b9068379v. Accessed 22 September 2021.

[185] Chavasse 1973, cxvii.

[186] Sermon MS *A 15*; for a description, see ibid., cxix. This MS is digitised: https://gallica.bnf.fr/ark:/12148/btv1b9067656k. Accessed 22 September 2021.

[187] Sermon MS *A 17*; for a description, see ibid., cxx.

[188] Sermon MS *A 18*; for a description, see ibid.

[189] This MS is digitised: http://bvmm.irht.cnrs.fr/resultRecherche/resultRecherche.php?COMPOSITION_ID = 11405 Accessed 22 September 2021.

with rubrication and red and green *litterae notabiliores* to mark new sections. After sermon collection *A*,[190] Leo's letters run fols 91ᵛ–151ᵛ. The *explicit* of the letter collection is in the outer margin of 151ᵛ. The rubric for the table of contents on 91ᵛ says that there are seventy-two letters in the manuscript, possibly a reflection of a time when Leo's letter to Januarius of Aquileia was included, given that it was struck out of the contents of *l* and added to those of *n*.

Chalon-sur-Saône, Bibliothèque municipale 12 (9) (saec. XII), from the abbey of La-Ferté-sur-Grosne.[191] Leo's letters run 72ʳᵇ-120ᵛ. The manuscript is damaged and cuts off partway through *Ep.* 15.16 at 'sacrilegiis aut(em) suis inueniant(ur)'.

Vitry-le-François, Bibliothèque municipale, 9 (16) (saec. XII), from the Cistercian abbey of Trois-Fontaines. This manuscript was destroyed during the Second World War, but Chavasse took notes from it based on the *Catalogue général des manuscrits*.[192] Leo's letters were on fols 122–204.

Paris, Assemblée nationale, 17 (saec. XIV).[193] Leo's letters are on fols 90–145ᵛ. There is a lacuna shortly after the beginning of *Ep.* 15. 146–47 give the table of contents.

Cesena, Biblioteca Malatestiana, Plut. d. XII, cod. 2 (saec. XV), written for the library of Domenico Malatesta, or Malatesta Novello, which was founded in 1452.[194]

Paris lat. 2158 (saec. XII), presumably from a nunnery since it includes the *Rule* of Augustine for women (165ᵛ–166ᵛ). This manuscript includes extracts from **24** after sermon collection *A* on fols 135–63. The letters included are *Epp.* 25, 28, 35, 165, 14, 108, 167, 15, and 1.[195] *Ep.* 25 is an addition from outside **24**.

Paris, Bibliothèque Mazarine, 587 (969) (saec. XIII). This manuscript is almost identical to Paris lat. 2158 above, includ-

---

[190] Sermon MS *A 19*.

[191] This manuscript is digitised: https://bvmm.irht.cnrs.fr/mirador/index.php?manifest = https://bvmm.irht.cnrs.fr/iiif/19625/manifest. Accessed 22 September 2021. Sermon MS *A 22*.

[192] Sermon MS *A 28*; for a description see Chavasse 1973, cxxiii.

[193] See ibid., cxxiii–cxxiv.

[194] Sermon MS *A 23*; for a description see ibid., cxxi–cxxii.

[195] See the Catalogue générale of the Bibliothèque nationale de France, https://archivesetmanuscrits.bnf.fr/ark:/12148/cc600478. Accessed 22 September 2021, and Chavasse 1973, cxxi. Sermon MS *A 20*.

ing the same dossier of Leo's letters extracted from **24** on fols 115ᵛ–139ᵛ.[196]

Paris, lat. 2160 (saec. XIIIⁱⁿ), from the Cistercian abbey of Foucarmont. This manuscript is primarily of sermon collection *A*,[197] with only a fragmentary triad of Leo's letters. Nonetheless, given the frequency of collection *A* being transmitted with **24**, at this juncture it is assumed that the three fragmentary letters derive from **24**. They are on fols 138ᵛ–143ᵛ, *Epp.* 59 (starting at PL 54.867B 8), 28 (PL 54.757B 6–777A 8), and 165 (PL 54.1161A 4–1169C 8).

Munich, Bayerische Staatsbibliothek, Clm 23458 (saec. XV), from Italy. This manuscript was written by Filippo de Arengaria (*d.* 1469) for the abbey of Monte Oliveto near Siena. It includes only a few of Leo's letters, possibly from **24**: *Epp.* 28, 31, and part of 167 on fols 65ᵛ–68.

f: Florence, Biblioteca Medicea Laurenziana, Fiesole 46,[198] which has 26 letters of this collection.[199] *f* was written in 1461, as noted on fol. 147ᵛ. It is written in a fine humanist script that mimics Caroline minuscule, and the pages are large with a wide margin, written in a single column of 31 lines. At the bottom of fol. 3ʳ there is a blue *fleur-de-lys* on a red field inside a green wreath flanked by Renaissance-style angels. The initials 'P. C. F.' ('Patres Canonici Faesulani') are below the wreath, and flowers mark off the bottom of the page, extending to either side of this seal; the same type of design adorns the top left corner which includes the L of the incipit illuminated with gold and a variety of interlocking floral designs that are also gilt and in blue, red, green, or uncoloured and outlined in blue. Furthermore, the parchment is very pale, smooth, and thin. The Lateran Canons of Fiesole evidently took care over this manuscript. The second hand of this manuscript seems either to be the same as that of Fiesole 48 or of approximate date, and the style of decoration is also similar; given that both are mid-fifteenth-century manuscripts from the Lateran Canons of Fiesole, it seems entirely likely that the same scribes could have been involved in their production.

---

[196] Sermon MS *A 21*; for a description, see ibid.

[197] Sermon MS *A 13*; for a description, see ibid., cxviii–cxix.

[198] Formerly of the Lateran Canons in Fiesole, Plut. 3, MS 10 (PL 54.575). Sermon MS *B 30*, Chavasse 1973, cxxxvi.

[199] Although the Ballerini say 25 (PL 54. 575).

Foll. 1ʳ–2ᵛ give the contents of the manuscript but only list 23 of Leo's letters, not all 26; it misses out *Epp.* 94 which is sandwiched between two letters to Pulcheria, 28, and 108, while further naming *Ep.* 127 as to 'nestoriano episcopo' when it should be 'iuliano', although the text of the letter herein does not include Julian's name. The letters themselves run fols 147ᵛ–180ᵛ, including: *Epp.* 12, 15, 24, 31, 94, 95, 93, 102, 104, 105, 113, 111, 112, 118, 121, 122, 123, 125, 120, 127, 130, 28, 108, 168, 2, 1. *Ep.* 108 cuts short at 'metuitur m(isericord)ia dei saluari cupientibus negetur'. 147ᵛ includes the explicit of the sermons as follows:

Expliciuunt [*sic*] sermones beati leonis pape deo gratias amen. Absoluit / N. die nona febr MCCCCLXI tu(n)c etatis annorum lxx duorum. [1 line blank] Iste fuit leo primus qui uirgo maria manum restituit: cuius festum celebratur in uigilia apostolorum.

The Ballerini also accessed a manuscript 'Caesanus Patrum Minorum Conventualium S. Francisci' and Quesnel used a manuscript from St-Martin in Auxerre (a church destroyed in the French Revolution), but I have no information as to their modern homes or shelfmarks.

6.3.e.iii. Manuscript Relations

Briefly, examining the **S** letters of *n* and *f* through the same select passages as we did in **S–ga** above at 5.2.e, we find first that, just as the order of the letters has been changed, so has the rubrication. We have, '**Item pla b(eat)i leonis pp ad o(mne)s episcopos per italiam**' in *n* at the start of *Ep.* 7, for example. *n* gives 'absoluerent' where **S/S–ga** gives 'absoluerentur', as well as the inclusion of 'hic' before 'ne'. Like many collections before it, *n* omits 'fratres charissimi' between 'uestra' and 'sollicitius'. These few variants—the different rubrication, the deviation from **S/S–ga** unity in the text—are enough to confirm that the text of *Ep.* 7 did not reach us in this twelfth-century Vatican text through Pseudo-Isidore (**I**). It may have begun there, due to the selection of letters and the Spanish features maintained throughout. But Leo's letters took a different course to reach us here, different from the one that brought them to the manuscript in Yale and its descendants. Therefore, this twelfth-century re-fashioning of the tradition of **I** would be worthy of inclusion in a full critical edition simply to see where it converges with which of the traditions, showing us how Leo's letters started to settle into different patterns during the twelfth-century Renaissance, patterns which would be the most popular means of ongoing transmission by the dawn of print when **24** *f.* was penned.

6.3.f. *Collectio Florentina* (Ballerini Collection 13; *m*)[200]

This collection was classed as Hinschius, Pseudo-Isidore A1, but that identification is false, as far as Leo is concerned. It is, instead, another high medieval descendant of Pseudo-Isidore, like those we have just observed. It includes twenty-four of Leo's letters, the last of which is damaged; there may formerly have been more. The pre-Leonine letters of this canonical collection are not even Pseudo-Isidorian, but the Ballerini say that Leo's letters clearly are, with the first eight, however, following the text of Cresconius.[201] These letters, of which twelve are decretals, are: 4, 7, 16, 18, 167, 14, 159, 12, 124, 59, 33, 44, 45, 29, 35, 31, 1, 2, 163, 135, 93, 19, the edict of Marcian to Palladius the Praetorian Prefect confirming the Council of Chalcedon: 'Tandem aliquando quod', 28, and 165. Leo's letters run fols 148^v–175^v. After *Ep.* 165 **m** closes with the *acta* of a synod.

Barberini Collection 13 (**m**) is the only source for the allegedly complete form of *Ep.* 12 as published by the Ballerini.[202] However, although **m** is, indeed, the only source for an integrated version of the two major recensions of *Ep.* 12, it is simply one recension of the text to which a good editor has added the chapters from the other (in this case the version called *decurtata* by the Ballerini because it is mutilated at the end). In a number of **I** manuscripts, the existence of the two very similar versions was identified, and the 'missing' chapters were appended to the end of the letter. Here, those chapters are transposed to a somewhat logical place in the text. Nevertheless, there never was a 'complete' text of *Ep.* 12. Rather, *Ep.* 12 is two letters, one of which repeats much of the other, as recently demonstrated.[203] The base text, then, is the form in **D–h**, and the added chapters are *decurtata*, added as chapters 6–8. A major piece of evidence for this not being an original 'complete' version is that the material that the **D–h** and *decurtata*

---

[200] PL 54.565, J1(xiii) (504).

[201] PL 54.563; repeated by Jalland 1941, 504.

[202] Edition in PL 54.645–56.

[203] Hoskin 2018.

recensions do not share in common is the material with proper names. A second piece of evidence is that Leo repeats himself on other occasions. It is not a great leap to assume two similar letters instead of two recensions of one letter.

If *m* is related to **I**, it is a highly contracted descendant of **I-a** rather **I-b**, since **I-a** includes the form of *Ep.* 12 with the 'missing' chapters appended to the end. As well, *m* does not include the same rubrics as the collections of **I**. Furthermore, in *Ep.* 28, the text of *m* is not sufficiently similar to **I-b** *c* to postulate a relationship; while they are more similar here than in the version of this letter added to manuscripts of **I-a**, such as **I-a** *o*, there are several differences, the most significant being that *m* writes, 'Beati quoque Iohannis apli testimonium resistat dicentis', while **I-b** *c*, along with Schwartz's text, writes, 'apostoli et euangelistae Iohannis expauit dicentis'. Another difference is the writing of 'desidentibus' in *m* against 'subsidentibus' in **I-b** *c*, in the phrase 'non desidentibus ambulare'. In *Ep.* 33, *m* gives the address as, 'Leo urbis romae eps dilectissimis fribs in ephesina synodo congregatis in dno salutem', against **I-b** *c*, 'Leo eps sanctae synodo quae apud Ephesum conuenit'. In the next sentence, it writes 'prouenire' against *c*, 'pertinere'; elsewhere in this letter, *m* omits: 'xpc' in Peter's response to Christ's question in Matthew 16:18, but *c* does not; *m* includes 'sunt' before 'placitura', but *c* omits the verb. Various other differences exist in *Ep.* 33, but they are small and subtle, and could merely speak of errors unique to any manuscript. The address in *Ep.* 44 once again differs between these manuscripts; in *m* we have 'Leo urbis romae eps et oms spi p(ro) sca religione in eade(m) urbe c(on)gregati theodosio augusto', as opposed to *c*, 'Leo eps et sancta synodus quae in urbe Roma conuenit, Theodosio augusto'. Later in that letter, *m* writes, 'datam defendite fidei' against *c*, 'date defendendae fidei'.

The collection of so-called 'decretals' at the beginning of *m* is a different story. Although in *Ep.* 7, *m* includes the **S**/**S-ga** variants 'quos ne absoluerentur', and omitting 'fratres charissimi', both are **D-h** variants. In fact, we should turn our attention for the source of the decretals in *m*, at least, from **I** to the **D** tradition, since the first eight letters of *m* are the letters of **D-h**. Without going needlessly into much more detail, the readings of *m* for the decretal portion of the manuscript are those of the **D** tradition. Interestingly, this tradition first gives us the damaged version of

Ep. 12, the entirety of which is found only here. It seems entirely likely that Pope Hadrian had access to a damaged copy of this decretal selection when he sent Charlemagne his augmented **D**, thus explaining the textual similarities and the presence of the undamaged *Ep.* 12 here but not there. In short, **m**'s opening Leo decretal collection comes from the **D/D-h** tradition.

6.3.g. Collection of 73 Letters (73)

6.3.g.i. Description and Context

This collection of letters was compiled in the High Middle Ages, with a possible connection to Le Grand Chartreuse, since Chavasse notes that the collection as it exists in the Brussels manuscript is in the 'forme du manuscrit de Grenoble, cf. variété *A*'.[204] Unfortunately, the Grenoble manuscript of sermon collection *A*, as described by R. Étaix, does not include a letter collection.[205] Regardless of that fact, this letter collection consists of Leo, *Epp.* 20, 24, 23, 22, 28, 25, 35, 29, 30, 9, 33, 59, 44, 45, 60, 61, 69, 70, 84, 71, 94, 82, 90, 83, 80, 155, 85, 93, 106, 104, 105, 115, 130, 134, 113, 111, 112, 79, 118, 123, 125, 124, 127, 163, 135, 114, 129, 97, 99, 102, 121, a letter to Eudoxia not in the Ballerini, 162, 165, 14, 2, a letter *ad metropolitam Venetie*, 168, 4, 159, 18, 19, 16, 7, 166, 12, JK † 551, 10, 41, 108, 167, 15.[206]

6.3.g.ii. Manuscripts

> Brussels, Bibliothèque Royale, cod. 1181 (593–94) (saec. XV).[207] From the Monastery of the Regular Canons of St-Martin of Louvain. This manuscript contains extracts from sermon collections *A* and *B*.[208] The collection of Leo's letters runs fols 113–86, and Leo, *Ep.* 93 is repeated on fol. 190^{r-v} after the anti-Pelagian dossier associated with **24**.

---

[204] Chavasse 1973, cxli.

[205] Grenoble, Bilbiothèque municipale, cod. 32 (101) and cod. 33 (102) (saec. XII). See Étaix 1962.

[206] Description of collection based upon Van den Gheyn 1902, 195.

[207] Ibid., 194–95.

[208] Chavasse 1973, cxli.

6.3.h. Ashburnham 1554[209]

6.3.h.i. Dating and Context

This manuscript is a twelfth-century Italian collection of patristic and canonical material. It is not, strictly speaking, a canonical collection, given its diverse nature, although it incorporates an epitome of the *Collectio in LXXIV titulos* on fols 9–69. Two items by Leo are included in the first eight folios. These first eight folios are designated in the catalogue as 'Prologus et excerpta', starting with the Prologue of Ivo of Chartres, then a passage from Isidore's *Etymologiae* about the Eucharist, an excerpt from Ambrose's *De mysteriis*, an excerpt from Leo, *Serm.* 91, then Leo, *Ep.* 80, followed by Augustine's *Contra epistulam Parmeniani*, Ivo, *Ep.* 187, and a passage from Gregory VII on liturgy. Leo, *Ep.* 80, is on fol. 6^v.

At the end of the manuscript, various hands have made additions in the twelfth or thirteenth century. The additions begin with Ambrose, *Ep.* 60; the rest are letters of Leo in the same order as **73**, but omitting *Ep.* 9, on fols 136–138^v: *Epp.* 28, 25, 35, 29, 30, 33, 59, 44, 45, and 60.[210] It would have been especially gratifying if the Leo additions were from **24**, to demonstrate an undeniable relationship between this manuscript and the other Clairvaux manuscript, Troyes 225.

6.3.h.ii. Manuscript

This collection exists in one manuscript:

> Florence, Biblioteca Medicea Laurenziana, Ashburnham 1554 (formerly Clairvaux I 25) (saec. XII, probably before 1124).

6.3.i. The Collection of Vat. Reg. lat. 293

6.3.i.i. Dating and Context

This collection of four of Leo's letters exists in a manuscript along with Isidore of Seville's *Quaestiones in Vetus Testamentum*, Prosper's *De Vocatione omnium gentium*, and is followed by Innocent I

---

[209] Bouhot and Genest 1997, 551–57.
[210] Ibid., 556.

to Decentius of Gubbio (JK 311). The Leo letters are: *Epp.* 139, 35, 31, and 165.

6.3.i.ii. Manuscript

Vat. Reg. lat. 293 (saec. XI–XII). Leo's letters are on fols 163ʳ–171ᵛ.

6.3.j. An Eleventh-century Pair of Leo's Letters

6.3.j.i. Context

This pair of letters, Leo, *Epp.* 28 and 27, is found in a manuscript otherwise devoted to St Augustine. Leo's so-called 'dogmatic' letters were circulating in the High Middle Ages and people found them useful and interesting enough to include in their theological compendia of short works by other authors.

6.3.j.ii. Manuscript

Vat. lat. 492 (saec. XIᵐᵉᵈ).[211] Leo's letters are on fols 55ʳ–60ᵛ.

6.3.k. The Milanese Collection with Sermon Collection D[212]

6.3.k.i. Description of Collection

This collection of letters is yet another high medieval re-casting of Pseudo-Isidore, this time deriving from Pseudo-Isidore A/B (**I–b**), with certain modifications. The first variation is the removal for *Ep.* 28 from its place in the collection and putting it at the start of sermon collection D which precedes the letter collection in its manuscript. There is no repetition of *Ep.* 108 after *Ep.* 168, and the *damnatio Vigilii* has been omitted. Moreover, the damaged, conflated *Ep.* 22a + *Ep.* 7b common to most descendents of **S–ga** has been fixed after the original copying of the manuscript. The text of *Ep* 7b has been scraped away, and the missing portion of *Ep.* 22 written. In the space that remains, *Ep.* 2 has been added. According Chavasse's analysis, *Ep.* 2 was added from **D–a**. After the text of **I–b** come *Epp.* 17, 145, and 119, likewise taken from **D–a**. These modifications and additions are in the original hand

---

[211] This MS is digitised: https://digi.vatlib.it/view/MSS_Vat.lat.492. Accessed 22 September 2021.

[212] See Chavasse 1978, lxxi.

of the manuscript. Given the home of the manuscript and the diffusion of **D-a** in northern Italy, Chavasse rightly surmises that the collection and manuscript originate there.

6.3.k.ii. Manuscript

Milan, Archivio Capitolare della Basilica di Sant Ambrogio (Museo S. Ambrogio), M.16 (saec. XII–XIII).

6.3.l. Milan, Ambrosiana C.50.inf

6.3.l.i. Description

Here we have another collection unique to its manuscript. It begins with sermon collection *B* and is followed, in a different hand, a selection of letters from the *Dionysiana adaucta* (**D-a**)—given the northern Italian origin of the manuscript and **D-a**, this is not surprising. The letters, on fols 147–151^v, are *Epp.* 119, 80, 145, and 165. *Ep.* 165 is incomplete, stopping in the middle of fol. 151^v.

6.3.l.ii. Manuscript

Milan, Biblioteca Ambrosiana, C.50.inf (saec. XIV–XV). Originally made for the Benedictine abbey of Sta-Giustina, Padua. After 1418–1419, it passed on to the abbey of San Benedetto in Polirone, according to a record on fol. 144.

6.3.m. Vat. Ross. 159[213]

Vat. Ross. 159 (1438) contains a unique collection of Leo's letters in fols 1–80^v.[214] It was produced at Ferrara at the beginning of 1438, as learnt on folio 228^v:

Anno domini millesimo quadringentesimo tricesimo octauo, indictione prima, die uero iouis tertiadecima mensis februarii, pontificatus sanctissimi in Christo patris et dni nri dni Eugenii diuina proudientia pape quarti anno septimo, congregato sacro generali concilio in ciuitate Ferrarien, scriptus et completus fuit per me Iohannem de Ghistella clericum Mormen. dioc. hic liber epistolarum necnon sermonum beati Leonis pape urbius Rome, pro Reuemo in Christo patre et dno dno D. sancte Romane ecclesie sancte Marie in Via lata diacono cardinali Firmano, Ferrarie,

---

[213] See ibid., cxxxviii. Sermon MS *B 33*.

[214] This MS is digitised: https://digi.vatlib.it/view/MSS_Ross.159 Accessed 22 September 2021.

> in domo prefati dni cardinalis. Laus Deo cui honor et gloria in
> secula seculorum. AMEN.

It begins with a copy of **I-a**, omitting *Epp.* 97, 99, and the *Damnatio Vigilii*, to which is added Chalcedonian collection **Ac**, omitting those items already present. The letter collection is followed by Leo's sermons, the *De Absalon*, and a table of the letters. The context of this collection is made clear by fol. 228ᵛ, cited above for the date. It was written for Firmanus, cardinal deacon of Sta-Maria in Via Lata, that is, Domenico Capranica, who was cardinal 1423–1458, during the Council of Ferrara—an event for which Leo's letters hold great import, as discussed in the introduction to this chapter.

6.3.n. Eugenius IV's Copy of Leo's letters

6.3.n. i. Description of collection

This collection of Leo's letters is a further re-working of Pseudo-Isidore's Leo collection, compiled, it seems, for Eugenius IV himself, yet another member of the Council of Ferrara-Florence. If it was not compiled for him, certainly its earliest manuscript, Vat. lat. 1326, was written for him. It is a rearrangement of most of the letters in **I-a** in three major batches. The first selection starts partway through the *testimonia* that accompany *Ep.* 165, then runs *Epp.* 15, 7, 28; the second selection runs: *Epp.* 120, 97, 99, 139, 31, 59, 124, 1, 35, 29, 114, 155, 162, 163, 135; the third selection runs: *Epp.* 25, 33, 44, 45, 60, 61, 69, 70, 71, 79, 80, 82, 83, 85, 90, 93, 104, 106, 19, 16, and 4. Note the placement of *Ep.* 19 before *Ep.* 16.

6.3.n. ii. Manuscripts

> Vat. lat. 1326 (saec. XV).[215] This manuscript was written by Domenico de Pollinis for Eugenius IV (1431–1447).

> Vat. lat. 1328 (saec. XV), provenance of Angelo Capranica, cardinal 1460–1478, and brother of Domenico Capranica, owner of Vat. Ross. 159, above. Leo's letters run fols 93ᵛ–124ʳ, 124ᵛ–125ʳ. Whereas Vat. lat. 1326 ends with the letter of John VIII, JE

---

[215] This MS is digitsed: https://digi.vatlib.it/view/MSS_Vat.lat.1326. Accessed 22 September 2021.

2986, this manuscript continues after JE 2986 with two more items from the Leonine corpus, letters from the western imperial family East, Leo, *Epp.* 58 (Galla Placidia to Pulcheria) and 55 (Valentinian III to Theodosius II).

Vat. lat. 4902 (saec. XVI).[216] The Leo portion of the manuscript has been copied from Vat. lat. 1326 above.[217] Leo's letters run 353ʳ–417ʳ.

6.3.o. Later Manuscripts of the *Tomus ad Flavianum*

Leo's most popular letter is, of course, *Ep.* 28, the *Tome*. *Ep.* 28 is often transmitted separately from the rest of his letters. We have seen above the Ragyndrudis Codex that contains only two of Leo's letters, one of which is *Ep.* 28. Regardless of where one believes Leo's best articulation of Christological dogma lies, the *Tome* is his most famous contribution to the debate, and it is the official position of the imperial church and its Catholic and Orthodox successors in the Middle Ages. Therefore, it is no surprise that through the ages, people have found it worth their time to copy this letter in particular, if none of the others. The following manuscripts contain Leo's *Tome* but none of his other letters:

Vat. Arch.Cap.S.Pietro.D.170 (saec. XI–XII).[218] This is a theological miscellany. The *Tome* appears on fols 11ʳ–15ʳ.

Vat. lat. 251 (saec. XV).[219] This manuscript begins with various works by Jerome of Stridon, the Leo, *Ep.* 28, fols 211ᵛ–213ᵛ, and closes with letters of Cyprian, Ambrose, and Jerome.

Vat. lat. 1267 (saec. XI).[220] Besides many of Leo's sermons, this patristic miscellany includes *Ep.* 28 on fols 44ʳ–46ʳ.

Vat. lat. 6450 (saec. XI–XII).[221] This patristic miscellany includes many of Leo's sermons as well as *Ep.* 28 at fols 11ᵛ–13ᵛ.

---

[216] Wrongly cited by the Ballerini as being **I-a**.

[217] See Dolezalek 2008.

[218] Kuttner 1986, 56–57. This MS is digitised: https://digi.vatlib.it/view/MSS_Arch.Cap.S.Pietro.D.170 Accessed 22 September 2021.

[219] This MS is digitised: https://digi.vatlib.it/view/MSS_Vat.lat.351. Accessed 22 September 2021.

[220] This MS is digitised: https://digi.vatlib.it/view/MSS_Vat.lat.1267. Accessed 22 September 2021.

[221] This MS is digitised: https://digi.vatlib.it/view/MSS_Vat.lat.6450. Accessed 22 September 2021.

Vat. lat. 549 (saec. XV).[222] This is a manuscript of Leo's sermons, collection *B*. The *Tome* comes between *Sermm.* 19 and 21.

Vat. lat. 550 (saec. XV).[223] This manuscript has the same contents as Vat. lat. 549, but neither is a copy of the other.

Paris, lat. 2161 (saec. XV),[224] this paper manuscript of sermon collection *B* also includes the *Tome* between *Sermm.* 19 and 21.

Vat. lat. 545 (saec. XV).[225] This manuscript of the sermons, like the three preceding, also includes *Ep.* 28 between *Sermm.* 19 and 21.

Vat. lat. 1276 (saec. XV).[226] This miscellany includes various sermons of Leo's amidst other patristic material along with *Ep.* 28 on fols 3ʳ–6ᵛ.

6.3.p. Other High and Late Medieval Manuscripts with Only One Leo Letter

6.3.p.i. Circumstances of these manuscripts

The *Tome* is not the only one of Leo's letters to find its solitary way into a copyist's hand. For each of the manuscripts below, I indicate which of the letters has been included and what other contents of note are to be found in each codex. The letters that receive this treatment are *Epp.* 16, 108, and 165. The first two found their way into the medieval concept of 'decretal' and are important for the history of canon law. The third is the 'second' *Tome*, to Emperor Leo I, Pope Leo's other letter outlining his teaching on the natures of Christ. They are, thus, not unsurprising choices to be excerpted without companions. The manuscripts are listed below in chronological order.

---

[222] Sermon MS *B 37*, Chavasse 1973, cxl. This MS is digitised: https://digi.vatlib.it/view/MSS_Vat.lat.549. Accessed 22 September 2021.

[223] Sermon MS *B 37bis*, ibid. This MS is digitised: https://digi.vatlib.it/view/MSS_Vat.lat.550. Accessed 22 September 2021.

[224] Sermon MS *B 38*, ibid., cxl–cxli.

[225] See ibid., cxliii. This MS is digitised: https://digi.vatlib.it/view/MSS_Vat.lat.545. Accessed 22 September 2021.

[226] This MS is digitised: https://digi.vatlib.it/view/MSS_Vat.lat.1276. Accessed 22 September 2021.

6.3.p.ii. The Manuscripts

Vat. lat. 202 (saec. XI^{ex}).[227] This manuscript includes Leo, *Ep.* 108 on fols 153^v–154^v. This manuscript includes the treatises of Cyprian of Carthage and a selection of his letters, several works by Peter Damian, a number of Augustine of Hippo's shorter works, a sermon of Caesarius of Arles on Psalm 50 (51), and Celestine I's letter to the Bishops of Vienne and Narbonne (JK 369), which immediately precedes Leo, *Ep.* 108. There is no common theme to the works included herein.

Vat. lat. 251 (saec. XI^{ex}).[228] This manuscript includes Leo, *Ep.* 16, ch. 6, on fol. 1$^{r–v}$, followed by Hilarius of Poitiers, *Tractatus super Psalmos*, and then the Pseudo-Seneca correspondence with St Paul.

Vatican, Arch. Cap. S. Pietro.D.210 (saec. XIV–XV).[229] This patristic miscellany was the property of Cardinal Giordano Orsini (card. 1405–1438), who opened the Council of Basel in 1431 and presided over a number of its sessions, including after its transfer to Ferrara. It includes one collection of Leo's sermons and some individual sermons, includes *Ep.* 165 on fols 229^r–233^r after a selection of works by Cyprian of Carthage.

6.4 Conclusion

A variety of socio-political and cultural factors led to the creation of more collections of Leo's letters during the rest of the Middle Ages. As I discussed in the Conclusion to Chapter 5, here we see the endurance of Pseudo-Isidore as a foundation for making more collections of Leo's letters, whether through expansion or selection. The main new trend in these centuries is the creation of more and more manuscripts devoted solely to Leo, whether just the letters or the letters and the sermons, whether because of interest in his work for canon law as a result of the reinvigorated papacy beginning in the eleventh century, or because of interest in the fathers of the church in the reforms of monasticism as found amongst Cistercians and Carthusians. Besides seeing the enduring influence of the Yale Pseudo-Isidore (**Y**), we also see fifteenth-century manu-

[227] Kuttner 1987, 317. This MS is digitised: https://digi.vatlib.it/view/MSS_Vat.lat.202. Accessed 22 September 2021.

[228] Kuttner 1987, 317. This MS is digitised: https://digi.vatlib.it/view/MSS_Vat.lat.251. Accessed 22 September 2021.

[229] This MS is digitised: https://digi.vatlib.it/view/MSS_Arch.Cap.S.Pietro.D.210. Accessed 22 September 2021.

scripts of Leo's work amongst the supporters of a strong papacy in the era of both conciliarism and East-West dialogue; Leo's letters speak directly to the context of papal-conciliar struggle and to the position of the Bishop of Rome in relation to the churches of the East. Notable amongst these fifteenth-century manuscripts are the copies of Leo's letters present at the Council of Ferrara-Florence in the possession of such prominent figures as Nicholas of Cusa, Bessarion, Juan de Torquemada, and Pope Eugenius IV himself. We have other beautiful late mediaeval/early Renaissance copies of Leo's works from fifteenth-century Italy.

Of this era's collections, the most important for editing Leo's letters are the collection of William of Malmesbury (**o**, see 6.2.c) and Ballerini Collection 24 (**24**, see 6.2.e). While the other collections and their manuscripts are important for understanding the reception and distribution of Leo the Great's letters throughout the high and late Middle Ages, it is the case that, due their derivation primarily from Pseudo-Isidore, we have many earlier manuscripts of high quality for those letters that they contain. However, William of Malmesbury's copy and Ballerini Collection 24, on the other hand, contain a number of rarities seldom found in other collections and, therefore, these manuscripts are worthy of attention for the editor of Leo's letters.

Chapter 7

Conspectus of the Letters of Pope Leo I

We have now examined the transmission of Leo's letters to our own day through the lens of their manuscripts and editions. This chapter inverts the paradigm, and we will now consider Leo's letters from the position of the letters themselves. Each section below deals with a different letter, the basic facts about it, the manuscripts that transmit it, and the modern editions where it may be found as well as the Ballerini reference in PL 54. As the lists of collections shrink and grow, the reader will see which of Leo's letters have had perennial popularity, and which have been rare. Moreover, connections between collections can possibly begin to be drawn, such as when rarities occur in **73**, *Grimanica*, and *Bobbiensis*. The letters are given, as throughout this book, in the numbering of the Ballerini, followed by their JK numbering from Jaffé's *Regesta Pontificum Romanorum*, the standard reference work for medieval papal letters. The opening words by which it may be known in canonistic literature are then given, as well as whether it has been classed as 'decretal' or not. This classification is, as argued elsewhere in this book, dubious, but it has merit at the level of reception, if not composition. Next is listed the recipient, a very brief outline of the contents, the letter collections that contain it, and the editions where it may be found. After the listing of the editions, any other important information that may assist the reader's interpretation and study of the text is given, such as whether it is spurious.

7.1 The Conspectus

Letter 1, JK 398 'Relatione sancti' – 'Decretal'

> Date: 442? (cf. PL 54.582–94)
>
> Recipient: A Bishop of Aquileia
>
> Contents: The bishop of Aquileia/Altinum has admitted Pelagians/Caelestians to the priesthood without recantation. This should be stopped.

In the following collections: Teatina, Vaticana, Sanblasiana, Quesnelliana (incl. Oriel College MS), Diessensis, Remensis, Dionysiana
adaucta, Ps.-Is. A1, Yale Pseudo-Isidore, Ps.-Is. C, Florentina,
Lanfranc, B20, **Y-a**, B22, B23, Eugenius IV

Editions: PL 54.593–97.

Further notes: PL 54.582–93 gives a thorough description of the
uncertain relationship this *ep* has with *Epp.* 2 & 18, to which it
bears a considerable resemblance, with some scholars considering this version spurious, others genuine. Given that Leo reuses
his own sermons in *Ep.* 28 and that the same issues can recur
in someone's lifetime, there is no textual reason to reject either
Ep. 2 or 18. The most likely situation is Leo reusing his own
material.

Letter 2, JK 399 'Lectis fraternitatis' – 'Decretal'

Date: 442

Recipient: Septimus, Bishop of Altinum

Contents: Covers much the same ground as *Ep.* 1.

In the following collections: Teatina, Sanblasiana, Quesnelliana
(incl. Oriel College MS), Diessensis, Remensis, Albigensis, Dionysiana adaucta, **I–c**, Florentina, Kues & Holkham **Y–a**, Milanese
Collection, B24, **73**.

Editions: PL 54.597–98.

Further notes: See 'Further notes' on Letter 1 above.

Letter 3, 'Apostolatus uestri scripta'

Date: 443

Recipient: Leo of Rome, from Paschasinus, Bishop of Lilybaeum

Contents: Paschasinus consults Leo concerning the date of Easter
444.

In the following collections: Oriel College MS of Quesnelliana, Albigensis

Editions: PL 54.606–10.

Letter 4, JK 402 'Ut nobis gratulationem' – 'Decretal'

Date: 10 October, 443

Recipient: All the bishops in Campania, Etruria, and all (Italian)
provinces

Contents: Leo deals with discipline: i. Slaves cannot be priests; ii. husbands neither of widows nor of multiple marriages can be priests; iii. neither clergy nor laity can lend at interest; iv. clergy are not to exact interest under another name; v. those who neglect Leo's or his predecessors' decrees are to be removed.

In the following collections: Frisingensis Prima, Diessensis, Quesnelliana (incl. Oriel College MS), Dionysiana, Cresconius, Corbeiensis, Pithouensis, Albigensis, Dionysio-Hadriana, Hadriano-Hispanica, Hispana, Hispana Gallica, Hispana Gallica Augustodunensis, all of Pseudo-Isidore (**I-a**, **I-b**, **I-c**, & **Y**), Florentina, Lanfranc, **Y-a**, Milanese collection, Vat. Ross. 159, B22, B23, B24, **73**, Eugenius IV, Vat. lat. 1347, Vat. Pal. lat. 579, Vat. Reg. lat. 849

Editions: Wurm 1939*b*, 82–93; PL 54.610–14.

Letter 5, JK 403 'Omnis admonitio'

Date: 12 January, 444

Recipient: Metropolitan Bishops of Illyricum

Contents: Leo places them under Anastasius, his *uicarius* and bishop of Thessalonica; they are to obey him, and the hierarchy is to be preserved.

In the following collections: Thessalonicensis

Editions: Silva-Tarouca (ST) 23, *Ep.* 24 (pp. 57–59); PL 54.614–16.

Letter 6, JK 404 'Omnium quidem litteras'

Date: 12 January, 444

Recipient: Anastasius, Bishop of Thessalonica

Contents: Leo declares Anastasius his *uicarius*, affirming his power to consecrate Illyrican Metropolitans and to convene synods, reserving weightier matters for himself. Priests and deacons are to be ordained on Sundays.

In the following collections: Thessalonicensis

Editions: ST 23, *Ep.* 23 (pp. 53–57); PL 54.616–20.

Letter 7, JK 405 'In consortium uos', – 'Decretal'

Date: 30 January, 444

Recipient: All Italian Bishops

Contents: Leo tells them to investigate for any Manichaeans, since a great number was found at Rome, of whom some returned to the faith, others were exiled, and others fled away.

In the following collections: Quesnelliana (incl. Oriel College MS), Dionysiana, Cresconius, Corbeiensis, Pithouensis, Albigensis, Dionysio-Hadriana, Hadriano-Hispanica, Hispana, Hispana Gallica, Hispana Gallica Augustodunesis, all of Pseudo-Isidore (**I-a**, **I-b**, **I-c**, & **Y**), Florentina, **Y-a**, Milanese collection, Vat. Ross. 159, B22, B23, B24, **73**, Eugenius IV, Vat. Reg. lat. 423.

Editions: CFM, Series Latina 1, pp. 46–48; PL 54.620–22.

Letter 8, 'Superstitio paganorum' Not Leonine

Date: 19 June, 445

Recipient: Albinus, praetorian prefect, from Theodosius II and Valentinian III (Valentinian III, *Novella* XVIII)

Contents: Manichaeans are abroad spreading their false beliefs and misdeeds; Manichaeism is a crime, and people who wish can expose Manichaeans with no fear of accusation. Manichaeans can neither inherit nor pass along inheritances; they are barred from military service.

In the following Leonine collections: Oriel MS of Quesnelliana

Editions: Corpus Fontium Manichaeorum, Series Latina 1, 48–50; Mommsen and Meyer 1905, 103–05; PL 54.622–24.

Letter 9, JK 406 'Quantum dilectioni' – 'Decretal'

Date: 21 June, 445

Recipient: Dioscorus, Bishop of Alexandria

Contents: Leo gives Dioscorus advice on how to be a good bishop: priests are to be ordained Saturday night or Sunday morning; both the consecrators and the one to be consecrated should fast; Eucharist can be celebrated twice on major feasts because of how many people who come.

In the following collections: Frisingensis Prima, Diessensis, Vaticana, Oriel College MS of Quesnelliana, Bobbiensis, Epitome Hispana, Hispana, Hispana Gallica, Hispana Gallica Augustodunensis, all of Pseudo-Isidore (**I-a**, **I-b**, **I-c**, & **Y**), Dionysiana adaucta, Lanfranc, **Y-a**, Milanese collection, Vat. Ross. 159, B22, B23, Vat. lat. 1343

Editions: PL 54.624–27.

Letter 10, JK 407 'Diuinae cultum' – 'Decretal'

Date: July, 445

Recipient: All bishops in the province of Viennensis

Contents: Leo writes against Hilary of Arles who, against Leo's wishes, acted as Metropolitan. Leo lists the grievances against Hilary, and annuls Hilary's metropolitical acts.

In the following collections: Corbeiensis, Pithouensis, Albigensis, Ps.-Is. C, B24, **73**

Editions: PL 54.628–36.

Letter 11, 'Certum est et nobis' Valentinian III, *Novella* XVII concerning Gallic Bishops – Not Leonine

Date: 8 July 445

Recipient: Aetius in Gaul

Contents: Hilary of Arles is not Metropolitan of Gaul.

In the following Leo manuscript: Oriel College Manuscript of **Q**.

Editions: PL 54.636–40; Mommsen and Meyer 1905, 101–03.

Letter 12, JK 410 'Cum de ordinationibus' – 'Decretal'

Date: 10 August, 446

Recipient: Bishops of Mauritania Caesariensis

Contents: Leo writes to them about the following concerns: Irregular ordinations are going on; bishops, priests, and deacons can only have been the husband of one wife; 'rudes' and recent converts are not to be ordained. Leo discusses a Donatist & a Novatianist who were reconciling to the Roman Church; where bishops ought to ordained; what to do about virgins violated by barbarians; and examines the case of Bishop Lupicinus. Major cases are to be referred to Rome.

This letter has been transmitted in four damaged and re-assembled forms. Hoskin 2018 demonstrates that *Ep.* 12 is not one letter with multiple recensions but two letters dealing with some of the same material, both of which are genuine. Therefore, the 'complete' form of the Ballerini is actually a conflation of two different texts. The posited letter JK 408 that was supposed to have come before *Ep.* 12 is, in fact, the first letter that came, thus rendering *Ep.* 12 both JK 408 and 410.

Ep. 12a in the following collections: Dionysio-Hadriana

Ep. 12b (so-called *decurtata* in Ballerini ed.) in the following collections: Frisingensis Prima, Diessensis, Teatina, Quesnelliana (incl. Oriel College MS), Vaticana, Sanblasiana, Remensis, Hispana, Hispana Gallica, Hispana Gallica Augustodunensis, Ps.-Is. A/B & B, Pseudo-Isidore C, Dionysiana adaucta, Bobbiensis

Composite form in the following collections: Ps.-Is. A1, Yale Pseudo-Isidore, Lanfranc, **Y–a**, B22, B23, B24

'Complete' form of Ballerini in the following collection: Florentina

Recension unknown to me: B20, Vat. Barb. lat. 77, **73**

Editions: PL 54.645–56 (Florentine version, text of 12a with additions from 12b); 656–63 (*decurtata*, 12b).

Letter 13, JK 409 'Grato animo epistolas'

Date: 6 January, 446

Recipient: Metropolitans of Illyricum

Contents: Leo reminds them that Anastasius of Thessalonica is to
oversee them. They are to go to his councils, and consecrations
require the consent of the people and cannot be in someone else's
jurisdiction.

In the following collection: Thessalonicensis

Editions: ST 23, *Ep.* 25 (pp. 60–62); PL 54.663–66.

Letter 14, JK 411 'Quanta fraternitati' – 'Decretal'

Date: 446

Recipient: Anastasius of Thessalonica

Contents: Anastasius has misused his authority and harmed Atticus of Old Epirus; Leo gives him rules for ordination—bishops
cannot be married, their election needs approval of both clergy
and people, and Leo discusses the consecration of metropolitans,
gathering of councils, not transferring bishops, not receiving for-
eign clerics without their bishops' invitation, summoning bishops
modestly, and the referral of weightier cases to himself.

In the following collections: Frisingensis Prima, Diessensis, Vaticana,
Quesnelliana (incl. Oriel College MS), Dionysiana, Cresconius,
Corbeiensis, Pithouensis, Remensis, Dionysio-Hadriana, Hadri-
ano-Hispanica, Epitome Hispana, Hispana, Hispana Gallica,
Hispana Gallica Augustodunesis, all of Pseudo-Isidore (**I–a**, **I–b**,
I–c, & **Y**), Florentina, Lanfranc, Bobbiensis, **Y–a**, Milanese col-
lection, Vat. Ross. 159, B22, B23, B24, **73**, Vat. Reg. lat. 423.

Editions: PL 54.666–77. There is also a fragment of this letter
edited in PL 54.1261, Mansi VI. 427.

Letter 15, JK 412 'Quam laudabiliter pro' – 'Decretal'

Date: 21 July, 447

Recipient: Turribius, Bishop of Astorga, Spain

Contents: Leo discusses how Turribius should deal with the Priscillianists and describes what the Priscillianists believe.

In the following collections: Frisingensis Prima, Diessensis, Teatina, Quesnelliana (incl. Oriel College MS), Corbeiensis, Pithouensis, Remensis, Epitome Hispana, Hispana, Hispana Gallica, Hispana Gallica Augustodunesis, all of Pseudo-Isidore (**I-a, I-b, I-c,** & **Y**), Dionysiana adaucta, Bobbiensis, Lanfranc, **Y-a**, Milanese collection, Vat. Ross. 159, B22, B23, B24, **73**, Eugenius IV

Editions: Vollmann 1965, 87–138, repr. CFM Series Latina 1, pp. 59–76; PL 54.677–92.

Further notes: Künstle 1905, 117–26, argues this letter is spuriously attributed to Leo. Künstle, however, is wrong; his argument is largely based on the information about Priscillianism being false. However, if it were wrong, it would be the fault of Turribius, not Leo. Furthermore, Chadwick 1976 has shown how many of these teachings are often attributed to Priscillianists.

Letter 16, JK 414 'Diuinis praeceptis et' – 'Decretal'

Date: 21 October, 447

Recipient: All the bishops of Sicily

Contents: Leo advises them not to baptise on Epiphany but at Easter and Pentecost instead.

In the following collections: Diessensis, Teatina, Vaticana, Quesnelliana (incl. Oriel College MS), Dionysiana, Cresconius, Remensis, Epitome Hispana, Hispana, Dionysio-Hadriana, Hadriano-Hispanica, Hispana Gallica, Hispana Gallica Augustodunesis, all of Pseudo-Isidore (**I-a, I-b, I-c,** & **Y**), Florentina, Bobbiensis, Lanfranc, **Y-a**, Milanese collection, Vat. Ross. 159, B22, B23, B24, **73**, Eugenius IV

Editions: PL 54.695–704.

Letter 17, JK 415 'Occasio specialium'

Date: 21 October, 447

Recipient: All the bishops of Sicily

Contents: Leo advises them not to sell church property if there is no advantage to the church in doing so.

In the following collections: Dionysiana adaucta, Kues & Holkham **Y-a**, Milanese collection, B23, Vat. lat. 1343

Editions: PL 54.703–06.

Letter 18, JK 416 'Lectis fraternitatis tuae' – 'Decretal'

Date: 30 December, 447

Recipient: Januarius, Bishop of Aquileia

Contents: If a cleric goes over to heresy and then recants, he cannot advance in the hierarchy once restored to catholic communion.

In the following collections: Quesnelliana (incl. Oriel College MS), Dionysiana, Cresconius, Dionysio-Hadriana, Hadriano-Hispanica, Hispana Gallica, Hispana Gallica Augustodunesis, all of Pseudo-Isidore (**I-a**, **I-b**, **I-c**, & **Y**), Florentina, Lanfranc, **Y-a**, Milanese collection, Vat. Ross. 159, B22, B23, B24, **73**

Editions: PL 54.706–09.

Letter 19, JK 417 'Iudicium, quod de te' – 'Decretal'

Date: 8 March, 448

Recipient: Dorus, Bishop of Beneventum

Contents: Leo is displeased with Dorus, who admitted some underage people to the priesthood. The priests thus ordained, rather than being defrocked, are to be last in rank amongst the priests of the province. Bishop Julius of Puteoli will carry out Leo's commands.

In the following collections: Quesnelliana (incl. Oriel College MS), Ps.-Is. A1, Yale Pseudo-Isidore, Florentina, Lanfranc, **Y-A**, B22, B23, B24, **73**, Eugenius IV

Editions: PL 54.709–14.

Letter 20, JK 418 'Ad notitiam nostram', 'Εἰς γνῶσιν'

Date: 1 June, 448

Recipient: Eutyches

Contents: Leo praises Eutyches for alerting him about an alleged Nestorian revival in Constantinople. Leo will gather more information and deal with the issue.

In the following collections: Vaticana, Casinensis, Hispana, Hispana Gallica, Hispana Gallica Augustodunesis, all of Pseudo-Isidore (**I-a**, **I-b**, **I-c**, & **Y**), Dionysiana adaucta, Grimanica, **Y-a**, Milanese collection, Vat. Ross. 159, **73**, Vat. lat. 1343, Greek Collections M B.

Editions: ACO 2.4, *Ep.* 1 (p. 3, Latin); ACO 2.1.2, p. 45 (Greek). PL 54.713 (Latin), 714 (Greek).

Letter 21, 'Domino uenerabili'

Date: After 22 November, 448

Recipient: Leo of Rome, from Eutyches

Contents: Eutyches denies two-nature Christology and gives his side of the events at the Home synod of Constantinople, 448.

In the following collections: Vat. lat. 1319; Novariensis

Editions: ACO 2.2.1, 33–35; PL 54.714–20.

Letter 22, 'Nulla res diaboli' 'Οὐδὲν ἵστησιν'

Date: Late 448, early 449

Recipient: Leo of Rome, from Flavian of Constantinople

Contents: Eutyches is a Valentinian & Apollinarian, he was excommunicated at the Home Synod.

In the following collections: Vaticana, Corbeiensis, Pithouensis, Coloniensis, Hispana, Dionysiana adaucta, Hispana Gallica, Hispana Gallica Augustodunesis, all of Pseudo-Isidore (**I-a, I-b, I-c,** & **Y**), Rusticus' Acta, *Versio Gestorum Chalcedonensium antiqua correcta*, Novariensis, **Y-a**, Milanese collection, Vat. Ross. 159, B22, B23, B24, **73**, Greek Collections M B H.

Editions: ACO 2.2.1, pp. 21–22 (Latin), ACO 2.1.1, 36–37 (Greek); PL 54.723–27 (Latin version 1), 727–32 (Latin version 2), 724–28 (Greek).

Letter 23, JK 420 'Cum Christianissimus', 'Ὁπότε ὁ'

Date: 18 February, 449

Recipient: Flavian of Constantinople

Contents: Leo is amazed that Flavian hadn't told him about the scandal sooner; Eutyches claims innocence, that he was wrongly excommunicated. Leo wishes to be made more certain of these events.

In the following collections: Vaticana, Hispana, Hispana Gallica, Hispana Gallica Augustodunesis, all of Pseudo-Isidore (**I-a, I-b, I-c,** & **Y**), Dionysiana adaucta, Rusticus' Acta, *Versio Gestorum Chalcedonensium antiqua correcta*, Ratisbonensis, Grimanica, **Y-a**, Milanese collection, Vat. Ross. 159, B22, B23, B24, **73**, Greek Collections M B.

Editions: ST 15, *Ep.* 2 (pp. 2–4); ACO 2.4, *Ep.* 3 (pp. 4–5, Latin), ACO 2.1, pp. 46–47 (Greek); PL 54.731–35 (Latin), 732–36 (Greek).

Letter 24, JK 421 'Quantum praesidii'

Date: 18 February, 449

Recipient: Theodosius II Augustus

Contents: A reply to Theodosius saying that Leo lacks sufficient knowledge to judge concerning Eutyches. He desires more accurate information so he can judge more easily.

In the following collections: Casinensis, Ps.-Is. C, Bobbiensis, Grimanica, Ratisbonensis, B24, **73**

Editions: ST 15, *Ep.* 1 (pp. 1–2); ACO 2.4, *Ep.* 2 (pp. 3–4); PL 54.735–36.

Letter 25, 'Tristis legi tristes' 'Στυγνῶς ἀνέγνων'

Date: *c.* February, 449

Recipient: Eutyches, from Peter Chrysologus

Contents: Eutyches should believe what the church has already decided on Christology, which he can learn from the pope.

In the following collections: Quesnelliana, Hispana, Hispana Gallica, Hispana Gallica Augustodunensis, all of Pseudo-Isidore (**I-a**, **I-b**, **I-c**, & **Y**), Rusticus' Acta, *Versio Gestorum Chalcedonensium Antiqua Correcta*, **Y-a**, Milanese collection, Vat. Ross. 159, B22, B23, **73**, Eugenius IV, Ashburnham 1554, Greek Collections M B.

Editions: ACO 2.3, pp. 6–7 (2 Latin versions), ACO 2.1.2, pp. 241–42 (Greek). PL 54.739–43 (Latin), 740–44 (Greek).

Letter 26, 'Pietate et recta uerbi'; 'Pie et recte' 'Εὐσεβείας καὶ'

Date: *c.* March, 449

Recipient: Leo of Rome, from Flavian of Constantinople

Contents: This is Flavian's second letter explaining Eutyches' condemnation. Eutyches' error, partly Apollinarian, partly Valentinian, is twofold—a. Before the Incarnation there were 2 natures, afterwards 1; b. Christ's body from the Blessed Virgin was not exactly the same nature as ours. Eutyches lied to Leo—there was no written appeal to the Home Synod of Constantinople or to Leo.

In the following collections: Albigensis, Rusticus' Acta, VGCAC, B22, Greek Collection H.

Editions: ACO 2.1.1, pp. 38–40 (Greek), ACO 2.3, pp. 9–11 (Latin version 1), ACO 2.2, 23–24 (Latin version 2, 'Pie et recte'); PL 54.743–47 (Latin version 1), 749–52 (Latin version 2), and 744–48 (Greek version).

Letter 27, JK 422 'Peruenisse ad nos'

Date: 21 May, 449

Recipient: Flavian of Constantinople

Contents: Leo has received Flavian's letter and praises him for his treatment of Eutyches. Promises a full response soon.

In the following collections: Albigensis, Grimanica, Vat. lat. 492.

Editions: ACO 2.4, p. 9; PL 54.752. Mansi V. 1359, Bull. Rom. T. E. App. I. 26.

Further notes: Silva-Tarouca 1931, p. 183, considers this letter suspect.

Letter 28, The *Tome*, JK 423 'Lectis dilectionis tuae', Ἀναγνόντες τὰ'

Date: 13 June, 449

Recipient: Flavian of Constantinople

Contents: Leo sets out in detail his view on the two natures of Christ in response to Eutyches.

In the following collections: Teatina, Corbeiensis, Vaticana, Quesnelliana (incl. Oriel College MS), Albigensis, Remensis, Coloniensis, Hispana, Ragyndrudis Codex, Hispana Gallica, Hispana Gallica Augustodunensis, all of Pseudo-Isidore (**I-a**, **I-b**, **I-c**, & **Y**), Florentina, Dionysiana adaucta, early Latin Acta, Rusticus' Acta, Novariensis, Ratisbonensis, Roman Homiliary *S*, Homiliary of Agimond, B20, **Y-a**, Milanese collection, Vat. Ross. 159, B22, B23, B24, **73**, Eugenius IV, Ashburnham 1554, various sermon MSS (see above 5.3.k), Verona 8, Verona 58, Verona LIX (57), Vat. lat. 492, Greek Collections M B H.

Editions: ST 9, *Ep.* 1 (pp. 20–33); ACO 2.2.1, pp. 24–33 (Latin), ACO 2.1.1, pp. 10–20 (Greek); PL 54.755–81 (Latin), 756–82 (Greek).

Letter 29, JK 424 'Quantum rebus' 'ὅσωι'

Date: 13 June, 449

Recipient: Theodosius II Augustus

Contents: Leo is sending *legati* to Eph2 & has sent the *Tome* to Flavin of Constantinople.

In the following collections: Corbeiensis, Pithouensis, Quesnelliana (incl. Oriel College MS), Ps.-Is. A1 (B10), Yale Pseudo-Isidore, Pseudo-Isidore C, Florentina, Rusticus' Acta, *Versio Gestorum Chalcedonensium Antiqua Correcta*, Grimanica, Bobbiensis, Ratisbonensis, **Y-a**, B22, B23, B24, **73**, Eugenius IV, Ashburnham 1554, Greek Collections M B H.

Editions: ST 15, *Ep.* 3 (pp. 4–5); ACO 2.4, p. 9 (Latin), ACO 2.1, p. 45 (Greek); PL 54.781–83 (Latin), 782–84 (Greek).

Letter 30, JK 425 'Quantum sibi fiduciae' 'ὅσην πεποίθησιν'

Date: 13 June, 449

Recipient: Pulcheria Augusta

Contents: About the same as *Ep.* 29.

In the following collections: Ps.-Is. C (B12), Rusticus' Acta, VGCAC, Ratisbonensis, Grimanica, B22, **73**, Ashburnham 1554, Greek Collections M B H.

Editions: ST 15, *Ep.* 4 (pp. 6–8); ACO 2.4, *Ep.* 8 (pp. 10–11, Latin), ACO 2.1, 45–47 (Greek); PL 54.785–89 (Latin), 786–90 (Greek).

This letter may be a recension of *Ep.* 31, which ST edits as 4b; JK lists both *Epp.* 30 and 31 as #425 with a preference for *Ep.* 31. Concerning *Ep.* 30, JK says: Altera in nonnullis locis abreviata et mutata recension cum versione graeca invenitur in Leonis M. Opp. I. 847 (Migne 54 p. 786), Mansi V. 1396, Bull. Rom. T. E. App. I. 35 ... Fortasse haec mutatio facta est a Leone M. ipso, cum Pulcheriae exemplar istius epistolae pridem ab eadem non acceptae transmisit cum litteris d. die. 13 m. Octobr. a. 449 (v. infra ep. 439).

Letter 31, JK 425 'Quantum praesidii'

Date: 13 June, 449

Recipient: Pulcheria Augusta

Contents: Leo goes into a deeper discussion of Eutyches' errors than in *Ep.* 30. He cannot be at Eph2.

In the following collections: Quesnelliana (incl. Oriel College MS), Corbeiensis, Pithouensis, Coloniensis, Ps.-Is. A1, Yale Pseudo-Isidore, Ps.-Is. C, Florentina, Bobbiensis, Grimanica, B20, **Y-a**, B22, B23, B24, Eugenius IV, Vat. Reg. lat. 293

Editions: ST 15, *Ep.* 4b (pp. 8–13); ACO 2.4, *Ep.* 11 (pp. 12–15); PL 54.789–96.

Further notes: See *Ep.* 30 concerns about its relationship with this letter.

Letter 32, JK 426 'Cum propter causam' 'ἐπειδὴ διὰ'

Date: 13 June, 449

Recipient: Faustus, Martinus, and the rest of the archimandrites of Constantinople

Contents: Leo condemns Eutyches, but wishes for mercy not to be denied Eutyches if he is penitent.

In the following collections: Rusticus' Acta, *Versio Gestorum Chalcedonensium Antiqua Correcta*, Grimanica, Ratisbonensis, B22, Montpellier H 308, Greek Collections M B H.

Editions: ST 15, *Ep.* 8; ACO 2.4, p. 10 (Latin); ACO 2.1, pp. 42–43 (Greek); PL 54.795–97 (Latin), 796–98 (Greek).

Letter 33, JK 427 'Religiosa clementissimi' 'ἡ τοῦ ἡμερωτάτου'

Date: 13 June, 449

Recipient: Council of Ephesus II

Contents: Leo asserts Petrine primacy (citing Mt. 16:13, 16–18), and encourages them to heed his *legati* whom he has sent to condemn Eutychianism and restored Eutyches if penitent.

In the following collections: Quesnelliana (incl. Oriel College MS), Hispana, Hispana Gallica, Hispana Gallica Augustodunensis, all of Pseudo-Isidore (**I-a, I-b, I-c,** & **Y**), Florentina, Rusticus' Acta, *Versio Gestorum Chalcedonensium Antiqua Correcta*, Grimanica, Ratisbonensis, **Y-a**, Milanese collection, Vat. Ross. 159, B22, B23, B24, **73**, Eugenius IV, Ashburnham 1554, Montpellier H 308, Greek Collections M B H.

Editions: ST 15, *Ep.* 8; ACO 2.4, p. 15 (Latin); ACO 2.1, pp. 43–44 (Greek); PL 54.797–99 (Latin), 798–800 (Greek).

Letter 34, JK 428 'Litterae dilectionis tuae'

Date: 13 June, 449

Recipient: Juvenal of Jerusalem (cf. ST 15, p. 18) or Julian of Cos (cf. PL 54.801, ACO 2.4, p. 16)

Contents: Leo praises his recipient's faith and tells him of the *legati* he is sending to Eph2 and states Eutyches' guilt.

In the following collections: Ps.-Is. C, Grimanica, Ratisbonensis

Editions: ST 15, *Ep.* 7; ACO 2.4, p. 16; PL 54.801–02.

Letter 35, JK 429 'Licet per nostros' 'Εἰ καὶ διὰ'

Date: 13 June, 449

Recipient: Julian of Cos

Contents: Leo expounds upon the errors of Eutyches

In the following collections: Oriel MS of Quesnelliana, Corbeiensis, Pithouensis, Ps.-Is. A1, Yale Pseudo-Isidore, Ps.-Is. C, Florentina, Rusticus' Acta, *Versio Gestorum Chalcedonensium Antiqua Correcta*, Grimanica, Ratisbonensis, B20, **Y-a**, B22, B23, B24, **73**, Eugenius IV, Ashburnham 1554, Vat. Reg. lat. 293, Leiden VLQ 122, Montpellier H 308, Greek Collections M B H.

Editions: ST 15, *Ep.* 6; ACO 2.4, pp. 6–8 (Latin); ACO 2.1, pp. 40–42 (Greek); PL 54.803–09 (Latin), 804–10 (Greek).

Letter 36, JK 430 'Litteras tuae dilectionis'

Date: 20 June, 449

Recipient: Flavian of Constantinople

Contents: Leo acknowledges receipt of *Ep.* 26. Although he sees no need for a council, he will send his *legati*.

In the following collections: Casinensis, Ps.-Is. C, Grimanica

Editions: ACO 2.4, p. 17; PL 54.809–11.

Further notes: Silva-Tarouca 1931, 183, thinks spurious.

Letter 37, JK 431 'Acceptis clementiae'

Date: 30 June, 449

Recipient: Theodosius II Augustus

Contents: Leo praises Theodosius' zeal but notes that a council is unnecessary. Nevertheless, he will send *legati*.

In the following collections: Casinensis, Ps.-Is. C, Grimanica, Ratisbonensis

Editions: ST 15, *Ep.* 10; ACO 2.4, p. 17; PL 54.811–12.

Letter 38, JK 432 'Profectis iam nostris'

Date: 23 July, 449

Recipient: Flavian of Constantinople

Contents: Leo encourages Flavian against those who are opposed to the truth, but encourages him to give leniency to the penitent.

In the following collections: Casinensis, Ps.-Is. C, Grimanica, Ratisbonensis

Editions: ST 15, *Ep.* 11; ACO 2.4, p. 18; PL 54.812–13.

Letter 39, JK 433 'Auget sollicitudines'

Date: 11 August, 449

Recipient: Flavian of Constantinople

Contents: Leo queries why Flavian is not sending him letters; he wants to know all about Eph2.

In the following collections: Casinensis, Ps.-Is. C, Grimanica

Editions: ACO 2.4, pp. 18–19; PL 54.813–14.

Further notes: Silva-Tarouca 1931, 183, thinks suspect

Letter 40, JK 434 'Iusta et rationabilis'

Date: 22 August, 449

Recipient: Constantine, Audentius, Rusticus, Auspicius, Nicetas, Nectarius, Florus, Asclepius, Iustus, Augustalis, Ynantius, and Chrysaphius, bishops of Arles

Contents: Leo congratulates them on the accession of Ravennius to the see of Arles.

In the following collections: Arelatensis, Albigensis

Editions: Gundlach 1892, 15; PL 54.814–15.

Letter 41, JK 435 'Prouectionem dilectionis'

Date: 22 August, 449

Recipient: Ravennius of Arles

Contents: Leo congratulates him on becoming bishop; encourages him to be moderate in governance and to consult Leo for advice often.

In the following collections: Arelatensis, Albigensis, Ps.-Is. C, B24, **73**

Editions: Gundlach 1892, 16–17; PL 54.815–16.

Letter 42, JK 436 'Circumspectum te'

Date: 26 August, 449

Recipient: Ravennius of Arles

Contents: Leo warns Ravennius to watch out for a certain Petronianus, a deacon who claims to be from Rome and is wandering about Gaul. Ravennius should check Petronianus' boldness if he crosses his path; he should excommunicate him if necessary.

In the following collections: Arelatensis, Britannica

Editions: Gundlach 1892, 16; PL 54.816–18.

Letter 43, JK 437 'Antea et ab' 'Olim et ab' 'ἄνωθεν'

Date: 26 August, 449

Recipient: Theodosius II Augustus

Contents: Leo queries about Eph2. He complains about how things transpired—they should have had a general synod in Italy.

In the following collections: Rusticus' Acta, VGCAC, Grimanica, B22, Greek Collections M B.

Editions: ST 15, *Ep.* 12b; ACO 2.4, pp. 26–27 (Latin), ACO 2.1.1, pp. 3–4 (Greek); PL 54.821–23 (Latin version 1), 823–26 (Latin version 2); 822–24 (Greek).

Further notes: Silva-Tarouca 1931, 150, 183, thinks spurious. In notes to his edition (TD 15), he writes, 'Versionem hanc falsatam epistulae XII [*Ep.* 44 in PL 54] Chrysaphio eunucho iubente, Constantinopoli statim post acceptam authenticam Leonis epistulam divulgatam fuisse exposui in *Nuovi Studi*, p. 150 ss. Finis et scopus fraudis fuit culpam omnem eorum quae Ephesi occurrerant, Flaviano adtribuere; quare eliminato Alexandrini antistitis nomine (supra XII, lin. 14), 'supra dicto sacerdoti' i.e. Flaviano (XII *b*) lin. 38, conf. 17) eius crimina tribuuntur' (p. 30, n. a). This theory is dependent upon Chrysaphius having done the modification/forgery, a theory in part hinged upon the idea that any such doings would necessarily be carried out by Chrysaphius. Traditionally, Chrysaphius has been seen as ruling over Theodosius II and forcing the emperor to do his will. However, as George Bevan's research from 2005 shows, Theodosius was a man of his own mind and his own will. Therefore, even if we can demonstrate this letter to be a modified forgery of *Ep.* 44, the identity of the forger is not necessarily Chrysaphius, as so easily assumed by an earlier generation.

Letter 44, JK 438 'Litteris clementiae uestrae' 'τοῖς γράμμασι'

Date: 13 October, 449

Recipient: Theodosius II Augustus, from both Leo and the recent Roman Synod

Contents: Leo and the Roman Synod set before the emperor the injuries done at Eph2, which Leo had already mentioned in earlier letters. Something must be done, and Leo and the Romans encourage Theodosius to be vigilant against heresy.

In the following collections: Quesnelliana, Hispana, Hispana Gallica, Hispana Gallica Augustodunensis, all of Pseudo-Isidore, Florentina, Rusticus' Acta, *Versio Gestorum Chalcedonensium Antiqua Correcta*, Grimanica, Ratisbonensis, Lanfranc, **Y–a**, B22, B23, B24, **73**, Eugenius IV, Ashburnham 1554, Greek Collections M B H.

Editions: ST 15, *Ep.* 12; ACO 2.4, pp. 19–21 (Latin), ACO 2.1, pp. 25–27 (Greek); PL 54.827–31 (Latin), 828–32 (Greek).

Letter 45, JK 439 'Si epistolae, quae' "Εἰ αἱ ἐπιστολαὶ'

Date: 13 October, 449

Recipient: Pulcheria Augusta

Contents: Leo and the synod send Pulcheria a copy of an earlier letter (*Ep.* 30) that never reached her. Leo wants a council in Italy.

In the following collections: Quesnelliana (incl. Oriel College MS),
Arelatensis, Hispana, Hispana Gallica, Hispana Gallica Augustodunensis, all of Pseudo-Isidore (**I-a**, **I-b**, **I-c**, & **Y**), Florentina, Rusticus' Acta, *Versio Gestorum Chalcedonensium Antiqua
Correcta*, Grimanica, Ratisbonensis, **Y-a**, Milanese collection,
Vat. Ross. 159, B22, B23, B24, **73**, Eugenius IV, Ashburnham
1554, Greek Collection H.

Editions: ST 15, *Ep.* 13; ACO 2.4, pp. 23–25 (Latin); ACO 2.1,
pp. 47–48 (Greek); PL 54.833–35 (Latin), 834–36 (Greek).

Letter 46, 'Studium mihi fuisse' 'Σπουδὴν μοι'

Date: 13 October, 449

Recipient: Pulcheria, from Hilarus the Deacon

Contents: Hilarus was not allowed to enter Eph2, and Dioscorus
sent back Leo's letters. He escaped Dioscorus' plots and returned
to Rome.

In the following collections: Grimanica, Rusticus' Acta, *Versio Gestorum Chalcedonensium Antiqua Correcta*, B22, Greek Collection H.

Editions: ACO 2.4, pp. 27–28 (Latin), ACO 2.1, 48–49 (Greek); PL
54.837–39 (Latin), 838–40 (Greek).

Letter 47, JK 440 'Quantum relatione'

Date: 13 October, 449

Recipient: Anastasius of Thessalonica

Contents: Leo congratulates Anastasius on avoiding Eph2; Anastasius is to keep the faith, following Flavian, and strengthening
other bishops.

In the following collections: Casinensis, Ps.-Is. C, Grimanica

Editions: ACO 2.4, pp. 22–23; PL 54.839–40.

Further notes: Silva-Tarouca 1931, 183, considers Epp. 47–49 suspect on stylistic grounds.

Letter 48, JK 441 'Cognitis, quae apud'

Date: 13 October, 449

Recipient: Julian of Cos

Contents: Leo consoles Julian and will write his plans to him through a messenger.

In the following collections: Ps.-Is. C, Grimanica

Editions: ACO 2.4, p. 23; PL 54.840.

Further notes: Silva-Tarouca 1931, 183, considers Epp. 47–49 suspect on stylistic grounds.

Letter 49, JK 442 'Quae et quanta'

Date: 13 October, 449

Recipient: Flavian of Constantinople – probably deceased at time of writing

Contents: Leo consoles Flavian in the matter of his sufferings Eph2 and encourages him to keep the faith.

In the following collections: Casinensis, Ps.-Is. C, B23, Grimanica

Editions: ACO 2.4, p. 23; PL 54.841–42.

Further notes: Silva-Tarouca 1931, 183, considers *Epp.* 47–49 suspect on stylistic grounds.

Letter 50, JK 443 'In notitiam nostram' 'Εἰς γνῶσιν'

Date: 15 (13?) October, 449 (cf. ACO 2.4, p. 22, app. crit. for *l.* 12)

Recipient: Clergy, nobles, and people in Constantinople

Contents: Leo and the Roman synod encourage them in the matter of the ill deeds of Dioscorus at Eph2. Leo encourages them to keep the faith.

In the following collections: Rusticus' Acta, *Versio Gestorum Chalcedonensium Antiqua Correcta*, Grimanica, Ratisbonensis, **Y-a**, B22, B23, B24, Greek Collection H.

Editions: ST 15, *Ep.* 15; ACO 2.4, pp. 21–22 (Latin); ACO 2.1, pp. 50–51 (Greek); PL 54.841–43 (Latin), 842–44 (Greek).

Letter 51, JK 444 'Quamuis ea, quae' 'Εἰ καὶ τὰ'

Date: 15 (13?) October, 449 (cf. ACO 2.4, p. 26, app. crit. for l. 4)

Recipient: Faustus, Martinus, Peter, and Emmanuel, presbyters and archimandrites in Constantinople

Contents: Leo warns them not to abandon Bishop Flavian or his faith. This letter from Leo and the Roman Synod.

In the following collections: Ps.-Is. C, Rusticus' Acta, *Versio Gestorum Chalcedonensium Antiqua Correcta*, Grimanica, Ratisbonensis, B22, B23, Greek Collection H.

Editions: ST 15, *Ep.* 14; ACO 2.4, pp. 25–26 (Latin); ACO 2.1, pp. 51–52 (Greek); PL 54.843–45 (Latin), 844–46 (Greek).

Letter 52, "Εἰ Παῦλος'

Date: September-October, 449

Recipient: Leo I Episcopus from Theodoret of Cyrrhus

Contents: Theodoret writes to Leo for instructions in the wake of his deposition at Eph2.

In the following collections: The letters of Theodoret of Cyrrhus

Editions: SC 111, pp. 56–67; PL 54.845–54 (Greek original with Ballerini Latin).

Letter 53, 'Καὶ γὰρ ὁ' 'Etenim piisimus et'

Date: Late 449

Recipient: Leo of Rome, from Anatolius of Constantinople

Contents: In this fragmentary letter Anatolius explains to Leo how he gained the see of Constantinople.

In the following collections: Vat. Reg. Gr. 940 (PL 54.853 simply calls it Cod. Regius 940).

Editions: PL 54.853–56 (Greek original with Ballerini Latin).

Letter 54, JK 445 'Pro integritate fidei'

Date: 25 December, 449

Recipient: Theodosius II Augustus

Contents: Leo maintains the Nicene faith and condemns Nestorianism. He urges the emperor to call a council in Italy.

In the following collections: Casinensis, Ps.-Is. C, Grimanica, Ratisbonensis

Editions: ST 15, *Ep.* 16; ACO 2.4, p. 11; PL 54.855–56.

Letter 55, 'Cum aduenissem' 'Παραγενομένου μου'

Date: February 450

Recipient: Theodosius II Augustus, from Valentinian III Augustus

Contents: If Theodosius were to hold a council in Italy, it would please Leo.

In the following collections: Rusticus' Acta, B22, Greek Collection M

Editions: ACO 2.3, pp. 13–14 (Latin), ACO 2.1.1, p. 5 (Greek); PL 54.857–59 (Latin), 858–60 (Greek).

Letter 56, 'Dum in ipso ingressu' 'Ὁπηνίκα ἐν αὐτῆι'

Date: 450

Recipient: Theodosius II Augustus, from Galla Placidia Augusta

Contents: At Leo's insistence, she mentions his complaints against Eph2 and call for Theodosius to follow Leo's lead in matters ecclesiastical.

In the following collections: Rusticus' Acta, B22, Greek Collection M

Editions: ACO 2.3, pp. 14–15 (Latin); ACO 2.1.1, pp. 5–6 (Greek); PL 54.859–61 (Latin), 860–62 (Greek).

Letter 57, 'Omnibus notum est' 'Πᾶσιν ἔγνωσται'

Date: 450

Recipient: Theodosius II Augustus, from Licinia Eudoxia

Contents: Leo knows what is best. Flavian of Constantinople suffered at the hands of the bishop of Alexandria. Theodosius should revoke Eph2.

In the following collections: Rusticus' Acta, B22, Greek Collection M

Editions: ACO 2.3, p. 15 (Latin), ACO 2.1.1, pp. 6–7 (Greek); PL 54.861–63 (Latin), 862–64 (Greek).

Letter 58, 'Ut Romam frequentibus' 'Ὅτι τὴν Ῥώμην'

Date: 450

Recipient: Pulcheria Augusta, from Galla Placidia Augusta

Contents: Leo is in a bad state about Eph2, where everything was conducted contrary to order. Galla Placidia encourages Pulcheria to work at overturning these actions.

In the following collections: Greek Collection H, Latin Acta (Veron. 57)

Editions: ACO 2.3.1, p. 13 (Latin), ACO 2.1.1, pp. 49–50 (Greek); PL 54.863–65 (Latin), 864–66 (Greek).

Letter 59, JK 447 'Licet de his quae'

Date: March 450 (ST thinks end of 449, TD 15, p. 40 n. a)

Recipient: Clergy and people of Constantinople

Contents: Leo congratulates them for not being heretics. He demonstrates Christ's real body from the Eucharist and that the Incarnation is needed to overcome Adam's sin.

In the following collections: Corbeiensis, Quesnelliana (incl. Oriel College MS), Ps.-Is. A1, Florentina, B20, **Y-a**, B22, B23, B24, **73**, Eugenius IV, Ashburnham 1554, Grimanica

Editions: ST 15, *Ep.* 15b; ACO 2.4, 34ff; PL 54.865–72.

Letter 60, JK 448 'Gaudere me plurimum'

Date: 17 March, 450

Recipient: Pulcheria Augusta

Contents: Leo praises her faith and requests her help to hold another synod.

In the following collections: Coloniensis, Hispana, Hispana Gallica, Hispana Gallica Augustodunensis, all of Pseudo-Isidore (**I-a, I-b, I-c, Y**), Grimanica, Ratisbonensis, **Y-a**, Milanese collection, Vat. Ross. 159, B22, B23, B24, **73**, Eugenius IV, Ashburnham 1554

Editions: ST 15, *Ep.* 17; ACO 2.4, p. 29; PL 54.873–74.

Letter 61, JK 449 'Bonorum operum'

Date: 17 March, 450

Recipient: Martinus and Faustus, presbyters and archimandrites

Contents: Leo reminds them of *Ep.* 51 and the need to preserve the faith and church from things contrary to piety and sense.

In the following collections: Hispana, Hispana Gallica, Hispana Gallica Augustodunensis, all of Pseudo-Isidore (**I-a, I-b, I-c, Y**), Grimanica, Ratisbonensis, Lanfranc, **Y-a**, Milanese collection, Vat. Ross. 159, B22, B23, B24, **73**, Eugenius IV

Editions: ST 15, *Ep.* 18; ACO 2.4, p. 28; PL 54.874–76.

Letter 62, 'Et Romae peruenisse' 'Καὶ ἐν τῆι Ῥώμηι'

Date: *c.* April 450 (cf. PL 54.875 n. *e*)

Recipient: Valentinian III, from Theodosius II

Contents: Theodosius responds to *Ep.* 55 that there has been no departure from the faith of the Fathers, and that Flavian was adding innovations. Now peace and harmony will reign in the Church.

In the following collections: Rusticus' Acta, B22, Greek Collection
M

Editions: ACO 2.3, pp. 15–16 (Latin); ACO 2.1.1, p. 7 (Greek); PL
54.875–77 (Latin), 876–78 (Greek).

Letter 63, 'Ex litteris tuae' 'ἐκ τῶν γραμμάτων'

Date: 450

Recipient: Galla Placidia Augusta, from Theodosius II

Contents: Despite Leo's concern, there has been no departure from
the faith of the Fathers decided at Nicaea. No new council will
be called, for all is well, and Flavian had been the innovator.

In the following collections: Rusticus' Acta, B22, Greek Collection
M.

Editions: ACO 2.3, p. 16 (Latin); ACO 2.1.1, pp. 7–8 (Greek); PL
54.877 (Latin), 878 (Greek).

Letter 64, 'Semper equidem tui' 'Ἀεῖ μὲν οὖν'

Date: 450

Recipient: Licinia Eudoxia, from Theodosius II

Contents: Although Theodosius receives her letter and requests with
sweetness, in the case of Flavian, nothing can be done. Flavian
was judged rightly at Eph2.

In the following collections: Rusticus' Acta, B22, Greek Collection
M

Editions: ACO 2.3, pp. 16–17 (Latin); ACO 2.1.1, p. 8 (Greek); PL
54.877–79 (Latin), 878–80 (Greek).

Letter 65, 'Memores quantum honoris'

Date: A while before May, 450 (PL 54.879, n. *d*)

Recipient: Leo of Rome, from all the bishops of Arles

Contents: The Arelatensians want old honours restored to the see
of Arles. Arles had various prerogatives, and St Trophimus
went there; there are civil rights and privileges given Arles; the
beseech Leo in various ways.

In the following collections: Arelatensis, Albigensis

Editions: Gundlach 1892, 17–20; PL 54.879–83.

Letter 66, JK 450 'Lectis dilectionis uestrae'

Date: 5 May, 450

Recipient: Bishops of the Province of Arles – all named

Contents: No. Leo has already presided over and judged this issue.

In the following collections: Arelatensis, Albigensis, Coloniensis, Britannica

Editions: Gundlach 1892, 20–21; PL 54.883–86.

Letter 67, JK 451 'Diu filios nostros'

Date: 5 May, 450 (PL 54.885)

Recipient: Ravennius of Arles

Contents: Leo commits Ravennius with the task of promoting the *Tome* and a letter of Cyril's (*II Ad Nestorium*?) in Gaul. Petronius the presbyter and Regulus the deacon will give him secret/unwritten insctructions.

In the following collections: Arelatensis

Editions: Gundlach 1892, 21–22; ST 15, p. 89; PL 54.886–87.

Letter 68, 'Recensita epistola beatitudinis uestrae'

Date: A little after May, 450 (PL 54.888, n. *c*)

Recipient: Leo, from Ceretius, Salonius, and Veranus, Bishops of Gaul

Contents: They thank Leo for the *Tome* and include a copy for him to make any corrections to and send back to them.

In the following collections: Oriel College MS of Quesnelliana, Ps.-Is. C.

Editions: PL 54.887–90.

Letter 69, JK 452 'Omnibus quidem uestrae' ('Credimus filium' – fragment, cf. below)

Date: 16 July, 450

Recipient: Theodosius II Augustus who died before the letter arrived

Contents: Leo has not yet acknowledged Anatolius as Bishop of Constantinople not out of spite but, rather, out of a concern for catholic doctrine. In all the trouble, he was waiting to be assured of Anatolius' catholicity. He urges Theodosius to secure and adhere to catholic teaching, which Leo and his predecessors maintained, through a council in Italy.

In the following collections: Oriel College MS of Quesnelliana, Hispana, Hispana Gallica, Hispana Gallica Augustodunensis, all of Pseudo-Isidore (**I-a**, **I-b**, **I-c**, **Y**), Grimanica, Ratisbonensis,

Y-a, Milanese collection, Vat. Ross. 159, B22, B23, B24, **73**, Eugenius IV

Editions: ST 15, *Ep.* 18 (pp. 51ff); ACO 2.4, pp. 30–31; PL 54.890–92.

Further notes: JK observes that there is a fragment in PL 54.1257, Mansi VI. 423, Bull. Rom. T. E. App. I. 198, that he believes to be from the same letter.

Letter 70, JK 453 'Gaudeo fidei clementiae'

Date: 16 July, 450

Recipient: Pulcheria Augusta

Contents: Leo has not heard back from the letters he sent to Anatolius to hear Anatolius' confession of faith. He stresses the importance of having a general council.

In the following collections: Oriel College MS of Quesnelliana, Hispana, Hispana Gallica, Hispana Gallica Augustodunensis, all of Pseudo-Isidore (**I-a, I-b, I-c, Y**), Grimanica, Ratisbonensis, Lanfranc, **Y-a**, Milanese collection, Vat. Ross. 159, B22, B23, B24, **73**, Eugenius IV

Editions: ST 15, *Ep.* 20 (pp. 54–55); ACO 2.4, p. 29; PL 54.893–95.

Letter 71, JK 454 'Causa fidei, in qua'

Date: 17 July, 450

Recipient: Faustus, Martinus, Petrus, Manuelus, Job, Antiochus, Abrahamius, Thedorus, Pientius, Eusebius, Helpidius, Paulus, Asterius, and Charosus, presbyters and archimandrites, and Jacobus the deacon and archimandrite in Constantinople

Contents: Leo complains of not having a confession of faith from Anatolius and the people whom he has ordained. Also, he commends his *legati* to the recipients.

In the following collections: Hispana, Hispana Gallica, Hispana Gallica Augustodunensis, all of Pseudo-Isidore (**I-a, I-b, I-c, Y**), Grimanica, **Y-a**, Milanese collection, Vat. Ross. 159, B22, B23, B24, **73**, Eugenius IV

Editions: ACO 2.4, pp. 31–32; PL 54.895–96.

Letter 72, JK 455 'Gratum semper est' 'Κεχαρισμένον ἐστὶν'

Date: Between March and November 450 (PL 54.897 n. *a*)

Recipient: Faustus the presbyter

Contents: Leo is answering Faustus, praising his faith and encouraging him not to be put to confusion concerning Jesus' incarnation.

In the following collections: Rusticus' Acta, *Versio Gestorum Chalcedonensium Antiqua Correcta*, Grimanica, B22, Greek Collections M B H.

Editions: ACO 2.4, pp. 5–6 (Latin), ACO 2.1.1, pp. 37–38 (Greek); PL 54.897 (Latin), 898 (Greek).

Letter 73, 'Ad hoc maximum imperium' Ἐἰς τοῦτο τὸ μέγιστον βασίλειον'

Date: Late August, early September 450 (PL 54.900, n. *a*)

Recipient: Leo of Rome, from Valentinian III and Marcian, Augusti (must be really fr Marcian)

Contents: The emperors promise to Leo that they will rid the world of heresy through another council.

In the following collections: Rusticus' Acta, VGCAC, B22, Greek Collection M

Editions: ACO 2.3, p. 17 (Latin), ACO 2.1.1, p. 10 (Greek); PL 54.899 (Latin), 900 (Greek).

Letter 74, JK 456 'Gratias agimus Deo'

Date: 13 September, 450

Recipient: Martinus, a presbyter

Contents: Leo encourages Martinus not to lack zeal for the destruction of heresy, for the right arm of God will break the weapons of the Devil. Leo hopes his *legati* are well in Constantinople.

In the following collections: Casinensis, Ps.-Is. C, Grimanica

Editions: ACO 2.4, p. 32; PL 54.899–901.

Further notes: ST, *NS* 183, thinks it spurious

Letter 75, JK 457 'Omnes scribendi'

Date: 9 or 8 November, 450 (cf. ACO 2.4, p. 33, app. crit. *l.* 36; ACO & ST = 9 November; PL 54 = 8 November)

Recipient: Faustus and Martinus, presbyters and archimandrites in Constantinople

Contents: Leo encourages them to take up constancy against Nestorius and Eutyches who are the precursors of Antichrist.

In the following collections: Grimanica, Ratisbonensis

Editions: ST 15, *Ep.* 21 (pp. 56–57); ACO 2.4, p. 33; PL 54.901–04.

Letter 76, 'De studio et oratione nostra' 'Περὶ τῆς σπουδῆς'

Date: 22 November, 450 (cf. PL 54.903, nn. *c* and *e*)

Recipient: Leo of Rome, from Marcian Augustus

Contents: Leo's envoys have arrived in Constantinople. Marcian agrees that a council should be held with all haste, but in the East, not the West.

In the following collections: Rusticus' Acta, *Versio Gestorum Chalce-donensium Antiqua Correcta*, B22, Greek Collection M

Editions: ACO 2.3, p. 18 (Latin), ACO 2.1.1, pp. 8–9 (Greek); PL 54.903–05 (Latin), 904–06 (Greek).

Letter 77, 'Litteras tuae beatitudinis' 'τὰ γράμματα τῆς σῆς μακαριότητος'

Date: Same time at *Ep.* 76 (22 November, 450)

Recipient: Leo of Rome, from Pulcheria Augusta

Contents: Anatolius has confirmed his orthodoxy, and Flavian of Constantinople's body has been returned and is buried in the Church of the Apostles. There should be a council in the East to decide the fates of those involved in Eph2.

In the following collections: Rusticus' Acta, *Versio Gestorum Chalce-donensium Antiqua Correcta*, B22, Greek Collection M

Editions: ACO 2.3, pp. 18–19 (Latin), ACO 2.1.1, pp. 9–10 (Greek); PL 54.905–07 (Latin), 906–08 (Greek).

Letter 78, JK 458 'Litteras pietatis uestrae'

Date: 13 April, 451

Recipient: Marcian Augustus

Contents: Leo responds to *Ep.* 76 that he is pleased with Marican's faith and encourages him to defend catholic truth. He adds that more letters will follow.

In the following collections: Casinensis, Ps.-Is. C, Grimanica, Ratis-bonensis

Editions: ST 15, *Ep.* 22 (pp. 57–58); ACO 2.4, p. 38; PL 54.907–09.

Letter 79, JK 459 'Quod semper de'

Date: 13 April, 451

Recipient: Pulcheria Augusta

Contents: In his response to *Ep.* 77, Leo congratulates Pulcheria for her victory over Nestorianism and Eutychianism. He praises her for aiding his *legati* and readmitting catholic priests ejected at Eph2, and returning Flavian to Constantinople. He commends Eusebius of Dorylaeum and Julian of Cos to her.

In the following collections: Oriel College MS of Quesnelliana, Hispana, Hispana Gallica, Hispana Gallica Augustodunensis, all of Pseudo-Isidore (**I-a**, **I-b**, **I-c**, **Y**), Ratisbonensis, Lanfranc, **Y-a**, Milanese collection, Vat. Ross. 159, B22, B23, B24, **73**, Eugenius IV

Editions: ST 15, *Ep.* 23 (pp. 58–60); ACO 2.4, pp. 37–38; PL 54.909–12.

Letter 80, JK 460 'Gaudemus in Dominio'

Date: 13 April, 451

Recipient: Anatolius of Constantinople

Contents: Leo rejoices in Anatolius' orthodoxy. He notes the error of the lapsed who are to be restored as are those condemned at Eph2. Dioscorus, Juvenal, and Eustathius are to be removed from the diptychs, and he commends Julian and Eusebius to him.

In the following collections: Vaticana, Oriel College MS of Quesnelliana, Hispana, Hispana Gallica, Hispana Gallica Augustodunensis, all of Pseudo-Isidore (**I-a**, **I-b**, **I-c**, **Y**), Dionysiana adaucta, Ratisbonensis, Lanfranc, **Y-a**, Milanese collection, Vat. Ross. 159, B22, B23, B24, **73**, Eugenius IV, Ashburnham 1554, Ambrosiana C.50.inf

Editions: ST 15, *Ep.* 24 (pp. 60–63); ACO 2.4, pp. 38–40; PL 54.912–15.

Letter 81, JK 461 'Litteras fraternitatis tuae'

Date: 13 April, 451

Recipient: Julian of Cos

Contents: Leo congratulates Julian for being freed from his miseries and encourages/urges him to put pressure more tightly upon treacherous heretics.

In the following collections: Ps.-Is. C, Grimanica, Ratisbonensis

Editions: ST 15, *Ep.* 25 (pp. 64–65); ACO 2.4, p. 40; PL 54.915–17.

Letter 82, JK 462 'Quamuis per Constantinopolitanos'

Date: 23 April, 451

Recipient: Marcian Augustus

Contents: Leo advises Marcian to guard the peace of the church against anything new insinuating itself contrary to evangelical and apostolic preaching. He will send *legati* to the new synod, which is to treat only of Dioscorus and Eutyches.

In the following collections: Hispana, Hispana Gallica, Hispana Gallica Augustodunensis, all of Pseudo-Isidore (**I-a**, **I-b**, **I-c**, **Y**), Grimanica, **Y-a**, Milanese collection, Vat. Ross. 159, B22, B23, B24, **73**, Eugenius IV

Editions: ACO 2.4, p. 41; PL 54.917–18.

Letter 83, JK 463 'Multam mihi fiduciam'

Date: 9 June, 451

Recipient: Marcian Augustus

Contents: Leo commends Lucentius a bishop and Basilius a presbyter to Marcian. They have been sent to Constantinople and are to receive penitent heretics. Leo wishes for the synod to be at a different time because bishops in places ravaged by war will not be able to travel.

In the following collections: Hispana, Hispana Gallica, Hispana Gallica Augustodunensis, all of Pseudo-Isidore (**I-a**, **I-b**, **I-c**, **Y**), Grimanica, Ratisbonensis, **Y-a**, Milanese collection, Vat. Ross. 159, B22, B23, B24, **73**, Eugenius IV

Editions: ST 15, *Ep.* 26 (pp. 65–67); ACO 2.4, 42–43; PL 54.919–21.

Letter 84, JK 464 'Religiosam pietatis'

Date: 9 June, 451

Recipient: Pulcheria Augusta

Contents: Leo commends his *legati* to her. Eutychianism is to be eliminated just like Nestorianism, wherever it may be—remove Eutyches from Constantinople so he won't pull others down with him, and replace him with a catholic abbot.

In the following collections: Casinensis, Ps.-Is. C, Grimanica, Ratisbonensis

Editions: ST 15, *Ep.* 27; ACO 2.4, pp. 43–44; PL 54.921–22.

Letter 85, JK 465 'Licet sperem dilectionem'

Date: 9 June, 451

Recipient: Anatolius of Constantinople

Contents: Leo urges Anatolius to be zealous and to act together with his *legati* so that neither benevolence nor justice will be neglected. Anatolius should receive those who were led to heresy out of fear, but the authors of impiety are to be reserved for the more mature judgement of the Apostolic See.

In the following collections: Casinensis, Hispana, Hispana Gallica, Hispana Gallica Augustodunensis, all of Pseudo-Isidore (**I-a**, **I-b**, **I-c**, **Y**), Grimanica, Ratisbonensis, **Y-a**, Milanese collection, Vat. Ross. 159, B22, B23, B24, **73**, Eugenius IV, Grimanica

Editions: ST 15, *Ep.* 28 (pp. 70–73); ACO 2.4, 44–45; PL 54.922–24.

Letter 86, JK 466 'Quam gratum mihi'

Date: 9 June, 451

Recipient: Julian of Cos

Contents: Leo urges Julian to aid his *legati* in the destruction of heresy through penitence.

In the following collections: Grimanica, Ratisbonensis

Editions: ST 15, *Ep.* 29 (p. 73); ACO 2.4, p. 42; PL 54.924–25.

Letter 87, JK 467 'Ad declinandam erroris'

Date: 19 June, 451

Recipient: Anatolius of Constantinople

Contents: Leo commends Basilius and John, presbyters, to Anatolius. By these men, both Nestorianism and Eutychianism were condemned at Rome.

In the following collections: Casinensis, Ps.-Is. C, Collection of Vat. lat. 1322, Grimanica

Editions: ACO 2.4, p. 45; PL 54.926.

Letter 88, JK 468 'Quamuis non dubitem'

Date: 24 June, 451

Recipient: Paschasinus, Bishop of Lilybaeum

Contents: Leo is sending Paschasinus a copy of the *Tome* and patristic testimonia to which all monasteries at Constantinople with many bishops and all bishops of Antioch have subscribed. He asks about the date of Easter, 455.

In the following collections: Grimanica, Ratisbonensis

Editions: ST 15, *Ep.* 30 (pp. 74–76); ACO 2.4, pp. 46–47; PL 54.927–29.

Letter 89, JK 469 'Credebamus, clementiam'

Date: 26 (ST, PL 54) or 24 (ACO 2.4) June, 451 (cf. ACO 2.4 p. 48, app. crit. *l.* 6)

Recipient: Marcian Augustus

Contents: Leo has sent Boniface the presbyter and Julian the bishop to join Paschasinus as his envoys at the council held at a time contrary to his wishes. He wants Paschasinus to preside at the council so that the catholic faith can hold strong.

In the following collections: Casinensis, Ps.-Is. C, Collection of Vat. lat. 1322, Grimanica

Editions: ST 15, *Ep.* 31b (pp. 79–80); ACO 2.4, pp. 47–48; PL 54.930–31.

Letter 90, JK 470 'Poposceram'

Date: 26 June, 451

Recipient: Marcian Augustus

Contents: Leo agrees to the council being held and asks for the faith not to be discussed as though doubtful.

In the following collections: Hispana, Hispana Gallica, Hispana Gallica Augustodunensis, all of Pseudo-Isidore (**I-a, I-b, I-c, Y**), Grimanica, Ratisbonensis, **Y-a**, Milanese collection, Vat. Ross. 159, B22, B23, B24, **73**, Eugenius IV

Editions: ST 15, *Ep.* 30 (pp. 77–78); ACO 2.4, p. 48; PL 54.932–34.

Letter 91, JK 471 'Cognita clementissimi'

Date: 26 June, 451

Recipient: Anatolius of Constantinople

Contents: Leo is amazed that the emperor is holding the council with such haste. Many bishops could not be summoned from various provinces.

In the following collections: Grimanica, Ratisbonensis

Editions: ST 15, *Ep.* 32 (p. 81); ACO 2.4, p. 49; PL 54.934–35.

Letter 92, JK 472 'Quid de dilectionis'

Date: 26 June, 451

Recipient: Julian of Cos

Contents: Leo gives Julian the mandate to support his *legati* at the council.

In the following collections: Grimanica, Ratisbonensis

Editions: ST 15, *Ep.* 33 (p. 82); ACO 2.4, p. 49; PL 54.936.

Letter 93, JK 473 'Optaueram quidem' 'ἐμοὶ μὲν'

Date: 26 June, 451

Recipient: Council to be gathered at Nicaea (Council of Chalcedon)

Contents: Although invited by the emperor, Leo cannot come, but will preside over the proceedings through his *legati*. He warns them not to acquiesce to the rejected boldness against the faith which out neither to be defended nor believed. He encourages them to embrace the *Tome* and take care to reinstate the exiled catholic bishops.

In the following collections: Quesnelliana (incl. Oriel College MS), Hispana, Hispana Gallica, Hispana Gallica Augustodunensis, all of Pseudo-Isidore (**I-a**, **I-b**, **I-c**, **Y**), Grimanica, Bobbiensis, Ratisbonensis, Collection of Vat. lat. 1322, Vallicelliana 18, **Y-a**, Milanese collection, Vat. Ross. 159, B22, B23, B24, **73**, Eugenius IV, Greek Collections M B H.

Editions: ST 15, *Ep.* 34 (pp. 83–84); ACO 2.4, 51–52 (Latin), ACO 2.1, 31–32 (Greek); PL 54.935–39 (Latin), 936–42 (Greek).

There are MS difficulties set out in PL 54.569–70 par. 36.

Letter 94, JK 474 'Sanctum clementiae uestrae'

Date: 20 July, 451

Recipient: Marcian Augustus

Contents: Leo encourages Marcian to remove the impiety of the few in the synod, not to admit any dispute nor to allow the foundations of the faith to seem infirm or doubtful.

In the following collections: Casinensis, Ps.-Is. C, Grimanica, Bobbiensis, Ratisbonensis, Collection of Vat. lat. 1322, B24, **73**

Editions: ST 15, *Ep.* 35 (pp. 85–86); ACO 2.4, pp. 49–50; PL 54.941–42.

Letter 95, JK 475 'Religiosam clementiae uestrae'

Date: 20 July, 451

Recipient: Pulcheria Augusta

Contents: Leo wishes the penitent heretics to be treated mercifully at the council, unlike how Catholics were treated 'in illo Ephesino non iudicio sed latricinio'—the first calling of Eph2 a 'latricinium'.

In the following collections: Ps.-Is. C, Florentina, Grimanica, Bobbiensis, Ratisbonensis, B24

Editions: ST 15, *Ep.* 36 (pp. 86–89); ACO 2.4, pp. 50–51; PL 54.942–44.

Letter 96, JK 477 'Ad praecipuum'

Date: July 451

Recipient: Ravennius of Arles

Contents: Leo requests Ravennius to celebrate Easter on 23 March in 452 since there should be no diversity in celebrating the feast.

In the following collections: Undetermined. Sirmond edited this letter from a manuscript of Bonneval, and the Ballerini reprinted his edition (PL 54.945, n. *b*). What manuscript this was remains a mystery.

Editions: PL 54.945.

Letter 97, 'Reuersis, Domino annuente'

Date: August or September 451 (PL 54.945, n. *c*)

Recipient: Leo of Rome from Eusebius, Bishop of Milan

Contents: Eusebius is glad that his fellows are back from the East. The *Tome* was read and signed at a Milanese synod; he and his bishops agree to the condemnation of Eutyches.

In the following collections: Oriel College MS of Quesnelliana, Ps.-Is. A1, Yale Pseudo-Isidore, **Y-a**, Vat. Ross. 159, B23, **73**, Eugenius IV

Editions: PL 54.945–50.

Letter 98, 'Repletum est gaudio' 'ἐπλήσθη χαρᾶς'

Date: Early November 451 (PL 54.951, n. *a*)

Recipient: Leo of Rome from the bishops at Chalcedon

Contents: Leo is congratulated for maintaining Catholic truth; Dioscorus' misdeeds are recounted; Eutyches has been deposed; they request that Leo ratify Canon 28 which his *legati* opposed.

In the following collections: Early Latin Acta (**Ac**), Vat. Ross. 159, Greek *Acta*

Editions: ACO 2.1, pp. 475–77 (Greek), ACO 2.3, pp. 355–60 (Latin); PL 54.951–60 (Latin), 952–60 (Greek), 959–65 (another Latin version).

Letter 99, 'Perlata ad nos'

Date: December 451 (PL 54.965, n. *c*)

Recipient: Leo of Rome from Ravennius of Arles

Contents: All the bishops of Gaul have received the *Tome* as the truth of the faith.

In the following collections: Oriel College MS of Quesnelliana, Ps.-Is. A1, Yale Pseudo-Isidore, **Y-a**, Vat. Ross. 159, B23, B24, **73**, Eugenius IV

Editions: PL 54.966–70.

Letter 100, 'Diuina humanaque scripta' Ἀἱ θεῖαι καὶ'

Date: 18 December, 451

Recipient: Leo of Rome from Marcian Augustus (& Valentinian III)

Contents: Marcian rejoices that the faith was restored at Chalcedon where the faith of the *Tome* was received. He asks for Constantinople to become second patriarchate, following Rome. He has asked Lucianus and Basilius for his consent in this matter.

In the following collections: Thessalonicensis, Greek Collection B

Editions: ST 23, *Ep.* 17 (pp. 46–47); ACO 2.1, pp. 251–52 (Greek), ACO 2.4, pp. 167–68 (Latin); PL 54.970–72 (Latin), 971–73 (Latin translation of Ballerini), 972–74 (Greek).

Letter 101, 'Vestrae sanctitatis zelus' Τῆς μὲν ὑμετέρας'

Date: December 451 (PL 54.975, n. *a*)

Recipient: Leo of Rome, from Anatolius of Constantinople

Contents: Anatolius approves Leo's zeal against heresy and mentions acts of Chalcedon gathered at Rome; his *legati* are bringing more. He speaks of Dioscorus' condemnation and says that the *Tome* was received by all as was the definition of faith produced at Chalcedon. He notes other business at Chalcedon after the definition, especially the privilege of Constantinople, the confirmation of which he seeks.

In the following collections: Greek Collection B

Editions: ACO 2.1, pp. 248–50 (Greek); PL 54.975–83 (Ballerini Latin), 976–84 (Greek original).

Letter 102, JK 479 'Optassemus quidem'

Date: 27 January, 452

Recipient: Various Gallic bishops, including Ravennius and Rusticus

Contents: Leo is glad that they approve of the heavenly teaching. Leo expounds on fleeing from Nestorian and Eutychian error. Dioscorus was condemned at Chalcedon, and Leo is expecting his own *legati*.

In the following collections: Ps.-Is. C, Grimanica, Bobbiensis, Ratis-bonensis, B24, **73**

Editions: ST 20, *Ep.* 44 (pp. 116–19); ACO 2.4, 53–54; PL 54.983–88.

Letter 103, JK 480 'Impletis per'

Date: February 452 (PL 54.987, n. *l*)

Recipient: Bishops of Gaul

Contents: Acts of Chalcedon have been gathered by Leo's *legati*, and he rejoices that the synod assented with him about the incarnation. Leo includes a copy of the sentence against Dioscorus and his associates.

In the following collections: Corbeiensis, Coloniensis, Ps.-Is. C

Editions: ACO 2.4, pp. 155–56; PL 54.988–92.

Letter 104, JK 481 'Magno munere' 'Μεγάληι χάριτι'

Date: 22 May, 452

Recipient: Marcian Augustus

Contents: Leo responds to Marcian, rejoicing at the extinction of error at Chalcedon but grieving over the ambition of Anatolius contrary to the ecclesiastical privileges established at Nicaea whereby he damages the dignity of Antioch.

In the following collections: Quesnelliana (incl. Oriel College MS), Thessalonicensis, Hispana, Hispana Gallica, Hispana Gallica Augustodunensis, all of Pseudo-Isidore (**I-a**, **I-b**, **I-c**, **Y**), Grimanica, Bobbiensis, Ratisbonensis, Lanfranc, **Y-a**, Milanese collection, Vat. Ross. 159, B22, B23, B24, **73**, Eugenius IV, Greek Collection B.

Editions: ST 20, *Ep.* 37 (pp. 93–97); ACO 2.4, pp. 55–57 (Latin), ACO 2.1.2, pp. 58–60/254–56 (Greek); PL 54.991–97 (Latin), 992–98 (Greek).

Further notes: ST replaces *Lucianus* with *Lucensius* in this letter and in *Ep.* 107. Hunt 1957 disagrees (181, n. 9).

Letter 105, JK 482 'Sanctis et Deo'

Date: 22 May, 452

Recipient: Pulcheria Augusta

Contents: Leo writes of the victory of the faith and the arrogance of Anatolius, which goes counter to the canons and ancient custom. This will cause trouble amongst the bishops.

In the following collections: Casinensis, Ps.-Is. C, Grimanica, Bobbiensis, Ratisbonensis, B24, **73**

Editions: ST 20, *Ep.* 38 (pp. 97–100); ACO 2.4, pp. 57–59; PL 54.997–1002.

Letter 106, JK 483 'Manifestato, sicut' 'Φανερωθέντος'

Date: 22 May, 452

Recipient: Anatolius of Constantinople

Contents: Leo values Anatolius' catholic faith but is harsh towards him over his abuses at Chalcedon, grieving that Anatolius has fallen into this situation, breaking the most holy canons of Nicaea and damaging the privileges of Antioch and Alexandria.

In the following collections: Quesnelliana (incl. Oriel College MS), Thessalonicensis, Hispana, Hispana Gallica, Hispana Gallica Augustodunensis, all of Pseudo-Isidore (**I-a**, **I-b**, **I-c**, **Y**), Grimanica, Ratisbonensis, Lanfranc, **Y-a**, Milanese collection, Vat. Ross. 159, B22, B23, B24, **73**, Eugenius IV, Vallicelliana 18, Greek Collection B.

Editions: ST 20, *Ep.* 39 (pp. 100–05); ACO 2.4, pp. 59–62 (Latin); ACO 2.1.2, 56–58/252–54 (Greek); PL 54.1001–1009 (Latin), 1002–1010 (Greek).

Letter 107, JK 484 'Cum frequentibus' (In some older edd., opens with, 'Dilectio tua', due to a misreading of the MS evidence [cf. PL 54.1009 n. *g*])

Date: 22 May, 452

Recipient: Julian of Cos

Contents: Leo reproves Julian because he sent him a letter on behalf of Anatolius of Constantinople

In the following collections: Grimanica, Ratisbonensis, B23

Editions: ST 20, *Ep.* 40 (pp. 105–06); ACO 2.4, p. 62; PL 54.1009–1010.

Letter 108, JK 485 'Sollicitudinis quidem tuae'

Date: 11 June, 452

Recipient: Theodore, Bishop of Forum Iulii (Fréjus)

Contents: Leo responds to Theodore concerning the status of penitents, first telling him to observe the hierarchy and go to his metropolitan first in the future.

In the following collections: Frisingensis Prima, Diessensis, Quesnel-liana, Oriel College MS 42, Hispana, Hispana Gallica, Hispana Gallica Augustodunensis, all of Pseudo-Isidore (**I-a**, **I-b**, **I-c**, **Y**), Dionysiana adaucta, Lanfranc, **Y-a**, Milanese collection, Vat. Ross. 159, B22, B23, B24, **73**, Vat. lat. 1343, Vat. lat. 202

Editions: PL 54.1011–1014.

Letter 109, JK 486 'Grauia sunt et'

Date: 25 November, 452

Recipient: Julian of Cos

Contents: Leo responds to Julian that the mobs of Palestinian monks are to be put down, that the emperor is to be moved to do something about it. Leo includes a copy of a letter from Athanasius to Epictetus which Cyril used against Nestorius at Eph1. Leo grieves for Juvenal of Jerusalem's calamity.

In the following collections: Ratisbonensis

Editions: ST 20, *Ep.* 43 (pp. 113–15); ACO 2.4, 137–38; PL 54.1014–1018.

Further notes: For *Ad Epictetum*, see ACO 1.5, pp. 321–34; PL 56.664–73.

Letter 110, 'Beatitudinem tuam ualere' 'Τὴν μακαριότατα τὴν'

Date: 15 February, 453

Recipient: Leo of Rome, from Valentinian III and Marcian Augusti

Contents: The emperors seek the necessary confirmation of Chalcedon from Leo and praise his constancy in protecting the canons and attacking innovations.

In the following collections: Greek Collection B.

Editions: ACO 2.1.2, p. 61/257 (Greek); PL 54.1017–1019 (Latin translation of Ballerini), 1018–1020 (Greek).

Letter 111, JK 487 'Quam excellenti'

Date: 10 March, 453

Recipient: Marcian Augustus

Contents: Anatolius has wrongly removed Aetius from archdiaconate and replaced with Andrew, a Eutychian. Leo urges Marcian to prevent Anatolius from such plots and commends Julian of Cos to him.

In the following collections: Casinensis, Ps.-Is. C, Grimanica, Bobbiensis, B24, **73**

Editions: ACO 2.4, pp. 62–64; PL 54.1019–1023.

Further notes: Silva-Tarouca 1931, 183, thinks it spurious

Letter 112, JK 488 'Multis exstantibus'

Date: 10 March, 453

Recipient: Pulcheria Augusta

Contents: As *Ep.* 111.

In the following collections: Ps.-Is. C, Grimanica, Bobbiensis, B24, **73**

Editions: ACO 2.4, pp. 64–65; PL 54.1023–1024.

Further notes: Silva-Tarouca 1931, 183, thinks spurious

Letter 113, JK 489 'Agnoui in dilectionis'

Date: 11 March, 453

Recipient: Julian of Cos

Contents: Leo praises Julian for relating to him ill deeds and encourages him to keep watching out for more impiety and heresy in Constantinople. He requests a letter on the causes of Palestinian and Egyptian monastic rebellion and on the state of Egypt.

In the following collections: Ps.-Is. C, Grimanica, Bobbiensis, B24, **73**, Bobbiensis, Grimanica

Editions: ACO 2.4, pp. 65–67; PL 54.1024–1028.

Further notes: Silva-Tarouca 1931, 183, thinks spurious

Letter 114, JK 490 'Omnem quidem fraternitatem' 'Πᾶσαν μὲν'

Recipient: Bishops who were at Chalcedon

Contents: Leo agrees to Chalcedon's defence of the truth but not its abrogation of the laws of Nicaea.

In the following collections: Quesnelliana (incl. Oriel College MS), Ps.-Is. A1, Yale Pseudo-Isidore, Rusticus' Acta, **Y-a**, B22, B23, B24, **73**, Eugenius IV, Greek Collection B.

Editions: ST 20, *Ep.* 41 (pp. 106–08); ACO 2.4, 70–71 (Latin), ACO 2.1.2, pp. 61–62/257–58 (Greek); PL 54.1027–1031 (Latin), 1028–1032 (Greek).

Letter 115, JK 491 'Multa mihi in omnibus' 'Πολλή μοι'

Date: 21 March, 453

Recipient: Marcian Augustus

Contents: Leo lets Marcian know of the letter sent to the bishops of Chalcedon. He praises his instructions concerning the monks and commends Julian of Cos to him.

In the following collections: Hispana, Hispana Gallica, Hispana Gallica Augustodunensis, all of Pseudo-Isidore (**I-a**, **I-b**, **I-c**, **Y**), Grimanica, Ratisbonensis, **Y-a**, Milanese collection, Vat. Ross. 159, B22, B23, B24, **73**, Greek Collection B.

Editions: ST 20, *Ep.* 45 (pp. 120–22); ACO 2.4, pp. 67–68 (Latin), 2.1.2, pp. 62–63/258–59 (Greek); PL 54.1031–1035 (Latin), 1032–1036 (Greek).

Letter 116, JK 492 'Quamuis nunc'

Date: 21 March, 453

Recipient: Pulcheria Augusta

Contents: Leo is pleased that something is being done about the rebellious monks and lets her know about his letter to the Chalcedonian bishops.

In the following collections: Casinensis, Ps.-Is. C, Grimanica, Ratisbonensis

Editions: ST 20, *Ep.* 46 (pp. 122–23); ACO 2.4, 69–70; PL 54.1035–1037.

Letter 117, JK 493 'Quam uigilanter'

Date: 21 March, 453

Recipient: Julian of Cos

Contents: Leo is sending Julian two copies of the letter he'd sent to the bishops from Chalcedon. One is attached to his letter to Anatolius, and the other is to be distributed to priests in the provinces. Leo is glad that Marcian and Pulcheria have done something about the Palestinian monks; he himself has called Eudocia back to orthodoxy. Julian should bear his injuries with a light spirit. It seems that Anatolius of Constantinople is intervening in Illyricum (the entirety of which Leo considers under his jurisdiction by old custom).

In the following collections: Grimanica, Ratisbonensis

Editions: ST 20, *Ep.* 47 (pp. 123–26); ACO 2.4, pp. 69–70; PL 54.1037–1039.

Letter 118, JK 494 'Litteras dilectionis tuae'

Date: 2 April, 453

Recipient: Julian of Cos

Contents: Leo encourages Julian to rouse Marcian to take real action against the Palestinian monks.

In the following collections: Ps.-Is. C (B12), VGCAC, B24, **73**, Bobbiensis, Grimanica

Editions: ACO 2.4, pp. 71–72; PL 54.1039–1040.

Further notes: Silva-Tarouca 1931, 183, thinks this spurious

Letter 119, JK 495 'Quantum dilectioni tuae'

Date: 11 June, 453

Recipient: Maximus, Bishop of Antioch

Contents: Leo write of the Nestorians and Eutychians, of Antioch's ecclesiastical privileges not being diminished, of preserving Nicene laws, and of his letter Anatolius.

In the following collections: Vaticana, Dionysiana adaucta, Kues & Holkham **Y-a**, Ps.-Is. C, Grimanica, Ratisbonensis, Ambrosiana C.50.inf, Milanese collection

Editions: ST 20, *Ep.* 42 (pp. 108–12); ACO 2.4, pp. 72–75; PL 54.1040–1046.

Letter 120, JK 496 'Remeantibus ad nos'

Date: 11 June, 453

Recipient: Theodoret of Cyrrhus

Contents: Leo commands Theodoret to reject the idea that the mystery of the incarnation is returned to earth. He expounds on both Nestorians and Eutychians and says that they are to be shunned and condemned.

In the following collections: Ps.-Is. A1, Yale Pseudo-Isidore, Grimanica, **Y-a**, B22, B23, B24, Eugenius IV

Editions: ST 20, pp. 169–75; ACO 2.4, pp. 78–81; PL 54.1046–1055.

Further notes: Silva-Tarouca 1931, 183, thinks it spurious.

Letter 121, JK 497 'Tam multis documentis'

Date: 15 June, 453

Recipient: Marcian Augustus

Contents: Dissension has arisen about the date of Easter. Leo wants Marcian to look into this.

In the following collections: Ps.-Is. C, Grimanica, Bobbiensis, Ratisbonensis, B24, **73**

Editions: ST 20, *Ep.* 48 (pp. 126–28); ACO 2.4, 75–76; PL 54.1055–1058.

Letter 122, JK 498 'De paschali'

Date: 15 June, 453

Recipient: Julian of Cos

Contents: Leo urges Julian to encourage the emperor to determine the date of Easter 455

In the following collections: Ps.-Is. C, Grimanica, Bobbiensis, Ratisbonensis, B24

Editions: ST 20, *Ep.* 49 (pp. 128–29); ACO 2.4, pp. 76–77; PL 54.1058–1060.

Letter 123, JK 499 'Quanta mihi catholicae'

Date: 15 June, 453

Recipient: Eudocia Augusta

Contents: Leo urges Eudocia to move the Palestinian monks back to orthodoxy

In the following collections: Ps.-Is. C, Grimanica, Bobbiensis, Ratisbonensis, B24, **73**

Editions: ST 20, *Ep.* 50 (pp. 130–31); ACO 2.4, p. 77; PL 54.1060–1061.

Letter 124, JK 500 'Sollicitudini meae, quam'

Date: *c.* 15 June, 453

Recipient: Palestinian monks

Contents: This letter contains Leo's recasting of two-nature Christology using 'substantia' over 'natura' as a way to reconcile Palestinian monks to Chalcedon and the *Tome*, which he understands to be circulating in a falsified version. The content is much the same as *Ep.* 165 without the *testimonia*.

In the following collections: Quesnelliana (incl. Oriel College MS), Ps.-Is. A1, Yale Pseudo-Isidore, Florentina, Lanfranc, B20, **Y-a**, B22, B23, B24, **73**, Eugenius IV

Editions: ACO 2.4, pp. 159–63; PL 54.1061–1068.

Letter 125, JK 501 'Saepissime dilectionem' 'Frequentissime' (Canisius 1546)

Date: 25 June, 453

Recipient: Julian of Cos

Contents: Leo chides Julian for not sending letters—he wants to know about the situation in the East.

In the following collections: Ps.-Is. C, Grimanica, Bobbiensis, B24, **73**

Editions: ACO 2.4, p. 78; PL 54.1068–1069.

Letter 126, JK 502 'Geminis clementiae'

Date: 9 January, 454

Recipient: Marcian Augustus

Contents: Leo congratulates Marcian for adhering to catholic teaching. He praises God for the final return of the Palestinian monks to orthodoxy—he prays for such a case in Egypt.

In the following collections: Grimanica, Ratisbonensis

Editions: ST 20, *Ep.* 51 (pp. 131–32); ACO 2.4, pp. 81–82; PL 54.1069–1070.

Letter 127, JK 503 'Christianissimi principis;

Date: 9 January, 454

Recipient: Julian of Cos

Contents: Leo lets Julian know of the letter he'd sent to the emperor (*Ep.* 126), and notes that he has accepted the letter of Proterius of Alexandria, and that it is full of faith. He advises Julian to take care concerning the date of Easter 455.

In the following collections: Ps.-Is. C (B12), Ratisbonensis, B24, **73**, Bobbiensis, Grimanica

Editions: ST 20, *Ep.* 52 (pp. 132–34); ACO 2.4, pp. 82–83; PL 54.1070–1073.

Letter 128, JK 504 'Si quantum uestra'

Date: 9 March, 454

Recipient: Marcian Augustus

Contents: Leo says that he will show favour to Anatolius and make friendship if Anatolius puts aside his ambition and association with heretics and answers his letters.

In the following collections: Grimanica, Bobbiensis

Editions: ST 20, *Ep.* 57 (pp. 144–46); ACO 2.4 p. 86; PL 54.1073–1074.

Letter 129, JK 505 'Laetificauerunt me'

Date: 10 March, 454

Recipient: Proterius of Alexandria

Contents: Leo responds to Proterius that he should watch carefully lest souls are led into heresy. He should teach the people, and there is nothing new in Leo's writings, just old things passed down from the Fathers.

In the following collections: Grimanica, Ratisbonensis, **73**

Editions: ST 20, *Ep.* 55 (pp. 140–43); ACO 2.4, 84–86; PL 54.1075–1078.

Letter 130, JK 506 'Puritatem fidei'

Date: 10 March, 454

Recipient: Marcian Augustus

Contents: Leo rejoices that Marcian favours Proterius and lets him know of his letter (*Ep.* 129). He requests that the *Tome*, which had been falsified by heretics, be translated into Greek by Julian of Cos or someone else suitable and sent to Alexandria with the imperial seal on it.

In the following collections: Hispana, Hispana Gallica, Hispana Gallica Augustodunensis, all of Pseudo-Isidore (**I-a**, **I-b**, **I-c**, **Y**), Grimanica, Bobbiensis, Ratisbonensis, **Y-a**, Milanese collection, Vat. Ross. 159, B22, B23, B24, **73**

Editions: ST 20, *Ep.* 54 (pp. 138–40); ACO 2.4, pp. 83–84; PL 54.1078–1080.

Letter 131, JK 507 'Sumptis fratris et'

Date: 10 March, 454

Recipient: Julian of Cos

Contents: Leo advises Julian about the *Tome*'s translation into Greek and wishes to know what the answer of the emperor was concerning the date of Easter 455.

In the following collections: Grimanica, Ratisbonensis

Editions: ST 20, *Ep.* 56 (pp. 143–44); ACO 2.4, p. 87; PL 54.1081–1082.

Letter 132, 'Omne quidem solacium'

Date: *c.* April, 454 (PL 54.1081 n. *f*)

Recipient: Leo of Rome, from Anatolius of Constantinople

Contents: Anatolius laments that he gets no letters while others do. He has restored Aetius and deposed Andrew. He says he has no ambition, and has published in the East Leo's approval of the *Gesta Chalcedonensia*.

In the following collections: Thessalonicensis

Editions: ST 23, *Ep.* 21 (pp. 48–50); PL 54.1082–1084.

Letter 133, 'Piissimus et fidelissimus'

Date: a little after 4 April, 454

Recipient: Leo of Rome, from Proterius of Alexandria

Contents: The date of Easter, 455, in Roman calendars is wrong. Proterius gives proof for 24 April, the Eastern date.

In the following collections: Oriel College MS of Quesnelliana

Editions: PL 54.1084–1094.

Further notes: See PL 54.1084 n. *j* concerning the two Latin translations of this letter.

Letter 134, JK 508 'Quod saepissime'

Date: 15 April, 454

Recipient: Marcian Augustus

Contents: Leo will show favour to Anatolius once Anatolius repents. Eutyches should be exiled further off, and Leo is still waiting on the correct date for Easter, 455.

In the following collections: Hispana, Hispana Gallica, Hispana Gallica Augustodunensis, all of Pseudo-Isidore (**I-a**, **I-b**, **I-c**, **Y**), Grimanica, **Y-a**, Milanese collection, Vat. Ross. 159, B23, B24, **73**

Editions: ACO 2.3, pp. 87–88; PL 54.1094–1096.

Letter 135, JK 509 'Si firmo incommutabilique'

Date: 29 May, 454

Recipient: Anatolius of Constantinople

Contents: Leo responds to *Ep.* 132. He praises Anatolius for reinstating Aetius. The lapsed are only to be taken up if they condemn their error.

In the following collections: Quesnelliana (incl. Oriel College MS), Thessalonicensis, Ps.-Is. A1, Yale Pseudo-Isidore, Ps.-Is. C, Florentina, Grimanica, **Y-a**, B22, B23, B24, **73**, Eugenius IV

Editions: ST 23, *Ep.* 22 (pp. 51–53); ACO 2.4, 88–89; PL 54.1096–1098.

Letter 136, JK 510 'Litterarum clementiae'

Date: 29 May, 454

Recipient: Marcian Augustus

Contents: Leo informs Marcian of his letter to Anatolius (*Ep.* 135) and requests him not to endure the condemned heresy of the monk Carosus being defended at Constantinople.

In the following collections: Thessalonicensis, Grimanica, Ratisbonensis

Editions: ST 20, *Ep.* 56 (pp. 143–44); ACO 2.4, p. 87; PL 54.1098–1100.

Letter 137, JK 511 'Sollicitudinem meam'

Date: 29 May, 454

Recipient: Marcian Augustus

Contents: Leo thanks Marcian for looking into the Easter matter which Proterius has made more certain for him. He then entreats Marcian that stewards of churches of Constantinople not be tried in public courts.

In the following collections: Grimanica

Editions: ACO 2.4, p. 89; PL 54.1100–1101.

Further notes: Silva-Tarouca 1931, 183, thinks it is spurious.

Letter 138, JK 512 'Cum in omnibus'

Date: 28 July, 454

Recipient: All the bishops in Gaul and Spain

Contents: Leo tells them that 24 April is the date for Easter in 455

In the following collections: Oriel College MS of Quesnelliana, Ps.-Is. C

Editions: PL 54.1101–1102.

Letter 139, JK 514 'Acceptis dilectionis tuae' 'Δεξάμενος'

Date: 4 September or 6 February 454 (ST 20, unlike PL & ACO, gives the date 'prid. non. <*feb.*>' with the note, 'Ita emandandum puto *Sep* codicis *M*, maxime cum epistula hic suo loco inserta videatur' [p. 137, n. *k*].)

Recipient: Juvenal of Jerusalem

Contents: Leo congratulates Juvenal on his restoration but is grieved when he recalls Juvenal's past as the cause of the troubles. He encourages Juvenal to stay in the faith.

In the following collections: Vaticana, Quesnelliana (incl. Oriel College MS), Corbeiensis, Pithouensis, Dionysiana adaucta, Ps.-Is. A1, Yale Pseudo-Isidore, Ps.-Is. C, Grimanica, Ratisbonensis, **Y-a**, B22, B23, B24, Eugenius IV, Vat. Reg. lat. 293, Greek Collection B.

Editions: ST 20, *Ep.* 53 (pp. 134–37); ACO 2.4, 91–93 (Latin); ACO 2.1.2, pp. 63–65/259–61 (Greek); PL 54.1101–1107 (Latin), 1104–1110 (Greek).

Letter 140, JK 515 'Litteras dilectionis tuae'

Date: 6 December, 454

Recipient: Julian of Cos

Contents: Leo hopes that with Dioscorus dead heresy can be more easily removed. He wishes to know more about affairs in Alexandria.

In the following collections: Grimanica

Editions: ACO 2.4, pp. 93–94; PL 54.1109–1110.

Letter 141, JK 516 'Per filium meum'

Date: 11 March, 455

Recipient: Julian of Cos

Contents: Leo inquires about Carosus, who had returned to the faith, and continues to avoid/shun communion with Anatolius. He also asks to be informed of the outcome of an embassy to Egypt undertaken by a certain John, and of the status of Maximus of Antioch.

In the following collections: Grimanica

Editions: ACO 2.4, pp. 94–95; PL 54.1110.

Further notes: Silva-Tarouca 1931, 183, thinks it spurious

Letter 142, JK 517 'Quanta sit in uestra'

Date: 13 March, 455

Recipient: Marcian Augustus

Contents: Leo lets Marcian know about the receiving of the date of Easter for 455 in the West. He is pleased that Carosus and Dorotheus, heretical monks, are in exile.

In the following collections: Grimanica, Ratisbonensis

Editions: ST 20, *Ep.* 58 (pp. 147–48); ACO 2.4, p. 95; PL 54.1110–1111.

Letter 143, JK 518 'Curae esse dilectioni'

Date: 13 March, 455

Recipient: Anatolius of Constantinople

Contents: Leo encourages Anatolius to get rid of the rest of the heretics in Constantinople.

In the following collections: Grimanica, Ratisbonensis

Editions: ST 20, *Ep.* 59 (p. 148); ACO 2.4, p. 94; PL 54.1111–1112.

Letter 144, JK 520, 'Gratias Deo, quod'

Date: 1 June, 457

Recipient: Julian of Cos

Contents: Leo is pleased that Eutychianism, softened by the Emperor Marcian, might be destroyed. He adds that uncertain men are telling things about actions dared at Alexandria.

In the following collections: Ratisbonensis, Collection of Vat. lat. 1322

Editions: ST 20, *Ep.* 60 (pp. 148–49); ACO 2.4, p. 138; PL 54.1112–1113.

Letter 145, JK 521 'Officiis, quae ad'

Date: 11 July, 457

Recipient: Leo I Augustus

Contents: Leo Episcopus encourages Leo Augustus to defend the church of Alexandria then stirred up by heretics, and that a catholic bishop should be installed there who would protect Chalcedonian decrees.

In the following collections: Vaticana, Casinensis, Dionysiana adaucta, Kues & Holkham **Y–a**, Ps.-Is. C, Grimanica, Ratisbonensis, Ambrosiana C.50.inf, Milanese collection

Editions: ST 20, *Ep.* 61 (pp. 150–51); ACO 2.3, pp. 95–96; PL 54.1113–1115.

Letter 146, JK 522 'Satis claret'

Date: 11 July, 457

Recipient: Anatolius of Constantinople

Contents: Leo responds to Anatolius with a notification that he had commended the church in Alexandria to the emperor.

In the following collections: Grimanica, Ratisbonensis

Editions: ST 20, *Ep.* 62 (pp. 151–52); ACO 2.4, p. 96; PL 54.1115.

Letter 147, JK 523 'Quamuis dudum'

Date: 11 July, 457

Recipient: Julian of Cos

Contents: Leo scolds Julian about the lack of letters from him and discusses matters at Alexandria.

In the following collections: Grimanica, Ratisbonensis

Editions; ST 20, *Ep.* 63 (pp. 152–53); ACO 2.4, p. 98; PL 54.1116.

Letter 148, JK 524 'Licet proxime'

Date: 1 September, 457

Recipient: Leo I Augustus

Contents: Leo Episcopus thanks Leo Augustus that he has professed himself to the guardian of peace in the world and of the Council of Chalcedon.

In the following collections: Casinensis, Ps.-Is. C, Ratisbonensis, Grimanica

Editions: ST 20, *Ep.* 64 (138–40); ACO 2.4, p. 98; PL 54.1117–1118.

Letter 149, JK 526 'Ordinationem quidem'

Date: 1 September, 457

Recipient: Basilius, Bishop of Antioch

Contents: Leo urges Basilius to resist Eutychianism, the madness that killed Proterius in Alexandria. He praises Leo Augustus for his support of Chalcedon.

In the following collections: Grimanica, Ratisbonensis

Editions: ST 20, *Ep.* 65 (pp. 155–56); ACO 2.4, pp. 97–98; PL 54.1119–1121.

Further notes: PL 54.1117–1118 notes that this and *Ep.* 150 are transmitted as a single letter in Ratisbonensis, but as two in Grimanica. Presumably these are different transmissions of the same circular sent East. ST 20, *Ep.* 65 based on Ratisbonensis, gives the single letter, letting the reader know where the

Ep. 149's independent material ends and *Ep.* 150 begins, as does ACO 2.4, pp. 97–98, based on Grimanica.

Letter 150, JK 525 'Cognitis, quae apud'

Date: 1 September, 457

Recipient: Exitheus of Thessalonica, Juvenal of Jerusalem, Peter of Corinth, Luke of Dyrrhachium

Contents: As *Ep.* 149 about Eutychians in Alexandria.

In the following collections: Grimanica, Ratisbonensis

Editions: ST 20, *Ep.* 65 (p. 155 l. 13-p. 156); ACO 2.4, p. 98 ll. 3–25; PL 54.1120–1121.

Further notes: See notes on *Ep.* 149 for the relationship between the two.

Letter 151, JK 529 'Fidem dilectionis tuae'

Date: 1 September, 457

Recipient: Anatolius of Constantinople

Contents: Leo advises Anatolius to maintain catholic purity and to either remove or correct Atticus, a heretical presbyter.

In the following collections: Ratisbonensis

Editions: ST 20, *Ep.* 66 (p. 157); ACO 2.4, 138–39; PL 54.1121–1122.

Letter 152, JK 527 'Existente occasione'

Date: 1 September, 457

Recipient: Julian of Cos

Contents: Leo commits Julian to take care that his earlier letter (*Epp.* 149–50) reaches its addressees. Notes his surprise at those who calumniate the *Tome*, a document which pleased the whole world; this calumniation makes the *Tome* appear obscure and in need of exposition.

In the following collections: Grimanica, Ratisbonensis

Editions: ST 20, *Ep.* 67 (pp. 157–58); ACO 2.4, *Ep.* 93, p. 99; PL 54.1122–1123.

Letter 153, JK 528 'Accepimus dilectionis'

Date: 1 September 457

Recipient: Aetius the Presbyter in Constantinople

Contents: Leo commands Aetius to send copies of his letter (*Epp.* 149–50) to the bishops of Antioch and Jerusalem. Leo also sends copies of letters from the bishops of Gaul (*Ep.* 99) and Italy (*Ep.* 97) so Aetius may know that western bishops agree with Leo's teachings.

In the following collections: Grimanica, Ratisbonensis

Editions: ST 20, *Ep.* 68 (pp. 158–59); ACO 2.4, *Ep.* 94, pp. 99–100; PL 54.1123–1124.

Letter 154, JK 530 'Licet laboribus'

Date: 11 October, 457

Recipient: Bishops of Egypt in exile at Constantinople

Contents: Leo consoles them and orders them to have hope. He is writing to the emperor to give him thanks for having taken them up humanely.

In the following collections: Grimanica

Editions: ACO 2.4, *Ep.* 98, pp. 104–05; PL 54.1124–1125.

Further notes: Silva-Tarouca 1931, 183, thinks spurious

Letter 155, JK 531 'Diligentiam necessariae'

Date: 11 October, 457

Recipient: Anatolius of Constantinople

Contents: Leo lets Anatolius know about the letter he sent to Egyptians (*Ep.* 154) and encourages him to be vigilant against heretics and their supporters.

In the following collections: Quesnelliana (incl. Oriel College MS), Ps.-Is. A1 (B11), **Y-a**, B22, B23, B24, **73**, Eugenius IV, Grimanica

Editions: ACO 2.4, *Ep.* 95, p. 100; PL 54.1125–1128.

Letter 156, JK 532 'Litteras clementiae tuae'

Date: 1 December, 457

Recipient: Leo I Augustus

Contents: Although he desires it, Leo Episcopus cannot visit Leo Augustus. He encourages him not to allow for retraction on things established at Chalcedon and that he should attempt to reconcile with Church of Alexandria, a 'spelunca latronum'. Heretics should be exiled from Constantinople and Leo commends Julian of Cos to the emperor.

In the following collections: Casinensis, Ps.-Is. C (B12), Grimanica, Codex Encyclius

Editions: ACO 2.4, *Ep.* 97, pp. 101–04; PL 54.1127–1132.

Letter 157, JK 534 'Rursus acceptis'

Date: December, 457

Recipient: Anatolius of Constantinople

Contents: Leo writes to Anatolius about troubles in Alexandria, asks him to write something about Atticus and Andrew, heretics in Constantinople.

In the following collections: Grimanica

Editions: ACO 2.4, pp. 109–10; PL 54.1132–1134.

Further notes: Silva-Tarouca 1931, 183, considers this letter suspect

Letter 158, JK 533 'Olim me commissorum'

Date: 1 December, 457

Recipient: Egyptian Bishops exiled in Constantinople

Contents: Leo exhorts them to be in good spirits and advises them to encourage the emperor to defend their common faith.

In the following collections: Grimanica

Editions: ACO 2.4, pp. 104–05; PL 54.1134–1135.

Further notes: Silva-Tarouca 1931, 183, considers it suspect

Letter 159, JK 536 'Regressus ad nos' – 'Decretal'

Date: 21 March, 458

Recipient: Nicetas, Bishop of Aquileia

Contents: The wife of a captured man who has remarried must, if her husband returns, go back to her first husband; people who ate sacrificial meat by force are not to be denied penitence; people baptised by heretics do not need to re-baptised but only get hands laid on them.

In the following collections: Frisingensis Prima, Diessensis, Teatina, Vaticana, Quesnelliana (incl. Oriel College MS), Dionysiana, Cresconius, Sancti Mauri, Ragyndrudis Codex, Dionysio-Hadriana, Epitome Hispana, Hispana, Hispana Gallica, Hispana Gallica Augustodunensis, all of Pseudo-Isidore (**I-a, I-b, I-c, Y**), Florentina, Bobbiensis, Lanfranc, **Y-a**, Milanese collection, Vat. Ross. 159, B22, B23, B24, **73**

Editions: PL 54.1135–1140.

Letter 160, JK 537 'Tribulationem, quam'

Date: 21 March, 458

Recipient: Bishops and clergy of Alexandria exiled at Constantinople

Contents: Leo hopes they will be restored, lets them know he has sent a *legatus* to the emperor. He encourages them not to allow the faith to be battled against.

In the following collections: Grimanica

Editions: ACO 2.4, pp. 107–08; PL 54.1140–1142.

Further notes: Silva-Tarouca 1931, 183, thinks suspect

Letter 161, JK 538 'Laetificatus ualde sum'

Date: 21 March, 458

Recipient: Presbyters, deacons, clerics of Constantinople

Contents: Leo urges them to preserve the catholic faith, that the decrees of Chalcedon are not to be violated, and Atticus and Andrew the Eutychians are to be corrected or removed.

In the following collections: Grimanica

Editions: ACO 2.4, *Ep.* 101, pp. 108–09; PL 54.1142–1143.

Further notes: Silva-Tarouca 1931, 183, considers it suspect

Letter 162, JK 539 'Multo gaudio mens'

Date: 21 March, 458

Recipient: Leo I Augustus

Contents: Leo Episcopus tells Leo Augusts that he is sending *legati* who will demonstrate what the rule of the apostolic faith is lest there be conflict with enemies of the faith since the affairs of Nicaea and Chalcedon ought not to be questioned.

In the following collections: Ps.-Is. A1, Yale Pseudo-Isidore, Ps.-Is. C, Grimanica, Ratisbonensis, **Y-a**, B22, **73**, Eugenius IV

Editions: ST 20, *Ep.* 72 (pp. 165–68); ACO 2.4, pp. 105–07; PL 54.1143–1146.

Letter 163, JK 540 'Lectis dilectionis tuae'

Date: 23 March, 458

Recipient: Anatolius of Constantinople

Contents: Leo answers Anatolius about being wary of heretics and asks for Atticus to be made to read a public statement condemning Eutyches.

In the following collections: Oriel College MS of Quesnelliana, Yale Pseudo-Isidore, Ps.-Is. C, Florentina, Lanfranc, B20, **Y-a**, B22, **73**, Eugenius IV

Editions: ACO 2.4, p. xxxxiiii; PL 54.1146–1148.

Letter 164, JK 541 'Multis manifestisque'

Date: 17 August (Grimanica, ACO, JK, PL 54) or 1 September (Ratisbonensis, Casinensis, ST), 458

Recipient: Leo I Augustus

Contents: Leo Episcopus commends to Leo Augustus Domitianus and Geminianus, his *legati*. Questionings of Chalcedon's integrity are not allowed. He encourages the emperor to free the Church of Alexandria and establish a catholic bishop there and reinstate exiled bishops.

In the following collections: Casinensis, Grimanica, Ratisbonensis

Editions: ST 20, *Ep.* 69 (pp. 160–64); ACO 2.4, pp. 110–12; PL 54.1148–1152.

Letter 165, JK 542 The 'Second' *Tome* 'Promisisse me' 'Ὑποσό-μενον'

Date: 17 August, 458

Recipient: Leo I Augustus

Contents: Leo Episcopus explains Eutyches' and Nestorius' errors to Leo Augustus, then expounds upon the incarnation at length with much the same content as *Ep.* 124. Then he appends patristic *testimonia*.

In the following collections: Vaticana, Quesnelliana (incl. Oriel College MS), Corbeiensis, Pithouensis, Hispana, Hispana Gallica, Hispana Gallica Augustodunensis, all of Pseudo-Isidore (**I-a, I-b, I-c, Y**), Florentina, Dionysiana adaucta, Codex encyclius, Grimanica, Ratisbonensis, B20, **Y-a**, Milanese collection, Vat. Ross. 159, B22, B23, B24, **73**, Ambrosiana C.50.inf, Vat. Reg. lat. 293, Paris lat. 3848b (*testimonia* only), Orsini's codex

Editions: ST 9, pp. 44–58 (letter), 34–43 (*testimonia*); ACO 2.4, pp. 113–31 (Latin); *Abhandlung d. Bayer. Ges. d. Wiss.* 32 (1927), 52–62 (Greek), ACO 2.1.1, pp. 20–25 (Greek *testimonia*); PL

54.1155–1173 (letter in Latin), 1156–1174 (letter in Greek), 1173–1190 (*testimonia*, Latin only).

Letter 166, JK 543 'Frequenter quidem'

Date: 24 October, 458

Recipient: Neon, Bishop of Ravenna

Contents: Leo says that, based on a recent synod, those returning from captivity amongst heretics who were taken when young and do not know if they were baptised are to be baptised. Those baptised by heretics are to be received by the laying on of hands.

In the following collections: Oriel College MS of Quesnelliana, Epitome Hispana, Hispana, Hispana Gallica, Hispana Gallica Augustodunensis, all of Pseudo-Isidore (**I–a**, **I–b**, **I–c**, **Y**), Lanfranc, **Y–a**, Milanese collection, Vat. Ross. 159, B22, B23, B24, **73**

Editions: PL 54.1191–1196.

Letter 167, JK 544 'Epistolas fraternitatis' – 'Decretal'

Date: 458–59?

Recipient: Rusticus, Bishop of Narbonne

Contents: Leo answers a series of questions from Rusticus on a wide range of issues, including episcopal elections, penance, marriage of clergy, monks and nuns returning to the world, heretical baptisms, and pagan feasts.

In the following collections: Diessensis, Teatina, Vaticana, Sanblasiana, Quesnelliana (incl. Oriel College MS), Dionysiana, Cresconius, Remensis, Dionysio-Hadriana, Hadriano-Hispanica, Epitome Hispana, Hispana, Hispana Gallica, Hispana Gallica Augustodunensis, all of Pseudo-Isidore (**I–a**, **I–b**, **I–c**, **Y**), Florentina, Bobbiensis, **Y–a**, Milanese collection, Vat. Ross. 159, B22, B23, B24, **73**, Verona 58, Verona LIX (57).

Editions: PL 54.1197–1209.

Letter 168, JK 545 'Magna indignatione' – 'Decretal'

Date: 6 March, 459

Recipient: All the bishops in Campania, Samnium, and Picenum

Contents: Leo informs them that they should baptise only in the seasons of Easter and Pentecost. They should not publish the written confessions of the faithful.

In the following collections: Sancti Mauri, Oriel College MS of Quesnelliana, Epitome Hispana, Hispana, Hispana Gallica,

Hispana Gallica Augustodunensis, all of Pseudo-Isidore (**I-a**, **I-b**, **I-c**, **Y**), Lanfranc, **Y-a**, Milanese collection, Vat. Ross. 159, B22, B23, B24, **73**

Editions: PL 54.1209–1211.

Letter 169, JK 546 'Si gloriosum pietatis'

Date: 17 June, 460

Recipient: Leo I Augustus

Contents: Leo Episcopus congratulates Leo Augustus on expelling Timothy Aelurus from Egypt. Care should be taken in placing a new catholic bishop in Alexandria.

In the following collections: Avellana

Editions: CSEL 35, *Ep.* 51 (pp. 117–19); PL 54.1212–1214.

Letter 170, JK 547 'Dilectionis tuae litteris'

Date: 17 June, 460

Recipient: Gennadius, Bishop of Constantinople

Contents: Leo complains to Gennadius that Timothy Aelurus had been allowed to go to Constantinople. Timothy's presence and speech should be fled, and Gennadius should take care to place a catholic bishop over the Church of Alexandria.

In the following collections: Avellana

Editions: CSEL 35, *Ep.* 52 (pp. 119–20); PL 54.1214–1215.

Letter 171, JK 548 'Euidenter apparet'

Date: 18 August, 460

Recipient: Timothy Wobblecap (Salophakiolus), Bishop of Alexandria

Contents: Leo writes to the new bishop of Alexandria congratulating him on his election and encouraging him to destroy the traces of Nestorian and Eutychian error. He asks him to write often.

In the following collections: Avellana

Editions: CSEL 35, *Ep.* 53 (pp. 120–21); PL 54.1215–1216.

Letter 172, JK 549 'Gaudeo exultanter'

Date: 18 August, 460

Recipient: Presbyters and deacons of Alexandria

Contents: Leo encourages them to preserve peace and concord and to restore heretics through penance.

In the following collections: Avellana

Editions: CSEL 35, *Ep.* 54 (pp. 121–22); PL 54.1216–1217.

Letter 173, JK 550 'Litteris fraternitatis uestrae'

Date: 18 August, 460

Recipient: Theophilus, John, Athanasius, Abraham, Daniel, Joahas, Paphnutius, Musaeaus, Panulvius, and Peter, Egyptian Bishops

Contents: Leo encourages them to help their newly-consecrated bishop, Timothy Wobblecop, in destroying scandal.

In the following collections: Avellana

Editions: CSEL 35, *Ep.* 55 (pp. 123–24); PL 54.1217–1218.

Cyril of Alexandria about Easter 444(?) (fragment)

Date: 443?

Recipient: Leo of Rome?

Contents: A discussion of the date of Easter and its calculation, a duty that belonged to the Bishop of Alexandria.

Collections: Paschal works of Dionysius Exiguus.

Edition: PL 54.601–06.

Further notes: The Ballerini are uncertain whether this letter was sent to Leo, although they believe it likely (PL 54.597–602). Something similar was sent to Africa as well. For this reason, they did not give it a number with the rest of the epistles. However, since it sheds light on Leo, *Ep.* 3, they included it in their edition just prior to that letter.

Two *libelli appellationis*: Two more items sent to Leo can be added to this corpus; these are the *libelli appellationis* from Flavian of Constantinople on the one hand and Eusebius of Dorylaeum on the other.

In the following collection: Novariensis is the only known source for these texts.

Editions: Amelli in *S. Leone Magno e l'Oriente*, 1882; Mommsen 1886, 362–68; ACO 2.2.1, 77–81.

The sacred letter of Marcian and Valentinian, 'Omnibus rebus oportet'. It is transmitted in Latin and Greek; the Greek manuscripts include Leo as a recipient although Schwartz deleted the inclusion of Leo's name in his edition.

462 — CONSPECTUS OF THE LETTERS OF POPE LEO I

In the following collections: *Versio Gestorum Chalcedonensium antiqua correcta*, Rusticus' *Acta*, Greek Collections M B H

Editions: ACO 2.3.1, p. 20 (Latin), ACO 2.1.1, pp. 27–28 (Greek).

7.2 Lost Letters of Leo (Arranged by JK Reference)

JK 400

Date: 442?

Recipient: Cyril of Alexandria

Subject: Date of Easter, 444

JK 401

Date: 442?

Recipient: Paschasinus of Lilybaeum

Subject: Date of Easter, 444

JK 413

Date: 447

Recipients: Bishops of Tarragona, Carthaginiensis, Lusitania, and Gallaecia

Subject: Priscillianism

JK 419

Date: 448

Recipient: Bassianus, Bishop of Ephesus

Subject: Leo condemns Bassianus for having been ordained outside canon law.

JK 476

Date: 451

Recipients: Paschasinus of Lilybaeum, Lucensius, and Boniface, Leo's legates

Subject: Theodoret of Cyrrhus is to be returned to communion

JK 478

Date: 451

Recipient: Eusebius of Milan

Subject: Leo sends a copy of *Ep.* 28 and lets Eusebius know that legates are going to the council in the East.

JK 496a

Date: 453

Recipient: Proterius of Alexandria

Subject: Date of Easter 455

JK 513

Date: 454

Recipients: The Britons.

Subject: A copy of *Ep.* 138 about the date of Easter 455

JK 519

Date: 457

Recipient: Leo I Augustus

Subject: Leo congratulates him on his accession.

Further notes: This is based on references in *Ep.* 145.

7.3 Known Spuria (Arranged by JK Reference)

JK † 446 'Quali pertinacia'

Alleged date: 450

Recipients: Bishops of the Gauls and Viennensis

Contents: Hilarius of Arles, who has fled Leo's judgement against him, is to have the privileges of Arles removed and transferred to Vienne.

In the following collections: Edited by Quesnel from a manuscript of Fleury. In *Collectio Caesaraugustana, c.* 1120.

Editions: PL 54.1237–1238.

Further notes: See PL 54.1235–1238 for arguments against its authenticity.

JK † 551 'Cum in Dei nomine'

Undated

Recipients: Bishops of the Germanies and Gauls

Contents: *Chorepiscopi* have been being consecrated and performing various sacramental duties contrary to the canons.

In the following collections: **S–ga**, **I–a**, **I–c**, **Y**, **Y–a**, Lanfranc, Oriel College MS 42, **22**, **73** Used by Ivo of Chartres,

Edition: PL 54.1238.

Further notes: Given that this letter appears no earlier than the *Hispana Gallica Augustodunensis*, a collection associated with the Pseudo-Isidorian forgeries, it may cautiously be ventured that it is one of their products. Its interest in *chorepiscopi* makes its later date evident.

'Tantam saeculi potestates'

Date: 453–61

Recipients: Sarmatio, Chariato, Desiderius, Bishops, from Leo of Bourges, Victorius of Le Mans, and Eustochius of Tours

Contents: Bishops should not be tried by secular courts for ecclesiastical/canonical offences.

In the following collections: Pithouensis (attrib. correctly to Leo of Bourges), **I–c** (attrib. to Leo the Great).

Editions: *Concilia Galliae*, ed. C. Munier, CCSL 148 (Turnhout, 1963), p. 136; PL 54.1239–1240; PL 130.922. NB: There is a forthcoming critical edition by Steven Schoenig, S. J., 'An Erased Canon and Roman Law in the Collectio Britannica'.[1]

Further notes: From Hincmar of Reims to the early editions of Leo the Great's letters, this was considered a text by the pope until Jacques Sirmond proved it was not by him in 1629 by finding its earliest attestation in *Collectio Pithouensis*. Unfortunately for the fate of this letter, it is mostly neglected as a *spurium*, despite being an authentic letter by Leo of Bourges and thus worthy of attention from scholars of the fifth century.

Sententia Papae Leonis de apocryphis Scripturis

This undated text is a combination of material from Leo, *Ep* 15, and spurious material.

In the following manuscripts: Rome, Biblioteca Vallicelliana T.XVIII and B.58; Vat. Pal. lat. 277.

Edition: PL 54.1239–1242.

Finally, there are three Greek fragments attributed to Leo, edited by the Ballerini in PL 54.1257–1262.

---

[1] My thanks to Charles West for showing me his work that uses this text and points the reader in its direction; Charles West, 'Pope Leo of Bourges, Clerical Immunity and the Early Medieval Secular', forthcoming.

Conclusion

This study has shown that Leo's letters were read and copied and reorganised time and again throughout the Middle Ages. For the later period, after the ninth century and even into the fifteenth, the *Collectio Hispana* (**S**, see 3.2.u) proved to be the most influential through the descendants of Pseudo-Isidore (**I**, see 5.2.f), even if modern scholars are often more interested in the work of early collections such as *Quesnelliana* (**Q**, see 3.2.c). Of the early collections, however, *Dionysiana* (**D**, see 3.2.f) is the most widespread and influential through the medium of the *Dionysio-Hadriana* (**D–h**, see 5.2.a) and its use by the various strands of Pseudo-Isidore (**I**). In fact, in Pseudo-Isidore (**I**), *Hispana* (**S**) and the *Dionysio-Hadriana* (**D–h**) come together. In the later collections, we also see the trend emerging of gathering as many letters as could come to hand—thus **I–c** and Ballerini Collection 24 (**24**) take their **S/D–h** base and bring in letters from *Grimanica* (**G**, see 4.1.g) and/or *Bobbiensis* (**B**, see 5.3.a) or even **Q**. The process of transmission, then, is not straightforward. We do not have a single corpus of letters descended from a single letter collection but many corpora born from many collections, extracted, rearranged, and amplified time and again as history progressed. A full stemma, which will not be attempted here, would look like a spider's web; it would probably require computer software to render it in three dimensions.

What we have seen in this book, however, is more than just a wildly contaminated tradition of interrelated collections and interrelated manuscripts, sometimes owned by people who knew each other. We have seen Leo the Great's position in the intellectual history of western Europe. First, we saw Leo himself in the Later Roman Empire with his own flurry of activity that generated not only so many letters but a legacy of such force that recipients kept and circulated those letters. This activity of Leo and his correspondents and archivists led on the one hand to his incorporation into books of canon law, and on the other to theological controversies guaranteeing him a readership and his letters survival and compilation into theological and canonical collections. The era of

codification, encyclopaedism, and compilation of the early sixth
century also helped ensure his transmission into the Merovingian
Age, and the Carolingians copied Leo in abundance, whether creating the second-largest of his letter collections (Pseudo-Isidore C,
I-c), or copying the sole manuscript of the largest (*Collectio Grimanica*, **G**)—his two-nature Christology found readers amongst
the Carolingians, as did his statements on canon law—and from
there, every time there was a cultural mixture of reform, renewal,
and 'Renaissance', Leo was amongst the authors copied, quoted,
and compiled.

He may have been called *magnus* because of his theology,
ensuring that his letters, especially the *Tome*, were copied and
re-copied, from the Carolingians to the attendees of the Council
of Ferrara-Florence, yet his greatness in terms of legacy comes
particularly through canon law, and thus his letters were gathered
and copied from the Carolingians to the high mediaeval reformers
and on through the later Middle Ages. The copyists of the majority of these manuscripts do not concern themselves overmuch with
the distinction, so important to the modern reader, between decretal and dogmatic letter. Both are copied and compiled together,
and Leo finds readers amongst kings such as Charlemagne, Bene-
dictines such as William of Malmesbury, Lanfranc and Anselm,
Cistercians throughout northern France, Lateran canons, and cardinals such as Nicholas of Cusa and Bessarion. Popes read him,
quoted him, and sought to emulate him, as did their advisers and
supporters. By studying these manuscripts, we gain a glimpse into
the readers as well. The story, then, needs its final chapters, and
Leo his new readers.

The case for the new edition has already been made in Chapter
2. With such a diverse array of texts, manuscripts, contaminations, and variants, it seems that an eclectic text is the only way
to move forward in editing—but an eclectic text with a proper,
full apparatus. The most important collections for the transmission of Leo's letters and for editing the text are as follows. The
main basis for editing Leo's letters will be those late fifth- and
early sixth-century collections (**Q**, **Te**, **Sa**, **C**, **P**, **D**, **Re**), as well
as *Hispana* (**S**) because of its influence, *Grimanica* (**G**) because of
its quality, size, and rarities, and *Ratisbonensis* (**E**, see 5.3.b) for
the same reasons as **G**. From these collections will come both the

earliest and best readings. The study of the tradition of the *Diony-siana* (**D**) must include the expanded versions in *Dionysiana Bobi-ensis* (**D–b**) and *Dionysio-Hadriana* (**D–h**). The collation of **S** and **I** will take into account the readings of **S–ga**, that intermediate text that grew from **S** and is the parent of **I**. Because of the rari-ties and unique items they include, the canonical collections *Thes-salonicensis* (**T**), *Arelatensis* (**Ar**), *Albigensis* (**Al**), and *Avellana* are also foundational for making a text and crucial for transmitting the entire surviving corpus of letters.

All of the major Chalcedonian collections are important for studying the transmission of Leo's text and redacting it—that is, Ballerini Collection 17 (**Ac**), the early Latin *Acta* (**A**), Rusticus' *Acta* (**Ru**), the old corrected version of the conciliar *acta* (**Ch**), the *Collectio Novariensis* (**N**), and *Collectio Grimanica* (**G**).

Later collections and manuscripts are not unimportant, of course. This is especially true for the earliest Pseudo-Isidore (**I**) manuscripts, the rare letters in the *Dionysiana adaucta* (**D–a**), William of Malmesbury, **24**, and **73**. Given how thin the trans-mission of certain letters in these collections is, and given the uniqueness of William's collection, they are worth considering in rendering Leo's text. On the other hand, there are later collections that are important because of their position in transmitting and propagating Leo's letters. The most important are **21** due to its popularity, and readings from Eugenius IV's collection because of who owned it. These are worth recording because of the story they tell, not necessarily because they cast light on Leo himself. As a Dante scholar remarked to this author on a train, when he reads Augustine, he does not want what Augustine *himself* said, but what Dante read. A balance must, therefore, be struck between overburdening the reader with notes and leaving too sparse an apparatus.

In an ideal world, one of the best ways to edit these letters would not be on paper but on-screen. Since they exist in so many different arrangements with variant readings, it is almost impos-sible to edit them according to collection. However, by program-ming them into a digital edition, the reader would have at his or her disposal the ability to change both the context of each letter and its readings based upon the letter collection desired. If such could be done for the whole corpus of pre-Carolingian papal letters, the task of studying and analysing decretals and their place in canon law would become much clearer than it is now, when we must rely upon old editions scattered about, often with imperfect apparatuses, or databases, or simply descriptions of these collections in books. With this tool at our disposal, we could see not just a list of which letters go together in the collections, but their contents and readings as well. Why did the compiler put these two or three together here? What story does each collection tell? That said, I believe there is still ample room for a traditional, printed codex of Leo's letters.

Finally, one important aspect of editing Leo's letters that we have not properly considered in this study is the question of *spuria*. Space did not allow treatment, but that such exist should be well known. Even in the Ballerini's day, JK † 446 and † 551 had been identified as pseudepigrapha.[2] Künstle argued that *Ep.* 15 was spurious; however, I disagree with his judgement.[3] Silva-Tarouca argued for the spuriousness of a large number of Leo's letters: *Epp.* 43, 74, 111, 112, 113, 118, 120, 137, 141, and 154.[4] I have not yet done a proper assessment of whether these letters are spurious or not; it would require an analysis of both the style and content of the letters, as well as an examination of Silva-Tarouca's historical contextualisation. For example, his reconstruction of *Ep.* 43's spurious origin hinges upon Theodosius II being the lackey of Chrysaphius, a theory now under scrutiny by the work of George Bevan.[5] Nonetheless, even if Silva-Tarouca is proven right, it is essential, in my mind, to edit the *spuria* alongside Leo's letters, but flag them for the reader; they have been read as his for centuries and deserve a good edition as well. If Nicholas of Cusa or William of Malmesbury read a text as Leo's, we should ourselves have access to it today.

[2] See PL 54.1237.
[3] See Künstle 1905, 117–26.
[4] See Silva-Tarouca 1931, 183.
[5] Bevan 2005, 405.

Appendix

Proto-Collections Analysed in This Book

proto-1: *Epp.* 28, 103, 31, 35, 139, 59, 165. Used by the *Collectiones Corbeiensis* (**C**), *Pithouensis* (**P**), and *Coloniensis* (**K**, omits *Ep.* 139)

proto-2: *Epp.* 4, 7, 15. Used by the *Collectiones Corbeiensis* (**C**), *Pithouensis* (**P**), and *Albigensis* (**Al**); *Quesnelliana* (**Q**) and *Dionysiana* (**D**) also include *Epp.* 4 and 7 in sequence but without *Ep.* 15, and **Q** without the same inscription as the rest

proto-3: *Epp.* 15, 16, 159, 1, 2. Used by the *Collectiones Teatina* (**Te**), *Diessensis* (**Di**), and *Remensis* (**Re**)

proto-4: *Epp.* 20, 23, 22, 28. Used by the *Collectiones Vaticana* (**L**), *Hispana* (**S**), and *Dionysiana adaucta* (**D-a**)

proto-5: *Epp.* 139, 119, 80, 145, 165. Used by the *Collectiones Vaticana* (**L**) and *Dionysiana adaucta* (**D-a**)

Bibliography

Primary Sources

Acts of the Council of Chalcedon. Ed. E. Schwartz. Greek *Acta* in ACO 2.1, Latin versions in ACO 2.2 (partial) and 2.3 (complete, Rusticus' *Acta*). Trans. R. Price and M. Gaddis. 2005–2007. *Acts of the Council of Chalcedon*. 3 vols. Liverpool.

Ad gallos episcopos. Ed. Y.-M. Duval. 2004. *La décrétale* Ad Gallos Episcopos: *son texte et son auteur*. Leiden.

Anselm of Canterbury. *Monologion*. Ed. F. S. Schmitt. 1946. In *Opera Omnia*, vol. 1, 1–88. Edinburgh.

Basil of Caesarea. Letters. Ed. Y. Courtonne. 2003. *Saint Basile. Correspondance*. Vol. 3. Paris.

Benedictus Levita. Ed. G. Schmitz. Online via MGH: http://www.benedictus.mgh.de/haupt.htm. Accessed 2 June 2015.

Biblia Sacra iuxta Vulgatam Versionem. Ed. R. Weber and R. Gryson. 2007. Fifth edition. Stuttgart.

Boniface. *Letters*. Ed. E. Dümmler. MGH Epist. III.230–433. Trans. E. Emerton. 2000. New York.

Capitularia Regum Francorum, vol. 1. Ed. A. Boretius. 1883. MGH Leges III.

Capitula Angilramni. Ed. K.-G. Schon. 2006. *Die Capitula Angilramni: eine prozessrechtliche Fälschung Pseudoisidors*. Hannover. Available online: http://www.pseudoisidor.mgh.de/html/capitula_angilramni.html. Accessed 2 June 2015.

Cassian, John. *Institutiones*. Ed. M. Petschenig, CSEL 17.

—. *De Incarnatione contra Nestorium*. Ed. M. Petschenig. CSEL 17.

Cassiodorus. *Chronicon*. Ed. T. Mommsen, MGH *Chronica Minora*, vol. 2: 109–61.

Charlemagne. *Admonitio Generalis*. Ed. A. Boretius, MGH, *Capitularia regum Francorum*, vol. 1, 53–62. Trans. P. D. King. 1987. In *Charlemagne: Translated Sources*, 209–20. Lambrigg.

Chronicon Paschale. Ed. L. A. Dindorf. 1832. Bonn. Trans. M. and M. Whitby. 1989. Liverpool.

Collectio Danieliana. Ed. K.-G. Schon. 2006. *Unbekannte Texte aus der Werkstatt Pseudoisidors: die Collectio Danieliana*. Hannover.

Collectio Vetus Gallica. Ed. H. Mordek. 1975. *Kirchenrecht und Reform im Frankreich. Die Collectio Vetus Gallica, die älteste systematische Kanonessammlung des fränkischen Gallien. Studien und Edition.* Berlin.

Constantine VII Porphyrogenitus. *De Administrando Imperio.* Ed. G. Moravcsik, trans. R. J. H. Jenkins. 1967. 2nd edition. Washington, DC.

Cresconius. *Concordia canonum.* Ed. K. Zechiel-Eckes. 1992. *Die Concordia canonum des Cresconius: Studien und Edition.* 2 volumes. Frankfurt.

Cyprian of Carthage. *Epistulae.* Ed. G. F. Diercks. 1994–1996. Turnhout. CCSL 3B and 3C.

Cyril of Alexandria. 'Laetentur Caeli' (*Ep.* 39). Ed. E. Schwartz, ACO 1.1.4, 15–20. Trans. J. I. McEnerney. 1987. In *Letters 1–50*, 147–52. Washington, DC.

—. *Select Letters.* Ed. and trans. L. R. Wickham. 1983. Oxford. Including the Second and Third Letters to Nestorius, 2–33.

—. *Quod Unus Sit Christus.* Ed. G. M. de Durand. 1964. In *Deux Dialogues Christologiques*, 302–515. Paris. Trans. J. A. McGuckin. 1995. *On the Unity of Christ.* Crestwood, N.Y.

Damasus of Rome, *Epigraphic Poetry.* Ed. D. Trout. 2015. *Damasus of Rome: The Epigraphic Poetry.* Oxford.

Demetrius. *On Style.* Ed. P. Chiron. 1993. *Démétrios: Du Style.* Paris.

Deusdedit. *Liber canonum.* Ed. V. W. von Glanvell. 1905. *Die Kanonessammlung des Kardinals Deusdedit.* Paderborn; repr. Aalen 1967. Dedicatory letter, trans. Robert Somerville and Bruce C. Brasington. 1998. *Prefaces to Canon Law Books in Latin Christianity: Selected Translations, 500–1245*, 122–29. New Haven.

Dionysius Exiguus. *Libellus de cyclo magno Paschae.* Ed. Br. Krusch. 1938. *Studien zur christlich-mittelalterlichen Chronologie*, vol. 2, 63–74. Berlin.

—. *Argumenta paschalia.* Ed. Br. Krusch. 1938. *Studien zur christlich-mittelalterlichen Chronologie*, vol. 2, 23–31. Berlin.

—. 'Epistula ad Bonifatium primicerium et Bonum secundicerium de ratione Paschae'. Ed. Br. Krusch. 1938. *Studien zur christlich-mittelalterlichen Chronologie*, vol. 2, 82–86. Berlin.

—. Prefaces. CCSL 87:31–51.

—. *Codex canonum ecclesiasticorum Dionysii Exigui.* Ed. C. Justel, 1628 and 1643. Paris. Repr. *Bibliotheca iuris canonici veteris* 1, ed. G. Voellius and H. Justellus, 1661. Paris. See also PL 67.137–316.

Eadmer of Canterbury. *Historia Novorum.* Ed. M. Rule. 1884. London.

Einhard. *The Life of Charlemagne.* Ed. O. Holder-Egger. 1911. MGH S.S. rer. Germ. 25. Trans. D. Ganz. 2008. In *Two Lives of Charlemagne,* 15–44. Harmondsworth.

Evagrius Scholasticus. *Ecclesiastical History.* Ed. J. Bidez and L. Parmentier. 2011. Paris. Trans. M. Whitby. 2000. Liverpool.

Eusebius of Caesarea. *Vita Constantini.* Ed. and trans. Av. Cameron and S. G. Hall. 1999. *Eusebius, Life of Constantine.* Oxford.

Facundus of Hermiane. *Pro Defensione Trium Capitulorum Libri XII.* Ed. I.-M. Clément and R. Vander Plaetse. CCSL 90A:1–398.

Faith in Formulae: A Collection of Early Christian Creeds and Creed-related Texts, 4 vols. Ed. W. Kinzig. 2017. Oxford.

Fulgentius of Ruspe. *Epistulae.* CCSL 91.

The Gallic Chronicle of 452. Ed. R. W. Burgess. 2001. In *Society and Culture in Late Antique Gaul,* ed. R. Mathisen, 52–84. Aldershot.

The Gallic Chronicle of 511. Ed. R. W. Burgess. 2001. In *Society and Culture in Late Antique Gaul,* ed. R. Mathisen, 85–100. Aldershot.

Gennadius of Constantinople. *Die Texte.* Ed. F. Diekamp. 1938. In *Analecta Patristica: Textue und Abhandlungen zur griechischen Patristik,* 73–84. Rome.

Gratian. *Decretum.* Ed. E. Friedberg. 1870. *Corpus Iuris Canonici, Pars Prior: Decretum Magistri Gratiani.* Leipzig.

Gregory of Nyssa. Letters. Ed. P. Maraval. 1990. *Grégoire de Nysse. Lettres, introduction, texte critique, traduction, notes et index.* SC 363.

Gregory of Tours. *History of the Franks.* Ed. B. Krusch and W. Levison. MGH SS Merov. rer. 1.1. Trans. L. Thorpe. 1974. Harmondsworth.

Gregory VII. *Registrum Epistolarum.* Ed. E. Caspar. MGH Epp. sel. 2,1–2. Trans. H. E. J. Cowdrey. 2002. *The Register of Pope Gregory VII, 1073–1085.* Oxford.

Hadrian I, Pope. *Epistulae.* Ed. W. Gundlach in *Codex Carolinus,* MGH Epist. 1, 469–657.

History and Hagiography from the Late Antique Sinai. Ed. and trans. D. F. Caner, 2010. Liverpool.

Honoratus of Marseille. *La Vie d'Hilaire d'Arles.* Ed. P.-A. Jacob. SC 404.

Hydatius. *Chronicle.* Ed. and trans. R. W. Burgess. 1993. *The Chronicle of Hydatius and the Consularia Constantinopolitana.* Oxford.

Isidore of Seville. *Etymologiae*. Ed. W. M. Lindsay. 1911. Oxford. Trans. S. A. Barney, W. J. Lewis, J. A. Beach, and O. Berghof. 2006. *Etymologies*. Cambridge.

Ivo of Chartres. *Prologue*. Ed. B. C. Brasington. 2004. *Ways of Mercy: The Prologue of Ivo of Chartres*. Münster.

Jerome of Stridon. *Epistulae*. Ed. I. Hilberg, vol. 1 & 2. CSEL 54, 55.

John Cassian. *See* Cassian, John.

John Moschus. *See* Moschus, John.

John Rufus. *See* Rufus, John.

Justinian. 'Edict on the Three Chapters'. Ed. E. Schwartz. 1939. In *Drei dogmatische Schriften Justinians*, 47–69. Munich. Trans. K. P. Wesche, 1991. *On the Person of Christ: The Christology of Emperor Justinian*, 161–98. Crestwood, N.Y.

—. Edict 'On the Orthodox Faith'. Ed. E. Schwartz. 1939. In *Drei dogmatische Schriften*, 72–111. Munich. Trans. Richard Price. 2009. *The Acts of the Council of Constantinople of 553*, 122–59. Liverpool.

Lactantius. *De Mortibus persecutorum*. Ed. J. L. Creed. 1984. Oxford.

Landulphus Sagax. *Historia Miscella*. Ed. F. Eyssenhardt. 1868. Berlin.

Lanfranc of Bec/Canterbury. *The Monastic Constitutions of Lanfranc*. Ed. and trans. D. Knowles, rev. C. N. L. Brooke. 2002. Oxford.

—. *Epistulae*. Ed. H. Clover and M. Gibson. 1979. *The Letters of Lanfranc Archbishop of Canterbury*. Oxford.

Leo the Great. *Episulae*. Ed. P. and G. Ballerini. PL 54.

—. *Sermones*. Ed. A. Chavasse. CCSL 148. Selection in *Select Sermons of S. Leo the Great*. 2nd edition. Trans. W. Bright. 1868. London.

Liber Pontificalis. Ed. L. Duchesne, 1886. Paris.

Liberatus of Carthage. *Breviarium*. Ed. E. Schwartz, ACO 2.5, 98–141.

Lucretius Carus, T. *De rerum natura*. Ed. W. H. D. Rouse, rev. M. F. Smith. 1982. Cambridge, MA.

Maier, I. 2012. *Latin Imperial Laws and Letters (A.D. 306–565) not Included in the Codes and Novels of Theodosius and Iustinianus*. Melbourne 2012. Online: https://www.notitiadignitatum.org/extracod. pdf. Accessed 23 September 2021.

Mansi, G. D. 1759–1798. *Sacrorum Conciliorum Nova et Amplissima Collectio*. 31 vols. Florence.

Martínez Diez, G., ed. 'El Epítome Hispánico. Una colección canónica Española del siglo VII', *Miscelanea Comillas* 37.2 (1962):322–466.

Moschus, John. *Pratum Spirituale*. PG 87.2852–3112. Trans. J. Wortley. Kalamazoo: Cistercian Press, 1992.

Paul the Deacon. *Historia Langobardorum*. Ed. L. K. Bethmann and G. Waitz. 1878. MGH SS rer. Germ. 48.

—. *Historia Romana*. Ed. H. Droysen. 1879. MGH SS rer. Germ. 49.

Pelagius the Deacon. *In Defensione trium capitulorum*. Ed. R. Devreesse. 1932. Vatican City.

Peter Damian. *Epistulae*. Ed. K. Reindel. 1983. *Die Briefe des Petrus Damiani*. Teil 1, 1–40. Munich. MGH *Epist*. 4.1.

Philoponos, John. *Commentary on Aristotle's Physics*. Ed. and trans. R. Sorabji. 2004. *The Philosophy of the Commentators 200–600 AD, A Sourcebook*. Vol. 2, *Physics*. London.

Pliny the Younger. *Epistularum Libri Decem*. Ed. R. Mynors. 1963. Oxford.

Price, R., trans. 2009. *The Acts of the Council of Constantinople of 553*. Liverpool.

Priscus of Panium. *Excerpta*. Ed. P. Carolla. 2000. Berlin.

Procopius of Caesarea. *Wars*. Ed. H. B. Dewing. 1916. Cambridge, MA.

Prosper Tiro (of Aquitaine). *Epitoma Chronicon*. Ed. T. Mommsen. 1892. In *Chronica Minora*, vol. I, 341–499. Berlin.

Rufus, John. *Plerophoriae*. Ed. F. Nau. PO 8, 5–208.

Salvian of Marseilles. *De Gubernatione dei*. Ed. C. Halm. 1877. Berlin. MGH AA 1.1.

Schon, K.-G., K. Zechiel Eckes, and W. Hartmann, edd. *Projekt Pseudoisidore*. Online edition under the auspices of MGH: http://www.pseudoisidor.mgh.de. Accessed 23 September 2021.

Sedulius. *Opera Omnia*. Ed. Iohannes Huemer, rev. Victoria Panagl. 2007. Vienna. CSEL 10.

Severus of Antioch. *Ad Nephalium*. Ed. CSCO 64: 10–21. Trans. P. Allen and C. T. R. Hayward. 2004. In *Severus of Antioch*, 59–66. London and New York.

—. 'Letter on His Flight', ed. S. H. Soumi. 2016. *Saint Sévère le Grand, 'La couronne des Syriaques', Lettre sur son exil. Texte inédit, édition critique du texte syriaque et traduction française*. Brussels. Trans. S. P. Brock. 2017. 'Patriarch Severos' Letter on His Flight from Antioch in 518', *Hugoye: Journal of Syriac Studies* 20: 25–50.

Sidonius Apollinaris. *Epistulae*. Ed. C. Luetjohan. 1887. Berlin. MGH AA 8.

—. *Letters 3–9*. Ed. and trans. W. B. Anderson. 1965. Cambridge, MA.

Siricius. Letter to Himerius of Tarragona. Ed. K. Zechiel-Eckes. 2013. *Die erste Dekretale: Der Brief Papst Siricius' an Bischof Himerius von Tarragona vom Jahr 385 (JK 255)*. Hannover.

Sorabji, R. 2004. *The Philosophy of the Commentators 200–600* AD, *A Sourcebook*. Vol. 2, *Physics*. London.

Symeon of Durham. *Liber de vexacione Willelmi episcopi*. Ed. T. Arnold. 1882–1885. *Symeonis Monachi Opera Omnia*. Vol. 1, 170–95. London.

—. *Liber de exordio*. Ed. D. Rollason. 2000. *Libellus de Exordio atque Procursu istius, hoc est Dunhelmensis, Ecclesie: Tract on the Origins and Progress of this the Church of Durham*. Oxford.

—. *Historia regum Anglorum et Danicorum*. Ed. T. Arnold. 1885. *Symeonis Monachi Opera Omnia*. Vol. 2. London.

Symmachus, Q. Aurelius. *Epistularum libri decem*. Ed. O. Seeck. 1882. Berlin, MGH AA 6.1.

Theophanes Confessor. *Chronographia*. Ed. J. Classen and I. Bekker. 1839–1841. Bonn. Trans. C. A. Mango and R. Scott. 1997. *The Chronicle of Theophanes Confessor*. Oxford.

Theophilus of Alexandria. 'Easter Prologue'. Ed. A. A. Mosshammer. 2017. *The Prologues on Easter of Theophilus of Alexandria and [Cyril]*. Oxford.

Timothy Aelurus, *Against Chalcedon*. Ed. and trans. R. Y. Ebied and L. R. Wickham. 1985. In *After Chalcedon*, 120–42 (Syriac text); 143–66 (English translation). Leuven.

Valentinian III. *Novellae*. Ed. T. Mommsen and P. M. Meyer. 1905. *Leges Novellae ad Theodosianum pertinentes*. Berlin.

Victor of Tunnuna. *Chronicon*. Ed. C. de Hartmann. 2001. Turnhout.

Victorius of Aquitaine. *Cursus Paschalis Annorum DXXXII*. Ed. T. Mommsen in *Chronica Minora*, vol. I, 667–735.

Vigilius. *Constitutum II*. Ed. E. Schwartz. ACO 4.2, 138–68. Trans. Richard Price. 2009. *The Acts of the Council of Constantinople 553*, vol. 2, 221–69. Liverpool.

—. Letter of excommunication to Theodore Ascidas and Menas of Constantinople. Ed. E. Schwartz. 1940. *Vigiliusbriefe*. Munich, 10–15. Trans. R. Price. 2009. *The Acts of the Council of Constantinople 553*, vol. 1, 161–65. Liverpool.

Vincentius of Lérins. *Commonitorium*. Ed. R. Demeulenaere. Turnhout: Brepols, 1985. CCSL 64, 147–95.

Zachariah Rhetor, *Historia Ecclesiastica*. Ed. E. W. Brooks. 1919-1924. *Historia ecclesiastica Zachariae rhetori vulgo adscripta; Accedit fragmentum Historiae ecclesiasticae Dionysii Telmahrensis*, CSCO 83–84/38–39. Paris.

Secondary Sources

Aaij, M. 2007. 'Boniface's Booklife: How the Ragyndrudis Codex Came to be a *Vita Bonifatii*', *The Heroic Age* 10. http://www.heroicage.org/issues/10/aaij.html Accessed 26 April 2018.

Abellán, S. I., and J. C. Martín-Iglesias. 2015. 'Turribius Episcopus Asturicensis'. In *Traditio Patrum I: Scriptores Hispaniae*, ed. E. Colombi, 373–81. Turnhout.

Adams, J. N. 2007. *The Regional Diversification of Latin 200 BC–AD 600*. Cambridge.

Allen, P. 2000. 'The Definition and Enforcement of Orthodoxy'. In *The Cambridge Ancient History Vol. 14*, ed. Av. Cameron, B. Ward-Perkins, and M. Whitby, 811–34. Cambridge.

Allen, P. and B. Neil. 2013. *Crisis Management in Late Antiquity (410–590): A Survey of the Evidence from Episcopal Letters*. Leiden.

—. 2014. *The Letters of Gelasius I (492–96): Pastor and Micro-Manager of the Church of Rome*. Turnhout.

Álvarez de las Asturias, N. 2008. *La 'Collectio Lanfranci': Origine e influenza di una collezione della chiesa anglo-normanna*. Milan.

Amelli, G. 1882. *S. Leone Magno e l'Oriente*, repr. 1908 as *Nuovi contributi alla teologia positiva. San Leone Magno e il primato del romano pontefice in Oriente*. Montecassino.

Armitage, J. M. 2005. *A Twofold Solidarity*. Strathfield, NSW.

Austin, G. 2009. *Shaping Church Law Around the Year 1000: The Decretum of Burchard of Worms*. Farnham.

Autenrieth, J. 1956. *Die Domschule von Konstanz zur Zeit des Investiturstreits*. Stuttgart.

Barclift, P. L. 1997. 'The Shifting Tones of Pope Leo the Great's Christological Vocabulary', *Church History* 66:221–39.

Barrow, R. H. 1973. *Prefect and Emperor: The Relationes of Symmachus A.D. 384*. Oxford.

Behr, J. 2011. *The Case Against Diodore and Theodore*. Oxford.

—. 2004. *The Nicene Faith*. 2 Parts. Crestwood, New York.

Beneto, C. 1500. *Illustrium virorum opuscula*. Paris.

Bethune-Baker, J. F. 1908. 'The Date of the Death of Nestorius: Schenute, Zacharias, Evagrius', *JTS* os 9:601–05.

Bevan, G. 2016. *The New Judas: The Case of Nestorius in Ecclesiastical Politics, 428–51 CE*. Leuven.

—. 2005. 'The Case of Nestorius: Ecclesiastical Politics in the East, 428–51 CE'. PhD diss., University of Toronto.

Bévenot, M. 1961. *The Tradition of Manuscripts: A Study in the Transmission of St Cyprian's Treatises.* Oxford.

Bischoff, B. 1998–2014. *Katalog der festländische Handschriften des neunten Jahrhunderts.* 3 volumes. Wiesbaden.

Bischoff, B. and J. Hofmann. 1952. *Libri Sancti Kyliani, Die Würzburger Schreibschule und die Dombibliothek im VIII. und IX. Jahrundert.* Würzburg.

Bjornlie, S. 2015. 'The Rhetoric of *Varietas* and Epistolary Encyclopedism in Cassiodorus *Variae*'. In *Shifting Genres in Late Antiquity*, ed. G. Greatrex and H. Elton with the assistance of L. McMahon, 289–303. Farnham.

Blanchard, F. 1647. *Les Presidens au mortier du Parlement de Paris.* Paris.

Blaudeau, P. 2012a. 'Between Petrine Ideology and Realpolitik: The See of Constantinople in Roman Geo-ecclesiology (449–536)'. In *Two Romes: Rome and Constantinople in Late Antiquity*, ed. L. Grig and G. Kelly, 364–84. New York.

—. 2012b. *Le Siège de Rome et l'Orient (448–536). Etude géo-ecclésiologique.* Rome.

—. 2001. '"*Vice mea*". Remarques sur les représentations pontificales auprès de l'empereur d'Orient dans la seconde moitié du Ve siècle (452–96)', *Mélanges de l'École Française de Rome Antiquité*, 113–12: 1059–1123.

Bouhot, J.-P. and J.-F. Genest. 1997. *La Bibliothèque de l'Abbaye de Clairvaux du XIIe au XVIIIe siècle*, vol. 2. Paris.

Brett, M. 1992. 'The *Collectio Lanfranci* and its Competitors'. In *Intellectual Life in the Middle Ages: Essays Presented to Margaret Gibson*, ed. Lesley Smith and Benedicta Ward, 157–74. London.

Brooke, Z. N. 1989. *The English Church and the Papacy.* Repr. of 1931 edition. Cambridge.

Brown, G. 1994. 'Introduction: the Carolingian Renaissance'. In *Carolingian Culture: Emulation and Innovation*, ed. R McKitterick, 1–51. Cambridge.

Brown, T. S. 2009. 'Lombard Religious Policy in the Late Sixth and Seventh Centuries: The Roman Dimension'. In *The Langobards Before the Frankish Conquest: An Ethnographic Perspective*, ed. G. Ausenda, P. Delogu, and C. Wickham, 289–308. Woodbridge.

Burgess, R. W. 1993. Introduction to *The Chronicle of Hydatius and the Consularia Constantinopolitana*, 3–66. Oxford.

—. 'The Accession of Marcian in the Light of Chalcedonian Apologetic and Monophysite Polemic'. In *Byzantinische Zeitschrift* 86:47–68. Repr. item XII in *Chronicles Consuls and Coins: Historiography and History in the Later Roman Empire*. Farnham, 2011.

Butterfield, D. 2013. *The Early Textual History of Lucretius'* De rerum natura. Oxford.

Butts, A. M. 2017. 'Manuscript Transmission as Reception History: The Case of Ephrem the Syrian (d. 373)'. *Journal of Early Christian Studies* 25, no. 2: 281–306.

Cain, A. 2009. *The Letters of Jerome: Asceticism, Biblical Exegesis, and the Construction of Christian Authority in Late Antiquity*. Oxford.

Callu, J. 1972. *Symmaque: Lettres Tome I*. Paris.

Cameron, Al. 2010. *The Last Pagans of Rome*. Oxford.

Campos, J. 1962. 'La epistola antipriscilianista de San León Magno', *Helmantica* 13:269–308.

Cappelli, A. 2011. *Dizionario di abbreviature Latine ed Italiane*. 7th edition. Milan.

Casiday, A. 2005. 'Grace and the humanity of Christ according to St Vincent of Lérins', *Vigiliae Christianae* 59: 298–314.

Chadwick, H. 1951. 'Eucharist and Christology in the Nestorian Controversy', *Journal of Theological Studies* ns 2:145–64.

—. 1955. 'The Exile and Death of Flavian of Constantinople: A Prologue to the Council of Chalcedon', *The Journal of Theological Studies*, ns 6: 17–34.

—. 1967. *The Early Church*. Harmondsworth.

—. 1976. *Priscillian of Avila: The Occult and the Charismatic in the Early Church*. Oxford.

Chadwick, O. 1968. *John Cassian*. 2nd edn. Cambridge.

Chavasse, A. 1964. 'Les lettres de Saint Léon le Grand dans le supplément de la Dionysiana et de l'Hadriana', *Revue des sciences religieuses* 38:154–76.

—. 1973. Introduction to *Sancti Leonis Magni Romani Pontificis Tractatus Septem et Nonaginta,* i–ccxviii. CCSL138. Turnhout.

—. 1975. 'Les lettres du Pape Léon le Grand (440–61) dans l'Hispana et la collection dite des Fausses Décrétales', *Revue de droit canonique* 25:28–39.

Chiron, P. 1993. *Démétrios, Du Style*. Paris.

Clément, J.-M. and R. Vander Plaeste. 1974. Einleitung to Facundus of Hermiane, *Opera Omnia*, vii–xxx. CCSL 90A. Turnhout.

Collins, R. 2004. *Visigothic Spain, 409–711*. Oxford.

Collura, P. 1943. *Studi paleografici. La pre-carolina e la carolina a Bobbio*. Milan.

Costambeys, M., M. Innes, and S. MacLean. 2011. *The Carolingian World*. Cambridge.

Cowdrey, H. E. J. 2003. *Lanfranc: Scholar, Monk, and Archishop*. Oxford.

Culler, J. 2011. *Literary Theory: A Very Short Introduction*. 2nd edn. Oxford.

Cushing, K. G. 2005. *Reform and the Papacy in the Eleventh Century: Spirituality and Social Change*. Manchester.

Damon, C. 2015. *Studies on the Text of Caesar's* Bellum ciuile. Oxford.

Davis, R. 2010. *The Book of Pontiffs*. Revised 3rd edition. Liverpool.

Davis, S. J. 2004. *The Early Coptic Papacy: The Egyptian Church and its Leadership in Late Antiquity*. Cairo.

de Jong, M. 2005. 'Charlemagne's Church'. In *Charlemagne: Empire and Society*, ed. J. Story, 103–35. Manchester and New York.

de Lubac, H. 1998. *Medieval Exegesis: Volume 1, The Four Senses of Scripture*. Trans. M. Sebanc. Grand Rapids.

Demacopoulos, G. 2013. *The Invention of Peter*. Philadelphia.

Devisse, J. 1975–1976. *Hincmar Archevêque de Reims 845–82*. 3 vols. Geneva.

Di Capua, F. 1934. 'De clausulis a S. Leone Magno adhibitis'. In *Textus et Documenta, Series Theologica 15: S. Leonis Magni Epistulae Contra Eutychis Haeresim*, Pars Prima, ed. C. Silva-Tarouca XXIII–XXXII. Rome. Repr. 1959 in *Scritti Minori* I, ed. F. di Capua, 431–40. Rome.

Dolezalek, G. 2008. 'Catalogue of Canon and Roman Law Manuscripts in the Vatican Library, vol. III resuscitated' https://home.uni-leipzig.de/jurarom/manuscr/VaticanCatalogue/indexvatican.html Accessed 23 September 2021.

Domínguez Bordona, J. 1930. *Spanish Illumination*. Florence.

Drobner, H. R. 2007. *The Fathers of the Church: A Comprehensive Introduction*. Trans. S. S. Schatzmann. Peabody.

Duchesne, L. 1886. Introduction to *Le Liber Pontificalis*, vol. 1, i–cclxii. Paris.

—. 1902. 'La première collection romaine des décrétale'. In *Atti del IIº congresso internazionale di archeologia cristiana*, 159–62. Rome.

—. 1907, 1910. *Fastes épiscopaux de l'ancienne Gaule*, vols 1 and 2, 2nd edition. Paris.

—. 1925. *L'Église au VIe siècle*. Paris.

Duggan, C. 1965. 'A Durham Canonical Manuscript of the Late Twelfth Century'. In *Studies in Church History Volume II*, 179–85. London.

—. 2008. 'Decretal Collections from Gratian's *Decretum* to the *Compilationes antiquae*: The Making of the New Case Law' In *The History of Medieval Canon Law in the Classical Period*, ed. W. Hartmann and K. Pennington, 246–91. Washington, DC.

Dunn, G. D. 2014. 'Is the Letter *Credbamus Post* from Boniface I or Leo I?', *Greek, Roman, and Byzantine Studies* 54:474–93.

—. 2015. '*Collectio Corbeiensis, Collectio Pithouensis* and the Earliest Collections of Papal Letters'. In *Collecting Early Christian Letters from the Apostle Paul to Late Antiquity*, ed. B. Neil and P. Allen, 175–205. Cambridge.

Dutton, M. L. 2010. Introduction to Aelred of Rievaulx, *Spiritual Friendship*. Trans. L. C. Braceland. Kalamazoo.

Dvornik, F. 1966. *Byzantium and the Roman Primacy*. New York.

Ebbeler, J. 2012. *Disciplining Christians: Correction and Community in Augustine's Letters*. Oxford.

Edwards, C. 2005. 'Epistolography'. In *A Companion to Latin Literature*, ed. S. Harrison, 270–83. Oxford.

Elliot, M. D. 2013. 'Canon Law Collections in England *ca* 600–1066: The Manuscript Evidence', Ph.D. Diss., University of Toronto.

Escribano, V. 2005. 'Heresy and Orthodoxy in Fifth-century Hispania'. In *Hispania in Late Antiquity: Current Perspectives*, ed. M. Kulikowski and K. Bowes. Leiden.

Étaix, R. 1962. 'L'homéliaire cartusien', *Sacris Erudiri* 13: 67–112.

Fanning, S. C. 1981. 'Lombard Arianism Reconsidered', *Speculum* 56:241–58.

Ferreiro, A. 2015. 'Pope Siricius and Himerius of Tarragona (385): Provincial Papal Intervention in the Fourth Century'. In *The Bishop of Rome in Late Antiquity*, ed. G. D. Dunn, 73–85. Farnham.

Firey, A. 2008. 'Collectio Dionysiana'. Part of the *Carolingian Canon Law Project*. https://ccl.rch.uky.edu/dionysiana-article. Accessed 24 September 2021.

—. 2015. 'Canon Law Studies at Corbie'. In *Fälschung als Mittel der Politik? Pseudoisidor im Licht der Neuen Forschung*, ed. K. Ubl and D. Ziemann, 19–79. Hannover.

Flechner, R. 2009. 'An Insular Tradition of Ecclesiastical Law: Fifth to Eighth Century'. In *Anglo-Saxon/Irish Relations Before the Vikings*, 23–46. Oxford; New York.

Fleming, R. 2010. *Britain After Rome: The Fall and Rise, 400 to 1070*. London.

Floyer, J. K., and S. G. Hamilton. 1906. *Catalogue of Manuscripts Preserved in the Chapter Library of Worcester Cathedral*. Oxford.

Fournier, P. and G. Le Bras. 1931–1932. *Histoire des collections canoniques en Occident depuis les Fausses Décrétales jusqu'au Décret de Gratien*. 2 Volumes. Paris. Repr. 1972, Aalen.

Fowler-Magerl, L. 2005. *Clavis Canonum: Selected Canon Law Collections Before 1140, Access with Data Processing*. Hannover. Book with CD-ROM.

Frend, W. H. C. 1972. *The Rise of the Monophysite Movement*. Cambridge.

Fuhrmann, H. 1972. *Einfluß und Verbreitung der pseudoisidorischen Fälschungen, von ihrem Auftauchen bis in die neuere Zeit*. Volume 1. Stuttgart.

—. 2001. 'The Pseudo-Isidorian Forgeries'. In *Papal Letters in the Early Middle Ages*, ed. D. Jasper and H. Fuhrmann, 137–95. Washington, DC.

Ganz, D. 1990. *Corbie in the Carolingian Renaissance*. Sigmaringen.

Gaudemet, J. 1985. *Les Sources du droit de l'église en occident du IIe au VIIe siècle*. Paris.

Gibson, R. 2012. 'On the nature of ancient letter collections', *Journal of Roman Studies* 102:56–78.

—. 2013. 'Pliny and the Letters of Sidonius: From Constantius and Clarus to Firminus and Fuscus' *Arethusa* 46: 333–55.

Gibson, R. K. and R. Morello. 2012. *Reading the Letters of Pliny the Younger: An Introduction*. Cambridge.

Gibson, R. K. and A. D. Morrison. 2007. 'Introduction: What Is a Letter?'. In *Ancient Letters: Classical and Late Antique Epistolography*, ed. R. Morello and A. D. Morrison, 1–16. Oxford.

Gilchrist, J. 1970. 'Was There a Gregorian Reform Movement in the Eleventh Century?', *The Canadian Catholic Historical Association: Study Sessions* 37:1–10.

—. 1980. *The Collection in Seventy-Four Titles: A Canon Law Manual: A Canon Law Manual of the Gregorian Reform*. Toronto.

Goldsworthy, A. 2009. *How Rome Fell: Death of a Superpower*. New Haven and London.

Gore, C. 1880. *Leo the Great*. London.

Gray, P. T. R. 1979. *The Defense of Chalcedon in the East (451–553)*. Leiden.

Green, B. 2008. *The Soteriology of Leo the Great*. Oxford.

Grégoire, R. 1966. *Les Homéliaires du Moyen Âge: Inventaire et analyse des manuscrits*. Rome.

—. 1980. *Homéliaires liturgiques médiévaux*. Spoleto.

Grillmeier, A. 1975. *Christ in Christian Tradition, Volume 1: From the Apostolic Age to Chalcedon (451)*. Second, revised edition. Trans. J. Bowden. London.

—. 1987. *Christ in Christian Tradition, Volume 2: From the Council of Chalcedon (451) to Gregory the Great (590–604)*, Part One. Trans. P. Allen and J. Cawte. London.

Guillermo, A. 1910. *Catálogo de los códices latinos de la Real biblioteca del Escorial*, Volume 1. Madrid.

—. 1911. *Catálogo de los códices latinos de la Real biblioteca del Escorial*, Volume 2. Madrid.

—. 1916. *Catálogo de los códices latinos de la Real biblioteca del Escorial*, Volume 4. Madrid.

Guilmain, J. 1960. 'Interlace Decoration and the Influence of the North on Mozarabic Illumination (in Notes)', *The Art Bulletin* 42:211–18.

Halsall, G. 2007. *Barbarian Migrations and the Roman West, 376–568*. Cambridge.

—. 2013. *Worlds of Arthur: Facts and Fictions of the Dark Ages*. New York.

Haring, N. M. 1950. 'The Character and Range of the Influence of St Cyril of Alexandria on Latin Theology (430–1260)', *Medieval Studies* 12:1–19.

Hinschius, P. 1863. *Decretales Pseudo-Isidorianae et Capitula Ingilramni*. Leipzig.

—. 1884. 'Die kanonistischen Handschriften der Hamiltonschen Sammlung', *ZKG* 6:193–246.

Hoffmann, H. and R. Pokorny. 1991. *Das Dekret des Bischofs Buchard von Worms: Textstufen – Frühe Verbreitung – Vorlagen*. Munich.

Holtzmann, W. 1979. *Studies in the Collections of Twelfth-century Decretals*. Ed., rev., and trans. C. R. Cheney and M. G. Cheney. Vatican.

Holum, K. G. 1982. *Theodosian Empresses: Women and Imperial Dominion in Late Antiquity*. Berkeley.

Hoskin, M. 2016. 'Pope Leo the Great's Rhetoric: Its Use and Misuse in *Ep.* 28, the "Tome", and the Impact upon "Leonine" Christology', *Studia Patristica* LXXIV: 317–28.

—. 2018. 'The Recensions of Leo the Great, *Ep.* 12', *Filologia Mediolatina* XXV: 45–62.

Hosp, E. 1936. 'Il sermonario di Alano di Farfa', *Ephemerides liturgicae* 50: 375–83.

—. 1937. 'Il sermonario di Alano di Farfa', *Ephemerides liturgicae* 51: 210–40.

Houghton, H. A. G., C. M. Kreinecker, R. F. MacLachlan, and C. J. Smith. 2019. *The Principal Pauline Epistles: A Collation of Old Latin Witnesses.* Leiden.

Humphries, M. 2007. 'From Emperor to Pope? Ceremonial, space, and authority in Rome from Constantine to Gregory the Great'. In *Religion, Dynasty, and Patronage in a Christian Capital: Rome, 300–900*, ed. K. Cooper and J. Hillner, 21–58. Cambridge.

—. 2012. 'Valentinian III and the City of Rome (425–55): Patronage, Politics, Power'. In *Two Romes: Rome and Constantinople in Late Antiquity*, ed. L. Grig and G. Kelly, 161–82. New York.

Hutchinson, G. O. 1998. *Cicero's Correspondence: A Literary Study.* Oxford.

Hwang, A. Y. 2010. 'Manifold grace in John Cassian and Prosper of Aquitaine', *Scottish Journal of Theology* 63: 93–108.

Jalland, T. 1941. *The Life and Times of St Leo the Great.* New York.

James, N. W. 1993. 'Leo the Great and Prosper of Aquitaine: A Fifth-century Pope and His Advisor', *JTS* ns 44:554–84.

Jankowiak, M. 2002. 'L'Accession au trône de Marcien vue de l'Occident: une usurpation légalisée'. In *Εὐεργεσίας Χαρίν: Studies Presented to Benedetto Bravo and Ewa Wipszycka by Their Disciples*, ed. T. Derda, J. Urbanik, and M. Węcowski, 87–129. Warsaw.

Jasper, D. 2001. 'The Beginning of the Decretal Tradition: Papal Letters from the Origin of the Genre through the Pontificate of Stephen V'. In *Papal Letters in the Early Middle Ages*, ed. D. Jasper and H. Fuhrmann, 3–133. Washington, DC.

Jemolo, V. and M. Palma. 1984. *Sessoriani dispersi: contributo all'identificazione di codici provenienti dalla Biblioteca Romana di S. Croce in Gerusalemme.* Rome.

Jenson, R. W. 2002. 'With No Qualifications: The Christological Maximalism of the Christian East'. In *Ancient and Postmodern Chrsitianity: Paleo-Orthodoxy in the 21ˢᵗ Century*, ed. K. Tanner and C. A. Hall, 13–22. Downers Grove.

Kaldellis, A. 2019. *Romanland: Ethnicity and Empire in Byzantium*. Cambridge, Massachusetts; London, England.

Kaster, R. A. 2010. *Studies on the Text of Macrobius' Saturnalia*. Oxford.

—, ed. 2011. Macrobius, *Saturnalia*. Oxford.

Kelly, C. 2015. 'Neither Conquest nor Settlement: Attila's Empire and Its Impact'. In *The Cambridge Companion to the Age of Attila*, ed. M. Maas, 193–208. Cambridge.

Kelly, G. 2013. 'Pliny and Symmachus'. *Arethusa* 46: 261–87.

—. 2015. 'The First Book of Symmachus' Correspondence As a Separate Collection'. In *Culture and Literature in Latin Late Antiquity. Continuities and Discontinuities*, ed. P. F. Moretti, Roberta Ricci, Chiara Torre, 197–220. Turnhout.

Ker, N. R. 1977. *Medieval Manuscripts in British Libraries*. Volume 2. Oxford.

Ker, N. R. and A. J. Piper. 1992. *Medieval Manuscripts in British Libraries*. Volume 4. Oxford.

Kéry, L. 1999. *Canonical Collections of the Early Middle Ages (ca. 400–1140): A Bibliographical Guide to the Manuscripts and Literature*. Washington, DC.

Knibbs, E. 2013. 'The Interpolated Hispana and the Origins of Pseudo-Isidore'. In *Zeitschrift der Savigny-Stiftung für Rechtsgeschichte: Kanonistische Abteilung* 99:1–71.

—. 2016a. 'Patzold and the Origins of the C Recension: I', http://pseudoisidore.blogspot.com/2016/08/patzold-and-origins-of-c-recension-i.html. Accessed 21 February 2020.

—. 2016b. 'Patzold and the Origins of the C Recension: III', http://pseudoisidore.blogspot.com/2016/08/patzold-and-origins-of-c-recension-iii.html. Accessed 21 February 2020.

Krautheimer, R. 2009. 'Damasus in His Time'. In *L'antica basilica di San Lorenzo in Damaso: Indagini acheologiche nel Palazzo della Cancelleria (1988–1993)*, ed. C. Frommel and M. Pentiricci, vol. 1, 313–27. Rome.

Krusch, Br. 1938. *Studien zur christlich-mittelalterlichen Chronologie*. Berlin.

Künstle, K. 1905. *Antipriscilliana*. Freiburg.

Kuttner, S. 1986–1987. *A catalogue of canon and Roman law manuscripts in the Vatican Library*. 2 vols. Vatican City.

Landau, P. 1989. 'Kanonessammlungen in der Lombardei im frühen und hohen Mittelalter'. In *Atti dell'11° congresso internazionale di studi sull'alto medioevo, Milano, 26–30 ottobre 1987*, volume 1, 425–57. Spoleto.

—. 2008. 'Gratian and the *Decretum Gratiani*'. In *The History of Medieval Canon Law in the Classical Period, 1140–1234: From Gratian to the Decretals of Pope Gregory IX*, ed. W. Hartmann and K. Pennington, 22–54. Washington, DC.

Lebon, J. 1909. *Le monophysisme sévérien: étude historique, littéraire et théologique sur la résistance monophysite au Concile de Chalcédoine jusqu'à la constitution de l'église Jacobite*. Louvain.

Le Bras, G. 1930. 'Notes pour servir à l'histoire des collections canoniques III: Un moment décisif dans l'histoire de l'Église et du droit canon: la Renaissance gélasienne', *Revue historique de droit français et étranger* 9:506–18.

Leclercq, J. 1982. *The Love of Learning and the Desire for God: A Study of Monastic Culture*. Trans. C. Misrahi. New York.

Lewis, C. S. 1967. *Studies in Words*. 2nd edition. Cambridge.

L'Huillier, P. 1996. *The Church of the Ancient Councils*. Crestwood, N.Y.

Lietzmann, H. 1921. *Das Sacramentarium Gregorianum nach dem Aachener Ur-exemplar*. Münster in Westf.

Louth, A. 2007. *Greek East and Latin West: The Church AD 681–1071*. Crestwood, NY.

—. 2019. Review of A. A. Mosshammer, *The Prologues on Easter of Theophilus of Alexandria and [Cyril]. Oxford Early Christian texts*. Oxford; New York: Oxford University Press, 2017. *The Bryn Mawr Classical Review*, January 2019. http://www.bmcreview.org/2019/01/20190118.html Accessed 30 October 2019.

Maassen, F. 1870. *Geschichte de Quellen und der Literatur des canonischen Rechts im Abendlande, 1: Die Rechtssammlungen bis zur Mitte des 9. Jahrhunderts*. Graz.

McEvoy, M. 2013. 'The mausoleum of Honorius: Late Roman Imperial Christianity and the City of Rome in the Fifth Century'. In *Old St Peter's, Rome*, ed. R. McKitterick, J. Osborne, C. M. Richardson, and J. Story, 119–36. Cambridge.

McGilll, S. 2012. 'Latin Poetry'. In *The Oxford Handbook to Late Antiquity*, ed. S. Fitzgerald Johnson, 335–60. Oxford.

McGuckin, J. A. 1994. *St Cyril of Alexandria: The Christological Controversy: Its History, Theology, and Texts*. Leiden.

—. 2017. *The Path of Christianity: The First Thousand Years*. Downers Grove.

McKitterick, R. 1977. *The Frankish Church and the Carolingian Reforms, 789–895*. London.

—. 1989. *The Carolingians and the Written Word.* Cambridge.

—. 1992. 'Royal patronage of culture in the Frankish kingdoms under the Carolingians: motives and consequences'. In *Committenti e produzione artistico-letteraria nell'alto medioevo occidentale,* 93–129. Spoleto.

—. 1994. 'Script and Book Production'. In *Carolingian Culture: Emulation and Innovation,* ed. R. McKitterick, 221–47. Cambridge.

—. 2004. *History and Memory in the Carolingian World.* Cambridge.

—. 2005. 'History, Law and Communication with the Past in the Carolingian Period', *Settimane di studio della fondazione centro italiano di studi sull'alto medioevo* 52: 943–82.

—. 2011. *Charlemagne: The Formation of a European Identity.* Cambridge.

McLynn, N. 2012. 'Two Romes, Beacons of the Whole World: Canonizing Constantinople'. In *Two Romes: Rome and Constantinople in Late Antiquity,* ed. L. Grig and G. Kelly, 345–65. Oxford.

Marchi, S. 1996. *I Manoscritti della Biblioteca Capitolare di Verona: Caralogo descrittivo redatto da don Antonio Spagnolo.* Verona.

Martínez-Díez, G. 1961. 'El Epítome Hispánico: Una colección canónica Española del siglo VII. Estudio y texto critico', *Miscelanea Comillas* 36:5–90.

—. 1962. 'El Epítome Hispánico. Una colección canónica Española del siglo VII', *Miscelanea Comillas* 37.2:322–466.

—. 1965. 'Prolegomenos a la edición critica de la Hispana'. In *Études d'histoire du droit canonique dediées à Gabriel Le Bras,* 263–72. Paris.

—. 1966. *La Colección Canónica Hispana,* vol. 1. Madrid.

—. 1976. *La Colección Canónica Hispana,* vol. 2.1. Madrid.

Massigli, R. 1912. 'Sur l'origine de la collection canonique dite Hadriana augmentée', *Mélanges d'archéologie et d'histoire* 32:363–83.

Mayer, R. 1994. *Horace: Epistles Book I.* Cambridge.

Melville, G. 2016. *The World of Medieval Monasticism.* Trans. J. Mixon. Collegeville.

Mentré, M. 1996. *The Illuminated Manuscripts of Medieval Spain.* London.

Menze, V. L. 2008. *Justinian and the Making of the Syrian Orthodox Church.* Oxford.

Merdinger, J. E. 1997. *Rome and the African Church in the Time of Augustine.* New Haven, London.

Meyendorff, J. 1989. *Imperial Unity and Christian Divisions*. Crestwood, N.Y.

Michelson, D. A. 2014. *The Practical Christology of Philoxenus of Mabbug*. Oxford.

Mommsen, T. 1886. 'Actenstücke zur Kirchengeschichte aus dem Cod. Cap. Novar. 30', *Neues Archiv der Gesselschaft für ältere deutsche Geschichtskunde* 11:361–68.

—. 1892. Prolegomena to *Epitoma Chronicon* by Prosper Tiro, 342–84, *Chronica Minora*, vol. I. Berlin.

—. 1898. Prolegomena to *Liber Pontificalis*, vii–cxxxix. MGH Gesta Pontificum Romanorum 1. Berlin.

Mommsen, T. and P. M. Meyer. 1905. Prolegomena to *Leges Novellae ad Theodosianum pertinentes*. Berlin.

Mordek, H. 1967. 'Zur handschriftlichen Überlieferung der Dacheriana', *Quellen und Forschungen aus italienischen Archiven und Bibliotheken* 47:574–95.

—. 1975. *Kirchenrecht und Reform im Frankreich. Die Collectio Vetus Gallica, die älteste systematische Kanonessammlung des fränkischen Gallien. Studien und Edition*. Berlin.

—. 1978. 'Codices Pseudo-Isidoriani: Addenda zu dem gleichnamigen Buch von Schafer Williams', *Archiv für katholisches Kirchenrecht* 147:471–78.

—. 1995. *Bibliotheca capitularium regun Francorum manuscripta: Überlieferung und Traditionszusammenhang der fränkischen Herrschererlasse*. Munich.

Moreau, D. 2015. '*Ipsis diebus Bonifatius, zelo et dolo ductus*: The Root Causes of the Double Papal Election of 22 September 530'. In *The Bishop of Rome in Late Antiquity*, ed. G. D. Dunn, 177–95. Farnham.

Mynors, R. A. B. 1969. Praefatio to P. Vergilius Maro, *Opera*, v–xiii. Oxford.

Mynors, R. A. B. and R. M. Thomson. 1993. *A Catalogue of the Manuscripts of Hereford Cathedral Library*. Cambridge.

Neil, B. 2009. *Leo the Great*. London and New York.

Nelson, J. L. 1995. 'The Frankish Kingdoms, 814–98: The West'. In *The New Cambridge Medieval History Vol. 2*, ed. R. McKitterick, 110–41. Cambridge.

Noble, T. F. X. 1990. 'Literacy and the Papal Government in the Early Middle Ages'. In *The Uses of Literacy in Early Medieval Europe*, ed. R. McKitterick, 82–108. Cambridge.

Pantarotto, M. 2007. 'La (ri)costruzione di un manoscritto nello scriptorium di Bobbio Al tempo dell'abate Agilulfo (887–96)', *Scriptorium* 61:48–71.

Patzold, S. 2015. *Gefälschtes Recht aus dem Frühmittelalter: Untersuchungen zur Herstellung und Überlieferung der pseudoisidorischen Dekretalen.* Heidelberg.

Pelikan, J. 1978. *The Christian Tradiiton: A History of the Development of Doctrine*, vol. 3, *The Growth of Medieval Theology (600–1300).* Chicago.

Pelttari, A. 2011. 'Approaches to the Writing of Greek in Late Antique Latin Texts', *Greek, Roman, and Byzantine Studies* 51:461–82.

Philpott, M. 1994. 'The *De iniusta vexacione Willelmi episcopi primi* and Canon Law in Anglo-Norman Durham'. In *Anglo-Norman Durham: 1093–1193*, ed. D. Rollason, M. Harvey, and M. Prestwich, 125–37. Woodbridg.

—. 1993. 'Lanfranc's Canonical Collection and "the Law of the Church"'. In *Lanfranco di Pavia e l'Europa del secolo XI. Nel IX centenario della morte (1089–1989). Atti del Convegno Internazionale di Studi (Pavia, Almo Collegio Borromeo, 21–24 settembre 1989)*, ed. G. D'Onofrio, 131–47. Padua.

Pietri, C. 1976. *Roma christiana: Recherches sur l'Église de Rome, son organisation, sa politique, son idéologie de Miltiade à Sixte III (311–440).*

Poole, R. L. 1915. *Lectures on the History of the Papal Chancery Down to the Time of Innocent III.* Cambridge.

Prestige, G. L. 1930. 'The Greek Translation of the *Tome* of St Leo', *JTS* os 31:183–84.

Price, R. 2009. *The Acts of the Council of Constantinople of 553.* Liverpool.

Price, R. and M. Gaddis. 2005–2007. *The Acts of the Council of Chalcedon.* 3 Volumes. Liverpool.

Quasten, J. 1986. *Patrology, Vol. IV: The Golden Age of Latin Patristic Literature from the Council of Nicea to the Council of Chalcedon.* Trans. P. Solari. Westminster, Maryland.

Ramsey, B. 1997. Introduction to *The Conferences* by John Cassian. Trans. B. Ramsey. New York.

Reifferscheid, A. 1976. *Bibliotheca patrum Latinorum Italica.* Hildesheim; New York.

Reynolds, L. D. 1983. *Texts and Transmission: A Survey of the Latin Classics.* Oxford.

Reynolds, L. D. and N. G. Wilson. 1991. *Scribes and Scholars: A Guide to the Transmission of Greek and Latin Literature*. Third edition. Oxford.

Reynolds, S. 2015. *A Catalogue of the Manuscripts in the Library at Holkham Hall. Volume 1. Manuscripts from Italy to 1500, Part 1. Shelfmarks 1–399*. Turnhout.

Richards, J. 1979. *The Popes and the Papacy in the Early Middle Ages, 476–752*. London, Boston.

Riché, P. 1977. *Education and Culture in the Barbarian West: Sixth through Eighth Centuries*. Trans. J. J. Contreni. Columbia, SC.

Risselada, R. 2013. 'Applying Text Linguistics to the Letters of Sidonius'. In *New Approches to Sidonius Apollinaris*, ed. J. A. van Waarden and G. Kelly. Leuven.

Roberts, E. D. 1934. 'Notes on Early Christian Libraries in Rome', *Speculum* 9:190–94.

Rolker, C. 2010. *Canon Law and the Letters of Ivo of Chartres*. Cambridge.

Ronnick, M. V. 2001. '"Honey-sweet Cups" in Lucretius, Jerome, and Alan of Lille: *Anticlaudianus* 7.442F', *Scholia: Studies in Classical Antiquity* 10: 92–93.

Russell, N. 2000. *Cyril of Alexandria*. London.

Salzman, M. R. 2012. Introduction to *The Letters of Symmachus: Book 1*, trans. M. R. Salzman and M. Roberts, xiii–lxviii. Leiden.

—. 2015. 'Reconsidering a Relationship: Pope Leo of Rome and Prosper of Aquitaine'. In *The Bishop of Rome in Late Antiquity*, ed. G. D. Dunn, 109–25. Farnham.

Schenkl, H. 1891. *Biblioteca Patrum Latinorum Britannica*. Vienna.

Schiaparelli, L. 1924. *Il Codice 490 della Biblioteca Capitolare di Lucca e la scuola scrittoria lucchese*. Rome.

Schipper, H. G. and J. van Oort. 2000. *Sancti Leonis Magni Romani Pontificis: Sermones et Epistulae Fragmenta Selecta*. Turnhout.

Schon, K.-G. 1978. 'Eine Redaktion der pseudoisidorischen Dekretalen aus der Zeit der Fälschung', *Deutsches Archiv für Erforschung des Mittelalters* 34:500–11.

—. 2006a. *Die Capitula Angilramni: eine prozessrechtliche Fälschung Pseudoisidors*. Hannover.

—. 2006b. *Unbekannte Texte aus der Werkstatt Pseudoisidors: die Collectio Danieliana*. Hannover.

Schwartz, E. 1930. 'Zum *Decretum Gelasianum*', *Zeitschrift für die neutestamentliche Wissenschaft und die Kunde der älteren Kirche* 29: 161–68.

—. 1931. 'Die sog. Sammlung der Kirche von Thessalonich'. In *Fest-schrift Richard Reitzenstein*, ed. E. Fraenkel et al, 137–59. Leipzig.

—. 1936. 'Die Kanonessammlungen der alten Reichskirche', *Zeitschrift der Savigny-Stiftung für Rechtsgeschichte: Kanonistische Abteilung* 25:1–114.

Sellers, R. V. 1953. *The Council of Chalcedon: A Historical and Doctrinal Survey*. London.

Sessa, K. 2012. *The Formation of Papal Authority in Late Antique Italy: Roman Bishops and the Domestic Sphere*. New York.

Shackleton Bailey, D. R. 1965. *Cicero's Letters to Atticus, Volume I, 68–59 B.C.* Cambridge.

—. 1971. *Cicero*. London.

Siecienski, A. E. 2017. *The Papacy and the Orthodox: Sources and History of a Debate*. New York.

Silva-Tarouca, C. 1926. 'Die Quellen der Briefsammlung Papst Leos des Großen'. In *Papsttum und Kaisertum: Forschungen zur politischen Geschichte und Geisteskultur des Mittelalters: P. Kehr zum 65. Geburtstag dargebracht*, ed. A. Brackmann, 23–47. Munich.

—. 1931. 'Nuovi studi sulle antiche lettere dei Papi', *Gregorianum* XII:3–56; 349–425; 547–98. Repr. 1932 as single volume. Rome.

Smith, J. C. 1990. 'The Side Chambers of San Giovanni Evangelista in Ravenna: Church Libraries of the Fifth Century', *Gesta* 29:86–97.

Smulders, P. 1979. Praefatio to Hilarius of Poitiers, *De Trinitate: Praefatio, Libri I–VII*, 1–78. Turnhout. CCSL 62.

Sogno, C., B. K. Storin, and E. J. Watts. 2017. *Late Antique Letter Collections: A Critical Introduction and Reference Guide*. Oakland.

Somerville, R. 1972. 'Lanfranc's Canonical Collection and Exeter', *The Bulletin of the Institute of Historical Research* 45:303–06.

Thomson, R. 1986. *William of Malmesbury*. Woodbridge.

—. 1989. *A Catalogue of the Manuscripts of Lincoln Cathedral Chapter Library*. Woodbridge.

Thurn, H. 1984. *Die Pergamenthandschriften der ehemaligen Dombibliothek*. Wiesbaden.

Torrance, I. R. 1988. *Christology After Chalcedon: Severus of Antioch & Sergius the Monophysite*. Norwich.

Torrance, T. F. 2008. *Incarnation: The Person and Life of Christ*. Downers Grove.

Trapp, M. 2003. *Greek and Latin Letters: An Anthology*. Cambridge.

Traube, L. 1898. *Textgeschichte der Regula S. Benedicti*. Munich.

—. 1909. Palaegraphical notes in *Facsimiles of the Creeds from Early Manuscripts*, ed. A. E. Burn, 27–37. London.

Trout, D. 2015. *Damasus of Rome: The Epigraphic Poetry: Introduction, Texts, Translations, and Commentary*. Oxford.

Turner, C. H. 1910. 'The Collection of the Dogmatic Letters of St Leo'. In *Miscelanea Ceriani*, ed. A. Ratti, 688–739. Milan.

—. 1916. 'Arles and Rome, the First Developments of Canon Law in Gaul', *JTS* o.s. 17:236–47.

—. 1929. 'Chapters in the History of Latin MSS of Canons IV: The Corbie MS(C) now Paris. lat. 12097', *JTS* o.s. 30:225–36.

Vaillancourt, M. G. 2009. Introduction to *Lanfranc of Canterbury: On the Body and Blood of the Lord and Guitmund of Aversa: On the Truth of the Body and Blood of Christ in the Eucharist*. Trans. M. G. Vaillancourt, 3–25. Washington, DC.

Valentinelli, J. 1868. *Bibliotheca manuscript ad S. Marci Venetiarum*. 2 volumes. Venice.

Van den Gheyn, J. 1902. *Catalogue des manuscrits de la Bibliothèque royale de Belgique, Tome 2*. Bruxelles.

Van der Speeten, J. 1985. 'Le dossier de Nicée dans la Quesnelliana', *Sacris erudiri* 28:383–450.

van Waarden, J. A. 2016. *Writing to Survive: A Commentary on Sidonius Apollinaris Letters Book 7, Volume 2: The Ascetic Letters 12–18*. Leuven.

Viezure, D. I. 2016. 'Collectio Avellana and the Unspoken Ostrogoths: Historical Reconstruction in the Sixth Century'. In *Shifting Genres in Late Antiquity*, ed. G. Greatrex, H. Elton, and L. McMahon. Farnham.

Voellius, G. and H. Justellus. 1661. *Appendix* to *Bibliotheca iuris canonici veteris*, 1, pp. xxxiii–cxii. Paris. PL 88.829–942.

Vollmann, B. 1965. *Studien zum Priszillianismus. Die Forschung, die Quellen, der fünfzehnte Brief Papst Leos des Grossen*. St Ottilien.

de Villanuño, M., ed. 1784. *Summa Conciliorum Hispaniae quotquot inveniri potuerunt ad usque saeculum proxime praeteritum, epistolarum ad Hispanos cum earum delectu*. Madrid.

Wallace-Hadrill, J. M. 1971. *Early Germanic Kingship in England and on the Continent*. Oxford.

—. 1983. *The Frankish Church*. Oxford.

Wallis, F. 1999. *Bede: The Reckoning of Time*. Liverpool.

Ward, B. 2007. *A True Easter: The Synod of Whitby 664 AD.* Oxford.

Ward-Perkins, B. 2005. *The Fall of Rome and the End of Civilization.* Oxford.

Wessell, S. 2000. *Cyril of Alexandria and the Nestorian Controversy: The Making of a Saint and of a Heretic.* London, New York.

—. 2008. *Leo the Great and the Spiritual Rebuilding of a Universal Rome.* Leiden.

—. 2015. 'Religious Doctrine and Ecclesiastical Change in the Time of Leo the Great'. In *The Cambridge Companion to the Age of Attila*, ed. M. Maas, 327–43. Cambridge.

Wickham, C. 2005. *Framing the Early Middle Ages: Europe and the Mediterranean 400 to 800.* Oxford.

—. 2009. *The Inheritance of Rome: A History of Europe from 400 to 1000.* London.

Williams, S. 1971. *Codices Pseudo-Isidoriani: A Paleographico-Historical Study*, New York.

Wilson, H. A. 1915. Introduction to *The Gregorian Sacramentary Under Charles the Great*, xv–xlv. London.

Winroth, A. 2000. *The Making of Gratian's* Decretum. Cambridge.

Wormald, P. 2005. 'Kings and Kingship'. In *The New Cambridge Medieval History Vol. 1*, ed. P. Fouracre, 571–604. Cambridge.

Wolff, É. and J. Soler. 2007. Introduction to *Rutilius Namatianus, Sur son retour*, ed. É. Wolff. Paris.

Wood, P. 2010. *We Have no King but Christ: Christian Political Thought in Greater Syria on the Eve of the Arab Conquest (c. 400–585).* Oxford.

Wurm, H. 1939a. *Studien und Texte zur Dekretalensammlung des Dionysius Exiguus.* Bonn.

—. 1939b. 'Decretales selectae ex antiquissimis Romanorum Pontificum epistulis decretalibus', *Apollinaris* 12: 40–93.

Zechiel-Eckes, K. 1992. *Die Concordia canonum des Cresconius: Studien und Edition.* 2 volumes. Frankfurt.

—. 2002. 'Aus Pseudoisidors Spur, Fortschritt durch Fälschungen?' MGH Studien und Texte 31.

Indices

Collections

Manuscripts

Persons

Collections

Manuscripts

Persons